Using Microsoft Dynamics 365 for Finance and Operations

Andreas Luszczak

Using Microsoft Dynamics 365 for Finance and Operations

Learn and understand the Dynamics 365 Supply Chain Management and Finance apps

2nd edition

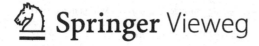

Springer Vieweg

Andreas Luszczak
Wien, Austria

ISBN 978-3-658-40452-9   ISBN 978-3-658-40453-6   (eBook)
https://doi.org/10.1007/978-3-658-40453-6

This Springer Vieweg imprint is published by the registered company Springer Fachmedien Wiesbaden GmbH, part of Springer Nature.
The registered company address is: Abraham-Lincoln-Str. 46, 65189 Wiesbaden, Germany

Preface

Reading this Book

The primary purpose of this book is to provide you with a good knowledge of the concept and functionality of Microsoft Dynamics 365 for Finance and Operations. As a result, you should be able you to execute business processes in the application on your own. It is primarily designed for users, students, and consultants who are interested in learning how to use the application.

Going beyond the operations on the user interface, you learn how the different parts of the application work together. For this reason, also system administrators, developers, IT executives, or consultants who do not know all the details of the application take advantage of getting to know the end-to-end concept.

The best way to learn an application is to use it. For that reason, this book includes exercises that build up on each other in a comprehensive case study. If you need support with the exercises, download the illustrated sample solutions.

Microsoft Dynamics 365 for Finance and Operations is a very comprehensive business solution, which makes it impossible to explain all parts of the application in a single book. In order to provide a profound understanding of the core application, this book addresses the essential functionality in the supply chain management (including trade and logistics, and production control) and the finance management. It covers the application but does not cover tasks in system administration and development.

Microsoft Dynamics 365 Product Version

This book is based on the product version 10.0.29 of Microsoft Dynamics 365 for Finance and Operations (released in October 2022) with all features enabled. It is an update of the initial book edition on Dynamics 365 for Finance and Operations. In order to avoid repeating the long name, the short name "Dynamics 365" is used in most parts of this book.

New in This Edition

Apart from updates in all chapters of the book, major additional topics in this edition include the Saved views feature and other changes of the user interface, the Credit management module, the Engineering change management module, the Planning optimization, the Rebate management module, new features like the advanced notes, and new options in the Warehouse management.

Applicable Settings

In Dynamics 365, you can individually select the language of your user interface. Descriptions and illustrations in this book refer to the language "EN-US" (United States English). Whereas it is obvious that the Dynamics 365 client shows different labels when you select languages like Spanish or Arabic, there are also differences when you select British English. For example, the label for the field "Sales tax" is "VAT" in British English. Other differences between your application and the descriptions in the book are possibly caused by permission settings, by local features, by settings in the feature management and in the license configuration, by later updates, or by modifications and add-ons in your application.

In order to benefit from the explanations, it is recommended to practice with Dynamics 365. A separate test application, which you can use to do the exercises, is required to avoid an impact on actual company data.

The illustrations and the exercises in this book refer to the Microsoft standard demo environment with the company "Contoso Entertainment System USA" ("USMF"). For the screenshots, the color theme "High contrast" and a small element size has been selected in the visual preferences of the user options. In order to grant a flexible choice of your training environment, the tasks in the exercises are specified in a way that you can use any Dynamics 365 test environment of your choice.

Available Support

You can download the exercise guide for the exercises in this book and other applicable resources from the online service of the publisher, or from my website:

http://D365book.addyn.com

If you have comments or questions regarding the book or the exercises, please contact me via this website or e-mail to *lua@addyn.com*.

Acknowledgments

Many people have been involved in finalizing this book, directly and indirectly, from the first to the current edition. Thank you to all of them. In particular, I would like to mention Matthias Gimbel (STZ IT Business Consulting), Ingo Maresch (Cegeka), and Finn Nielsen-Friis (AXcademy).

Thank you also to the editor, Petra Steinmüller, and to my family – Sonja, Felix, and Caroline.

Andreas Luszczak

Table of Contents

1   What is Microsoft Dynamics 365? 1

1.1   Dynamics 365, Dynamics AX and Axapta 1

1.2   Dynamics 365 for Finance and Operations at a Glance.............. 2

    1.2.1 Functional Capabilities.. 2

    1.2.2 Implementation... 3

    1.2.3 Data Structure 4

    1.2.4 Voucher Principle 4

2   Getting Started: Navigation and General Options............................... 5

2.1   User Interface and Common Tasks 5

    2.1.1 Login and Authentication 5

    2.1.2 Navigation... 6

    2.1.3 Elements of the User Interface 9

    2.1.4 Working with Records.. 17

    2.1.5 Filtering and Sorting... 23

    2.1.6 Help System 28

    2.1.7 Case Study Exercises 29

2.2   Printing and Reporting 30

    2.2.1 Printing Documents.. 31

    2.2.2 Microsoft Office Integration.. 34

    2.2.3 Case Study Exercise 36

2.3   Advanced Options.. 36

    2.3.1 User Options 36

    2.3.2 Personalization and Saved Views............................... 38

    2.3.3 Record Information and Templates.............................. 42

    2.3.4 Case Study Exercises 45

2.4   Global Address Book.. 45

    2.4.1 Parties and Addresses 45

    2.4.2 Address Books 47

    2.4.3 Case Study Exercise.. 48

3   Purchase Management... 49

3.1   Business Processes in Purchasing... 49

    3.1.1 Basic Approach 49

        3.1.2 At a Glance: Purchase Order Processing 52

3.2   Vendor Management 54
        3.2.1 Vendor Records 54
        3.2.2 Payment Terms and Cash Discounts 60
        3.2.3 Ledger Integration 63
        3.2.4 Case Study Exercises 64

3.3   Product Management in Purchasing 65
        3.3.1 Product Categories and Procurement Categories 65
        3.3.2 Basic Product Data 67
        3.3.3 Purchase Price Setup 72
        3.3.4 Case Study Exercises 73

3.4   Purchase Order Management 74
        3.4.1 Basics of Purchase Order Processing 74
        3.4.2 Purchase Order Registration 76
        3.4.3 Change Management and Purchase Order Approval 84
        3.4.4 Canceling and Deleting Purchase Orders 85
        3.4.5 Purchase Inquiries and Order Confirmations 86
        3.4.6 Case Study Exercises 90

3.5   Item Receipt 91
        3.5.1 Basics of Item Receipts 91
        3.5.2 Receipts Lists 92
        3.5.3 Inventory Registration 92
        3.5.4 Product Receipts 95
        3.5.5 Partial Delivery, Underdelivery, and Overdelivery 97
        3.5.6 Order Status and Inquiries 100
        3.5.7 Case Study Exercises 103

3.6   Vendor Invoice 103
        3.6.1 Processing Vendor Invoices 104
        3.6.2 Order Status and Inquiries 109
        3.6.3 Case Study Exercises 111

3.7   Vendor Credit Note and Item Return 112
        3.7.1 Crediting and Returning 112
        3.7.2 Credit Notes without Item Return 114
        3.7.3 Case Study Exercise 115

3.8   Purchase Agreement, Requisition, and Quotation Request 115
        3.8.1 Purchase Agreements 116
        3.8.2 Purchase Requisitions 118
        3.8.3 Requests for Quotation 120
        3.8.4 Case Study Exercise 122

4 Sales and Distribution 123

4.1 Business Processes in Sales and Distribution 123
4.1.1 Basic Approach 123
4.1.2 At a Glance: Sales Order Processing........................... 126

4.2 Customer Management.. 128
4.2.1 Core Data in the Customer Records 128
4.2.2 Case Study Exercise 133

4.3 Product Management in Sales 133
4.3.1 Product Data and Sales Categories............................. 133
4.3.2 Sales Price and Discount Setup................................... 135
4.3.3 Case Study Exercises 142

4.4 Sales Order Management.. 143
4.4.1 Basics of Sales Order Processing................................. 143
4.4.2 Sales Quotations... 144
4.4.3 Sales Order Registration... 146
4.4.4 Order Prices and Discounts 153
4.4.5 Surcharge Management... 155
4.4.6 Sales Order Confirmations... 157
4.4.7 Case Study Exercises 158

4.5 Order Picking and Shipment 158
4.5.1 Basics of Picking and Shipping................................... 158
4.5.2 Pick Form and Picking Lists... 160
4.5.3 Picking Workbench... 163
4.5.4 Packing Slips 165
4.5.5 Case Study Exercises 167

4.6 Sales Invoice... 168
4.6.1 Sales Order Invoices 168
4.6.2 Collective Invoices.. 170
4.6.3 Free Text Invoices 172
4.6.4 Case Study Exercises 173

4.7 Sales Credit Note and Item Return... 174
4.7.1 Return Order Management.. 175
4.7.2 Simple Credit Notes.. 177
4.7.3 Case Study Exercise.. 178

4.8 Direct Delivery.. 179
4.8.1 Processing Direct Deliveries... 179
4.8.2 Case Study Exercise.. 181

4.9 Rebate Management and Trade Allowances 182

4.9.1 Trade Allowances 182

4.9.2 Broker Contracts 188

4.9.3 Royalty Agreements 189

4.9.4 Vendor Rebates 189

4.9.5 Rebate Management Deals 190

5   Production Control... 193

5.1 Business Processes in Manufacturing 193

5.1.1 Basic Approach 193

5.1.2 At a Glance: Production Order Processing 196

5.2 Product Management and Bill of Materials........................... 198

5.2.1 Product Data in Manufacturing.................................... 198

5.2.2 Bills of Materials (BOM) 200

5.2.3 Case Study Exercises 207

5.3 Resource and Route Management... 208

5.3.1 Working Time Calendars and Templates..................... 208

5.3.2 Resource Groups and Resource Management 209

5.3.3 Routes and Operations 215

5.3.4 Case Study Exercises 223

5.4 Production Order Management.. 225

5.4.1 Basics of Production Order Processing......................... 225

5.4.2 Production Order Registration...................................... 226

5.4.3 Processing Production Orders 229

5.4.4 Case Study Exercises 235

5.5 Consumption of Material and Resource Capacity................. 236

5.5.1 Journal Setup and Ledger Integration 236

5.5.2 Picking Lists 237

5.5.3 Resource Usage... 239

5.5.4 Case Study Exercises 240

5.6 Reporting as Finished and Ending Production 240

5.6.1 Reporting as Finished 241

5.6.2 Ending and Costing 243

5.6.3 Case Study Exercise 245

5.7 Subcontracting.. 245

5.7.1 External Resources.. 245

5.7.2 Purchased Services 246

5.7.3 Case Study Exercise 249

5.8 Formula and Batch Production Order..................................... 250

5.8.1 Formula Management 250

5.8.2 Batch Production Orders.. 252

6   Forecasts and Master Planning... 253

    6.1   Business Processes in Master Planning.. 253
          6.1.1 Basic Approach.. 253
          6.1.2 At a Glance: Master Planning 254
    6.2   Forecasting.. 255
          6.2.1 Basics of Forecasting... 255
          6.2.2 Forecast Settings 256
          6.2.3 Forecasts and Forecast Planning... 258
          6.2.4 Case Study Exercises 260
    6.3   Master Planning and Planning Optimization................................. 260
          6.3.1 Basics of Master Planning 261
          6.3.2 Planning Optimization.. 263
          6.3.3 Master Planning Setup 264
          6.3.4 Item Coverage and Item Settings... 267
          6.3.5 Master Planning and Planned Orders 271
          6.3.6 Case Study Exercises 276

7   Inventory and Product Management... 277

    7.1   Principles of Inventory Transactions... 277
          7.1.1 Basic Approach.. 277
          7.1.2 At a Glance: Inventory Journal Transactions......................... 280
    7.2   Product Information Management.. 282
          7.2.1 General Product Data 282
          7.2.2 Inventory Dimension Groups... 291
          7.2.3 Item Model Groups 296
          7.2.4 Transactions and Inventory Quantity 298
          7.2.5 Engineering Change Management.. 302
          7.2.6 Case Study Exercises 306
    7.3   Inventory Valuation and Cost Management 307
          7.3.1 Valuation and Cost Flow... 307
          7.3.2 Inventory Closing and Adjustment.. 312
          7.3.3 Product Cost Management.. 314
          7.3.4 Case Study Exercises 318
    7.4   Business Processes in Inventory 320
          7.4.1 Inventory Structures and Parameters..................................... 320
          7.4.2 Inventory Journals 322
          7.4.3 Inventory Counting 325

       7.4.4 Transfer Orders.. 328
       7.4.5 Item Reservation 330
       7.4.6 Quarantine and Inventory Blocking.............................. 333
       7.4.7 Quality Management.. 335
       7.4.8 Consignment Inventory... 337
       7.4.9 Case Study Exercises 339

8   Warehouse and Transportation Management...................................... 341
    8.1   Advanced Warehouse Management.. 341
          8.1.1 Core Setup for Warehouse Management 341
          8.1.2 Core Warehouse Processes... 353
          8.1.3 Advanced Options for Inbound and Outbound Processes........ 360
          8.1.4 Tasks within the Warehouse.. 369
          8.1.5 Case Study Exercises 376
    8.2   Transportation Management 379
          8.2.1 Core Setup for Transportation Management 379
          8.2.2 Managing Transportation Processes.............................. 385
          8.2.3 Case Study Exercises 391

9   Financial Management.. 393
    9.1   Business Processes in Finance... 393
          9.1.1 Basic Approach 393
          9.1.2 At a Glance: Ledger Journal Transactions..................... 394
    9.2   Core Setup for Finance... 395
          9.2.1 Fiscal and Ledger Calendars.. 395
          9.2.2 Currencies and Exchange Rates..................................... 397
          9.2.3 Financial Dimensions 399
          9.2.4 Account Structures and Chart of Accounts................... 401
          9.2.5 Customers, Vendors, and Bank Accounts...................... 408
          9.2.6 Customer Credit Management 409
          9.2.7 Sales Tax / VAT Settings.. 412
          9.2.8 Basic Setup for Journal Transactions 416
          9.2.9 Case Study Exercises 417
    9.3   Transactions in Finance.. 418
          9.3.1 General Journals.. 418
          9.3.2 Invoice Posting.. 423
          9.3.3 Payments 428
          9.3.4 Transaction Reversal and Reversing Entries................. 432
          9.3.5 Case Study Exercises 434
    9.4   Ledger Integration.. 435

9.4.1 Basics of Ledger Integration.. 435
9.4.2 Ledger Integration in Inventory 437
9.4.3 Ledger Integration in Production 441

10 Core Setup and Essential Features 443

10.1 Organizational Structures... 443

10.1.1 Organization Model Architecture... 443
10.1.2 Organization Units 444
10.1.3 Organization Hierarchy Structures 446
10.1.4 Legal Entities (Company Accounts)... 448
10.1.5 Cross-Company Data Sharing 450
10.1.6 Sites.. 450

10.2 User and Security Management 452

10.2.1 Access Control 452
10.2.2 Users and Employees 453
10.2.3 Role-Based Security 456

10.3 Common Settings 458

10.3.1 Number Sequences 459
10.3.2 Calendars... 461
10.3.3 Address Setup... 461
10.3.4 Parameters... 462

10.4 Alerts and Workflow Management... 462

10.4.1 Alert Rules and Notifications... 463
10.4.2 Configuring Workflows 464
10.4.3 Working with Workflows 467

10.5 Other Features 469

10.5.1 Document Management.. 469
10.5.2 Case Management... 471
10.5.3 Task Recorder and Task Guide... 474
10.5.4 Feature Management and License Configuration 475

Appendix.. 477

Setup Checklist.. 477

Commands and Keyboard Shortcuts... 482

Bibliography... 483

Index... 485

1 What is Microsoft Dynamics 365?

Microsoft Dynamics 365 is a cloud-based business platform which comprises the functionality of ERP and CRM solutions. Within Dynamics 365, there are several applications for the different areas of business. In that regard, Dynamics 365 for Finance and Operation, the solution which is covered by this book, includes the ERP functionality for mid-sized and multinational enterprises. Based on state-of-the-art architecture, it offers high usability and comprehensive functionality.

While Dynamics 365 for Finance and Operations is a complete ERP solution, in terms of licensing and product management it is broken into separate applications for Finance, Supply Chain Management, and Commerce. It is a cloud-based solution on the Microsoft Azure platform, but an on-premise deployment on customer infrastructure is possible. The browser-based client can run on most operating systems and browsers.

1.1 Dynamics 365, Dynamics AX and Axapta

Dynamics 365 for Finance and Operations has been initially developed under the name "Axapta" by Damgaard A/S, a Danish software company. The founders of Damgaard have before been co-founders of PC&C, the company that has developed Navision (later "Dynamics NAV").

The first official version of Axapta, version 1.0, was released in March 1998 for Denmark and the USA. Version 1.5, published in October 1998, added the country-specific functionality for several European countries. With the release of version 2.0 in July 1999 and version 3.0 in October 2002, Axapta was introduced in further countries with a wide range of functional enhancements.

Based on a merger agreement in November 2000, Damgaard A/S united with the local rival Navision A/S, the successor of PC&C. Microsoft subsequently acquired Navision-Damgaard in May 2002 and accepted the main products of this company, Navision and Axapta, as core business solutions in the software portfolio. Navision was positioned as the solution for small, Axapta for large companies.

With version 4.0 in June 2006, Microsoft rebranded Axapta to Dynamics AX. Apart from functional enhancements, Dynamics AX 4.0 introduced a redesigned user interface with a Microsoft Office-like look and feel.

Dynamics AX 2009, which was published in June 2008, added the role centers, the workflow functionality, and substantial functional features (including the multisite foundation and new modules) that ensure an end-to-end support for the supply chain requirements of global organizations.

© Springer Fachmedien Wiesbaden GmbH, part of Springer Nature 2023
A. Luszczak, *Using Microsoft Dynamics 365 for Finance and Operations*,
https://doi.org/10.1007/978-3-658-40453-6_1

In August 2011, Dynamics AX 2012 was published, which introduced a further update of the user interface with list pages and action panes across the whole application. New features included the role-based security, the accounting framework with segmented account structures, the enhanced use of shared data structures, and further options for the collaboration across legal entities within the application. Updated versions of Dynamics AX 2012 were released later: The Feature Pack in February 2012 (adding industry features for retail and process manufacturing), R2 in December 2012 (adding data partitions, additional country features, and Windows 8 support), and R3 in May 2014 (adding the advanced warehouse and transportation management solution).

In March 2016, the first version of the current solution – a cloud-based application with a web client – was published with the name Dynamics AX 7. In comparison to Dynamics AX 2012, the technical foundation was completely new, but initially the functionality remained unchanged for the most part. In line with the principle of a cloud-based solution, technical and functional updates have been continuously published since then. With the integration into the Dynamics 365 platform in November 2016, the new name "Dynamics 365 for Operations", later "Dynamics 365 for Finance and Operations", was given to Dynamics AX.

Starting with the product version 10 in April 2019, the "one version" policy has been implemented which means that all customers are on the current product version. In line with this policy, customer environments need to be updated to the newest version continuously. With the feature management, new functionality that is included in a product update usually remains deactivated until you activate it in the Feature management workspace.

1.2   Dynamics 365 for Finance and Operations at a Glance

Microsoft Dynamics 365 for Finance and Operations is a business solution that meets the complex requirements of multinational enterprises, but is easy to use.

Because of its intuitive user interface, most people feel comfortable with Dynamics 365 from the very beginning. Along with the tight integration of other Microsoft cloud services, this helps to start working in Dynamics 365 easily and efficiently. Dashboards, which are the start page when opening Dynamics 365, grant an easy and fast access to all required areas of the application.

1.2.1   Functional Capabilities

The end-to-end support of business processes across the organization enables the integration of internal organization units (e.g., companies or departments) and external business partners (e.g., customers or vendors).

Multi-language, multi-country, and multi-currency capabilities, the organization model that includes multiple hierarchies of operating units and legal entities, and the option to manage multiple sites within one legal entity, make it possible to manage complex global organizations within a common environment.

The functional capabilities of Dynamics 365 for Finance and Operations include the following main areas in Finance and Supply Chain Management:

> **Sales and marketing**
> **Supply chain management**
> **Procurement and sourcing**
> **Production control**
> **MRP (Material requirements planning / Master planning)**
> **Warehouse management**
> **Financial management**
> **Cost accounting and cost management**
> **Budgeting**
> **Project management and accounting**
> **Asset management**

In addition to the core ERP functionality, industry-specific features for distribution, manufacturing, retail and commerce, services, and the public sector are included in the standard application and provide a broad industry foundation. Local features meet the particular requirements of different countries. By default, local features are controlled by the country in the primary address of the company (legal entity).

The integrated reporting features and the option to embed business intelligence reports and visualizations grant a fast and reliable presentation of business data. Business intelligence features are not only available to users in finance, but to the users in all areas of Dynamics 365 who need to analyze their data.

In line with the one-version policy for Dynamics 365, application and platform improvements are periodically published in a single version that covers the entire update. New features, which are included in an update, are shown in the Feature management workspace and must be activated there to make them available.

1.2.2 Implementation

You can deploy Dynamics 365 for Finance and Operations on Microsoft Azure in the cloud, or on-premise in a data center of your company.

The Microsoft Dynamics Lifecycle Services – a portal solution on Microsoft Azure that includes a collaborative environment and continuously updated services for the management of Dynamics 365 deployments – are the starting point for a Dynamics 365 implementation.

Microsoft usually does not sell Dynamics 365 directly to customers but offers an indirect sales channel. Customers purchase licenses from certified partners, who provide their services for the implementation. These services include application consulting, system setup, and the development of enhancements.

1.2.3   Data Structure

In Dynamics 365, you work with data that describe transactions – for example, the inventory transactions of an item. As a prerequisite for the transactions, you need to manage data which describe the objects in transactions – for example, the item itself. Including the data that control the configuration, there are three data types:

➢ **Setup data**
➢ **Master data**
➢ **Transaction data**

Setup data specify the way in which business processes work in Dynamics 365. The setup determines, for example, whether warehouse locations or serial numbers are used. Apart from the development of enhancements, the setup is the primary way to adapt the application to the requirements. Setup data are entered with the initial setup of the application. Later changes need to be checked carefully.

Master data describe objects like customers or products. They are not updated periodically, but at the time when there are changes on the object – for example, when a customer changes the delivery address. Master data are entered or imported initially before a company starts working in the application. Depending on the business, there are only occasional updates of master data later on.

Transaction data are continuously updated with the activities in business processes. Examples of transaction data are sales orders, invoices, or inventory transactions. Dynamics 365 generates transaction data with each business activity. The registration and the posting of transactions comply with the voucher principle.

1.2.4   Voucher Principle

If you want to post a transaction, you have to register a voucher with a header and one or more lines. Processing a voucher includes two steps:

➢ **Registration** – Enter the voucher (create the initial document).
➢ **Posting** – Post the voucher (create the posted document).

Vouchers are based on master data – for example, the main accounts, customers, or products. It is not possible to post a voucher as long as it does not comply with the rules that are defined by setup data or given by the internal business logic of Dynamics 365 (which, for example, requires that an inventory transaction has to include a serial number if serial number control is active). Once a voucher is posted, it is not possible to change it anymore. Depending on the setup, approval in a Dynamics 365 workflow may be required before it is possible to post the transaction. Examples of vouchers are orders in sales and purchasing, or journals in finance and inventory management. The related posted documents are packing slips, invoices, ledger transactions, or inventory transactions.

Note: Some minor vouchers like quarantine orders show an exception regarding the voucher structure – they do not consist of a header and separate lines.

2   Getting Started: Navigation and General Options

Microsoft Dynamics 365 provides an intuitive and smooth user experience. But business software supports business processes which may be quite complex. For this reason, it is important to know the basics.

2.1   User Interface and Common Tasks

Whereas the subsequent chapters give a description of the business processes in Dynamics 365, this section gives an overview of the general functionality.

2.1.1   Login and Authentication

Before you can log on to Microsoft Dynamics 365, an administrator must set up your Dynamics 365 user with appropriate permissions. In addition, a worker record (see section 10.2.2) assigned to your user is required in some areas of the application.

Once your user has been set up, you can sign in with a Microsoft Azure Active Directory user account (Microsoft Office 365 account). Dynamics 365 provides three different ways of access:

➢ **Web client** – As described below, with full access to all functional areas.
➢ **Power Apps portals** – Websites for external and internal users, which are based on the Power Platform and can be easily created using templates (e.g., the customer portal template).
➢ **Mobile apps** – For particular areas (e.g., project timesheet entry)

In order to access the Dynamics 365 web client, start a supported web browser like Microsoft Edge or Google Chrome and open the web address (URL) of your Dynamics 365 application. The browser subsequently shows the login dialog, in which you enter your Azure Active Directory user ID (Email) and password.

Settings in your user options determine the current company (legal entity) and the language in Dynamics 365 after logging on. Parameters in the web address of the Dynamics 365 application may override these user settings, and they provide further options. The web address *https://XXX.com/?cmp=FRSI&lng=fr* (*XXX.com* = Dynamics 365 URL), for example, opens the company "FRSI" in French.

If you want to log off, click the icon with your user initials on the right of the Dynamics 365 navigation bar and select the option *Sign out*.

<u>Note</u>: The **Finance and Operations (Dynamics 365) mobile app** and the related mobile workspaces have been deprecated. Some mobile workspaces are already or will be replaced by new mobile apps like the Project timesheet mobile app.

© Springer Fachmedien Wiesbaden GmbH, part of Springer Nature 2023
A. Luszczak, *Using Microsoft Dynamics 365 for Finance and Operations*,
https://doi.org/10.1007/978-3-658-40453-6_2

2.1.2   Navigation

Within the Dynamics 365 web client, there the following ways to access the different pages and forms:

➢ **Dashboard and workspaces**
➢ **Navigation pane**
➢ **Navigation search**
➢ **Favorites**
➢ **Parameter "mi" in the web address (URL)**

With the parameter "mi" in the web address, you can directly access a page within Dynamics 365. The web address *https://XXX.com/?cmp=USSI&mi=CustTableListPage* (*XXX.com* = Dynamics 365 URL), for example, opens the Customer list page in the company "USSI".

The Dynamics 365 dashboard (see section 2.1.3) is the default initial page in Microsoft Dynamics 365. It contains all workspaces which are available to the current user. In the dashboard, you can open a workspace, and in the workspace, you can subsequently access the related list pages and detail forms.

2.1.2.1 Navigation Pane

The navigation pane provides access to all workspaces, list pages, and forms, for which you have got appropriate permissions. Apart from the *Modules* section, which contains all your menu items, and the *Workspaces* section, which contains your workspaces, it includes the *Favorites* section, in which you can place a limited number of menu items for frequent use.

Figure 2-1:   Navigation pane and menu in Dynamics 365

If you want to display the complete navigation pane, press the keyboard shortcut *Alt+F1* or click the button ▤ (*Show navigation pane*) in the sidebar on the left of the Dynamics 365 client. Dynamics 365 will show the following navigation elements then (see Figure 2-1):

> **Navigation pane** [1]
> **Home** [2] – Opens the home page (dashboard, see section 2.1.3).
> **Favorites** [3] – Shows the favorites.
> **Recent** [4] – Shows workspaces and pages which you have visited recently.
> **Workspaces** [5] – Shows the workspaces, see section 2.1.3.
> **Modules** [6]
> **Menu for the selected module** [7]

If you want to view the navigation pane permanently, click the button ⊞ (*Pin navigation pane open*) at the top right of the navigation pane. With the button ⊠ at the top right of the (permanently shown) navigation pane, you can subsequently collapse the navigation pane again.

2.1.2.2 Modules and Menu Structure

The structure of the modules complies with functional areas like *Accounts payable* or *Production control* and refers to standard roles in the industry. The modules *Organization administration* and *System administration* include basic settings and tasks which are not related to a specific functional area.

The *Common* module contains menu items which not related to a functional role, but which are relevant for all users. These menu items include the *Global address book* (see section 2.4), the *Work items* (workflow management, see section 10.4.3), the *Cases* (see section 10.5.2), and the *Document management* (see section 10.5.1).

Within each module, the menu shows all menu items which you can access with your permissions. The menu items and folders in the menu comply with the following common structure:

The first folder in the menu is the folder *Workspaces*. It is only shown if the selected module contains one or more workspaces and contains all workspaces that refer to the selected module.

Below the workspaces, there are folders and menu items which provide access to pages for frequent tasks in the particular module (e.g., the vendor management in the Accounts payable module).

The folder *Inquiries and reports* contains menu items for analysis and reporting. Inquires show the result directly on the screen whereas reports generate a printout on paper. For reports, you can also select to display a print preview or to save the output to a file instead of a printed hard copy.

The folder *Periodic tasks* contains menu items, which are not in use every day – for example, the menu items for summary updates or month end closing.

Depending on the module, one or more *Setup* folders provide access to the configuration data of the particular module. Configuration data are entered when initially setting up a company (legal entity). Later on, configuration data are only updated if changes in the business require changes in the setup. Some settings should not be changed without a deep knowledge of the Dynamics 365 functionality. For this reason, the permissions for the *Setup* folders usually are set in a way that regular users cannot edit crucial configuration data.

2.1.2.3 Recent Pages

The section *Recent* in the navigation pane contains the Dynamics 365 pages and workspaces which you have visited most recently. When you access a menu item, Dynamics 365 automatically adds it to the section *Recent*. This way you can quickly return to a form which you have opened lately.

2.1.2.4 Navigation Search

The navigation search is a way to access menu items by typing the name or part of the name (similar to the search feature in Windows).

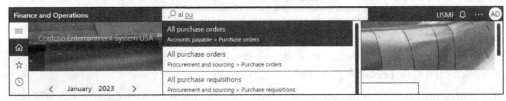

Figure 2-2:   Using the navigation search

If you want to open the navigation search, press the shortcut *Alt+G* or click in the search field button ⊘ in the navigation bar. In the search field, enter the page title or a part of the navigation path. You can limit the text, which you enter, to the first characters of the words of the page title or the navigation path. For example, the page *All purchase orders* is shown as the first result when you type "al pu" in the navigation search. In the drop-down menu that pops up automatically, click on the respective menu item or simply press the *Enter* key to access the page.

2.1.2.5 Favorites and Shared Links

Whereas the module structure and menu items in the navigation pane are given by the system, the personal Dynamics 365 favorites provide an option to collect menu items according to the preferences of the individual user.

If you want to add a workspace or a page to your Dynamics 365 favorites, open the navigation pane and move the mouse to the menu item which you want to add to the favorites. A click on the empty star ☆ which is then shown on the right of the menu item adds it to the favorites. A full star ★ on the right of the menu item indicates that it is included in the favorites.

Once a menu item is included in the favorites, it is shown in the *Favorites* section of the navigation pane. If you want to remove an item from the favorites, click on the full star ★ that is shown on the right of the menu item.

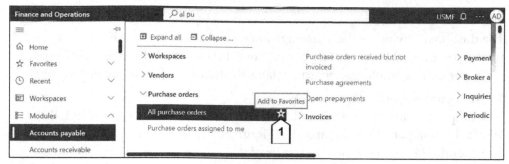

Figure 2-3: Adding a menu item to the Dynamics 365 favorites

Apart from the favorites within Dynamics 365, you can use shared links to access a page in Dynamics 365. In the action pane of all list pages and forms, there is the button *Options/Share/Get a link*. If you click this button, a dialog with the web address of the current form is shown. You can copy this link and send it to other users of Dynamics 365 in your enterprise, or add it to the browser start page or the browser favorites.

2.1.2.6 Switching the Current Company

You can use the company lookup, which you open with a click on the company field in the navigation bar or with the shortcut *Ctrl+Shift+O*, if you want to switch from one legal entity to another. Once you select a company in the lookup, Dynamics 365 immediately switches to this company. You are viewing and editing data in that company then.

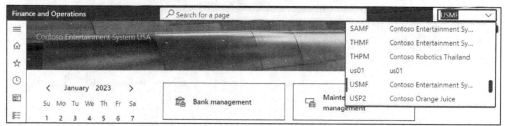

Figure 2-4: Switching the current company

2.1.3 Elements of the User Interface

Microsoft Dynamics 365 contains the following types of standard pages:

- ➢ **Dashboard**
- ➢ **Workspaces**
- ➢ **List pages**
- ➢ **Detail forms and transaction forms**
- ➢ **Journals, inquiries, and setup forms**

This section explains the elements in these pages.

2.1.3.1 Dashboard

The dashboard, which is the start page in Dynamics 365, shows all workspaces, for which you have got appropriate permissions. It is designed to give an overview of your work. The default dashboard contains the following items (see Figure 2-5):

➢ **Navigation bar** [1] – Described below.
➢ **Company banner** [2] – Specified in the company setup (see section 10.1.4).
➢ **Navigation pane** [3] – Collapsed in Figure 2-5.
➢ **Calendar** [4] – Determines the session date.
➢ **Work items** [5] – Refer to the workflow management (see section 10.4.3).
➢ **Workspaces** [6] – For the different functional areas.

Workspace tiles, for example the tile *Bank management* in Figure 2-5, provide access to the related workspaces. The calendar in the dashboard highlights the *Session date* of the current session, which is the default value for the posting date in journals and orders. The initial value for the session date is the current date. If you want set it to a different date, click on the respective date in the dashboard calendar or select it in the menu item *Common> Common> Session date and time*.

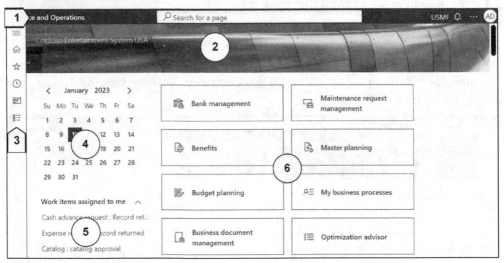

Figure 2-5:   The Dynamics 365 dashboard

The link *Finance and Operations* on the left of the navigation bar provides the option to return to the dashboard (initial page) from every workspace or form.

Note: You can select an alternative page (e.g., the employee self-service portal) instead of the dashboard as *Initial page* on the tab *Preferences* in your user options.

2.1.3.2 Navigation Bar

The navigation bar at the top of the Dynamics 365 client contains the following elements for global Dynamics 365 features (see Figure 2-6):

> **Office 365 portal** [1] – Access to Microsoft Office 365.
> **Finance and Operations** [2] – Opens the home page (dashboard).
> **Navigation search** [3] – See section 2.1.2.
> **Company lookup** [4] – Switch between companies, see section 2.1.2.
> **Messages** [5] – See section 2.1.4.
> **Settings** [6] – User options and other general settings.
> **Help & Support** [7] – See section 2.1.6.
> **User initials** [8] – Sign out.

If the browser window with the Dynamics 365 client is not wide enough to show all elements, there is the button ▦ (*More*) on the right of the Navigation bar to access to the missing elements.

The options within the button ⚙ (*Settings*) [6] include the *User options* (see section 2.3.1), the *Task recorder* (see section 10.5.3), and access to the personalization toolbar (see section 2.3.2). Within the button ❓ (*Help & Support*) [7], you can find the buttons *Help*, *Trace* (capturing a trace for problem diagnosis and performance analysis), *About* (product information), and buttons for submitting feedback and ideas.

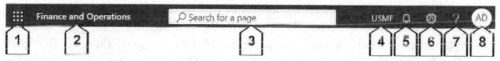

Figure 2-6: Navigation bar in Dynamics 365

Note: If the slider *Enable legacy navigation bar* in the Client performance options form is set to "Yes", the navigation bar shows the navigation path and looks slightly different from the screenshots in this book.

2.1.3.3 Workspaces

The dashboard, and the section *Workspaces* in the navigation pane, contain all workspaces for which you have got appropriate permissions.

Workspaces are designed as a starting point for the daily work in a particular job. They are pages which collect all the information and functionality required to perform this job. In the example of the workspace *Purchase order receipt and follow-up* in Figure 2-7, a list of delayed receipts is shown in the center. Tiles on the left and on the right of the workspace provide access to related forms and indicate the corresponding number of records, for example the orders that are not yet invoiced.

In general, a workspace contains the following sections (compare Figure 2-7):

> **Summary section** [1]
> **Tabbed list section** [2]
> **Further sections as applicable** [3]
> **Related links** [4]

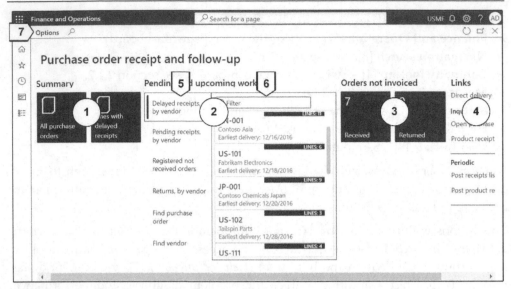

Figure 2-7:   Workspace for purchase order receipt and follow-up

The tabbed list section [2] in the center of a workspace is the main place for the daily work. If you select a list on the left [5] of this section, the grid on the right [6] displays the related list of records. The filter field above the grid provides the option to enter a filter. A click on a key field (shown as a link) in the grid immediately opens the related detail form. Depending on the particular workspace, buttons in the action pane [7] and, if applicable, in the toolbar above the grid in the tabbed list section [2] (the example in Figure 2-7 does not include such a toolbar) provide the option to execute actions immediately.

Tiles are rectangular buttons which open pages (in the same way as a menu item button), and optionally display data like counts or key performance indicators. The summary section [1] on the left contains tiles which provide the option to start new tasks or to access pages which are important with regard to the selected workspace (e.g., purchase orders in Figure 2-7).

Depending on the particular workspace, there are further sections [3] on the right, which contain tiles, charts, or graphs. The rightmost section [4] contains links to further pages with reference to the selected workspace.

2.1.3.4 List Pages

A list page shows the list of records in a Dynamics 365 table. It is primarily designed for viewing records, but you can activate the *Edit mode* to edit records immediately, and with the buttons in the action pane you can execute tasks on the selected record.

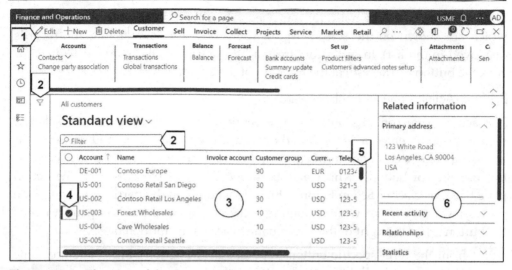

Figure 2-8: Elements of the Customer list page (in Read mode)

While list pages have got a common structure, the particular elements and features are depending on the respective page. The common structure includes the following basic elements (see Figure 2-8):

➢ **Action pane** [1] – Contains the action buttons.
➢ **Filter options** [?] – With a filter button and a quick filter field (see section 2.1.5).
➢ **Grid** [3] – Displays the list of records.
➢ **Grid checkboxes** [4] – Select one, or multiple, or, with the checkbox in the grid header, all records.
➢ **Scrollbar** [5] – Scroll through records (alternatively press the shortcuts *PgUp*, *PgDn*, *Ctrl+Home*, and *Ctrl+End*).
➢ **FactBoxes** [6] – Show additional information on the selected record (e.g., the primary address of the customer) in the *Related information* pane on the right.

With the button *Edit* in the action pane, you can activate the Edit mode and update record data in the list page immediately.

If a page is shown with the full action pane and you need additional space for viewing more lines in the grid, click the button ⌃ (*Collapse*) at the bottom right of the action pane. Once collapsed, the action pane automatically expands whenever you click a tab of the action pane (e.g., *Customer* in the action pane in Figure 2-8). If you want to show the full action pane permanently, click the button 🔄 (*Pin open*) at the bottom right of the action pane when expanded.

If the *Related information* pane is collapsed and you want to view the FactBoxes [6], press the shortcut *Ctrl+F2* or click on the collapsed *Related information* pane on the right. Once expanded, you can click the button ▷ at the top of the pane if you want to collapse the *Related information* pane again. As a prerequisite for the use of FactBoxes, the FactBoxes have to be activated in the client performance options (*System administration> Setup> Client performance options*).

List pages are not automatically refreshed when there is an update of the data which are shown on the screen (e.g., if somebody else is changing the records displayed in the list). In order to refresh a list page, press the shortcut *Shift+F5* or click the button ⊙ (*Refresh*) at the top right of the action pane.

2.1.3.5 Action Pane and Action Search

The action pane contains buttons for executing activities related to the selected record (e.g., to enter a sales order from a customer record) and buttons for accessing connected detail forms (to display more information). The number and functionality of buttons, which may be shown on multiple tabs (e.g., the action pane tabs *Customer* or *Sell* in Figure 2-8), is depending on the particular page. If the browser window is not wide enough to show all tabs of the action pane, there is the button ⊡ on the right of the action pane to access the hidden tabs.

Apart from the form-specific buttons and tabs in the action pane, there are some general buttons on the right:

> ⊗ **[Power Apps]** – Add a PowerApp.
> ⓐ **[Open in Microsoft Office]** – See section 2.2.2.
> ℗ **[Attach]** – Document handling/attachment, see section 10.5.1.
> ⊙ **[Refresh]** – Refresh the screen.
> ⊡ **[Open in new window]** – Connected windows, as described further below.
> ⊠ **[Close]** – Close the page or form within the Dynamics 365 client.

As an alternative to the buttons in the action pane, you can use the action search to execute an activity. Click the search button ⊘ in the action pane (not in the navigation bar – this would start the navigation search) or press the shortcut *Alt+Q* for this purpose, and enter the action name or the action pane button path in the search field. Like in the navigation search, you can limit the entered text to the first characters of the words of the name. You can, for example, use of the action search to access the customer balance from the Customer list page as follows: First press the shortcut *Alt+Q*, then type "b" and finally press the *Enter* key (you might need to wait for a few seconds before the search result is shown).

2.1.3.6 Detail Forms for Master Data

Unlike list pages, which are primarily designed for viewing a list of records, the primary use of detail forms is inserting, modifying and viewing the details of individual records.

In order to access a detail form from the related list page, click on a key field in the grid of the list page or press the *Enter* key when the field is active. Key fields are shown as a link in list pages, usually in the first column of the grid – in the example of Figure 2-8, this is the column *Account*. The button *Options/Page options/ Go to/Details* in the action pane of list pages provides an alternative way to access the detail form.

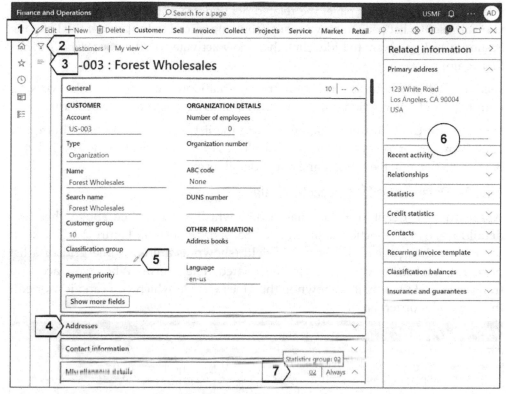

Figure 2-9: Elements of the Customer detail form (in Read mode)

Detail forms have got a similar structure to list pages, and like in list pages, the elements and functions are depending on the particular form. The Customer detail form (accessed from the list page *Accounts receivable> Customers> All customers*) in Figure 2-9 is an example of the structure of detail forms. The common structure of detail forms includes the following basic elements:

➢ **Action pane** [1] – Like in list pages (collapsed in Figure 2-9).
➢ **Filter button** [2] – Opens the filter pane (see section 2.1.5).
➢ **List button** [3] – Opens the list pane with the list of records.
➢ **Tabs** [4] – Group fields in line with the functional area.
➢ **Edit button** [5] – Activates the Edit mode (shown in Read mode).
➢ **FactBoxes** [6] – Show related information (in the same way as in a list page).

You can expand a tab with a click on the particular tab. If you right-click a tab, the context menu will display the options for expanding or collapsing all tabs of the form. **Summary fields** on a tab [7] show core data directly on the tab. If you want to know the field name of a summary field, hover with the mouse over it. In the example of Figure 2-9, you can view the statistics group "02" in a summary field on the tab *Miscellaneous details*.

With the shortcut *Ctrl+F8* or the button ▤ (*Show list/Hide list*) [3] in the sidebar on the left of detail forms, you can show the list pane with the list of records. If you select a record in the list pane, the related detail data are shown immediately, and you can use the list pane to move easily from one record to the next. If the list pane is shown and you want to hide, click the – now activate – button ■ (*Show list/Hide list*) again.

Section 2.1.4 in this book contains more information on editing records, working with tabs, and other options which are available in list pages and detail forms.

If you want to return from a detail form to the list page, click the *Back* button of your browser, or press the shortcut *Alt+Back Arrow* or the *Esc* key, or click the button ⊠ (*Close*) in the action pane of the detail form.

2.1.3.7   Detail Forms for Transaction Data

Apart from the detail forms for master data which are described above, there are detail forms for transaction data (e.g., the Sales order form in Figure 2-10). Like in the master data pages, click on a key field (shown as a link) in the grid of a list page for transaction data to open the related detail form. When you access a transaction detail form, it is shown in the Lines view in which you can view or edit the (e.g., sales order) lines.

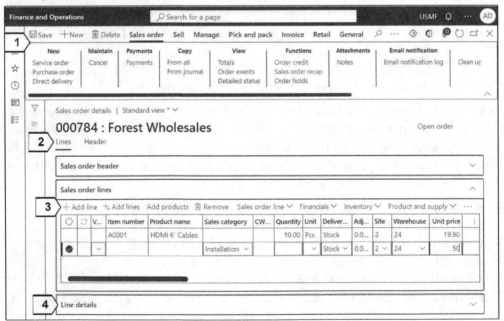

Figure 2-10:   Elements in the transaction detail form for sales orders

In the **toolbar** [3] above the grid with the lines, there are buttons for actions on the selected line – for example, the button *Remove* to delete the record in that line. The **action pane** [1] at the top of the form contains the buttons for actions at header level – for example, the button *Delete* to delete a complete order.

If you want to view or to edit details that are not shown in the line grid, expand the tab **Line details** [4]. The tab *Line details* contains multiple sub-tabs which structure the fields of the line.

Some basic header data are shown on the tab *Header* in the Lines view. In order to access all available fields of the header record, open the Header view with the button **Header** [2] or with the shortcut *Ctrl+Shift+H*. In the Header view, the button **Lines** (or the shortcut *Ctrl+Shift+L*) takes you back to the Lines view.

2.1.3.8 Inquiries and Setup Forms

In comparison to detail forms, inquiries and setup forms have got a simple layout. In Dynamics 365, there are following types of simple forms:

➤ **Simple lists** – Contain all relevant fields directly in the grid (e.g., the form *Accounts receivable> Setup> Customer groups*).
➤ **Detail forms with list pane** – Detail forms, which you can directly access from the menu and which show the list pane by default, include the same functionality as the master data detail forms described above (e.g., the form *Accounts receivable> Payment setup> Terms of payment*).
➤ **Parameter forms** – Show a table of contents with sections on the left and related data on the right (e.g., the form *Accounts payable> Setup> Accounts payable parameters*).

2.1.3.9 Connected Browser Windows

Connected browser windows provide the option to view connected information side by side. You can use them, for example, if you want to view the related vendor transactions when switching between vendor records.

In the example of the vendor transactions, open the Vendor list page (*Accounts payable> Vendors> All vendors*) and click the button *Vendor/Transactions/Transactions* in the action pane. In the vendor transactions, click the button ⊡ (*Open in new window*) in the action pane. The vendor transactions are subsequently shown in a new browser window. The new browser window is dynamically linked to the main browser window, which is showing the previous form (the Vendor list page in the example). Moving from one vendor to another in the main window then automatically updates the data shown in the connected transaction window.

2.1.4   Working with Records

In Microsoft Dynamics 365, you can work with the mouse, but you can also use the keyboard for many actions. Apart from keyboard shortcuts, the navigation search and the action search enable entering data quickly without a mouse.

In the context menu, which you can open with a right-click on a control (e.g., a button or a field name) in a detail form or a list page, the option *View shortcuts* opens a window which shows all available shortcuts. In the appendix of this book, you can find an overview of the basic shortcuts in Dynamics 365.

2.1.4.1   Structure of Pages and Forms

When you open a regular form, no matter whether you access it from a tile, or a link in a workspace, or a menu item in the navigation pane, Dynamics 365 shows the related list page.

List pages are the starting point for the work in a particular area. You can search and filter records in a list page, and buttons in the action pane provide the option to edit, delete, and insert data in line with your permissions.

The columns in a list page only show a limited number of fields. Detail forms include all available fields of the selected record. If you want to access the detail form from a list page, click the related key field (shown as a link in the grid).

You can expand a tab in a detail form with a click on the tab or – after switching to the particular tab with the *Tab* key – with the *Enter* key. If you want to collapse a particular tab, click the tab header again (or press the shortcut *Alt+0*). Further options are shown after a right-click on a tab. If you expand all tabs, you can easily scroll the complete record (e.g., with your mouse wheel) without additional mouse clicks. Some tabs contain less important fields, which are not immediately shown when you expand the tab. You can show these fields with the link *Show more fields* in such tabs.

2.1.4.2   Edit Mode and Read Mode

When you open a list page or a detail form, by default it is shown in Read mode (also called "View mode") to prevent unintended changes of data.

In Read mode, editable fields show the icon ⌀ (*Edit*) on the right. If you want to switch to the Edit mode (in which you can update records), click on this icon. Apart from the icon, you can also use the *F2* key or the button *Edit* in the action pane to switch to the Edit mode. If the Edit mode is active in a list page and you access the related detail form, the detail form is also opened in Edit mode. If you want to return to the Read mode, press the *F2* key again (or click the button *Options/Edit/Read mode* in the action pane).

If you want to start a particular form in Edit mode all the time, click the button *Options/Personalize/Always open for editing* in the action pane of the form. You can also set your general default mode to the Edit mode or to the Read mode (setting in the field *Default view/edit mode* on the tab *Preferences* in your user options).

2.1.4.3   Inserting Records

If you want to insert a record in a list page or a detail form (e.g., a new customer in the Customer form), press the shortcut *Alt+N* or click the button *New* in the action pane. Apart from list pages and detail forms, some workspaces also contain a button in the action pane for creating new records.

In many forms, a *Quick create* dialog (see Figure 2-11) is shown on the right when you create a new record. This dialog contains the core fields of the record and helps inserting records in an easy way. Once you close the dialog with the button *Save* at the bottom, Dynamics 365 opens the related detail form in which you can enter additional data. Depending on the page, a button *Save and open* with further options is shown in the dialog. With this button, you can, for example, directly switch from the *Create customer* dialog to a new sales quotation.

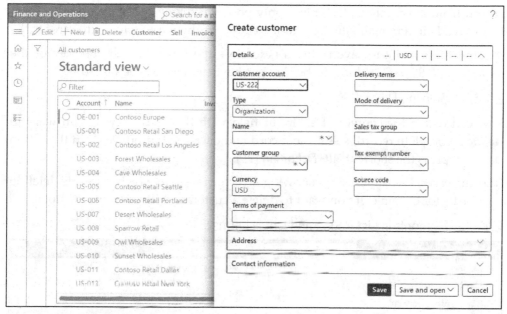

Figure 2-11: The *Quick create* dialog for a new customer

If there is no *Quick create* dialog in a particular page, inserting a new record opens the detail form with an empty record, in which you can enter the required data. If you use a template (see section 2.3.3), the new record is not empty but receives default values for the field content from the template.

In the lines of a transaction form (e.g., in the sales order lines), you can press the *Down Arrow* key in the last line of the grid to create a new record.

If you have started inserting a record with a mandatory field and you want to cancel the action, you might need to delete the record, even if you have not entered any data. Alternatively, press the *Esc* key and close the form without saving. If you are in a *Quick create* dialog, click the button *Cancel* at the bottom.

2.1.4.4 Editing Data

Before you can edit a record in a list page or a detail form, you have to make sure that you are in the Edit mode. In order to switch between the fields of the form, you can use the mouse, or the *Tab* key, or the shortcut *Shift+Tab*.

You can manually save a record with the shortcut *Alt+S* (or *Ctrl+S*), or with the button *Save* in the action pane. But it is not required to save a record explicitly. Dynamics 365 saves every change of a record automatically when you leave the record – switching to another record or closing the form with the *Back* button of the browser or with the button ☒ (*Close*) in the action pane. If you close a form with the *Esc* key, a dialog will ask whether you want to save the changes.

If you have entered or modified data and you do not want to save the update, press the shortcut *Ctrl+Shift+F5* or click the button *Options/Edit/Revert* to restore the record from the database. But this is only possible as long as the changes have not been saved already manually or automatically (e.g., by moving to another record).

Another option not to save changes is to close the form with the *Esc* key or the shortcut *Alt+Shift+Q* (as long as the changes have not been saved already).

2.1.4.5 Deleting Data

You can delete the content of an input field with the *Delete* key. If you want to delete a complete record, select the record and click the button *Delete* in the action pane (or press the shortcut *Alt+Del* or *Alt+F9*).

In some cases, Dynamics 365 is showing an error message which prevents deleting a record – for example, if you want to delete a customer with open transactions.

2.1.4.6 Elements in List Pages and Detail Forms

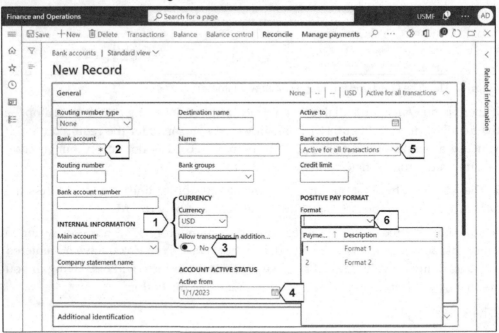

Figure 2-12:   Types of fields in the Bank account detail form

List pages and detail forms contain the following elements as shown in Figure 2-12 on the example of the Bank account detail form (*Cash and bank management> Bank accounts> Bank accounts*):

➢ **Field groups** [1] – Group fields by functional areas.
➢ **Mandatory fields** [2] – Show a red frame and the icon ⊠ (*Required field indicator*). The required content must be entered before you can save the record.
➢ **Sliders** [3] – Sliders and checkboxes are used for a binary choice (Yes/No). If you want to select a checkbox (set a slider to "Yes"), click it with the mouse or press the *Spacebar* key while the cursor is on the field.
➢ **Date fields** [4]
➢ **Lookup fields with a fixed list of values** [5]
➢ **Lookup fields with a related main table** [6]

Date fields contain a calendar icon 📅 which you can use to select a particular date. In your user options, the lookup field *Date, time, and number format* on the tab *Preferences* determines the format in which all date and number fields are shown in your web client. If you enter a date manually, date separators like "." or "/" are not required. For a date in the current year, you can optionally enter only day and month (e.g., "0523" if you use the US date format). If you want to insert the current date, you can enter the character "t" (or "d" for the session date) instead of a date.

Numeric fields support basic arithmetical expressions. You can, for example, type "= 55 * 1.1" instead of "60.50"to enter an amount of "55.00 plus 10 %".

<u>Note</u>: Before version 10.0.29, the use of mathematical expressions has only been possible in the numeric cells of a grid.

2.1.4.7 Lookup Fields and Table Reference

In a lookup field, you can only enter or select a value which is included in a predefined list of values. With regard to the setup of this list of values, there are two types of lookup fields:

➢ **Lookup fields with a fixed list of values**, which is given by Dynamics 365 enumerable types (*Enums*) – e.g., *Bank account status* [5] in Figure 2-12.
➢ **Lookup fields with a related main table**, which contains permitted values – e.g., *Pay format* [6] in Figure 2-12.

In Edit mode, both types of lookup fields show the lookup button ⌄ on the right of the field. Lookup fields with a related main table are shown as a link (similar to Internet links), both in Edit mode and in Read mode. This link provides access to the corresponding main table form (in the example of Figure 2-12, to the Pay format form).

When you start typing characters into a lookup field, a drop-down menu (lookup) which uses the typed characters as a filter on the key field of the related table will pop up automatically. In many lookups, this filter also includes the column *Name*. If you enter, for example, the character "F" in the field *Customer account* of a sales order, the lookup which pops up automatically will show all records which start with "F" in the customer name (if there is no customer number starting with "F").

If you want to open the lookup manually, click the lookup button ⌄ on the right of the respective field (or press the shortcut *Alt + Down*).

In the lookup, you can select a record with a mouse click (or with the *Enter* key once the respective line in the lookup is active). If a lookup is showing numerous lines and you want to reduce the number of lines which are displayed, you can use the grid column filter and the sorting options described in section 2.1.5. In the example of Figure 2-12, you can click on the column header field *Description* in the lookup to enter a filter on the field *Description* of the pay formats.

In addition to the lookup, the table reference of fields with a related main table provides the option to access the detail form of the related main table. If you want to insert a new bank group in the example of Figure 2-12, you can open the Pay format form directly from the field *Format*. For this purpose, the table reference is shown as a link which you can use to access the related detail form with a mouse click. Alternatively, you can access the related detail form with the option *View details* in the context menu of the field. In order to open the context menu, select the field and press the shortcut *Ctrl+F10*, or right-click the lookup button ⌄ or the field label (not the field itself).

After opening the related detail form, you can edit records in the same way as after accessing the form from the navigation pane. Apart from using the table reference as an easy way to insert and to edit related data, you can use it to view the details of related records – you can, e.g., click on a sales order number in the invoice inquiry to access the corresponding sales order immediately.

2.1.4.8   Product Information Dialog

In some forms, for example in the Sales order form or in the Purchase order form, the link (and the option *View details*) in the item number field does not directly open the Item form (Released product form), but the *Product information* dialog. This dialog displays the core data of the item. In many cases, these core data are sufficient, and you don't need to access the details in the Released product form. But if you need to access more details, click the link in the field *Item number* of the dialog to open the related Released product detail form.

2.1.4.9   Segmented Entry Control

A special type of lookups is used in ledger account fields, for example in the lines of financial journals. Since the ledger account is one field with multiple segments (the main account and applicable financial dimensions), there is a special control for lookup and data entry – the segmented entry control (see section 9.3.1).

2.1.4.10 Message Bar and Action Center

If there is an issue with an action that you execute in Dynamics 365 (e.g., if you try to enter a main account which does not exist, or to delete a customer with open transactions), an error message is immediately shown in the message bar (below the action pane of the form).

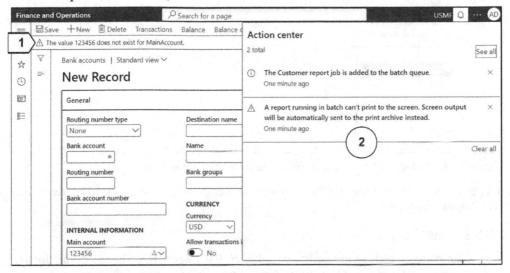

Figure 2-13: Viewing notifications in the message bar [1] and in the action center [2]

If there is an error or a warning that is generated by an asynchronous operation (processing a batch job), the message is sent to the action center (message center). The button 🔳 (*Show messages*) in the navigation bar then indicates the number of unread notifications, and you can click this button to view the recent messages.

The example of Figure 2-13 shows an error message in the message bar and – irrespective of this message – messages in the action center.

2.1.5   Filtering and Sorting

In order to work efficiently in tables with numerous records, it is important to find the right records quickly. For this purpose, Dynamics 365 offers various features for filtering and sorting in list pages and detail forms.

2.1.5.1   Quick Filter

In list pages, the quick filter is the easiest way to enter a filter. When you type characters into the quick filter field, a drop-down menu, in which you can select the column that you want to use for filtering, pops up automatically.

After activating the filter with the *Enter* key or with the button 🔳 (*Apply filter*) on the left of the quick filter field, the page only displays records in which the content of the selected column starts with the characters entered in the quick filter field. An asterisk (*) which appears next to the current view name indicates that you have modified the view (see section 2.3.2), in this case by applying a filter.

Figure 2-14 shows an example of using of the quick filter. The filter on customers with a name beginning with the characters "co" is not yet executed.

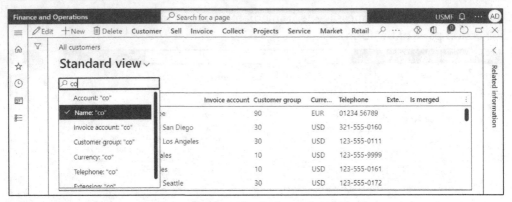

Figure 2-14:   Selecting the filter column in the lookup of a quick filter

If you want to clear a quick filter, remove the content in the quick filter field and press the *Enter* key.

2.1.5.2 Filter Pane

The filter pane, which is not only available in list pages, but also in detail forms, provides the option to apply multiple filter criteria in parallel.

If you want to show the filter pane in a form, click the filter button ⧖ in the sidebar on the left (or press the shortcut *Ctrl+F3*). Then enter the characters which you want to use for filtering in the respective field of the filter pane. In the operator selection on the right above the filter field, you can select whether to use these characters together with the operator "begins with", "contains", "is one of", or one of the other operators. If you want to filter on additional fields, click the button *Add* at the top right of the filter pane and select the respective field. Then activate the filter with the button *Apply*.

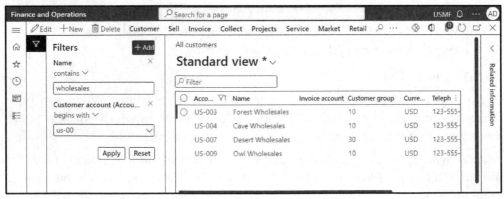

Figure 2-15:   Using the filter pane in a list page

Instead of the operator "contains", you can also use the asterisk (*) wildcard together with the "begins with" operator (which is the default operator). This way you can, for example, enter "*ab" in a filter field to filter on all records which contain "ab" in any part of the field – without the need to change the operator.

The operator "matches" provides the option to use manual wildcards and filter expressions as described further below.

If you want to hide the filter pane again, click the – now active – filter button 📑 in the sidebar on the left again, or click in a field in the filter pane and press the *Esc* key. Hiding the filter pane does not clear the filter.

If you want to clear the filter, click the button *Reset* in the filter pane.

2.1.5.3 Grid Column Filter

The grid column filter, which is available in list pages and in the grid of other forms (also in the grid of lookups), is another option for filtering.

You can access the grid column filter with a click on the header field of the respective column. Alternatively, select a field in the column of the grid and press the shortcut *Ctrl+G*. In the drop-down menu which is displayed next, you can enter the filter. The operator works the same way as described for the filter pane above.

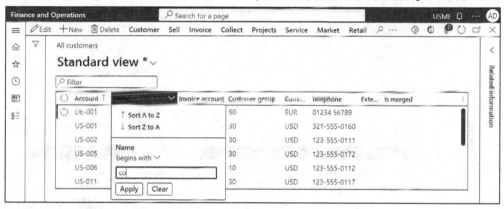

Figure 2-16:   Entering a grid column filter in a list page

Once the grid column filter is active, the filter icon 📑 is shown next to the particular column header.

If you want to clear the grid column filter, click on the header field of the respective column to show the drop-down menu again. In the drop-down menu, click the button *Clear*. Another way for clearing the filter is to open the filter pane and to click the button *Reset*.

2.1.5.4 Advanced Filter

The advanced filter in list pages and in detail forms provides the option to enter complex filter criteria. You can access the advanced filter, which is shown in a separate dialog on the right, with the shortcut *Ctrl+Shift+F3* (or with the button *Options/Page options/Advanced Filter or sort* in the action pane). Like the filter pane, the advanced filter provides the option to set a filter on fields which are not shown in the list page or detail form.

When you open the *Advanced filter* dialog, it shows the most common filter fields of the particular form. If you need to enter a criterion on a field which is not shown in the dialog, insert a record in the dialog (press the shortcut *Alt+N* or click the button *Add*). In the new filter line, enter the filter instruction in the columns *Table, Derived table, Field,* and *Criteria.*

The fields *Table* and *Derived table* in a new line by default contain the base table of the page or form in which you have opened the advanced filter. In case of a simple criterion (i.e., not filtering on a related table), you don't have to change the content of these fields. Select the field, to which you want to apply the filter, in the column *Field* (you can use the lookup for the field name) and enter the filter criterion in the column *Criteria.* If the selected field in the filter line is a lookup field, you can use a lookup in the column *Criteria* (open the lookup with the button ⊞ on the right of the field). The way for entering filter expressions in the criteria of an advanced filter, which provides more options but is more complex, is described below.

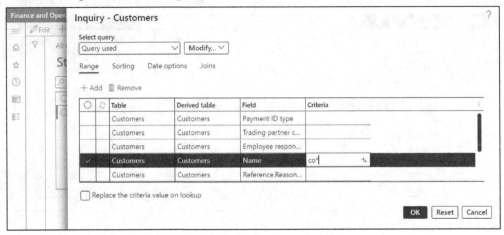

Figure 2-17:   Entering filter criteria in the *Advanced filter* dialog

Once you have entered the filter criteria, close the *Advanced filter* dialog with the button *OK.* The filter is active now, and the page only shows matching records.

2.1.5.5 Saving a Filter

If you frequently need particular filter criteria, you can save them in the *Advanced filter* dialog. For this purpose, click the button *Modify/Save as* in the dialog and enter a filter name in a second dialog which is displayed then.

Saved filters are stored in your *Usage data,* which means that nobody else can use your saved filters. If you want to apply a saved filter, select it in the lookup field *Select query* of the *Advanced filter* dialog (see Figure 2-18).

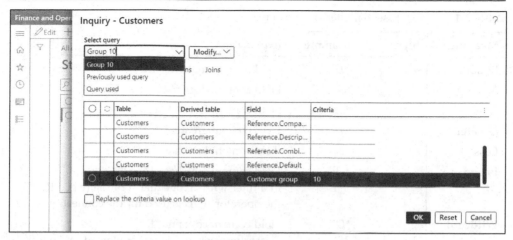

Figure 2-18: Selecting a saved filter in the *Advanced filter* dialog

In addition to the filters which you have saved manually, the filter which you have used the last time is saved automatically and is available in every page (select the option *Previously used query* in the lookup field *Select query*).

2.1.5.6 Sorting

The grid column filter in list pages does not only provide the option to filter records, but you can also sort records. If you sort the records in a list page and open the related detail form, the detail form applies the sorting of the list page.

Alternatively, you can specify sorting criteria in the *Advanced filter* dialog which contains the tab *Sorting* for this purpose. On this tab, you can enter sorting criteria with table name and field name in one or more lines (similar to a filter criterion).

2.1.5.7 Drop-down menu

You should not confuse a filter in a list page or a detail form with the drop-down menu (lookup) described in section 2.1.4. You use the drop-down menu to select the content of a field. The filter features that are described in the current section aim to select the records which are shown in the list page or detail form.

2.1.5.8 Filter Expressions

If you use the quick filter in a list page, the page shows all records which start with the characters which you have entered in the quick filter field (in the column, which you have selected for the filter).

In all other filter options, you can use further filter expressions – the filter pane and the grid column filter include the operator "matches" for this purpose. The table below gives an overview of the most important filter expressions.

Table 2-1:   Essential filter expressions

Meaning	Sign	Example	Explanation
Equal	=	*EU*	Field content matches "EU"
Not equal	*!*	*!GB*	Field content does not match "GB"
Interval	*..*	*1..2*	Field content from "1" to "2" (incl.)
Greater	>	*>1*	Field content greater than "1"
Less	<	*<2*	Field content less than "2"
Is one of	*,*	*1,2*	Field content matches "1" or "2"; in a filter with "Not equal" criteria (e.g., "!1,!2"), the operator *AND* is used for the connection
Wildcard	*	**E**	Field content contains "E"
	?	*?B**	First character unknown, followed by a "B", subsequent characters unknown
Date field		*<123122*	Field content less than 12/31/2022; insert a date in a filter like in any date field (see section 2.1.4), including "t" for "today"; filter operators work like in any other filter field
Relative date	*(Day(XX))*	*(Day(-1))*	Yesterday (*XX* is calculated from today's date); include outer parentheses in the filter expression
Relative date range	*(DayRange (XX,YY))*	*(DayRange (-2,1))*	From the day before yesterday till tomorrow (the date range is calculated from today's date)

2.1.6   Help System

If you need help on the functionality, open the Dynamics 365 *Help* which is available within the whole application. In the help pane, there are two areas:

➢ **Help** – Links to Microsoft help texts and videos.
➢ **Task Guides** – From the Microsoft Dynamics Lifecycle Services (LCS).

Whereas task guides describe how to use Dynamics 365 in business processes, the help articles explain the functionality of standard features.

Basic parameters for the help system are specified in the System parameters (*System administration> Setup> System parameters*, section *Help*).

2.1.6.1   Accessing Help

As shown in Figure 2-19 on the example of the *Item model group*, you can view a short help after pointing the mouse on a field label. If you want to access the full help content, click the button 🔲 / *Help* in the navigation bar. The help pane subsequently displays the links to the help articles and the task guides that refer to the particular form.

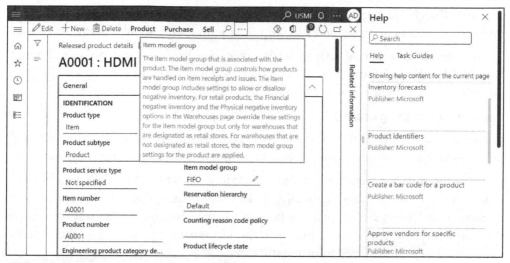

Figure 2-19: Viewing the Dynamics 365 help in the Released product form

2.1.6.2 Custom Help with Task Guides

The task recorder (see section 10.5.3) provides the option to create recordings which are based on the particular business processes in your enterprise. If you save a recording to a Lifecycle Services (LCS) Business Process Library which is selected in the section *Help* of the System parameters, the recording will be shown on the tab *Task guides* in the help pane of the related forms.

2.1.7 Case Study Exercises

Exercise 2.1 – Login and Navigation

As a first task, you should access a Dynamics 365 training environment. In this environment, switch to a company which is different from your default company.

Open the list page *All vendors*, first from the *Accounts payable* menu in the navigation pane, and then with the navigation search. Check if there are vendors with a name which starts with an "A". Then open the workspace *Purchase order preparation* and try to find a vendor with a name starting with an "A".

Finally, log out from Dynamics 365.

Exercise 2.2 – Favorites

Start a web client session in Dynamics 365, select the training company, and show the navigation pane. Add the list page *Released products*, which you can find in the *Product information management* module, to your favorites. Then open this page from the favorites.

Exercise 2.3 – Detail Forms

As an example of detail forms in Dynamics 365, review the Vendor detail form which you access from the Vendor list page (*Accounts payable> Vendors> All vendors*). Check the details of the vendor in the third line of the list page and show an example of a field group and a lookup field with and without a main table.

Then show an example of a slider and a checkbox field. What can you tell about tabs and FactBoxes? How do you proceed if you want to edit the vendor? Is there an option to edit multiple vendors in this form?

Exercise 2.4 – Inserting Records

Create a new vendor with the name "##-Exercise 2.4 Inc." (## = your user ID) and any vendor group of your choice. Do not use record templates in this exercise.

Notes: If the number sequence for vendor accounts is set to "Manual", you have to enter the vendor number manually. If the sales tax group or the tax-exempt number (VAT registration number) is mandatory according to the settings in the Accounts payable parameters, switch to the tab *Invoice and delivery* in the Vendor form and enter the required information.

Exercise 2.5 – Lookup Fields

You want to assign a *Buyer group* to the vendor of exercise 2.4. In the lookup of the corresponding field on the tab *Miscellaneous details* in the Vendor form, you notice that the required group is not there. Create the buyer group B-## (## = your user ID) with the *View details* option and select this group for the vendor.

Exercise 2.6 – Filtering

In order to get practice with filtering, enter the filters given below in the Vendor list page. Use the quick filter and the grid column filter for the first and the second filter task. For the other filter tasks, use the filter pane and the advanced filter.

Filter on following criteria one after another and clear the filter after each task:

➢ All vendors with a name which starts with "T".
➢ All vendors assigned to the vendor group that you have selected in exercise 2.4.
➢ All vendors with a name which contains "in".
➢ Vendors with a number from US-101 to US-103 or higher than US-108
  (use a similar filter if these vendor accounts do not exist).
➢ Vendors with a number that ends with "1" and a name which contains "of".
➢ Vendors with an "e" on the second character of the name.
➢ Vendors with a name which does not start with "C".

Once you have completed these filter tasks, open the advanced filter and select all vendors who are not assigned to the *Terms of payment* "Net 30 days".

2.2   Printing and Reporting

Depending on the requirements, you have got several options for viewing and analyzing data. These options include the Dynamics 365 standard reports, the Microsoft Office integration, and the Business Intelligence tools (including Microsoft Power BI).

2.2.1   Printing Documents

In Dynamics 365, there are the following options for printing:

> **Print browser pages** – Print any list page or form as a web page with the page printing features of your browser.
> **Download report previews** – Print a report to the screen (print preview) and export a PDF or Word file from the preview.
> **Print reports directly** – Send a report directly to a local or network printer.

Printing a Dynamics 365 page (that is the content currently shown in the browser) from the browser, which works like printing any other web page, does not require print settings in Dynamics 365. The print layout may be different in different browsers (Microsoft Edge, Google Chrome, or other).

Standard reports in Dynamics 365 are formatted documents which are generated with the Microsoft SQL Server Reporting Services (SSRS). When you print a standard report, you can either download a PDF/Word file from the print preview or send the document directly to a local printer or a network printer. If you want to send documents directly to a printer, the *Document Routing Agent* has to be installed and configured.

2.2.1.1   Network Printer Setup

In a cloud hosted Dynamics 365 environment, the Document Reporting Services that are required to print standard reports, are hosted in Microsoft Azure. If you want to connect your printers to the Azure services, you have to install the *Document Routing Agent* on one or more computers/servers in your network.

You can download the *Document Routing Agent* from the Network printer form (*Organization administration> Setup> Network printers*). Click the button *Options/ Application/Download document routing agent installer* in this form and install the *Document Routing Agent*. Then open the document routing agent and click the button *Settings* in the toolbar of the routing agent. In the settings, enter the *Dynamics 365 URL* (web address of your Dynamics 365 application) and the *Azure AD Tenant* (tenant of your organization in the Azure Active Directory) before you click the button *OK* and *Sign In*. Finally, click the button *Printers* and put a checkmark in front of the printers which you want to use in Dynamics 365.

The Network printer form then shows the printers which have been enabled by one or more *Document Routing Agents*. In Edit mode, select the option "Yes" in the column *Active* of this form for all printers which should be available in the current company.

2.2.1.2   Printing Standard Reports

In the Dynamics 365 modules, the standard reports are included in the folder *Inquiries and reports*. In addition, some list pages and detail forms contain buttons to start particular standard reports – you can, for example, print a customer account statement with the button *Collect/Customer balances/Statements* in the Customer list page (*Accounts receivable> Customers> All customers*).

If you start a standard report in the menu, or in a list page or detail form, the report dialog, in which you can specify filter criteria and the print destination, is shown first. In the example of Figure 2-20, you can view the dialog of the report in the menu item *Accounts receivable> Inquiries and reports> Customers> Customer report* with a filter on the customer group.

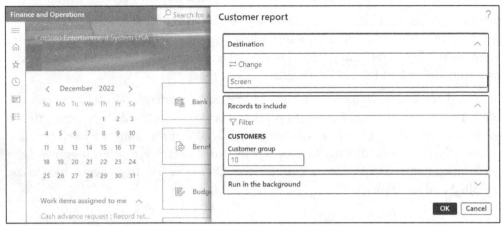

Figure 2-20:   Report dialog for the customer report

It is not possible to enter filter criteria directly in the report dialog. Click the button *Filter* on the tab *Records to include* of the report dialog to open a filter dialog for this purpose. The filter dialog for reports works similar to the advanced filter in list pages and detail forms. Apart from filter criteria on the tab *Range*, there is the option to enter sorting criteria on the tab *Sorting*. Once you close the filter dialog, the selected filter is shown in the report dialog.

On the tab *Destination* of the report dialog, the button *Change* opens the *Print destination* dialog, in which you can select the destination for the printout:

➢ **Print archive** – Saves the report selection to the print archive.
➢ **Screen** – Shows a report preview on the screen.
➢ **Printer** – Prints the report on the selected printer (available printers are specified in the Network printer form as described above).
➢ **File** – Downloads the report to a CSV, Excel, Word, HTML, XML, or PDF file.
➢ **E-mail** – Sends the report to an e-mail recipient.

Once you have entered the print destination and the filter criteria in the report dialog, click the button *OK* to print the report. The settings in the report dialog are automatically stored in your user options and initialize the report dialog when you print the selected report again. You can change the filter criteria and the print destination as required then.

2.2.1.3 Print Preview

If you select the option "Screen" as the print destination, Dynamics 365 will show a print preview.

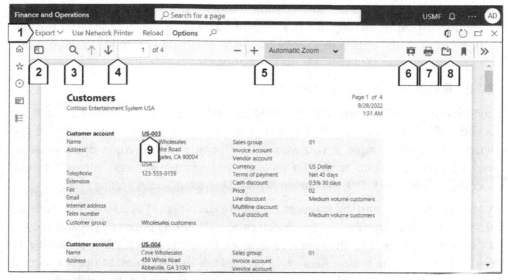

Figure 2-21: Elements in the print preview

The preview contains the following elements (see Figure 2-21):

➢ **Export** [1] – Export the preview to different file formats (PDF, Excel, Word, CSV, XML, HTML, TIFF).
➢ **Show sidebar** [2] – Overview of the content of the report.
➢ **Find** [3] – Search text in the report.
➢ **Switch page** [4] – Enter the page number, or click the button for the previous page ⬆ or the next page ⬇.
➢ **Zoom** [5] – Zoom in and out.
➢ **Presentation mode** [6] – Switch to the presentation mode.
➢ **Print** [7] – Send the preview to a local printer of your client.
➢ **Download** [8] – Download a PDF file of the preview.
➢ **Link** [9] – Link to the detail form of the particular field.

2.2.1.4 Print Archive

The print archive provides the option to save a report within Dynamics 365. If you want to save a report to the archive, select the print archive as the destination in the *Print destination* dialog or – if you choose a different destination – set the slider *Save in print archive* in the *Print destination* dialog to "Yes".

When saving to the archive, the report is stored in the print archive. The form *Common> Inquiries> Print archive* shows your print archive and provides the option to reprint the report later. If you want to access the print archives of all users, open the menu item *Organization administration> Inquiries and reports> Print archive*.

2.2.1.5 Post and Print

When you post an external document (e.g., an invoice or a packing slip), you need a printout in many cases. For this reason, there is a parameter for printing the corresponding document in most posting dialogs – for example, the slider *Print invoice* in the posting dialog for sales invoices. The button *Printer setup* in posting dialogs provides the option to specify the print destination (similar to the options when printing a standard report from the menu).

2.2.1.6 Reprinting and Batch Processing

If printing a posted document is required at a later time (e.g., if you have not set the slider *Print* to "Yes" when posting), you can print it from the inquiry of the document. As an example, if you want to (re-)print a sales invoice, open the sales invoice journal (*Accounts receivable> Inquiries and reports> Invoices> Invoice journal*), select the invoice, and click the button *Invoice/Document/View/Original preview*.

If you want to run a particular report (or a periodic activity) at a later time and not immediately, you can submit it to a batch process. For this purpose, expand the tab *Run in the background* in the report dialog and set the slider *Batch processing* to "Yes". Then click the button *Recurrence* on this tab in the dialog to open a second dialog, in which you can enter the start time and repetitions for the batch job.

As a prerequisite for batch processing, at least one batch server has to be set up in the server configuration (*System administration> Setup> Server configuration*). If you want to categorize batch jobs, you can use batch groups (*System administration> Setup> Batch group*).

You can check and edit the status of batch jobs in the menu item *System administration> Inquiries> Batch jobs*.

2.2.2 Microsoft Office Integration

The Microsoft Office integration in Dynamics 365 makes it easy to exchange data between Dynamics 365 and Office. There are two options for this data exchange:

➢ **Static export** – Export data from Dynamics 365 to Microsoft Excel.
➢ **Opening and editing** – Update Dynamics 365 data from Microsoft Office.

Apart from the standard workbooks for updating Dynamics 365 data from Office, you can use your own Excel workbooks to edit Dynamics 365 data in Excel.

In addition to the Microsoft Office integration, there are export and import features in the Data management workspace, especially for regular data export and import.

2.2.2.1 Static Export to Excel

The static export to Microsoft Excel supports copying data from the grid of a list page or detail form to an Excel sheet. Any update of data in the Excel sheet has no impact on the data in Dynamics 365.

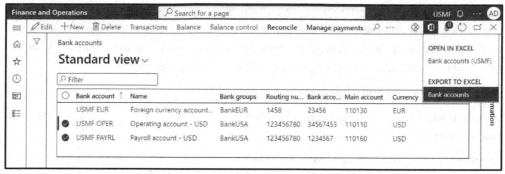

Figure 2-22:   Starting the export to Excel

In order to execute a static export, open the respective page in Dynamics 365 and select the lines which you want to export. If you want to select all lines, select the checkbox on the left in the grid header or do not select any line (if no line is explicitly selected, it also means all lines). Then click the button 🗋 (*Open in Microsoft Office*) / *Export to Excel* in the action pane (see Figure 2-22), or select the option *Export marked rows* in the context menu which you can access with a right-click on the grid header. In the next step, the *Export to Excel* dialog is shown. In this dialog, select to download the Excel file to your local computer, or to save it to OneDrive or SharePoint.

Note: By default, you can export 50,000 rows, but the limit can be increased in the Client performance options form.

2.2.2.2 Opening Data in Excel

Unlike the static export, which you can only use to retrieve data from Dynamics 365, the option *Open in Microsoft Office* enables the use of Excel to update Dynamics 365 data from Excel.

In order to start editing data with Excel, open the relevant list page or detail form in Dynamics 365. Then click the button 🗋 (*Open in Microsoft Office*) in the action pane and select the appropriate option in the button group *Open in Excel*. Some forms, for example the general journals (*General ledger> Journal entries> General journals*), also contain a dedicated button in the action pane for editing in Excel.

The *Open in Excel* dialog is shown next. Select to download the Excel file to your computer, or to save it to OneDrive or SharePoint (like in the static export).

Microsoft Excel, which shows up next, includes the *Data Connector* in the task pane. You have to sign in with your Azure Active Directory account in the Data Connector before you can retrieve data. Once the Dynamics 365 data are shown, you can edit the records and – with the button *New* in the Data Connector – insert additional records. If required, you can temporarily work offline in Excel.

If you want to retrieve current data from Dynamics 365, including new lines with new records, click the button *Refresh* in the Excel Data Connector. In order to transfer data from Excel to Dynamics 365, click the button *Publish*. If the Excel workbook contains incorrect data, an error message in the Excel Data Connector will show the issue and prevent the update. You can click the icon ▣ at the bottom of the Data Connector to view the details of the error message.

2.2.2.3 Document Templates for Excel Integration

In addition to the standard Excel worksheets in Dynamics 365, you can create and use your own Excel workbooks to update Dynamics 365 data.

In order to create such an Excel workbook, open the Excel workbook designer (*Common> Common> Office integration> Excel workbook designer*) and select the Dynamics 365 table which you want to edit in Excel. In the workbook designer, move the fields, which should be included in the Excel workbook, from the pane *Available fields* to the pane *Selected fields*. Then click the button *Create workbook* in the action pane to open a dialog in which you select whether to export the Excel workbook to your local computer, or to OneDrive, or to SharePoint. After logging in to the Excel Data Connector, you can update Dynamics 365 data from the new worksheet (like in a Dynamics 365 standard worksheet described above).

You can save the Excel worksheet and upload it as document template if you want to make it available as an additional option in the button ▣ (*Open in Microsoft Office*) of the related Dynamics 365 form. Open the document templates (*Common> Common> Office integration> Document templates*) for this purpose, click the button *New* in the action pane, and upload the Excel file which you have saved before.

2.2.3   Case Study Exercise

Exercise 2.7 – Printing

Print a vendor list (*Accounts payable> Inquiries and reports> Vendor reports> Vendors*) and select the print preview as the print destination.

Then close the print preview and print the vendor list again. Filter on any vendor group of your choice and select a PDF-file as the print destination this time.

2.3   Advanced Options

In addition to the core options in the user interface, the personalization features and settings in the user options help working efficiently in Dynamics 365.

2.3.1   User Options

The user options contain the individual personal settings for the user interface, which are stored for each user.

2.3.1.1 Settings in the User Options

If you want to access your user options, click the button ⚙ (*Settings*) / *User options* in the navigation bar, or open the menu item *Common> Setup> User options* (with appropriate permissions). Administrators can manage the user options of all users in the user management (*System administration> Users> Users*, button *User options*).

The section *Preferences* in the User options form (see Figure 2-23) contains the following main settings for the user environment:

➤ **Company** – Company which you access when logging on.
➤ **Default view/edit mode** – Personal option to set the Read mode or the Edit mode as the default mode for all pages and forms.
➤ **Language** – Language of the user interface.
➤ **Date, time, and number format** – Personal setting for the display format of date and number fields.
➤ **Country/region** – Default for the country/region when entering an address.
➤ **Document handling** – See section 10.5.1.

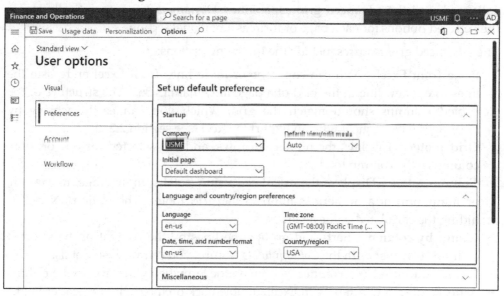

Figure 2-23: Managing preferences in the User options form

In addition, you can choose an element size and a color theme in the section *Visual*, and settings for workflow management (see section 10.4) in the section *Workflow*.

2.3.1.2 Usage Data

In order to access the Usage data form with detailed settings of the particular user, click the button *Usage data* in the action pane of the user options. The usage data, which have been stored automatically or manually, include filter settings, form settings, and record templates (user templates).

In the usage data, switch from the section *General* to the other sections if you want to view the usage data of a particular area. The button *Data* provides access to the details of the selected record in the usage data. It is not possible to modify usage data, but with the button *Delete* or the shortcut *Alt+Del* you can delete usage data records. The button *Reset* in the section *General* deletes all usage data of the user.

2.3.2   Personalization and Saved Views

Apart from modifications in the development environment that affect all users, changes of the user interface are also possible at a personal level. For this purpose, each user with appropriate permissions can adjust list pages and forms according to the personal preferences.

2.3.2.1   Restricted Personalization and Advanced Grid Capabilities

At the restricted personalization access level, available options include the change of the column width (drag and drop the borders in the grid header), the settings whether the action pane, the tabs, and the FactBoxes are shown in full size or collapsed, and the advanced grid capabilities. Dynamics 365 automatically stores the selected options for each page or form as a personal setting.

The advanced grid features include the following options:

➢ **Paste from Excel** – You can copy one or more lines from Excel and paste the lines into a new line in the grid of a page in Dynamics 365. The structure of the copied columns should match the grid, which you can easily achieve by creating the Excel sheet with an Export to Excel (see section 2.2.2).

➢ **Grid footer** – Displays the number of rows, and – if selected for one or more columns – the column totals.

➢ **Column totals** – Displays the calculated value (total sum, average, maximum, or minimum) of a numeric column in the grid footer. The option "None" is hiding the calculated value again.

➢ **Group by column** – Sorts and groups the lines by the content of the selected column. Together with the *Column totals* feature, you can view subtotals.

➢ **Freeze column** – Keep columns shown on the left when you scroll to the right.

➢ **Autofit column width** – As in Excel, double-click on the right in a header field.

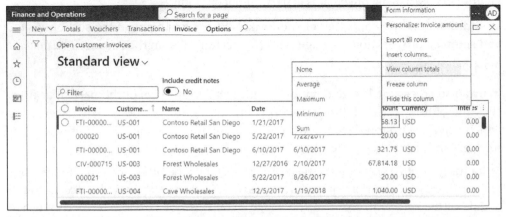

Figure 2-24:   Selecting to *View column totals* in a grid (right-click on the column header)

In order to display or to hide the **Grid footer**, click the button ⊞ (*Grid options*) on the very right in the grid header and select the option *Show footer*. The footer is automatically shown if you select to show column totals.

If you want to use the features which refer to a particular column (**Column totals, Group by column, Freeze column**), right-click the column header field and select the respective option in the drop-down menu (see Figure 2-24).

Note: Before version 10.0.29, the sum is the only option for column totals.

2.3.2.2 Full Personalization

If you need enhanced options to adjust a form according to your preferences, you can use the personalization window and the personalization toolbar (see Figure 2-25). The personalization options are available in each list page, detail form, workspace, and dashboard.

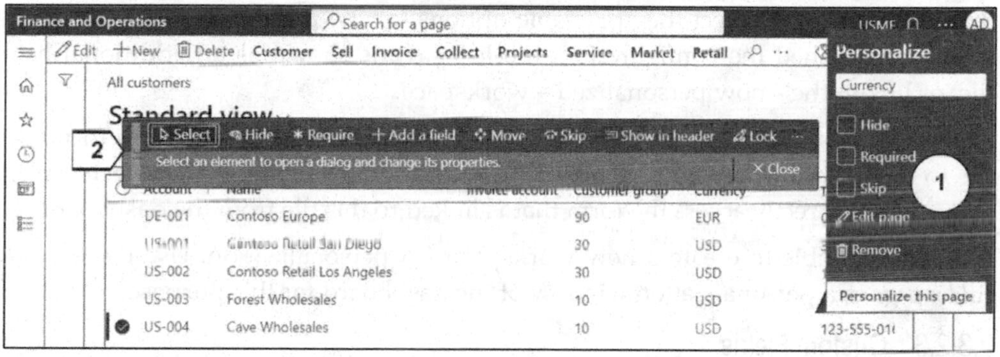

Figure 2-25: Viewing the personalization window [1] and the personalization toolbar [2]

In order to access the personalization window, select the option *Personalize* in the context menu of an element – you can open the context menu with a right-click on an element label (e.g., a field label), or with the shortcut *Ctrl+F10*. In the personalization window of the element (field or button), you can override several standard settings – for example, by entering a personal field label, by hiding the element, or by setting a field as mandatory.

The personalization toolbar, which you can access with the link *Personalize this page* in the personalization window or with the button *Options/Personalize/Personalize this page* in the action pane, provides additional personalization options.

In order to adjust a form with the personalization toolbar, click the applicable button in the personalization toolbar first and then select the element (field, field group, tab, button) which you want to personalize. The personalization toolbar includes the button *Select* (show the personalization window for the selected element), *Hide* (hide the element from the page), *Require* (designate a required data entry for the field), *Add a field* (show one or more additional fields), *Move* (change the location of the element), *Skip* (skip in the tab sequence), *Show in header* (in forms with tabs, show the field as summary field on the tab), and *Lock* (prevent editing).

When you click a button in the personalization toolbar, the next step is to click on the element (field or button in the page) on which you want to execute the action. If you click the button *Add a field*, select the page area to which you want to add the field first. Then select the respective field (adding multiple fields is possible) in the dialog that is shown next.

Settings in the personalization apply immediately. If you click the button ▦ (*More*) on the right of the personalization toolbar, you can access the option to reset the form to the standard layout (button *Clear*) or to import/export a personalization.

Apart from changing the layout of list pages and detail forms, personalization also allows adding a list page to a workspace. For this purpose, click the button *Options/ Personalize/Add to workspace* in the action pane of the list page which you want to add, and select the appropriate *Workspace* and *Presentation* (tile, list, or link) in the related drop-down menu before you click the button *Configure* there. In the dialog that is shown next, select the applicable options for the presentation layout. Once you have finished the configuration, the list page is shown as an additional list, tile, or link in the – now personalized – workspace.

In workspaces, the personalization window for tiles includes the option to pin a tile to the dashboard. Your dashboard then additionally contains the selected tile, and you can directly access the form that is linked to this tile from the dashboard.

It is also possible to create a new workspace via personalization. Use the option *Add a page* in a personalization window of the dashboard for this purpose.

2.3.2.3 Custom Fields

In addition to the adjustment of the layout of the user interface, the personalization includes the option to create new fields for a form. The dialog for adding fields, which you can open with the button *Add a field* in the personalization toolbar, includes the button *Create new field* for this purpose (see Figure 2-26).

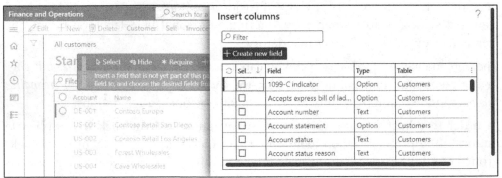

Figure 2-26:   Creating a new field with the personalization

If you click this button, a second dialog is shown in which you enter the *Table name*, *Name prefix*, *Type*, and *Label* for the new field. Once you confirm the update, the new field is included in the *Insert fields* personalization dialog of the list page or detail form which you have started to personalize.

You can manage all custom fields in the menu item *System administration> Setup> Custom fields* (select the relevant *Table* in the list pane on the left).

If other users should have access to the new field, they have to use personalized views. For this purpose, it is also possible to publish, export/import saved views.

2.3.2.4 Saved Views

With the Saved views feature, you can store multiple personalized versions of a page or form as personalized views, and distribute these views to other users.

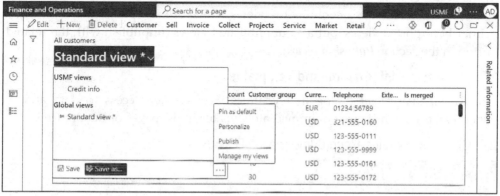

Figure 2-27:   Changing and managing personal views

When you access a form in Dynamics 365, the *Standard view* is the general default for the view name which determines the screen layout. A click on the view name (in Figure 2-27, the default *Standard view*) opens the View selector lookup in which you can select a different view.

If you personalize or filter a form, an asterisk (*) appears next to the current view name. In case you want to use the modified view again at a later time, either save the changes to the current view name (click the button *Save* in the View selector) or to a new view name (click the button *Save as*). When saving to a new name, a dialog is shown in which you can enter the name, a short description, and optionally set the slider *Pin as default view* (personal default) to "Yes". The section *Legal entity access* in this dialog provides the option to select whether the new view should be available in all, or only in selected companies.

With the button ⊡ / *Manage my views* in the View selector, you can change the initial settings later on. If you want to make a view available for others and got appropriate permissions, click the button *Publish* to release the view at the level of user roles (security roles, see section 10.2.2).

2.3.2.5 Personalization Setup and Management

In the personalization setup (*System administration> Setup> Personalization*), settings in the section *System settings* control whether personalization is allowed in general. In the section *User settings*, there is the option to override the general settings at the level of individual users.

The section *Personal views* contains the views which have been created by the users. With the buttons in the toolbar above the grid, you can *Publish, Export,* or *Delete* the personal views. If you want to import exported views, click the button *Import views* in the action pane.

In the section *Published views*, you can manage all views which are published. The section *Unpublished views* contains the views which are not published currently – primarily imported views, but also unpublished views (unpublish with the related button in the section *Published views*).

2.3.3 Record Information and Templates

The *Record information* dialog in Dynamics 365 provides access to data and to general features which are not immediately visible in list pages or detail forms.

2.3.3.1 Options in the Record Information Dialog

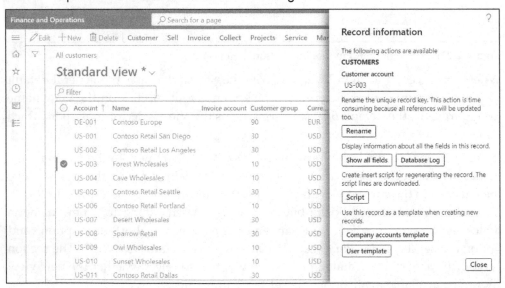

Figure 2-28: The *Record information* dialog in the Customer list page

In order to open the *Record information* for a record in a list page or detail form, select the record and click the button *Options/Page options/Record info*. In the *Record information* dialog that is shown next, you can select to execute the following actions on the selected record:

➢ **Rename** – Change the content of the key field in the current record.

➢ **Show all fields** and **Database log** – View detail data of the current record.

> **Script** – Create an insert script with data of the current record.
> **Company accounts template** and **User template** – Create a record template.

Note: Depending on your permissions and the Dynamics 365 configuration, not all of these options are available.

2.3.3.2 Renaming

The button *Rename* in the *Record information* dialog provides the option to change the content of the key field of the selected record. Renaming opens a second dialog, in which you enter the new field value (e.g., the new customer number).

Processing a request for renaming can be a time-consuming activity. The reason is that all references to the record in Dynamics 365 are updated in parallel. If you modify, for example, a customer number, the update does not only include the customer table itself, but also the customer transactions, the sales orders, and all other tables which contain the customer number. You should take into account, that the update only includes references within Dynamics 365. Other applications and external partners (e.g., customers) have to execute the update separately.

For this reason, renaming is an exceptional activity which should be coordinated with the system administrator, and which is usually secured by appropriate permission settings.

2.3.3.3 Show All Fields and the Database Log

The button *Show all fields* in the *Record information* dialog displays the content of all fields of the selected record. You can use this feature if you want to know the content of table fields which are not shown in the regular interface of a particular list page or detail form.

The button *Database log* in the *Record information* dialog opens a log file which shows the updates on the selected record. As a prerequisite, logging for the particular table has to be enabled in the menu item *System administration> Setup> Database log> Database log setup*.

2.3.3.4 Record Templates

Based on the record which you have selected when accessing the *Record information* dialog, you can set up a template. If you subsequently create a new record in the original form, you can select this (or another) template to initialize the record with the content of the template. You can, for example, set up a template for domestic vendors and a template for foreign vendors in the Vendor form to initialize new vendors with correct posting groups.

Within the record templates, you can distinguish the following types:

> **User templates** – Only available to the current user.
> **Company accounts templates** – Available to all users.

A user template is only available to the user who has created the template. You can create a user template with the button *User template* in the *Record information* dialog. In a second dialog, enter the name and a short description of the template. The new template is a copy of the record which you have selected when opening the *Record information* dialog.

User templates are stored in your usage data, and it is not possible to modify them. If a user template is not required anymore, you can delete it in the usage data. For this purpose, click the button ⚙ (*Settings*) / *User options* in the navigation bar, then click the button *Usage data* in the user options, and in the usage data switch to the section *Record templates*. Alternatively, you can delete a user template with the shortcut *Alt+Del* or *Alt+F9* in the *Template selection* dialog shown in Figure 2-29.

Company accounts templates, unlike user templates, are available to all users. You can create a company accounts template with the button *Company accounts template* in the *Record information* dialog.

If you want to view or modify a company accounts template later, open the menu item *Common> Setup> Record templates*. On the tab *Overview* in the Record template form, select the table to which the template refers. Then switch to the tab *Templates*, in which you can edit or delete the template.

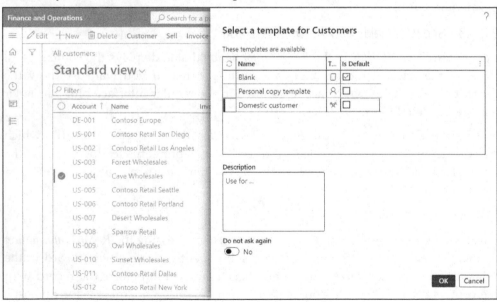

Figure 2-29:   Selecting a template in the *Template selection* dialog

If there are record templates for a particular form, they are shown in a *Template selection* dialog whenever you create a record in this form. Figure 2-29 shows the *Template selection* dialog which is displayed when you create a customer in the Customer form (in case there is a customer template).

In the *Template selection* dialog, select the appropriate template and click the button *OK* to apply it to the new record. You can recognize company accounts templates by the icon ▣ and user templates by the icon ▣. If you do not want to apply a template, select the template "Blank". In the column on the right of the template selection, you can optionally select a template which you want to make the default template. If you set the slider *Do not ask again* at the bottom of the *Template selection* dialog to "Yes", the default template is automatically used without showing the template selection dialog when inserting further records. If you want to view the template selection dialog when creating new records again, click the button *Show template selection* which is displayed in the *Record information* dialog in this case.

2.3.4   Case Study Exercises

Exercise 2.8 – User Options

Review the username and other settings in your user options. In the visual options, select the high-contrast color theme and the small element size. Then select the training company as the company which you access when you log on.

Exercise 2.9 – Record Templates

Set up a user template which is based on the vendor of exercise 2.4. Then create a new vendor with default data from this template.

2.4   Global Address Book

Dynamics 365 contains a common table with all business partners of your enterprise – internal and external relationships, companies and persons. This common table is the global address book. Business partners are called "Parties" in the global address book. They are shared across companies and include customers, sales leads, vendors, organization units, employees, and other contacts.

2.4.1   Parties and Addresses

Whenever you create a new customer, vendor, or any other kind of party, Dynamics 365 inserts a corresponding record in the global address book. A party, which may contain one or more (postal) addresses and contact data, is not the same as an address – it is an organization or person characterized by its name.

2.4.1.1 Creating Parties in the Global Address Book

Depending on permission settings, you can manage all parties in the Global address book list page (*Common> Common> Global address book*).

In order to insert a party in the Global address book page, click the button *New* in the action pane. In the new party, the *Party ID* derives from the corresponding number sequence. The party type (lookup field *Type*) with the options "Organization" and "Person" controls the fields which are displayed in the Party form (e.g., the field *First name* is only shown for persons).

Enter the party name in the field *Name* (for an organization) or in the fields *First name* and *Last name* (for a person) before you register additional data, including the postal address on the tab *Addresses* and contact data like e-mail addresses and phone numbers on the tab *Contact information*. Section 3.2.1 in this book contains – on the example of the vendor management – more details on how to manage postal addresses and contact data.

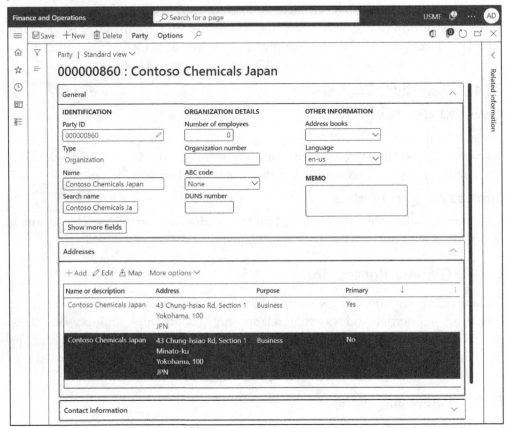

Figure 2-30:   Managing a party with multiple addresses in the Party detail form

2.4.1.2 Indirectly Creating Parties

Apart from directly creating a party in the global address book, you can indirectly create a party by entering a customer, a vendor, or any other kind of party in any module. In all forms, in which parties are created indirectly, the field *Name* is a lookup field in which you can search an existing party. If you select a party in this field, this party receives an additional role. If you do not select a party, but type a new name, Dynamics 365 creates a new party with this name automatically.

If you insert a new customer in the Customer form and <u>type a name</u> in the lookup field *Name* of the *Create* dialog, a new party is created. However, if you <u>select a party</u> in the lookup field *Name*, the new role "Customer" is assigned to this party.

Since a party may already exist in the global address book (e.g., if a customer is already a vendor in your or an affiliated company within a common Dynamics 365 environment), you should – in order to avoid duplicate parties – check the existing parties before creating a new party. In case the duplicate check is activated in the Global address book parameters, and you enter a duplicate party anyhow, a confirmation dialog shows the existing party before saving the new party.

2.4.1.3 Internal Organizations

Apart from external organizations and persons, internal organizations (e.g., operating units and legal entities, see section 10.1.2) are also parties in the global address book. You can recognize internal organizations by the party type (e.g., "Legal entities"). The related party types are reserved for internal organizations and not included in the options when entering a party in the global address book.

2.4.2   Address Books

An address book is a collection of party records. You can set up one or more address books in the menu item *Organization administration> Global address book> Address books* – for example, one address book for sales and one for purchasing.

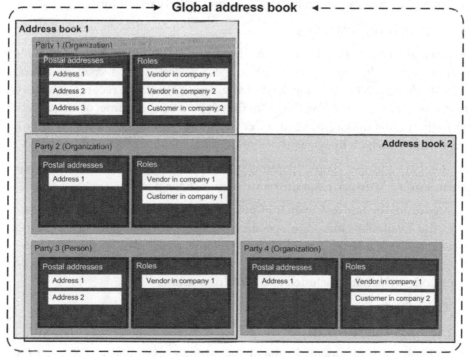

Figure 2-31:   Conceptual structure of the global address book

Independent of the individual address books, the global address book is the collection of all parties in all companies within a Dynamics 365 environment (see Figure 2-31).

If you want to link a party to one or more address books, open the lookup of the field *Address books* on the tab *General* in the Party detail form and put a checkmark in front of the applicable address books.

You can use address books for searching and filtering parties (e.g., with the filter field *Address books* in the Global address book list page), and as a basis for security settings (restrict accessing the parties of an address books, see section 10.1.2).

2.4.2.1 Party Roles

A party role – e.g., "Vendor" or "Customer" – describes the relationship between your enterprise and the party. A party can be assigned to one or more roles in one or more companies. There are two ways of assigning a role to a party:

➢ **Indirectly** – Entering a record in other areas (e.g., a customer in the Customer form) automatically creates a party with the corresponding role in the global address book.

➢ **Directly** – Buttons in the Global address book form (e.g., *Party/New/Customer*) create a record in the selected area (e.g., a customer record) and assign the corresponding role to the selected party.

The roles of a party are shown on the tab *Roles* in the Party detail form.

2.4.2.2 Address Book Parameters

If the duplicate check is activated in the Global address book parameters (*Organization administration> Global address book> Global address book parameters*, slider *Use duplicate check*), a dialog is showing duplicate party records whenever you try to create a party (directly or indirectly) with the name of an already existing party. In this dialog, you can select whether to use the existing party or to create a new party, which by chance has got the same name as the existing party.

Further Global address book parameters include the default party type ("Organization" or "Person") and the name sequence for persons (first/last name).

Settings regarding the address format of postal addresses, the available ZIP/postal codes, or the available cities, are specified in the address setup (*Organization administration> Global address book> Addresses> Address setup*). The section *Parameters* in the Address setup form contains the setting whether you can only enter ZIP/postal codes which are included in the address setup.

2.4.3   Case Study Exercise

Exercise 2.10 – Global Address Book

In order to learn the functionality of the global address book, check if you can find the party that is assigned to the vendor of exercise 2.4.

Then insert a new party with the name "##-Exercise 2.10" (## = your user ID) and a postal address in London. This new party becomes a vendor in your company later on. What do you do in Dynamics 365?

3   Purchase Management

The primary responsibility of purchasing is to manage the supply of goods and services from vendors. The related process includes the following activities:

➢ Determine material requirements
➢ Process purchase requisitions, requests for quotations, and purchase orders
➢ Post item receipts and purchase invoices

3.1   Business Processes in Purchasing

Before we start to go into details, the lines below give an overview of the business processes in purchasing.

3.1.1   Basic Approach

As a prerequisite for procurement, correct master data are required – in particular the vendor and the product data. For purchased services and non-inventoried commodities, it is possible to use procurement categories instead of products.

3.1.1.1   Master Data and Transactions in Purchasing

Vendors and products are master data, which are created once and only occasionally updated later. In the course of the purchasing process, planned and actual purchase orders (transaction data) receive default values from vendor and product records (master data). You can override these data in the transaction – for example, if you agree to special payment terms in a particular purchase order.

If you modify data in a transaction, it does not update the related master data. If you agree with a vendor on some general changes, for example on new payment terms, you have to update the vendor record accordingly.

Based on correct master data, the purchasing process – along with the required predecessor and successor activities – includes the steps shown in Figure 3-1.

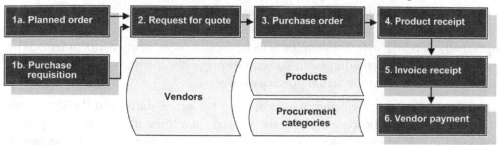

Figure 3-1:   Purchase order processing in Dynamics 365

© Springer Fachmedien Wiesbaden GmbH, part of Springer Nature 2023
A. Luszczak, *Using Microsoft Dynamics 365 for Finance and Operations*,
https://doi.org/10.1007/978-3-658-40453-6_3

3.1.1.2 Material Requirement, Purchase Requisition, and Request for Quotation

Determining the material requirements is the starting point for the purchasing process. Depending on the particular product and on the business processes, there are two alternative origins for purchase orders:

➢ **Planned orders** – Generated automatically from known demand within Dynamics 365 (e.g., sales orders, forecasts, or materials for production).
➢ **Purchase requisitions** – Entered manually for other demand.

Planned orders, which are generated in master planning (see section 6.3), require accurate figures on inventory quantity, sales orders, purchase orders, and forecasts. In addition, appropriate item coverage settings are necessary.

Purchase requisitions are internal documents which ask the procurement department to purchase specific items (like consumables and office supplies). Unlike planned orders, which are created automatically, requisitions are entered manually by the person who needs the material or service. A requisition runs through an approval workflow before it is released to a purchase order.

Requests for quotation are sent to vendors to receive information on prices and delivery times. The purchasing department enters requests for quotation manually, or generates them from planned purchase orders or purchase requisitions.

3.1.1.3 Purchase Order

You can create purchase orders either automatically (from planned orders, purchase requisitions, or requests for quotation) or manually.

A purchase order consists of a header, which contains the common data of the whole order (e.g., the vendor data), and one or more lines, which contain the ordered items. Once you have completed the order entry, you have to start the approval workflow (in case change management is active). If change management is not active, the order immediately gets the status "Approved". After approval, you can optionally post a purchase inquiry and send it to the vendor so that he can validate and confirm it.

Before you can continue with order processing and the product receipt, you have to post a purchase order confirmation. Posting the confirmation means to save it, optionally sending it to the vendor (electronically or as printed document). The purchase order confirmation is stored with its original content, no matter if there is a later modification of the actual purchase order.

The status of a purchase order is indicated by the order status and the document status in the order header, and by the posted quantities in the lines. Inquiries, workspace information, and periodic reports provide the option to recognize issues like late shipments.

3.1.1.4   Product Receipt, Vendor Invoice, and Vendor Payment

Once you receive the items or services, you need to record the product receipt. Posting the product receipt reduces the open quantity in the purchase order and increases – for inventoried items – the physical quantity in inventory.

The invoice from the vendor arrives together with the items or at a later time. When you register the invoice in the Pending vendor invoice form, invoice control features support matching the invoice with the purchase order and the product receipt. If an invoice does not refer to a purchase order, you can enter it in an invoice journal or in the Pending vendor invoice form (see section 9.3.2).

After posting the invoice, you can record a payment to the vendor manually or as a result of a payment proposal. The calculation of payment proposals is based on the due date and the cash discount period. Payment processing is independent of purchase orders and usually a responsibility of the finance department. You can find a description on vendor payments in section 9.3.3 of this book.

3.1.1.5   Ledger Integration and Voucher Principle

Based on the deep integration of finance with the business processes in all areas of Dynamics 365, the inventory and vendor transactions in purchasing are posted to ledger accounts as specified in the setup (see section 9.4).

In order to keep track of the whole business process, Dynamics 365 comprehensively applies the voucher principle to transactions: You have to register a transaction in a document (voucher) before you can post it. After posting, it is not possible to modify the document anymore. Figure 3-2 gives an overview of the documents in purchase order processing.

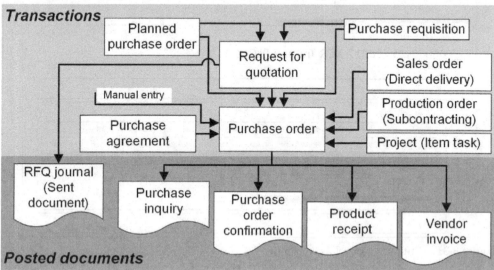

Figure 3-2:   Transactions and posted documents in purchasing

3.1.2   At a Glance: Purchase Order Processing

The following example demonstrates the main steps in purchase order processing. It starts with creating the order in the workspace *Purchase order preparation* and shows all transactions directly in the Purchase order form. Alternatively, you can create the order from the Vendor form, or directly in the Purchase order list page.

In the workspace *Purchase order preparation*, which you can access from the dashboard or from the Procurement and sourcing module, click the button *New purchase order* in the action pane to create an order. In the *Create purchase order* dialog which is shown next, select a vendor in the field *Vendor account* (you can trigger the search in this field by typing the first characters of the vendor name) before you click the button *OK*. Dynamics 365 then creates an order header with default data (e.g., for the language and the currency) from the selected vendor and opens the Purchase order detail form in the Lines view.

If you are in Read mode, click the button *Edit* or press the *F2* key to switch to the Edit mode. Then enter the first order line with the item number, the quantity, and the price on the tab *Purchase order lines*. When you select the item, the quantity, the price, and other fields are initialized with default values from the item. If you want to enter another line, press the *Down Arrow* key or click the button *Add line* in the toolbar of the lines. The button *Header* (or *Lines*) below the action pane provides the option to switch between the Lines view (see Figure 3-3) and the Header view.

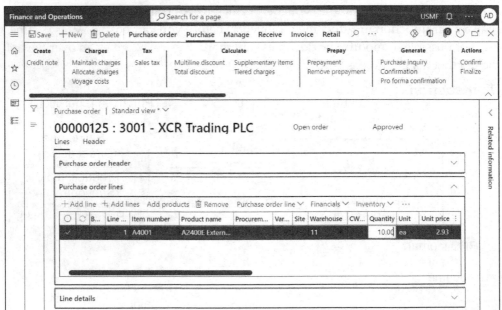

Figure 3-3:   Entering a purchase order line

If change management is activated, the *Approval status* (shown on the right above the header) is "Draft" after entering the order. In an order with this status, click the button *Workflow/Submit* (shown in the action pane then) and process the approval.

Then click the button *Purchase/Generate/Confirmation* in the action pane to post the purchase order confirmation. If you want to print the purchase order, do not only set the slider *Posting* in the posting dialog to "Yes", but also the slider *Print purchase order*. The button *Printer setup* in the dialog provides the option to select a printer for the printout (see section 2.2.1).

Figure 3-4:   Confirming and printing the purchase order

When you receive the item, click the button *Receive/Generate/Product receipt* in the purchase order to post the product receipt. Posting the receipt works similar to the purchase order confirmation described above. But unlike an order confirmation, a product receipt usually is not printed. If there is no prior item arrival registration, select the option "Ordered quantity" in the lookup field *Quantity* and enter the vendor's packing slip number in the column *Product receipt* on the tab *Overview* of the posting dialog before you click the button *OK*. The product receipt increases the physical quantity in inventory and updates the order status to "Received".

If you want to post the vendor invoice directly from the Purchase order form, click the button *Invoice/Generate/Invoice* in this form. With an action pane and FactBoxes, the form for vendor invoice posting is different from the other posting dialogs. In a FactBox on the right, or with the button *Totals* in the action pane, you can review the totals. If invoice matching validation is active, click the button *Update match status* to validate the invoice data against the purchase order and product receipt. After entering the vendor invoice number in the field *Number* (*Invoice identification*), click the button *Post* to post the invoice. Invoice posting generates an open vendor transaction (waiting for the payment) and updates the order status to "Invoiced".

Note: If you want to quit the Pending invoice form without saving, delete the invoice – do not simply close the form (this would save a pending invoice).

3.2   Vendor Management

Vendor records are required in purchasing and in accounts payable. In line with the deep integration of Dynamics 365, there is one common record for each vendor, which is used in all areas of the application. If you want to restrict access to the fields and field groups of the Vendor form, you can set appropriate permissions.

3.2.1   Vendor Records

In order to check existing vendors or to create new vendors, open the Vendor list page in the Procurement module (*Procurement and sourcing> Vendors> All vendors*) or in the Accounts payable module (*Accounts payable> Vendors> All vendors*). Alternatively, use the navigation search to access this page. According to the general structure of list pages, the Vendor list page is showing a list of all vendors. In the Vendor detail form, which you open with a click on the link in the field *Vendor account* of a line, you can view the details of the respective vendor.

Apart from the menu items, also the workspace *Purchase order preparation* provides access to the Vendor detail form (there is the list *Find vendor* in the center section).

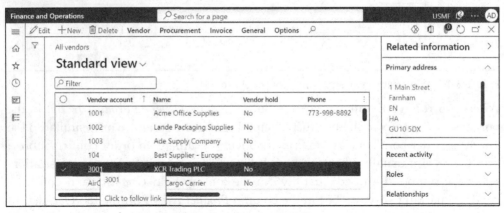

Figure 3-5:   Selecting a vendor in the Vendor list page

If you want to update data in the Vendor detail form, switch to the Edit mode (press the *F2* key or click the button *Edit* in the action pane for this purpose). If already the list page is in Edit mode before you access the detail form, the detail form is also opened in Edit mode.

The Vendor detail form contains numerous fields. The following description covers the core data in the vendor record. More information is available in the online help.

3.2.1.1   Entering New Vendors

If you want to create a new vendor in the Vendor list page or the detail form, press the shortcut *Alt+N* or click the button *New* in the action pane. If templates for vendors are set up, you can populate the fields of the new record from a template (see section 2.3.3).

Depending on settings in the corresponding number sequence, the unique vendor number in the field *Vendor account* is assigned automatically or has to be entered manually. By default, the number sequence in the Accounts payable parameters is used, but you can override this number sequence in the vendor groups (personalize the Vendor group form to shown the column *Vendor account number sequence*).

3.2.1.2   Global Address Book Integration

The party type (field *Type* in the field group *Identification*) on the tab *General* of the Vendor detail form determines if the vendor is a company (organization) or a person. Depending on the party type, the tab *General* will show different fields – for example, the fields *First name* and *Last name* for the type "Person".

Vendors are parties in the global address book. For this reason, the field *Name* is a lookup field in which you can select an existing party from the global address book when creating a new vendor. If you enter the name of a new vendor manually, a confirmation dialog is shown in case an existing party has got the same name as the new vendor (as a prerequisite, the duplicate check has to be activated in the Global address book parameters). The confirmation dialog provides the option to link the vendor to the existing party or to create a new party, which by chance has got the same name.

After saving the vendor record, you can use the table reference (*View details*) in the vendor name field to access the related party in the global address book.

As an alternative to the Vendor form, you can create new vendors in the global address book (*Common> Common> Global address book*, see section 2.4) in order to reduce the risk of duplicate party records. In the global address book, it is easy to check if a new vendor is already a party (e.g., if the new vendor is a vendor in an affiliated company) before creating a new record. If the vendor is a party, select the party and click the button *Party/New/Vendor* to convert it to a vendor in the current company. If not, first create the party and then convert it to a vendor.

3.2.1.3   General Data

The search name in the vendor record is initialized with the vendor name, but you can modify it. Apart from the name, mandatory data in the vendor record include the lookup field *Group* (vendor group, usually controlling the ledger integration, see section 3.2.3), and the *Currency* on the tab *Purchasing demographics* (initialized with the accounting currency).

Further core fields on the tab *General* are the *Language*, which determines the language for printing purchase orders or other documents, and, in case address books are used (e.g., for access control) the *Address books* linked to the vendor.

The display field *Vendor hold* on the tab *Miscellaneous details* shows whether the vendor is blocked. If you want to change the hold status, click the button *Vendor/*

Maintain/On hold in the action pane. The vendor hold status "All" prevents entering or posting any purchase order or other transaction for the vendor. The options "No" and "Never" enable all transactions ("Never" prevents automatic blocking of the vendor after a period of inactivity).

3.2.1.4 Input Tax

Tax settings for the vendor have to be entered on the tab *Invoice and delivery*. The *Sales tax group* (*VAT group*, initialized from the vendor group) on this tab determines the tax duty depending on the vendor location. A correct sales tax group is necessary to distinguish between domestic vendors, who charge sales tax or VAT, and foreign vendors, who do not. The setup of the sales tax groups and the tax calculation depends on the current company and its location. Section 9.2.7 contains more information on the tax setup in Dynamics 365.

If your company is located within the European Union and you need to record the VAT registration number of vendors for tax purposes, enter it in the field *Tax exempt number* (*VAT number*) next to the sales tax group. Since it is a lookup field, you have to insert a new tax-exempt number in the main table (use the option *View details* in the context menu, or the menu item *Tax> Setup> Sales tax> Tax exempt numbers*) before you can select it in the vendor record.

The setting *Tax exempt number requirement* and the *Mandatory tax group* in the Accounts payable parameters (*Accounts payable> Setup> Accounts payable parameters*, section *General*, tab *Vendor*) determine whether the tax-exempt number or the sales tax group are mandatory when creating a vendor.

3.2.1.5 Settings for Delivery and Payment

The field *Delivery terms* on the tab *Invoice and delivery* of the Vendor detail form specifies the usual delivery terms of the particular vendor. You can set up the required delivery terms, including a translation into foreign languages, in the menu item *Procurement and sourcing> Setup> Distribution> Terms of delivery*. The delivery terms reflect the agreed incoterms (standardized contractual rules that determine the tasks, costs, and risks for transportation and delivery).

The field *Mode of delivery* below the delivery terms specifies the way of delivery (e.g., "Truck" or "Parcel"). You can set up the modes of delivery in the menu item *Procurement and sourcing> Setup> Distribution> Modes of delivery*.

Delivery terms and modes of delivery are a common setup for vendors and customers.

The tab *Payment* in the Vendor detail form contains settings on payment terms and cash discount. You can find more details on these settings in section 3.2.2.

3.2.1.6 Postal Addresses

You can manage one or more addresses of a vendor on the tab *Addresses* of the Vendor detail form. Addresses and contact data are stored in the global address book, which is why you can find a party record for each vendor. Address and contact data in the global address book are shared with the other roles of the party (e.g., if the vendor is also a customer or vendor in another company in Dynamics 365).

In order to enter the postal address of a vendor, click the button *Add* in the toolbar of the tab *Addresses* in the Vendor form. In the *New address* dialog that is shown next, enter an identification (which helps to select the right address in the address search) for the address in the field *Name or description*. If the address is the primary address of the vendor, make sure that the slider *Primary* is set to "Yes" and the slider *Private* to "No". The field *Purpose* in the *Address* dialog controls, which transactions should use the current address as default value. In a primary address, select the purpose "Business". In an additional address, select an alternative purpose – e.g., the purpose "Payment" for an alternative payee address whose name is printed on checks. One postal address can have multiple purposes at the same time. If no specific address is specified for a particular purpose, the primary address is used.

The form *Organization administration> Global address book> Address and contact information purpose* shows the available standard address purposes. If required, you can set up additional purposes.

Another important setting in a postal address is the *Country/region*, which is the basis for the address format and for reports to the authorities – including sales tax and Intrastat reports.

Once you have selected the country code, only postal codes of this country are shown in the lookup of the field *ZIP/postal Code*. Depending on the settings in the Address setup (*Organization administration> Global address book> Addresses> Address setup*, tab *Parameters*), postal codes are validated against the ZIP/postal code table when entering an address. If the ZIP/postal code validation is activated, you have to insert a new postal code in the ZIP/postal code table before you can enter it in an address. You can manage the postal codes in the Address setup form (open the section *ZIP/postal codes*), or with the option *View details* in the context menu of the ZIP/postal code field.

After closing the *Address* dialog, you can click the button *More options/Advanced* in the toolbar of the tab *Addresses* in the Vendor form if you want to access further address details. The tab *Contact information* in the Manage addresses form contains the contact data, which are specific to the particular address (e.g., the phone number of the payee address), and not general contact data of the vendor.

If a vendor has multiple addresses with the same purpose and you want to specify a default value for a purpose, click the button *More options/Set defaults* in the toolbar of the tab *Addresses* in the Vendor form.

3.2.1.7 Contact Information

In order to enter general contact data of a vendor (e.g., the vendor telephone number or the general e-mail address), click the button *Add* in the toolbar of the tab *Contact information* of the Vendor detail form. On the tab *Purchasing demographics* of the Vendor detail form, you can select a main contact person in the field *Primary contact*. If you want to specify a new main contact, first enter the data of this person (use the button *Vendor/Set up/Contacts/Add contacts* in the Vendor form).

3.2.1.8 Features in the Vendor Page

The buttons in the action pane of the Vendor list page or detail form provide access to various inquiries and activities on the selected vendor:

➢ **Action pane tab** *Vendor*:
  o *Set up/Contacts* – Manage vendor contact persons.
  o *Set up/Bank accounts* – Manage vendor bank accounts for payment.
  o *Transactions/Transactions* – Show vendor invoices and payments.
  o *Transactions/Balance* – Show the total of open liabilities.
➢ **Action pane tab** *Procurement*:
  o *New/Purchase order* – Enter a purchase order, see section 3.4.2.
  o *Related information/Purchase orders* – View current orders.
  o *Agreements/Purchase agreements* – Blanket orders, see section 3.8.1.
➢ **Action pane tab** *Invoice*:
  o *New/Invoice* – Enter a vendor invoice, see section 9.3.2.
  o *Settle/Settle transactions* – Settle invoices, see section 9.2.5.
  o *Related information/Invoice* – View posted invoices.

3.2.1.9 Vendor Approval

In case an approval workflow for updates in particular vendor fields is required, enable vendor approvals in the Accounts payable parameters (section *General*, tab *Vendor approval*) and set up a workflow with the type "Proposed vendor changes workflow" in the menu item *Accounts payable> Setup> Accounts payable workflows*.

With this setup, updates in the selected vendor fields have to be submitted to the workflow and only after approval, the changes are applied to the vendor. While the approval is pending, the additional button *Proposed changes* (opens a dialog in which you can view and, if necessary, discard the changes) is shown in the action pane of the Vendor form.

You can find details on the workflow management in section 10.4.3.

3.2.1.10 One-time Vendors

One-time vendors provide the option to keep master data of regular suppliers separate from vendors, who supply items rarely or only once.

The tab *Vendor* in the section *General* in the Accounts payable parameters includes the vendor number of a vendor who is used as the template for one-time vendors.

In addition, there is a separate number sequence for one-time vendors in the section *Number sequences* of the parameters.

If you want to use a one-time vendor in a purchase order, do not select an existing vendor when you create the order (e.g., in the menu item *Procurement and sourcing> Purchase orders> All purchase orders*), but set the slider *One-time supplier* in the *Create purchase order* dialog to "Yes" (see Figure 3-6). With this setting, a new vendor is created in parallel to the order.

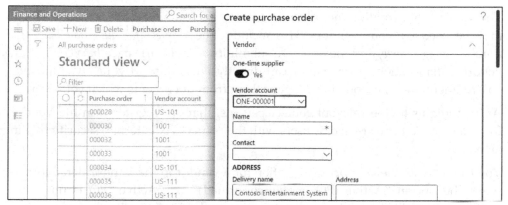

Figure 3-6:   Creating a one time vendor in a new purchase order

The vendor account number of this vendor derives from the number-sequence for one-time vendors, and the checkbox *One-time supplier* on the tab *Vendor profile* of the Vendor form is selected. If you want to convert the one-time vendor into a regular vendor, clear this checkbox (but clearing the checkbox does not change the vendor number).

3.2.1.11 Sharing Vendors across Companies

Since vendors are parties in the global address book and the global address book is shared across companies, the party details (address and contact data) are shared automatically if you link the vendor records in two or more companies to a common party in the global address book.

The button *Vendor/Copy/Add vendor to another legal entity* in the Vendor form, which opens a drop-down in which you can enter the target company, vendor group, currency, and vendor hold information, provides an easy way to create a vendor – which is linked to the same party as the selected vendor – in another company.

If you want to share the data in the vendor table in addition to the data in the party table, you can use cross-company data sharing (see section 10.1.5) for the vendor table. With cross-company data sharing, make sure that the referenced data which you enter (e.g., the vendor groups) are consistent across the selected companies.

If cross-company data sharing is not enabled and you want to initialize a new vendor from the vendor record in another company, access the Vendor form in the company in which you want to create the vendor, click the button *New* and, in the field *Name* on the tab *General*, search the vendor (party) which you want to copy. If the selected party is a vendor in another company, the party lookup will show the additional slider *Existing vendor. Copy vendor?* on the right which enables copying the vendor data. As a prerequisite, the two companies must use a shared number sequence (see section 10.3.1) for vendor numbers, which ensures a common vendor number across the companies.

3.2.1.12 Vendor Collaboration

The Vendor collaboration module in Dynamics 365 contains the menu items which may be used by your vendors. This includes the *Request for quotation bids*, the *Purchase order review*, and the option to submit invoices (workspace *Invoicing*). With vendor collaboration, your vendor can directly enter data in your Dynamics 365 environment and you don't have to type them from documents which you receive.

As a prerequisite, the relevant contact persons, that are registered in the Vendor form, also have to be created as users with the respective (external) security role in Dynamics 365.

You can activate the vendor collaboration for a vendor in the Vendor detail form – select the option "Active (PO is auto-confirmed)" or "Active (PO is not auto-confirmed)" in the field *Collaboration activation* on the tab *General*.

If a vendor uses the vendor collaboration, the following steps in purchase order processing are different from the common procedure (see section 3.4): Instead of the (optional) purchase inquiry, you send a confirmation request to the vendor once the purchase order is internally approved – click the button *Purchase/Vendor/Send for confirmation* in the Purchase order form for this purpose. The vendor then accepts the inquiry in the vendor collaboration portal (*Vendor collaboration> Purchase orders> Purchase orders for review*). If the *Collaboration activation* option "Active (PO is auto-confirmed)" in the Vendor form is selected for the vendor, the purchase order confirmation is posted automatically then (requires the job *Procurement and sourcing> Purchase orders> Purchase order confirmation> Confirm accepted purchase orders*, which should run as a recurring batch job).

3.2.2   Payment Terms and Cash Discounts

Unlike other business applications, which include cash discount settings in the payment terms, Dynamics 365 keeps payment terms and cash discounts separately.

Payment terms and cash discounts in Dynamics 365 are a common setup for vendors and customers. For this reason, the administration is included in both, the Accounts payable module and the Accounts receivable module. The calculation of the due date and the cash discount date starts from the document date, which you can enter in an invoice. If you leave the document date empty, Dynamics 365 uses the posting date as the start date for due date calculation. But particularly in purchase invoices, the document date may deviate from the posting date.

If necessary, you can modify the due date and the cash discount date when posting an invoice or when settling it in the Settle transactions form (see section 9.2.5).

3.2.2.1 Terms of Payment

You can manage the payment terms in the Accounts payable module (*Accounts payable> Payment setup> Terms of payment*) and in the Accounts receivable module (*Accounts receivable> Payment setup> Terms of payment*).

Figure 3-7:   Settings for the due date calculation in the payment terms

The list pane on the left of this form shows the available payment terms with their ID and description. The settings for the due date calculation of the selected payment term are shown on the right.

The lookup field *Payment method* on the tab *Setup* determines the start date for due date calculation: "Net" means starting from the document date, "Current month" means starting from month end. The fields *Days* and *Months* determine the period length for the due date calculation.

The button *Translations* provides the option to enter a longer description (text) in different languages. When you print an external document (e.g., a printed purchase order), the text of the payment terms is printed in the language of the document. If no translation to this language has been entered for the particular payment terms, the content of the field *Description* of the payment terms is printed.

3.2.2.2 Cash on Delivery

If you want to create payment terms for cash on delivery, select the *Payment method* "COD", set the slider *Cash payment* to "Yes", and select the appropriate main account for petty cash in the field *Cash*.

When you post an invoice with payment terms "Cash on delivery", the payment, and a settlement of the invoice with the petty cash account in the payment terms, is posted in parallel. There is no open vendor transaction in this case.

3.2.2.3 Cash Discounts

Like the setup of the payment terms, the cash discount setup is included in both, the Accounts payable module and the Accounts receivable module (*Accounts payable> Payment setup> Cash discounts* and *Accounts receivable> Payment setup> Cash discounts*). When you create a cash discount, there are details that are similar to the details in the payment terms. In addition, you have to specify the cash discount percentage and settings that control posting cash discount to the general ledger.

Figure 3-8:   Setting up a cash discount

Cash discounts are a common setup in accounts payable and accounts receivable. Nevertheless, there are different settings for posting the cash discount deduction for vendors and for customers (the settings apply when the payment is posted):

➢ **Accounts receivable** – Field *Main account for customer discounts*.
➢ **Accounts payable** – The main account is depending on the selected option in the lookup field *Discount offset accounts* of the cash discount:
   o *Use main account for vendor discounts* – Posting to the *Main account for vendor discounts* entered in the field below.
   o *Accounts on the invoice lines* – Posting to the accounts of the invoice lines (offsetting part of the invoiced expense amount with the cash discount).

If required, you can apply a setup that posts the cash discount to ledger accounts which are depending on the applicable sales tax – enter the applicable main accounts in the fields *Vendor cash discount* and *Customer cash discount* of the sales tax ledger posting groups (*Sales tax> Setup> Sales tax> Ledger posting groups*) for this purpose. In this way you can, for example, distinguish between cash discounts which you receive from domestic vendors and from foreign vendors.

3.2.3 Ledger Integration

Whenever you post a purchase order invoice, it generates financial transactions. These financial transactions include the general ledger and subledgers for accounts payable, sales tax, inventory, and other areas as applicable.

3.2.3.1 Subledger and General Ledger

Vendor invoices, credit notes, and payments generate vendor transactions in accounts payable. In addition to these subledger postings, Dynamics 365 is posting transactions in the general ledger (see section 9.4). Two settings are relevant for the automatic selection of main accounts in the ledger transactions:

➤ **Posting setup** (see section 9.4.2) – Determines the applicable main accounts in the ledger transactions posted with the product (or service) receipt and the invoice (with reference to the vendor and the item or procurement category).
➤ **Vendor posting profiles** – Determine the applicable vendor summary account in the ledger transaction posted with the invoice (with reference to the vendor).

Both references, the reference to the item and to the vendor, are not only available at the level of individual items and vendors, but also at the group level.

3.2.3.2 Settings for Vendor Transactions

Vendor groups (*Accounts payable> Vendors> Vendor groups*) are a primary setting for vendor transactions. In addition to the ID and the description, you can optionally enter a *Default tax group* (for the input tax) in the vendor group. When you create a vendor, the default tax group of the vendor group initializes the sales tax group of the vendor.

Vendor posting profiles (*Accounts payable> Setup> Vendor posting profiles*) control the assignment of vendors to summary accounts. As a prerequisite for posting a purchase transaction, at least one posting profile has to be specified. In addition, the default *Posting profile* for regular purchase transactions has to be specified in the Accounts payable parameters (section *Ledger and sales tax*, tab *Posting*).

The field *Summary account* on the tab *Setup* in the posting profile determines the liability account for the assigned vendors. The assignment of summary accounts is available at three different levels as specified in the *Account code*:

➤ **Table** – Assigns a summary account to a particular vendor (enter the vendor number in the field *Account/Group number*).
➤ **Group** – Assigns a summary account to a vendor group (enter the vendor group in the field *Account/Group number*).
➤ **All** – Assigns a general summary account (the field *Account/Group number* remains empty).

If there are settings at multiple levels, Dynamics 365 uses the most specific setting. The search for this setting starts with the vendor number, and the level "All" has got the lowest priority.

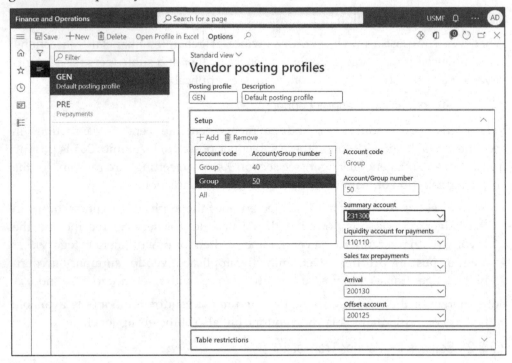

Figure 3-9:   Setting up a vendor posting profile

If you want to use alternative profile settings for special purposes like prepayment, set up additional posting profiles with account assignments that are different from the settings in the default posting profile. In order to use such a posting profile in a transaction, select it in the particular transaction (e.g., in the Purchase order detail form on the tab *Setup* of the Header view). For prepayment, the posting profile is specified in the Accounts payable parameters.

3.2.4   Case Study Exercises

Exercise 3.1 – Terms of Payment

New terms of payment "60 days net" are required in your company. Enter these payment terms in Dynamics 365 with a code P-## (## = your user ID).

In addition, a new cash discount D-## for "14 days with 3 percent discount" is required. Be sure to enter the details for the due date and the cash discount date calculation correctly, and select main accounts which correspond to the accounts in existing cash discounts.

Exercise 3.2 – Vendor Record

A new domestic vendor is accepted. Do not use a template when you create this vendor with a name (starting with your user ID) and a primary address of your choice. Select the payment terms and the cash discount of exercise 3.1, and an appropriate vendor group and sales tax group for domestic vendors. Vendor collaboration is not used with this vendor.

Exercise 3.3 – Ledger Integration

You want to investigate the ledger integration. Can you tell which summary account is used in ledger transactions which are posted with an invoice of the vendor of exercise 3.2?

3.3   Product Management in Purchasing

Purchased items include physical products and intangible goods (e.g., services, fees, licenses). For both types of items, you have to ensure correct and complete master data for the following purposes:

> **Identification** – Clearly describe the item to make sure that the vendor ships the right product.
> **Internal settings** – Multiple settings in the item master data control the way in which the particular item works in Dynamics 365.

For inventoried items, required master data include the product (at shared level) and the released product (at company level). For intangible goods, you can also use an item (if you want to manage details like prices in the master data) or, without details, a procurement category.

Along with an introduction to the basics of product management, this section primarily contains an explanation of the product data which are necessary for purchasing. In section 7.2 of this book, you can find a general description of product management in Dynamics 365.

3.3.1   Product Categories and Procurement Categories

Product categories are used to group the products and services in a hierarchical structure. Depending on the requirements, you can set up multiple hierarchies in parallel and assign an item to a different category in each hierarchy.

The hierarchy structure of product categories can be simple or contain multiple levels. Depending on the hierarchy type, a particular category hierarchy is only used in procurement, or also in sales or other areas.

You can use product categories independently of items. When you purchase a service or intangible item, which is not tracked in inventory, simply enter a product category (instead of an item) in the purchase order line in this case.

3.3.1.1 Category Hierarchies and Product Categories

The list page *Product information management> Setup> Categories and attributes> Category hierarchies* displays the product category hierarchies. The link in the field *Name* of a hierarchy provides access to the Category hierarchy detail form that shows the structure of the hierarchy.

If you want to set up a completely new category hierarchy, click the button *New* in the Category hierarchy list page. In the *Create* dialog that is shown next, enter a name and a description for the hierarchy before you click the button *Create*. Dynamics 365 then shows the Category hierarchy detail form. If you want to add a new category or a new category folder to a hierarchy, select the parent node in the tree structure on the left and click the button *New category node* in the action pane. In the new category, enter at least the *Name*, the *Code*, and the *Friendly name*.

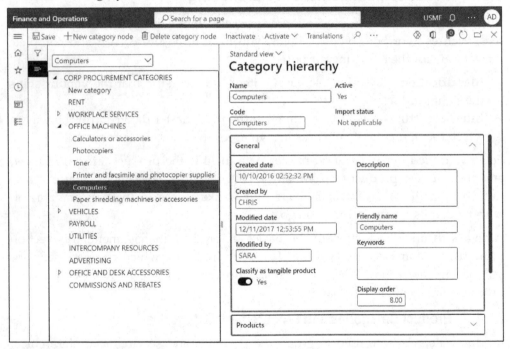

Figure 3-10: Editing a product category in the Category hierarchy detail form

The purpose of a hierarchy is given by the hierarchy role. Available roles include the "Procurement category hierarchy" for purchasing and the "Sales category hierarchy" for sales. In order to assign a hierarchy to a hierarchy role, open the Category hierarchy role association form (*Product information management> Setup> Categories and attributes> Category hierarchy role associations*) and enter a line with a *Category hierarchy type* (select the hierarchy role) and the respective *Category hierarchy*. You can select the same hierarchy in multiple lines.

The purchasing-related data of a procurement category (a category in a hierarchy with the role "Procurement category hierarchy") are specified in separate form, the Procurement categories form.

3.3.1.2 Procurement Categories

Procurement categories are product categories which belong to the hierarchy with the type "Procurement category hierarchy". You can select a procurement category instead of a product number in the lines of purchase transactions (purchase orders, purchase requisitions, purchase agreements).

The Procurement category form (*Procurement and sourcing> Procurement categories*), which shows the purchasing-related settings of these categories, includes the item sales tax group on the tab *Item sales tax groups* as a core setting.

As a prerequisite for the use of procurement categories in purchase transactions, the posting setup (see section 9.4.2) has to include settings for categories (*Cost management> Ledger integration policies setup> Posting*, tab *Purchase order*, option *Purchase expenditure for expense*).

3.3.2 Basic Product Data

In order to support multi-company enterprises, the structure of product data in Dynamics 365 has got two levels:

> **Products ("Shared products")** – Include the common data in all companies.
> **Released products ("Items")** – Include the company-specific data.

Shared products are a mandatory element in the data structure. But in a small enterprise with only one company, it is possible to manage and create the products directly in the Released product form.

Note: Creating a product works different if your enterprise uses engineering change management (see section 7.2.5).

3.3.2.1 Shared Products

The aim of the shared products in Dynamics 365 is to establish a common table with all products in all companies. Apart from the product number and the name, shared products do not contain extensive information.

The form *Product information management> Products> All products and product masters* shows all items at the enterprise level – including regular products, configurable products, and service items. If you want to create a new product, click the button *New* and enter following data in the *Create product* dialog:

> **Product type** – "Item" for stocked products, "Service" for services.
> **Product subtype** – "Product" for regular items, "Product master" for items with variants (see section 7.2.1).
> **Product number** – Enter manually, if there is no automatic number from the number sequence.

- ➤ **Product name** – Short description in system language.
- ➤ **Search name** – Internal text for searching the item.
- ➤ **Retail category** – Product categorization in the Retail and commerce module.
- ➤ **Catch weight** – Usually "No", for catch weight items "Yes" (see section 7.2.1).

Note: If activated in the feature management, the field *Product service type* is shown additionally.

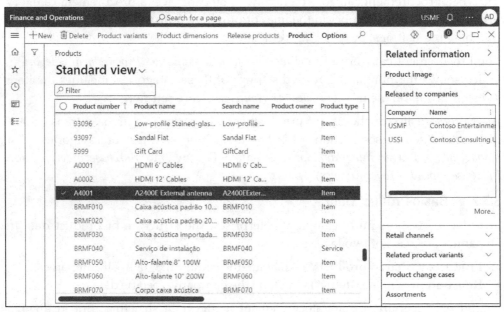

Figure 3-11: Selecting an item in the list page *All products and product masters*

For a regular item that is stored in inventory, select the *Product type* "Item" and the *Product subtype* "Product". For an intangible item or a service, select the *Product type* "Service". Alternatively, you can also select the *Product type* "Item" for an intangible item in case you select an item model group for non-inventoried products in the related released product(s) later (see section 7.2.1).

Once you close the *Create* dialog with the button *OK*, Dynamics 365 creates a shared product and shows the (shared) Product detail form. In the detail form, you can enter further optional settings.

Apart from the fields *Product name* and *Description* in the detail form, which both have to be entered in the *System language* (specified in the System parameters), there is a separate form for item descriptions in foreign languages (access with the button *Product/Languages/Translations* in the action pane).

In order to assign the inventory dimensions that you want to use for the product, click the button *Product/Set up/Dimension groups* in the shared product. The inventory dimensions are divided into three groups:

> **Product dimension group** – For the product subtype "Product master", specifies whether the item has versions, styles, sizes, colors, or configurations.
> **Storage dimension group** – Specifies whether the item inventory is tracked at the level of sites, warehouses, locations, inventory status, or license plates.
> **Tracking dimension group** – Specifies whether batch or serial numbers are used. The dimension "Owner" refers to vendor consignment (see section 7.4.8).

The button *Product/Set up/Product categories* in the shared product provides access to the category assignment, in which you can link the product to categories. Product categories, which are optional, provide the option to manage hierarchical product structures (widely used in the Retail and commerce module).

Except for the product dimension group (for product masters), you can leave the dimension groups in the shared product empty. Dimension groups, which are not specified in the shared product, have to be entered in the related released product(s) at the company level. You should specify the dimension groups at the company level (in the released product, and not in the shared product) if there are different dimension settings per company (e.g., if only one company in the enterprise uses locations).

3.3.2.2 Releasing a Product

Before you can register a transaction for a new shared product, you have to release it with the button *Release products* in the action pane of the All products page (you can select multiple products at the same time). The selected product(s) are shown in the *Release products* wizard next. Once you switch to the *Select companies* page of the wizard, put a checkmark in front of all applicable companies. Then confirm the selection with the button *Finish* on the last page.

If applicable (e.g., in a single-company implementation), you can skip creating a shared product and immediately create a new product in the Released product form. If you create a product with the button *New* in the Released product form, the released product and the shared product are created in parallel.

3.3.2.3 Managing Released Products

The released product, also called "Item" in some areas of Dynamics 365, contains the item details. Apart from the menu item *Product information management> Products> Released products*, the workspace *Released product maintenance* provides access to the Released product form.

In the shared product, you can directly access the related released product with the link in the field *Item number* on the right of the FactBox *Released to companies* (select the line with the appropriate company) and the link in the field *Item number* of the *Product information* dialog which is shown next.

After releasing a new product, you have to populate the following mandatory fields in the Released product form:

➢ **Item group** (tab *Manage costs*) – Determines the main accounts for ledger integration.

➢ **Item model group** (tab *General*) – Determines item handling and inventory valuation.

➢ **Dimension groups** (button *Product/Set up/Dimension groups*) – Required if not specified in the shared product.

➢ **Unit of measure** – For purchasing, sales, and inventory.

The default for the inventory unit of measure (field *Unit* on the tab *Manage inventory* in the Released product form) of new items is specified in the Inventory parameters (*Inventory management> Setup> Inventory and warehouse management parameters*, field *Unit* in the section *General*). After specifying an applicable unit conversion to the inventory unit, you can select different units for sales (on the tab *Sell*) and purchasing (on the tab *Purchase*).

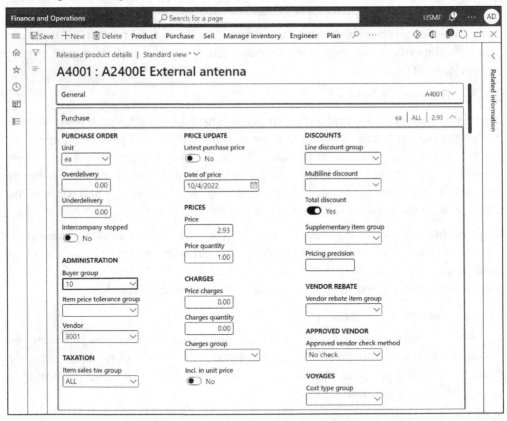

Figure 3-12: Viewing the tab *Purchase* in the Released product detail form

In addition, you should enter the *Item sales tax group* on the tab *Sell* and on the tab *Purchase* (mandatory, if the slider *Mandatory item sales tax group* in the section *General* of the Inventory parameters is set to "Yes"). A default value for the item sales tax group is specified on the tab *Setup* in the item group.

In the field *Price* on the tab *Manage costs*, you can enter a base cost price for the item. If the item applies a standard cost valuation (according to selected item model group), click the button *Manage costs/Set up/Item price* in the action pane and enter a cost price per site as described in section 7.3.3.

3.3.2.4   Purchasing Related Data and Default Order Settings

The tab *Purchase* in the Released product detail form contains core purchasing data, including the item sales tax group already mentioned. The *Buyer group* provides the option to specify the purchasing responsibility for the item. The lookup field *Approved vendor check method*, initialized from the corresponding field in the item model group, controls if you can purchase the item only from approved vendors. If you decide to use approved vendors for the item (with the option "Warning only" or "Not allowed"), enter allowed vendors with the button *Purchase/Approved vendor/Setup* in the action pane.

Essential order-related settings of a released product are specified in the default order settings, which you can access with the button *Manage inventory/Order settings/Default order settings* in the Released product form. In the default order settings, the record with a blank *Site* and the *Rank* "0" determines the default order settings at the company level.

The field *Default order type*, which is only editable at the company level, controls the way to supply the item. The default order type "Purchase order" determines that the item is purchased externally, whereas the default order types "Production" (for discrete manufacturing and process manufacturing) and "Kanban" (for lean manufacturing) specify internal production. You can override the default order type with settings in the item coverage (see section 6.3.4).

The tab *Purchase order* in the default order settings contains the purchasing-related settings – including default values for lot size (field *Multiple*) and order quantity (field *Standard order quantity*). A checkmark in the checkbox *Stopped* on this tab blocks the item for purchase transactions.

If you want to specify order settings at the level of sites (for subsidiaries, see section 10.1.6), insert an additional record in the default order setting with the *Site* in the respective field. The field *Rank*, which determines the search priority within the default order settings, is automatically populated with the next number. In order to override the default order settings at the company level with settings at the level of sites, set the applicable slider *Override default settings* in the site-specific order settings to "Yes".

If the item is a product master (product with variants, see section 7.2.1), you can also enter default order setting at variant level.

When you enter an order (e.g., a purchase order), the default order settings initialize various fields in the order line (e.g., the order quantity). You can override the default values in the order line afterward.

3.3.3   Purchase Price Setup

The functionality for pricing in purchasing and in sales is very similar. Pricing in purchase management includes a multi-stage calculation of prices and discounts, which starts with the base price in the Released product form and continues with trade agreements at the level of vendor groups and individual vendors.

Since many companies use a comprehensive setup for prices and discounts rather in sales than in purchasing, the section below only covers the base prices. You can find details on trade agreements for prices and discounts in section 4.3.2.

Apart from discounts which are deducted immediately, there is the option to manage vendor rebate contracts with a retrospective discount depending on the purchasing volume in a given period (see section 4.9.4).

3.3.3.1   Base Purchase Price

The base purchase price is specified in the field *Price* on the tab *Purchase* of the Released product form. This price is the price per purchase unit (field *Unit* on the tab *Purchase*). The field *Price quantity* determines the quantity which is the basis for this price. With a price quantity "100", for example, the price for 100 units (e.g., for screws).

If you want to record different base purchase prices per site (subsidiary), click the button *Manage costs/Set up/Item price* in the released product to open the Item price form. In this form, you can enter and activate a price per site as described in section 7.3.3 (use the *Price type* "Purchase price").

The base purchase price is used in purchase orders if there is no applicable trade agreement for the particular vendor and item. Since prices (and price charges) in the Released product form are shown in the accounting currency of the current company, there is a conversion of the base purchase price to the currency of the purchase order if the order is in a foreign currency.

3.3.3.2   Automatic Price Update

If the slider *Latest purchase price* on the tab *Purchase* of the released product is set to "Yes", the base purchase price in the released product is updated with the invoiced price whenever you post a purchase order invoice for the item. With this setting, not only the field *Price* on the tab *Purchase* of the released product (which is the default value for the next order if no other price is applicable) is updated with the latest purchase price, the Item price form (access with the button *Manage costs/Set up/Item price* in the released product) also shows this price update.

If you want to track the history of price updates, activate the price history (Inventory parameters, slider *Last price history* in the section *Inventory accounting*). If the price history is activated, the Item price form will insert new item price records in case of price changes (instead of updating existing item price records).

3.3.3.3   Price Charges

In order to record charges (like fees and freight), which are added to the base price, you can optionally enter *Price charges* on the tab *Purchase* of the released product.

If the slider *Incl. in unit price* is set to "No", the amount entered in the field *Price charges* is added to the total of an order line, irrespective of the quantity. An example for this setting: If an item got a *Price* of USD 3.00 and *Price charges* of USD 1.00 in the Released product form, a purchase order line with 10 units of this item will show a unit price of USD 3.00 and a line amount of USD 31.00. The price charges are not shown in a separate field on printed purchasing documents.

If the slider *Incl. in unit price* is set to "Yes", Dynamics 365 adds the price charges to the unit price. In this case, the field *Charges quantity* determines the quantity basis for allocating the price charges to the unit price. An example for this setting: If an item got a *Price* of USD 3.00, a *Charges quantity* of 0.00 (or 1.00), and *Price charges* of USD 1.00 in the Released product form, a purchase order line with 10 units of this item will show a unit price of USD 4.00 and a line amount of USD 40.00.

Apart from the general price charges in the Released product form, you can manage site-specific price charges for an item in the Item price form.

In the context of charges, do not confuse the price charges in the released product with charges codes and charges transactions, which are managed separately in orders. You can find more details on charges management in section 4.4.5.

3.3.4   Case Study Exercises

Exercise 3.4 – Procurement Categories

Your company wants to purchase a new kind of services, for which you have to set up appropriate product categories in the procurement category hierarchy. Enter a new category node "##-services" with the categories "##-assembling" and "##-fees" (## = your user ID). The procurement categories refer to the standard tax rate.

Exercise 3.5 – Product Record

In order to process purchase orders in the following exercises, you want to set up a new product. Create a shared product with the product number I-## and the name "##-merchandise" (## = your user ID). It is a stocked product with inventory control at the level of site and warehouse. Variants and serial/batch numbers are not required. Select the appropriate dimension groups in the shared product.

Then release the product to your test company. In the released product, select an appropriate item group for merchandise and an item model group with FIFO-valuation. The item does not require approved vendors.

The item sales tax group for sales and for purchasing should refer to the standard tax rate. The unit of measurement for the item is "Pieces" in all areas, and the main vendor is the vendor of exercise 3.2. The base purchase price and the base cost price is USD 50, and the base sales price is USD 100.

In the default order settings for purchasing and for sales, enter default quantities (*Multiple* 20, *Min. order quantity* 40, *Standard order quantity* 100) and select the main site and the main warehouse.

Note: If the number sequence for product numbers is set up for automatic numbering, you don't have to enter a product number.

3.4   Purchase Order Management

An order is a firm commitment to supply/accept goods or services on agreed terms. For this reason, purchase orders have to include at least following details: Vendor (name, address), commercial terms (currency, payment terms, terms of delivery), product (identification, quantity, unit of measure), price (price, discount), delivery date, and delivery address.

3.4.1   Basics of Purchase Order Processing

Apart from manually entering a new purchase order, there are the following options to generate an order automatically:

➢ **Master planning** – Generate an order from a planned order, see section 6.3.5.
➢ **Purchase requisition** – Generate an order from a requisition, see section 3.8.2.
➢ **Request for quotation** – Generate an order from a quote, see section 3.8.3.
➢ **Purchase agreement** – Generate an order as a release order, see section 3.8.1.
➢ **Direct delivery** – Generate an order from a sales order, see section 4.8.
➢ **Subcontracting** – Generate an order from a production order, see section 5.7.2.
➢ **Inventory ownership change** – For consignment inventory, see section 7.4.8.
➢ **Project accounting** – Generate an order from an item task in the Project module.
➢ **Purchase journal** – Generate an order from an order with the type "Journal".

Planned purchase orders are a result of master planning. You can create an actual purchase order by firming the planned purchase order then. Depending on the master planning setup (firming time fence), master planning may skip planned orders and immediately create purchase orders.

Purchase requisitions are internal documents which request purchasing an item. They have to be entered or initiated by the person who wants the item (e.g., for items like office supplies).

Requests for quotation are required if you want to obtain and compare quotes from multiple vendors. You can create a request for quotation either automatically from a purchase requisition or a planned order, or enter it manually.

Purchase order processing related to projects is part of the Project management and accounting module.

Other ways for creating purchase orders in Dynamics 365 are automatic transfers with an import from external applications, or the intercompany functionality (purchasing from an affiliated company in a common Dynamics 365 environment).

After creating and, if required, approving a purchase order, you can process the order from the start to the end as shown in Figure 3-13. Depending on the setup, confirming the purchase order and posting the vendor invoice are the only mandatory steps in order processing.

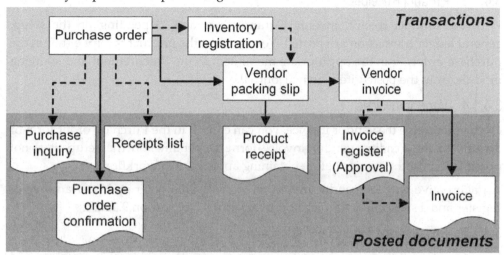

Figure 3-13: Purchase order processing in Dynamics 365

3.4.1.1 Approving and Confirming Purchase Orders

In a purchase order which is subject to change management, you have to submit the order for approval. Depending on the order and the approval workflow, there is an automatic or a manual approval. If change management does not apply, the approval status of the order is immediately "Approved".

Once the order is approved, you can optionally post a purchase inquiry which is a document for the vendor to review and confirm the order from his side.

The next mandatory step in order processing is the order confirmation, which usually includes sending a hardcopy or electronic order document to the vendor.

3.4.1.2 Receipts List and Inventory Registration

If your warehouse requires a list of purchased items for information purposes and for preparing the item arrival, you can post and print a receipts list.

Unlike the receipts list, inventory registration as the next step updates the on-hand quantity in inventory. The inventory registration, which contains all required inventory dimensions (depending on the item, this includes the warehouse, serial number, or batch number), is an optional step before posting the product receipt. Depending on the business processes in the warehouse, there are the following alternatives for the inventory registration:

➢ **Registration form** – Inventory registration in the purchase order line.
➢ **Item arrival journal** – Inventory registration with a journal in inventory.
➢ **Mobile device transactions** – In the advanced warehouse management.

If the checkbox *Registration requirements* is selected in the item model group of the purchased item, inventory registration is not optional, but a mandatory step before posting the product receipt.

3.4.1.3   Product Receipts

With the product receipt, inventory transactions and, depending on the setup, general ledger transaction are posted. You can post the product receipt either in the purchase order, or in the appropriate menu item in the Procurement and sourcing module, or in the posted item arrival journal.

3.4.1.4   Vendor Invoices

Once you receive the vendor invoice, you can enter it in the Purchase order form or directly in the Pending vendor invoice form. Depending on the setup, it is not possible to post the invoice before obtaining approval in a workflow.

An alternative way for vendor invoice processing is to enter and post an invoice register and a subsequent invoice approval journal (see section 9.3.2).

3.4.1.5   Physical and Financial Transactions

Inventory transactions consist of two components: The physical transaction and the financial transactions. Generally speaking, packing slips (product receipts) are physical transactions, and invoices are financial transactions. You should distinguish these transactions, in particular with regard to inventory valuation and ledger posting. Section 7.2.4 in this book contains more details on this subject.

3.4.2   Purchase Order Registration

Like all documents, purchase orders consist of a header and one or more lines. The header contains the common data of the order, including the order number, vendor, language, currency, and payment terms.

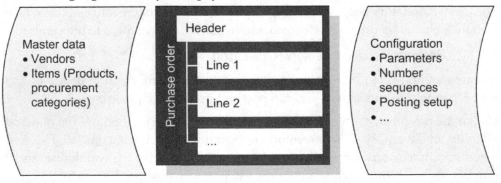

Figure 3-14:   Structure of purchase orders

Some other fields in the order header (e.g., the delivery date) are not managed at the order header level, but are a default value for the order lines – you can override them at the line level. If you modify header data after creating order lines, Procurement parameter settings (*Procurement and sourcing> Setup> Procurement and sourcing parameters*, section *General*, button *Update order lines* in the toolbar of the tab *Default values and parameters*) control whether the present order lines are updated automatically.

The default value for the *Purchase type* in the purchase order header is specified in the section *General* of the Procurement parameters (usually "Purchase order" for regular purchase orders). There are the following options for the purchase type in a purchase order:

➢ **Purchase order** – Regular purchase order.
➢ **Journal** – Draft or template, with no impact on inventory or finance.
➢ **Returned order** – Credit note, see section 3.7.

Data in the order lines include the item number (or procurement category), text (initialized from the item description), quantity, price, discount, delivery date, and other data as applicable. When ordering an inventoried item, select the item number of a released product. For non-inventoried items (e.g., services), you can enter the item number of an intangible item, or skip the item number and select a procurement category.

When you create a purchase order header or line, Dynamics 365 initializes numerous fields with default values from the vendor in the header and the item in the line. Depending on your permissions, you can subsequently update the content of the fields in the purchase order. If you agree, for example, to particular payment terms in a purchase order, change the terms of payment in the order header. If the new payment terms apply to all future orders, you should also change the terms of payment in the vendor record to make sure that you receive the right default value when entering the next order with this vendor.

3.4.2.1 Entering a Purchase Order

Depending on your personal preferences, you can start from one of the following forms to create or update a purchase order manually:

➢ **Vendor form** – Preferable, if you want to start with a vendor search.
➢ **Purchase order form** – Preferable, if you want to edit an existing order (e.g., if you look for all orders that are not yet approved).
➢ **Purchase order preparation workspace** – Several filtered lists with orders.

In the Vendor form (*Procurement and sourcing> Vendors> All vendors*), you can click the button *Procurement/New/Purchase order* to create an order. Dynamics 365 creates a purchase order header with default data from the selected vendor and switches to the Lines view of the Purchase order detail form, in which you can enter the first order line immediately. If you want to access the current orders of a vendor from the Vendor list page or detail form, click the button *Procurement/Related information/ Purchase orders/All purchase orders*. Dynamics 365 shows the Purchase order list page filtered on the selected vendor then.

In the workspace *Purchase order preparation*, which you can access from the dashboard or from the folder *Workspaces* in the *Procurement and sourcing* menu, the center section contains several lists with purchase orders grouped by approval status. Click on a purchase order number shown as a link in the grid if you want to view the order in the Purchase order detail form. If you want to create a new order from the workspace, click the button *New purchase order* in the action pane. The subsequent steps are the same as when creating an order from the Purchase order list page.

The Purchase order list page (*Procurement and sourcing> Purchase orders> All purchase orders*) shows a list of all purchase orders. In order to view the details of a purchase order, click the link in the field *Purchase order* in the grid.

If you want to enter a new purchase order in the Purchase order list page, press the shortcut *Alt+N* or click the button *New* in the action pane. In the *Create purchase order* dialog, select the vendor in the field *Vendor account* first. You can search the vendor by typing the first characters of the vendor number (or the name), or by explicitly opening the lookup in which you can use a grid column filter (e.g., for a filter on the column *Name* of the lookup).

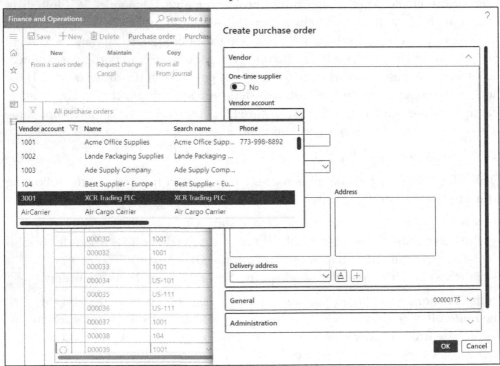

Figure 3-15:   Creating a new order in the Purchase order list page

Once you select a vendor, the *Create* dialog retrieves various default values from the vendor record. You can expand the tabs *General* and *Administration* in the dialog to access additional fields of the new order header. If you want to change data like the vendor number, purchase type, or currency, you can update the particular field in the dialog or – after closing the dialog – in the Header view of the Purchase order detail form.

When you close the dialog with the button *OK*, Dynamics 365 creates the order header and switches to the Purchase order detail form in the Lines view.

3.4.2.2 Purchase Order Lines

In order to create an order line in the Lines view of the Purchase order detail form, click the button *Add line* in the toolbar of the tab *Purchase order lines* or simply click the first line in the grid and select an *Item number* (released product) or a *Procurement category*. Data in the released product initialize numerous fields in the order line – e.g., the *Quantity*, the *Unit*, the *Unit price*, or the Site and the *Warehouse*. If site and warehouse are specified in the order header, they take priority over the default values from the item.

Trade agreements can override the primary default for the *Unit price*, which is the base price specified in the Released product form. They also provide a default for the discount fields (see section 4.3.2). The net amount in a line is calculated from the quantity, unit price, and discounts. You can update the field *Net amount* manually – Dynamics 365 clears the unit price and discount in this case.

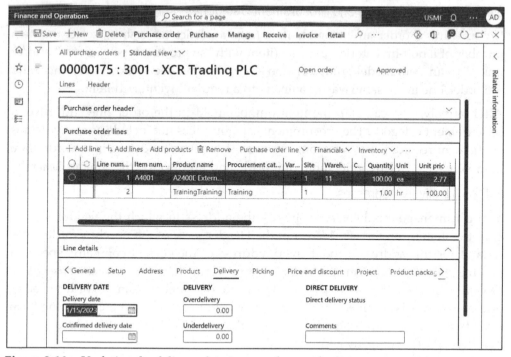

Figure 3-16: Updating the delivery date in a purchase order line

The *Line number* is automatically populated when you save the order line. The default for line numbers derives from the field *Increment* in the System parameters (*System administration> Setup> System parameters*).

If you want to view additional line data (e.g., the delivery date), expand the tab *Line details* and switch to the appropriate sub-tab. The delivery date on the sub-tab *Delivery* in the line details receives its default value from the purchase order header if this date is after the lead time of the item. Otherwise, the default for the delivery date of the line is the lead time added to the session date. You can specify the purchase lead time of the item at different levels – in the default order settings of the item, in a purchase price trade agreement, or in the item coverage.

3.4.2.3   Inventory Transactions

When you enter a line with an inventoried product in a regular purchase order, Dynamics 365 creates a corresponding inventory transaction. You can view this transaction with the button *Inventory/Transactions* in the toolbar of the order line. The receipt status of the transaction is "Ordered" (or, for lines with a negative quantity, the issue status is "On order"), and the fields *Physical date* and *Financial date* are empty. In the course of purchase order processing, the product receipt and the vendor invoice update this inventory transaction (see section 7.2.4).

3.4.2.4   Intangible Items and Procurement Categories

If you want to order an intangible item (e.g., a particular service), select the item number of a non-inventoried product (item with the product type "Service" and/or linked to an item model group for non-stocked items, see section 7.2.1) and enter the order line in the same way as a line with a regular inventoried item.

Alternatively, you can skip the item number field in the order line and select a procurement category. The procurement category does not include as many details as the item record. For this reason, you have to enter many details in the order line manually – e.g., the quantity, unit, unit price, and line text (on the sub-tab *General*).

3.4.2.5   Delivery Addresses

You can manage the delivery address – the address to which the vendor should ship the items – on the tab *Address* in the Header view of the purchase order. The default for this address is the delivery address of the current company, specified on the tab *Addresses* in the Legal entity form (*Organization administration> Organizations> Legal entities*). If you select a site or warehouse in the order header, and an address is specified for this site or warehouse (for warehouses, in the form *Inventory management> Setup> Inventory breakdown> Warehouses*), this address takes priority over the company address.

There are two options to change the delivery address in a purchase order:

➢ **Select an existing address** – If already included in the global address book.
➢ **Insert a new address** – If the address is completely new.

You can select the address of the current company, the site, or the warehouse in the field *Delivery address* on the tab *Address* in the Header view of the purchase order. If you want to select another address from the global address book (e.g., a customer address), click the button ⊠ on the right of the field *Delivery address*. The *Address selection* dialog then provides the option to select an address from the global address book.

If you want to specify a completely new address, click the button ⊞ on the right of the field *Delivery address*. In the *New address* dialog that is shown next, enter the delivery address (similar to a vendor address, see section 3.2.1) and set the slider *One-time* to "Yes".

If you need separate delivery addresses at the line level, open the sub-tab *Address* on the tab *Line details* in the purchase order lines. In the lines, you can select existing addresses or create new addresses (like in the header).

Note: If the slider *One-time* in the *New address* dialog is set to "No" and you select the option "Delivery" in the field *Purpose* when creating a new address, the address is a standard receipt address of the current company.

3.4.2.6 Input Tax (Sales Tax)

The applicable input tax (Sales tax/VAT) is depending on the vendor and the item:

➢ **Sales tax group** – The vendor record contains the *Sales tax group* (VAT group), which usually distinguishes between domestic vendors and foreign vendors. For companies within the European Union, "EU vendors" is another group.

➢ **Item sales tax group** – The item record contains the *Item sales tax group* (item VAT group) which distinguishes between items at a regular tax rate and other items, which are subject to a reduced rate (e.g., food in many countries).

Purchase order header and lines retrieve the tax groups from the vendor and the item. Based on these groups and related settings, the applicable tax is calculated automatically. You can edit the *Sales tax group* on the tab *Setup* in the Header view. From the header, the sales tax group is copied to the lines. In the lines, you can edit the *Sales tax group* and the *Item sales tax group* on the sub-tab *Setup* of the tab *Line details*. If you want to view the calculated sales tax, click the button *Purchase/Tax/ Sales tax* in the Purchase order form.

3.4.2.7 Charges

If an order includes additional costs like freight or insurance, you can use charges at order header level or at line level. The functionality of charges in purchasing corresponds to charges in sales (see section 4.4.5). With the button *Purchase/ Charges/Maintain charges* in the action pane of a purchase order, you can access the charges that refer to the order header. In order to access the line charges, select the respective order line and click the button *Financials/Maintain charges* in the toolbar of the tab *Purchase order lines*.

3.4.2.8   Delivery Schedule

If you got a purchase order with an item, which you want to receive in multiple deliveries, enter multiple lines with the same item but different delivery dates. In order to simplify administration, you can use the delivery schedule functionality for managing order lines with common commercial conditions (price, discounts) but multiple deliveries.

Entering a delivery schedule starts by inserting a regular order line with the total quantity of all deliveries. Then click the button *Purchase order line/Delivery schedule* in the toolbar of the order lines. In the *Delivery schedule* dialog, enter the lines for the individual deliveries with quantity and delivery date. Once you close the dialog with the button *OK*, Dynamics 365 creates additional purchase order lines for the deliveries. Only these delivery lines are included in the product receipt and the invoice, and in the calculation of the item availability. The original order line can be used to manage a common price and discount for the delivery lines.

The column *Type* on the left in the purchase order lines indicates whether an order line is the total quantity line or a delivery line.

3.4.2.9   Header View and Lines View

When you access the Purchase order detail form, it is shown in the Lines view. At the top of the page, a header line displays the order number and the vendor on the left, and the order status and the approval status on the right. After expanding the tab *Purchase order header* in the Lines view, it shows selected header fields (e.g., the delivery date).

If you want to view the complete header, click the button *Header* above the tabs in the detail form, or press the shortcut *Ctrl+Shift+H*. In order to switch back from the Header view to the Lines view, click the button *Lines* or press the shortcut *Ctrl+Shift+L*.

3.4.2.10 Copying a Purchase Order

When entering a purchase order which is similar to an existing order, you can copy the existing order. This order does not need to be of the same purchase type. You can, for example, copy an order with the type "Journal" into a regular purchase order.

In order to copy a purchase order into a new order, create a new order header into which you want to copy. In the new order, click the button *Purchase order/Copy/ From all* in the action pane. The *Copy from other document* dialog, which is shown next, displays a list of orders on the tab *Purchase orders*, and of other documents on the lower tabs. Select the checkbox in the left-most column as shown in Figure 3-17 to mark the records which you want to copy – entire orders in the section *Headers*, or individual order lines in the section *Lines*.

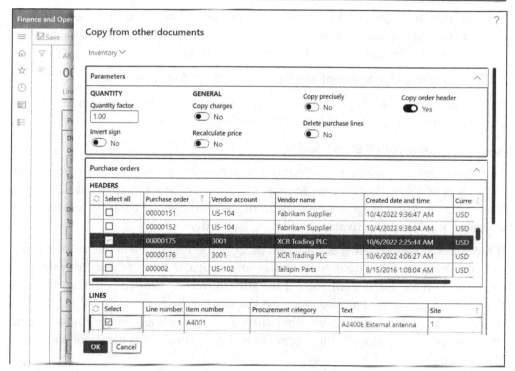

Figure 3-17: Selecting orders and order lines in the *Copy from other documents* dialog

When you copy an order, be aware of the slider *Delete purchase lines* on the tab *Parameters*. If this slider is set to "Yes", all lines of the new order are deleted before the copied lines are inserted. This does not matter for a new order, but it might be unintended if you only want to copy additional lines to an existing order.

Once you have selected the order headers and the lines (lines can refer to different headers), click the button *OK* to close the *Copy* dialog. Dynamics 365 copies the selected lines, depending on the slider *Copy order header* including header data like the payment terms (if you want to copy header data, select one header).

In addition to the *Copy from all* button, there is another button for copying in the Purchase order form – the button *Purchase order/Copy/From journal*. You can use this button if there is a purchase order with posted documents (e.g., vendor invoices) and you want to transfer the posted lines into the order again.

In addition to the copy buttons in the action pane, the copy features are also available within the button *Purchase order line* in the toolbar of the order lines.

3.4.2.11 Purchase Journal Orders

Purchase orders with the type "Journal" are used as draft or template. It is not possible to post a document (e.g., an order confirmation or a product receipt) in orders with this purchase type, and the order lines do not generate inventory transactions. Apart from copying a purchase journal to a regular purchase order, you can transfer a journal to a purchase order by simply changing the purchase type in the order header, or with the periodic activity *Procurement and sourcing> Purchase orders> Purchase journal> Post purchase journal*.

3.4.3   Change Management and Purchase Order Approval

Depending on the settings for change management, a purchase order has to be approved in an approval workflow after creating the order.

3.4.3.1   Change Management Settings

The Procurement parameters (*Procurement and sourcing> Setup> Procurement and sourcing parameters*) contain core settings for purchase order change management: The slider *Activate change management* in the section *General* controls whether the approval workflow is activated for all purchase orders.

If the slider *Allow override of settings per vendor* in the Procurement parameters is set to "Yes", you can enter divergent settings for particular vendors. For this purpose, open the Vendor detail form and set the slider *Override settings* in the field group *Change management for purchase orders* on the tab *Purchase order defaults* to "Yes" to override the general setting in either direction: Activating change management only for specific vendors (while approval is not required in general), or the other way around.

The purchase order approval process is based on the workflow system (see section 10.4). You can manage the workflows in the menu item *Procurement and Sourcing> Setup> Procurement and sourcing workflows*. Purchase order workflows refer to the workflow type "Purchase order workflow" and "Purchase order line workflow".

3.4.3.2   Approval Status

The purchase order header contains the *Approval status*, which is displayed in a separate column in the Purchase order list page. Depending on the approval workflow, a purchase order has got the following approval status:

➤ **Draft** – Initial approval status, before submitting for approval.
➤ **In review** – After submitting, while the order is waiting for approval.
➤ **Rejected** – After the reviewer rejects approval (resubmit or recall in this case).
➤ **Approved** – After approval (the next step is the order confirmation).
➤ **In external review** – After posting the purchase inquiry (optional step).
➤ **Confirmed** – After posting the purchase order confirmation.

In addition, there is the approval status "Finalized". This status, which you can set with the button *Purchase/Actions/Finalize* in the purchase order, is only available after posting the invoice. Finalizing is an optional last step in order processing which blocks the order for any changes. It is only necessary when working with budget control and encumbrances.

If change management is not activate for a purchase order, the approval status of the order immediately is "Approved", and you can continue order processing and confirm the order.

3.4.3.3 Approval Workflow for Purchase Orders

In a purchase order with activated change management, the button *Workflow* is shown in the action pane, and the initial approval status of the order is "Draft". Click the button *Workflow/Submit* to submit the order for approval after entering the order in this case. Approval is also required after modifying an order which has been approved already.

After submitting for approval, the approval status switches to "In review" and the workflow system starts processing the approval workflow in a batch process.

Because of this batch process, it is not possible to post the order confirmation for a purchase order immediately if change management is active. Even if a workflow with automatic approval applies, you have to wait until the workflow system has finished the batch process. If a manual approval is required, the responsible person has to decide whether to approve the purchase order. The work items assigned to this person (see section 10.4.3) are the usual starting point for manual approvals.

3.4.3.4 Request Changes

If you want to edit a purchase order after approval, click the button *Purchase order/ Maintain/Request change* in the purchase order. Once you have finished the changes on the purchase order, you have to submit the order for approval again.

When deciding on the approval of a modified order, the responsible person can click the button *Manage/History/Compare to recent versions* to compare the current purchase order with the last confirmed version. If you want to compare all precedent versions, click the button *Manage/History/View purchase order versions*.

3.4.4   Canceling and Deleting Purchase Orders

There is a difference between canceling and deleting a purchase order: Whereas canceling removes the open quantity (the expected quantity for future product receipts), deleting eliminates the order line or the entire order.

Deleting an order is not possible after posting the order confirmation, or, if change management applies, after approval. But you can still cancel the order.

3.4.4.1 Canceling an Order or Order Line

You should cancel a purchase order line if you do not expect any further deliveries for the line. For this purpose, select the respective order line and click the button *Update line/Deliver remainder* in the toolbar of the purchase order lines. In the *Update remaining quantity* dialog, which is shown next, you can change or cancel the remaining quantity (deliver remainder). If you want to cancel the deliver remainder, click the button *Cancel quantity* in the dialog to set the deliver remainder to zero.

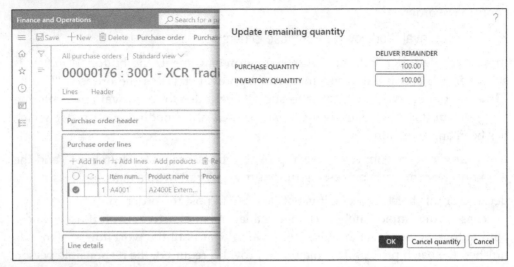

Figure 3-18: Modifying or canceling a remaining line quantity in the *Update quantity* dialog

Once you click the button *OK* in the dialog, the deliver remainder in the order line is adjusted. If partial deliveries have been received already, canceling has not got an impact on these receipts – you just do not expect any further receipt.

If the purchase order confirmation has been posted already, you can cancel the complete order with the button *Purchase order/Maintain/Cancel* in the action pane of the purchase order. After canceling a complete order (that is, all lines of the order), the order status is "Canceled".

3.4.4.2 Deleting Purchase Orders and Order Lines

Unlike canceling, which reduces the open quantity of an order line, deleting a purchase order line removes it from Dynamics 365. In order to delete a purchase order line, select it and click the button *Remove* in the toolbar of the order lines, or press the shortcut *Alt+Del*.

If you want to delete a complete order, click the button *Delete* in the action pane at the top of the detail form or – after selecting the order header – press the shortcut *Alt+Del*.

Once you have posted the order confirmation or submitted the order for approval, it is not possible to delete the order completely. If you want to delete an order line in an approved order which is subject to change management, you have to request a change (button *Purchase order/Maintain/Request change*, see section 3.4.3).

3.4.5   Purchase Inquiries and Order Confirmations

Once the order entry and – if required – the approval process is completed, the approval status of the purchase order is "Approved". In this status, you can optionally post a purchase inquiry before you post the required purchase order confirmation. If you use the vendor portal in Dynamics 365, post a *Confirmation request* (instead of the purchase inquiry) for requesting the vendor validation in the portal.

3.4.5.1 Purchase Inquiries

The purchase inquiry is an optional document which you can send to the vendor for validation. It does not create physical or financial transactions. Posting the purchase inquiry sets the approval status of the order to "In external review".

In order to post the purchase inquiry, click the button *Purchase/Generate/Purchase inquiry* in the purchase order. In the *Purchase inquiry* dialog, you can select settings for posting and printing as described below for the order confirmation.

If the vendor wants you to apply changes to the purchase order, you can update the order and – if change management is activated – approve the changes in the approval workflow before posting another purchase inquiry for the same order.

Note: Purchase inquiries are available for vendors without vendor collaboration (see section 3.2.1). If the vendor collaboration is active, use the option *Send for confirmation* instead of the purchase inquiry in the purchase order.

3.4.5.2 Purchase Order Confirmations

The purchase order confirmation is a mandatory document which you have to post before you can record a product receipt. In parallel to posting the confirmation, you usually print it (physically or electronically) and send it to the vendor.

Confirming a purchase order means to save it unchangeably and separately from the current purchase order. The confirmation shows the document which has been agreed with the vendor. It does not create physical or financial transactions.

In order to confirm a purchase order, select the order and click the button *Purchase/ Generate/Confirmation* in the Purchase order form. Alternatively, you can click the button *Purchase/Actions/Confirm* which executes the same functionality (without showing the posting dialog).

The option to confirm a purchase order is also available on applicable tabs in the center section of the workspace *Purchase order preparation*.

3.4.5.3 Posting Dialog for Order Updates

Whenever you post a document for a purchase order (confirming the order also is posting a document), a posting dialog with the following options is shown:

➢ **Parameters / Quantity** – "Ordered quantity" is the only option for the purchase order confirmation, posting the total quantity of all lines. Additional options are available for other transactions (e.g., for the receipts list described below).

➢ **Parameters / Posting** – If set to "Yes", the document is posted. If set to "No", the output is a pro forma document.

> ➢ **Parameters / Late selection** – Relevant for the filter selection of summary updates which are submitted to a batch process (as described further below).
> ➢ **Print options / Print** – If you select multiple orders for a summary update, the option "Current" prints each document separately while posting, whereas "After" starts printing after the last document has been posted.
> ➢ **Print options / Print purchase order** – If set to "Yes", the document is printed. Otherwise, the document is posted is without printing (reprinting is possible).
> ➢ **Print options / Use print management destination** – If set to "Yes", the settings specified in the print management are used. Otherwise, settings which you specify with the button *Printer setup* in the toolbar of the posting dialog apply.

You can access the print management settings in the menu item *Procurement and sourcing> Setup> Forms> Form setup* (click the button *Print management* in the section *General*) or, at vendor level, in the Vendor form (click the button *General/Set up/ Print management* in the action pane). For details on the general functionality of print management and on advanced notes, see section 4.2.1.

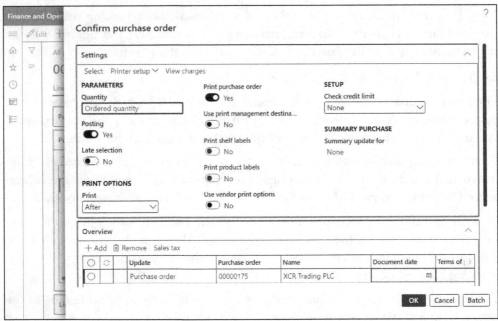

Figure 3-19:   Accessing the printer setup in the *Confirm purchase order* dialog

In order to post the document finally, click the button *OK* in the posting dialog. If the slider for printing is set to "Yes" in the dialog, the document is printed on a printer, or saved as a file, or shown in a print preview (depending on the selected settings for printing).

3.4.5.4   Pro Forma Documents

In the *Confirm purchase order* dialog, you can select to print a document while the slider *Posting* is set to "No". Dynamics 365 generates a pro forma document in this case. A pro forma document, which can be required for purposes like the customs declaration, is not a posted document. For this reason, it is not possible to reprint or display the document independent of the purchase order.

Instead of the regular button for posting order confirmations, you can also use the button *Purchase/Generate/Pro forma confirmation* in the purchase order to generate a pro forma confirmation. In the posting dialog for pro forma documents, the slider *Posting* is always set to "No".

3.4.5.5 Summary Updates

Apart from the button in the Purchase order form, the related periodic activity for summary updates is another option to post a document.

The summary order confirmation (*Procurement and sourcing> Purchase orders> Purchase order confirmation> Confirm purchase orders*) opens the same posting dialog as the button for the order confirmation in the purchase order. But whereas a filter on the current order is automatically set when you access the posting dialog from a purchase order, the summary update requires manually entering a filter. You can set this filter with the button *Select* in the toolbar of the tab *Settings* in the posting dialog. A dialog with an advanced filter, in which you can select the applicable purchase orders, is shown then. Once you close the filter dialog with the button *OK*, the selected orders are shown on the tab *Overview* of the posting dialog. If you do not want to post a particular order which is listed on this tab, delete the respective line in the dialog. Then post the document(s) with the button *OK*.

The slider *Late selection* in the posting dialog is relevant if you submit the order confirmation to a batch process (see section 2.2.1): If this slider is set to "Yes", Dynamics 365 searches for orders which meet the filter criteria at the time when executing the batch process. Otherwise, posting is executed for the orders that are selected at the time when originally entering the filter (in a recurring batch process this would mean that always the same orders are selected).

3.4.5.6 Inquiries and Document Reprint

After posting a document in the purchase order, the posted document is stored separate from the purchase order. Later amendments of the order have no impact on the posted document.

If you want to view a posted purchase order confirmation, click the button *Purchase/Journals/Purchase order confirmations* in the Purchase order form or open the menu item *Procurement and sourcing> Purchase orders> Purchase order confirmation> Purchase order confirmations*.

If you want to view a posted *Purchase inquiry* document, click the button *Purchase/Journals/Purchase inquiry* in the purchase order.

The tab *Overview* in the Purchase order confirmation inquiry shows the posted purchase order confirmations. Select an order confirmation header on this tab and switch to the tab *Lines* if you want to view the related lines.

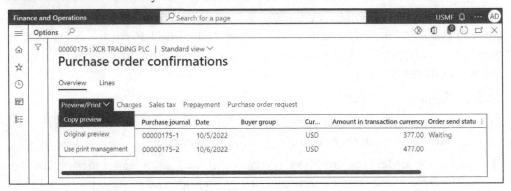

Figure 3-20: Reprint options in the purchase order confirmation inquiry

If you want to display a print preview of the posted order confirmation, click the button *Preview/Print> Copy preview* or *Preview/Print> Original preview* in the toolbar of the tab *Overview* in the inquiry. From the preview, you can reprint the document. Alternatively, use the button *Preview/Print> Use print management* to print one or more order confirmations from the order confirmation inquiry (printing to the printer specified in the print management).

3.4.6   Case Study Exercises

Exercise 3.6 – Purchase Order

In order to avoid purchase order approvals, make sure that change management does not apply to the vendor of exercise 3.2.

You want to order the item of exercise 3.5 from the vendor of exercise 3.2. Enter the purchase order in the workspace *Purchase order preparation*. Which quantity and which price is shown in the order line? Then enter a second order line with two hours of the procurement category "##-assembling" (entered in exercise 3.4) for a price of USD 100.

In the next step, check all orders with the vendor of exercise 3.2. How do you proceed and how many orders are shown?

Exercise 3.7 – Order Confirmation

Post and print the purchase order confirmation for the order which you have created in exercise 3.6. Generate a PDF file for the order confirmation.

Then change the quantity in the first line of the order of exercise 3.6 to 120 units. How do you proceed? Post the confirmation and display it as a print preview.

3.5   Item Receipt

Once an ordered item arrives in the warehouse, you post an item receipt. The item is available in inventory then.

3.5.1   Basics of Item Receipts

The workspace *Purchase order receipt and follow-up* is there to check whether the required items arrive on time. It shows the delayed and the pending receipts on lists in the center section, and it provides access to the related backorder lines.

Apart from the workspace, there are inquiries and reports which are designed to review open purchase order lines. These inquiries include:

➢ *Procurement and sourcing> Purchase orders> Purchase order follow-up> Backorder purchase lines* – List page showing open order lines with a confirmed delivery date on or before the *To date* in the filter area of the list page.

➢ *Procurement and sourcing> Purchase orders> Purchase order follow-up> Open purchase order lines* – Inquiry showing all open order lines (use the filter pane, the grid column filter, or the advanced filter to select relevant records).

You can optionally print a receipts list if you need to prepare the item receipt. This list is only used for information purposes (e.g., for the responsible in your warehouse). Apart from the receipts list, the warehouse responsible can also use the Arrival overview form to view and to prepare expected receipts.

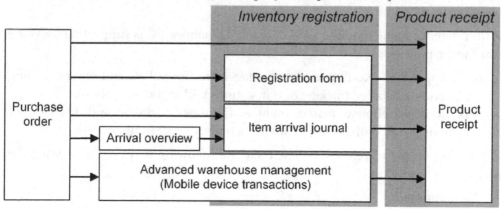

Figure 3-21:   Options for processing the item receipt

The item receipt in inventory includes two consecutive steps (see Figure 3-21):

➢ **Inventory registration** – You can record the inventory registration, which preliminarily increases the on-hand quantity in inventory, from the purchase order line, or in an item arrival journal, or in mobile device transactions (with the advanced warehouse management).

➢ **Product receipt** – The product receipt is posting the final physical inventory transaction and – depending on the setup – general ledger transactions for the item receipt. The inventory registration before the product receipt is optional.

Whereas you can execute the inventory registration before posting a purchase order confirmation, is not possible to post the product receipt before the purchase order confirmation.

Depending on the particular requirements and on the setup, it is possible to skip the inventory registration and the product receipt for a purchase order. If you skip the product receipt, a receipt is posted when you post the vendor invoice.

3.5.2   Receipts Lists

The way of posting a receipts list is similar to a purchase order confirmation: If you want to generate a receipts list, open the related posting dialog. The receipts list is optional, and it does not create transactions in inventory or in finance.

In order to post and print a receipts list, open the Purchase order list page, select the order and click the button *Receive/Generate/Receipts list*. Alternatively, you can open the posting dialog with the menu item *Procurement and sourcing> Purchase orders> Receiving products> Post receipts list* and enter a filter with the button *Select*.

The receipts list is not a very common document, but you can use it for information purposes on an expected item receipt.

3.5.3   Inventory Registration

Inventory registration is a preliminary step before posting the product receipt. The options, which are available for inventory registration, are depending on the warehouse policy.

With reference to the required level of detail, Dynamics 365 is supporting two core warehouse policies:

➢ **Basic approach** – No license plate management (for pallets and other handling units) and no detailed tracking of transactions within the warehouse.
➢ **Advanced warehouse management** – Detailed planning and tracking of warehouse work with license plates (which represent handling units).

Depending on the warehouse policy, there are following ways for processing the inventory registration:

➢ **Basic approach**
   o **Registration form** – From the order line (e.g., for entering serial numbers).
   o **Item arrival journal** – In inventory, separate from the Purchase order form.
   o **Arrival overview** – Optional prior step to item arrival journals.
➢ **Advanced warehouse management**
   o **Mobile device** – Record transactions on the mobile device.

Inventory registration is only possible for inventoried items (product type "Item", item model group with *Stocked product* enabled). The item model group of the purchased item also controls whether you have to post a registration before the product receipt (checkbox *Registration requirements* on the tab *Inventory policies* in the item model group).

It is not possible to use the inventory registration for order lines which contain a procurement category or a non-stocked item. But you can post a product receipt for these lines.

This section explains the inventory registration in the basic approach for warehouse management. Section 8.1.2 contains details on how to process item receipts with the advanced warehouse management.

3.5.3.1 Registration in a Purchase Order Line

If it is required to register the item quantity before posting the product receipt, the usual approach is to post an item arrival journal or, in the advanced warehouse management, to register mobile device transactions.

But you can also record the inventory registration without these advanced options – for example, if you need to split the transaction of a single order line into multiple lines with different locations, batch numbers, or serial numbers.

In order to access the inventory registration from the Purchase order form, select the respective order line and click the button *Update line/Registration* in the toolbar of the tab *Purchase order lines*. The Registration form is divided among two tabs: The tab *Transactions* in the upper pane, which shows the status of the inventory transaction(s) that are linked to the selected order line, and the tab *Registration lines* in the lower pane, in which you can post the registration.

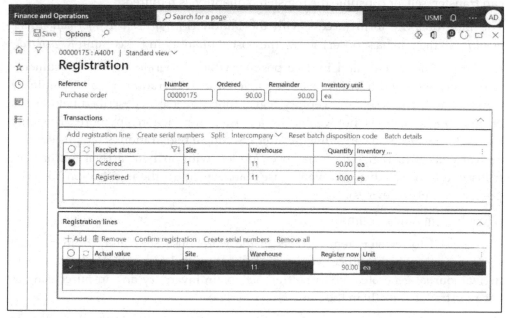

Figure 3-22: Registering a receipt in the Registration form

When you access the inventory registration from a purchase order line, the tab *Transactions* initially shows a single inventory transaction, which has been created when entering the order line. This transaction is split into multiple lines if you post partial deliveries, or if you split the line manually. If you want to register inventory dimensions for batch or serial numbers (if applicable), you can split a line with the button *Split* or *Create serial numbers* in the toolbar of the tab *Transactions*.

In order to record the inventory registration, insert appropriate lines on the tab *Registration lines* manually with the button *Add* on this tab, or with the button *Add registration line* in the toolbar of the tab *Transactions* (see Figure 3-22).

Before posting the registration with the button *Confirm registration* on the tab *Registration lines*, you can change the warehouse, the quantity, and applicable inventory dimensions as required. You can record a partial registration by entering a smaller than the original quantity on the tab *Registration lines*. In this case, the inventory transaction is split into two lines – one with the registered quantity, and one with the remaining quantity.

If you have already started the registration on the tab *Registration lines* and you want to cancel it before posting, click the button *Remove all*. Removing registration lines restores the registration as it has been before starting the current registration.

3.5.3.2   Registration Status

Once the inventory registration is posted, the registered quantity is available in inventory, and the status of this quantity is "Registered". After registration, you can transfer, sell, or consume the registered quantity as required.

The Line quantity form (access with the button *General/Related information/Line quantity* in the purchase order) shows the posted quantity in the column *Registered*.

Unlike product receipt and invoice posting, which generate voucher documents with unchangeable transactions, the inventory registration is a preliminary transaction. If you reset an inventory registration (reverse as described below), the original registration is not visible as a posted transaction anymore. The only transaction which you can still view after resetting a registration is the posted item arrival journal (if registration has been posted with an item arrival journal), or transactions in the advanced warehouse management (if the registration has been posted on mobile devices).

3.5.3.3   Item Arrival Journals

If you need to register item receipts in the warehouse separately from product receipt posting in the office, you can use item arrival journals. Posting an item arrival journal generates the same transactions in inventory and in purchasing as the registration directly in the purchase order line.

Registering and posting an item arrival journal works similar to the procedure in other inventory journals (see section 7.4.2).

3.5.3.4   Arrival Overview

The form *Inventory management> Inbound orders> Arrival overview* gives an overview of the expected item arrivals. On the tabs *Arrival options* and *Arrival query details* of this form, you can enter filter criteria like the date range of expected receipts (*Days back, Days forward*), the warehouse, or the vendor (*Account number*). The button *Update* in the action pane then applies the selected criteria. If you want to use the same filter criteria repeatedly, create one or more profiles with appropriate filter settings (click the button *Arrival overview profiles* or *New arrival overview profile* for this purpose). On the tab *Arrival options* of the arrival overview, you can subsequently select an *Arrival overview profile name*.

Then select the receipts or lines for which you actually want to register an arrival (use the checkbox in the column *Select for arrival* on the tab *Receipts* or the tab *Lines*) and click the button *Start arrival* in the toolbar of the tab *Receipts*. Starting the arrival creates, but does not post, an item arrival journal for the selected lines (the journal name is given on the tab *Arrival options*).

In order to post the arrival journal, open the item arrival journals (*Inventory management> Journal entries> Item arrival> Item arrival*). Alternatively, click the button *Journals/Show arrivals from receipts* in the toolbar of tab *Receipts* in the arrival overview after selecting the receipt, for which you have started the arrival.

With the button *Journals/Product receipt ready journals* in the arrival overview, you can show posted arrival journals, for which the product receipt (see section 3.5.4 below) has not been posted yet.

3.5.3.5   Reversing an Inventory Registration

In order to reverse (cancel) a registration, which has been posted in the item arrival journal or in the Registration form, select the respective order line in the Purchase order form and open the Registration form.

On the tab *Transactions* of the Registration form, click the button *Add registration line* for the particular transaction. Then post the transaction like a regular inventory registration, but with a negative quantity.

3.5.4   Product Receipts

Whereas the inventory registration is a preliminary transaction, the product receipt is the commercial acknowledgement that you have actually received the items. In line with this, posting a product receipt generates a physical inventory transaction, which finally receives the item in an unchangeable voucher document.

3.5.4.1   Posting Dialog for Product Receipts

The way to post a product receipt is similar to a purchase order confirmation. If you want to post the product receipt from the Purchase order form, select the order and click the button *Receive/Generate/Product receipt*.

The posting dialog then shows the familiar format. In the lookup field *Quantity* on the tab *Settings*, select the applicable option depending on the prior process:

➢ **Registered quantity** – Select this option, if an inventory registration (item arrival) has been posted before the product receipt. Dynamics 365 initializes the posting lines with the registered (not yet received) quantity.

➢ **Registered quantity and services** – In addition to the registered quantity for order lines with inventoried items, the ordered quantity is the receipt quantity for order lines with procurement categories and non-inventoried items.

➢ **Ordered quantity** – Dynamics 365 inserts the total remaining order quantity.

➢ **Receive now quantity** – Dynamics 365 inserts the quantity of the order line column *Receive now*.

The posting quantity is shown in the column *Quantity* on the tab *Lines* in the lower pane of the posting dialog. If required, edit the quantities before you post the receipt finally.

The other parameters in the posting dialog are similar to the purchase order confirmation parameters (see section 3.4.5), except for the following fields/options:

➢ **Product receipt** – Column on the tab *Overview* of the posting dialog, in which you have to enter the packing slip number of the vendor.

➢ **Print product receipt** – Slider on the tab *Parameters* of the posting dialog, which is usually set to "No" because you probably don't print your own document when receiving the vendor's packing slip.

If an exclamation mark (!) is shown in front of a product receipt record on the tab *Overview* of the posting dialog, it indicates an issue with posting. A common reason is that the selected quantity in the posting dialog is "Registered quantity", but there has not been an inventory registration before the product receipt. Depending on the circumstances, you can select the option "Ordered quantity" in the lookup field *Quantity* of the posting dialog to solve this issue.

3.5.4.2 Product Receipts in Summary Updates and Item Arrival Journals

Similar to the options for the purchase order confirmation, the posting dialog for product receipts is also available as a periodic activity in the menu (for summary updates). If you access the posting dialog from the menu (menu item *Procurement and sourcing> Purchase orders> Receiving products> Post product receipt*), you have to enter a filter with the button *Select*. After closing the filter dialog, you can optionally collect multiple purchase orders into one collective product receipt (click the button *Arrange* for this purpose). You can find more details on how to arrange orders into collective documents in section 4.6.2.

If an item arrival journal has been posted for the purchase order, you can also open the *Posting product receipt* dialog with the button *Functions/Product receipt* in the action pane of the item arrival journal. If a *Packing slip* number has been entered on the tab *Journal header details* of the item arrival journal before posting, it is the default value for the *Product receipt* number in the *Posting product receipt* dialog. This way the warehouse responsible can immediately post the product receipt after the item arrival without accessing the purchase order or a separate menu item.

3.5.4.3 Canceling a Product Receipt

If you want to cancel a posted product receipt, use the *Cancel* feature in the product receipt inquiry. Open the product receipt inquiry (e.g., with the button *Receive/ Journals/Product receipt* in the Purchase order form) for this purpose and select the respective receipt. Then click the button *Cancel* in the toolbar of the tab *Overview*. If you only want to reduce the posted quantity, click the button *Correct* in the product receipt inquiry.

Canceling or correcting a product receipt does not change the original transaction, but posts a new transaction which offsets the original one.

3.5.4.4 Ledger Integration and Settings for Product Receipt Posting

If ledger integration is activated for the product receipt, Dynamics 365 posts general ledger transactions in parallel to the inventory transactions. These ledger transactions are reversed when posting the related invoice.

There are two relevant settings, which enable the posting of product receipts to the general ledger:

➢ **Accounts payable parameters** – The slider *Post product receipt in ledger* (section *General*, tab *Product receipt*) has to be set to "Yes".
➢ **Item model group** – The checkbox *Post physical inventory* on the tab *Costing method & cost recognition* in the item model group of the item has to be selected.

Irrespective of the parameter setting, product receipt transactions of items with the inventory model "Standard costs" are always posted to the ledger.

In addition to the setting on ledger integration, the item model group contains two more relevant settings for product receipts: The checkbox *Registration requirements* in the item model group controls whether you have to post the inventory registration before posting the product receipt. The checkbox *Receiving requirements* controls whether posting the product receipt is required before posting the invoice.

3.5.5 Partial Delivery, Underdelivery, and Overdelivery

You have to post a partial delivery if you do not receive the entire quantity of a purchase order line in one shipment, but split into multiple shipments.

In case the slider *Prevent partial delivery* on the sub-tab *General* in the purchase order line is set to "Yes", it is not possible to post partial deliveries.

3.5.5.1 Inventory Registration of Partial Deliveries

In the inventory registration, you can record partial deliveries in the Registration form or, if the inventory registration is posted with an item arrival journal, enter the partial quantity in the arrival journal lines (see section 3.5.3). When you post a product receipt which refers to the inventory registration afterward, select the option "Registered quantity" in the quantity lookup field of the posting dialog.

3.5.5.2 Product Receipt of Partial Deliveries

If you do not use inventory registration, you can optionally enter a *Receive now* quantity in the purchase order line in order to prepare a partial product receipt.

The *Receive now* quantity is one of the rightmost columns on the tab *Purchase order lines* of the Purchase order form. Apart from the column in the purchase order lines, the *Receive now* quantity is also shown on the tab *Receive now* of the Line quantity form (see Figure 3-23). In order to access the Line quantity form, click the button *General/Related information/Line quantity* in the purchase order.

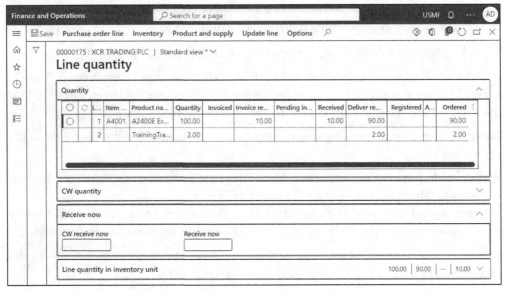

Figure 3-23: Line quantity form for a purchase order after the receipt of a partial delivery

When posting the product receipt later, select the option "Receive now quantity" in the quantity lookup field of the *Posting product receipt* dialog to refer to the previously entered *Receive now* quantity.

Alternatively, you can skip the *Receive now* quantity and select the option "Ordered quantity" in the quantity lookup field of the *Posting product receipt* dialog. In this case, enter the received quantities in the column *Quantity* on the tab *Lines* further down the posting dialog.

After posting a partial receipt, the remaining quantity for further product receipts is shown in the column *Deliver remainder* of the Line quantity form (see Figure 3-23). The received quantity (total of multiple partial receipts, if applicable) is shown in the column *Received*.

When you receive further partial deliveries, you can post the product receipts in the same way as described for the first delivery until the total of the received quantity matches the ordered quantity.

3.5.5.3   Underdelivery and Overdelivery

If you record a quantity in a product receipt, which is less than the ordered quantity, Dynamics 365 posts a partial delivery unless you characterize the receipt as underdelivery (which means that you do not expect further receipts). In order to register underdelivery, select the checkbox in the column *Close for receipt* on the tab *Lines* of the posting dialog and enter the received quantity in the column *Quantity* (see Figure 3-24).

As an alternative to the underdelivery in the product receipt, you can set the open quantity to zero by canceling the deliver remainder quantity (see section 3.4.4). But unlike the underdelivery option in the product receipt, canceling the deliver remainder does not execute a check whether the quantity reduction is within the allowed range for the underdelivery percentage of the order line.

When you post an item receipt (inventory registration or product receipt), the transaction is an overdelivery in case the total received quantity exceeds the ordered quantity. Dynamics 365 accepts overdelivery if the exceeding quantity is less than the allowed overdelivery specified in the overdelivery percentage of the order line.

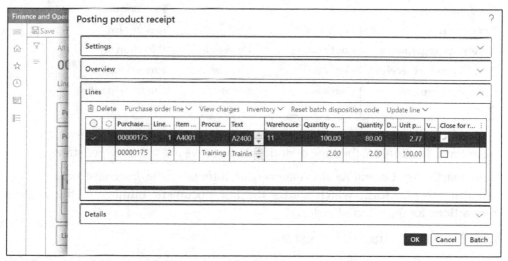

Figure 3-24:   Marking a receipt as underdelivery in the *Posting product receipt* dialog

You can only post underdelivery or overdelivery if the slider *Accept underdelivery* or *Accept overdelivery* in the section *Delivery* of the Procurement parameters is set to "Yes". In the Released product detail form (*Product information management> Products> Released products*), the maximum percentage for underdelivery and overdelivery in purchase orders and sales orders is specified on the tabs *Purchase* and *Sell*. The percentages in the released product are the default for the order lines. In the order lines, you can adjust the maximum underdelivery and overdelivery percentage as needed (on the sub-tab *Delivery* of the *Line details*).

3.5.6 Order Status and Inquiries

Posting an item receipt updates the order status and the quantity in inventory.

3.5.6.1 Purchase Order Status

The Purchase order list page contains the column *Approval status* (see section 3.4.3) and the column *Purchase order status*. The Header view of the Purchase order detail form additionally shows the *Document status* on the tab *General*. Whereas the order status indicates the order progress as given by the lowest status of the purchase order lines, the document status shows the highest status of a posted document.

For this reason, the order status of a purchase order may still be "Open order" while the document status is "Invoiced" (in case of partial deliveries and invoices). Table 3-1 below gives an overview of receipt transactions and the related status.

Table 3-1:   Order status, approval status, and document status for receipt transactions

Transaction	Approval status	Order status	Document status
(Approval)	*Approved*	*Open order*	*None*
Purchase inquiry	*In external review*	*Open order*	*Purchase inquiry*
Confirmation	*Confirmed*	*Open order*	*Purchase order*
Receipts list	*Confirmed*	*Open order*	*Receipts list*
Inventory registration	*Confirmed*	*Open order*	(No change)
Partial product receipt	*Confirmed*	*Open order*	*Product receipt*
Complete product receipt	*Confirmed*	*Received*	*Product receipt*

At line level, the status is shown in the field *Line status* on the sub-tab *General* of the order lines. In addition, the Line quantity form shows the quantity per status.

With the button *General/Related information/Postings* in the Purchase order form, you can access a form which shows the last document number of the posted transactions for the selected order.

3.5.6.2 Inventory Transaction Status

Both, the inventory registration and the product receipt, change the on-hand quantity with an inventory transaction.

When you enter a new purchase order line with an inventoried item, Dynamics 365 creates an inventory transaction with the *Receipt* status "Ordered". You can view this transaction with the button *Inventory/Transactions* in the toolbar of the tab *Purchase order lines*.

When you post an inventory registration, the receipt status of the inventory transaction changes to "Registered". The registration date is stored in the field *Inventory date*, which you can view on the tab *General* of the Transaction details form (click the button *Transaction details* in the inventory transaction to access the details). If you reverse an inventory registration, the inventory date is cleared.

Figure 3-25: Inventory transactions for an order line with two partial product receipts

When you post a product receipt, with or without a prior inventory registration, the receipt status of the inventory transaction changes to "Received". The posting date of the product receipt is shown in the column *Physical date* of the inventory transaction. The *Financial date* in the inventory transaction remains empty until the vendor invoice is posted. Additional detail data of the transaction (e.g., the packing slip number) are shown on the tab *Updates* of the Transaction details form.

Since you can only reverse a product receipt by posting an offset transaction, the physical date in the inventory transaction never changes after posting the receipt.

If there are partial receipts, the original inventory transaction is split into two (or more) transactions with a status which refers to the respective quantity. In the example of Figure 3-25, you can view the inventory transactions for a purchase order line after posting the product receipts of two partial deliveries.

3.5.6.3 Product Receipt Inquiry

If you want to view the posted product receipts, open the menu item *Procurement and sourcing> Purchase orders> Receiving products> Product receipt* or click the button *Receive/Journals/Product receipt* in the Purchase order form.

Select a product receipt on the tab *Overview* of the inquiry and switch to the tab *Lines* if you want to view the related receipt lines. The button *Inventory/Lot transactions* in the toolbar of the tab *Lines* provides an alternative way to access the inventory transactions.

3.5.6.4 Ledger Transactions and Transaction Origin

If the ledger integration is activated for the product receipt, you can click the button *Ledger/Vouchers/Physical voucher* in the inventory transaction inquiry to view the related transactions in the general ledger. If you want to view all ledger transactions that refer to a product receipt, open the product receipt inquiry and click the button *Vouchers* in the toolbar of the tab *Overview*.

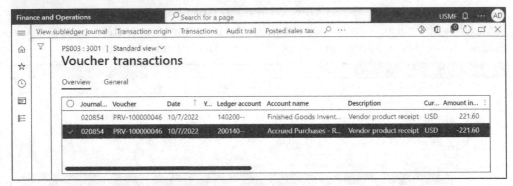

Figure 3-26:   General ledger transactions related to a product receipt

The main accounts in the ledger transactions are given by the posting setup – for the product receipt of inventoried items, the accounts for the options "Cost of purchased materials received" and "Purchase, accrual" on the tab *Purchase order* are relevant (see section 9.4.2).

The button *Transaction origin* in the action pane of the Voucher transactions form provides access to the Transaction origin form, which shows related transactions in all modules. Depending on integration settings, the product receipt is posting transactions in inventory and in the general ledger. In the example of Figure 3-27, you can view the transaction origin of the voucher in Figure 3-26.

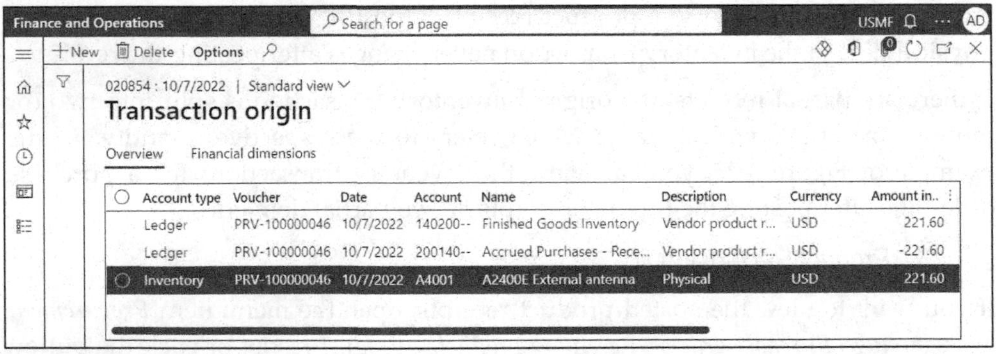

Figure 3-27:   Transaction origin form with all transactions for a product receipt

Note: For source documents like the product receipt, settings for subledger accounting in the General ledger parameters (see section 9.4.1) determine when the transactions are posted to the general ledger. If the Voucher transactions form is empty, you can access the form *General ledger> Periodic tasks> Subledger journal entries not yet transferred*, select the product receipt and click the button *Transfer now* to speed up the general ledger posting.

3.5.7   Case Study Exercises

Exercise 3.8 – Product Receipt

Your vendor ships the goods and services ordered in exercise 3.6 with packing slip
PS308. Before posting the receipt, check following items in the purchase order:

> ➢ Order status and document status.
> ➢ Inventory quantity of the ordered item.
> ➢ Inventory transaction for the order line of the product.

Then post a product receipt for the complete order quantity (120 units for the first
line after the update in exercise 3.7) with the vendor packing slip number given
above. You can post the receipt directly from the Purchase order form.

Now review the status of the items in the list above again. What is different after
product receipt posting?

Exercise 3.9 – Partial Delivery and Inventory Registration

You want to order the item of exercise 3.5 from the vendor of exercise 3.2 one more
time, this time with a quantity of 80 units. Enter and confirm the purchase order.

With the packing slip PS309, you receive a partial delivery of 50 units from the
vendor. Post the corresponding product receipt.

Next you receive a second shipment PS309 2 with 10 units. Due to organizational
reasons, you should record an inventory registration for this receipt. Open the
Registration form from the purchase order line and post the registration.

Do you know how to show the remaining quantity? Check the order status, the
inventory quantity, and the inventory transactions like you did in exercise 3.8.
What is different in comparison to exercise 3.8?

Post the product receipt for the second shipment PS309-2 afterward.

Exercise 3.10 – Product Receipt Inquiry

You are asked to review the product receipt of exercise 3.8. For this purpose, open
the product receipt inquiry, first from the Purchase order form and then from the
navigation pane. Review the product receipt header and lines, and check if there
are related ledger transactions.

Note: If the Voucher transactions form is empty, the subledger transfer probably
has not been executed yet. In this case, open the form _General ledger> Periodic tasks>
Subledger journal entries not yet transferred_, select the product receipt and click the
button _Transfer now_ in the action pane to speed up the general ledger posting.

3.6   Vendor Invoice

Together with the shipment, or at a later stage, the vendor transmits an invoice.
Before posting the invoice, you can check it in an invoice matching procedure.

Whereas product receipts update the preliminary (physical) inventory value, vendor invoices update the actual (financial) value. For this reason, posting a vendor invoice which you receive does not only increase the open vendor balance, but it also increases the financial value in inventory.

Once all lines of a purchase order are invoiced, purchase order processing is completed. The payment of vendor invoices is a separate process which is described in section 9.3.3 of this book.

3.6.1   Processing Vendor Invoices

With regard to the line content and the way of processing the invoice, there are two types of vendor invoices:

> **Invoices related to products and procurement categories** – With or without reference to a purchase order.
> **Invoices related to ledger accounts** – For example, with reference to an expense account for office rent or legal fees (see section 9.3.2).

Vendor invoices, which refer to products or procurement categories, have to be registered and posted in the Pending vendor invoices form as described below. Pending vendor invoices are not only used for invoices which refer to purchase orders, but also for invoices which do not refer to orders (these invoices may only include lines with non-stocked products or procurement categories). For inventoried items, you must process a purchase order before registering an invoice.

If a vendor invoice refers to a purchase order, both is possible – registering the invoice with reference to a prior product receipt, or posting the invoice and the receipt of the items or services at the same time (in one common step). Invoice posting without a prior product receipt is applicable if you receive goods or services together with the invoice and do not post an item receipt in the warehouse separately. For inventoried items, the checkbox *Receiving requirements* in the item model group of the item may not be activated in this case (see section 7.2.3).

If required, you can pre-register a vendor invoice in an invoice journal (invoice register, invoice approval journal). You can find more details on invoice journals in section 9.3.2 of this book.

3.6.1.1   Registering a Vendor Invoice

When you receive a vendor invoice, you enter it separately from purchase orders in the Pending vendor invoice form (*Accounts payable> Invoices> Pending vendor invoices*). This form shows all vendor invoices, which have been entered but not yet posted.

In order to switch from the Pending vendor invoice list page to the related detail form, select a particular invoice and click the link in the field *Number* (invoice number) or click the button *Edit* in the action pane.

If you want to create a new pending vendor invoice, you can start in the following pages:

> ➢ **Vendor invoice entry workspace**
> ➢ **(Pending) Vendor invoice form**
> ➢ **Vendor form**
> ➢ **Purchase order form**

The workspace *Vendor invoice entry* provides an overview of billable documents (purchase orders and product receipts) and registered invoices, which have not been posted. You can create a pending vendor invoice with the button *New vendor invoice* in this workspace.

If you start in the Pending vendor invoices form, click the button *New* in the action pane to create a new pending invoice. If you rather want to enter a new invoice in the Vendor form, click the button *Invoice/New/Invoice/Vendor invoice* in the action pane of this form.

When you register an invoice in the Pending vendor invoice form, select the vendor number in the field *Invoice account* first. Then select the purchase order number in the lookup field *Purchase order*. If you select the order number first, Dynamics 365 automatically retrieves the corresponding vendor.

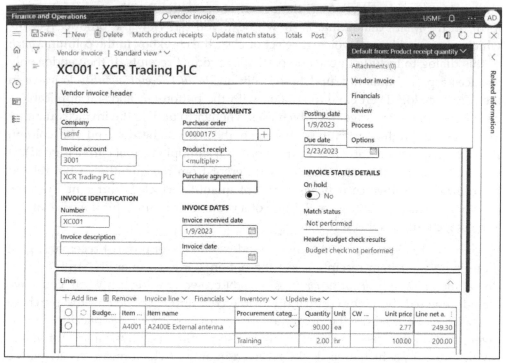

Figure 3-28:   Registering a vendor invoice for a purchase order

If you are working in the Purchase order form, you can register a vendor invoice directly from the order. The button *Invoice/Generate/Invoice* in the Purchase order form opens the Vendor invoice form and creates an invoice which is already linked to the selected order. The workspace *Vendor invoice entry* provides a similar option: Select a purchase order or a product receipt in the respective list in the center section and click the button *Invoice now* in the toolbar of the list for this purpose.

While the Pending vendor invoice form looks different from the other posting dialogs (e.g., the product receipt), the functionality is similar. Like in the other posting dialogs, the prior business process determines which option you choose in the quantity selection (button *Default from* in the action pane of the pending vendor invoice):

➤ **Product receipt quantity** – Common option (for invoices linked to a product receipt).

➤ **Ordered quantity** or **Receive now quantity** – For invoices which are not related to a product receipt.

If you select the option "Product receipt quantity" in the drop-down menu *Default quantity for lines* (access with the button *Default from* in the action pane), the quantity that is received but not invoiced is used as the default value in the column *Quantity* on the tab *Lines* of the pending vendor invoice.

In order to review the product receipts which are covered by the invoice, click the button *Match product receipts* in the action pane of the Pending vendor invoice form. In the *Match* dialog that is shown next, you can view the product receipts which are available for invoicing. Select or clear the checkbox in the column *Match* of this dialog to include or exclude particular product receipts. If the vendor only invoices a partial quantity, update the column *Product receipt quantity to match* in the *Match* dialog. Then close the dialog with the button *OK* and – if applicable – click "Yes" in the message box which asks whether to update the invoice quantity. The selected product receipt is shown in the invoice header and the column *Product receipt* on the tab *Lines* ("<multiple>", if multiple receipts are assigned). If the *Product receipt quantity to match* is different from the quantity in the related invoice line, the invoice matches a receipt quantity which is different from the quantity on the invoice (e.g., in the case of a promotion "3 units for the price of 2"). A message indicates this situation.

If you want to register a vendor invoice independently of product receipts (e.g., if there is no prior item receipt), select the option "Ordered quantity" in the drop-down menu *Default quantity for lines* – or "Receive now quantity", if you have already entered the invoiced quantity in the column *Receive now* of the purchase order lines. Then adjust the quantities in the invoice lines as applicable. But be aware that, in this case, invoice posting is also posting the physical receipt of any invoice quantity which exceeds the received quantity (which means receiving the total quantity if there is no prior product receipt).

The invoice number given by the vendor (mandatory field *Number* in the field group *Invoice identification*), the *Posting date* (for your ledger posting), the *Invoice date* (for the date on which the vendor has issued the invoice), and the *Due date* (receiving the default value from the payment terms calculation) are shown on the tab *Vendor invoice header*. If you want to prevent posting a particular invoice for some time, set the slider *On hold* to "Yes".

If you create an invoice and close the Pending vendor invoice form before posting, the invoice is stored for later posting (and approval, if applicable). You can still view and edit the invoice in the pending vendor invoices. For this reason, delete the invoice with the button *Delete* if you want to completely cancel invoice registration once you have started to enter an invoice.

Note: Simply closing the Pending vendor invoice form after starting to register a vendor invoice saves the invoice. If product receipts are assigned to the invoice, you can't assign them to a second invoice before deleting the first pending invoice.

3.6.1.2 Collective Vendor Invoices

If a vendor invoice refers to multiple purchase orders, you have to post a collective invoice. Entering collective invoices in the Pending vendor invoice form is different from registering collective documents for other document types (e.g., collective product receipts).

In the Pending vendor invoice form, click the button ⊞ next to the field *Purchase order* to access the *Retrieve purchase orders* dialog. When you select purchase orders in this dialog, pay attention to the option that is selected in the button *Default from* in the action pane of the Invoice form. This option controls whether you can select a purchase order without a prior product receipt. In addition, Summary update parameters (*Accounts payable> Setup> Summary update parameters*) and settings at vendor level determine requirements on orders which are collected to a common invoice (similar to accounts receivable, see section 4.6.2).

3.6.1.3 Invoice Matching

The details, which you enter in the Pending vendor invoice form, have to match the invoice which you receive from the vendor. For this reason, it is useful to compare the totals on the actual vendor invoice with the totals in the Invoice detail form – review the *Totals* dialog (access with the button *Totals*) or the FactBox *Invoice totals* – before posting the invoice. If necessary, adjust the quantities, prices, discounts, and line amounts on the tab *Lines* or *Line details* in the Pending vendor invoice detail form.

Apart from a manual invoice validation, there are features for automatic invoice matching. Primary settings for invoice matching are available in the section *Invoice validation* of the Accounts payable parameters. Invoice matching is only active if the slider *Enable invoice matching validation* in the parameters is set to "Yes". In this case, the parameter *Automatically update invoice header status* controls whether invoice matching is executed automatically or if it is necessary to start it manually.

If invoice matching is active, you can specify various tolerances and types of matching in the Accounts payable parameters:

➢ **Invoice totals matching** – Compares invoice total fields (invoice amount, sales tax, charges) with the purchase order.
➢ **Price and quantity matching**
   o **Line matching policy** – "Two-way matching" compares the prices and discounts on the invoice with the order line; "Three-way matching" also compares the quantity in product receipts.
   o **Match price totals** – Tolerance ("Percentage" or "Amount") for matching the total on purchase order lines with the total on invoice lines.
➢ **Charges matching** – Separate settings for matching charges.

Depending on the settings in the field *Allow matching policy override* of the Accounts payable parameters, you can override invoice validation criteria at vendor level or item level in the forms of the menu folder *Accounts payable> Invoice matching setup*. In addition, you can use business policies (menu items in the folder *Accounts payable> Policy setup*) to specify matching rules which are different from the standard invoice validation settings.

If invoice matching is activated (and not executed automatically), you have to click the button *Update match status* in the action pane of the Pending vendor invoice form to execute invoice matching before you can post the invoice. In case the vendor invoice exceeds the tolerances specified in the invoice matching setup, the Pending vendor invoice form shows the status "Failed" in the field *Match status* on the invoice header and in the related column on the tab *Lines*. Click the button *Review/Matching/Matching details* in the Pending vendor invoice form if you want to view the detailed results of invoice matching.

3.6.1.4 Posting a Vendor Invoice

Once you have entered a pending vendor invoice, you can optionally leave it pending and post it later – for example, if you have to obtain approval in an approval workflow first.

If your enterprise wants to use approval workflows for pending vendor invoices, set up an appropriate workflow (with the workflow type "Vendor invoice workflow" or "Vendor invoice line workflow") in the menu item *Accounts payable> Setup> Accounts payable workflows*. With this setup, you can post a pending vendor invoice only after approval.

Once the vendor invoice is ready to be posted, click the button *Post* in the action pane of the Pending vendor invoice form. After posting, the invoice is not shown as a pending vendor invoice anymore. It is shown in the Open vendor invoice form (*Accounts payable> Invoices> Open vendor invoices*) then, which contains all invoices that are not yet paid.

Posting a vendor invoice generates general ledger transactions, inventory transactions, vendor transactions, and transactions in other subledgers (e.g., sales tax if applicable). The vendor posting profile determines the summary account which is used in the vendor transaction (see section 3.2.3). The posting setup contains the settings for the main accounts which are related to the inventory transactions (see section 9.4.2).

3.6.1.5 Invoices without Order Reference

Registering an invoice, which does not refer to a purchase order, is similar to entering an order in the Purchase order form. Once you select a vendor in the Pending vendor invoice form, the invoice retrieves numerous default values from the vendor record. You can view and edit the corresponding fields in the Pending vendor invoice form. But unlike purchase order lines, the lines which you enter in the Invoice form may only contain non-stocked items and procurement categories.

Posting such an invoice works similar to posting any other vendor invoice.

3.6.2   Order Status and Inquiries

Similar to a product receipt, a vendor invoice updates the order status and posts inventory transactions and general ledger transactions. But an invoice additionally generates a vendor transaction.

3.6.2.1 Purchase Order Status and Transaction Status

Depending on whether you have posted a partial or a complete invoice, the purchase order has got the following status:

➢ **Partial invoice** – Order status "Received" or "Open order", document status "Invoice".

➢ **Complete invoice or last partial invoice** – Order status "Invoiced", document status "Invoice".

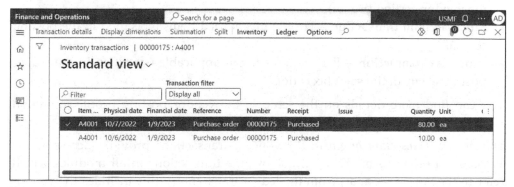

Figure 3-29:   Inventory transactions after posting the vendor invoice

If you want to view the inventory transactions which refer to an order line, select the respective line in the purchase order and click the button *Inventory/Transactions* in the toolbar of the tab *Purchase order lines*. After posting the invoice, the *Receipt* status of the inventory transaction is "Purchased", and the posting date of the invoice is shown in the column *Financial date*. The invoice number is shown on the tab *Updates* of the Transaction details form (click the button *Transaction details* in the inventory transaction to access the details).

In the example of Figure 3-29, there are two inventory transactions which refer to one common purchase order line and which are included in a posted invoice.

3.6.2.2 Invoice Inquiry

In order to view the posted invoice, open the menu item *Accounts payable> Inquiries and reports> Invoice> Invoice journal* or click the button *Invoice/Journals/Invoice* in the Purchase order form.

Select an invoice on the tab *Overview* of the inquiry and switch to the tab *Lines* if you want to view the related invoice lines. The button *Inventory/Lot transactions* in the toolbar of the tab *Lines* provides an alternative way to access the inventory transactions described above.

3.6.2.3 Ledger Transactions and Transaction Origin

If you want to view the general ledger transactions which refer to a vendor invoice, click the button *Voucher* in the toolbar of the tab *Overview* in the invoice inquiry to open the Voucher transaction form. Alternatively, you can access the voucher transactions with the button *Ledger/Financial voucher* in the inventory transaction inquiry (in this case, only the ledger transactions related to the particular inventory transaction are shown).

The Voucher transaction form displays all general ledger transactions related to the posted invoice, including the following transactions:

➢ **Transactions which reverse the packing slip**.
➢ **Vendor summary account transaction** – For the vendor balance (specified in the vendor posting profile).
➢ **Stock account transaction** – For the inventoried items (specified in the posting setup).
➢ **Input tax transaction** – For the sales tax, if applicable (specified in the ledger posting group of the sales tax code).

You can find more details on the setup of the vendor posting profile in section 3.2.3, and on the posting setup in section 9.4.2.

The button *Transaction origin* in the voucher transactions provides access to the Transaction origin form. This form shows the transactions in all modules which refer to the voucher – apart from the ledger transactions, this includes the vendor transactions, the inventory transactions, and the tax transactions as applicable.

Note: Like for the product receipt, settings for subledger accounting in the General ledger parameters determine when the transactions are posted to the general ledger. If the Voucher transactions form is empty, you can access the form *General ledger> Periodic tasks> Subledger journal entries not yet transferred*, select the vendor invoice and click the button *Transfer now* to speed up the general ledger posting.

3.6.3   Case Study Exercises

Exercise 3.11 – Purchase Order Invoice

Your vendor transmits the invoice VI311 which covers the goods and services received in exercise 3.8. Before posting the invoice, check following items:

➢ Order status and document status of the purchase order.
➢ Inventory transaction for the order line with the product.

Then register and post the vendor invoice with the received quantity in the Pending vendor invoice page. Check the invoice total before you post the invoice.

Now review the status of the items in the list above again. What is different?

Exercise 3.12 – Partial Invoice for a Purchase Order

You receive the invoice VI312 which covers the goods that you have received with packing slip PS309 in exercise 3.9. Post the vendor invoice from the Purchase order form and make sure that the posted invoice only contains the items received with packing slip PS309.

Exercise 3.13 – Vendor Invoice Not Related to an Order

Your vendor now submits the invoice VI313, which contains a line with one hour of the procurement category "##-assembling" (created in exercise 3.4) for a price of USD 105. The invoice does not refer to a purchase order.

You accept this invoice and want to register it in the Pending vendor invoice page. Check the invoice total before you post the invoice.

Exercise 3.14 – Invoice Inquiry

You want to review the invoice which you have posted in exercise 3.11. For this purpose, open the invoice inquiry, first from the Purchase order form and then from the navigation pane. Check the invoice header, the lines, and the related ledger transactions.

In exercise 3.3, you have been looking for the vendor summary account. Can you find the ledger transaction for this account? Then open the Transaction origin form and check in which modules the invoice has posted transactions.

<u>Note</u>: If the Voucher transactions form is empty, the subledger transfer probably has not been executed yet. In this case, open the form *General ledger> Periodic tasks> Subledger journal entries not yet transferred*, select the vendor invoice and click the button *Transfer now* in the action pane to speed up the general ledger posting.

3.7   Vendor Credit Note and Item Return

If you receive a credit note from a supplier, you want to register and to post it. Posting a vendor credit note works similar to posting a vendor invoice, except that credit notes are registered with a negative quantity. Like vendor invoices, vendor credit notes are classified into the following categories:

➢ **Credit notes for inventoried items** – In case items are returned to the vendor.
➢ **Credit notes for intangible items** – For crediting services, fees, or licenses.

For inventoried items, vendor credit notes have to be registered in the Purchase order form. Processing the purchase order includes the (negative) product receipt for the item return and the (negative) invoice for the credit note. If you do not post the item return separately, posting the invoice (credit note) posts the item return of inventoried items in parallel. If the item model group does not allow a negative physical inventory, you can only post the return if the item is still in stock.

In case you have to reverse a product receipt, but not a vendor invoice, use the functionality for canceling product receipts (see section 3.5.4).

For intangible items, you can register a vendor credit note in the following forms (similar to invoices for intangible items):

➢ **Purchase order** – Order lines with non-stocked items or procurement categories and a negative quantity.
➢ **Pending vendor invoice** – Invoice lines with non-stocked items or procurement categories and a negative quantity.
➢ **Invoice journal** – Journal lines with offset ledger accounts (see section 9.3.2).

In the Purchase order form or in the Pending vendor invoice form, processing a credit note for intangible items works similar to credit notes for inventoried items, but there is no inventory transaction and no inventory value for intangible items.

3.7.1   Crediting and Returning

In the Purchase order form, you have to process credit notes for inventoried items in one of the following ways:

➢ **Original purchase order** – Register a new line in the original order.
➢ **New purchase order** – Purchase type "Purchase order" or "Returned order".

The first option – using the original purchase order for the credit note – is not available, if the approval status of the order is "Finalized", or if the order is completely invoiced, and the Procurement parameter *Safety level of invoiced orders* (*Procurement and sourcing> Setup> Procurement and sourcing parameters*, section *Delivery*) is set to "Locked".

3.7.1.1   Credit Note in the Original Purchase Order

If you want to record a credit note in a new line of the original purchase order, open this purchase order in Edit mode and insert a regular order line – but with a negative sign in the column *Quantity*. If you expect a replacement from the vendor, you can enter another purchase order line with a positive quantity for the replacement.

Depending on change management settings, the purchase order may be subject to approval before it is possible to confirm it. Once you have posted the confirmation, you can optionally post the (negative) product receipt which records the item return, before you start posting the credit note with the button *Invoice/Generate/ Invoice* in the purchase order. In the Pending vendor invoice form, be aware of the posting quantity: In most cases, you can simply click the button *Default from* in the action pane of the Invoice form and select the option "Ordered quantity" – in particular, if you haven't posted the (negative) product receipt before.

If there is no other order line with an open quantity apart from the line with the negative quantity, only this line is shown on the tab *Lines* of the Invoice form. Otherwise, you have to delete the lines in the posting dialog which you do not want to post. Enter the credit note number in the invoice number (field *Number* in the field group *Invoice identification*) before you finally post the credit note with the button *Post* in the action pane of the Pending vendor invoice form.

If the checkbox *Deductions requirement* in the item model group of the credited item is selected, you have to post a (negative) product receipt for the item return before you can post the credit note (negative invoice).

3.7.1.2 Credit Note in a New Order

If you want to use a new order for the credit note, you can enter a regular purchase order (*Purchase type* "Purchase order") that contains lines with a negative quantity.

Alternatively, you can select the *Purchase type* "Returned order" when you create the order (field on the tab *General* in the *Create purchase order* dialog). If you use the purchase type "Returned order", there are the following characteristics:

➢ **RMA number** – The return merchandise authorization provided by the vendor has to be entered in the field *RMA number* in the *Create purchase order* dialog.
➢ **Quantity** – Has to be negative in all order lines.
➢ **Return action** – For information purposes, displayed on the sub-tab *Setup* of the purchase order lines (you can specify a default in the Procurement parameters).

In order to facilitate entering the credit note, you can create the order lines in the new purchase order with the button *Purchase/Create/Credit note* in the action pane of the Purchase order form, or with the button *Purchase order line/Credit note* in the toolbar of the order lines. The *Create credit note* feature is a special version of the copy feature for purchase orders (see section 3.4.2), in which you can only copy invoices or invoice lines. Compared to the regular copy feature, creating a credit note reverses the quantity sign, creates a reservation, and applies inventory marking (exactly offsetting the inventory value of the original line). Depending on whether you add credit note lines to an existing or a new order, you have to pay attention to the checkbox *Delete purchase lines* in the *Create credit note* dialog.

3.7.1.3   Inventory Marking

In order to avoid unintended changes of the inventory value, you can use inventory marking to assign the value of the returned/credited item to the corresponding original receipt.

For this purpose, select the new order line (credit note line) in the Purchase order form and click the button *Inventory/Marking* in the toolbar of the purchase order lines. In the *Marking* dialog that is shown next, select the checkbox in the column *Set mark now* (marking the original order line now returned) and click the button *Apply*. The inventory value of the new line entered for crediting now exactly offsets the inventory value received from the original line. When you apply marking to a transaction which is not posted yet, a corresponding reservation (see section 7.4.5) is set automatically.

Without marking, Dynamics 365 calculates the (outbound) inventory value of the credit note according to the item model group of the item – e.g., applying a FIFO calculation for an item with a FIFO valuation model. Depending on the valuation model, the value of the transaction is not known finally before inventory closing (see section 7.3.2).

3.7.1.4   Transaction Settlement

If the original invoice has not been paid and settled yet, you can immediately close the open vendor transaction of the original invoice when posting the credit note.

For this purpose, click the button *Invoice/Settle/Open transaction* in the action pane of the crediting purchase order. In the *Settle transaction* dialog that is shown next, select the checkbox in the column *Mark* for the respective invoice and click the button *OK*. Posting the credit note then closes the open vendor transaction of the invoice.

If you do not settle the invoice when registering the crediting purchase order, the responsible person has to settle the invoice and the credit note in the open transactions later on (see section 9.2.5).

When working with settlements, be aware that there is no manual settlement if the automatic settlement is enabled in the applicable vendor posting profile (tab *Table restrictions*) or the Accounts payable parameters (section *Settlement*).

3.7.2   Credit Notes without Item Return

If you receive a credit note from a vendor that covers a price reduction (e.g., a refund for slightly damaged goods), there is no actual physical return of an item.

3.7.2.1 Crediting and Re-Invoicing

The easiest way to process such a refund is to register and to post a purchase order with two lines: One line with a negative quantity and the original price (credit note) and one line with a positive quantity and the new price (invoice).

3.7.2.2 Crediting and Allocating Charges

If this is not suitable (e.g., if you have already shipped or consumed the credited item), you have to post a credit note which does not directly refer to the item. The credit amount has to be allocated to the item separately in this case. There are two ways to enter the credit note:

➢ **Pending vendor invoice form** – Enter an invoice line with negative quantity and an appropriate procurement category.
➢ **Invoice journal** – Enter a journal line with a negative amount and an appropriate ledger account (see section 9.3.2).

Once you have posted the credit note, you can record a charges transaction to adjust inventory value if applicable. For this purpose, select the original invoice in the invoice inquiry (*Accounts payable> Inquiries and reports> Invoice> Invoice journal*) and click the button *Charges/Adjustment* in the toolbar of the tab *Overview*. In the *Allocate charges* dialog that is shown next, enter a line for the charges transaction. The lookup in the field *Charges code* of this dialog only shows charges with the *Debit type* "Item" and the *Credit type* "Ledger account". You can offset the balance on the credit ledger account – select a charges code which refers to the same ledger account that you have used in the credit note. The ledger account on the credit note is either determined by the procurement category (in the Pending vendor invoice form) or entered as offset account in the invoice journal.

Section 4.4.5 in this book contains more details on the general use of charges.

3.7.3　Case Study Exercise

Exercise 3.15 – Vendor Credit Note

The goods received in exercise 3.8 show serious defects. You return them to the vendor and receive the credit note VC315. The vendor does not send a replacement. Which ways do you know for registering the credit note?

You decide to register the credit note in the original order. Enter the required data and post the credit note.

3.8　Purchase Agreement, Requisition, and Quotation Request

Purchase orders are the only documents which can be used a basis for product receipts and vendor invoices in procurement. Other documents in purchasing are used in business processes which prepare creating a purchase order.

3.8.1 Purchase Agreements

Purchase agreements provide the option to register and to follow up on blanket orders. Apart from agreements at the level of product number and quantity, there are agreements which specify the total amount per product (and not the quantity), and agreements at the level of product categories or vendor totals.

3.8.1.1 Managing Purchase Agreements

In order to create a purchase agreement, open the menu item *Procurement and sourcing> Purchase agreements> Purchase agreements* and click the button *New* in the action pane. In the *Create* dialog, you have to select a *Purchase agreement classification* for the new agreement. Agreement classifications (*Procurement and sourcing> Setup> Purchase agreement classification*) are only used for grouping and reporting purposes and do not refer to a particular functionality.

The field *Default commitment* on the tab *General* in the dialog determines the level of the agreement:

➢ **Product quantity commitment** – Product number and quantity.
➢ **Product value commitment** – Product number and value.
➢ **Product category value commitment** – Value of a product category.
➢ **Value commitment** – Total value for a vendor.

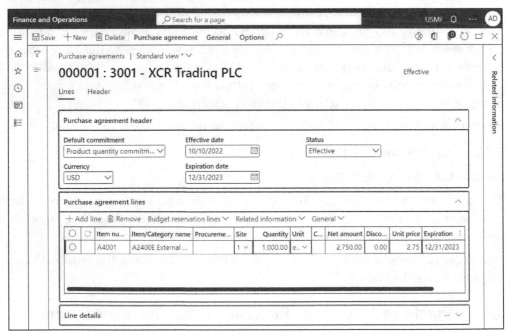

Figure 3-30:   Managing a purchase agreement

The fields *Effective date* (start date of the contract) and *Expiration date* (end date) in the dialog initialize the related fields in the agreement lines. Once you close the dialog with the button *OK*, Dynamics 365 creates the purchase agreement header and switches to the Purchase agreement detail form in the Lines view.

In the agreement lines, enter a new line with the *Item number*, *Quantity*, *Unit price*, and *Discount percent* (or *Net amount* and *Procurement category*, depending on the option selected in the *Default commitment*). If you want to prevent, that the total quantity of related release order lines exceeds the quantity in the agreement, set the slider *Max is enforced* on the sub-tab *General* of the *Line details* to "Yes".

Once you have completed the agreement lines, you can click the button *Purchase agreement/Generate/Confirmation* in the action pane to confirm the agreement. In the *Confirm purchase agreement* dialog, set the slider *Print report* to "Yes" if you want to print the confirmation. In addition, you can set the slider *Mark agreement as effective* to "Yes" if you want to set the *Status* in the agreement header to "Effective".

If you do not set the agreement to effective when posting the confirmation, you have to manually change the *Status* in the agreement header from "On hold" to "Effective" before you can generate a release order. The status "Closed" can be used to deactivate an agreement irrespective of the expiration date.

3.8.1.2 Release Orders

In order to create a release order in the Purchase agreement form, select the agreement and click the button *Purchase agreement/New/Release order*. In the *Create release order* dialog which is shown next, select the items for the release order by entering the *Purchase quantity* and the *Delivery date*. Then click the button *Create* in the dialog to generate the new release order (which is a regular purchase order with the type "Purchase order").

Instead of creating a release order in the Purchase agreement form, you can start by creating a regular order in the workspace *Purchase order preparation* or in the Purchase order form. On the tab *General* in the *Create purchase order* dialog, select the *Purchase agreement* to indicate that the order is a release order for the respective agreement. When you enter an order line with an item which is covered by the agreement, Dynamics 365 generates a link automatically.

If you create a new purchase order in the Vendor form and there is an applicable agreement, a dialog is shown in which you can select the agreement.

In the release order, you can post the order confirmation, the product receipt, and the vendor invoice like in any other purchase order. When you post the product receipt or the invoice, the order fulfillment in the related purchase agreement is updated. The fulfillment is shown on the sub-tab *Fulfillment* of the lines in the purchase agreement. If you want to check the link from a purchase order line to the purchase agreement, click the button *Update line/Purchase agreement/Attached* in the toolbar. At header level, there is the button *General/Related information/Purchase agreement* in the action pane.

3.8.2   Purchase Requisitions

A purchase requisition is an internal document which asks the purchasing department to supply particular goods or services. Unlike a planned order, which is created automatically in master planning because of an applicable item demand, a purchase requisition has to be entered manually.

3.8.2.1   Prerequisites for Processing Purchase Requisitions

Users, who enter purchase requisitions, have to be assigned to respective worker records (see section 10.2.2). The worker is shown in the field *Preparer* of the purchase requisition then.

Before you can transfer a purchase requisition to a purchase order, an approval process has to be completed. This approval process is based on the workflow management in Dynamics 365. In order to configure the purchase requisition workflow, open the menu item *Procurement and Sourcing> Setup> Procurement and sourcing workflows*. Workflows for purchase requisitions refer to the workflow type "Purchase requisition review" and, if necessary for the approval process, "Purchase requisition line review".

In the purchasing policies (*Procurement and Sourcing> Setup> Policies> Purchasing policies*), the *Policy rule* "Requisition purpose rule" of the policy which applies to your organization determines the *Requisition purpose* of the purchase requisitions:

> **Consumption** – for internal demand; approved purchase requisitions are directly transferred to purchase orders.
> **Replenishment** – for replenishing inventory; master planning needs to be executed to generate purchase/production/transfer orders for approved purchase requisitions.

If the slider "Allow manual override" in this policy rule is set to "Yes", you can override the requisition purpose in the particular purchase requisitions.

For purchase requisitions with the requisition purpose "Consumption", available products and categories have to be registered and activated in an appropriate procurement catalog (*Procurement and Sourcing> Catalogs> Procurement catalog*). Make sure that this catalog is selected in the purchasing policies for the *Policy rule* "Catalog policy rule".

For purchase requisitions with the requisition purpose "Replenishment", the policy rule "Replenishment category access policy" determines the available procurement categories with the items assigned to these procurement categories.

3.8.2.2   Entering Purchase Requisitions

In order to create a purchase requisition, open the menu item *Procurement and Sourcing> Purchase Requisitions> All purchase requisitions* and click the button *New* in the action pane. In the *Create* dialog, enter a name for the requisition before you click the button *OK*.

In the requisition lines, you can enter a released product, which is included in the active procurement catalog, in the column *Item number*. In requisitions with the *Requisition purpose* "Consumption", you can also enter a *Procurement category* and a *Product name* (description) instead of an item number if you want to request a service or a product without an item number.

If external catalogs (*Procurement and Sourcing> Catalogs> External catalogs*) and the integration settings with the vendor have been set up, you can click the button *External catalogs* in the toolbar of the requisition lines to access the vendor website, in which you order products which are transferred to the purchase requisition.

Depending on purchasing policy settings, you can enter a requisition line on behalf of another person or organization – select the appropriate *Requester, Buying legal entity,* or *Receiving operating unit* in this case.

3.8.2.3 Approval Workflow

The initial status of a purchase requisition is "Draft". Once you have completed the purchase requisition registration, click the button *Workflow/Submit* in the action pane to start the purchase requisition workflow. The requisition status switches to "In review" and the workflow system starts processing the submitted requisition in a batch process.

The further approval process is depending on the workflow configuration of the purchase requisition workflow. Section 10.4 in this book contains a brief description on how to configure and to process workflows.

As long as a purchase requisition shows the status "In review", you can create a related request for quotation (see section 3.8.3) with the button *Purchase requisition/ New/Request for quotation* in the purchase requisition.

3.8.2.4 Creating a Purchase Order

Once a purchase requisition is approved, the status changes to "Approved" and you can release the requisition to a purchase order. If purchase requisitions are released automatically, Dynamics 365 skips the status "Approved" and sets the status "Closed" immediately.

In the purchasing policies, the *Policy rule* "Purchase order creation and demand consolidation" (in the policy for your organization) determines if purchase orders are generated automatically or if they have to be released manually.

If manual releasing is necessary, click the button *Release/New/Purchase order* in the list page *Procurement and sourcing> Purchase requisitions> Approved purchase requisition processing> Release approved purchase requisitions* to release an approved purchase requisition to a purchase order.

3.8.3   Requests for Quotation

A request for quotation (RFQ) is an external document which asks vendors to submit a quotation. One request for quotation can include multiple vendors. Once you receive a quotation from a vendor, register it in a "Request for quotation reply" as a preparation for comparing quotations. If you accept a quotation, you can transfer it to a purchase order.

3.8.3.1   Entering Requests for Quotation

You can create a request for quotation manually in the Request for quotation form, or generate it from planned purchase orders or purchase requisitions.

In the Request for quotation form (*Procurement and sourcing> Requests for quotations> All requests for quotations*), you can create a new request for quotations with the button *New*. Select the *Purchase type* "Purchase order" in the *Create* dialog, if you want to enter a request which should finally create a regular purchase order, or "Purchase agreement" if you want to prepare a purchase agreement. The *Purchase type* "Purchase requisition", which you can't select manually, indicates that the request for quotation derives from a purchase requisition. Enter the delivery date and the expiration date in the dialog before you close it with the button *OK*.

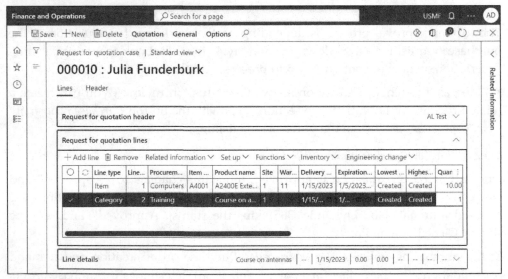

Figure 3-31:   Entering RFQ lines in the Request for quotation form

Requests for quotation consist of a header and one or more lines. The header contains common data like the language and the quotation deadline (*Expiration date*). The lines contain the items with quantity and price. Both, header and lines, include the fields *Lowest status* and *Highest status* which show the status of the request ("Created", "Sent", "Received", "Accepted", or "Rejected") and of the related quotations.

Like in the lines of purchase requisitions or purchase orders, a line in the request for quotation either contains an item number or a procurement category. In the Request for quotation form, the column *Line type* controls whether the line contains an item or a procurement category. Data like the delivery date and the address in the lines are initialized with a default value from the header. The document management (see section 10.5.1) provides the option to add details like data sheets or drawings to the request header or lines.

In order to specify the vendors, who receive the request for quotation, switch to the tab *Vendor* in the Header view and insert a line for each vendor.

3.8.3.2 Sending Requests to Vendors

Once you have entered all required vendors, click the button *Quotation/Process/ Send* in the action pane. In the *Sending request for quotation* dialog that is shown next, click the button *Print* in the upper toolbar and set the slider *Print request for quotation* in the print dialog to "Yes" if you want to print the request. Then click the button *OK* in the prior dialog to post and print the request.

If you want to view the vendors who have received the request for quotation, click the button *Quotation/Journals/Request for quotation journals* in the Request for quotation form afterward.

3.8.3.3 Request for Quotation Replies

In order to enable regular users with appropriate permissions to register RFQ replies (vendor bids), the slider *Purchaser can edit vendors bid* in the Procurement parameters (*Procurement and sourcing> Setup> Procurement and sourcing parameters*, section *Request for quotation*) has to be set to "Yes".

The button *Quotation/Replies/Set RFQ reply defaults* in the Request for quotation form provides access to a form, in which you can specify the fields which have to be included in a reply (vendor bid). These fields are shown on the RFQ reply sheet, which you can print when sending the request for quotation (there is a corresponding slider in the printing options). The default for the reply field settings is specified in the Procurement parameters (access with the button *Default request for quotation reply fields* in the toolbar of the section *Request for quotation*).

Once a vendor replies to a request by sending a quotation, open the menu item *Procurement and sourcing> Requests for quotations> Requests for quotations follow-up> Request for quotation*, select the line which shows the particular RFQ (in the column *Request for quotation case*) and vendor, and open the Reply detail form with the link in the field *Request for quotation case* or with the button *Reply/Maintain/Edit*. Alternatively, you can open the Reply detail form with the button *Quotation/ Replies/Manage replies* in the request for quotation.

In the Reply detail form, click the button *Edit/Edit RFQ reply* to access the *RFQ bid*. In this form, you can enter the header and line data of the vendor quotation before you click the button *Submit* to set the reply status to "Received".

3.8.3.4 Approving and Rejecting Replies

If you want to compare the replies (quotations) which you receive from the vendors, click the button *Quotation/Replies/Compare replies* in the Request for quotation form to access the *Compare request for quotation replies* form. In this form, you can select the checkbox in the column *Mark* and click the button *Accept* in the action pane to accept a quotation. Alternatively, you can accept a quotation in the Reply detail form (click the button *Reply/Process/Accept* in this form).

When you accept a quotation for an RFQ with the *Purchase type* "Purchase order", a purchase order is created. If you accept all lines of an RFQ, Dynamics 365 suggests rejecting the other replies for the request. But you can also reject a request with the button *Reply/Process/Reject* in the Reply detail form.

If you want to create a purchase price trade agreement (section 4.3.2 in this book contains more details on price agreements) from a quotation, click the button *General/Trade agreements/Create price agreement journal line* in the Reply detail form to generate a trade agreement journal (with a journal name specified in the Procurement parameters) which you can post subsequently.

3.8.4   Case Study Exercise

Exercise 3.16 – Purchase Agreement

In a long-term contract with the vendor of exercise 3.2, you agree that you purchase 500 units of the item of exercise 3.5 within the next 6 months for a price of USD 44. The contract is valid starting from today. Enter and confirm a corresponding purchase agreement.

The first release order related to this agreement is required today. Create this order and check the fulfillment of the agreement then.

Exercise 3.17 – Request for Quotation

You want to receive vendor quotations for the item of exercise 3.5. For this purpose, enter a request for quotation with this item. The RFQ reply defaults for the request should include the header field *Reply valid to* and the line fields *Quantity* and *Unit price*. Send the request to the vendor of exercise 3.2 and another vendor of your choice.

After a while, you receive quotations with quantities and prices of your choice from both vendors. Enter these quotations in the request for quotation replies assigned to the original request. The vendor of exercise 3.2 has submitted the better quotation, which you want to accept. Reject the quotation of the other vendor.

4 Sales and Distribution

The primary responsibility in sales and distribution is to provide customers with goods and services. In order to perform this task, the sales order process includes the order entry, picking, shipping, and invoicing.

4.1 Business Processes in Sales and Distribution

Before we start to go into details, the lines below give an overview of the business processes in sales and distribution.

4.1.1 Basic Approach

As a prerequisite for order processing, correct master data are required, particularly the customer and the product data. For services and non-inventoried items, it is possible to use sales categories instead of products.

4.1.1.1 Master Data and Transactions in Sales

Customers and products are master data, which are created once and only occasionally updated later. In the course of sales order processing, default values from customer and product records (master data) initialize the respective fields in sales quotations and sales orders (transaction data). You can override these data in the transaction – for example, if the customer requires a different delivery address in a particular sales order. If such an update should also apply to future orders, you should modify the customer record accordingly.

Since the sales process is mirroring the purchasing process, sales order processing is very similar to purchase order processing. Figure 4-1 shows the primary steps of sales order processing (including predecessor and successor activities).

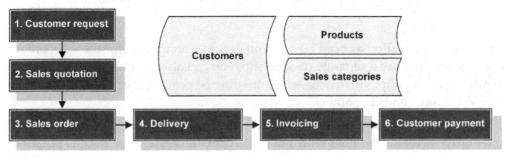

Figure 4-1:   Sales order processing in Dynamics 365

© Springer Fachmedien Wiesbaden GmbH, part of Springer Nature 2023
A. Luszczak, *Using Microsoft Dynamics 365 for Finance and Operations*,
https://doi.org/10.1007/978-3-658-40453-6_4

4.1.1.2 Sales Quotation

If we disregard prior marketing activities, the sales cycle starts with a request from a prospect or customer. The sales team then creates a quotation as an answer to this request and sends it to the potential or actual customer. Depending on applicable parameter settings, Dynamics 365 will generate activities for following up on this sales quotation.

4.1.1.3 Sales Order

If the customer agrees to the proposal and orders the goods or services, create a sales order as the basis for order fulfillment. Like a purchase order, a sales order consists of a header, which contains the common data of the whole order (e.g., customer data), and one or more lines, which contain the ordered items (products or sales categories).

Optionally, you can post an order confirmation and send it to the customer electronically or as a printed document. Posting the order confirmation stores the confirmation. For this reason, you can always view the order confirmation with its original content, no matter if the sales order has been modified later.

In order to manage long-term contracts (blanket orders), you can use sales agreements in Dynamics 365. If you later want to issue a shipment related to the blanket order, create a release order with a partial quantity of the sales agreement. Release orders are regular sales orders which are assigned to the agreement.

4.1.1.4 Picking and Shipment

Depending on the settings of the item, master planning determines the material supply (in purchasing or production) and makes sure that you can ship the sales order in time.

Before shipping the item, you can print a picking list to prepare the delivery. After finishing the internal picking process, you can post the packing slip. If no picking list is needed, you can also post a packing slip without a prior picking list.

4.1.1.5 Invoicing

Once the packing slip has been posted, you can post an invoice for the sales order. If you do not require a separate packing slip, you can also post the invoice without a prior packing slip. In this case, the invoice is posting the physical and the financial transactions in parallel.

If you want to sell services or non-inventoried items, you can process a regular sales order – enter order lines with a sales category or service item for this purpose. Alternatively, you can use a free text invoice in case you just need an invoice and no other sales document. In the lines of a free text invoice, you have to enter ledger accounts instead of products or sales categories.

4.1.1.6 Customer Payment

Before the due date, the customer has to pay the invoice with or without cash discount deduction. Section 9.3.3 contains a description on how to post the customer payment and to settle the invoice in the customer transactions.

If the customer does not pay in time, you can create payment reminders in Dynamics 365.

4.1.1.7 Ledger Integration and Voucher Principle

Based on the deep integration of finance with the business processes in all areas of Dynamics 365, the inventory and customer transactions in sales are posted to ledger accounts as specified in the setup (see section 9.4).

In order to keep track of the whole business process, Dynamics 365 comprehensively applies the voucher principle which means that you have to register a document (voucher) before posting the transaction. The transactions in sales order processing are similar to the respective purchasing transactions.

For your guidance, the Figure 4-2 below shows a comparison of purchase documents and sales documents in order processing.

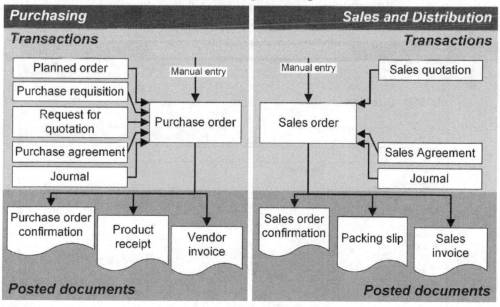

Figure 4-2: Comparison of purchasing and sales documents

4.1.2   At a Glance: Sales Order Processing

The following example demonstrates the main steps in sales order processing. It starts with creating the order in the workspace *Sales order processing and inquiry* and shows how to post all transactions directly in the Sales order form. Alternatively, you can create an order from the Customer form or in the Sales order form.

In the workspace *Sales order processing and inquiry*, click the button *New/Sales order* in the action pane to create the order. In the *Create sales order* dialog which is shown next, select a customer in the field *Customer account* (you can trigger the search in this field by typing the first characters of the customer name). Once you close the dialog with the button *OK*, Dynamics 365 creates an order header with default data (e.g., for the currency) from the customer.

The Sales order detail form is shown in the Lines view then. If you are in Read mode, click the button *Edit*, or press the *F2* key, to switch to the Edit mode. Then enter the first order line with the item number (or sales category), the quantity, and the price on the tab *Sales order lines*. When you select the item, Dynamics 365 initializes the quantity, the price, and other fields with default values from the item. If you want to enter another line, press the *Down Arrow*, or click the button *Add line* in the toolbar. The button *Header* (or *Lines*) below the action pane provides the option to switch between the Header view (see Figure 4-3) and the Lines view.

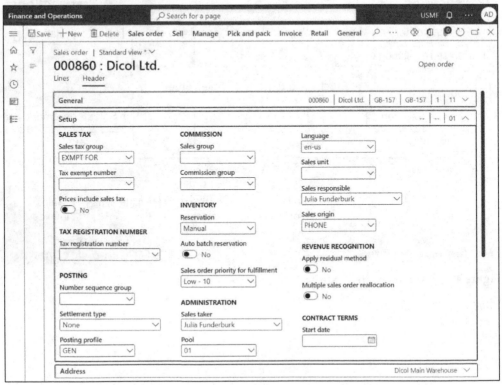

Figure 4-3:   Entering header data in the sales order Header view

If you want to print the order confirmation, click the button *Sell/Generate/Confirm sales order* in the action pane and make sure that the sliders *Posting* and *Print confirmation* on the tab *Parameters* in the dialog are set to "Yes". Optionally, click the button *Printer setup* in the dialog to select a printer.

Then click the button *Pick and pack/Generate/Post packing slip* in the action pane of the Sales order form to start posting the packing slip. In the posting dialog, select the option "All" in the field *Quantity* to ship the entire quantity and make sure that the sliders *Posting* and *Print packing slip* are set to "Yes". Then click the button *OK* to post and print the packing slip. Packing slip posting reduces the physical quantity in inventory and sets the order status to "Delivered".

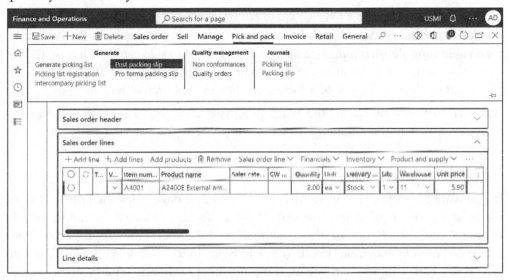

Figure 4-4: Posting the packing slip in the sales order

Posting the sales invoice with the button *Invoice/Generate/Invoice* in the Sales order form is similar to packing slip posting. In order to invoice only shipped items, make sure to select the option "Packing slip" in the lookup field *Quantity* of the posting dialog. If you select the option "All", invoice posting ships the deliver remainder quantity (open quantity, which is not included in prior packing slips) in parallel. Invoice posting generates an open customer transaction, which needs to be paid, and updates the order status to "Invoiced".

Notes: If an order contains only one line, you might need to refresh the form with the shortcut *Shift+F5* to activate the button for the order confirmation. And depending on the requirements, you can skip transactions in the process described above. The most streamlined process is to post the invoice immediately after entering the sales order (select "All" in the field *Quantity* of the *Posting invoice* dialog in this case).

4.2   Customer Management

Business partners, who receive goods or services, have to be registered as customers in Dynamics 365. As long as the business partner only receives quotations, you can optionally use a prospect instead of a customer.

Customer records in sales are similar to vendor records in purchasing, and the list pages and detail forms for both areas contain similar features. Examples of these features are one-time customers, payment terms, posting profiles, and the global address book.

4.2.1   Core Data in the Customer Records

In order to edit existing or to create new customers, open the Customer list page in the Sales module (*Sales and marketing> Customers> All customers*) or in the Accounts receivable module (*Accounts receivable> Customers> All customers*). In line with the general structure of list pages, the Customer page shows a list of all customers. If you want to view the details of a customer, click the link in the field *Account*.

Apart from the menu items, the workspace *Sales order processing and inquiry* also provides access to the Customer detail form (there is the list *Find customer* in the center section).

4.2.1.1   Create Customer Dialog

If you want to create a new customer in the Customer page, click the button *New* in the action pane or press the shortcut *Alt+N*. In the *Create customer* dialog, which contains the core fields of the customer record, select the appropriate *Type* ("Person" or "Organization") first. The field *Name* in the dialog is a lookup field in which you can enter a new name or, if the customer is already a party in the global address book, select an existing party. Depending on settings in the corresponding number sequence, the unique customer number in the field *Customer account* is assigned automatically or has to be entered manually. By default, the number sequence in the Accounts receivable parameters is used, but you can override this number sequence in the customer groups (personalize the Customer group form to shown the column *Customer account number sequence*).

Customer records are linked to the global address book in the same way as vendor records, which is why features like the duplicate check and the options to share customers across companies work similar to the options in the vendor form (see section 3.2.1).

If you want to create a sales order immediately when creating the customer, click the button *Save and open/Sales order* in the dialog.

4.2.1.2   Customer Detail Form

The Customer detail form contains numerous fields, which are used as default values in sales orders. Like the vendor group in the Vendor form, the *Customer group* on the tab *General* in the Customer form is a core setting which controls the ledger integration via customer posting profiles (compare section 3.2.3). Further important fields include the *Sales tax group* (*VAT group*, default from the customer group), the *Delivery terms*, and the *Mode of delivery* on the tab *Invoice and delivery*, the *Currency* on the tab *Sales demographics*, the *Terms of payment* on the tab *Payment defaults*, and settings for blocking (lookup field *Invoicing and delivery on hold* on the tab *Credit and collections*).

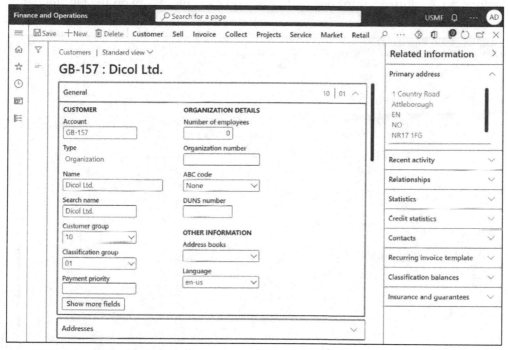

Figure 4-5:   Editing a customer in the Customer detail form

Since the structure, the fields, and the options in the Customer form are similar to the Vendor from (corresponding to the vendor approval, there is also a customer approval), the description below only covers the differences and, in addition, the elements that are primarily relevant for customer records and have not been explained for vendor records.

4.2.1.3 Invoice Account

Sometimes it is necessary to send an invoice to a customer, who is not the order customer – for example, if the head office of an affiliated group should receive the invoice for subsidiaries. In order to deal with this, you can select the customer number of the invoice customer in the field *Invoice account* on the tab *Invoice and delivery*. The invoice customer in the customer record – or, if empty, the customer number itself – is the default for the field *Invoice account* in related sales order headers, but you can override the invoice account in the sales order. The customer in the open customer transaction is the invoice account of the sales order.

Unless chosen differently in the lookup field *Invoice address* on the tab *Invoice and delivery* in the customer record, the printed invoice shows the name and address of the invoice customer.

4.2.1.4   Alternative Addresses and Global Address Book Integration

The invoice account in the Customer form refers to another customer, who needs to be entered as a separate customer with all required details. If you only need several postal addresses for one customer, you can enter them on the tab *Addresses* of the Customer form.

Figure 4-6:   Editing a customer delivery address in the *Edit address* dialog

Like the postal addresses for vendors (see section 3.2.1), customer addresses are shared with the related party in the global address book.

In order to create a new customer address, click the button *Add* in the toolbar of the tab *Addresses*. In the *New address* dialog that is shown next, enter the address name and select one or more purposes. If the address is the primary customer address, make sure that the slider *Primary* is set to "Yes" and the slider *Private* to "No".

If you enter an address with the purpose "Invoice", invoices for the customer show this address instead of the primary address. An address with the purpose "Delivery" is a delivery address in sales orders.

Whereas the button *Edit* in the toolbar of the tab *Addresses* in the Customer form provides access to the fields that are also shown in the *New address* dialog, the button *More options/Advanced* in the toolbar provides access to all address details. If a customer has multiple addresses with the same purpose – e.g., multiple delivery addresses – and you want to specify a default value for the particular purpose, click the button *More options/Set defaults* in the toolbar of the tab *Addresses*.

If you want to ship a sales order to an address, which is different from the default delivery address and from the primary address (which is the default if there is no particular delivery address), you can select one of the other customer addresses or enter a completely new address in the sales order then.

4.2.1.5 Credit Limit

In order to reduce the risk of unpaid invoices, many companies apply credit limits to customers. For this purpose, the Credit and collections module includes detailed settings which control the usage of credit limits (see section 9.2.6).

In the Customer form, the tab *Credit and collections* contains the core fields *Credit limit* (credit limit amount of the customer) and *Credit limit expiration date* (validity of the credit limit) for the credit limit. Irrespective of these settings, there is no credit limit check if the slider *Exclude from credit management* for the customer is set to "Yes".

When you enter a sales order or post a transaction, there is a check whether the customer exceeds the credit limit and the order is put on hold if applicable. In case of an order hold, you can click the button *Credit management/Credit management/ Credit management hold list* in the Sales order form and release the hold in the hold list (similar to managing an order hold, see section 4.4.3).

4.2.1.6 Print Management

The *Form setup* form in the Accounts receivable module (*Accounts receivable> Setup> Forms> Form setup*) contains some basic settings for the layout of sales documents – for example, if the external item number is printed on documents. Sections like *Quotation* or *Confirmation* (for the order confirmation) on the left determine for the related document, which inventory dimensions are printed in the lines, and – in the field group *Note* – if attachments (using the document management, see section 10.5.1) with the *Document type* which is selected in the field *Include documents of type* should be printed on the document.

In the Accounts receivable parameters, the slider *Copy notes when transferring to sales order* (in the section *General*, tab *Sales setup*) controls whether attachments are automatically copied from the customer or the released product to the sales order.

Base settings for printing sales documents – e.g., the destination (printer), the number of copies, or a footer text – are specified in the Print management setup form, which you can access with the button *Print management* in the toolbar of the section *General* in the Form setup form. If there are no settings for a document and you want to set it up, right-click on the respective document in the left pane of the Print management setup form and select the option *New* in the drop-down menu.

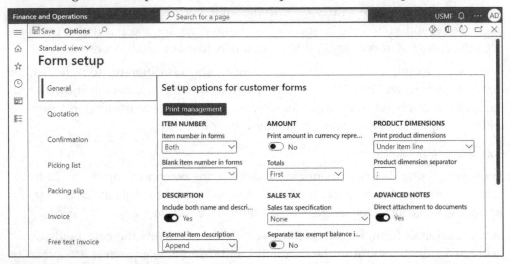

Figure 4-7:   Configuring the form setup for sales documents

At customer level, you can override these settings with the button *General/Set up/ Print management* in the Customer form: Right-click the respective original or copy document in the left pane of the Print management setup form, and then select the option *Override* in the drop-down menu before you enter the individual settings. Customer print management settings are transferred to the related sales orders. In the sales orders, you can override the settings again.

The print management settings for the print destination (printer) are used when printing a document, if the slider *Use print management destination* in the particular posting dialog is set to "Yes" (see section 3.4.5).

If you want to include some general lines in the printed documents, you can specify a standard text per document and language in the form notes (*Accounts receivable> Setup> Forms> Form notes*).

4.2.1.7 Advanced Notes

Advanced notes, which are also available in purchasing, are a more detailed option for specifying text elements which should be printed on sales documents. In order to set up advanced notes for customers, open the form *Accounts receivable> Setup> Forms> Customers advanced notes setup* and create a line – per customer, customer group, or all customers – in the upper pane with the applicable text in the lower pane (select the *Restriction* "External" in the upper pane for printing on external documents). If you use groups, create the groups in the form *Accounts receivable> Setup> Forms> Customers advanced notes groups* and assign them to the respective customers on the tab *Sales order defaults* in the Customer form. Advanced notes on line level can be entered on the tab *Lines* of the Advanced notes setup form.

In addition, some prerequisite settings for advanced notes are included in the *Form setup* form (described above). The sections for the applicable documents (e.g., *Confirmation* for the order confirmation) contain the following relevant fields:

> **Include document on sheets** – Controls whether header level or line level notes are included.
> **Include documents of type** – Specifies the document type which is used for attaching the advanced note to the posted documents.

On the tab *General* in the *Form setup* form, the slider *Direct attachment to documents* controls whether advanced notes are directly attached to the posted documents.

Note: Advanced notes for vendors and released products got a similar setup.

4.2.2   Case Study Exercise

Exercise 4.1 – Customer Record

A new domestic customer wants to place an order. Create a record for this customer with a name (starting with your user ID) and a primary address of your choice. Select the payment terms and the cash discount of exercise 3.1, and an appropriate customer group and sales tax group for domestic customers. For this customer, the credit limit should not be checked.

The customer wants you to ship ordered goods to a separate delivery address. Enter a domestic delivery address of your choice for this purpose, which should be the default for orders of this customer.

4.3   Product Management in Sales

Whereas the customer records are the main data source for sales order headers, products and sales categories are the main data source for sales order lines.

For inventoried items, product and released product records are required. For intangible items (e.g., services, fees, licenses), you can either use items (with the product type "Service" or a specific item model group) or sales categories.

This section primarily explains the product data that are necessary for sales and distribution. In section 7.2 of this book, you can find a general description of product management in Dynamics 365.

4.3.1   Product Data and Sales Categories

When entering a sales order line, you have to select an item number or a sales category to identify the item or service which you are selling.

4.3.1.1 Sales Categories

A product category (see section 3.3.1) is a group of similar products or services. Sales categories are product categories which belong to the hierarchy with the type "Sales category hierarchy". You can manage the sales-related settings of these product categories in the Sales category form (*Sales and marketing> Setup> Categories> Sales categories*). In this form, the item sales tax group on the tab *Item sales tax groups* is one of the core settings.

4.3.1.2 Entering New Products

The product management in Dynamics 365 has got two levels: The shared products (*Product information management> Products> All products and product masters*), which contain the common data of the items in all companies, and the released products (*Product information management> Products> Released products*), which contain the company-specific data.

In order to create a new product, open form *Product information management> Products> All products and product masters* (which contains the shared products) and click the button *New* to insert a record. Once you have completed the shared product, click the button *Release products* in the action pane of the shared product to create the released product. In the released product, you have to enter at least the item group, the item model group, the dimension groups (if not specified in the shared product) and the unit of measure for purchasing, sales, and inventory (a default unit is specified in the section *General* of the Inventory parameters).

As an alternative to creating a shared product and releasing it, you can create a released product with the button *New* directly in the Released product form. The *New released product* dialog, which includes data for the shared and for the released product, then creates the shared product and the released product in parallel.

4.3.1.3 Sales Related Data

Core sales data, including the *Item sales tax group* (which determines whether regular sales tax / VAT or a reduced rate applies), are available on the tab *Sell* of the Released product form.

Settings for order quantities and lot sizes are specified in the default order settings, which you can access with the button *Manage inventory/Order settings/Default order settings* in the released product. Apart from sales-related data on the tab *Sales order*, the default order settings contain further tabs with data for purchasing and inventory. A checkmark in the checkbox *Stopped* on the tab *Sales order* blocks the item for sales transactions.

In the default order settings, the record with a blank *Site* and the *Rank* "0" determines the settings at the company level. If you want to specify order settings at the level of sites, insert an additional record in which you enter the *Site* in the respective field. In order to override the default order settings at the company level with default order settings at the level of sites, set the applicable slider *Override default settings* in the site-specific order settings to "Yes".

4.3.2 Sales Price and Discount Setup

Apart from the base sales price, which you can enter in the released product, there are the trade agreements that cover price lists and discount agreements.

4.3.2.1 Base Sales Price

The base sales price is used in sales orders with no applicable trade agreement for the respective customer and item. You can edit the base sales price on the tab *Sell* in the Released product form.

It is possible to enable an automatic update of this base sales price (based on the purchase price or the cost price). The field group *Price update* on the tab *Sell* in the released product contains the settings for this price calculation. The first setting in this field group is the lookup field *Sales price model* which determines if the price calculation refers to the field *Contribution ratio* or to the field *Charges percentage*. The *Sales price model* "None" means that there is no automatic calculation of the base sales price. The lookup field *Base price* determines the basis for the price calculation and includes two options:

➤ **Purchase price** – Sales price based on the base purchase price (tab *Purchase*).
➤ **Cost** – Sales price based on the base cost price (tab *Manage costs*).

The other settings related to the base sales price (including the price quantity and price charges) are similar to the base purchase price settings (see section 3.3.3).

In addition to the base sales price on the tab *Sell* in the Released product form, you can enter base prices at the level of sites in the Item price form. In order to access the Item price form, click the button *Manage costs/Set up/Item price* in the released product. For manufactured items, you can run a sales price calculation which is based on the bill of materials and the route (see section 7.3.3).

Trade agreements enable more detailed settings for prices and discounts. If you want to view the trade agreements with the sales prices of an item, click the button *Sell/View/Sales price* in the Released product form.

4.3.2.2 Discount Groups

In the Released product form, the tab *Sell* contains (apart from the *Base sales price*) settings for discounts which are specified in trade agreements – the *Line discount group*, the group for *Multiline discount*, and the slider *Total discount*. If the slider *Total discount* is set to "No", the respective product is excluded from the basis of the total discount calculation.

In the discount calculation, the line discount is calculated on the basis of the individual order line whereas the calculation of multiline discounts includes all order lines with the same multiline discount group (which is relevant, if the discount is depending on the quantity). Total discounts (invoice discounts), which are specified at the order header level, are calculated on the order total.

In the Customer form, the tab *Sales order defaults* contains the price group and the discount groups (line discount, multiline discount, total discount) which you can use to group customers for pricing purposes. In sales orders, the price group of the customer is the default value, but you can override the price group on the tab *Price and discount* in the Header view of the Sales order detail form. The discount groups work the same way.

For purchasing, settings for trade agreements are available on the tab *Purchase* in the Released product form and on the tab *Purchase order defaults* in the Vendor form.

4.3.2.3 Structure of Trade Agreements

Trade agreements in sales determine prices and discounts depending on customers and released products. Trade agreements in purchasing work similar (with reference to vendors).

In Dynamics 365, there are the following types of trade agreements:

➢ **Prices**
➢ **Line discounts**
➢ **Multiline discounts**
➢ **Total discounts** (Invoice discounts)

Whereas trade agreements for prices, line discounts and multiline discounts refer to the order lines, the total discounts relate to the order header.

Trade agreements for prices and discounts can be specified at different levels. You can, for example, enter a line discount agreement for a particular customer, for a customer discount group, or for all customers. In addition to the customer selection, line discount agreements contain an item selection (particular item, item discount group, or all items). Table 4-1 shows the options for a line discount agreement in sales with regard to the customer and the item selection.

Table 4-1:   Discount selection levels for sales line discounts

	Item number	Item discount group	All items
Customer number	X	X	X
Customer discount group	X	X	X
All customers	X	X	X

As a result, you can enter a line discount agreement for a particular item and a particular customer, and another agreement for an item discount group and all customers.

For multiline discounts, the same principle is true, except that you can't enter a multiline discount at the level of an item number.

In trade agreements for prices and in trade agreements for total discounts, the item selection is limited to one option: Prices are specified per item, which restricts the item selection to "Item number", and total discounts refer to the order header, which restricts the item selection to "All items".

In addition to the customer/vendor level and the item level, trade agreements include the following selection criteria:

➤ **Period of validity** – *From date / To date*; the parameter field *Date type* in the section *Prices* of the Accounts receivable parameters (or, for purchasing, the Procurement parameters) controls whether the date refers to the order entry or to the receipt date.

➤ **Quantity** – Columns *From* and *To* (for quantity-dependent agreements).

➤ **Unit of measure** – Column *Unit*.

➤ **Currency** – Currency of the price (or a discount specified as discount amount).

In addition to the selection criteria mentioned above, inventory dimensions are another specification level for trade agreements. You can use inventory dimensions in trade agreements if there are different prices or discounts per site, or per warehouse, or related to product dimensions like size or color. As a prerequisite for the use of dimensions in pricing, the dimension group of the particular item has to include the selected dimensions as a price search criterion (see section 7.2.2).

The price search runs from the most specific to the general agreement, in other words from customer prices to customer group prices to general prices (in case of a sales price agreement). If the checkbox *Find next* in the rightmost column of the trade agreements is selected, Dynamics 365 searches for the lowest price in trade agreements – a lower group price overrides a higher customer-specific price in this case. You can stop this search by clearing the checkbox *Find next* (set the slider *Find next* to "No" when entering the respective trade agreement journal line).

An option which is only available in sales price agreements and not in purchase price agreements is the use of a *Generic currency* and an *Exchange rate type* which is specified in the Accounts receivable parameters (section *Prices*, tab *Generic currency and smart rounding*). If a generic currency is specified, prices in trade agreements with this currency (if the slider *Include in generic currency* in the agreement line is set to "Yes") are automatically converted to other currencies if there is no other applicable trade agreement when entering a sales order line.

4.3.2.4 Managing Trade Agreements for Sales Prices

If you want to record a sales price agreement, enter and post a trade agreement journal. In order to access the trade agreement journal, open the menu item *Sales and marketing> Prices and discounts> Trade agreement journals* or click the button *Sell/ Trade agreements/Create trade agreements* in the Released product form.

A trade agreement journal consists of a header and at least one line. The lookup field *Show* in the upper pane of the Trade agreement journal list page provides the option to select whether to view only open journals or to include posted journals. In order to create a new journal, click the button *New* in the action pane and select a journal name. From the journal name setup, the content of the field *Relation* – e.g., "Price (sales)" – initializes the *Default relation* in the journal header, which, in turn, is used as default value for field *Relation* in the journal lines.

In the journal header, click the button *Lines* to access the Journal lines form with the trade agreement lines. In the journal line for a sales price agreement, make sure that the option "Price (sales)" is selected in the column *Relation*. The *Party code type* determines if the price refers to a specific customer ("Table"), a customer price group ("Group"), or all customers. Depending on this selection, the customer or the customer price group has to be entered in the column *Account selection*. In the price agreement line, you can only use the option "Table" in the column *Product code type*. Enter the product number in the column *Item relation*.

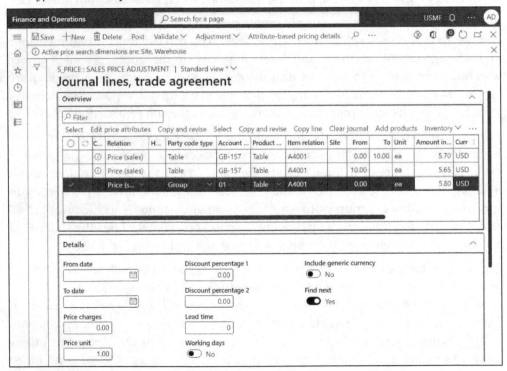

Figure 4-8:   Registering purchase prices in the trade agreement journal lines

Apart from the fields in the journal lines grid, additional data for the selected line are shown on the tab *Details*. These data include the *From date*, the *To date*, the *Price unit* (refers to the column *Unit* in the journal line, equivalent to the *Price quantity* and the sales unit in the Released product form), and the *Lead time*.

When you enter an order line, the price, price unit, and lead time of the applicable trade agreement override the default values from the released product.

At the top of the Journal lines form, a message bar indicates the inventory dimensions which are applicable for prices of the selected item. In Figure 4-8, the message tells that price agreements for the selected item can be entered at the level of site and warehouse. With the button *Inventory/Display dimensions* in the toolbar of the tab *Overview*, you can show or hide the inventory dimension columns in the journal lines.

Once you have entered the journal lines, click the button *Post* in the action pane to activate the agreement.

4.3.2.5 Updating or Deleting Trade Agreements

In order to record a new price for an item, enter and post a trade agreement with the new price, the from-date, and the to-date.

If you want to edit (e.g., update the to-date of the old agreement) or delete an active agreement, open the trade agreement inquiry – for example, with the button *Sell/View/Sales price* or the button *Sell/Trade agreement/View trade agreements* in the released product. Select one or more trade agreement lines and click the button *Edit selected lines* in the action pane next. In the confirmation dialog which is subsequently shown, select a journal name for the new journal (which is used for the update) and click the button *OK*.

The new trade agreement journal contains one line per original trade agreement line. This new line is connected to the original trade agreement. Edit the data in the line(s) according to your requirements before you click the button *Post* to update the agreement. If you want to delete the old agreement instead of updating it, click the button *Select all agreements to be deleted* in the toolbar above the grid in the new trade agreement journal and post the journal.

4.3.2.6 Managing Line Discount Agreements

In order to view sales line discount agreements, you can access the line discounts from different menu items (depending on the basis of the discount):

➢ **For an item** (including the line discount group of the item) – In the Released product form, click the button *Sell/View/Line discount*.

➢ **For a customer** (including the line discount group of the customer) – In the Customer form, click the button *Sell/Trade agreements/Discounts/Line discount*.

➢ **For an item discount group** – In the Item discount group form (*Sales and marketing> Prices and discounts> Item discount groups*), make sure that the option "Line discount group" is selected in the lookup field *Show* and click the button *Trade agreements/Sales/View line discount*.

➢ **For a customer discount group** – In the Customer price/discount group form (*Sales and marketing> Prices and discounts> Customer price/discount groups*), select the option "Line discount group" in the lookup field *Show* and click the button *Trade agreements/Sales/View line discount*.

In discount agreements, the column *Discount* (or *Amount in transaction currency*) specifies a discount amount (only applicable if the discount is an amount and not a percentage). The *Discount percentage 1* is shown in a separate column and in the footer pane of the form. The *Discount percentage 2* is only shown in the footer pane. If both, the discount percentage-1 and the percentage-2, are specified in a trade agreement, the multiplied total of these discounts is transferred to the field *Discount percent* in applicable order lines. If a trade agreement contains, for example, a percentage-1 of 10 % and a percentage-2 of 10 %, the discount percent in the order line is 19 %.

Another important setting for discount calculation is the column *Find next* on the right of the trade agreement lines. The checkbox in this column should only be selected for discounts, which apply in addition to discounts entered at another level. In the example of the trade agreements shown in Figure 4-9, the discount in a sales order line with a quantity of 100 units (or more) is 17 percent for a customer with the applicable line discount group, if the checkbox *Find next* is marked for the 12 percent discount line and if the item is assigned to the item discount group with a discount of 5 percent in the other agreement line.

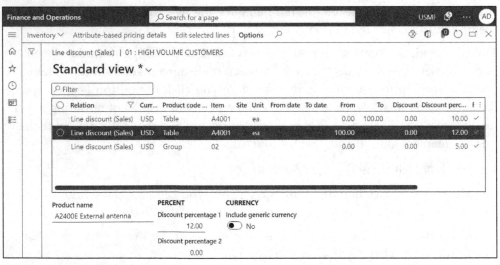

Figure 4-9:   Viewing the line discounts for a customer line discount group

Like registering price agreement, registering line discount agreement requires to enter and to post a trade agreement journal (*Sales and marketing> Prices and discounts> Trade agreement journals*). After creating a journal with the button *New* in the agreement journal header, click the button *Lines* in the action pane to access the journal lines. When you enter a sales line discount in an agreement journal line, make sure to select the option "Line discount (Sales)" in the column *Relation* and keep in mind that discount percentages are shown in the footer pane of the journal lines. If entered, a discount in the column *Amount in currency* is a discount amount.

Once you have entered the line discounts in the agreement journal completely, you can click the button *Post* to activate the agreement.

If you want to update or to delete an active trade agreement, open the respective trade agreement inquiry (e.g., the line discount inquiry that you access with the button *Sell/View/Line discount* in the Released product form), select the agreement, and click the button *Edit selected lines*. Like when updating prices, the update or deletion is posted in a new journal which is linked to the selected agreement.

4.3.2.7 Managing Multiline Discounts and Total Discounts

Whereas the basis for the calculation of line discounts is the individual order line, the basis for the calculation of multiline discounts are all lines within a sales order, in which the items are assigned to the same multiline discount group. You can use multiline discounts if you want to grant a discount based on the total quantity of several similar items (e.g., for a discount on all items of a group "Accessories"). Managing multiline discounts works similar to managing line discounts.

Unlike line discounts, total discounts (invoice discounts) do not refer to items or item groups. Total discounts refer to a complete invoice and provide the option to enter a discount based on the invoice total.

4.3.2.8 Required Setup for Prices and Discounts

As a prerequisite for trade agreements, you have to set up at least one trade agreement journal name (*Sales and marketing> Setup> Prices and discounts> Trade agreement journal names* or *Procurement and sourcing> Setup> Prices and discounts> Trade agreement journal names*). Trade agreement journal names are a common setup for sales and for purchasing. The field *Relation* in a journal name determines the default value for the column *Relation* in the agreement journals.

If you want to use trade agreements at the level of groups, you have to set up the required price and discount groups and assign them to the customers or vendors or released products.

Trade agreements are only used in the price and discount calculation, if the appropriate combination is selected in the price/discount activation (*Sales and marketing> Setup> Prices and discounts> Activate price/discount* for sales, and *Procurement and sourcing> Setup> Prices and discounts> Activate price/discount* for purchasing).

Within the activated elements, the discount calculation searches from the specific to the general level – first the customer and item number level, then the group level, and finally the general discount level ("All"). Depending on the setting of the checkbox *Find next* in the applicable trade agreements, only one discount or the total of several applicable discounts is used in the respective order lines.

If line discount and multiline discount apply to a particular sales order line in parallel, the Accounts receivable parameters (field *Discount* in the section *Prices*) control how to calculate the total of line and multiline discount.

4.3.2.9   Ledger Integration for Discounts

Discounts are reflected in the financial transactions. With regard to ledger transactions and sales revenue calculation, you have to distinguish between line and multiline discounts on the one hand, and total discounts on the other hand.

Line and multiline discounts in sales are included in the item revenue calculation – they reduce the revenue and the gross margin. Settings for the ledger integration of line and multiline discounts in sales control, if the discount is posted to a separate account or if it reduces the amount which is posted to the revenue account. Dynamics 365 will post to a separate account, if there is an applicable main account for discounts in the posting setup (*Cost management> Ledger integration policies setup> Posting*, tab *Sales order*, option *Discount*).

Unlike line and multiline discounts, total discounts are always posted to a separate account and, at the level of items, do not reduce the revenue – or, in purchasing, the cost of purchased materials (which gives the inventory value). In addition, it is not possible to post total discounts to main accounts that depend on the customer. The main account for total discount transactions is specified in the accounts for automatic transaction (*General ledger> Posting setup> Accounts for automatic transactions*, line with the posting type "Customer invoice discount" and "Vendor invoice discount").

4.3.3   Case Study Exercises

Exercise 4.2 – Sales Categories

Your company offers installation services to the customers. For this purpose, enter a new category "##-installation" (## = your user ID) in the sales category hierarchy. The sales category should refer to the standard tax rate.

Exercise 4.3 – Price List

Your company requires an additional price list for new sales markets. Enter a new customer price group P-## (## = your user ID) for this price list and attach it to the customer of exercise 4.1.

The new price list shows a price of USD 90, which is valid from now on, for the item of exercise 3.5. Enter and post this price in a trade agreement journal. Then check if the price is shown correctly for the customer.

Exercise 4.4 – Line Discount

You agree to a line discount of 10 percent on all items for the customer of exercise 4.1. Enter and post a trade agreement with this discount, which only applies to this customer. Which setting is required to use the discount in sales orders?

4.4   Sales Order Management

The first document in the sales cycle often is a sales quotation, which you can send to a prospect or customer in reply to a request for quotation. Once the customer orders the requested goods or services, you can enter an appropriate sales order.

With regard to the functionality and the structure of forms and list pages, sales orders work similar to purchase orders. For this reason, the focus in this section is on the subjects in sales which are different from purchasing.

4.4.1   Basics of Sales Order Processing

Unlike purchase orders, which are primarily based on material requirements which are known within Dynamics 365, sales orders in most cases originate from sources outside the application. Apart from manually entering a sales order, there are only a few other options to generate a sales order from within Dynamics 365. These possible options for generating a sales order include:

➢ **Sales quotations** – After acceptance, quotations are transferred to orders.
➢ **Sales agreements** – Blanket orders are the basis for release orders.
➢ **Data import/export framework** – Exchanging data with other applications.
➢ **Intercompany functionality** – From purchase orders in another legal entity.
➢ **Project module** – Create project sales orders or item requirements

In Dynamics 365, blanket orders are covered by sales agreements (*Sales and marketing> Sales agreements> Sales agreements*), which do not only contain contracts at the level of product number and quantity, but also at the level of the total sales amount for a product, or at the level of the total sales volume for a customer. In order to ship and invoice a delivery with reference to a sales agreement, create a release order (regular sales order which is linked to the sales agreement). In general, sales agreements work similar to purchase agreements (see section 3.8.1).

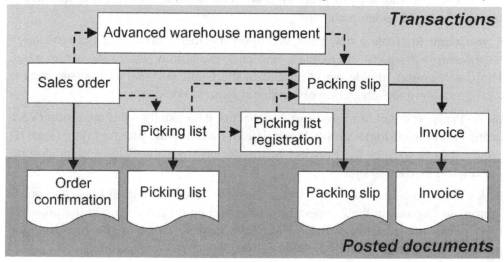

Figure 4-10:   Sales order processing in Dynamics 365

Once you have entered a new sales order – either manually or transferring a prior document like the sales agreement – you can post and print the order confirmation. The further proceeding is depending on the requirements and the related settings on how and which transactions should be registered in inventory and in sales.

In the warehouse, there are the following options for processing a sales order (see Figure 4-10):

➢ **Packing slip** – Immediately post the packing slip.
➢ **Picking list** – Post a picking list before posting the packing slip.
➢ **Picking list registration** – Confirm the picking list before packing slip posting.
➢ **Advanced warehouse management** – See section 8.1.

Another way for the warehouse process is to execute picking in the Pick form (accessed from the sales order line). Usually, you work in this way if you have to register serial numbers or batch numbers, but do not process picking as a separate step in the warehouse.

After posting the packing slip, you can post the invoice. If no packing slip is required, you can also post the invoice immediately after entering the order.

4.4.2   Sales Quotations

In a sales quotation, the business partner does not need to be a customer, it can also be a prospect. But since sales orders require a customer, you have to convert the prospect to a customer before you can transfer an accepted quotation to an order.

4.4.2.1 Managing Prospects

Prospects are parties – companies or persons – in sales, who are not customers yet. It is not possible to register transactions for prospects, which have an impact on the general ledger or generate customer transactions – this is only possible for customers. You can use prospects in CRM activities like mailings and marketing campaigns, and in sales quotations.

If you want to create a new prospect, open the menu item *Sales and marketing> Relationships> Prospects> All prospects* and click the button *New* in the action pane. The *Create prospect* dialog works similar to the *Create customer* dialog (see section 4.2.1), including the integration of the global address book.

In the Prospect detail form, you can update core data like the sales tax group (VAT group) and the customer group. Some default data like the prospect type (*Type ID* on the tab *General* in the Prospect form) derive from the Sales and marketing parameters (section *Prospects*).

If you want to convert a prospect to a customer, click the button *General/Convert/ Convert to customer* in the Prospect form. Depending on the setting in the prospect type (*Sales and marketing> Setup> Prospects> Relation types*) of the prospect, the prospect is deleted automatically after converting.

4.4.2.2 Processing Sales Quotations

In order to create a new sales quotation, open the Quotation form (*Sales and marketing> Sales quotations> All quotations*) and click the button *New* in the action pane. Alternatively, you can create a quotation with the button *Sell/New/Sales quotation* in the Customer form or in the Prospect form.

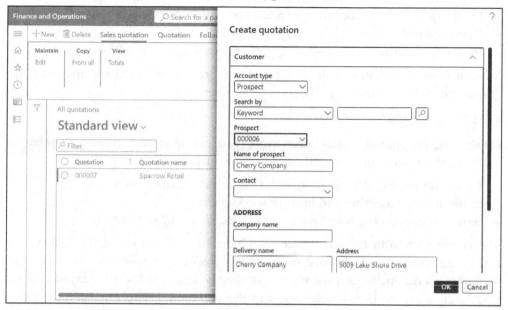

Figure 4-11: Creating a new quotation for a prospect

If you create a quotation in the Quotation form, the *Create quotation* dialog is shown in which you have to select the *Account type* ("Customer" or "Prospect"). Depending on the selected account type, select a customer or a prospect in the respective lookup field. The sales quotation is initialized with default values from the selected customer or prospect then. Once you close the dialog with the button *OK*, Dynamics 365 creates the quotation header and switches to the Quotation detail form in the Lines view.

In the Quotation detail form, you can click the button *Add line* in the toolbar of the tab *Lines* or simply click on the first line in the grid to create a line. Then select an item number (or a sales category) and enter other line details as required.

Once you have completed the quotation lines, click the button *Quotation/ Generate/Send quotation* in the action pane to post and print the quotation (similar to an order confirmation in a sales order). Depending on the decision of the customer or prospect, you can confirm the quotation with the button *Follow up/Generate/ Confirm* in the action pane later (which generates a sales order automatically).

If the quotation refers to a prospect, you have to convert the prospect to a customer before you can create the sales order. Click the button *Follow up/Modify/Convert to customer* in the Quotation form for this purpose.

4.4.3   Sales Order Registration

Like in a purchase order, the order type is a core characteristic in a sales order. In a sales order, there are the following order types:

➢ **Sales order** – Regular sales order.
➢ **Journal** – Draft or template, without impact on inventory or finance.
➢ **Subscription** – Periodic order, remains open after invoicing.
➢ **Returned order** – Credit note, see section 4.7.1.
➢ **Item requirements** – Representing project demand from the Project module.

It is not possible to enter a sales order with the order type "Item requirements" or "Returned order" manually in the Sales order form.

4.4.3.1   Entering a Sales Order

Depending on your personal preferences, you can manually create or update a sales order starting from one of the following forms:

➢ **Customer form** (*Sales and marketing> Customers> All customers*)
➢ **Sales order processing and inquiry workspace**
➢ **Sales order form** (*Sales and marketing> Sales orders> All sales orders*)

The center section in the workspace *Sales order processing and inquiry*, which you can access from the dashboard or from the folder *Workspaces* in the *Sales and marketing* menu, includes a list with unconfirmed and a list with delayed orders. With a click on the tile *All sales orders* in the workspace, you can open the Sales order list page with all orders. If you want to create a new order in the workspace, click the button *New/Sales order* in the action pane. The following steps are the same as when creating the order in the Sales order form.

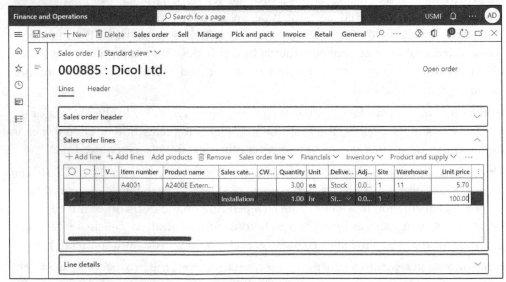

Figure 4-12:   Entering a sales order line with a sales category

In the *Create sales order* dialog, select a customer in the field *Customer account*. You can search the customer by typing the first characters of the customer number (or the name), or by explicitly opening the lookup. In the lookup, you can use a grid column filter, for example on the column *Name*. The sales order then accepts various default values from the selected customer, which you can override in the dialog. When you click the button *OK* in the dialog, the sales order header is created and the Sales order detail form is shown in the Lines view.

In the Sales order detail form, you can click the button *Add line* in the toolbar of the tab *Sales order lines* or simply click on the first line in the grid to create a line. Then select an item number (or a sales category) and enter other line details as required.

Sales orders work similar to purchase orders for the most part. For this reason, you can refer to section 3.4 and 3.5 on the following topics:

➢ **Layout and features of the order form** – See section 3.4.2.
➢ **Sales tax / VAT** – See also section 9.2.7.
➢ **Delivery schedule** – See section 3.4.2.
➢ **Order cancelation** – See section 3.4.4.
➢ **Partial delivery, underdelivery, and overdelivery** – See section 3.5.5.
➢ **Order status and inquiries** – See section 3.5.6 and 3.6.2.

With regard to deleting a sales order, the following settings in the *Accounts receivable parameters* are relevant:

➢ **Mark order as voided** (in the section *General*, tab *Sales setup*) – If set to "Yes", deleted sales orders are shown in the menu item *Sales and marketing> Inquiries and reports> History> Voided sales orders*.
➢ **Delete order line invoiced in total** and **Delete order after invoicing** (in the section *Updates*, tab *Invoice*) – If set to "Yes", orders (order lines) are deleted when posting the invoice (but transactions in inventory and finance are kept).

Unlike purchase orders, sales orders do not include features for change management and order approval.

4.4.3.2 Keyword Search

The keyword search is an enhanced search functionality which facilitates selecting customers, prospects, and products in sales orders.

Before you can use the keyword search, the Search parameters (*Sales and marketing> Setup> Search> Search parameters*) have to be set up. In addition, the fields which should be included in the search have to be defined in the search criteria (*Sales and marketing> Setup> Search> Define criteria*). Click the button *Customer* (or *Product*, or *Prospect*) in the action pane of the *Define criteria* form to access the search fields for the customer search, the product search, or the prospect search.

When you create a new sales order, you can select the option "Keyword" in the lookup field *Search by* of the *Create sales order* dialog to execute a customer search with the specified search criteria.

The keyword search for products is executed in a new a sales order line if you enter a part of the product name, or another search field specified in the criteria, in the item number field and press the *Tab* key (ignoring the lookup that pops up automatically). If you want to search by product name, the search criteria for products have to include the field "ProductName".

4.4.3.3   Sales Order Holds and Line Blocking

At order line level, an easy way to block transactions (picking list, packing slip, invoice) is available with the slider *Stopped* on the sub-tab *General* in the *Line details*. Simply set the slider *Stopped* to "Yes" to block a line (or "No" to unblock).

At order header level, you can use the sales order holds to put a complete order on hold and to give a reason for the hold. As a prerequisite, set up hold codes (*Sales and Marketing> Setup> Sales orders> Order hold codes*) which indicate the different hold reasons.

If you want to set an order hold, click the button *Sales order/Functions/Order holds* in the Sales order form. In the Order hold form which is shown next, click the button *New* and select the respective *Hold code*. The Sales order list page then shows a checkmark in the column *Do not process* for the order. Processing the order is prevented.

In order to clear the hold, open the Order hold form again – click the button *Sales order/Functions/Order holds* in the Sales order form, or access the menu item *Sales and marketing> Sales orders> Open orders> Order holds*. In the Order hold form, click the button *Clear hold/Clear hold/Clear holds* in the action pane.

If you want to assign the decision to somebody else, click the button *Hold checkout/ Hold checkout/Override checkout* in the Order hold form and select the other user in the dialog. The selected user then is the only person who may work on the hold. If you want to transfer the checkout to another user, click the button *Override checkout* again. The checkout is cleared when you clear the order hold, or manually with the button *Hold checkout/Hold checkout/Clear checkout*.

4.4.3.4   Delivery Address and Invoice Address

The delivery address in a sales order is initialized with the primary address or, if specified, with the separate delivery address of the customer. Like in a purchase order (see section 3.4.2), you can override the delivery address on the tab *Address* in the Header view or – at line level – on the sub-tab *Address* in the order lines. In this context, the Accounts receivable parameters (section *Summary update*, tab *Split based on*) determine whether posted documents (e.g., delivery notes) are split automatically based on different delivery addresses in the order lines.

Unlike the delivery address, the invoice address is not directly editable in a sales order. If the option "Invoice account" (which is the default value) is selected in the lookup field *Invoice address* on the tab *Invoice and delivery* in the Customer form, the name and address on the invoice is the *Invoice account* in the sales order (on the tab *General* in the Header view). The option the option "Order account" in the field *Invoice address* of the customer record means that the name and address of the order customer (*Customer account* in the order) is printed on the invoice.

If the customer record of the invoice account contains an address with the purpose "Invoice", this address is printed on documents.

4.4.3.5 Item Lists

If a customer frequently orders the same products, you can facilitate the order entry with the use of item lists. An item list is a copy template, and the lines of an item list only specify the item number and quantity.

In the Item list form (*Sales and marketing> Setup> Items> Item list*), you can click the button *New* to create a new list with *Item list* ID and *Description*. Then click the button *Add* in the toolbar of the tab *Items* and add the items (including product dimensions if applicable) with the default order quantity. Alternatively, you can generate customer-specific item lists (based on past sales orders) with the button *Item list generation* in the action pane.

In order to use an item list in a sales order, click the button *Sales order line/Copy/ From item list* in the toolbar of the order lines. In the *Item list* dialog, select one or more items and optionally override the quantity before you click the button *Copy and close*. If the slider *Prompt for item list* in the Accounts receivable parameters (section *General*, tab *Sales setup*) is set to "Yes", the *Item list* dialog is automatically shown when you create a sales order.

4.4.3.6 Delivery Date Control

Determining the possible delivery date is an important task in order management. A number of aspects control the calculation of delivery dates in sales:

➢ **Item availability**
➢ **Order entry deadlines**
➢ **Sales lead time**
➢ **Delivery date control settings**
➢ **Calendar settings**

In Dynamics 365, there is a difference between the shipping date and the customer receipt date on the one hand, and between the requested and the confirmed date on the other hand. As a result, there are four different fields related to the delivery date on the sub-tab *Delivery* in the *Line details* of the sales order line.

If you want to execute an automatic calculation of the delivery date when entering a sales order line, activate the delivery date control. For this purpose, you can select one of the following options in the lookup field *Delivery date control* in the Accounts receivable parameters (section *Shipments*, tab *Delivery control*):

> **None** – No delivery date control.
> **Sales lead time** – Delivery date based on the lead time and calendar settings.
> **ATP** ("Available to promise") – Delivery date based on the item availability.
> **ATP + Issue margin** – Adds the safety margin for the item (specified in the coverage group) to the delivery date calculated from ATP.
> **CTP** ("Capable to promise") – Immediately executes local master planning.

If the option "Sales lead time" is selected, the delivery date calculation in sales order lines is only based on the applicable sales lead time and calendars (the slider *Working days* in the parameters controls whether the calculation only includes working days). The sales lead time determines the number of days that are required internally until shipping the item. A general default for the sales lead time is specified in the section *Shipments* of the Accounts receivable parameters. The lead time specified there is used as default value for the ship date in the order header. Order lines accept the ship date of the header if the calculated delivery date based on the sales lead time of the item is not after the header ship date. You can specify sales lead times at item level in the default order settings and in trade agreements for sales prices.

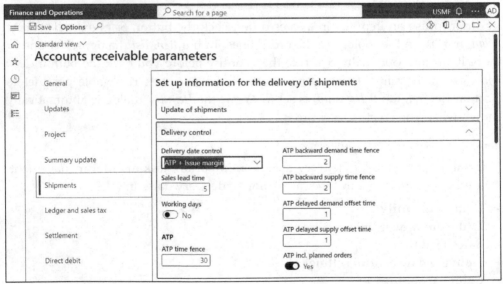

Figure 4-13:   Delivery control settings in the Accounts receivable parameters

If the option "ATP" is selected, the delivery date calculation is based on the item availability within the *ATP time fence* (in the field group *ATP* of the parameters). Existing planned orders are included in the ATP calculation if the slider *ATP incl. planned orders* is set to "Yes". If you enter a quantity in a sales order line which is not available (the calculation includes the on-hand quantity and the transactions within the ATP time fence), the shipping date is the first day after the ATP time fence. In order to avoid that the delivery date is later than the earliest possible date, the ATP time fence should match the lead time of the item for this reason. In order to deal with delayed shipments and receipts of current orders, the *ATP delayed demand offset time* and the *ATP delayed supply offset time* in the Accounts receivable parameters determine whether a transaction, which is scheduled for a past date (but within the *ATP backward demand time fence* and the *ATP backward supply time fence*) and has not been posted yet, is included in the calculation.

If the option "CTP" is selected, the delivery date calculation immediately executes local master planning in the current dynamic master plan (see section 6.3.1) and creates planned purchase orders and production orders as required. For planned production orders, the delivery date which results from the planned order includes the delivery time for components.

In the default order settings of the released product, the lookup field *Delivery date control* on the tab *Sales order* provides the option to override the base settings for delivery date control in the Accounts receivable parameters. If you want to activate or deactivate delivery control in a specific sales order or sales order line, you can select the appropriate option in the lookup field *Delivery date control* on the (sub-) tab *Delivery* of the order header or line.

The calculation of the delivery date in an order line includes the following calendar and transport time settings:

➢ **General shipping calendar of the company** – *Organization administration> Organizations> Legal entities*, tab *Foreign trade and logistics* (field *Shipping calendar*).

➢ **Calendar of the shipping warehouse** – *Inventory management> Setup> Inventory breakdown> Warehouses*, tab *Master planning* (field *Calendar*).

➢ **Receipt calendar of the customer** – *Sales and marketing> Customers> All customers*, field *Receipt calendar* on the tab *Invoice and delivery* (or a *Receipt calendar* in the delivery address details, which you access with the button *More options/Advanced* on the tab *Addresses* in the Customer form).

➢ **Transport calendar per delivery mode and (optionally) warehouse** – *Sales and marketing> Setup> Distribution> Modes of delivery*, button *Transport calendar*.

➢ **Transport days** – *Inventory management> Setup> Distribution> Transport days* (with reference to the delivery mode, shipping warehouse, and receipt address).

Order entry deadlines (*Inventory management> Setup> Distribution> Order entry deadlines*) determine the latest time for entering same-day shipments in sales order lines. After the deadline, delivery date calculation starts with the next day.

In case delivery date control is activated, Dynamics 365 checks if the item in the order line is available at the entered delivery date. In order to receive a proposal of possible delivery dates, click the link *Simulate delivery date* below the field *Requested receipt date* on the (sub-)tab *Delivery* in the order header or line.

If necessary, you can deactivate delivery date control – select the option "None" in the lookup field *Delivery date control* of the order header or line for this purpose. Once delivery date control is deactivated, you can enter a date which is not included in the regular dates for possible deliveries.

4.4.3.7   Item Availability and Delivery Alternatives

As a prerequisite for shipping a stocked product, it must be available in inventory. You can use manual or automatic reservation (see section 7.4.5) to make sure that the required quantity is reserved for the order and it is not possible to consume it for any other purpose.

Inquiries in the Sales order form provide the option to check the item availability. If you only want to view the current inventory quantity of an item with the dimensions of the order line (e.g., site/warehouse), click the button *Inventory/View/On-hand inventory* in the toolbar of the order line. If you want to check the item quantity in other warehouses (and further inventory dimensions), click the button *Overview* in the *On-hand* dialog. In the on-hand inquiry that is shown, you can click the button *Dimensions* to select the displayed inventory dimensions.

The Net requirements form, which you can access the with the button *Product and supply/Net requirements* in the toolbar of the sales order lines, gives a more detailed view of the future availability. In the net requirements, you can start local master planning (see section 6.3) to calculate possible delivery dates.

The Explosion form shows the item availability at multiple BOM levels. You can access this form with the button *Product and supply/Explosion* in the toolbar of the order lines.

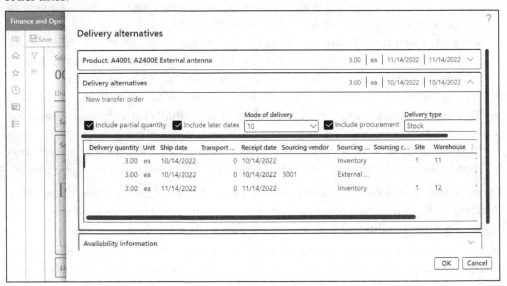

Figure 4-14:   Delivery options in the *Delivery alternatives* dialog

In case there are issues to meet the required delivery date of an order line, you can search for other delivery options – warehouses, product variants (for product masters), and modes of delivery – in the *Delivery alternatives* dialog, which you can open with the button *Product and supply/Delivery alternatives* in the toolbar of the sales order lines. On the tab *Delivery alternatives* in the *Delivery alternatives* dialog, select a new mode of delivery or a supply line with a different warehouse or variant before you click the button *OK* to transfer the selected alternative to the order line. The options in the dialog depend on the selected *Delivery date control* (sales lead time, ATP, CTP) on the sub-tab *Delivery* of the order line.

4.4.4 Order Prices and Discounts

Based on the price groups and discount groups in the order header (copied from the customer) and in the order lines (copied from the products), and on applicable trade agreements, Dynamics 365 determines the price and discounts. Apart from the prices and discounts which are immediately shown in the sales order, trade allowances, which specify a discount that depends on the sales volume in a period (see section 4.9.1), have a later impact on the revenue and profitability of the order.

4.4.4.1 Sales Price Calculation

The sales price in an order line derives from the base price in the released product, or from an applicable trade agreement. Trade agreements for prices at customer level take priority over prices at price group level.

The price group (which represents a price list in Dynamics 365) of a customer is specified in the field *Price* on the tab *Sales order defaults* in the Customer form. When you enter a sales order, the price group of the customer is the default for the price group in the order (shown on the tab *Price and discount* in the Header view of the Sales order form). If required, you can change the price group in the order.

In the sales order lines, you can override the calculated sales price and enter a new price manually.

If you enter a sales price or a discount manually and later modify data in fields of the order line which are among the basis of price calculation (e.g., the quantity), Dynamics 365 may override the manual price and discount with an applicable trade agreement. A confirmation dialog is shown before overriding the manual price or discount, if specified in the Accounts receivable parameters (the dialog is shown if the source "Manual entry" is included in the list on the tab *Trade agreement evaluation* in the section *Prices*).

If the margin percentage (based on the sales amount and the cost price) is too low, a margin alert icon is shown in the column *Margin alert* of the order lines next to the *Estimated margin %*. As a prerequisite, margin alerts have to be enabled in the section *Margin alerts* of the Accounts receivable parameters (together with settings for the acceptable and the questionable margin).

4.4.4.2 Discount Calculation

Sales orders inherit the discounts from the applicable trade agreements for total discounts, multiline discounts, or line discounts as default value. If you want to change a discount group at header level, select the appropriate group on the tab *Price and discount* in the sales order header.

Since the total discount is a discount at the header level, the discount group and the discount percentage for the total discount are included in the order header.

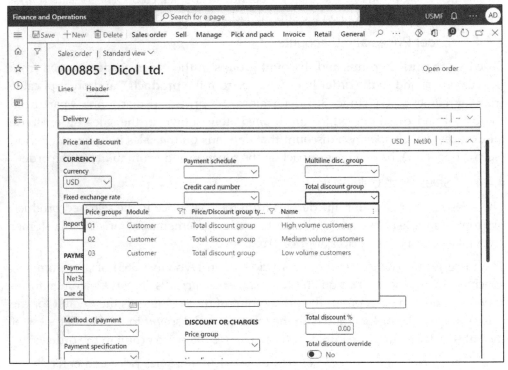

Figure 4-15: Price and discount groups in the sales order header

The percentage of a line discount is shown in a separate column in the sales order lines. In addition, the line discount – and the multiline discount – is shown on the sub-tab *Price and discount* in the order line. Apart from the percentage fields, there are fields for the line discount amount and the multiline discount amount. Be aware not to confuse the percentage and the amount fields.

The line discount for an order line is calculated whenever you save the line. Unlike the line discount calculation, the calculation of the multiline discount and the total discount needs to be started manually with the button *Sell/Calculate/Multiline discount* or *Sell/Calculate/Total discount* in the Sales order form.

For the total discount, you can skip the manual calculation if the slider *Calculate total discount on posting* in the Accounts receivable parameters (section *Prices*, tab *Total discounts*) is set to "Yes". In this case, the total discount is calculated whenever you print or post an order.

If the slider *Enable price details* in the Accounts receivable parameters (section *Prices*, tab *Price details*) is set to "Yes", you can click the button *Sales order line/Price details* in the toolbar of a sales order line to view extended price and discount information – including the trade agreement that has been used.

4.4.5   Surcharge Management

Charges in sales orders and in purchase orders are used for expenses, which are not covered by the sales price or purchase price itself – for example, fees for freight and insurance.

You can enter charges manually in a sales order or a purchase order at header level and at line level. In addition, there are charges which automatically apply when entering an order header or line.

Standard documents like the order confirmation only print the total charges amount, no matter if the applicable charges refer to the header or to a line.

4.4.5.1   Charges Codes

As a prerequisite for the use of charges in orders, you have to set up the required charges codes. Charges codes in sales and in purchasing are independent of each other. For sales charges, use the form *Accounts receivable> Charges setup> Charges code*, and for purchasing the form *Accounts payable> Charges setup> Charges code*.

When you create a new charges code, enter the charges code ID, the description, and – if applicable – the item sales tax group before you switch to the tab *Posting*. On this tab, you have to specify appropriate ledger integration settings.

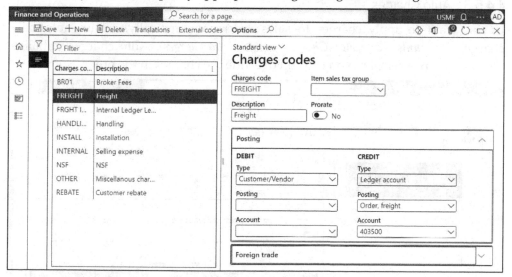

Figure 4-16:   Editing a sales charges code

For sales charges, select the *Debit/Type* "Customer/Vendor" and the *Credit/Type* "Ledger account" (and a related revenue account in the field *Account*) if you want to add the charges on top of the item sales amount. The charges amount is printed separately on documents (e.g., invoices).

For purchasing charges which are shown separately on the vendor invoice, select the option "Customer/Vendor" in the *Credit/Type*. In the field *Debit/Type*, select the option "Ledger account" if you want to post the charges to a separate ledger account, or "Item" if you want to include the charges amount in the cost price (inventory value) of the item.

In addition to charges with the *Debit/Type* (or *Credit/Type*) "Customer/Vendor", which are shown separately on documents, it is also possible to set up charges codes which only generate internal transactions in finance. The codes for these charges include the type "Ledger account" or "Item" for *Debit* and for *Credit*.

4.4.5.2 Manual Charges

If you want to enter surcharges in a sales order or in a purchase order, open the form *Maintain charges*. At header level, you can access the Maintain charges form with the button *Sell/Charges/Charges* in the Sales order form. In purchase orders, click the button *Purchase/Charges/Maintain charges*. In order to enter line charges in a sales order line or a purchase order line, click the button *Financials/Maintain charges* in the toolbar of the order lines.

In the Maintain charges form, select the charges code first. Then select in the column *Category*, whether the charge is a fixed total amount, or an amount per sales unit, or a percentage of the line amount.

4.4.5.3 Auto Charges

If you want to apply charges to sales orders automatically, set up automatic charges (*Accounts receivable> Charges setup> Auto charges*). Auto charges initialize the charges in orders, but you can still override the charges in the order.

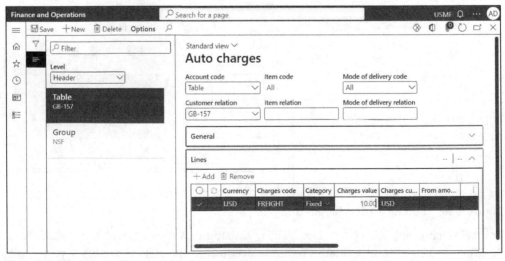

Figure 4-17: Managing auto charges

When setting up auto charges in the Auto-charges form, first select in the lookup field *Level* (in the filter pane on the left) whether the charges are specified at order header or at order line level.

In the right pane, the settings at the top determine the customers, the items, and the modes of delivery to which the charges apply. You can enter line charges with reference to the customer (customer number, customer charge group, or all), the item (item number, item charge group, or all), and the mode of delivery (mode of delivery, delivery charges group, or all). For header charges, the item selection is fixed to "All". In order to specify the calculation details for an auto charge, switch to the tab *Lines* and select the *Category* (determining whether the charges value is a fixed amount, or an amount per sales unit, or a percentage of the line amount) before you enter the *Charges value*.

As a prerequisite for the use of auto charges in sales orders, the sliders *Find auto charges for header* or *Find auto charges for line* in the section *Prices* of the Accounts receivable parameters have to be set to "Yes".

If you want to maintain auto charges at group level, set up the *Customer charge groups*, *Item charge groups*, or *Delivery charges groups* which you want to use and assign them in the Customer form, the Released product form, or the Modes of delivery form (similar to the price/discount groups for trade agreements).

For purchasing, the form *Procurement and sourcing> Setup> Charges> Automatic charges* and the Procurement parameters contain similar settings.

4.4.6 Sales Order Confirmations

Printing an order confirmation requires to post it, which saves the document unchangeable and separate from the actual sales order. Within Dynamics 365, it is the evidence of the document which has been sent to the customer.

Like purchase order confirmations, sales order confirmations do not create transactions in inventory or in finance.

4.4.6.1 Posting Dialog for Sales Order Confirmations

In order to generate an order confirmation, click the button *Sell/Generate/ Confirmation* in the Sales order list page (or *Sell/Generate/Confirm sales order* in the detail form). The dialog for the sales order confirmation is similar to the posting dialogs in purchasing (see section 3.4.5). Like in the *Confirm purchase order* dialog, you can – once you have set the slider *Print confirmation* to "Yes" – manually select the printer (click the button *Printer setup*) or use the printer specified in the print management setup (set the slider *Use print management destination* to "Yes" for this purpose). If you want to post and print the confirmation, make sure that both sliders, *Posting* and *Print confirmation*, in the posting dialog are set to "Yes" before you click the button *OK*.

Apart from the Sales order form, further options for posting the order confirmation include the workspace *Sales order processing and inquiry* (there is the button *Confirm* in the toolbar of the list *Unconfirmed* in the center section) and the summary update in the menu (*Sales and marketing> Sales orders> Order confirmation> Confirm sales order*). If you access the posting dialog from the menu, be aware that you have to enter a filter (click the button *Select* to open the filter dialog).

4.4.6.2 Order Confirmation Inquiry

After posting an order confirmation in the sales order, the posted document is saved. Later amendments of the order have no impact on the posted document.

If you want to view a posted order confirmation, click the button *Sell/Journals/Sales order confirmation* in the Sales order form, or open the menu item *Sales and marketing> Sales orders> Order confirmation> Sales order confirmations*.

4.4.7   Case Study Exercises

Exercise 4.5 – Sales Order

The customer of exercise 4.1 orders 20 units of the item of exercise 3.5. Enter this sales order in the Customer form. Which quantity and which price is shown by default, where do these settings come from?

Switch to the Header view of the sales order and review the delivery address and the price group afterward.

Exercise 4.6 – Surcharges

Your company wants to invoice a handling fee to customers. Create an appropriate charges code C-## (## = your user ID) with the standard tax rate, the posting type "Customer revenue", and an appropriate revenue account for credit posting.

In the header of the sales order of exercise 4.5, add this new handling fee with an amount of USD 10 as a fixed charge to the customer.

Exercise 4.7 – Order Confirmation

Post the order confirmation for the order of exercise 4.5 in the workspace *Sales order processing and inquiry* and print it as a print preview. Check the amount in the order line. In the order confirmation, where do you find the charges?

4.5   Order Picking and Shipment

Delivery management includes all activities in the process of picking and shipping the ordered items. Picking, as a preparation for shipping, is the internal process of collecting items within the warehouse.

4.5.1   Basics of Picking and Shipping

As a preparation for picking and shipping, the upcoming deliveries should be monitored continuously. For this purpose, the workspace *Sales order processing and inquiry* shows delayed orders, and orders with delivery date changes, in related lists in the center section. Apart from the workspace, there are particular inquiries which are designed to review pending shipments:

> *Sales and marketing> Sales orders> Open orders> Backorder lines*
> *Sales and marketing> Sales orders> Open orders> Open sales order lines*

In addition, the pending shipments are shown in the posting dialog of picking lists and packing slips when you filter on the delivery date or the ship date.

4.5.1.1 Picking Policy

In Dynamics 365, it is not required to process picking as a separate step. Depending on the setup, you can skip picking and immediately ship an item by posting the packing slip or the invoice.

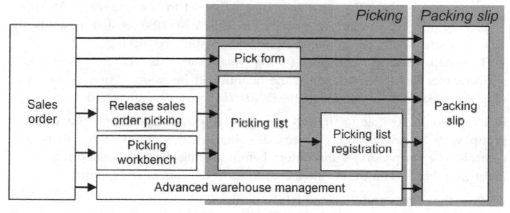

Figure 4-18:   Options for sales order picking in Dynamics 365

If you want to process picking, the warehouse policy (which distinguishes between the basic approach and the advanced warehouse management) determines the available options. Depending on the warehouse policy, there are the following options for the picking process:

> **One-step picking**
> o **Pick form** – Manual recording in the Pick form.
> o **Picking list** – With automatic picking list registration.
> **Two-step picking**
> o **Order picking** – Picking list, followed by a picking list registration.
> o **Advanced warehouse management** – Picking wave, followed by mobile device transactions.

One-step picking is a process that includes picking but does not require a confirmation of the picked quantity. This way of picking is only used in the basic approach for warehouse management.

Two-step picking requires confirming the quantity that has been actually picked. In a warehouse with the basic approach, this is done by entering the picking list registration (on the basis of the picking list which has been posted before). In a warehouse with advanced warehouse management, the confirmation is done with mobile device transactions (based on preassigned picking wave work).

This section explains the picking process in the basic approach for warehouse management. You can find a description on how to process picking with advanced warehouse management in section 8.1.2 of this book.

4.5.1.2 Core Settings for Picking

As a prerequisite for the picking process, the setup has to be completed. If the basic approach for warehouse management is used, the Accounts receivable parameters determine whether there is one-step or two-step picking:

➢ **One-step picking** – If the *Picking route status* in the Accounts receivable parameters (section *Updates*, tab *Picking list*) is set to "Completed", automatic picking list registration is enabled. In this case, the posted quantity is immediately deducted from inventory when posting the picking list.

➢ **Two-step picking** – If the *Picking route status* is set to "Activated", Dynamics 365 does not change the quantity in inventory when posting the picking list. In this case, update the *Picking list registration* afterward.

Picking is only possible for inventoried items (product type "Item", item model group with *Stocked product* enabled). The item model group of the item also controls whether picking is mandatory before posting the packing slip (checkbox *Picking requirements* on the tab *Inventory policies* of the item model group).

4.5.2   Pick Form and Picking Lists

Picking in sales matches the inventory registration in purchasing: The picked quantity reduces the on-hand inventory, and the status of this quantity is "Picked". Like the inventory registration in purchasing, picking is a preliminary transaction which is not shown separately in the inventory transaction.

4.5.2.1 Pick Form

The first option for picking, using the Pick form, is a manual registration in the sales order. The Pick form in sales works similar to the Registration form in purchasing (see section 3.5.3). In a similar way to the inventory registration, the Pick form can be used, for example, to split the transaction of a single order line into lines with different locations, batch numbers, or serial numbers.

In order to access the Pick form, click the button *Update line/Pick* in the toolbar of the order lines in the Sales order form. In the Pick form, you can insert lines for picking in the lower pane (*Picking lines*). Apart from manually creating records with the button *Add* in the lower pane, the button *Add picking line* in the toolbar of the upper pane is another way to insert lines. Edit the quantity, the warehouse, or other inventory dimensions in the lower pane as applicable before you post the transaction with the button *Confirm pick all* in the toolbar of the lower pane.

4.5.2.2 Picking Lists

If you need a printed report for the picking work in the warehouse, post and print a picking list. In sales order processing, picking lists are another way to register a pick transaction.

There are the following ways to post the picking list:

➢ **Sales order** – Sales order form, button *Pick and pack/Generate/Generate picking list* in the action pane.

➢ **Summary update** – *Sales and marketing> Sales orders> Order shipping> Generate picking list*.

➢ **Release picking** – Start from the *Release sales order picking* form, see below.

➢ **Picking workbench** – Group picking lists to batches, see section 4.5.3.

If the warehouse usually picks all items immediately, it is useful to enable one-step picking (the field *Picking route status* in the Accounts receivable parameters has to be set to "Completed" for this purpose). With this setup, no manual picking list registration is required, and the next step is packing slip posting.

4.5.2.3 Picking List Registration

In case two-step picking is enabled (Accounts receivable parameters, field *Picking route status* set to "Activated"), you have to execute the picking list registration after posting a picking list and actually doing the picking work in the warehouse.

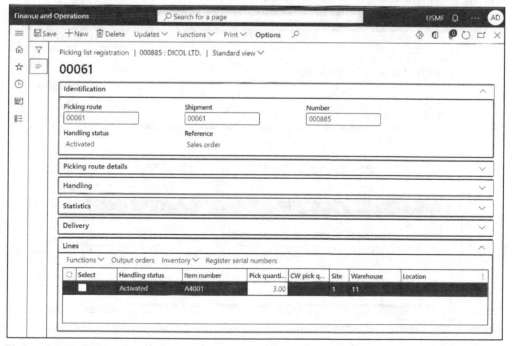

Figure 4-19:   Picking list registration accessed from a sales order

In order to access the Picking list registration form, click the button *Pick and pack/ Generate/Picking list registration* in the Sales order form, or open the menu item *Sales and marketing> Sales orders> Order shipping> Picking list registration*, or the menu item *Inventory management> Outbound orders> Picking list registration*.

If you access the picking list registration from them menu, the list page with all posted picking lists is shown and you have to enter a filter on the applicable sales order number. If you open the picking list registration from the sales order, the detail form with the picking list for the order is immediately shown. If there is more than one picking list for the order, you should expand the list pane on the left in the Picking list registration detail form to select the respective picking list.

On the tab *Lines* in the Picking list registration detail form, select the checkbox in the column *Select* in the lines which you want to update (see Figure 4-19). Before you confirm the picked quantity of the selected lines with the button *Functions/ Update selected* in the toolbar of this tab (or the button *Updates/Update all* in the action pane of the form for all lines), you can adjust the quantity in the column *Pick quantity* as applicable.

4.5.2.4 Release Sales Order Picking

If you want to start picking from an overview that shows the order lines which are ready for shipping, use the Release picking form. The Release picking form only shows items which currently are in stock.

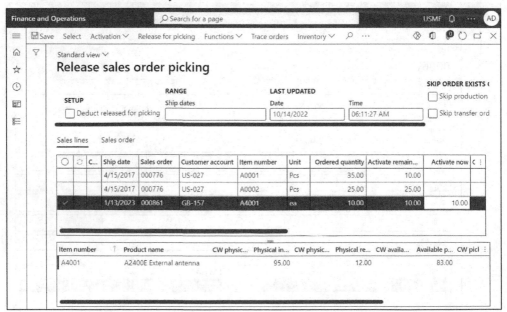

Figure 4-20:   Entering an *Activate now* quantity in the Release sales order picking form

When you open the Release picking form (*Inventory management> Periodic tasks> Release sales order picking*), an advanced filter is shown in which you can enter filter criteria on order lines. If you need to change this filter later, click the button *Select* in the action pane of the Release picking form.

In order to start the picking process, activate the items which should be picked. You can do this with the button *Activation* in the action pane (select the appropriate option within this button), or manually by entering a quantity in the column *Activate now*. Activation also reserves the respective quantity.

For the quantities in the column *Activate now*, you can subsequently post the picking list with the button *Release for picking* in the action pane. The further process with one-step picking or two-step picking is the same as when posting the picking list directly from the order.

If you want to use picking priorities for customers, you can enter a *Classification group* on the tab *General* of the Customer form. The customer classification group is shown in the left-most column of the Release picking form, and you can set a filter on this group.

4.5.2.5 Reverse Pick Transactions

If you want to reverse a pick transaction that has been posted in the Pick form or in a picking list, you can use the Pick form. In the Pick form, which you can access with the button *Update line/Pick* in the toolbar of the respective sales order line, first select the transaction which you want to reverse in the upper pane and then click the button *Add picking line*. Posting the reversal with the button *Confirm pick all* works similar to regular picking, but with a negative quantity.

If the original pick transaction has been posted with a picking list, you can alternatively use the picking list registration to reverse picking. Open the Picking list registration form from the menu or with the button *Pick and pack/Generate/ Picking list registration* in the Sales order form for this purpose. In the Picking list registration form, click the button *Functions/Unpick* in the toolbar of the tab *Lines* to cancel the picking list registration. In a second step, click the button *Functions/ Cancel picking route* in the action pane of the picking list registration to cancel the picking list completely. You can skip the second step if you already set the slider *Cancel unpicked quantity* in the *Unpick* dialog to "Yes".

Note: If you have posted more than one picking list for an order, expand the list pane on the left in the Picking list registration detail form to select the picking list.

4.5.3 Picking Workbench

The Picking workbench is an enhancement for sales order picking in paper-based warehouse processes, which you can use if you need to group picking lists to batches (picking waves).

If the picking process includes putting the items into boxes, you can optionally apply a boxing logic to collect items in boxes or carts. Dynamics 365 then suggests boxes of an appropriate size for picking.

You can use the Picking workbench as an alternative to the *Release sales order picking* functionality.

4.5.3.1 Setup for the Picking Workbench

As a prerequisite for the Picking workbench, the respective number sequences have to be specified in the Inventory parameters. And if you want to use the boxing logic, the slider *Boxing logic for picking workbench* in the section *General* of the Inventory parameters has to be set to "Yes".

In the workbench profiles (*Inventory management> Setup> Picking workbench> Workbench profiles*), you can set up one or more profiles which are used as filter criteria in the Picking workbench.

In the Warehouse form (*Inventory management> Setup> Inventory breakdown> Warehouses*), the tab *Picking workbench* contains settings (e.g., the maximum number of lines per picking list) on how to split picking waves (workbench sessions).

If you want to use the boxing logic in the Picking workbench, enter the individual boxes with their physical dimensions and weight in the menu item *Inventory management> Setup> Picking workbench> Box definitions*. The slider *Active* controls whether a box is available for picking.

In the Released product detail form, the slider *Apply boxing logic for picking workbench* on the tab *Deliver* has to be set to "Yes" for items which should use the boxing logic. The selection of applicable boxes for an item is only based on the physical dimensions and the weight of the item (specified on the tab *Manage inventory* of the released product). If the slider *Ship alone* on the tab *Deliver* of the released product is set to "Yes", the item is picked separately without boxing.

4.5.3.2 Working with the Picking Workbench

The starting point for picking in the Picking workbench are sales orders which should be shipped. In the Picking workbench (*Inventory management> Outbound orders> Picking workbench*), you can start the picking process and create a new picking session with the button *New* in the action pane. In the next step, enter filter criteria (e.g., on the *Ship date* of the order line) on the tab *Criteria* which determine the sales orders which are included in the current picking session. The field *Profile* on this tab provides the option to select a workbench profile with default values for the criteria fields.

Once you have entered appropriate filter criteria, click the button *Picking session/ Picking session/Generate picking batches* in the action pane of the Picking workbench. Depending on the criteria, on the settings for splitting picking batches in the Warehouse form, and on the settings for boxing (box size and item size/weight), Dynamics 365 creates one or more picking batches which are shown on the tab *Picking batches*. When you generate picking batches, corresponding picking lists are posted. You can view the picking lists that are linked to a picking batch on the tab *Picking list* in the workbench.

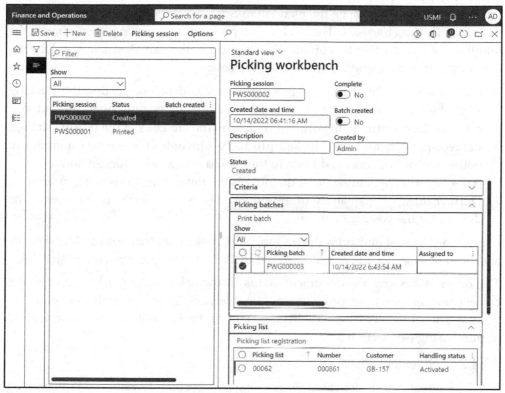

Figure 4-21:   Managing a picking batch in the Picking workbench

Printing the picking batch label and the picking list is a required step, which you can execute with the button *Print batch* in the toolbar of the tab *Picking batches* in the workbench (or the button *Picking session/Picking session/Print session* in the action pane). For items which apply the boxing logic, the selected box name is printed in the picking list header.

After printing all picking lists of a picking batch, select the checkbox *Complete* in the picking batch. Alternatively, set the slider *Complete* in the picking session to "Yes" to complete all picking batches of the session at the same time.

The further process with one-step picking or two-step picking is the same as when posting the picking list directly from the order (see section 4.5.2). In case of two-step picking, you can directly access the picking list registration with the button *Picking list registration* in the toolbar of the tab *Picking list* in the Picking workbench.

4.5.4   Packing Slips

Posting the packing slip (delivery note) is the last step in the picking and shipping process.

4.5.4.1 Posting Dialog for Packing Slips

In order to post a packing slip, click the button *Pick and pack/Generate/Packing slip* in the Sales order form or open the menu item *Sales and marketing> Sales orders> Order shipping> Post packing slip*. The dialog for packing slip posting then shows the familiar format. In the lookup field *Quantity* on the tab *Parameters*, select the applicable option depending on the prior process:

➤ **Picked** – Select this option, if picking is executed before posting the packing slip. The picked quantity then is the default for the posting quantity, but you can edit the quantity in the column *Update* on the tab *Lines* of the posting dialog.

➤ **Picked quantity and non-stocked products** – Includes the ordered quantity of non-stocked products in addition to the picked quantity of stocked items.

➤ **All** – The total remaining order quantity is the default for the posting quantity.

➤ **Deliver now** – The quantity of the column *Deliver now* in the order lines is the default for the posting quantity.

If you want to post and print the packing slip, make sure that both sliders, *Posting* and *Print packing slip*, in the dialog are set to "Yes" before you click the button *OK*.

The order status and the document status in the sales order work similar to the corresponding purchase order status (see section 3.5.6). In addition, you can process partial deliveries, overdeliveries, and underdeliveries in the same way as in purchasing (see section 3.5.5).

4.5.4.2 Ledger Integration

If ledger integration is activated for packing slip posting, Dynamics 365 is posting general ledger transactions in parallel to the inventory transactions. These ledger transactions are reversed when posting the related invoice.

The following core settings control packing slip posting to the general ledger:

➤ **Accounts receivable parameters** – The slider *Post packing slip in ledger* (section *Updates*, tab *Packing slip*) has to be set to "Yes" to enable ledger posting (not required for standard cost items).

➤ **Item model group** – The checkbox *Post physical inventory* on the tab *Costing method & cost recognition* in the item model group of the item has to be selected.

These settings work similar to the corresponding settings for the ledger integration of product receipts in purchasing.

4.5.4.3 Transaction Inquiry

If you want to view the inventory transactions that refer to an order line, select the respective line in the sales order and click the button *Inventory/Transactions* in the toolbar of the order lines. After posting the packing slip, the issue status of the inventory transaction is "Deducted". The posting date of the packing slip is shown in the column *Physical date* whereas the *Financial date* remains empty until posting the invoice. The packing slip number is shown on the tab *Updates* of the *Transaction details* form (access with the button *Transaction details* in the inventory transaction).

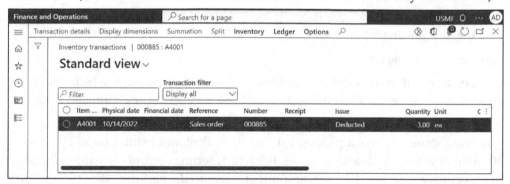

Figure 4-22: Inventory transaction after packing slip posting

In order to view a posted packing slip, open the menu item *Sales and marketing> Sales orders> Order shipping> Packing slip* or click the button *Pick and pack/Journals/ Packing slip* in the Sales order form. Select a packing slip on the tab *Overview* of the inquiry and switch to the tab *Lines* if you want to view the related packing slip lines.

You can view the related ledger transactions in the Voucher transaction form, which you open with the button *Vouchers* in the action pane of the packing slip inquiry (or with the button *Ledger/Physical voucher* in the inventory transactions).

4.5.4.4 Canceling a Packing Slip

If you want to cancel a posted packing slip, use the *Cancel* feature in the packing slip inquiry. Open the packing slip inquiry with the button *Pick and pack/Journals/ Packing slip* in the Sales order form for this purpose, select the respective packing slip and click the button *Cancel* in the action pane. If you only want to reduce the posted quantity, click the button *Correct*.

Canceling and correcting a packing slip does not change the original transaction, but posts a new transaction which offsets the original transaction.

4.5.5 Case Study Exercises

Exercise 4.8 – Packing Slip

You are asked to review the order lines which are available for shipping. The inquiry should not be limited to your orders, but include all applicable orders in your company. Which options do you know?

Your order of exercise 4.5 is among the orders which are ready to be shipped. Check following items in this order before you post the packing slip:

➢ Order status and document status.
➢ Inventory quantity of the ordered item.
➢ Inventory transactions for the order line.

Post and print a packing slip for the complete order quantity in the Sales order form and select a print preview as the print destination.

Then review the status of the items in the list above again. What is different after packing slip posting?

Exercise 4.9 – Picking List

The customer of exercise 4.1 orders another 20 units of the item which you have created in exercise 3.5. Only 10 units should be shipped at the moment. Enter an appropriate sales order first.

The warehouse requires a picking list this time. Post and print a picking list with 10 units of the ordered item. Can you tell which setting controls whether you need to execute a picking list registration? If required, perform the picking list registration.

Then post the packing slip for the picked items.

Exercise 4.10 – Packing Slip Inquiry

Review the packing slip of exercise 4.9 in the packing slip inquiry, which you access from the Sales order form first, and then from the navigation pane. Is it possible to update the posted packing slip?

4.6   Sales Invoice

Posting the sales invoice is the last step in sales order processing. The invoice increases the open customer balance and reduces the financial value in inventory. After invoicing all lines of a sales order, the sales order is completed. The payment of invoices is processed separately in finance (see section 9.3.3).

If you want to invoice a stocked product, you have to process a sales order. But it is not required to perform the complete sales process with order confirmation, picking, and shipping – you can post the sales order invoice immediately after entering the order (if no restrictions are specified in the item model group).

You can use a free text invoice if you want to post an invoice which is not related to products or sales categories. In the lines of a free text invoice, ledger accounts are entered instead of item numbers. Free text invoices have no reference to items and no impact on inventory and supply chain management.

4.6.1   Sales Order Invoices

The way of posting a sales invoice is similar to posting a packing slip.

4.6.1.1   Posting Dialog for Sales Order Invoices

In order to post a sales invoice, click the button *Invoice/Generate/Invoice* in the Sales order form or open the menu item *Accounts receivable> Invoices> Batch invoicing> Invoice*. The posting dialog then shows the familiar format. In the lookup field

Quantity on the tab *Parameters*, select the applicable option depending on the prior process:

➢ **Packing Slip** – Usual option, since in most cases a packing slip is posted first and you want to invoice the shipped quantity.

➢ **All** or **Deliver now** – If selected, Dynamics 365 does not initialize the column *Update* in the invoice lines with the shipped quantity. For any quantity not shipped yet, the physical transaction is posted in parallel to the invoice.

If you select the option "Packing Slip" in the lookup field *Quantity*, you can select or deselect particular packing slips for invoicing. Click the button *Select packing slip* in the toolbar of the tab *Overview* in the posting dialog for this purpose.

Before posting, you check the totals with the button *Totals* on the tab *Overview* of the posting dialog. In order to post and print the invoice, make sure that both sliders, *Posting* and *Print invoice*, in the dialog are set to "Yes" before you click the button *OK*.

4.6.1.2 Transaction Inquiry

Posting the invoice generates general ledger transactions, inventory transactions, customer transactions, and transactions in other subledgers like the sales tax as applicable. Once all lines of a sales order are completely invoiced, the order status is "Invoiced".

If you want to view the inventory transactions that refer to an order line, select the respective line in the sales order and click the button *Inventory/Transactions* in the toolbar of the order lines. After posting the invoice, the issue status of the inventory transaction is "Sold" and the posting date of the invoice is shown in the column *Financial date*.

In order to view the posted sales invoices, open the menu item *Accounts receivable> Inquiries and reports> Invoices> Invoice journal* or click the button *Invoice/Journals/ Invoice* in the Sales order form. Click on an invoice number shown as a link in the grid if you want to open the related Invoice detail form. In the Invoice detail form, you can view the invoice lines on the tab *Lines*.

4.6.1.3 Ledger Transactions and Transaction Origin

If you want to view the ledger transactions that refer to a posted invoice, open the Voucher transaction form with the button *Voucher* in the invoice inquiry or with the button *Ledger/Financial voucher* in the inventory transactions.

The button *Transaction origin* in the Voucher transaction form provides access to the Transaction origin form, which shows the related transactions in all modules.

The particular ledger accounts in the transactions depend on the actual procedure and on the setup. The customer summary account for the customer transaction is specified in the applicable customer posting profile, which works similar to the vendor posting profile (see section 3.2.3). The settings for the main account in the other transactions – except for the sales tax transaction – are specified in the posting setup (see section 9.4.2).

4.6.2   Collective Invoices

If you want to post an invoice which covers multiple sales orders (e.g., a monthly invoice), post a collective invoice in a summary update. Collective documents are available for all document types. Apart from collective invoices, you can, for example, also post collective packing slips.

Apart from the fact that it covers multiple orders, posting a collective document is not different from posting an individual document.

The setup for summary updates at the company level and at the customer level controls whether it is possible to combine orders into collective documents.

4.6.2.1   Setup for Summary Updates

The section *Summary update* in the Accounts receivable parameters contains basic configuration settings for collective sales documents. The lookup field *Default values for summary update* in this section is a core setting for summary updates. In most cases, the option "Automatic summary" is selected, which makes it possible to deselect orders from a collective document already in the order. If the option "Invoice account" is selected, you can only exclude a particular order by removing it in the posting dialog.

The Summary update parameter form, which you can access with the button *Summary update parameters* in the toolbar of the tab *Summary update* in the Accounts receivable parameters, contains a separate section per document type. For each document type, you can specify, which fields in a sales order must have the same content to join a collective document.

If the option "Automatic summary" is selected in the parameter field *Default values for summary update*, you have to enable the automatic summary per customer (click the button *Customer/Set up/Summary update* in the Customer form). The setting in the customer is the default for related sales orders. In the Sales order form, you can access and edit this setting with the button *General/Set up/Summary*.

4.6.2.2   Posting Collective Invoices

In order to post a collective invoice, open the menu item *Accounts receivable> Invoices> Batch invoicing> Invoice*. In the lookup field *Quantity* of the posting dialog, select the option "Packing slip" if you want to make sure that the invoice only covers items that have been shipped.

Then click the button *Select* [1] in the posting dialog (see Figure 4-23) and select applicable sales orders in the Advanced filter dialog. After closing the filter dialog, the selected orders are shown on the tab *Overview* of the posting dialog.

If there are sales orders which you do not want to include in the invoice, select the respective records on the tab *Overview* of the posting dialog and delete them (click the button *Remove* in the toolbar of this tab). Deleting a record in the posting dialog only removes the selection. It does not delete the order or the packing slip, which is why the order is shown again when you select orders for posting the next invoice.

Figure 4-23: Posting a collective sales invoice

If you want to include or exclude particular packing slips from invoice posting, click the button *Select packing slip* [2].

Once you have selected the respective sales orders and packing slips, click the button *Arrange* [3]. Arranging combines the orders into a common invoice as specified in the Summary update parameters. If the setting in the Accounts receivable parameters is not suitable for a particular invoice, you can select a different option in the lookup field *Summary update for* [4] on the tab *Parameters* of the posting dialog before arranging.

In the example of Figure 4-23, the *Arrange* feature merges the two orders into one common line. You can subsequently post the collective invoice with the button *OK* in the posting dialog.

4.6.3   Free Text Invoices

Free text invoices are independent of sales orders, shipments, and inventory. You can use free text invoices to sell intangible items or fixed assets.

The structure of free text invoices is similar to sales orders – a free text invoice consists of a header and one or more lines. Instead of product numbers and sales categories, the lines of a free text invoice contain main accounts.

If you want to create a credit note, enter a negative amount in the free text invoice. Item statistics and inventory valuation do not include free text invoices and free text credit notes.

Once you have entered the free text invoice, you can post and print it. The invoice is the only document which you can generate in a free text invoice. It is not possible to generate other documents (e.g., order confirmations).

4.6.3.1   Registering Free Text Invoices

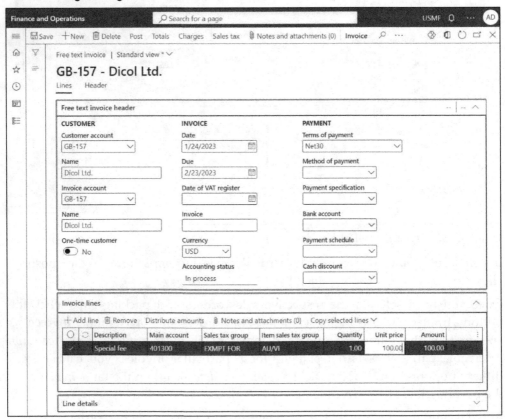

Figure 4-24:   Registering an invoice line in a free text invoice

In order to enter a free text invoice, open the menu item *Accounts receivable> Invoices> All free text invoices* and click the button *New* in the action pane.

Alternatively, you can access the Customer form and create a free text invoice with the button *Invoice/New/Free text invoice* in action pane of this form.

Unlike the Sales order form, the Free text invoice form does not open a separate *Create* dialog when you create a new record. But the fields *Customer account* and *Invoice account*, in which you select the respective customer, are not only shown in the Header view of the Free text invoice form, they are also included on the tab *Free text invoice header* in the Lines view.

After entering the header data, insert the lines with *Description, Main account*, and *Amount* (or *Quantity* and *Unit price*). If a line requires a longer description, you can use the field *Invoice text* on the sub-tab *General* of the tab *Line details*. If sales tax (VAT) applies, make sure to select a correct *Sales tax group* and *Item sales tax group*.

If you sell a fixed asset, enter the *Fixed asset number* on the sub-tab *General* of the tab *Line details*.

You can update the financial dimensions (e.g., the department or cost center) on the sub-tab *Financial dimensions line* of the tab *Line details* – enter applicable dimension values individually or select a financial dimension default template in the lookup field *Template ID*.

4.6.3.2 Posting and Inquiry

In order to post the free text invoice, click the button *Post* in the action pane of the Free text invoice form. You can view the posted invoice with the button *Invoice/ Related information/Invoice journal* afterward.

In the invoice inquiry (*Accounts receivable> Inquiries and reports> Invoices> Invoice journal*), free text invoices are shown in parallel with the sales order invoices. For free text invoices, there is no order number that is shown in this inquiry.

4.6.3.3 Recurring Free Text Invoices

If you want to issue a particular free text invoice periodically, you can use recurring free text invoices. As a prerequisite for this kind of invoices, set up free text invoice templates (*Accounts receivable> Invoices> Recurring invoices> Free text invoice templates*). In the Customer form, you can assign customers to one or more templates with the button *Invoice/Set up/Recurring invoices*.

In order to generate a periodical free text invoice based on these settings, open the menu item *Accounts receivable> Invoices> Recurring invoices> Generate recurring invoices*. The periodic activity generates regular free text invoices, which you can review in the Free text invoice form before posting.

4.6.4   Case Study Exercises

Exercise 4.11 – Sales Invoice

The items which you have shipped in exercise 4.8 need to be invoiced. Before posting the invoice, review following items:

> ➤ Order status and document status of the sales order.
> ➤ Inventory transaction for the order line.

Post and print the invoice directly in the Sales order form and check the invoice total in the posting dialog.

Then review the status of the items in the list above again. What is different now?

Exercise 4.12 – Partial Invoice

Invoice the items which you have picked and shipped in exercise 4.9. Post and print the invoice in the Sales order form and make sure to invoice only the items which you have shipped.

Exercise 4.13 – Shipping with Invoice

The customer of exercise 4.1 orders another unit of the product of exercise 3.5. In addition, he wants to order one hour of the installation service of exercise 4.2 for a price of USD 110. This time you do not post a packing slip, but you want to ship the items with the invoice.

Enter an appropriate sales order and immediately post the invoice. After posting the invoice, review the order status, the document status, and the inventory transaction of the product.

Exercise 4.14 – Invoice Inquiry

Review the invoice which you have posted in exercise 4.11 in the invoice inquiry. Check the invoice header and the invoice lines.

Exercise 4.15 – Free Text Invoice

Invoice a service to the customer of exercise 4.1. There is no product or sales category for this service. For this reason, enter and post a free text invoice with an appropriate revenue account.

What is the difference between a free text invoice and a sales order invoice?

4.7   Sales Credit Note and Item Return

A credit note is a document which you issue if a customer returns an item to your company and receives a financial compensation. You can also post a credit note if the customer does not actually return the defective item, or if you have to credit a price discrepancy.

In order to manage customer returns, you can use the return order management in Dynamics 365. In case of a simple return process, you can alternatively use regular sales orders instead of return orders.

If a credit note does not cover inventoried items, you can use a free text invoice.

4.7.1   Return Order Management

Return orders support a proper procedure for item returns which makes sure, that a customer must contact you to receive a return merchandise authorization (RMA) before returning a product.

4.7.1.1 Disposition Codes and Required Setup

As a prerequisite for the use of return orders, you have to set up disposition codes (*Sales and marketing> Setup> Returns> Disposition codes*). In the Disposition code form, the field *Action* is a core setting for the return process. It controls the handling of returned items and includes the following options:

> **Credit only** – Credit without item return.
> **Credit** – Return items and credit.
> **Scrap** – Return items and credit, scrap immediately.
> **Replace and credit** (or **Replace and scrap**) – Return items and replace.
> **Return to customer** – Do not credit.

Except for the option "Credit only", an item receipt has to be posted in all cases, no matter if the products are returned to stock or if they are scrapped. But in case of scrap, an inventory transaction for scrapping is posted parallel to the receipt of the return order.

4.7.1.2 Return Order Registration

Return orders are sales orders with the order type "Returned order". The sales order number of a return order is shown in the return order header. But except for return orders with the disposition code "Credit only", return orders are not shown in the regular Sales order form until the item arrival is posted.

The workspace *Sales return processing* gives an overview of the current return orders. The tile *All return orders* on the left provides access to the Return order list page. If you want to create a new return order in the workspace, click the button *New/Return order* in the action pane. The following steps are the same as when you create a return order from the Return order form.

In order to access the return orders from the menu, open the list page *Sales and marketing> Sales returns> All return orders*. When you create a new return order, you can optionally select a *Return reason code* on the tab *General* in the *Create* dialog or in the return order header. The return reason code is used for statistical purposes and, if applicable, for the automatic assignment of charges.

If you want to copy an original sales order (in fact, sales invoice lines) to the new return order, click the button *Return order/Return/Find sales order* in the action pane. Alternatively, you can enter return order lines with a negative quantity manually. The *Disposition code* of a line is shown on the sub-tab *General* of the tab *Line details*. But except for disposition codes with the *Action* "Credit only" (crediting without physical return), you do not enter the disposition code before item arrival.

Optionally, you can click the button *Return order/Send/Return order* in the return order to print an RMA document which you can send to the customer.

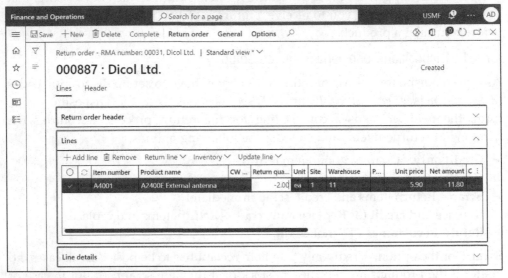

Figure 4-25:   Registering a line in the Return order form

If you want to send an up-front replacement for the returned item to the customer, you can create the respective sales order with the button *Return order/New/ Replacement order* in the return order.

4.7.1.3 Return Orders without Physical Returns

If you do not want the customer to return the item, select a disposition code without item return ("Credit only") on the sub-tab *General* of the tab *Line details* in the return order. In this case, you can immediately post the credit note in the Sales order form (*Sales and marketing> Sales Orders> All sales orders*) or in the summary update for invoices (*Accounts receivable> Invoices> Batch invoicing> Invoice*).

4.7.1.4 Return Orders – Item Arrival and Credit Note

When you receive an item of a return order, you have to record an inventory registration. Like the inventory registration in purchasing (see section 3.5.3), the registration for return orders can be done in the Registration form (access with the button *Update line/Registration* in the return order lines) or in an item arrival journal. In a warehouse with advanced warehouse management, inventory registration is done with mobile device transactions.

If you use an item arrival journal (*Inventory management> Journal entries> Item arrival> Item arrival*, see section 7.4.2), select the option "Sales order" in the lookup field *Reference* and enter the *RMA number* in the dialog which is shown when creating a new journal. You can update this reference, which is a default for the journal lines, on the tab *Default values* in the Header view of the Journal form. In addition, you can enter a *Disposition code* in the header which is used as default value for the journal lines.

In order to create journal lines in the item arrival journal, either click the button *Functions/Create lines* in the action pane or manually enter the lines in the Lines view of the journal.

The disposition code has to be specified in the journal lines before you can post the item return. If it is not possible to decide upon the disposition code at the time when you receive the item, set the slider *Quarantine management* in the journal line to "Yes" (you can enter a default value in the journal header) and leave the disposition code empty. In this case, a quarantine order (see section 7.4.6) is created when you post the item arrival, and it is not required to enter the disposition code before ending quarantine.

After posting the item arrival journal with the button *Post*, the status of the return order line is updated to "Registered".

Once you have finished inventory registration, you can optionally print a receipt acknowledgment with the button *Return order/Send/Acknowledgement* in the Return order form.

Then post the packing slip (with a negative quantity) in the Return order form (button *Return order/Generate/Post packing slip*) or in the Sales order form (button *Pick and pack/Generate/Packing slip*) and make sure to select an appropriate option (usually "All" since you have posted an inbound registration and not an outbound picking) in the lookup field *Quantity* of the posting dialog.

In order to credit the customer financially, open the Sales order form, select the respective order and click the button *Invoice/Generate/Invoice* in the action pane. Alternatively, you can use the summary update for invoices (*Accounts receivable> Invoices> Batch invoicing> Invoice*).

4.7.2   Simple Credit Notes

If you do not want to process a customer return in a return order, you can use a regular sales order to credit a customer. If it is not required to track the physical and financial process at the level of the item, you can also use a free text invoice.

The credit note is processed as an invoice with a negative quantity/amount then.

4.7.2.1   Credit Note from a Sales Order

In the Sales order form, there are the following options for crediting:

➤ **Original order line** – Negative *Deliver now* quantity.
➤ **New order line** – Order line with a negative quantity in the original order.
➤ **New order** – Order line with a negative quantity in a new sales order.

The way to enter a new order or a new order line for a credit note in sales is similar to entering an order for a credit note in purchasing (see section 3.7.1). But since it is not possible to select the order type "Returned order" in a sales order manually, the order header of an order which you enter for crediting in the Sales order form looks like the header of any regular sales order.

If you want to record a credit note in the original sales order line, enter a negative quantity in the column *Deliver now* in that line. When you post the credit note (by posting an invoice), select the option "Deliver now" – which refers to the column *Deliver now* – in the lookup field *Quantity* of the *Posting invoice* dialog.

4.7.2.2 Inventory Valuation for Returned Items

If you register a credit note in a new order or order line, you should select the original invoice transaction in the lookup field *Return lot ID* (on the sub-tab *Setup* of the tab *Line details*) of the order line before posting. This link to the return lot makes sure that the inventory value of the crediting line exactly matches the inventory value of the original delivery.

Dynamics 365 automatically inserts the return lot ID when you create a credit note line with the button *Return order/Return/Find sales order* in the Return order form or with the button *Sell/Create/Credit note* in the Sales order form.

If you do not select a return lot ID, Dynamics 365 uses the *Return cost price* on the sub-tab *Setup* of the crediting order line for inventory valuation.

4.7.2.3 Scrapping Items

If you do not want the customer to return a defective item, set the slider *Scrap* on the sub-tab *Setup* of the order line to "Yes". When you post the invoice (credit note), Dynamics 365 posts the item receipt and a related inventory loss at the same time. In return orders, the slider *Scrap* in the order line is controlled by the disposition code.

4.7.2.4 Refunds not Related to Item Returns

The free text invoice (see section 4.6.3) is another option to register and post customer refunds. But if a refund refers to an item, you should not use a free text invoice, since this kind of invoicing is not included in item statistics and inventory valuation.

If you need to credit a price discrepancy, rather enter a new sales order which contains a line with a negative quantity and the old price and a line with a positive quantity and the actual price. You can link both transactions (in order to offset the inventory value) with the button *Inventory/Marking* (see section 3.7.1).

4.7.3   Case Study Exercise

Exercise 4.16 – Sales Credit Note

Your customer complains about defects on the items which you have invoiced in exercise 4.11. You agree to accept an item return and to credit the invoice. Enter a return order and post the item receipt with an appropriate disposition code. Then post the packing slip for the item return, and finally post and print the credit note.

4.8   Direct Delivery

Direct delivery is the process of shipping goods directly from the vendor to the customer. This means there is no purchase receipt and sales shipment in the warehouse, which saves time and expenses for transportation and stocking.

4.8.1   Processing Direct Deliveries

The functionality for direct delivery in Dynamics 365 is based on a purchase order which is created from a related sales order. There are the following options for creating this purchase order:

➤ **Purchase order from a sales order** – Create a regular purchase order.
➤ **Direct delivery from a sales order** – Create a direct delivery purchase order.
➤ **Direct delivery type in a sales order line** – Automatically creates a direct delivery purchase order.
➤ **Direct delivery workbench** – Create a direct delivery from the workbench.

Whereas creating a regular purchase order or a direct delivery purchase order from a sales order does not require specific settings, the Direct delivery workbench requires that direct delivery is enabled in the sales order line.

4.8.1.1   Regular Purchase Order from a Sales Order

You can create a regular purchase order from a sales order if you want to process the purchase order with reference to the sales order (separate from other orders), but nevertheless receive and ship it in a warehouse of your company.

As a starting point, enter a regular sales order. Once you have completed the sales order, click the button *Sales order/New/Purchase order* in the action pane to create a related purchase order. In the *Create purchase order* dialog, select the checkbox *Include* in the respective lines and choose a vendor (if no main vendor is specified for the item). Processing the purchase order and the sales order works like processing regular orders, including change management for the purchase order.

In the purchase order, the delivery address for the vendor is your warehouse or company address (like in any regular purchase order). You can post the product receipt in your warehouse and then perform picking and shipping to the customer.

4.8.1.2   Direct Delivery Purchase Order from a Sales Order

If you want a direct delivery from the vendor to the customer, also start with a regular sales order. But it is useful to select a separate warehouse for direct deliveries to avoid confusing inventory transactions in a regular warehouse with transactions for direct delivery which never actually affect this warehouse.

Figure 4-26:   Printing a sales packing slip for direct delivery with product receipt posting

Click the button *Sales order/New/Direct delivery* in the sales order to create a direct delivery purchase order, which has got a tight link to the sales order. The delivery address of the purchase order is the customer address, modifications of the address and of other data in the sales order which are relevant to purchasing (e.g., the quantity or the delivery date) are synchronized to the purchase order. In case of changes, you have to observe the purchase order change management, which at least requires a confirmation of the modified purchase order.

When you post the product receipt for direct delivery in purchasing, Dynamics 365 automatically posts the related sales packing slip. If you need to print a packing slip for the customer, set the slider *Print sales documents* in the posting dialog for the product receipt to "Yes" (see Figure 4-26).

Invoice posting in sales is independent of the purchase invoice.

4.8.1.3   Delivery Type for Direct Delivery

If you select the option "Direct delivery" in the column *Delivery type* of a sales order line (or in the corresponding field on the sub-tab *Sourcing* of the *Line details*), a direct delivery purchase order is immediately created when saving the order line. The vendor for the direct delivery purchase order is specified in the field *Sourcing vendor* on the sub-tab *Sourcing* of the sales order line.

With this setting, you do not need to create the purchase order manually (with the button *Direct delivery*), but it is created automatically. The further proceeding with product receipt and invoice posting for the direct delivery is the same as described above.

4.8.1.4   Settings in the Released Product

If an item is usually distributed with direct delivery, you can set the slider *Delivery type* on the tab *Deliver* in the Released product form to "Yes". When entering a sales order line for such an item, the setting for the *Delivery type*, the *Direct delivery warehouse*, and the main vendor in the released product initialize the column *Delivery type*, the warehouse, and the *Sourcing vendor* in the order line.

4.8.1.5   Direct Delivery Workbench

If you do not want to create direct delivery purchase orders straight from the sales orders (e.g., because the purchasing department should create all purchase orders), set slider *Direct delivery* on the sub-tab *Delivery* of the sales order line to "Yes" (and do not set the *Delivery type* to "Direct delivery").

The Direct delivery workbench (*Procurement and sourcing> Purchase orders> Direct delivery processing> Direct delivery*) gives an overview of all sales orders which are marked as "Direct delivery" this way. In the Direct delivery workbench, these sales orders are initially shown on the tab *Direct delivery*. Click the button *Create direct delivery* in the toolbar of this tab to create a purchase order.

This purchase order – and any other direct delivery purchase order which is created independently of the workbench – is then shown on the tab *Confirmation* of the workbench. You can post the purchase order confirmation on this tab. On the tab *Delivery* in the workbench, you can post the product receipt (together with the packing slip).

4.8.1.6   Links between Purchase and Sales Order

The field group *Item reference* on the sub-tab *Product* of a sales order line shows the purchase order which is linked to the sales order line. The same reference is also available in the other direction, from the purchase order line to the sales order. In addition, the reference is shown in the *Related orders* dialog (access with the button *General/Related information/Related orders* in the action pane of the purchase order or the sales order). In the Sales order form, you can click the button *General/Related information/Purchase order* to directly access the assigned purchase order.

4.8.2   Case Study Exercise

Exercise 4.17 – Direct Delivery

The customer of exercise 4.1 orders 100 units of the item of exercise 3.5. In order to avoid stocking this large quantity in the warehouse, you want to process a direct delivery. Enter an appropriate sales order and create a direct delivery purchase order which you send to the vendor of exercise 3.2.

Your vendor confirms shipping the item with packing slip PS417. Post this product receipt in the purchase order. In the next step, review the status of the sales order before you post and print the sales invoice. Finally, you receive the purchase invoice VI417 which you post in the pending vendor invoices.

4.9   Rebate Management and Trade Allowances

Customer rebates are contracts which specify a discount depending on the actual sales volume. With rebates, the customer usually receives a credit note or a payment at the end of a period if the total sales amount or quantity meets the target as agreed in the rebate contract.

Apart from customer rebates, Dynamics 365 also covers agreements with vendors, broker contracts, and royalty contracts:

> **Customer rebates** – Rebate contracts with customers.
> **Trade allowances** – Enhanced customer rebate functionality.
> **Vendor rebates** – Rebate functionality in purchasing (similar to sales).
> **Broker contracts** – Reimbursement of agents (set up as vendors) based on the sales revenue with particular customers.
> **Royalty contracts** – Reimbursement of royalty owners (set up as vendors) based on the sales volume of particular items.
> **Rebate management deals** – Extended features for customer rebates, vendor rebates, and royalties in the Rebate management module.

The Rebate management module, which works independent of the customer and vendor rebates and the related setup, provides extended rebate features.

4.9.1   Trade Allowances

Trade allowance agreements in Dynamics 365 are used for the calculation and the payment of rebates, and for the analysis of the profitability of promotions. You can group trade allowances in Dynamics 365 into three categories:

> **Bill back** – Allowances based on the posted invoices in a period, paid to the order customer or the invoice customer.
> **Lump sum** – Allowances paid upfront to an agent (vendor or customer).
> **Invoicing rebate** – Allowance immediately deducted from the sales invoice.

Customer rebate agreements (*Sales and marketing> Customer rebates> Rebate agreements*) with the rebate program type "Rebate" and "TMA" work similar to the bill back trade allowance agreement which is described in this section.

4.9.1.1   Required Setup for Trade Allowances

As a prerequisite for trade allowance agreements, you have to set up a customer hierarchy (*Sales and marketing> Trade allowances> Customer category hierarchy*) with the customers who use trade allowances. In order to create a hierarchy, click the button *New* in the action pane of the Customer hierarchy form. With the button *New category node* in the toolbar of the tab *Categories*, you can optionally create a multilevel hierarchy structure as applicable. Then, with the button *Add/remove customer* in the action pane, assign the customers to the top category or the lower nodes. In trade allowance agreements, you can only select customers who are assigned to a hierarchy.

In the merchandising event categories (*Sales and marketing> Setup> Trade allowance> Merchandising event category*), at least one category per trade allowance type is required:

➢ **Bill back** – Category with *Default type* "Bill back".
➢ **Lump sum** – Category with *Default type* "Lump sum".
➢ **Invoicing rebate** – Category with *Default type* "Off invoice".

For bill back trade allowance agreements, at least one program type with the *Rebate program type* "Bill back" has to be set up in the rebate program types (*Sales and marketing> Customer rebates> Rebate program types*).

Following parameter settings are required prerequisites for trade allowances:

➢ **Accounts receivable parameters** – Select an *AR consumption journal* and a *Rebate accrual journal* (section *Rebate program*, tab *Journals*). Optionally set the slider *Rebates at invoicing* to "Yes" (if you want to generate a rebate claim immediately when posting an applicable sales invoice). In the section *Number sequences*, enter number sequences for the *Reference* "Rebate ID" and "Rebate agreement ID".
➢ **Trade allowance management parameters** (*Sales and marketing> Setup> Trade allowance> Trade allowance management parameters*) – Enter the required number sequences and optionally select a default *Customer hierarchy* and a *Default rebate program ID*. If you want to use lump sum allowances, optionally select an *Expense account* or a *Procurement category* for lump sum transactions.

4.9.1.2 Funds and Other Optional Settings

Trade allowance funds are used to specify the budget for the costs of trade allowance rebates. Although funds are not a mandatory precondition for trade allowances, it is nevertheless useful to specify the monetary funds as a basis for the check of the profitability of sales promotions with rebates.

You can set up trade allowance funds in the menu item *Sales and marketing> Trade allowances> Funds> Funds* with the applicable validity period (*From date* and *To date*) and the budget amount (*Fund budgeted*). Before you activate the fund (change the *Status* to "Approved"), switch to the tab *Customers* and the tab *Items*, and enter the customers and the items that are covered by the fund.

Trade allowance agreement periods (*Sales and marketing> Setup> Trade allowance> Trade allowance agreement period*) provide the option to specify date intervals which you can use as the default value when entering trade allowance agreements.

If you want to apply an approval process for trade allowance agreements, configure the required approval workflows in the menu item *Sales and marketing> Setup> Trade allowance> Trade allowance workflows*.

4.9.1.3 Managing Trade Allowance Agreements

Trade allowance agreements specify rebates for customers. In order to create a new agreement, open the menu item *Sales and marketing> Trade allowances> Trade allowance agreements* and click the button *New* in the action pane. Then enter a description and the validity dates (mandatory fields *Order from* and *Order to*, optionally initialized with a default from the field *Trade allowance agreement period*). In the field group *Analysis*, you have to select the *Unit*. Then optionally specify the sales target of the agreement – enter the usual sales quantity without trade allowances in the field *Base units*, and the intended increase in the field *Lift percent*.

The contract customers have to be specified on the tab *Customers*. The tabs *Items* and *Funds* in the Header view of the trade allowances contain default values for the trade allowance lines.

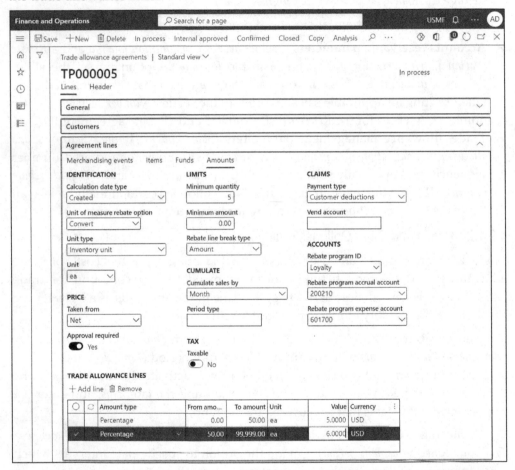

Figure 4-27:   Amount calculation settings in a bill back trade allowance agreement line

In the Lines view of the agreement, the tabs *General* and *Customers* include core header data. On the tab *Agreement lines*, the first sub-tab is the *Merchandising event*, which contains the agreement lines with their *Category* (merchandising event category). The other sub-tabs contain the details of each agreement line, including the allowance calculation on the sub-tab *Amounts*. The fields on this sub-tab depend on the *Category* in the agreement line ("Bill back", "Lump sum", or "Off invoice").

In a "Bill back" agreement line, the *Minimum quantity* and *Minimum amount* on the sub-tab *Amounts* determine the required minimum sales volume within the cumulating period (selected in the field *Cumulate sales by*) for being eligible to deduct a rebate. The *Payment type* determines whether the customer receives a credit note or a payment:

> ➤ **Payment type "Customer deductions"** – Credit note in the form of a (negative) invoice to the order customer (for orders that are covered by the agreement).
> ➤ **Payment type "Invoice customer deductions"** – Credit note to the invoice customer (for the orders that are covered by the agreement).
> ➤ **Payment type "Pay using account payable"** – Reimbursement via accounts payable, i.e., by paying the vendor in the field *Vend account* of the agreement line or the vendor who is linked to the order customer (field *Vendor account* on the tab *Miscellaneous details* in the Customer form).

The pane *Trade allowance lines* on the sub-tab *Amounts* in a "Bill back" agreement line contains the rebate calculation. The column *Amount type* in this pane specifies whether the number in the column *Value* is an amount or a percentage. You can enter multiple trade allowance lines in case the allowance percentage or amount is depending on the sales volume. The field *Rebate line break type* in the field group *Limits* determines whether the *From qty* and the *To qty* in the lines is a quantity or an amount.

Once you have completed the trade allowance agreement, click the button *Confirmed* in the action pane to activate the agreement.

If you want to set up multiple similar trade allowance agreements, you can create a template (*Sales and marketing> Trade allowances> Templates*) in a similar way to a regular trade allowance. In the template, you can click the button *Create trade allowances* to create a new trade allowance as a copy of the template.

4.9.1.4 Lump Sum Agreements

Lump sum agreements are one-time payments or credit notes, which should support sales promotion activities for customers or vendors. In order to set up a lump sum agreement, enter an agreement line in a trade allowance agreement as described above, but with the *Category* "Lump sum". In a lump sum agreement line, the sub-tab *Amounts* contains the core fields *Amount* (for the claim amount) and *Payment type* (customer credit note, or reimbursement as a vendor payment).

Once you have set the status of the trade allowance agreement to "Confirmed", you can click the button *Approve* in the toolbar of the sub-tab *Amounts* to credit or pay the rebate (depending on the *Payment type* in the agreement line):

➢ **Payment type "Customer deductions" or "Invoice customer deductions"** – Credit note to the customer in the field *Pay to* of the agreement line (offset account is the expense account specified in the Trade allowance parameters).

➢ **Payment type "Pay using account payable"** – Reimbursement by a vendor invoice with the vendor in the field *Pay to* (offset account from the procurement category as specified in the Trade allowance parameters).

You can view the posted customer or vendor invoice for the rebate in the open transactions of the particular customer or vendor.

4.9.1.5 Processing Bill Back Agreements

Rebate claims from a bill back agreement (trade allowance agreement line "Bill back") are based on sales invoices with the customers and the items that are specified in the agreement.

The rebate claims are immediately created when posting a sales invoice if the slider *Rebates at invoicing* in the Accounts receivable parameters (section *Rebate program*, tab *Invoicing*) is set to "Yes". If this slider is set to "No", execute the periodic activity *Sales and marketing> Customer rebate> Rebate update> Calculate rebates* to generate rebate claims.

Rebate claims, which refer to a bill back agreement, are shown in the Bill back workbench (*Sales and marketing> Trade allowances> Bill back workbench*).

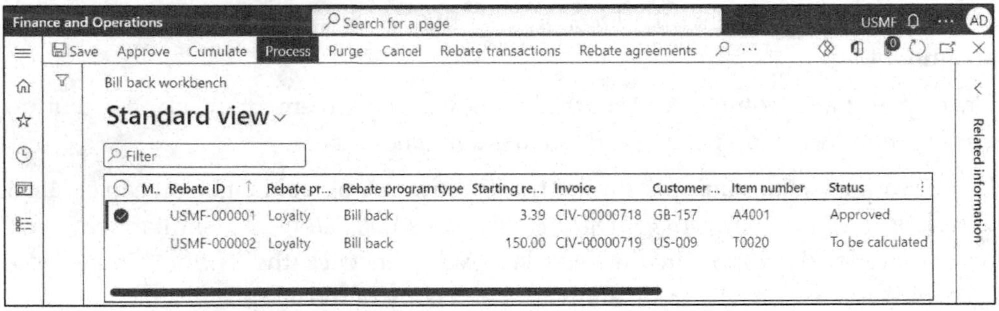

Figure 4-28:   Processing a rebate in the Bill back workbench

For the rebate claims that have been generated, the rebate amounts need to be cumulated (based on the period revenue) at the end of each cumulating period (given by the field *Cumulate sales by* on the sub-tab *Amounts* of the trade allowance agreement line). This cumulation can be done with the button *Cumulate* in the workbench or with the periodic activity *Sales and marketing> Customer rebate> Rebate update> Cumulate rebates*.

Once the rebates are cumulated, you can approve them. Select the lines for approval in the grid of the workbench and approve the rebates with the button *Approve*. Then click the button *Process* to generate rebate transactions. Processing sets the rebate status to "Mark" and posts accrual transactions.

For a trade allowance agreement line with the cumulating period "Invoice" (field *Cumulate sales by* on the sub-tab *Amounts*) and the slider *Approval required* (on this sub-tab) set to "No", all rebate claims are processed immediately. There is no need to cumulate, approve, and process the claims.

You can credit or pay a rebate claim in the open transactions of the customer who receives the rebate. In order to access the open transactions, click the button *Collect/Settle/Settle transactions* in the Customer form. In the *Settle transactions* dialog that is shown next, click the button *Functions/Bill back program* to open the Rebate form in which you select the checkbox *Mark* of applicable rebate lines. Then click the button *Functions/Create credit note* to create a sales credit note (in an *AR consumption journal* specified in the Accounts receivable parameter), or the button *Functions/Pass to AP* to create a vendor invoice that is included in the next payment proposal.

Once you have created the sales credit note or vendor invoice, the status of the related rebate claim is "Completed".

4.9.1.6 Canceling and Purging Rebates

If there is a rebate claim from a trade allowance agreement which you do not want to pay or credit, you can cancel the rebate claim after processing it (in the status "Mark"). Click the button *Cancel* in the Bill back workbench for this purpose and enter an appropriate filter in the related dialog. Canceling sets the status of the rebate claim to "Canceled" and reverses the accrual transactions.

With the button *Purge* in the Bill back workbench, you can clean up the workbench. Purging deletes all finished transactions (status "Completed" or "Canceled").

4.9.1.7 Deductions and One-Time Promotions

You can use trade allowance deductions if a customer only pays a reduced amount for an invoice and indicates, that the deduction is an anticipation of an allowance (and will be included in the rebate payout at period end anyhow). The following setup is required as a prerequisite for deductions:

➢ **Deduction journal name** – Select a journal name (used for the posting of deductions) in the Trade allowance parameters.
➢ **Deduction types** (*Sales and marketing> Trade allowances> Deductions> Deduction types*) – Create at least one type with the related offset account.
➢ **Deduction denial reasons** (*Sales and marketing> Trade allowances> Deductions> Deduction denial reasons*) – If you deny deductions, a reason code is required.

Deductions are recorded together with the customer payment in a payment journal (*Accounts receivable> Payments> Payment journal*, see section 9.3.3). Enter a payment journal line which does not fully match the invoice amount (because of the deduction) and click the button *Deductions* in the toolbar of the tab *List* in the journal lines. In the Deduction form that is shown next, insert a new line with the deduction type, the deduction amount, and the trade allowance ID. The fields in the field group *Balance* at the bottom of the Deduction form show the balance of settled amount, payment, and deduction. After closing the Deduction form, the payment journal shows an additional line with the deduction. Posting the payment journal generates a separate transaction for the payment and for the deduction.

You can manage the open deductions after posting the payment journal in the Deduction workbench (*Sales and marketing> Trade allowances> Deductions> Deduction workbench*). When you select a deduction line in the upper pane of the workbench, the open transactions (credit notes generated in the trade allowances process) for the related customer are shown in the lower pane. In order to match a deduction with a credit transaction in the Deduction workbench, select the checkbox *Mark* in the appropriate deduction first, and mark applicable rebate transactions in the lower pane next. Then click the button *Maintain/Match* to post the match transaction.

In case a customer has applied a deduction incorrectly, click the button *Maintain/ Deny* in the action pane of the Deduction workbench to reverse the deduction. The denied amount is shown as an open customer transaction then.

The button *Maintain/Split* provides the option to split a deduction line – for example, if you want to deny only part of the deduction.

A one-time deduction enables the deduction of an amount which exceeds the trade allowance agreement. You can post it with the button *Maintain/Settle deduction as one-time promotion* in the workbench. The one-time promotion is posted as a lump sum transaction (as additional promotion) with the trade allowance template that is selected as *One-time promotion template* in the Trade allowance parameters.

4.9.2   Broker Contracts

Broker contracts are agreements with agents (set up as vendors), which require to pay the agent based on the sales volume with selected customers and items.

4.9.2.1   Required Setup for Broker Contracts

As a prerequisite for broker contracts, you have to set up at least one charges code (Ledger – Ledger) for broker charges in the sales charges (*Accounts receivable> Charges setup> Charges code*). This code is used for posting the broker charges ledger transaction when posting a sales invoice.

In the Accounts payable parameters (section *Broker and royalty*, tab *Brokerage*), select a procurement category for broker claim expenses and applicable journal names. A number sequence for the *Broker claim invoice* is required in the section *Number sequences* of the parameters.

4.9.2.2   Entering and Processing Broker Contracts

Since a broker is a vendor, the broker contracts are included in the Accounts payable module (*Accounts payable> Broker and royalties> Broker contracts*). When you set up a broker contract, select the broker and a default for the *Charges code* and the

Category in the upper pane of the form. In the lower pane, specify the items and customers which are covered by the broker agreement. The *Break type* and *Break in* a line determine the minimum quantity or amount which is required to apply a broker charge. Depending on the *Category* in the line, the *Charges value* is a percentage or an amount. You can enter multiple lines in the lower pane in case there are charges which depend on the sales quantity or amount. When you are finished, select the option "Approved" in the column *Status* of the upper pane to activate the contract.

In a sales order line that is covered by a broker contract, you can click the button *Sales order line/Broker commission* in the toolbar of the lines to view the calculated broker commission. The button *Financials/Maintain charges* in the sales order line provides access to the related charges transaction. Posting the sales order invoice generates an accrual (based on the charges transaction) and a broker claim.

In the broker claims (*Accounts payable> Broker and royalties> Broker claims*), you can view the claims that are generated from sales invoices. In order to pay a claim, make sure that the checkbox *Mark* is selected in the applicable lines and click the button *Approve*. The approval is posting a reversal of the accrual and a new vendor invoice with the broker expense.

4.9.3 Royalty Agreements

Royalty agreements in Dynamics 365 support contracts with royalty owners (set up as vendors), which require to pay a fee (e.g., a license fee) to the royalty owner based on the sales volume with selected items. Royalty contracts work similar to vendor rebate agreements, but they are based on the customer invoice transactions covered by the royalty agreement.

The required setup for royalty contracts in the Accounts payable parameters includes settings in the sections *Broker and royalty* and *Number sequences*.

Based on the royalty contracts, which you enter in the menu item *Accounts payable> Broker and royalties> Royalty agreements*, you can process the claims in the menu item *Accounts payable> Broker and royalties> Royalty claims*.

4.9.4 Vendor Rebates

Rebate and trade allowance agreements are not only available in the Sales module. You can also manage rebate agreements with vendors in Dynamics 365. Vendor rebate agreements (*Procurement and sourcing> Vendor rebates> Rebate agreements*) have to be entered in a similar way to customer rebate agreements and trade allowance agreements. You can process the claims subsequently in the menu item *Procurement and sourcing> Vendor rebates> Rebate claims*. The required setup for vendor rebate agreements includes the Procurement and sourcing parameters (section *Rebate program*) and the setup forms in the menu folder *Procurement and sourcing> Vendor rebates*.

4.9.5   Rebate Management Deals

The Rebate management module, which you can use instead of the trade allowances, customer rebates, vendor rebates, and royalties, provides extended features for rebates. It is shared across companies, and you can specify for each deal in which companies it should be used. Apart from a financial rebate in the form of a payment or a credit note, a rebate may also grant a free item delivery.

4.9.5.1   Setup for Rebate Management

If you use the Rebate management module, set in set the slider *Activate* in the section *Feature visibility* of the Rebate management parameters (*Rebate management> Setup> Rebate management parameters*) to "Yes". The applicable rebate management features are shown in all modules then. The tab *Rebate management* in the parameters includes further settings like the option to post rebates automatically.

Different from the trade allowance agreements with an optional approval workflow, all rebate management deals must be approved in an approval process. Configure the required approval workflows in the menu item *Rebate management> Setup> Rebate management workflows*.

Optional settings include the rebate reduction principles (*Rebate management> Setup> Rebate reduction principles*), which control how rebates are calculated if multiple rebate management deals apply to a sales transaction, and the rebate status (*Rebate management> Setup> Status> Status*), which enables characterizing the status of a deal – e.g., active or completed.

Rebate management groups for customers, vendors, and items, which you can set up and assign in the menu items of the folder *Rebate management> Rebate management groups setup*, are also optional.

The rebate management posting profiles (*Rebate management> Rebate management posting setup> Rebate management posting profiles*) control the way in which rebates are calculated and posted. The field *Module* in this form specifies whether the profile is for customer transactions or for vendor transactions. The available options for the *Payment type* are similar to the options in a trade allowances bill back agreement (with the options "Customer deductions" and "Pay using account payable"), but with the additional option "Tax invoice customer deductions" which you can use to post a free text invoice for the rebate (instead of just posting a journal with the option "Customer deductions"). The *Credit account* on the tab *Posting* is the accrual account, and the *Debit account* at the bottom of the form specifies the expense account for rebates. In the field *Use account source*, select the option "Deal line account" (and "Customer/Vendor" in the field *Type*) to award the rebate to the customer in the sales order, or the option "Fixed account" to award it to a fixed customer or ledger account irrespective of the sales customer.

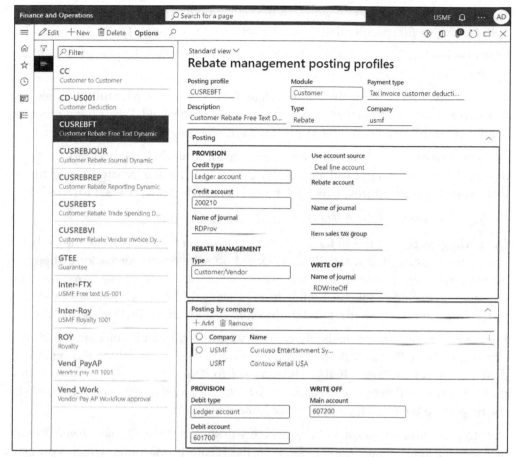

Figure 4-29: Rebate settings in the rebate management posting profile

4.9.5.2 Managing Rebate Management Deals

Rebate Management deals (*Rebate management> Rebate management deals> All rebate management deals*) include customer rebates, vendor rebates, and royalties.

When you create a new deal with the button *New* in the action pane, a *Create* dialog is shown, in which you enter several fields including *Module* ("Customer" for customer rebates), *Type* ("Rebate" for rebates), *Reconcile by* ("Line" for processing rebates on line level; the *Posting profile* is specified on deal line level in this case). In the field *Rebate output*, make sure that the option "Financial" is selected for a rebate which is granted in the form of a payment or a credit note.

In the rebate deal lines, enter one or more lines with reference to the customer (customer number, customer rebate group, or all), the item (item number, item rebate group, or all), and inventory dimensions as applicable.

On the sub-tab *General* in the tab *Rebate management details* of a rebate management deal line, select the *Calculation method* and the *Basis*. Whereas the trade allowances are only based on invoices, rebate deals can also refer to orders or to deliveries –

select the applicable *Transaction type* in the rebate management details. The lookup field *Posting profile* specifies the applicable settings for posting.

On the sub-tab *Date* in the tab *Rebate management details*, enter the period of validity for the deal line.

The sub-tab *Lines* contains the rebate calculation. You can enter multiple lines on this sub-tab in case the rebate amount or – only if the field *Rebate output* in the header is set to "Financial" – the percentage is depending on the sales volume.

Once you have completed the rebate management deal, click the button *Workflow/ Submit*. The further approval process is depending on the rebate management workflow. With the approval, the slider *Active* in the deal header is set to "Yes".

4.9.5.3   Processing Rebate Management Deals for Customers

Depending on the settings in the deal (field *Transaction type* in the deal line), rebate claims from a customer rebate deal are based on sales orders, or packing slips, or invoices with the customers and the items that are specified in the agreement. If you want to exclude a sales order line from rebate calculation, set the slider *Exclude from rebate management* on the sub-tab *Price and discount* in the line details to "Yes".

Rebate provisions are immediately created when posting an invoice or a packing slip if the slider *Process at posting* on the sub-tab *Dates* in the rebate management deal line is set to "Yes". If this slider is set to "No", you have to execute the periodic activity *Rebate management> Periodic tasks> Process> Provision* (or the click the respective button in the rebate management deal).

Rebate provisions are shown in the Rebate workbench (*Rebate management> Rebate management deals> Rebate workbench*) or in the rebate transactions, which you can access with the button *Rebate management deals/Transactions/Transactions* in the Rebate management deal form. With the button *Rebate workbench/View/Source transactions* (or the respective button in the rebate transactions) you can view the basis (sales transaction) for the rebate transaction. Depending on the Rebate management settings on automatic posting, you have to post the provision (click the button *Rebate workbench/Processing/Post*) to generate the target transaction (accrual journal).

In order to process actually paying or refunding the rebate, process the rebate with the periodic activity *Rebate management> Periodic tasks> Process> Rebate management* (or the click the respective button in the Rebate workbench). When you post the rebate transaction which has been created then, a deduction journal (credit note), or a vendor invoice (for payment), or a free text invoice (credit note which can be printed) will be created as target transaction (depending on the *Payment type* in the rebate management deal line) and offset the accrual.

5 Production Control

The primary responsibility of production control is to manufacture products. In manufacturing, materials and resource capacity are consumed.

5.1 Business Processes in Manufacturing

Depending on the requirements in your enterprise, you can apply the following manufacturing concepts in Dynamics 365:

➤ **Discrete manufacturing** – Core production functionality with bills of materials (BOMs), resources, routes, and production orders.
➤ **Process manufacturing** – Covers the additional requirements of batch-producing industries (e.g., the chemical industry) with formulas.
➤ **Lean manufacturing** – Covers production flows and Kanbans (completely independent of routes and production orders).

You can apply the concepts in a mixed mode and, for example, use process manufacturing for components and lean manufacturing for finished products.

This book addresses the core functionality in discrete manufacturing and includes an outline of process manufacturing. Before we start to go into details, the lines below give an overview of the processes in discrete manufacturing.

5.1.1 Basic Approach

Like in purchasing and sales, correct master data are an essential prerequisite for order processing in production control.

5.1.1.1 Master Data and Transactions in Production Control

The released product record contains the main characteristics of an item. The structure of a finished (or semi-finished) item with a list of components (materials, or lower-level semi-finished items) is given by the bill of materials (BOM).

Resources (machines or workers) are another basic element – they provide the required capacity for manufacturing. Routes and operations, which describe the activities to manufacture an item, determine the required resources.

Products, BOMs, resources, and routes are master data, which are created once and only occasionally updated later. In the course of production order processing, default values from the master data initialize the planned and actual production orders (transaction data). You can override these data in the transaction – e.g., if you need a non-standard bill of materials in a particular production order.

Figure 5-1 below shows the main steps in production order processing.

© Springer Fachmedien Wiesbaden GmbH, part of Springer Nature 2023
A. Luszczak, *Using Microsoft Dynamics 365 for Finance and Operations*,
https://doi.org/10.1007/978-3-658-40453-6_5

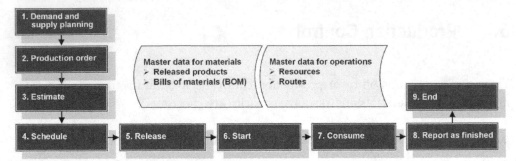

Figure 5-1:   Production order processing in Dynamics 365

5.1.1.2 Demand and Supply Planning

Since it calculates the required quantity of finished products, master planning (see section 6.3) often is the starting point for the manufacturing process. Depending on the settings for scheduling, the calculated item demand (required quantity) derives from sources like forecasts, sales quotations, sales orders, or a minimum stock.

5.1.1.3 Creating Production Orders

Master planning generates planned production orders, which you can transfer to actual production orders. Including the option to transfer planned orders, there are the following ways to generate a production order:

➢ **Manual** – Enter an order in the Production order form.
➢ **Planned production order** – Transfer a planned order.
➢ **Sales order** – Create a production order from a sales order line.
➢ **Pegged supply** – Automatically creating a production order for a semi-finished product (sub-production) from the production order of a finished product.
➢ **Project** – Create a production order from a project (Project accounting module).

A production order consists of an order header, which contains the manufactured item, and lines. Unlike purchase orders or sales orders, which only include order lines with items, a production order contains two types of lines: BOM lines with items and route operations. These different line types are shown in separate forms.

After creating a production order, you have to execute all subsequent steps – from estimating to ending – one after another. But depending on parameter settings, you can skip steps when processing a production order.

5.1.1.4 Estimation and Scheduling

Once you have created a production order, estimation is the first step in order processing. The estimation determines the quantity and the cost of the items and resources which are required to manufacture the product.

Whereas the estimation calculates the item and resource demand without a date or time, scheduling as the next step determines exact production dates.

5.1.1.5 Releasing and Starting

Releasing a production order means to hand it over from the front office to the shop floor. At this stage, you can print the production papers as required.

Once you want to start activities on the shop floor, set the order status to "Started". You can't consume items or resources before the order has got this status. When starting an order, you can print the picking list and post the automatic consumption of items and resource capacity.

5.1.1.6 Production Journals

In the manufacturing process, the shop floor consumes materials and resource capacity. This consumption is reported in production journals. Depending on the requirements, you can post the journals manually or backflush automatically (with estimation data). Alternatively, you can use the Dynamics 365 Manufacturing execution features to report the consumption on terminals and mobile devices.

5.1.1.7 Reporting as Finished and Ending

Once you have produced a partial or the entire quantity of the manufactured item, post a "Report as finished" transaction. Reporting as finished increases the physical inventory of the manufactured item. Ending the production order is the last step in production order processing. It calculates the actual costs of production and posts the financial transactions to the general ledger.

5.1.1.8 Ledger Integration and Voucher Principle

Production journals, which record the consumption of materials or resources and the receipt of manufactured items, post physical transactions to the general ledger. The financial transactions are posted when ending the order (see section 9.4.3).

The voucher principle, which is the general principle for processing transactions in Dynamics 365, also applies to transactions in manufacturing: You have to register a transaction in a journal before you can post it.

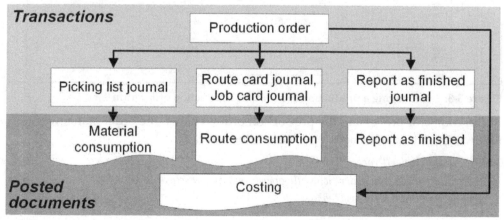

Figure 5-2:   Transactions and posted documents in production control

5.1.2   At a Glance: Production Order Processing

The following example demonstrates the main steps in production order processing. It starts with creating the order in the workspace *Production floor management* and shows how to post all transactions directly in the Production order form. Alternatively, you can create the order in the Production order form.

In the workspace *Production floor management*, click the button *Create new/Production order* in the action pane to create a regular order (for discrete manufacturing). In the *Create production order* dialog which is shown next, select the *Item number* of the manufactured item. The quantity, the BOM, and the route in the production order are initialized with default values from this item. Click the button *Create* in the dialog to create the production order with these data then.

If the Production order detail form is in Read mode, click the button *Edit*, or press the *F2* key, to switch to the Edit mode. If you want to view or edit the BOM or the route of the order, click the button *Production order/Order details/BOM* or *Production order/Order details/Route* in the action pane.

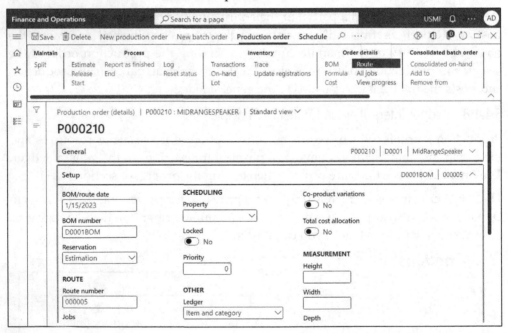

Figure 5-3:   Managing a production order in the Production order form

In the course of processing the production order, change the order status with the following buttons in the action pane one after another:

➢ *Production order/Process/Estimate*
➢ *Schedule/Production order/Schedule operations* or …/*Schedule jobs*
➢ *Production order/Process/Release*

When changing the status, you can select applicable parameters on the first tab (or on the tab *General*) of each update dialog – for example, if you want to select the scheduling direction when scheduling, or to print the production papers when releasing. If you skip a step, it is automatically executed with the next step. Once you want to execute the work for the order on the shop floor, start the order with the button *Production order/Process/Start*. Starting posts automatic material and route consumption as applicable. In addition, you can print the picking list.

In order to record the consumption of items with the flushing principle "Manual", click the button *View/Journals/Picking list* in the production order. If you want to generate a proposal with picking list lines, click the button *Picking list/Create lines* in the Journal list page. In the *Create lines* dialog that is shown in this case, select the option "Remaining quantity" in the lookup field *Proposal* to initialize the journal lines with the open quantity. In the Lines view of the Journal detail form (shown automatically after generating the proposal, or manually with a click on the journal ID shown as a link in the list page), you can edit the quantity, the warehouse, and other data before you post the journal with the button *Post*.

Depending on the setup and on the scheduling type (*Operations scheduling* or *Job scheduling*) which you have selected when scheduling the production order, you can enter the actual working time consumption either at route level or at job level (click the button *View/Journals/Route card* or *View/Journals/Job card* in the order). In route card journals and job card journals, there is no proposal which initializes the lines with default values when you manually enter a journal. Click the button *New* in the route card (or job card) journal and select the journal name in the *Create production journal* dialog before you close the dialog with the button *OK*. In the Lines view of the Journal detail form that is shown next, enter one or more lines with the date, operation/job number, resource, hours, and good quantity before you click the button *Post*.

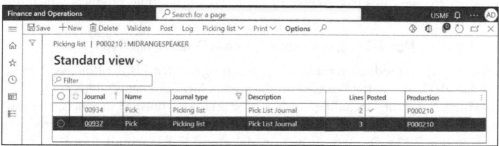

Figure 5-4:   Picking list journal page with a journal which is not yet posted

In order to receive the manufactured item in inventory, click the button *Production order/Process/Report as finished* in the production order. If you want to ignore missing consumption postings, set the slider *Accept error* on the tab *General* of the update dialog to "Yes". Once all transactions of the production order are posted, close the order with the button *Production order/Process/End*.

5.2   Product Management and Bill of Materials

All items, which are involved in the manufacturing process, have to be set up in the shared and in the released products. Apart from inventoried items like finished products, semi-finished products, and raw materials or parts, product records are also required for phantom items or purchased services.

The bill of materials (BOM) specifies the materials which are included in a manufactured item. You can assign one or more bills of materials to an item, but you can also assign one common bill of materials to multiple items. A single item is assigned to multiple bills of materials, if the applicable bill of materials is, for example, depending on the lot size or on the production date.

5.2.1   Product Data in Manufacturing

The form for shared products (*Product information management> Products> All products and product masters*) and the Released product form (*Product information management> Products> Released products*) include all products – finished products, semi-finished products, and raw materials or parts. The workspace *Released product maintenance* is another place to manage the released products.

You can find a general description on the product management in Dynamics 365 in section 7.2 of this book. The following section contains an explanation of the product data which are necessary for production control. Except for the product type and the product subtype, which are specified in the shared product, these data are stored in the released product.

The engineering change management with product versions (see section 7.2.5) provides a structured way to manage the process of creating new and changing existing products, in particular for manufacturing. If you do not need the advanced engineering change management functionality, you can alternatively use the product change cases (see section 10.5.2) to collect multiple products which are affected by a change.

5.2.1.1   Item Model Group, Production Type and Default Order Type

With regard to production control, a core setting for items is the *Item model group* on the tab *General* in the Released product detail form. All items which are used in production control – including finished products, semi-finished products, and raw materials or parts – have to be linked to an item model group for stocked products (see section 7.2.1). This type of item model group is also required for BOM-lines with non-inventoried items (e.g., subcontractor work), which is why you select the *Product type* "Service" in the shared product records of non-inventoried items that you want to include in a BOM (this way avoiding inventory control for the items).

In the lookup field *Production type* on the tab *Engineer*, select the option "BOM" for finished or semi-finished products. If you select the production type "Formula" or "Planning item", you can assign a formula (related to process manufacturing) instead of a BOM to the item. The production type "None" prevents assigning a BOM to the item. This means you can only purchase the item, not produce it. But you can also purchase an item with another production type because the default order type – and not the production type – determines the primary sourcing strategy for the item.

The field *Default order type*, which controls item sourcing, is shown on the tab *General* in the default order settings. In order to access the default order settings, click the button *Manage inventory/Order settings/Default order settings* in the Released product form. There are the following options for the default order type:

➤ **Purchase order** – Purchase orders are used to supply the item.
➤ **Production** – Production orders are used to supply the item.
➤ **Kanban** – Kanbans (lean manufacturing) are used to supply the item.

If you need to override the default order type at the level of a particular site, or warehouse, or another inventory dimension, click the button *Plan/Coverage/Item coverage* in the released product to open the Item coverage form. On the tab *General* in the item coverage, you have to select the checkbox *Change planned order type* before you can select a dimension-specific order type in the field *Planned order type*.

5.2.1.2 Settings for Quantity and Price

Apart from the default order type on the tab *General*, the tab *Inventory* in the default order settings contains data which are also used for production orders – including default values for the lot size (field *Multiple*) and the order quantity (field *Standard order quantity*). You can override the default order settings at the company level (which is the record with a blank *Site*) with order settings at the site level (create additional records with the respective *Site*).

On the tab *Manage costs* in the Released product form, the field *Price* specifies the general cost price of the item. In the Item price form, which you can access with the button *Manage costs/Set up/Item price* in the released product, you can register site-specific cost prices (see section 7.3.3).

In a released product with an item model group with the valuation model "Standard cost", a cost price with a costing version with the costing type "Standard cost" has to be activated in the Item price form before you can record transactions.

5.2.1.3 Phantom Items

The slider *Phantom* on the tab *Engineer* in the Released product form determines the default for the *Line type* when inserting the item as a component in a BOM line. Phantom items are semi-finished products with a bill of materials and (optionally) a route. When you estimate a production order, BOM lines with the type "Phantom" are exploded. The production order then contains BOM lines with the components of the phantom item (instead of a line with the phantom item itself).

5.2.1.4 Flushing Principle

The *Flushing principle* on the tab *Engineer* in the Released product detail form controls whether automatic consumption is posted in production orders (for the BOM lines with the respective item). There are four different options for the flushing principle:

➢ **Start** – Automatic consumption when starting the production order.
➢ **Finish** – Automatic consumption when reporting as finished.
➢ **Manual** – No automatic consumption.
➢ **Available on location** – Only used with the advanced warehouse management (automatic consumption if available on the production input location).

In the BOM lines, you can override the flushing principle that is specified in the released product record of the respective item.

As a prerequisite for the automatic consumption based on the flushing principle in the released product or in the BOM line, you have to select the option "Flushing principle" in the update dialog when starting a production order or when reporting as finished (see section 5.4.3).

5.2.2 Bills of Materials (BOM)

A bill of materials (BOM), which is a list of items, specifies the components of a manufactured item (finished or semi-finished product).

5.2.2.1 Bill of Materials Structure

In Dynamics 365, the components (raw materials, parts) of a manufactured item are not directly assigned to the product, but to a bill of materials. This bill of materials is then separately assigned to the manufactured item (see Figure 5-5). The assignment of a BOM to a manufactured item is called "BOM version" in Dynamics 365. You can assign one or more BOMs to a manufactured item.

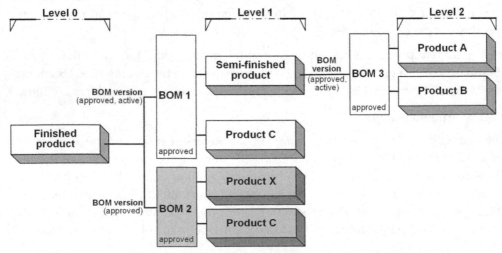

Figure 5-5:   Example of a multi-level product structure with BOMs and BOM versions

Items in a BOM line may consist of other items and therefore refer to a lower-level BOM. Such items are semi-finished items. With semi-finished items, there is a multi-level product structure.

The BOM level shows the number of product levels between the selected product and the final finished product. Products, which are not a component in any BOM, show the level "0". Semi-finished products, which are only included in the most upper-level BOM of finished products, show the level "1".

The BOM level is relevant for master planning (should first calculate the demand for finished products, because this demand determines the demand for lower-level components) and for cost calculation (should first calculate the price of lower-level components to use already updated prices for calculating upper levels).

A product can be a component in the BOMs of multiple products with different levels. A screw, for example, may be directly used in a finished product and in parallel be a component of a semifinished product. For this reason, there are different fields for the BOM level on the tab *Engineer* of the Released product form – the *Costing level*, the *Planning level*, and the *Cost calculation level*. The difference between the *Costing level* and the *Cost calculation level* is that the *Costing level* includes production BOMs (BOMs, which are assigned to the individual production orders and can be modified there) in the calculation, whereas the *Cost calculation level* only includes BOMs which are assigned to released products.

You can update the BOM level with the periodic activity *Product information management> Periodic tasks> Recalculate BOM levels*. In addition, the BOM level is recalculated in parallel with other relevant periodic tasks.

In order to make use of a bill of materials in production control, the BOM and the BOM version have to be approved. In addition, the BOM version has to be activated if it should be used as the default value in production orders and in master planning. An active BOM version for an item has to be unique per date, from-quantity, and site.

5.2.2.2 Entering Bills of Materials and BOM Versions

You can access the bills of materials in the following way:

➢ **From the released product** (*Product information management> Products> Released products*, button *Engineer/BOM/BOM versions*)
➢ **From the menu** (*Product information management> Bills of materials and formulas> Bills of materials*)

The workspace *Product readiness for discrete manufacturing* is another place, from which you can access (use the link *Bills of materials* on the very right) and create (click the button *New/BOM* in the action pane) bills of materials. The BOM form is the same, no matter whether you access it from the workspace or from the menu.

Although the BOM form (accessed from the menu or the workspace) and the BOM version form (accessed from the released product) update the same BOM and BOM version data, the functionality and the structure of these forms is different.

Since understanding the data structure is easier if you start from the menu, the lines below first explain the BOM form in the menu. If you open the menu item *Product information management> Bills of materials and formulas> Bills of materials*, a list page with the bills of materials is displayed. Click on a BOM ID shown as a link in the grid to open the related detail form in the Lines view. The Lines view of the BOM detail form shows the BOM lines. The BOM versions (assignment of manufactured items to the BOM) are shown in the Header view, which you can access with the button *Header* (below the action pane) in the detail form.

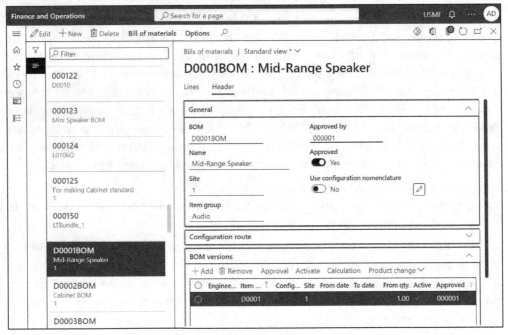

Figure 5-6:   BOM versions in the Header view of the BOM form (accessed from the menu)

In order to create a new bill of materials, click the button *New* in the action pane of the BOM form. The BOM detail form then shows the Lines view with an empty record in the tab *Bill of materials header*, in which you enter the *Name* of the BOM (e.g., identical with the product name). Depending on the settings of the applicable number sequence, the BOM ID is assigned automatically or has to be entered manually.

If the bill of materials is site-specific, enter the site in the field *Site*. If you leave the site empty, it is a common bill of materials for all sites.

In order to assign a finished (or semi-finished) product to the BOM, switch to the Header view and click the button *Add* in the toolbar of the tab *BOM versions* (see Figure 5-6). In the BOM version line, enter the *Item number* of the manufactured item. If the BOM assignment is only valid for a particular period, enter the *From date* and the *To date*. If the BOM assignment is depending on the lot size, enter a *From qty*. And if the BOM assignment is depending on the site, enter the *Site*.

If you want to assign the BOM to a second manufactured item in parallel (which is not very common), create another BOM version on the tab *BOM versions* for the selected BOM.

5.2.2.3 BOM Lines

In the Lines view of the BOM form, you can view and edit the components (raw materials/parts, semi-finished products) which are assigned to the bill of materials.

When you insert a new BOM line with the button *New* in the toolbar of the tab *Bill of materials lines*, enter at least the *Item number* and the *Quantity* of the component. The column *Per series* specifies the number of manufactured items which is produced with the *Quantity* of components in the BOM line – for example, 5 (*Quantity*) boxes (*Unit*) to produce 10 (*Per series*) manufactured items.

On the sub-tab *Setup* of the tab *Line details*, select the option "Constant" in the field *Consumption is* (instead of the default value "Variable") if the consumption (specified in the field *Quantity*) is independent of the production quantity. If you want to specify an additional consumption that covers inevitable scrap, enter a percentage in the field *Variable scrap*, or a fixed quantity in the field *Constant scrap*.

In addition, you can select a *Flushing principle* for automatic consumption. If the flushing principle in the BOM line is empty, the setting in the released product of the BOM line item will be used.

In a site-specific bill of materials, you can enter a picking warehouse in the column *Warehouse* of the BOM lines. In a bill of materials which is not assigned to a particular site, it is not possible to specify the picking warehouse in the BOM lines. In both cases, you can select the checkbox *Resource consumption*, which means that the picking warehouse in a production order is determined by scheduling. With this setting, the *Input warehouse* (specified in the resource group or, if empty, in the production unit) of the resource/resource group in the route operation which consumes the BOM line is used as picking warehouse.

The *Line type* (on the sub-tab *General* of the tab *Line details)* determines the supply strategy of a BOM line. You can choose between the following options:

➢ **Item** – Semi-finished or purchased item, considered as demand in inventory.
➢ **Phantom** – Virtual semi-finished item, replaced by its components when estimating the production order.
➢ **Pegged supply** – Semi-finished or purchased item, creating a referenced sub-production or purchase order when estimating the production order.
➢ **Vendor** – For subcontracting, works like "Pegged supply".

BOM lines with the line type "Item" are considered as a regular demand in inventory. When creating planned production or purchase orders, master planning may consolidate the demand from different sources (orders and warehouse replenishment proposals) according to the item coverage settings. The default order type (or the order type in the item coverage) controls, if master planning creates a planned purchase order, a planned production order, or a Kanban. Unlike the line type "Pegged supply" or "Vendor", the line type "Item" does not establish a close link between the order with the semi-finished product and the original production order with the upper-level finished product.

Production order scheduling and master planning calculate the item demand in a way that all components have to be available at the start date of the production order. If this is not necessary for some components because they are required at a later date, you can assign components to the respective route operation (enter the operation number in the BOM line for this purpose). Available operation numbers are depending on the route which is assigned to the manufactured item. For this reason, the field *Oper.No.* on the sub-tab *General* of the tab *Line details* only shows a lookup in the BOM version form which you access from the released product.

Instead of manually entering all lines in a BOM from scratch, you can copy an existing BOM, which is similar to the new BOM, with the button *Bill of materials/ Maintain/Copy* in the BOM form.

5.2.2.4 Approving and Activating Bills of Materials

In a production order, you can only use approved BOM versions. As a prerequisite for approving a BOM version, the BOM itself has to be approved.

You can approve a BOM with the button *Bill of materials/Maintain/Approval* in the action pane of the BOM form. Next, you can approve the BOM version – click the button *Approve* in the toolbar of the tab *BOM versions* in the Header view of the detail form. If you approve the BOM version before you approve the BOM itself, an additional slider, which enables approving the BOM and the BOM version in parallel, is displayed in the *Approve version* dialog.

If you want to use a particular bill of materials as default value for production orders, for the item price calculation, and for master planning, activate the BOM version with the button *Activate* in the toolbar of the tab *BOM versions*. Active BOM versions show a checkmark in the column *Active* and have to be unique per date, from-quantity, and site.

In order to support approval and activation, the workspace *Product readiness for discrete manufacturing* includes the list *Missing active BOM versions*. This list shows items with the default order type "Production" but no active BOM version.

You can remove the activation and the approval if required. For this purpose, click the button for approval or activation again. When you remove an approval, set the slider *Remove approval* in the dialog to "Yes".

5.2.2.5 Bills of Materials in the Released Product

Apart from the menu item for bills of materials, you can also use the Released product form to access the bills of materials. Select an item with the *Production type* "BOM" in the Released product form, and click the button *Engineer/BOM/BOM versions* to open the BOM version form. The BOM version form shows the bills of materials which are assigned to the selected item. In the rare case that a bill of materials is assigned to multiple items, keep in mind that modifying the bill of materials in this form also affects the other items with a BOM version assignment to the BOM.

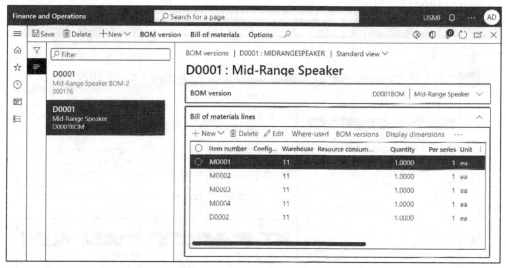

Figure 5-7: Working in the BOM version form (accessed from the released product)

The BOM version form (see Figure 5-7) has got a different structure than the BOM form accessed from the menu: Instead of a Header view and a Lines view, there is a tab *BOM version* (with the fields of the BOM version) and a tab *Bill of materials lines* (with the BOM lines of the BOM which is assigned to the BOM version).

If you want to enter a new bill of materials in this form, click the button *New/BOM and BOM version* in the action pane. In the *Create BOM* dialog, enter the *Name* of the BOM and, in case the bill of materials is site-specific, the *Site* before you click the button *OK*. The BOM form is shown next. Enter the components on the tab *Bill of materials lines* of this form. Once you close the BOM form, the BOM is shown in the BOM version form.

In the BOM version form, you can edit the details of a BOM line in a separate dialog which you access with the button *Edit* in the toolbar of the tab *Bill of materials lines*. If you want to access the BOM form from the BOM version form, click the button *Bill of materials/Maintain BOM/Bill of materials*.

With the button *BOM version/Maintain BOM version/Approve* in the BOM version form, you can approve a BOM version (if necessary, set the slider to also approve the BOM itself in the dialog to "Yes"). With the button *BOM version/Maintain BOM version/Activate*, you can subsequently activate the BOM version.

Note: Use the button *New/BOM version* in the BOM version form if you want to assign the item to an existing bill of materials (which only creates a BOM version).

5.2.2.6 BOM Designer

The BOM designer is an alternative option for viewing and editing BOMs and BOM versions. You can access the BOM designer with the button *Engineer/BOM/ Designer* in the Released product form, or with the button *Bill of materials/Maintain/ Designer* in the BOM form.

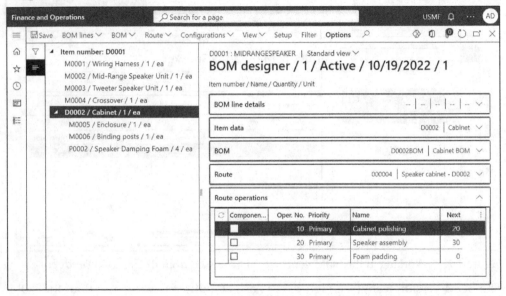

Figure 5-8:   Working with the BOM designer (accessed from the released product)

The BOM designer shows a multi-level structure of the bill of materials in the list pane on the left, and related detail data in tabs on the right. In the action pane of the BOM designer, there are buttons to edit, insert, and delete BOM lines and to create new bills of materials (together with the related BOM version). On the tab *Route operations*, you can select the checkbox *Component needed at* to assign a BOM line to a route operation (which fills the field *Oper.No.* in a BOM line).

If you want to change the display settings in the BOM designer, click the button *Setup* in the action pane. In the *Setup* dialog that is shown next, select the fields which you want to view in the left pane of the BOM designer (e.g., the quantity).

The button *Filter* in the BOM designer provides access to a dialog, in which you can select the BOM/BOM version that you want to view. If you select the *Display principle* "Active" in this dialog, it is the active BOM version for the selected site, date and quantity in the dialog (initialized with the session date and the default order settings of the item). With the *Display principle* "Selected/Active" (or

"Selected"), you can view a BOM version which is different from the active BOM version. In order to select a BOM version for the display principle "Selected", click the button *BOM/BOM versions* in the BOM designer to access the BOM versions selection form. In this form, highlight the BOM version which you want to view and click the button *Select* before you close the form.

5.2.2.7 Block BOM for Editing

Depending on the setup, you can update an approved bill of materials at any time. In some industries, it is required to protect an approved BOM against any changes. For this purpose, there are the following settings in the Inventory parameters (*Inventory management> Setup> Inventory and warehouse management parameters*, section *Bill of materials*):

➢ **Block editing** – If this slider is set to "Yes", no changes are possible once a BOM is approved (remove approval and re-approve afterward in this case).
➢ **Block removal of approval** – If set to "Yes" in parallel to *Block editing*, you can't change a BOM once it is approved.

5.2.2.8 Where-Used

The bill of materials shows the components of an item. If you want to know for a component, in which finished or semi-finished products it is included, access the Where-used form. For this purpose, select the respective item (component) in the Released product form and click the button *Engineer/BOM/Where-used*. If you need the where-used information across multiple BOM levels, run the report *Product information management> Inquiries and reports> Bill of materials where-used*.

5.2.3   Case Study Exercises

Exercise 5.1 – Components

Your company wants to manufacture a new product which consists of two components. Create these components in the Released product form – an item with the product number I-##-C1 and the name "##-Component 1" (## = your user ID) and an item with the number I-##-C2 and the name "##-Component 2". Variants and serial/batch numbers are not required. Inventory control is at the level of site and warehouse.

For both items, choose proper settings for the product type, product subtype, dimension groups, item group (raw materials/parts), and production type. The item model group should refer to the inventory model "FIFO". Approved vendors are not required.

The base purchase price and the base cost price for both items are USD 100. Your vendor of exercise 3.2 is the main vendor for the items and the flushing principle is "Manual". For purchasing and inventory, enter the main site and the main warehouse in the *Default order settings*.

Note: If the number sequence for product numbers is set up for automatic numbering, don't enter a product number.

Exercise 5.2 – Finished Product

For the finished product, create an item with the product number I-##-F (if no automatic number sequence applies) and the name "##-Finished product" in the Released product form. Variants and serial/batch numbers are not required. Inventory control is at the level of site and warehouse.

Select applicable settings for the product type, product subtype, dimension groups, item group (finished product), and production type. The item model group should refer to the inventory model "FIFO". The base cost price is USD 500, and the base sales price is USD 1,000. In the *Default order settings*, make sure that the appropriate *Default order type* is selected and enter the main site and the main warehouse in the settings for inventory and sales.

Exercise 5.3 – Bill of Materials

Once the item records for the finished product and its components are set up in the previous exercises, you can enter the bill of materials for the item of exercise 5.2.

Create a site-specific BOM for the main site with two units of the first and one unit of the second item of exercise 5.1. Components should be picked from the main warehouse. Once you have completed the BOM lines, approve and activate the BOM version.

5.3   Resource and Route Management

Resources include operating personnel, machines, tools, working places, and vendors (subcontractors). They execute the operations and provide the available capacity in manufacturing. Apart from the calculation of the item availability, scheduling and master planning also match the available capacity of resources with the capacity demand.

Routes are the basis for calculating the capacity demand. They specify the necessary resources and the working time for producing a particular item.

Along with items and bills of materials, resources and routes are the second area of master data that are required for production control.

5.3.1   Working Time Calendars and Templates

The working time calendar of a resource or resource group determines the hours of operation. You can manage the working time calendars in the Calendar form (*Production control> Setup> Calendars> Calendars*).

If you need a new calendar (for example, if a resource has working times which do not match any existing calendar), insert a new record with ID and name in the Calendar form. Then click the button *Working times* to access the Working time form. The Working time form shows the calendar days in the upper pane and the working hours of the selected day (with the start time and the end time in editable fields) in the lower pane. If you want to create working days and hours for the selected calendar, click the button *Compose working times* in the Working time form. In the *Compose working times* dialog that is shown next, select a *Working time template* which determines the default values for the daily working hours.

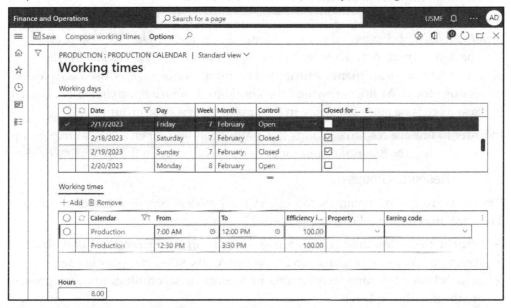

Figure 5-9:   Editing the working times in the calendar

The working time templates (*Production control> Setup> Calendars> Working time templates*) specify the usual working hours per weekday on the tabs *Monday* to *Sunday*.

The base calendar is an alternative way to specify the working times. In the Calendar form, you can link each calendar to another calendar by selecting this calendar in the field *Base calendar* of the first calendar. With this setting, you can set the slider *Use base calendar* in the *Compose working time* dialog to "Yes". Dynamics 365 then initializes the column *Control* in the Working time form with the option "Base calendar". This option means that the working time is given by the base calendar. You can override the working times of a calendar for a day – select the option "Open" or "Closed" in the column *Control* for this purpose.

5.3.2   Resource Groups and Resource Management

Production units represent plants in capacity management. Within a production unit, resource groups collect the resources according to the physical organization on the shop floor. Resources within a resource group can have different capabilities and do not need to be interchangeable.

5.3.2.1 Production Units

Production units, which are an optional setup for capacity management, are independent of the storage dimension "Site", which is used in material management. They are not included in the inventory transactions of items, but in the capacity reservations and route transactions of resources and resource groups. You can link multiple production units to one common site.

If you want to create a production unit, open the menu item *Production control> Setup> Production> Production units* and enter a new record with ID, name, and site. On the tab *General*, optionally enter an *Input warehouse* (the *Output warehouse* is only relevant for lean manufacturing). The input warehouse is used as picking warehouse for BOM lines in which the checkbox *Resource consumption* is selected (in case there is no *Input warehouse* in the applicable resource group).

In order to link the resource groups to a production unit, open the Resource group form and select the *Production unit* for each resource group in the respective field.

5.3.2.2 Resource Groups

Resource groups in Dynamics 365 reflect the physical organization of resources. They are used for the following purposes:

➢ **Structuring** – Resource groups are an element in the hierarchical organization structure. They link resources to production units, sites, and warehouses.
➢ **Scheduling** – For capacity planning in operations scheduling, resource groups are the scheduling level.

The capacity of a resource group is the total capacity of the assigned resources. Since the assignment of resources to resource groups is date effective, you can adjust the resource assignment in line with organizational and seasonal changes. But on each day, a resource can only be linked to one resource group.

If a resource is not assigned to a resource group on a given day, it is not available for manufacturing on that day. Resource scheduling only includes resources which are assigned to a resource group.

If you want to edit the resource groups, open the menu item *Production control> Setup> Resources> Resource groups*. In order to create a new resource group, click the button *New* in the action pane and enter the ID, name, and site.

On the tab *Resources* of the Resource group form, you can manage the resources which are assigned to the resource group. In order to assign an additional resource, click the button *Add* in the toolbar of this tab. If you want to view past assignments or to enter an assignment with a future start date (which you enter in the column *Effective*), click the button *View/All* in the toolbar of this tab.

You can assign resources to a resource group in the Resource group form as described, but you can also work the other way around – open the Resource form and select the resource group there.

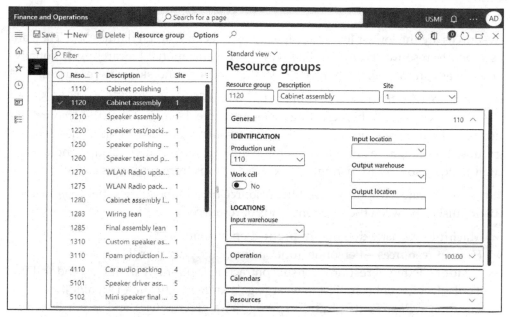

Figure 5-10: Editing a resource group

On the tab *General* of the Resource group form, you can optionally assign a production unit to the resource group. The *Input warehouse* on this tab specifies the picking warehouse for BOM lines with *Resource consumption* (see section 5.2.2).

If the slider *Work cell* on the tab *General* is set to "Yes", the resource group is a work cell in lean manufacturing and not available for operations and production orders in discrete manufacturing. On the tab *Work cell capacity*, you can specify the capacity for the work cell in lean manufacturing then.

Settings on the tab *Operation* of the Resource group form correspond to equivalent settings on the tab *Operation* in the Resource form (see below).

The calendar of a resource group is specified on the tab *Calendars* in the Resource group form. The calendar assignment is date effective, which means that you can record a future change of the working times by entering an additional line with the start date on the tab *Calendars* of the resource group – for example, if you want to change the regular working times for the resource group from two shifts to three shifts. In order to show the required column *Effective* (for the start date), click the button *View/All* in the toolbar of this tab.

If you need to override the working times of a resource group for a particular day, click the button *Resource group/Maintain/Calendar deviations* in the resource group and assign an alternative calendar for this day (e.g., a calendar without working times if a resource is not available temporarily).

5.3.2.3   Resources

Resources are the lowest level for capacity management in Dynamics 365. They are assigned to resource groups in line with the organizational hierarchy. Optionally, you can assign capabilities (which reflect the functions and skills) to resources.

In order to edit the resources, open the menu item *Production control> Setup> Resources> Resources*. When creating a new resource, be aware that the resource ID needs to be unique – not only within the resources but also within the resource groups. You can, for example, use a three-digit ID for resource groups and a four-digit ID for resources to distinguish resource groups from resources easily.

When you create a resource, select the resource type in the lookup field *Type* which distinguishes between the different kinds of resources:

> **Machine** – General default, for production machines.
> **Human resources** – Personnel (optionally assign a worker ID).
> **Vendor** – External resource for subcontracting (optionally assign a vendor ID).
> **Tool** – Device, often subject to wear (e.g., a knife in a turning machine).
> **Location** – Represents physical space (e.g., a greenhouse) and is not linked to warehouse locations.
> **Facility** – Similar functionality to "Machine", but for a group of machines and workers.

If you do not need to schedule and to report the activities of a machine and its operating staff separately, you can use a common resource with the type "Facility" or "Machine" and avoid setting up resources with the type "Human resources". If you want to manage tools, enter the usage of a tool as a secondary operation in routes (see section 5.3.3 below).

On the tab *Calendars* of the Resource form, you can assign a working time calendar to the resource (similar to assigning a calendar to a resource group). The calendar, together with the efficiency percentage, determines the capacity of the resource.

On the tab *Resource groups*, you can manage the resource group to which the resource is assigned. In order to assign a resource group, click the button *Add* in the toolbar of this tab. If you want to view past assignments or to enter an assignment with a future start date (which you enter in the column *Effective*), click the button *View/All* in the toolbar of this tab.

If needed, you can assign multiple resources to a resource group in a single step: Select the resources in the Resource form, then click the button *Resource/ Maintain/Add to resource group* in the action pane and select the applicable resource group in the lookup.

5.3.2.4   Resource Capacity and Operation Settings

The capacity of a resource is given by its working time calendar and efficiency percentage. For a resource group, the capacity is the total capacity of its resources.

In the Capacity load form, which you can open with the button *Resource/View/ Capacity load* in the Resource form, you can view the totals of available capacity and capacity reservations per day. For resource groups, a similar inquiry is available in the Resource group form.

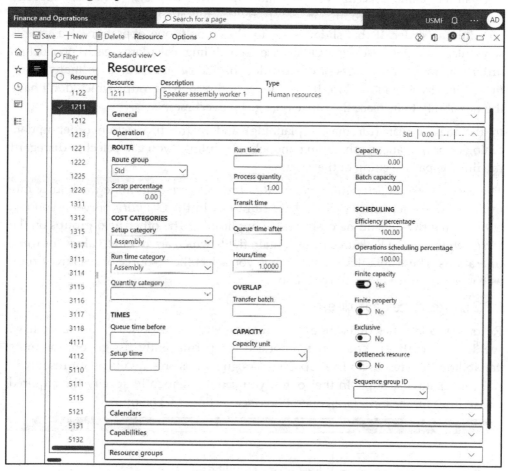

Figure 5-11: Managing the capacity and operation settings of a resource

The time unit for resource scheduling is hours. If a different unit of time is required for a resource, enter a conversion factor in the field *Hours/time* on the tab *Operation* of the Resource form. If you want to specify the time in route operations, for example, in minutes, enter $1/60 = 0.0167$ in the *Hours/time*.

If the unit of measure for a particular resource is not a unit of time, you can select an alternative *Capacity unit* (e.g., "Strokes/hour") on the tab *Operation*. The field *Capacity* then contains the conversion factor to hours. In the related route operations, select the option "Capacity" in the field *Formula* on the tab *Setup*.

The field *Efficiency percentage* on the tab *Operation* of the Resource form enables adapting the scheduled time for route operations by a factor. The default for the efficiency percentage is 100. If, for example, a particular resource is 25 percent faster than a standard resource, enter 125 in the efficiency percentage. With this setting, the scheduled time of a route operation with 10 hours (for other resources) is only 8 hours (= 10 * 100/125) on this resource.

The slider *Finite capacity* on the tab *Operation* controls, whether capacity reservations of other production orders reduce the available capacity when you schedule an order. If this slider is set to "Yes", only one operation at a time is scheduled on this resource. Otherwise, scheduling calculates each production order separately, regardless of other orders on the same resource. In many cases, finite capacity is only used for the resources and resource groups which don't have the possibility to increase the capacity (e.g., by overtime).

In the master plan (for master planning) and in the production order update dialogs (for operations scheduling and job scheduling), you can select to disregard the finite capacity setting of the resource.

The cost categories *Setup category* and *Run time category* determine the hourly rate of the resource for setup time and for run time. In the *Quantity category*, you can enter a quantity-depending cost price (if applicable). The other field groups on the tab *Operation* in the Resource form contain fields which are default values for route operations. These defaults are used when you select the resource or resource group as costing resource in a route operation.

5.3.2.5 Resource Capabilities

Resource capabilities determine the activities which a resource is able to do (e.g., welding or cutting). You can temporarily or permanently assign one or more capabilities to a resource. The capability assignment is only available for resources, not for resource groups. In the routes, you can subsequently specify the required capabilities for the individual operations (see section 5.3.3 below).

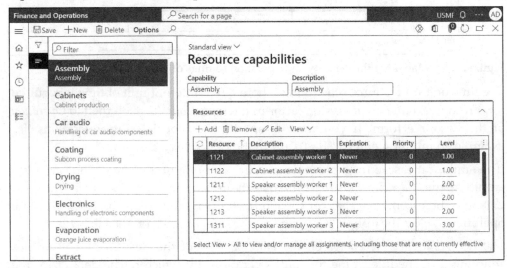

Figure 5-12:   Managing the resource capability assignment in the Capability form

In order to create a capability (shared across companies), open the menu item *Production control> Setup> Resources> Resource capabilities* and click the button *New* in the action pane. Enter the ID and description of the new capability and switch to the tab *Resources*. On this tab, assign the applicable resources to the capability.

It is not only possible to assign resources to a capability in the Resource capability form, you can also open the Resource form and assign the capabilities to the resource with the button *Add* in the toolbar of the tab *Capabilities* there. If needed, assign multiple resources to a capability in a single step – select the resources and click the button *Resource/Maintain/Add capability* in the Resource form.

The capability assignment is date effective, which means that you can record a future capability of a resource in an additional line on the tab *Capabilities* of the resource (with a start date which you can show with the *View/All* in the toolbar of this tab). In addition, there is the field *Priority* in the assignment line: Depending on the Scheduling parameters (see section 5.4.1), job scheduling is searching for the applicable resources with the higher priority (this is the lower priority number, priority "1" is the highest priority) first.

5.3.2.6   Settings for Ledger Integration

The tab *Ledger postings* in the Resource form and the Resource group form contains the main accounts which are used for route consumption. When you post a route card or job card journal for a production order, the costs for the use of the resource (usually measured by the working time) are posted to the general ledger. The applicable main accounts are specified in the field group *Accounts-Physical* of the resource. When you cost and end a production order, ledger transactions are posted to the accounts in the field group *Accounts-Financial*.

The account settings in the resource only apply, if the option "Item and resource" is selected in the lookup field *Ledger posting* of the production order (see section 9.4.3). If the option "Item and category" is selected, applicable main accounts derive from the cost categories.

5.3.3   Routes and Operations

Routes determine the operations which are required to manufacture an item. In addition to the bills of materials, which contain the required components, routes are the second area of required setup for production.

Like bills of materials, routes contain planned data which determine the target for production. In the course of manufacturing, the workshop reports actual figures in production journal transactions. You can subsequently compare and analyze the target and actual figures to determine possible improvements.

In order to describe the operations in manufacturing, a route has to contain at least the following data:

➢ **Activity** – Specified in the field *Operation*.
➢ **Resource** – Specified on the tab *Resource requirements*.
➢ **Sequence of operations** – Specified by the next operation (field *Next*).
➢ **Time consumption** – Specified in the fields *Setup time* and *Run time*.
➢ **Manufactured item** – Specified by the *Item number* in the route version.
➢ **Required material** – Specified in the BOM lines, optionally linked to operations.

If the workshop does not need all components of the bill of materials when starting the first operation, you can link BOM lines to the applicable route operations (see section 5.2.2).

5.3.3.1 Setup of Operations

As a prerequisite for routes, you have to set up operations (*Production control> Setup> Routes> Operations*). You can use one operation in multiple routes.

Operations are separate from routes and only contain a unique ID and a name. Other details which are necessary to execute an operation (e.g., the expected time/duration, or the required resource) are not included in the operation record itself, but in the operation relations.

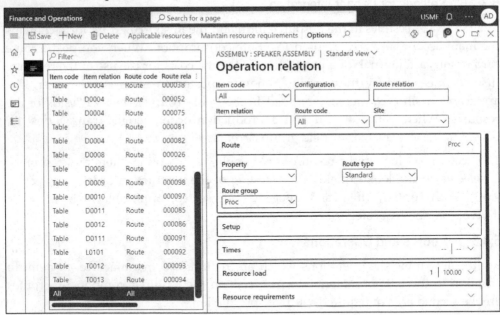

Figure 5-13:   Managing general operation relations for an operation

In order to view and to edit the details of an operation (specified in the operation relations), click the button *Relations* in the Operation form. Depending on the requirements, you can enter the operation relations at a general level or at a route-specific level:

➤ **General** – For operation details at a general level, select the option "All" in the field *Item code* and *Route code* of the operation relation (see Figure 5-13).

➤ **Route-specific** – Route-specific operation details contain the option "Route" in the *Route code* and the route number in the field *Route relation*.

On the other tabs of the Operation relation form, you can enter the details of the particular operation relation (including applicable resources and times). You can find more details on operation relations in the explanation of route operations further down this section.

5.3.3.2 Operation Sequence

The sequence of operations is not specified in the operation, but in the route. There are two types of operation sequences:

➤ **Simple sequence** – One operation after the other.

➤ **Complex sequence** – Multiple predecessors for an operation are possible.

Simple operation sequences are used, if the slider *Route network* in the Production control parameters (section *General*) is set to "No". In this case, routes only contain operations that are executed one after another.

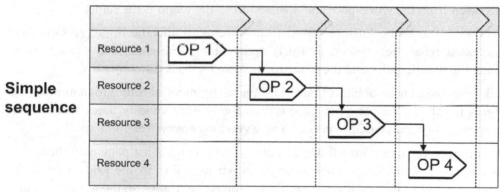

Figure 5-14:   Example of a simple operation sequence

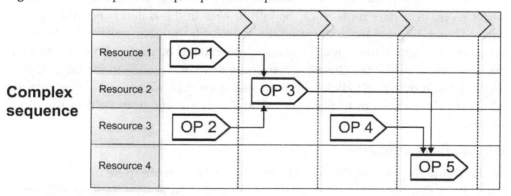

Figure 5-15:   Example of a complex operation sequence

If the parameter *Route network* is set to "Yes", you have to enter the next operation in each operation of a route. This setting enables complex operation sequences with multiple independent prior operations for a route operation.

Irrespective of the setting on simple or complex operation sequences, you can use secondary operations in routes for operations that can be executed on multiple resources in parallel (select the *Priority* "Secondary" in the respective route operation).

5.3.3.3 Entering Routes and Route Versions

Managing routes in Dynamics 365 is similar to managing bills of materials, including the way in which you can access the Route form:

➢ **From the released product** (*Product information management> Products> Released products,* button *Engineer/View/Route*)
➢ **From the menu** (*Production control> All routes*)

The workspace *Product readiness for discrete manufacturing* is another place, from which you can access (use the link *All routes* in the pane on the very right) and create (click the button *New/Route* in the action pane) routes. The Route form accessed from the workspace and accessed from the menu is the same.

Although the Route form (accessed from the menu) and the Route version form (accessed from the released product) update the same route and route version data, the functionality and the structure of these forms is different.

Like the assignment of bills of materials, the assignment of routes to manufactured items is called "Version" (with the option the specify validity dates and a from-quantity). But unlike BOM versions, route versions always refer to a site.

If you open the menu item *Production control> All routes,* a list page with the routes is displayed. Click on a route number shown as a link in the grid to open the related detail form. The Route form shows the route header on the tab *General* and one or more assigned manufactured items ("Versions") on the tab *Versions*. In order to create a new route, click the button *New* in the action pane of the Route form. Depending on the settings of the applicable number sequence, the route number is assigned automatically or has to be entered manually. Enter a *Name* for the new route on the tab *General* of the Route form and switch to the tab *Versions*. In the toolbar of this tab, click the button *Add* to create a route version (assignment of a manufactured item to the route). The *Site* is a mandatory field in the route version.

5.3.3.4 Route Operations

In the Route list page or the detail form, you can access the route operations with the button *Route/Maintain/Route details* in the action pane. The Route details form then shows the sequence of the route operations in the upper pane and the operation relations (operation details) of the selected operation in the lower pane.

Click the button *New* in the action pane if you want to insert a new route operation. If required, you can override the operation number (column *Oper.No.*). Then select the applicable operation in the column *Operation*. If the Production control parameters specify complex operation sequences , you have to enter the number of the next route operation in the column *Next* of the upper pane (for the last operation, the *Next* number is "0").

If the shop floor should execute some operations in parallel (e.g., if the work of the machine and of the operating personnel should be reported separately), enter two or more operations with the same operation number, but with a different *Priority*. In the example of Figure 5-16, there are two parallel operations with operation number 30 – one with *Priority* "Primary" and one with *Priority* "Secondary 1".

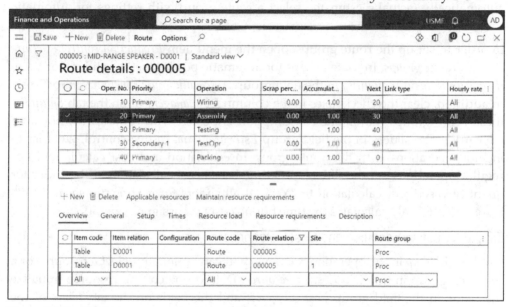

Figure 5-16: Editing a route operation with a general operation relation (All/All)

In case additional time and material consumption for inevitable scrap – caused by the operation – should be included, enter a *Scrap percentage*. If there is scrap in more than one route operation, the total scrap is calculated by multiplication. If there is, for example, a route with two operations and each of them has got 10 % scrap, the material and resource demand for the first operation is 123 % of the demand without scrap – 10 % scrap for this operation produce an output of 111 %, which is subsequently reduced to an output of 100 % by the second operation.

If the operation (in the column *Operation*) which you select in a new route operation has got a general operation relation (indicated by the option "All" in the column *Route code*), this general operation relation is shown in the lower pane of the Route details form when you save the record. If you change the data of a general operation relation in the Operation relation form (accessed from the menu), keep in mind that these changes apply to all routes which use the selected general operation relation.

If you want to enter route-specific operation details (independent of a general operation relation), insert a line with a new operation relation in the lower pane of the Route operation form. In the operation relation, select the option "Route" in the column *Route code* and enter the required data on the other tabs of the lower pane.

5.3.3.5 Route Groups

The *Route group* on the tab *Overview* (and the tab *General*) in the operation relations (the lower pane of the Route details form) controls if the resource usage is posted automatically or manually. If the resource usage for an operation should be posted automatically (actual = estimate), select a route group with settings for automatic route consumption.

In order to set up the route groups, open the menu item *Production control> Setup> Routes> Route groups*. In route groups for automatic posting, set the sliders for *Setup time*, *Run time* and *Quantity* in the field group *Automatic route consumption* to "Yes". In addition, clear the checkboxes in the column *Job management* on the tab *Setup* for these route groups (automatic consumption is posted with route cards, not with job cards). The sliders in the field group *Estimation and costing* control, whether to include operations with this route group in estimation and cost calculation. For regular operations, set the sliders for a time-based cost calculation or the slider for quantity-based cost calculation to "Yes". If all sliders for costing are set to "No", Dynamics 365 only calculates the time but no costs for assigned operations.

5.3.3.6 Costing Resource and Cost Categories

On the tab *Setup* in the operation relations, you can optionally select a resource or a resource group in the field *Costing resource*. Data of the costing resource initialize the fields in the field group *Cost categories* and the fields on the tab *Times* of the route operation.

Cost categories are, apart from the route group, another setting which controls cost estimation and cost calculation. You can assign different cost categories for setup time, run time, and quantity. When you assign a cost category, make sure that the related slider in the route group (the field group *Estimation and costing* controls whether time or quantity are included in the calculation) is set to "Yes".

Before you can create a new cost category, you have to create a related shared category in the menu item *Production control> Setup> Routes> Shared categories*. Shared categories ensure common category definitions across companies. For categories in production control, set the slider *Can be used in Production* in the shared category to "Yes".

Cost categories for production control (*Production control> Setup> Routes> Cost categories*) contain three core settings:

➢ **Cost price** – Determines the hourly rate (for setup time and run time).

➢ **Cost group** – Classifies the cost types in the cost calculation (see section 7.3.3).

➢ **Ledger postings** – The settings on this tab determine the main accounts which are used for route consumption (in case the option "Item and category" is selected in lookup field *Ledger* of the production order).

If you want to enter the cost price for a category, click the button *Category setup/ Category setup/Price* in the Cost categories form to access the Cost category price form. In this form, enter a cost price with a costing version (see section 7.3.3) for the category per site or – if you leave the field *Site* empty – at the company level. Then click the button *Activate* (which is active after saving the record) in the Cost category price form to activate the price.

In a production order, the (upfront) estimation applies the cost price of the cost categories in the route operation. The later calculation of the actual costs applies the cost categories of the resource in the actual transaction.

5.3.3.7 Operation Times

The fields on the tab *Times* in the operation relations show the expected time for the operation. You can distinguish between the setup time, the run time, the queue times, and the transit time. The *Setup time* is the required time for preparing the operation. The *Run time* is the time which it takes to produce the quantity in the field *Process qty.* This quantity refers to the manufactured product (specified via the route version).

If the *Process qty.* is 1.00, the run time is the required time in hours to produce one unit. If necessary, you can use other units than hours for the time: Enter a conversion factor *Hours/time* in the route operation or select a capacity unit in the resource (see section 5.3.2) for this purpose.

The processing time of an operation is the result of the following formula:

$$PROCESSING\ TIME = \frac{Setup\ time + \left(Run\ time \times Quantity\right)}{Efficiency\ percentage\ of\ the\ resource}$$

In addition to the processing time, queue times and transit times are included in the total lead time.

5.3.3.8 Resource Requirements and Resource Load

On the tab *Resource load* in the operation relations, the field *Quantity* specifies the number of required resources (for resources which are used in parallel). The calculation of the required capacity then multiplies the operation time with the load quantity. As a prerequisite for the use of the load quantity, a resource requirement with the *Requirement type* "Resource group" has to be selected in the operation relation.

The settings on the tab *Resource requirements* of the operation relation determine the resources which can execute the operation. From a functional point of view, these settings are independent of the costing resource. If there are multiple lines in the resource requirements, an applicable resource must comply with all of them.

The checkboxes in the respective columns determine separate requirements for *Operations scheduling* and for *Job scheduling*. In the column *Requirement type*, you can select if a requirement refers to a resource group, a resource, a resource type, or a capability. The options "Skill", "Courses", "Certificate" and "Title" are only used for job scheduling with resources of the resource type "Human resource" (related to worker data in human resource management).

If you want to view the resources which meet the requirements for a route operation, click the button *Applicable resources* in the toolbar of the lower pane in the Route details form (or in the action pane of the Operation relation form). Since the assignment of resources to resource groups and to capabilities is date effective, you have to specify the date for which you want to view the applicable resources (today's date is the default). In addition, select whether to show the resources for operations scheduling or for job scheduling.

If you want to get an overview of all operations with the applicable resources, click the button *Route feasibility* in the toolbar of the tab *Versions* in the Route form (the button is not available in the Route details form with the operations).

5.3.3.9 Approving and Activating Routes

Like bills of materials, routes and route versions have to be approved before you can use them in production orders. You can approve a route with the button *Route/ Maintain/Approve* in the action pane of the Route form. In order to approve a route version, click the button *Approve* in the toolbar of the tab *Versions* in the Route form. If you approve the route version before you approve the route itself, a slider for simultaneously approving the route and the route version is shown in the approval dialog.

If you want to use a route as default value for production orders, for item price calculations, and for master planning, activate the route version with the button *Activation* in the toolbar of the tab *Versions*. Active route versions show a checkmark in the column *Active* and have to be unique per date, quantity, and site.

Depending on the Production control parameters (sliders *Block editing* and *Block removal of approval* in the section *General*, similar to the settings for BOMs), you can update an approved route at any time.

You can remove the activation and the approval if required. For this purpose, click the button for approval or activation again. When you remove an approval, set the slider *Remove approval* in the dialog to "Yes".

5.3.3.10 Routes in the Released Product

Apart from the menu item for routes, you can also use the Released product form for accessing a route. Select the respective item in the Released product form and click the button *Engineer/View/Route* to open the Route version form.

The Route version form (accessed from the released product) shows all routes that are assigned to the selected item. It has got a different structure than the Route form accessed from the menu – the route versions are shown in the upper pane and the route operations with the operation number and the operation relations (operation details) in the lower pane.

If you want to create a new route in this form, click the button *New/Route and route version* in the action pane. Alternatively, click the button *New/Route version* (which just creates a route version and not a new route in parallel) if you only want to assign the item to an existing route.

In order to create a route operation for a route in the Route version form, select the route in the upper pane and click the button *New* in the toolbar of the lower pane.

If the operation (in the column *Operation*) which you select in the new route operation has got a general operation relation (indicated by the option "All" in the column *Route code*), this general operation relation is shown on the tabs in the lower pane of the Route operation form when you save the record. Unlike the functionality in the Route form accessed from the menu, overriding the data of a general operation relation in this form creates a route-specific operation relation automatically – indicated by the option "Route" in the column *Route code*. You can alternatively click the button *Copy and edit relation* in the toolbar of the lower pane if you want to enter route-specific operation details which are independent of the general operation relation (same result as simply overriding data). If you want to delete a route-specific operation relation and to apply an applicable general operation relation again, click the button *Delete relation* in the toolbar.

If there is no general operation relation for a route operation, you have to enter a new operation relation with all required data in the lower pane manually.

In the Route version form, you can approve a route version with the button *Route version/Maintain route version/Approve* (if necessary, set the slider to approve also the route itself in the dialog to "Yes"). With the button *Route version/Maintain route version/Activate,* you can subsequently activate the route version.

5.3.4   Case Study Exercises

Exercise 5.4 – Setup for Routes

In order to investigate the use of capabilities, route groups, and cost categories, you want to set up an example. As a start, create a capability C-## (## = your user ID) with the name "##-specific". Then enter a route group R-## with settings which require a manual posting of the actual working time. Estimation and costing should only be based on setup time and run time.

Next, set up a new cost category G-## (and the related shared category) for production. In the cost category, select an appropriate cost group of your choice and enter main accounts similar to the settings in existing cost categories. For the hourly rate, enter and activate a cost price of USD 100 at the company level (select a costing version with the costing type "Planned cost").

Exercise 5.5 – Resource Groups and Resources

New resources are required to manufacture the finished product of exercise 5.2. Enter a new resource group W-## with the name "##-assembly", which is assigned to the main site and an appropriate production unit. The resource group applies the cost category of exercise 5.4 for setup time and for run time. In the resource group calendar, select a regular calendar of your choice.

Then create two new resources, W-##-1 and W-##-2, with the type "Machine". For both resources, the route group and – for setup time and for run time – the cost category of exercise 5.4 is used. Select main accounts for the resources which are similar to the settings in existing resources. Both resources are assigned to the new resource group W-##, but only the resource W-##-2 has got the capability of exercise 5.4. The resources use the same calendar as the resource group.

Exercise 5.6 – Operation and Operation Relations

As a prerequisite for production, a new operation is required. Create the operation O-## (## = your user ID) with the name "##-processing". In general, the setup time for this operation is one hour and the run time is two hours per unit. Select the resource W-##-1 of exercise 5.5 as costing resource which specifies default values for the route group and the cost categories. Only resources of the resource group W-## and the capability C-## of exercise 5.4 can execute the operation.

Exercise 5.7 – Route

In order to manufacture the finished product, a new route which is based on the setup in the previous exercises is required. Select the item I-##-F of exercise 5.2 in the Released product form and access the route from the released product. Create a new route with the operation O-## of exercise 5.6 as the only route operation. There is no setup time, and the run time for the operation is one hour per unit. The other settings in the route operation – including costing resource, route group, cost categories, and resource requirements – are the same as the applicable settings in the general operation relation which you have entered in exercise 5.6.

Once you have completed the details, approve and activate the route and the route version. Can you check which resources can execute the route operation? Finally, check which operation relations are assigned to the operation of exercise 5.6.

5.4 Production Order Management

A production order is a request to manufacture a particular product. Apart from the item number and the quantity of the manufactured item, production orders include data on the required materials and resources.

The order status, which is updated with every step in the sequential flow of order processing, shows the progress of a production order.

5.4.1 Basics of Production Order Processing

Apart from manually entering a production order, there are the following options to create an order:

➢ **Sales order** – Create a production order from a sales order line.
➢ **Project** – Create a production order from a project (Project accounting module).
➢ **Master planning** – Generates a planned production order which you firm to convert it to an actual production order (see section 6.3.5).
➢ **Pegged supply** – Automatically generates a production order from the BOM line of an upper-level production order (sub-production, see section 5.4.3).

5.4.1.1 Production Order Status

When you create a production order manually, the first status is "Created". This is the only status in which you can delete a production order. If you need to delete a production order in a later status, you have to reset the status to "Created" first. The manufacturing cycle, which updates the order status, includes the following steps:

➢ **Created** – Temporary status after creating a new order.
➢ **Estimated** – Material and resource demand is calculated.
➢ **Scheduled** – Start/end dates are calculated, and resources are assigned.
➢ **Released** – The order is transferred to the shop floor.
➢ **Started** – Posting of actual consumption is possible.
➢ **Reported as finished** – The manufactured item is received in inventory.
➢ **Ended** – The order is finally closed.

The order status is updated when you process the order with the corresponding button in the Production order form or with the related periodic activity in the menu folder *Production control> Periodic tasks> Production order status update*.

You can skip steps in the order processing cycle – Dynamics 365 then automatically executes the steps which you omit (using the settings in the section *Automatic update* of the Production control parameters). If you want to reset the status of a production order, click the button *Production order/Process/Reset status* in the Production order form. Dynamics 365 then reverses all posted transactions (automatic and manual postings) which refer to the reversed status.

Settings in the section *Status* of the Production control parameters determine from which status you can move to which status. There are different checkboxes for both directions, for skipping a status and for reversing a status.

5.4.1.2 Production Control Parameters

Unlike parameter settings in other areas, Production control parameters are not only available at the company level, but also at the site level. The field *Parameter usage* in the section *General* of the Production control parameters at the company level (*Production control> Setup> Production control parameters*) determines whether the site-specific parameters are used. You can manage the site-specific parameters in the menu item *Production control> Setup> Production control parameters by site*.

5.4.1.3 Scheduling Parameters

Scheduling parameters (*Master planning> Setup> Scheduling> Scheduling parameters*) determine default values in the update dialogs for production order scheduling. Essential Scheduling parameters include the *Primary resource selection*, which determines if capability-based scheduling is based on the priority or on the shortest duration. Like the Production control parameters, the Scheduling parameters are available at the company level and at the site level.

5.4.2   Production Order Registration

Data in a production order include the header data, the production BOM, and the production route. When you create a production order, an inventory transaction for the manufactured item with the status "Ordered" in the column *Receipt* is created (similar to the inventory transaction for a purchase order line). The inventory transactions for the components of the production order (BOM lines) are only created when you execute the order estimation. As long as the status of the production order is "Created", master planning only recognizes a supply of the manufactured item (from the inventory transaction), but there is no component demand (the corresponding inventory transactions are not created yet). For this reason, you should estimate a production order soon after creating it.

If a production order is created automatically from a planned order, settings in the applicable coverage group determine the initial status (usually "Scheduled").

5.4.2.1 Entering a New Production Order

You can manually create a production order with the button *Create new/Production order* in the workspace *Production floor management*. Alternatively, open the Production order form (*Production control> Production Orders> All production orders*) and click the button *New production order* in this form. In a sales order, you can click the button *Product and supply/New/Production order* in the toolbar of the order lines to create a production order which is – with reservation and marking – linked to the sales order line.

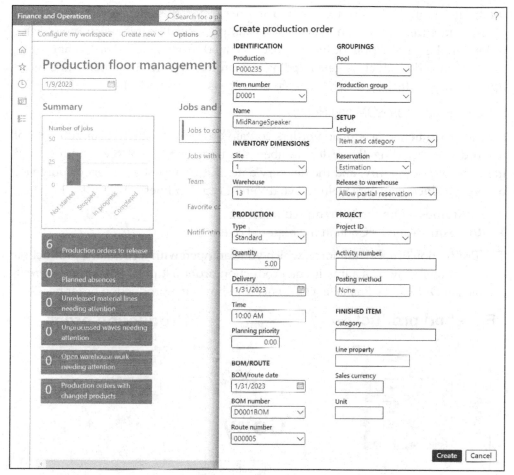

Figure 5-17:   Creating a production order in the production floor management workspace

In the *Create production order* dialog, select the item number of the manufactured product first. Depending on the selected item, several fields are initialized with default values which you can override as required (for example, if you want to select a different BOM). Once you click the button *Create* in the dialog, the production order is generated and shows the initial status "Created".

When you process the order, it switches to a subsequent status. A summary of the status updates is shown on the tab *Update* of the Production order detail form.

You can still update the settings in a production order later – for example, if you need to modify the BOM or the route in the order. If you change a production order which is already estimated or scheduled, you should run the estimation or scheduling again to ensure consistent data. If the production papers have been printed already, you might need to reprint them with the updated data.

For production orders, which have been created in another area of the application, the tab *References* of the Production order detail form shows the reference to the origin. If the production order refers to another order, this original order is shown in the reference type and number – for example, with the reference type "Sales order" if the production order has been created from a sales order line. In a production order which is generated as sub-production from the BOM line of an upper-level production order, the reference type is "Production line".

5.4.2.2 Production BOM and Route

Like all documents, production orders contain a header with the common data of the order – including the order number, the item number of the manufactured item, the order quantity, and the delivery date. But unlike sales orders or purchase orders, production orders include two different types of lines:

➢ **BOM lines** – Contain the required materials.
➢ **Route operations** – Contain the required operations.

The Production order detail form, which you can open with a click on a production order number shown as a link in the Production order list page (*Production control> Production Orders> All Production Orders*), only shows the production order header.

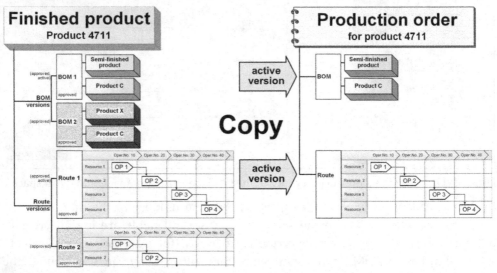

Figure 5-18: The active BOM/route version is the default for the production BOM/route

In order to access the BOM lines of a particular production order, click the button *Production order/Production details/BOM* in the action pane. If you want to access to the production BOM line details, click on the respective item number shown as a link in the production BOM lines.

If you want to access the production route with its operations, click the button *Production order/Production details/Route* in the production order.

When you create a new a production order, the production order receives a copy of the BOM and the route of the manufactured item. The order subsequently has got its own production BOM and route, which you can edit separately from the BOM and the route of the manufactured item.

By default, the BOM and the route which is copied into the production order is given by the active BOM version and route version for the item, site, date, and quantity of the production order. The date which is used for this BOM and route selection is specified in the field *BOM/route date* in the *Create production order* dialog (the default in this field is the delivery date).

If you do not want to use the active BOM version or route version in a particular production order, you can select any other approved BOM version or route version for the manufactured item in the *Create production order* dialog (e.g., an alternative BOM for subcontracting).

5.4.3 Processing Production Orders

Once a production order is created, preparing the order for starting the work on the shop floor has to be done in a few steps which update the status.

5.4.3.1 Default Values in Update Dialogs

When you update the status of a production order, an update dialog is shown. In the update dialog, you can click the button *Default values* if you want to specify default values which are different from the standard defaults. In the default values dialog, you can optionally click the button *Make default for all users* to apply your customized default values to all users.

The default values are stored in the *Usage data*, which you can access from the user options. Be aware that new users who are created later receive the standard settings (the button *Make default for all users* only copies to the usage data of existing users) and that resetting the usage data resets the default values.

5.4.3.2 Estimation

Estimation is the first step after creating a production order. The primary task of estimation is to calculate the required material and resource capacity for the production order. The basis for this calculation is the bill of materials and the route of the order.

In order to run the estimation, click the button *Production order/Process/Estimate* in the Production order form or execute the related periodic activity. In parallel to the calculation of the required quantities and times, estimation determines the expected costs (based on the cost price of materials and route operations).

If you want to view the cost estimation subsequently, click the button *Manage costs/Calculations/View calculation details* in the Production order form. The tab *Overview estimation* in the Price calculation form shows the estimation lines. If you want to view a summary according to the costing sheet setup, switch to the tab *Costing sheet* in the Price calculation form.

For the BOM lines of the production order, estimation creates inventory transactions which are similar to the inventory transactions of open sales order lines. You can view these transactions with the button *Inventory/Transactions* in the production BOM form (access with the button *Production order/Production details/ BOM* in the Production order form). All inventory transactions related to a production order are shown in the inquiry, which you can access with the button *Manage costs/Cost transactions/Inventory transactions* in the Production order form.

Since there are no inventory transactions related to BOM lines before estimation, this status is the earliest order status in which you can execute a manual or an automatic reservation (see section 7.4.5).

If the *Line type* in a production BOM line is "Pegged supply", estimation creates a related order:

➢ **Sub-production order** (regular production order which is linked to the main production order) – For BOM lines with an item with the default order type "Production".
➢ **Purchase order** – For BOM lines with an item with the default order type "Purchase order".

For BOM lines with the line type "Phantom", estimation replaces the production BOM line by the components of the phantom item (and, if applicable, adds the route operations of the phantom item to the production route).

5.4.3.3 Scheduling

Production order scheduling determines the exact date and time of material and resource demand and reserves resource capacity. In Dynamics 365, there are two types of scheduling:

➢ **Operations scheduling** – At the level of resource groups and dates.
➢ **Job scheduling** – At the level of individual resources and exact times.

Depending on the setup, you can execute either operations scheduling, or job scheduling, or both (first operations scheduling, and then job scheduling).

Operations scheduling is a rough scheduling process, which calculates the required time per day. Based on the resource requirements in the route operation (capabilities, resource groups, resource types), operation scheduling selects a resource group and reserves the required capacity. Only if the operation contains a resource requirement with the *Requirement type* "Resource", operations scheduling reserves capacity on the resource (and not at group level).

The available capacity of a resource group is the total capacity of its resources. Current capacity reservations are deducted from the available capacity if scheduling is executed with finite capacity and if the slider *Finite capacity* in the resource group is set to "Yes". Depending on the setting of the slider *Planned order* in the section *General* of the Production control parameters, the deducted capacity reservations include planned orders or only actual production orders.

Job scheduling at a later stage calculates the capacity at the level of individual resources and reserves capacity with exact start and end times. In addition to the calculation of exact start and end times, job scheduling generates jobs which split the route operations of a production order into individual tasks. These individual tasks show different job types, corresponding to the different time fields on the tab *Times* of the route operation (e.g., *Setup time* and *Run time*). The available job types for a particular operation are determined by the *Route group* of the operation (column *Job management* on the tab *Setup* in the Route group form).

Job transactions (which are generated with job scheduling) are independent of route transactions (which refer to operations scheduling). For this reason, you have to decide whether to schedule the capacity and to post the actual resource usage at the operations level or at the detailed job level. There are no job transactions in a production order if you skip job scheduling.

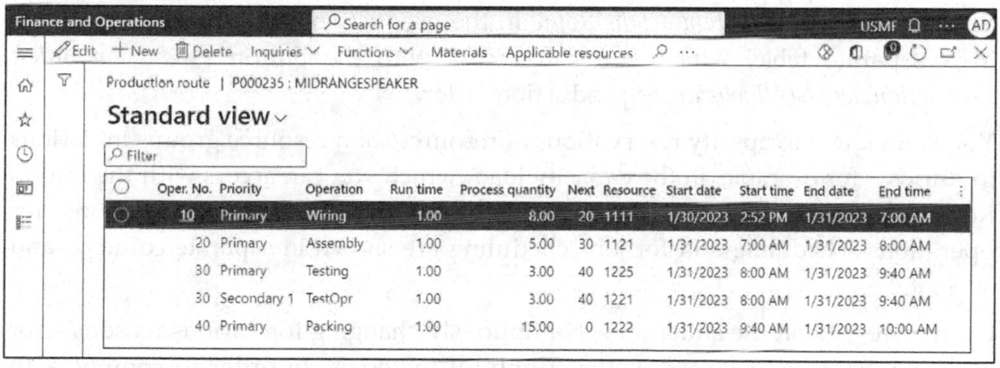

Figure 5-19: Production route transactions after job scheduling

In order to execute operations scheduling or job scheduling, click the button *Schedule/Production order/Schedule operations* or *Schedule/Production order/Schedule jobs* in the Production order form. If you want to schedule multiple orders, execute the corresponding periodic activity in the menu folder *Production control> Periodic tasks> Scheduling*.

On the tab *Scheduling parameters* of the update dialog for scheduling, the following parameters are available:

➢ **Scheduling direction** – Select one of the various options for forward or backward scheduling ("Forward from today" is used in case the field is empty).
➢ **Primary resource selection** (for job scheduling) – Specifies whether a capability-based resource selection primarily searches the shortest duration (latest start date when scheduling backward) or the highest priority (priority "1" is the highest priority).
➢ **Finite capacity** and **Finite material** – Observe the resource or item availability.

➢ **Keep warehouse from resource** – Only a resource, which is assigned to the same input warehouse as the original resource, is selected when you re-schedule an order (applicable if the checkbox *Resource consumption* in the BOM lines is selected).

➢ **Schedule references** – Includes scheduling of sub-production orders.

If required, you can skip particular job types (set the applicable sliders in the field group *Cancellation* on the tab *Parameters per order* to "Yes"). With this setting you can, for example, skip the setup time if you produce the same product in sequence, or skip the queue time for a production order of high importance.

If you do not execute scheduling in a separate step, it is automatically executed when you update the order to a later status (e.g., if you skip scheduling and immediately release the order). In this case, the *Scheduling method* in the Production control parameters (section *Automatic update*) specifies whether Dynamics 365 runs operations scheduling or job scheduling.

In order to view the route transactions with the scheduled dates, click the button *Production order/Production details/Route* in the production order. Jobs are recorded in a separate table, which you can access with the button *Production order/ Production details/All jobs* in the production order.

You can view the capacity reservations of resources and resource groups in various inquiries – for example, in the capacity load, which you can access with the button *Resource/View/Capacity load* in the Resource form. Capacity reservations for operations scheduling and for job scheduling are shown in separate columns and as a total.

On the shop floor, the situation is continuously changing for various reasons – for example, because of delays in the supply of materials. In order to comply with these changes, you can reschedule the orders on a regular basis. For job scheduling, use the periodic activity *Production control> Periodic tasks> Scheduling> Job scheduling* and enter a filter – e.g., on the production order status "Created .. Scheduled" (in the scheduling dialog, click the button *Filter* in the toolbar of the tab *Parameters per order* to access the filter). If you reschedule orders with the status "Released" (or a later status) and you have printed the production papers, make sure to replace the papers on the shop floor with papers that show the new dates.

When you reschedule production orders, the capacity reservations of the selected orders are deleted and replaced by new reservations. If you want to lock the dates and the resource assignments for a particular order, set the slider *Locked* on the tab *Setup* in the Production order detail form to "Yes" (alternatively, click the button *Schedule/Production order/Locked for rescheduling*) to prevent rescheduling.

If required, you can manually reassign a job to a particular resource. Select the job in the list *Jobs to complete* in the center section of the workspace *Production floor management* for this purpose, click the button *Reassign* in the toolbar of this list, and select the new resource.

5.4.3.4 Gantt Chart

The Gant chart is a graphical representation of the jobs which are generated with job scheduling. It is not only possible to view the current jobs, but you can also use drag and drop features in the Gantt chart to reschedule jobs.

In order to open the Gantt chart, click the button *Schedule/View/Gantt chart* in the action pane of the production order. In the Gantt chart, you can select and move jobs as required, and you can use the buttons in the button group *Activity/Maintain* to schedule the previous and subsequent jobs automatically. Once you have finished the updates, click the button *Save* in the Gantt chart to save the updates to the jobs. You can manage the layout of the Gantt chart with the buttons in the button group *Gantt chart/Setup*.

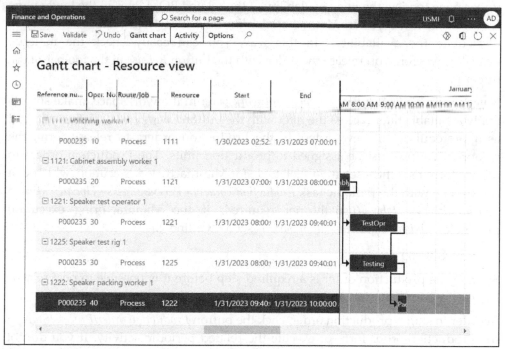

Figure 5-20: Updating the Gantt chart for a production order

It is not only possible to access the Gantt chart from the production order, but you can also use the respective button in the Resource form, or in the list *Jobs to complete* in the workspace *Production floor management*, or in the form *Production control> Setup> Resources> Gantt chart* (if you want to use this form., first create a setup which specifies the resource groups and resources which you want to view).

5.4.3.5 Releasing

In order to transfer the production order to the shop floor, you have to release it. Once released, the production order is shown in the Dynamics 365 Manufacturing execution pages (Production floor execution and Job card terminal).

You can release an order with the button *Production order/Process/Release* directly in the production order. On the tab *General* of the *Release* dialog, you can specify whether to print production papers (job or route cards). In addition, the slider *References* on this tab controls whether referenced sub-production orders are released in parallel.

The workspace *Production floor management* provides a convenient alternative to release an order: The tile *Production orders to release* on the left of the workspace opens the Production orders to release form. This form shows the production orders, which have been job scheduled but not yet released. Select an order in the upper pane to view the item availability of the related BOM lines in the lower pane (you can click the button *Material availability check* and *Update critical on-hand* to recalculate the availability). In this way, you can easily check the material availability before you release the order with the button *Release* in the toolbar of the upper pane.

Notes on the Production floor management workspace: In the workspace, make sure to apply a suitable filter (access the filter with the button *Configure my workspace*). And as a prerequisite to view orders in the Production orders to release form, the resource groups must be assigned to production units. The Production orders to release form uses the – separate – job table for Manufacturing execution, which you can update with the periodic task *Production control> Periodic tasks> Update entities> Synchronize job table* (usually not required, if the Manufacturing execution parameter *Job table synchronization mode* is set to "Online").

5.4.3.6 Starting

Starting the production order is a required step before it is possible to post related transactions for materials and resources.

In order to start a production order, click the button *Production order/Process/Start* in the Production order form or execute the related periodic activity. If you do not want to start the entire production quantity, you can enter a partial quantity on the tab *General* of the update dialog for starting. If you enter a *From Oper.No.* and a *To Oper.No.*, only the selected operations are started.

The automatic posting of the resource usage (working time consumption) is controlled by the field group *Route card journal* on the tab *General* of the update dialog. The field *Route card* on this tab specifies the journal name for posting. In the lookup field *Automatic route consumption*, the following options are available for automatic posting:

➤ **Route group dependent** – Automatic consumption depending on the route group of the operation (see section 5.3.3).

➤ **Always** – Automatic consumption of all route operations.

➤ **Never** – No automatic consumption.

The slider *Post route card now* controls whether the consumption journal is posted immediately. If automatic route consumption is selected and this slider is set to "No", a route card journal for manual editing is generated (but not posted yet).

The automatic consumption of resource capacity is posted with a route card, which is why the route group of operations with automatic consumption should be set up in a way that jobs are not created for these operations.

The automatic BOM consumption settings in the field group *Picking list journal* of the update dialog work similar to the automatic route consumption settings. If you want to post automatic consumption with reference to the settings in the BOM lines, select the option "Flushing principle" (see section 5.2.1) in the lookup field *Automatic BOM consumption*. This option refers to the corresponding field on the tab *Setup* in the production BOM line details.

If you set the slider *Print picking list* in the update dialog to "Yes", the picking list is printed in parallel to starting the order. If you want to print a complete picking list, set the slider *Complete picking list journal* to "Yes". The picking list otherwise only shows the items in the picking list journal that is generated for automatic consumption.

5.4.4 Case Study Exercises

Exercise 5.8 – Production Order

Your company needs five pieces of the finished product of exercise 5.2. Enter a corresponding production order and check the BOM and the route in the order.

Exercise 5.9 – Purchase Components

In order to process the production order of exercise 5.8, the required components have to be available in inventory.

Enter a purchase order with the vendor of exercise 3.2, which includes nine units of the first and five units of the second item of exercise 5.1. Confirm the purchase order and post the product receipt.

Exercise 5.10 – Release and Start the Order

You are asked to process the production order of exercise 5.8. Start with the estimation and check the price calculation afterward. Then execute operations scheduling and job scheduling one after another. Once you have completed scheduling, release the order from the Production order form or from the Production floor management workspace.

Finally, start the order and print the complete picking list (displayed in a print preview). You do not want to post the picking list. Is it possible to apply these settings as a default for all users?

5.5   Consumption of Material and Resource Capacity

In order to know the inventory quantity and to analyze production performance, the actual material consumption and the resource usage must be reported. This reporting is always done in production journals, but there are different ways in which you can create and post the journals:

> **Manually** – Enter and post journals in the respective forms (companies working this way usually do it in the office, based on paper reports from the shop floor).
> **Automatically** – Create journals automatically (e.g., when starting the order).
> **With terminals or devices** – The Manufacturing execution pages (Production floor execution and Job card terminal) also generate journals when you report consumption on terminals or mobile devices on the shop floor.

If you use the advanced warehouse management, the consumption of material and the receipt of the manufactured item is registered with mobile device transactions in the warehouse (see section 8.1.3).

Apart from the options in Dynamics 365, you can use the Manufacturing execution integration feature to integrate third-party manufacturing execution systems.

5.5.1   Journal Setup and Ledger Integration

In discrete manufacturing, there are the following types of production journals for posting consumption with reference to a production order:

> **Picking list** – Post item consumption.
> **Route card** – Post the use of resources at the level of operations.
> **Job card** – Post the use of resources at the level of jobs.

If item consumption and resource usage are posted automatically (controlled by the *Route group* and the *Flushing principle*), Dynamics 365 creates production journals automatically when starting a production order or when reporting as finished. Production journals are also automatically generated when registrations are transferred from the Manufacturing execution (Production floor execution and Job card terminal).

For BOM lines or route operations which are not posted automatically, you have to create production journals manually and enter the transactions as described below.

5.5.1.1   Journal Setup

As a prerequisite for transactions in manufacturing, you have to set up the required journals in the menu item *Production control> Setup> Production journal names*. Picking lists, route cards, job cards, and report as finished journals refer to different journal names, which you have to set up with the appropriate *Journal type*.

The journal type "Report as finished" does not refer to item consumption, but to the receipt of manufactured items in inventory.

5.5.1.2 Ledger Integration

When you post a production journal, the consumption is posted to clearing accounts for WIP (work in progress). Posting to the final ledger accounts is done when you end and cost the production order.

As a prerequisite for posting the item consumption to WIP accounts, the slider *Post picking list in ledger* in the Production control parameters (section *General*) has to be set to "Yes" (not required for standard cost items). In addition, the checkbox *Post physical inventory* in the item model group of the picked item has to be selected.

Like the general ledger transactions with reference to product receipts (in purchasing) and to packing slips (in sales), which are reversed when posting the related invoice, the ledger transactions with reference to picking lists, route card journals, and job card journals are reversed when ending the production order.

5.5.2 Picking Lists

Picking list journals are used to register the item consumption related to production orders. In order to access the picking list journals, click the button *View/ Journals/Picking list* in the Production order form or open the menu item *Production control> Adjustments> Picking list*.

Like all journals, picking lists are documents which consist of a header and lines. If you access the picking list journals from the menu, the list page shows all open journals which are not posted yet. If you want to view the posted journals, apply an appropriate filter in the column *Posted* (use the filter pane, the grid column filter, or the advanced filter). If you access the picking list journal directly from the Production order form, it shows the posted journals immediately.

5.5.2.1 Creating Picking List Journals

If you want to create a new journal, click the button *New* in the action pane of the list page. Select a journal name and click the button *OK* in the *Create* dialog. The Journal detail form with the new journal is shown in the Lines view then.

In order to facilitate the picking list registration, you can click the button *Picking list/Create lines* instead of the button *New* in the list page or the detail form. In the *Create lines* dialog, specify the way in which the production BOM lines should initialize the journal lines. For this purpose, select the option "Remaining quantity" in the field *Proposal* if you want to use the open quantity as default for the column *Proposal* in the picking list lines. If you set the slider *Consumption=Proposal* to "Yes", the column *Consumption* in the journal lines is also initialized with the proposal quantity. In this case, you can immediately post the journal without manual data entry (consuming the estimated quantity).

5.5.2.2   Journal Lines

In the Journal list page, you can access the detail form with a click on a journal ID shown as a link in the list page. In the Journal detail form, click the button *Header* (below the action pane) if you want to switch to the Header view, which shows the complete journal header.

When you manually enter a line in the Lines view of a picking list journal, select the *Lot ID* (which links the consumption to a production BOM line) before you enter the *Consumption* quantity. The checkbox in the column *End* of the journal line sets the production BOM line to finished and clears the remaining quantity (select the checkbox, if the final consumption is less than the estimated quantity).

If you consume an item which is not included in the BOM lines of the production order, insert a picking list line in which you enter the item number (leave the lot ID empty). Dynamics 365 in this case automatically creates a corresponding BOM line in the production order and applies the lot ID to the picking list line.

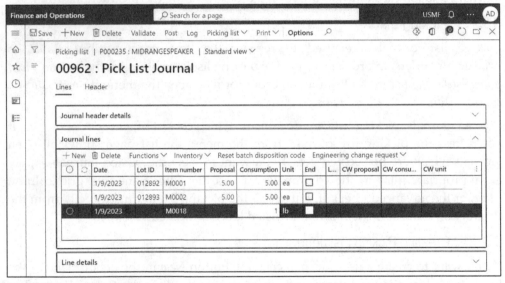

Figure 5-21:   Entering an additional picking list line in a picking list journal

Figure 5-21 shows an example of lines in a picking list journal which are generated by a consumption proposal. The column *Consumption* in the lines contains a default value for the actual quantity (the slider *Consumption=Proposal* in the *Create lines* dialog has been set to "Yes" when creating the proposal). The last line in Figure 5-21 shows a manual entry for an item which is not included in the BOM. The columns *Proposal* and – only before saving the line – *Lot ID* in this line are empty.

Once you have completed the picking list, you can post the journal with the button *Post* in the Journal list page or detail form. Posting the picking list deducts the quantity from inventory (similar to the packing slip transactions in a sales orders).

Inventory valuation applies a preliminary physical value when posting the picking list journal. The financial valuation is posted later when ending and costing the production order.

5.5.2.3 Inquiries and Reversal

If you want to view a posted journal, access the Picking list journal form and enter an appropriate filter in the column *Posted*. The posted journal shows a checkmark in the column *Posted* and does not allow modifications.

Alternatively, you can view the posted transactions in the Production posting form. In order to access this form, click the button *Manage costs/Production accounting/Production posting* in the production order form or open the menu item *Production control> Inquiries and reports> Production> Production posting*.

If you want to reverse a posted picking list journal, register and post a picking list journal with negative quantities. You can easily create an appropriate picking list proposal with the button *Picking list/Create lines* in the picking list journal (select the option "Full reversal" in the field *Proposal* of the *Create lines* dialog).

5.5.3 Resource Usage

Depending on the route group settings and on the way of scheduling the order, you have to use route cards or job cards to record the usage of resources (usually measured by the working time).

5.5.3.1 Route Cards and Job Cards

Route card journals record the use of resources at the operation level. You should use route cards if you execute only operations scheduling but not job scheduling, or if the setting in the route group (column *Job management* on the tab *Setup*) of an operation prevents the use of job cards.

Job card journals record the use of resources at the job level. Jobs are created when you execute job scheduling. Depending on the route group setting, you should use job cards instead of route cards when jobs have been created for an operation.

The automatic consumption of resource capacity when starting or reporting as finished is posted in route card journals. For registrations which are transferred from the Manufacturing execution features, a parameter setting (*Production control> Setup> Manufacturing execution> Production order defaults*, lookup field *Job level* in the section *Operations*) determines whether job card or route card journals are posted.

5.5.3.2 Journal Registration of Resource Usage

In order to access the route card journals, open the menu item *Production control> Adjustments> Route card* or click the button *View/Journals/Route card* in the Production order form. For job cards, open the menu item *Production control> Adjustments> Job card* or click the button *View/Journals/Job card* in the production order.

Journal headers and lines in route card journals and job card journals work similar to picking list journals. But except for the automatic consumption when starting or reporting as finished, there is no consumption proposal in route cards or job cards.

When you insert a journal line in a route card or job card journal, select the operation number (or the job identification) first. Then enter the resource, the task type (only in route cards, in job cards it is derived from the job), the number of hours, the produced quantity (*Good quantity*, only for the task type "Process"), and other data as applicable – for example, the scrap quantity (*Error quantity*) of the manufactured item. In a job card, you should additionally enter the start time, the end time, and the worker.

Once you have completed the journal lines, you can post the journal with the button *Post* in the Journal list page or detail form.

If you want to view the posted journal afterward, open the route card journal or the job card journal and enter an appropriate filter in the column *Posted*. In addition, you can view the posted transactions in the route transactions inquiry (button *Manage costs/Cost transactions/Route transactions* in the production order) or in the posting inquiry (*Manage costs/Production accounting/Production posting*).

5.5.3.3 Reporting as Finished in Route Cards and Job Cards

When you register the last operation or job in a journal line, you can select the checkbox in the column *Production report as finished* to post a report as finished journal for the manufactured item (*Good quantity*) in parallel to the route card or job card. The default for the report as finished setting in journal lines is specified in the Production control parameters (slider *Automatic report as finished* in the section *Journals*).

5.5.4   Case Study Exercises

Exercise 5.11 – Picking List

You can pick the components of the production order of exercise 5.8 now. Enter and post a picking list journal which includes nine units of the first and five units of the second component. You do not expect any additional consumption. Pick from the warehouse in which you have received the items in exercise 5.9.

Exercise 5.12 – Job Card

Record the actual working time for the operation in the production order of exercise 5.8. For this purpose, enter and post a job card which refers to this production order. Record the production of five units in the time between 8:00 AM and 2:00 PM. You do not want to report the order as finished in parallel.

5.6   Reporting as Finished and Ending Production

In the cycle of production order processing, reporting as finished and ending are the last steps. Reporting as finished posts physical transactions and increases the inventory quantity of the manufactured item. Ending the order then performs costing and posts the financial transactions.

5.6.1   Reporting as Finished

Reporting as finished physically receives the manufactured item in inventory. In Dynamics 365, there are following options to report a production order as finished:

> **Order status update** – Update the status of the production order.
> **Production journal** – Post a report as finished journal.
> **Last operation** – Report as finished in parallel when posting the route card or job card for the last operation.
> **Advanced warehouse management** – Post transactions on the mobile device (see section 8.1.3).

Optionally, you can use a production input journal (*Inventory management> Journal entries> Item arrival> Production input*) to post an inventory registration before reporting as finished. This works similar to the arrival journal in purchasing (see section 3.5.3).

5.6.1.1   Order Status Updates

In order to report as finished by updating the order status, click the button *Production order/Process/Report as finished* in the Production order form or execute the periodic activity *Production control> Periodic tasks> Production order status update> Report as finished*.

If you only want to report a part of the entire order quantity, edit the *Good quantity* on the tab *Overview* (or the tab *General*) and deselect the checkbox *End job* in the update dialog before you click the button *OK*. Select the checkbox *End job* in the dialog (which clears the remaining open quantity) in case you do not expect any additional report as finished transaction for the order.

If you are confident, that the actual consumption of items and resources has been posted completely already, and you do not want to receive messages on open consumption (estimated consumption, which has not been reported or – e.g., with the checkbox *End* in the picking list line – cleared), set the slider *Accept error* on the tab *General* to "Yes".

5.6.1.2   Production Journals

Apart from the status update, reporting as finished is also possible by posting a production journal. In order to access this journal, click the button *View/Journals/ Report as finished* in the Production order form or open the menu item *Production control> Adjustments> Report as finished*.

The way of registering and posting a report as finished journal is similar to the options in a picking list journal (see section 5.5.2), but includes the order status update settings as described above. A report as finished journal is also created and posted if you report as finished with the order status update.

Posting a report as finished journal generates transactions which are similar to product receipts in purchase orders: Inventory physically receives the item with a preliminary value and increases the on-hand quantity.

5.6.1.3   Automatic Consumption

When reporting as finished, an automatic posting of the item consumption and the resource usage is possible in the same way as when starting the production order. On the tab *General* in the *Report as finished* dialog, the field groups *Route card journal* and *Picking list journal* control automatic consumption in this context.

If you post an automatic consumption when starting and when reporting as finished, select the flushing principle "Start" in the BOM lines that should be consumed when starting the production order, and "Finish" in the BOM lines that should be consumed when reporting as finished. With this setting, you can consume some items when starting and other items when finishing the order.

Route operations do not include this option. The automatic posting is executed for all "automatic posting" operations in a production order at the same time – either when starting or when reporting as finished. In order to avoid duplicate posting, select the option "Route group dependent" in the lookup field *Automatic route consumption* only in the *Start* dialog or only in the *Report as finished* dialog – not in both dialogs.

5.6.1.4   Ledger Integration

If you want to post to clearing accounts (deducting from WIP) when reporting as finished, ledger integration has to be active for the report as finished transactions. For this purpose, the slider *Post report as finished in ledger* in the section *General* of the Production control parameters has to be set to "Yes" (not required for standard cost items) and the checkbox *Post physical inventory* in the item model group of the manufactured item has to be selected.

The ledger transactions with reference to the report as finished transactions are reversed when you end and cost the production order.

5.6.1.5   Reporting Scrap

Scrap, which is specified in the BOM or in the route, is planned scrap that is included in the estimated consumption of items and resources. For this reason, the cost analysis does not show this scrap as a deviation between the estimated and the actual consumption. A deviation is only visible if the total actual consumption does not match the estimated consumption. In this context, data in the field group *Scrap* in the line details of the picking list journal are only used for information purposes and do not generate a separate transaction.

Scrapping a (partly or completely) manufactured item in the course of production order processing is unplanned scrap. You can report this scrap in the field *Error quantity* when reporting as finished. The default for the error quantity when reporting as finished is the total of the reported error quantity of all operations (entered in route card or job card journals). If the slider *Increase remain qty with err qty* in the Production control parameters (section *General*) is set to "No", the open quantity of the production order is reduced by the scrap quantity, which means that you accept a lower good quantity.

From a financial perspective, you can allocate the costs for scrapping the manufactured item to the good quantity (which means that the good quantity carries all costs of the production order). Alternatively, you can post the costs for scrapping to a separate scrap account (you can specify a default scrap account in the section *Standard update* of the Production control parameters). If you apply a scrap account, an inventory receipt and an immediate consumption for scrap (crediting the scrap account) is posted when ending the order. Only when you use a scrap account, you can scrap an order completely (with no good quantity).

The scrap account option is not used for manufactured items with standard costs.

5.6.2 Ending and Costing

Ending a production order is required to post the final costs and to close the order. At the same time, WIP ledger transactions for production journals are reversed. The consumption of materials and resources and the receipt of the manufactured item are posted to the final ledger accounts.

You should end a production order in time. Before ending, the WIP account balance for the production order is not cleared and the manufactured item is only included in the physical inventory, not in the financial inventory (see section 7.2.4).

5.6.2.1 Ending

Ending a production order closes the order and executes costing in one step. Since it is not possible to post any further transaction for a closed production order, you should not end the order until you are confident that all transactions are posted.

In order to end the production order, click the button *Production order/Process/End* in the Production order form. If you want to end multiple orders (e.g., in a month-end procedure), execute the corresponding periodic activity in the menu item *Production control> Periodic tasks> Production order status update> End*.

In the inventory transactions, the ending date of the production order is shown in the field *Financial date*. The receipt status in the transaction of the manufactured item is "Purchased". For consumed items (BOM lines), the issue status is "Sold".

5.6.2.2 Costing

From a financial perspective, costing a production order is the equivalent action to invoicing a purchase order or sales order. When you cost the order (which is done automatically in the course of the ending routine), Dynamics 365 calculates the actual costs of all item consumption and resource usage transactions (including indirect costs). Based on these actual costs of the production order, the cost price of the manufactured item is calculated. If the manufactured item applies a standard cost valuation, costing posts the cost price differences to variance accounts.

If you want to compare the actual and the estimated consumption, click the button *Manage costs/Calculations/View calculation details* in the Production order form. The tab *Overview costing* in the Price calculation form shows – at item and operation line level – a comparison of the estimated and the actual quantity consumption, and of the estimated and the actual costs. If you want a summary of the estimation or the actual consumption, switch to the tab *Costing sheet*.

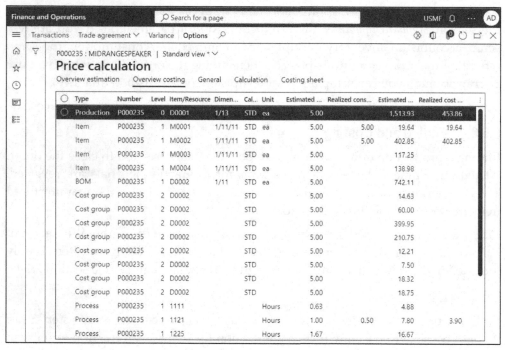

Figure 5-22: Viewing the estimation and the actual consumption in the price calculation

5.6.2.3 Ledger Integration and Inquiries

Like invoice posting in a purchasing or sales order, costing a production order generates financial transactions for the items which have been consumed or reported as finished. In this context, costing reverses the WIP ledger transactions that have been posted in picking list journals, route card journals, job card journals, and report as finished journals. In a second step, costing posts the following ledger transactions which close the order financially:

➤ **Consumption of components** – To the stock accounts of the BOM line items.
➤ **Consumption of resource capacity** – To the costing accounts of the resources.
➤ **Receipt of the produced item** – To the stock account of the manufactured item.
➤ **Indirect costs** – To the financial accounts specified in the costing sheet.

For the item transactions, applicable main accounts are specified in the posting setup (*Cost management> Ledger integration policies setup> Posting*). For the resource usage, main accounts can derive from settings in the resource/resource group or in the applicable cost category. Apart from these settings, applicable main accounts for item and resource transactions can also derive from the production group.

The lookup field *Ledger* on the tab *Setup* of the Production order detail form (initialized from the Production control parameters) determines which of these settings for the main accounts are used (see section 9.4.3).

In order to view the transactions that are generated when ending and costing the order, click the button *Manage costs/Production accounting/Production posting* in the Production order form or open the menu item *Production control> Inquiries and reports> Production> Production posting*. In the production posting inquiry, the ending and costing transactions show the type "Costing". If you want to view the related ledger transactions, select the respective line and click the button *Voucher*.

5.6.3   Case Study Exercise

Exercise 5.13 – End Production

Report the entire quantity of the production order in exercise 5.8 as finished. Then end the production order and check the price calculation inquiry to compare estimation and costing.

5.7   Subcontracting

If it is not possible or advisable to process a particular operation internally (e.g., for technical reasons or because of insufficient internal capacity), you can subcontract the operation to an external vendor. The BOM and/or route of the manufactured item has to include the subcontracted service in this case.

Sometimes, there is the situation that you can execute an operation alternatively internally or externally – for example, small orders internally, and large quantities with a subcontractor. In order to manage these options, set up a route/BOM version for the manufactured item with the internal operation and an alternative route/BOM version with the subcontracted operation.

In Dynamics 365, there are two basic options for subcontracting:

> **External resource** – Resource with the type "Vendor" in a route operation.
> **Purchased service** – Service item with the line type "Vendor" in a BOM line.

Since a purchase order line needs to contain a physical item or a service item (it is not possible to purchase a route operation), a purchase order is only created with the second option ("Purchased service").

5.7.1   External Resources

You can use an external resource in an operation which is not linked to a BOM line with a service item if you do not need to generate a purchase order – for example, if there is a contract to use a fixed subcontractor capacity for a given monthly fee.

In this case, create a separate resource group and resource for the subcontractor. The external resource is similar to a regular internal resource (see section 5.3.2), but with the *Type* "Vendor". In resources with this type, you can select the vendor number in the field *Vendor* on the tab *General* of the Resource form. In addition, make sure to select appropriate cost categories (depending on the contract, maybe only a *Quantity category*) and main accounts for subcontracting. Settings for the calendar and for finite capacity depend on the contract. In the route operation, select the *Route type* "Vendor" on the tab *General* and enter the external resource in the field *Costing resource* on the tab *Setup*. On the tab *Resource requirements*, specify the requirements in a way that the external resource is selected.

Processing the operation with the external resource in a production order works similar to processing an internal operation. There is no automatic purchase order.

5.7.2   Purchased Services

If you need a purchase order for the outsourced operation, create a service item and include it in the BOM of the manufactured item. For scheduling purposes, you can link the BOM line with the service item to an external operation.

5.7.2.1 Master Data for Purchased Services

The required service item is a product with the *Product type* "Service", an *Item model group* that generates inventory transactions ("Stocked product"), and the *Default order type* "Purchase order". In the field *Cost group* on the tab *Manage costs* of the released product, you can select a cost group with the type "Direct outsourcing". The *Flushing principle* on the tab *Engineer* should be "Finish". Other relevant settings in the released product include the item group, the cost price, the dimension groups, the units of measure, the purchase price, the main vendor, and the default order settings. In the BOM of the manufactured item, insert a BOM line with the service item and the *Line type* "Vendor". You can optionally enter a *Vendor account* in the field group *Subcontractor* of the BOM line, which overrides the main vendor that is specified in the released product.

If you need an outsourced operation for scheduling purposes, you can set it up as described in the previous section. But unlike an outsourced operation which is not linked to a BOM line with a service item, this operation should contain a route group with automatic consumption and – if all subcontracting costs are included in the service item – deactivated cost calculation (the sliders in the field group *Estimation and costing* of the route group are set to "No"). In order to assign the outsourced operation (for scheduling the subcontracted activity) to the BOM line with the service item (for purchasing the subcontracted activity), select the relevant operation number in the field *Oper.No.* on the tab *General* of the BOM line and make sure that the slider *End* is set to "Yes" (you do not consume the service item before the operation is finished).

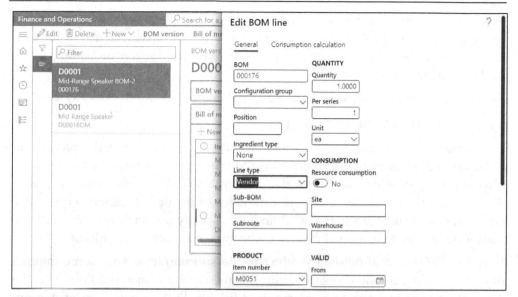

Figure 5-23: Managing the settings in a BOM line for a subcontracted service

If material is supplied to the subcontractor, assign the BOM lines of the related components to the outsourced operation in the same way as you link BOM lines to an internal operation.

5.7.2.2 Production Orders with Purchased Services

You can manually or automatically create a production order with subcontracted service items in the same way as a regular internal production order. Estimating the order creates a purchase order for the BOM line with the service item (triggered by the BOM line type "Vendor" and the default order type "Purchase order"). The production BOM, which you can access with the button *Production order/Production details/BOM* in the production order, shows the reference to the purchase order in the columns *Reference type* and *Number*. Like any other purchase order, the order has to be confirmed before you can receive the service item.

Scheduling and releasing a production order with a subcontracted service is not different from the way you process an internal order.

But you can start a production order with a subcontracted service in the list page *Production control> Subcontracted work*, which includes the button *Start* in the action pane for this purpose. On the tab *General* in the *Start* dialog, make sure to apply appropriate settings for automatic consumption (when starting, do not consume the BOM lines which are consumed when you receive the purchase order). In the print options for the picking list, which you can access with the button *Print options* on the tab *General* in the *Start* dialog, you can set the slider *Use delivery note layout* for the picking list to "Yes" if you supply BOM line items to the subcontractor.

When you post the product receipt for the purchase order afterward, settings in the field group *Receive purchase order* of the Production control parameters (section

Automatic update) determine if BOM and route consumption are posted in parallel to the product receipt. The settings have to be selected in a way, that consumption is not posted two times – both when starting the production order and when posting the product receipt.

Reporting the production order as finished and ending the order works as usual.

5.7.2.3   Item Transfer to Subcontractors

If you want to keep control of the materials that are included in the production BOM and supplied from your warehouse to the subcontractor, you can set up a separate warehouse or location for the subcontractor. When you send an item to the subcontractor, register and post a transfer order or a transfer journal. The consumption of the items in the BOM lines that specify materials consumed by the subcontractor has to be posted from the subcontractor warehouse or location then.

If you transfer a semi-finished product to the subcontractor after some internal operations and you want to keep control of the complete material flow with the subcontractor, you have to implement additional BOM levels: Create a semi-finished item which contains all items and operations before the external operation, and a second semi-finished item after the external operation. Both items got the default order type "Production". The BOM of the second semi-finished item contains the first semi-finished item, the subcontracting service item, and – if applicable – additional materials directly supplied to the subcontractor. The BOM of the final manufactured product contains the second semi-finished item and the material required for later operations.

With this setup, master planning generates a (planned) production order for the first semi-finished item, which you receive in inventory by reporting as finished. You can use a regular transfer order to transfer the item afterward and consume it in the upper-level production order of the second semi-finished item. Processing the production order of the second semi-finished item works as described in the section for production orders with purchased services above. When you receive the second semi-finished item from the subcontractor, report it as finished and consume it in the upper-level production order for the finished product.

In order to specify that the first semi-finished item needs to be transferred to the subcontractor warehouse, you can access the item coverage of this item and set up a record with the subcontractor warehouse. In this record, mark the checkbox *Change planned order type* on the tab *General* and select the *Planned order type* "Transfer" and the *Main warehouse* which is your warehouse from which you supply the semi-finished item. For the second semi-finished item, you can set up an item coverage in the other direction (with a record with your warehouse, the subcontractor warehouse is the *Main warehouse* from which the item is shipped). Based on these item coverage settings, master planning generates (planned) transfer orders for the semi-finished items. With similar item coverage settings for the materials supplied to the subcontractor, master planning also generates planned orders for these items.

5.7.3 Case Study Exercise

Exercise 5.14 – Setup for Subcontracting

Because of limited internal capacity, the operation which you have set up in exercise 5.6 should be executed by a subcontractor for production orders with the item of exercise 5.2 and a quantity of 10 units or more.

Set up a subcontractor resource and resource group (similar to the resource in exercise 5.5) with a vendor of your choice. Then create an alternative route and route version to the route of exercise 5.7. This new route, in which you enter the subcontractor resource and applicable settings for subcontracting, should be the default when producing 10 units or more. When posting a route card or job card with the route operation, the good quantity should also be reported as finished.

Next, create a service item with the required settings for subcontracting and the product number I-##-SRV, the name "##-processing", the main vendor which you have selected in the resource, and a base purchase price of USD 150. Then create an alternative BOM and BOM version to the BOM of exercise 5.3, which should be the default when producing 10 units or more. Compared to the BOM of exercise 5.3, this new BOM includes a line with the subcontracting service. In order to facilitate production posting, the BOM lines with physical products in this BOM should be consumed automatically when starting a production order.

In order to avoid a duplicate posting of consumption, make sure that the Production control parameter for *Automatic BOM consumption* when receiving assigned purchase orders (in the field group *Receive purchase order* of the section *Automatic update*) is set to "Flushing principle" and for *Automatic route consumption* to "Route group dependent".

Exercise 5.15 – Production Order with Subcontracting

A production order with 10 units of the finished product of exercise 5.2 is required and should be processed immediately.

Enter a corresponding production order and check the BOM and the route in the order. Then enter a purchase order with the vendor of exercise 3.2, which includes 20 units of the first and 10 units of the second item of exercise 5.1. Confirm the purchase order and post the product receipt. In the next step, estimate the production order and check the production BOM afterward. It contains a link to the purchase order for subcontracting – confirm this purchase order. In the production order, you can skip scheduling and start the order. Check the status and the transactions of the production order afterward.

The subcontractor then completes his services and you post the related product receipt. Check the status and the transactions of the production order again.

5.8   Formula and Batch Production Order

In discrete manufacturing, a distinct item is produced from multiple components. Process manufacturing, in contrast to discrete manufacturing, covers a continuous process which produces a batch-controlled item together with its co-products.

Production control in Dynamics 365 meets the requirements of process industries by the use of formulas for material management (instead of the bills of materials in discrete manufacturing). For resource management, process manufacturing and discrete manufacturing share the same functionality.

If you work in a discrete manufacturing environment and there are requirements that are covered by process manufacturing features, you can also use formulas. You can, for example, apply a formula with co-products for a cutting operation, even if the items are not batch-controlled. But it is not possible to use formulas in the product configurator.

5.8.1   Formula Management

Formula management is based on bills of materials. Formulas (with formula lines and formula versions) and bills of materials (with BOM lines and BOM versions) share the same concepts and functionality. But in addition to the functionality in bills of materials, formulas include the following core features:

➢ **Co-products and by-products** – Produce more than one product in parallel.
➢ **Catch weight items** (see section 7.2.1) – Can be included as a finished product or component.

In addition, there are features which help managing the quantity in formula lines (e.g., with the columns *Scalable* and *Percent controlled*) and other options which support item substitution (with the column *Plan group*).

5.8.1.1   Product Data for Formulas

In the Released product form, items which are produced with a formula have got similar settings to items which are manufactured with a BOM (including the default order type "Production"). There are settings which are more common in process industry than in discrete manufacturing (e.g., weight as inventory unit), but the only mandatory difference is the setting in the field *Production type* on the tab *Engineer* of the released product. The following options in the *Production type* refer to formula management:

➢ **Formula** – For the main item which is produced with a formula.
➢ **Co-product** – Item produced with a formula in parallel to the main item.
➢ **By-product** – Like a co-product, but undesirable (causing costs, not value).
➢ **Planning item** – Virtual main item, if a formula only produces co-products.

Planning items are used if there is no clear physical main item in a formula, but co-products with similar importance (e.g., gasoline and diesel in a refinery plant).

You can assign a formula only to an item with the production type "Formula" or "Planning item". Co-products and by-products are produced in a production order for the related formula or planning item. If a co-product is always produced with the same formula or planning item, enter the respective item number in the field *Planning formula* of the co-product (on the tab *Engineer* in the released product).

5.8.1.2 Working with Formulas

You can access the Formula form in a similar way to accessing the BOM form:

> ➤ **From the released product** (*Product information management> Products> Released products*, button *Engineer/Formula/Formula versions*)
> ➤ **From the menu** (*Product information management> Bills of materials and formulas> Formulas*)

Like the assignment of BOMs, the assignment of formulas to manufactured items is called "Version". The formula version – like the BOM version – can be specified at the level of the site, date (from/to), and quantity.

In the Released product form, you can only access the formula management for items with the production type "Formula" or "Planning item". If you access the Formula form from the menu, the list page shows all formulas. Click on a formula ID shown as a link in the grid of the list page to open the Formula detail form in the Lines view, which shows the formula lines. The formula versions (assignment of formula items or planning items to the formula) are shown in the Header view, which you can access with the button *Header* in the detail form.

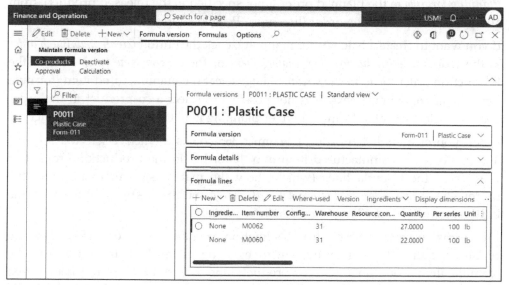

Figure 5-24:   Accessing co-products from the Formula version form

The field *Formula size* in the formula version provides the default for the column *Per series* in the formula lines and is the default quantity for production orders with the particular product. You can optionally record co-products and by-products in the Header view of the Formula detail form – click the button *Co-products* on the tab *Formula versions* (or the button *Formula version/Maintain formula version/Co-products* in the action pane of the Formula version form accessed from the released product) for this purpose. In the lower pane of the Co-product form, you can add co-products and by-products with the respective quantity. For a co-product, you can select the *Co-product cost allocation* "Manual" and enter the *Cost allocation percent*. This percentage, which is the percentage of the total production costs which is allocated to the co-product, determines the inventory value of the co-product. For a by-product, select the appropriate option for additional production costs (e.g., covering the disposal) in the *By-product cost allocation*.

Like bill of materials, formulas and formula versions have to be approved before they are available for production orders. And the active formula version is the default for production orders, the item price calculation, and master planning.

5.8.2   Batch Production Orders

Batch orders are production orders for items that are linked to a formula. There is no separate form for batch orders – they use the regular Production order form. In the Production control parameters, you can select a separate number sequence for batch orders (or use the same number sequence as for regular production orders).

The ways for creating a batch order are the same as for creating a regular discrete production order: Apart from manually entering it, you can create it automatically from master planning (including co-product demand in the calculation – select a *Planning formula* in the planned order if not specified in the released product), from an upper-level production order (line type "Pegged supply"), or from a sales order.

If you want to create a batch order manually, click the button *Create new/Batch order* in the workspace *Production floor management* or the button *New batch order* in the Production order form. In the *Create* dialog, select the manufactured item (formula item or planning item) next. It is not possible to select a co-product in the order header – select a related formula item or planning item to produce a co-product.

When you create a batch order, Dynamics 365 copies the active/selected formula and route of the manufactured item into the order. In the production order, you can access the formula lines (which show the materials/components) with the button *Production order/Production details/Formula* and the co-/by-products with the button *Production order/Production details/Co-products*.

Processing the batch order – from estimation to ending – is not different from a regular production order except when reporting as finished: In addition to the formula item, you can report co-products and by-products as finished. When ending a batch order with co-products or by-products, the production costs are allocated to the co-products according to the settings in the formula, and the additional costs from by-products are posted as a route transaction with a *Burden cost category* (specified in the Production control parameters).

6   Forecasts and Master Planning

The aim of master planning is to ensure item availability and economic efficiency. For this reason, master planning has to deal with the conflicting priorities of high supply readiness and low inventory quantity and value.

6.1   Business Processes in Master Planning

In Dynamics 365, long-term forecasting and short-term master planning are covered by the Master planning module.

6.1.1   Basic Approach

The task of forecasting is to identify the item demand on a long-term basis. Master planning calculates the supply and demand on a short-term basis.

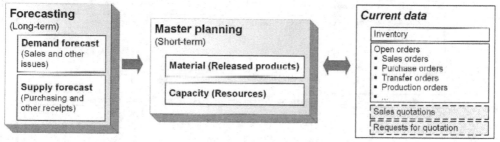

Figure 6-1:   Forecasting and master planning in Dynamics 365

6.1.1.1 Forecasting

Forecasting is a long-term prognosis for planning and budgeting purposes. It includes demand forecasts that cover sales and other demand (e.g., manufacturing materials) and supply forecasts that cover purchasing and other supply. Forecast versions enable multiple parallel scenarios.

6.1.1.2 Master Planning and Planning Optimization

Master planning is the short-term planning in the day-to-day business. Based on current orders, on-hand inventory, sales quotations, and forecasts, master planning calculates the item demand and supply. As a result, actual and planned orders for purchasing, transfer, and production are generated. Master planning, like forecasting, provides the option to use multiple scenarios in parallel.

With the Planning Optimization service, the calculation is executed in a separate service. This service reduces the impact of the master planning calculation on the performance of the transactional database, and eliminates the requirement to run master planning outside the regular business hours.

© Springer Fachmedien Wiesbaden GmbH, part of Springer Nature 2023
A. Luszczak, *Using Microsoft Dynamics 365 for Finance and Operations*,
https://doi.org/10.1007/978-3-658-40453-6_6

6.1.2   At a Glance: Master Planning

The following example demonstrates the main steps in master planning on the example of the net requirements calculation for a manufactured item.

As a basis for the net requirements calculation, enter a sales order with a line with a manufactured item (default order type "Production") which should be shipped today, but is out of stock. In the toolbar of the order lines, click the button *Product and supply/Net requirements* to access to the Net requirements form that shows the item availability. In order to update the net requirements based on current data, click the button *Update/Master planning* to execute local master planning.

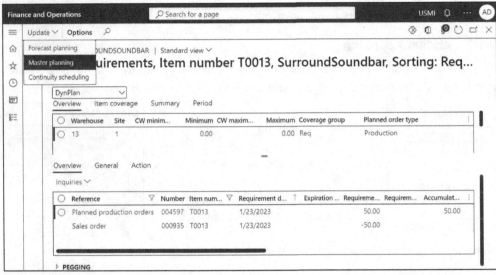

Figure 6-2:   The Net requirements form after executing local master planning

In the described scenario, master planning generates a planned production order for the manufactured item. Since the planned order needs to start in the past in order to meet the delivery date in the sales order, the requirement date in this line is adjusted to the earliest possible date (depending on the related setting for calculated delays in the master plan). The column *Delay (days)* in the requirement line with the sales order shows the calculated delay.

In master planning, you can manage multiple parallel scenarios – for example, a static plan and a dynamic plan. In the Net requirements form, the dynamic plan (used for simulation and order promising) is the default for the planned orders which are shown. The static plan is used for scheduling and firming orders in the planning or purchasing department. In order to switch between the different plans, select the appropriate option in the lookup field *Plan* at the top of the Net requirements form.

6.2 Forecasting

A forecast is a long-term prognosis, which you use for estimating and amending future capacities in resource and material management. In addition, you can use forecasts as a basis for budgeting in finance. You can maintain multiple forecasts, which represent alternative scenarios for the business development, in parallel.

Forecasts in Dynamics 365 do not only include sales forecasts, but you can include further sources of item demand. In addition, you can manage supply forecasts – e.g., to manage a prognosis of long-term vendor contracts.

6.2.1   Basics of Forecasting

Forecast models represent the planning scenarios. When you enter or calculate a forecast in Dynamics 365, you have to select a forecast model which holds the forecast data. A forecast plan, which is the scenario in which a forecast is calculated, then refers to a particular forecast model. You can include a forecast plan in master planning as a source of supply and demand.

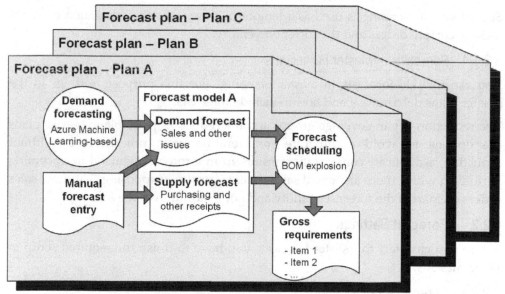

Figure 6-3:   Forecasting in Dynamics 365

6.2.1.1 Demand Forecasts

Estimated sales figures are the starting point for the forecast of the future demand. Apart from the sales demand, demand forecasts may also include other demand – for example, the demand for semi-finished items (instead of finished items) if it is not possible to give reliable forecasts at the detail level of finished products.

Forecast planning and master planning are based on released products. If it is not feasible or possible to enter forecasts at the level of individual items, you can use item allocation keys. An item allocation key contains several items and determines the percentage distribution between these items.

6.2.1.2 Supply Forecasts

Separately from demand forecasts, you can optionally manage supply forecasts with purchasing transactions and other types of item receipts. The inventory forecast then provides the option to align demand forecasts and supply forecasts.

6.2.1.3 Forecast Planning

The aim of forecast planning, which is an optional feature, is to calculate the demand for components and materials based on the forecast demand for finished products (using the active BOM versions). As a result, Dynamics 365 creates planned purchase and production orders in the selected forecast plan.

If there is a supply forecast, it determines the minimum quantities for the planned purchase or production orders, no matter if these quantities exceed the direct and indirect demand from the demand forecast.

Since forecast planning is used as a long-term prognosis, the calculation does not include current orders and the current inventory.

6.2.1.4 Forecasts in Master Planning

You can include forecasts in master planning. For this purpose, settings in the master plans determine if and how to include forecasts.

The reduction key in coverage groups and the reduction principle in master plans are options to avoid a duplicate consideration of future demand. Without reduction, a duplicate consideration results from a forecast demand in upcoming periods in which there are actual sales orders already – supposing that these sales orders are part of the forecast quantity and not in addition to the forecast.

6.2.2 Forecast Settings

Before you can start to register forecasts, you have to finish the required setup in Dynamics 365.

6.2.2.1 Forecast Models

Forecast models represent the different scenarios in forecasting. In order to use forecasts, you have to set up at least one forecast model in the menu item *Master planning> Setup> Demand forecasting> Forecast models*.

If you want to structure forecasts (e.g., group forecasts by region), you can configure a two-stage forecast with submodels. Create the submodels like regular forecast models for this purpose first, and subsequently create the main model, to which you assign the submodels (on the tab *Submodel* of the Forecast model form).

If you want to protect forecasts against changes, set the slider *Stopped* in the forecast model to "Yes". You can use blocking, for example, if you do not want any changes on an annual forecast once it is completed (use a separate forecast model per year in this case).

6.2.2.2 Forecast Plans

When you update or enter a forecast, you select a forecast model which represents the forecast scenario. Forecast planning does not directly refer to a forecast model, but to a forecast plan. In order to assign a forecast model to a forecast plan, open the menu item *Master planning> Setup> Plans> Forecast plans* and select the forecast model in the lookup field *Forecast model* of the respective forecast plan.

The forecast plan also contains settings on whether to include supply forecasts or demand forecasts. The tab *Time fences in days* contains the periods which should be covered by forecast planning (starting from the day of calculation).

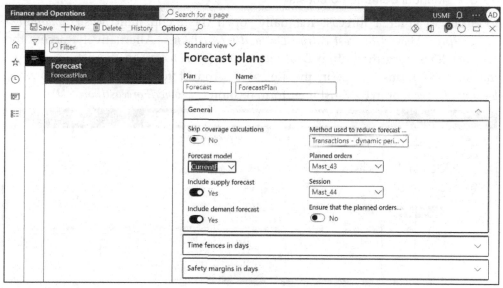

Figure 6-4:   Selecting a forecast model in the forecast plan

6.2.2.3 Parameters and Item Allocation Keys

As a prerequisite for the use of forecasts, the slider *Disable all planning processes* in the Master planning parameters (*Master planning> Setup> Master planning parameters*) has to be set to "No". The Master planning parameters also contain the field *Current forecast plan*, which determines the default forecast plan in the inquiries and dialogs for forecast planning.

Another important setting for item forecasts is the coverage group, which specifies how to summarize net requirements. The *Forecast plan time fence* on the tab *Other* in the coverage groups determines the applicable period for forecast planning. You can find more details on coverage groups in section 6.3.4.

If you do not want to enter forecasts at the level of individual items, you can use item allocation keys. With an item allocation key, you can enter a forecast total for a group of items. In order to set up item allocation keys, open the menu item *Master planning> Setup> Demand forecasting> Item allocation keys*. The tab *Item allocation* in this form contains the assigned items with their percentage.

Demand forecasting parameters (*Master planning> Setup> Demand forecasting> Demand forecasting parameters*) are required if you want to use Azure Machine Learning-based demand forecasting.

6.2.3   Forecasts and Forecast Planning

You can enter forecasts manually (including the option to import forecast data from Excel with the Microsoft Office integration), but it is also possible to generate demand forecasts with Azure Machine Learning features automatically.

6.2.3.1   Manual Demand Forecasts

In order to enter a forecast manually, open the menu item *Master planning> Forecasting> Manual forecast entry> Demand forecast lines*. Alternatively, access the forecast lines with the button *Demand forecast* (or *Forecast*) in the action pane of master data forms – e.g., in the Released product form (button *Plan/Forecast/ Demand forecast*) or in the Customer form (button *Customer/Forecast/Forecast*).

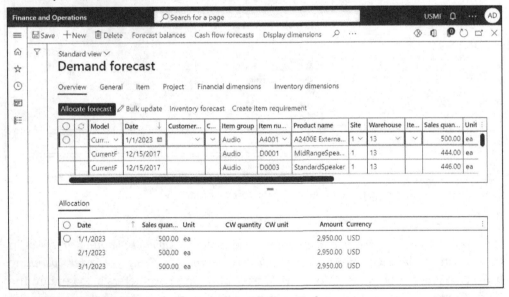

Figure 6-5:   Allocating a sales forecast line across periods

When you insert a demand forecast line, select the applicable forecast model in the column *Model* first. You can record different scenarios with different models in separate lines. In the column *Date*, enter the start date of the particular forecast period – for example, the first day of a month if you enter a line per month. If you want to record a forecast per customer or customer group, select the *Customer account* or *Customer group* in the respective column. Then select the *Item number* or the *Item allocation key* before you enter the *Sales quantity* and the *Amount* (or, if it is possible to calculate the amount from the quantity and the price, the *Sales quantity* and the *Sales price*). If you want to allocate a forecast line across periods, click the button *Allocate forecast* in the toolbar of the tab *Overview* and enter the allocation details in the following dialog.

You can facilitate the manual forecast entry with bulk updates (click the button *Bulk update* in the toolbar of the tab *Overview*) or with the Excel integration. In order to use Excel, click the button 🔲 /*Demand forecast entries in Excel* in the action pane, change and add lines in Excel as appropriate, and publish the data back to Dynamics 365.

6.2.3.2   Azure Machine Learning-Based Demand Forecasting

As an alternative to the manual entry of demand forecast lines, you can create demand forecast lines with Azure Machine Learning (Azure ML). With Azure ML-based demand forecasting, you can calculate forecasts based on historical demand (originating from inventory transactions in Dynamics 365).

Once item allocation keys and Demand forecasting parameters are set up, you can access the Adjusted demand forecast form (*Master planning> Forecasting> Demand forecasting> Adjusted demand forecast*) and click the button *Generate statistical baseline forecast* to calculate the forecast using Azure ML. You can edit the forecast data in the Adjusted demand forecast form as required before you click the button *Authorize adjusted demand forecast* to create the actual demand forecast lines.

6.2.3.3   Supply Forecasts and Inventory Forecasts

If you want to manage a supply forecast separately from the demand forecast, open the menu item *Master planning> Forecasting> Supply forecast lines* or click the button *Supply forecast* or *Forecast* in the action pane of the respective master data form (released product, vendor) and enter the supply forecast in a similar way to the demand forecast. Depending on the setup, forecast planning then includes the supply forecast in parallel to the demand forecast.

Inventory forecasts show the result of supply and demand forecasts at the level of item numbers and periods. You can access the inventory forecasts with the button *Inventory forecast* in applicable master data forms.

6.2.3.4   Forecast Planning

The results of the forecasts for trade items, manufactured items, and raw materials are a valuable basis for the preparation of future production and purchasing.

In order to identify forecast data on multiple BOM levels, you can execute forecast planning (*Master planning> Forecasting> Forecast planning*). The update dialog for forecast planning includes the lookup field *Forecast plan*, which determines the forecast plan that is calculated.

The results of forecast planning are shown in the Gross requirements form, which you can access with the button *Plan/Requirement/Gross requirement* in the Released product form. By default, this form shows the forecast plan which is selected as the current forecast plan in the Master planning parameters. But you can also select a different plan in the lookup field *Plan* at the top of the Gross requirements form.

Apart from the Gross requirements form, all master planning inquiries (e.g., the list page *Master planning> Master planning> Planned orders*) also show the results of forecast planning if you select a forecast plan instead of a master plan in the lookup field *Plan* at the top of the respective form.

6.2.3.5 Budget Transfer

If you want to use demand or supply forecasts as a basis for financial budgets, you can execute the periodic activity *Budgeting> Periodic> Generate budget plan from demand forecasts* (or *Generate budget plan from supply forecast*) to transfer the forecast figures to budgeting.

6.2.4   Case Study Exercises

Exercise 6.1 – Forecast Settings

You are asked to enter a new sales forecast for items which you have set up in the previous exercises. This forecast should be included in a scenario which is separate from other forecast scenarios.

In order to meet this requirement, create a forecast plan Y-## and a forecast model F-## (## = your user ID) without submodels. Assign the forecast model to the forecast plan and make sure that demand forecasts are included in this plan. In the forecast plan, select a number sequence for *Planned orders* and for the *Session* which is similar to the settings in existing forecast plans.

Exercise 6.2 – Demand Forecast

You expect the customer of exercise 4.1 to order 200 units of the merchandise item of exercise 3.5 and 100 units of the finished product of exercise 5.2 on the first day of each of the next three months.

Enter this demand in a demand forecast with the forecast model of exercise 6.1. Then execute forecast planning with the forecast plan of exercise 6.1 and check the results.

6.3   Master Planning and Planning Optimization

Master planning in Dynamics 365 covers the short-term calculation of material and capacity requirements. It is the basis for the day-to-day work in purchasing and production management.

The calculation in master planning is based on data related to released products and to resources all across Dynamics 365. Depending on the setup, these data include sales orders, purchase orders, production orders, transfer orders, current inventory, forecasts, and master data (released products, resources).

Master planning generates planned orders for purchasing, production (including Kanbans), and inventory transfer. In addition, action messages and notifications on calculated delays support the manual adjustment of current orders.

6.3.1 Basics of Master Planning

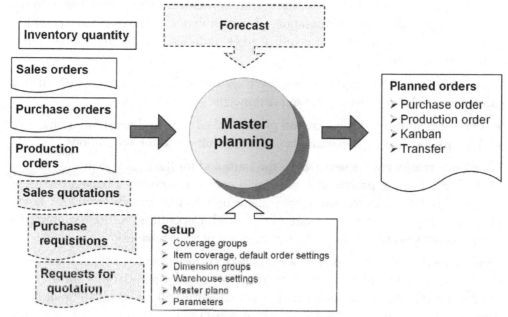

Figure 6-6: Elements of master planning

Inventory transactions, sales orders, purchase orders, production orders, and the on-hand quantity in inventory are an essential basis for master planning. In addition, master planning can include sales quotations, requests for quotation, approved purchase requisitions, and forecasts.

Like in forecasting, you can maintain multiple parallel scenarios in master planning. A scenario is represented by a master plan, which contains the particular settings for the scenario. Relevant settings in the plan relate to the elements that are included in master planning and the calculation principles for planned orders.

6.3.1.1 Master Planning Strategies

In a legacy environment without Planning Optimization (see section 6.3.2), master planning occurs within the transactional database and puts a heavy load on the database engine. For this reason, master planning is usually executed in a batch job which calculates the net requirements for all items every night. The result of this calculation is available in a scenario called "static master plan".

If you work with the Planning Optimization service, performance considerations are not the reason for recalculating the static plan only in the night. But still there may be organizational reasons to restrict it to a night job, avoiding planned orders in that plan to be automatically updated during the day.

The static plan is the master plan which is used for scheduling planned orders in purchasing and in production control. It is the default plan which is used when you open a Planned order form.

Apart from the master plan which is used for purchase and production scheduling, the sales department needs a plan to run simulations that identify possible delivery dates in sales orders and in quotations. This simulation requires master planning only for a particular item. The result of the simulation is available in a scenario called "dynamic master plan".

In order to meet these requirements, there are two different strategies which you can determine in the Master planning parameters:

➢ **One-plan strategy** – One common plan for scheduling and for simulations.
➢ **Two-plan strategy** – Separate plans for scheduling and for simulations.

If the same master plan is selected for the static and for the dynamic master plan in the Master planning parameters, you run a one-plan strategy. Planned orders of current simulations in the sales department update the static plan, which is the plan used in purchasing and production control. Depending on the requirements of your enterprise, this strategy does or does not fit your business.

If you want to apply a two-plan strategy, select a different master plan for the static and for the dynamic plan. In order to keep the basis for simulations current, you can specify that the result of the static plan, which usually is calculating all items every night, is copied into the dynamic plan every time.

With this setting, simulation in sales starts with the same data basis as purchasing and production scheduling in the morning. Simulations throughout the day do not modify the planned orders in the static plan, which avoids confusion in purchasing and production control caused by continuous changes in planned orders.

6.3.1.2 Customer Order Decoupling Point

Depending on the structure of the products, there are two key supply policies in production control for fulfilling the customer demand:

➢ **Make-to-Stock** – Produce based on sales forecasts and historical demand.
➢ **Make-to-Order** – Produce based on confirmed sales orders.

In addition, there are hybrid supply strategies that apply a make-to-stock strategy for purchased or semi-finished items with a long lead time, and a make-to-order strategy for finished products. If you apply a hybrid strategy, the customer order decoupling point (push/pull point) determines the level in the product structure, to which the items are built to stock.

With the use of appropriate coverage groups (see section 6.3.4), you can apply all of these strategies. In case of a hybrid supply strategy, enter forecasts at the semi-finished product level (which is the customer order decoupling point for these items). The reduction principle (field *Method used to reduce forecast requirements*) in the master plan determines the way in which master planning offsets forecasted demand with actual sales orders. You do not sell the semi-finished product which is why sales orders do not directly offset forecasts of semi-finished products. For this reason, you should select to include all inventory transactions – including BOM line demand from production orders – in the coverage groups of applicable semi-finished items. In the Coverage group form, the lookup field *Reduce forecast by* contains the required option for this purpose.

6.3.1.3 Master Planning and Planned Orders

Master planning generates planned purchase orders, planned production orders, planned Kanbans, and planned transfers based on the item demand and settings for master planning. Depending on the planning method (see section 6.3.5), master planning initially deletes existing planned orders which are not in the status "Approved" before creating new planned orders.

You can review and edit the planned orders before you convert them to actual purchase orders, production orders, Kanbans, and transfer orders (or, if selected in the Site form, transfer journals).

6.3.2 Planning Optimization

The Planning Optimization add-in provides the option to execute master planning as a separate service outside the transactional Dynamics 365 environment. Unlike the built-in master planning engine, Planning Optimization this way enables to continuously run master planning without a negative impact on the performance.

The Planning Optimization service replaces the built-in master planning engine. While the built-in engine is deprecated and will not receive updates anymore, you can still use it until a few features, which are available in the built-in engine but not yet in the Planning Optimization, are also included in the Planning Optimization.

6.3.2.1 Technical Overview and Implementation

Planning Optimization, which is only available for cloud-hosted environments, is a separate service which is designed for a fast calculation of large data volumes. It receives the required data and the execution trigger from the transactional Dynamics 365 environment and returns the calculation results.

As a prerequisite for using the Planning Optimization, it must be enabled in the feature management and in the license configuration. In order to check whether there are features required by your company, which are available in the built-in master planning engine but not in the Planning Optimization, check the differences (see below). Note that additional Planning Optimization features will be released in the course of time.

If all required features are available, install the Planning Optimization add-in, which acts as connector, in the Microsoft Dynamics Lifecycle Services (LCS). Then activate the Planning Optimization in the parameters (*Master planning> Setup> Planning Optimization parameters*).

6.3.2.2   Differences to the Built-In Master Planning Engine

While the technical implementation of the Planning Optimization is different from the built-in master planning engine, the implemented functionality matches for the most part. In the Feature management workspace, there are multiple Planning Optimization features which have been added with the Dynamics 365 updates.

With all these features enabled, there are still differences currently – in particular related to production control.

In order to check whether these differences are relevant for you, open the form *Master planning> Setup> Planning Optimization fit analysis* and click the button *Run analysis* in the action pane. Apart from the items listed in this form, there are individual features which are not listed in this analysis and which are documented in the Microsoft documentation on the Planning Optimization.

6.3.2.3   Using the Planning Optimization

On the user interface, there is no big difference between working with the Planning Optimization and the built-in master planning. You can use the same menu items for the setup and the execution of master planning, no matter if the built-in engine or the Planning Optimization service runs the calculation.

The main difference is that the Planning Optimization returns the results much faster and that you can run it at any time without a negative impact on the system performance.

If you want to view the master planning job history and the Planning Optimization logs, which eventually show important warnings, open the form *Master planning> Setup> Plans> Master plans*, select the respective plan and click the button *History* in the action pane. In the History form, the button *Logs* provides access to the warnings which have been generated (in case there are any).

6.3.3   Master Planning Setup

Before you can execute master planning, an appropriate setup needs to be done in Dynamics 365.

6.3.3.1   Master Plans

A master plan is a scenario with supply and demand calculation data which are separate from the scenarios in other master plans. Depending on the planning strategy, only one or two master plans are used. If you need more simulation scenarios, you can set up additional master plans.

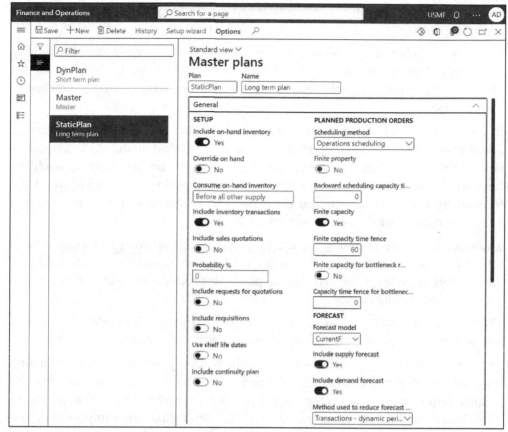

Figure 6-7:   Editing a master plan in the Master plan form

You can manage the master plans in the menu item *Master planning> Setup> Plans> Master plans*. Sliders on the tab *General* determine for each master plan, which items are included in the calculation:

➢ **Include on-hand inventory** – Refers to the current inventory.
➢ **Include inventory transactions** – This is "open orders" (e.g., purchase, sales).
➢ **Include sales quotations** – Optionally restricted by a minimum probability.
➢ **Include requests for quotation** – Entered in procurement and sourcing.
➢ **Include requisitions** – Only approved purchase requisitions with the requisition purpose "Replenishment" (see section 3.8.2).
➢ **Use shelf life dates** – For batch-controlled items.
➢ **Include continuity plans** – Related to the Retail and commerce module.
➢ **Include demand forecast** – For the *Forecast model* in the master plan.

The slider *Override on hand,* and the related lookup field *Consume on-hand inventory,* are relevant for sales order lines with the delivery date control "CTP" (see section 4.4.3). In the end this setting controls, whether the item availability for a sales order is verified in the sequence of the order entry or in the sequence of the delivery dates (or, in other words, whether a later order with an earlier date consumes the inventory first).

For sales quotations, you can optionally specify a minimum probability percentage. Only quotations with at least this probability are included in master planning. The quotation probability is given by the opportunity that is attached to the quotation.

If you want to include sales forecasts in master planning, set the slider *Include demand forecast* to "Yes" and select the appropriate forecast model in the respective field of the master plan. In order to avoid excessive demand resulting from adding forecasts for a period to actual orders in the same period, you should offset the forecast by the current orders in this case. The related setting is the reduction principle in the master plan (see section 6.3.4).

The field *Scheduling method* in the master plan controls whether to run operations scheduling or job scheduling (see section 5.4.3) for planned production orders. Among other settings for scheduling planned production orders, there is the option to apply finite capacity.

On the tab *Time fences in days* in the Master plan form, you can override the time fences which are specified in the coverage groups or in the item coverage.

The tab *Calculated delays* contains settings which specify, whether master planning may set the requirement date in planned orders to a date, which is after the original requirement date in case it is not possible to meet the original requirement date (based on the applicable lead times). This setting prevents impossible dates like a delivery date before today.

Note: Not all these settings are also covered by the Planning Optimization. If you are using the Planning Optimization, check whether you got unsupported settings in the Planning Optimization fit analysis form.

6.3.3.2 Master Planning Parameters

In the Master planning parameters (*Master planning> Setup> Master planning parameters*), there are general settings for master planning. As a prerequisite for master planning, the slider *Disable all planning processes* in the parameters has to be set to "No".

Further core parameter settings control the planning strategy: If you want to apply a one-plan strategy, enter the same master plan in the fields *Current static master plan* and *Current dynamic master plan*.

If you want to apply a two-plan strategy, select two different master plans. In a two-plan strategy, you can optionally set the slider *Copy the complete and updated static master plan...* to "Yes". In this case, the data in the dynamic plan are updated with the static plan when you execute master planning for the static plan

Note: The setting to copy the data from the static plan to the dynamic plan is only applicable with the built-in master planning engine.

6.3.3.3 Warehouse and Site Settings

If a particular warehouse (for example, a consignment warehouse that is managed by the customer) should be excluded from master planning, set the slider *Manual* for the warehouse (*Inventory management> Setup> Inventory breakdown> Warehouses,* tab *Master planning*) to "Yes".

The tab *Master planning* in the Warehouse form also contains the slider *Refilling* and the related field *Main warehouse* that control, whether the warehouse should be refilled from another warehouse (main warehouse). If selected, master planning generates item transfer proposals. As a prerequisite, the item has to contain a storage dimension group in which the checkbox *Coverage plan by dimension* is selected for the dimension "Warehouse".

If you don't need the functionality of transfer orders for transfers within a particular site, you can set the slider *Use transfer journals for movements within site* on the tab *General* in the Site form (*Inventory management> Setup> Inventory breakdown> Sites*) to "Yes". Master planning then generates a transfer journal instead of a transfer order for transfers within the site.

6.3.4   Item Coverage and Item Settings

Coverage groups and settings in the released product control the calculation of the quantity and the delivery date in planned orders.

6.3.4.1 Coverage Principle

The coverage principle, which is specified by the *Coverage code* in the coverage groups, is the primary setting for the item coverage. It controls the way in which requirements are summarized into a planned order.

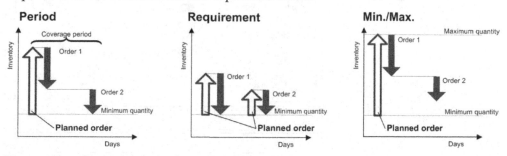

Figure 6-8:   Coverage principles in Dynamics 365

Dynamics 365 includes the following coverage principles (compare Figure 6-8):

➢ **Period** – Summarizes requirements within the coverage period (specified in the coverage group).
➢ **Requirement** – Creates a planned order per requirement.

➢ **Min./Max.** – Replenishes to the maximum quantity when inventory drops below the minimum quantity.

➢ **Manual** – Planned orders are not generated in master planning.

➢ **Priority** – Observes the field *Planning priority* in order lines and forecasts (only with Planning Optimization, requires the feature "Priority driven MRP support for Planning Optimization").

Master planning generates a planned order, if the calculated inventory at a date is below the minimum quantity (or below zero, if there is no minimum quantity in the item coverage of the released product).

6.3.4.2 Managing Coverage Groups

The coverage groups (*Master planning> Setup> Coverage> Coverage groups*) determine the coverage principle and further settings for the calculation of the quantity and the delivery date. The main setting in a coverage group is the *Coverage code*, which specifies the coverage principle. For the *Coverage code* "Period", the *Coverage period* below this field determines the number of days for aggregating demand into one planned order.

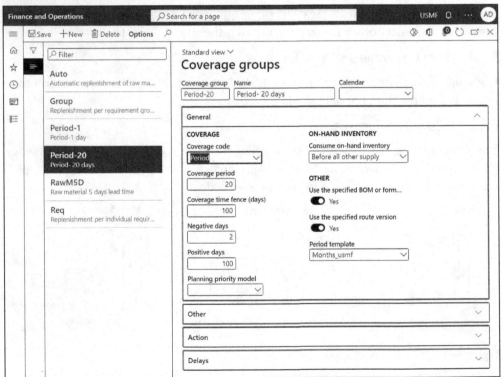

Figure 6-9:   Selecting the coverage code in a coverage group

The field *Positive days* on the tab *General* determines the time fence for including the on-hand quantity in the calculation. It should correspond to the lead time or the coverage time fence (depending on the order history).

The *Coverage time fence* on the tab *General* and the time fence fields on the tab *Other* determine the periods which are included in master planning. Depending on the planning strategy and the lead time of the items, the number of days entered in the time fence fields should cover an applicable number of weeks or months.

The *Automatic firming time fence* on the tab *Other* determines the period, in which master planning does not create a planned order but an actual purchase order or production order. If no main supplier is entered in the released product or specified in an applicable trade agreement for the purchased item, master planning still generates a planned purchase order (in which you can select the vendor). As a prerequisite for the use of vendors from trade agreements in master planning, the slider *Find trade agreement* in the Master planning parameters has to be set to "Yes".

<u>Note</u>: When specifying an *Automatic firming time fence*, be aware that auto-firming is based on the order date (start date) with Planning Optimization whereas it is based on the requirement date (end date) with the built-in master planning engine.

6.3.4.3   Forecasts and Reduction Keys

On the tab *Other* of the coverage groups, the *Forecast plan time fence* and forecast reduction settings determine how to include forecasts in master planning.

The reduction principle (field *Method used to reduce forecast requirements*) in the master plan controls the way in which forecasts are reduced when they are included as demand. If the reduction principle refers to a reduction key, a *Reduction key* has to be selected on the tab *Other* in the applicable coverage groups.

Reduction keys (*Master planning> Setup> Coverage> Reduction keys*) control the periods and percentages which are used to reduce the forecast figures in the course of time. You can, for example, use a reduction key with a reduction of 75 percent for a period of 7 days, if 75 percent of the sales orders (in terms of the quantity) for the next 7 days usually are created already and you only want to include 25 percent of the forecast demand to cover short term orders. As a prerequisite for the use of the reduction key in the coverage group, the reduction principle in the master plan has to refer to reduction keys.

If forecasts are entered for semi-finished items (hybrid supply strategy with a customer order decoupling point, see section 6.3.1), the reduction for the semi-finished product should not only include direct sales orders but also demand that derives from the finished product. Select the option "All transactions" in the lookup field *Reduce forecast by* of the coverage group to offset forecasts by all issue transactions (including production BOM line demand) in this case.

6.3.4.4   Settings for Calculated Delays and Action Messages

Action messages, which are activated on the tab *Action* in the Coverage group form, are messages from master planning which require an adjustment of actual or planned purchase and production orders. The aim of action messages is to support adjustments, which may not be done automatically – for example, postponing a purchase order which is not required at the delivery date of the order. They show optimization proposals for receipt quantities and dates. Item availability is granted, no matter if you disregard action messages.

Unlike action messages, calculated delays (activated on the tab *Delays* in the Coverage group form) show actual issues with the item availability. A calculated delay is created, if the lead time of the required items at all BOM levels results in a necessary supply before today (which causes a delay in the order fulfillment).

If both options, calculated delays and action messages, are activated, you can select the option "Delayed date" in the lookup field *Basis date* on the tab *Action* in the coverage group. With this setting, action messages are based on the earliest possible date and not on the original – perhaps impossible – requirement date.

6.3.4.5   Assigning Coverage Groups to Items

There are three levels for the assignment of a coverage group to an item:

> **Master planning parameters** – *General coverage group* in the section *General*.
> **Released product** – On the tab *Plan* in the Released product detail form.
> **Item coverage** – On the tab *General* in the Item coverage form (access with the button *Plan/Coverage/Item coverage* in the released product).

The coverage group controls the method for the calculation of order quantities. If there is a big difference in the lead time or in the cost price of the items, assign different coverage groups – based on the inventory value or the lead time – to the released products.

6.3.4.6   Dimension Group Settings

Settings in the storage and tracking dimension groups control the inventory dimensions which are kept separately in the coverage calculation. Accordingly, the dimension groups of the item determine the available dimensions in the Item coverage form and the dimensions which are calculated separately in master planning (for the supply and demand calculation per, e.g., warehouse).

You can manage the dimension groups in the menu folder *Product information management> Setup> Dimension and variant groups* (see section 7.2.2). Select the checkbox *Coverage plan by dimension* in the dimension groups of storage and tracking dimensions which should be calculated separately in master planning. Product dimensions (for product masters) and the dimension *Site* are always calculated separately.

6.3.4.7   Item Coverage

Apart from the coverage group and the dimension groups, the item coverage in the released product is another important setting for master planning.

You can access the Item coverage form with the button *Plan/Coverage/Item coverage* in the action pane of the released product. In the item coverage, you can insert records that specify a minimum and – if applicable – a maximum quantity for the item. Depending on the dimension groups of the item and the coverage settings in these dimension groups, you have to enter the item coverage per site, warehouse, or other dimensions like color or configuration.

The Item coverage form contains settings for the item at dimension level. These settings may override settings specified in the item or in the coverage group. You can, for example, select a coverage group for a particular warehouse which is different from the coverage group in the released product (for this purpose, select the checkbox *Use specific settings* above the field *Coverage group* on the tab *General* in the item coverage). You can also select a particular main vendor and planned order type – for example, if you purchase an item from an external vendor for one warehouse, but produce it internally for the other warehouses.

If you enter a minimum quantity, you can specify a seasonal distribution with the lookup field *Minimum key* on the tab *General*. The results of the minimum key are shown on the tab *Min./Max.* in the Item coverage form. In the minimum keys (*Master planning> Setup> Coverage> Minimum/Maximum keys*), you can specify a percentage per period on the tab *Periods*.

6.3.5 Master Planning and Planned Orders

Based on item requirements and coverage settings, master planning generates planned orders for purchasing, production and inventory transfer. There are two different types of master planning:

> **Local master planning** – Availability check (e.g., in a sales order line).
> **Global master planning** – Regular master planning for all items.

6.3.5.1 Global Master Planning

Global master planning generates proposals for purchase and production orders in the day-to-day business of the planning department. Depending on the company size and the item structure, master planning involves extensive calculations.

In order to start global master planning, open the menu item *Master planning> Master planning> Run> Master planning* or click the corresponding tile in the workspace *Master planning*. In the following dialog, select the applicable *Master plan* (for global master planning usually the current static master plan). The other options in the dialog are depending on whether the Planning Optimization is used.

With the Planning Optimization, the only other setting is the slider *Enable auto-firming* for enabling or preventing automatic firming within the corresponding time fence. The Planning Optimization always executes a complete calculation.

With the built-in master planning engine, the lookup *Planning method* determines the calculation principle. You can choose between the following options:

➢ **Regeneration** – Complete calculation, deleting all planned orders (except approved planned orders).
➢ **Net change** – Generates action messages and calculated delays for all requirements, but planned orders only for new requirements.
➢ **Net change minimized** – Like net change, limiting new messages to new requirements.

If the current static plan is selected, "Regeneration" is the only available planning method. For dynamic plans, also select the option "Regeneration" if there are changes in the coverage settings (e.g., a new minimum quantity for an item).

6.3.5.2 Local Master Planning

The aim of local master planning is to check the item availability and the possible delivery dates for a particular item when entering data – for example, a new sales order line. You can execute local master planning in the Net requirements form, which you can access with the button *Plan/Requirement/Net requirements* in the action pane of the released product or with the button *Product and supply/Net requirements* in the toolbar of order lines.

The Net requirements form shows the result of the last master planning cycle, by default for the dynamic master plan. If a one master plan strategy is in place, the net requirements lines for the dynamic plan are identical to those for the static plan (which is used in purchasing and production control). With the lookup field *Plan* at the top of the Net requirements form, you can switch between plans if required.

The button *Update/Master planning* in the action pane of the Net requirements form starts local master planning in the selected plan. In case you use the built-in master planning engine, take into account that not all dependencies with other items are covered by the calculation, particularly with regard to the resource capacities.

6.3.5.3 Action Messages and Calculated Delays

If calculated delays (which show availability issues) and action messages (which show optimization proposals that require manual decisions) are activated in the applicable coverage groups, master planning generates corresponding messages. These messages are shown in respective columns of the Net requirements form.

The list page *Master planning> Master planning> Calculated delays* (also included as a tile in the workspace *Master planning*) gives an overview of the calculated delays. When you open this form, select the appropriate (static or dynamic) plan in the lookup field *Plan* at the top first. If you want to access a particular order, click on the order number shown as a link in the column *Number* of the list page or click the button *Calculated delays/Open/Reference*.

The list page *Master planning> Master planning> Actions> Actions* gives an overview of the action messages. Like in the calculated delays, select a plan in the lookup field *Plan* first. With a click on the order number shown as a link in the column

Number, you can access the details of the order. If you want to execute the action message of a particular line (e.g., the action of deleting a purchase order), click the button *Apply action* in the action pane of the Action form. The button *Action graph* in the Action form provides access to a chart which shows the dependencies between related action messages.

6.3.5.4 Working with Planned Orders

Master planning generates planned orders, which you can view in the list page *Master planning> Master planning> Planned orders* and in the center section of the workspace *Master planning* (e.g., in the list *Urgent*). In order to restrict the displayed planned orders to a particular master plan, select the master plan (e.g., the static plan) in the lookup field *Plan* at the top of the list page or the workspace.

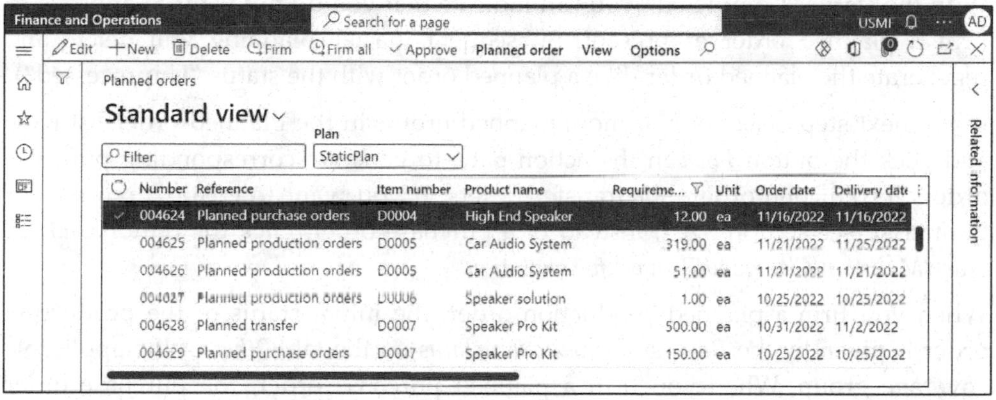

Figure 6-10: Working with planned orders

The Planned order list page in the Master planning module (and the workspace *Master planning*) show planned orders in all areas – for purchasing, for production, and for inventory transfers (indicated by the column *Reference*). A filtered view of planned orders is available in all relevant modules (e.g., *Procurement and sourcing> Purchase orders> Planned purchase orders> Planned purchase orders*).

If the master planning calculation shows that it is not possible to meet a required date and the slider *Add the calculated delay to the requirement date* on the tab *Calculated delays* in the selected master plan is set to "Yes" for the relevant order type, the *Delivery date* in the planned order is adjusted to the earliest possible date. The original – impossible – requirement date is shown in the column *Requested date*.

Apart from the delivery date and the requirement quantity, the Planned order page displays action messages and calculated delays in separate columns. The Planned order detail form, which you can open with a click on the order number shown as a link in the column *Number*, shows the details on the action message and calculated delays on the tabs *Action* and *Delays*. The tab *Pegging* in the detail form shows the demand (including sales orders, BOM lines of production orders, demand forecasts, or safety stock) that is covered by the selected planned order.

6.3.5.5 Firming Planned Orders

On the tab *Planned supply* of the Planned order detail form, you can edit the delivery date and the quantity. For planned purchase orders, make sure that a vendor number is entered in the lookup field *Vendor*. If you want to add a planned order as an additional line to an existing purchase order (instead of creating an additional purchase order), select this order in the field *Purchase order number*.

In case you do not want to firm a planned order immediately, but together with other planned orders, click the button *Approve* or *Planned order/Process/Change status* in the action pane to change the planned order status to "Approved". Subsequent master planning does not update or delete approved planned orders (important when Planning Optimization continuously updates the selected plan). With the status "Completed" you can indicate that you do not want to approve or firm a planned order at present. Subsequent master planning will delete and regenerate the planned order (like a planned order with the status "Unprocessed").

In the next step, select one or more planned orders in the Planned order list page and click the button *Firm* in the action pane to generate corresponding purchase orders, production orders, or transfer orders. If you want to create a request for quotation (see section 3.8.3) instead of a purchase order, click the button *Planned order/Maintain/Change to/Request for quotation*.

When you firm a planned production order, the initial status of the production order is given by the *Requested production status* on the tab *Other* of the applicable coverage group. When you firm a planned purchase order, the purchase order always receives the approval status "Approved" (irrespective of change management settings).

The firming history (*Master planning> Inquiries and reports> Master planning> Firming history*) displays a log of firming activities.

Apart from the Planned order form, the workspace *Master planning* also includes lists (e.g., the list *Urgent*) which you can use to edit and to firm planned orders.

6.3.5.6 Net Requirements and Explosion

In order to get an overview of the net requirements related to a planned order, click the button *View/Requirements/Requirement profile* in the action pane of the Planned order form. The requirement profile shows the Net requirements form, which you can also access from the Released product form or from the order lines.

The button *View/Requirements/Explosion* in the action pane of the Planned order form provides access to another inquiry, the Explosion form. This form, which you can also access with the button *Product and supply/Explosion* in the toolbar of sales order lines, shows the item availability including components at all BOM levels.

With the button *Setup* in the action pane of the Explosion form, you can change the display settings. The button *Explosion view* in the action pane determines the direction of the explosion: If you select "Down", the form shows the semi-finished items and components of the selected item. If you select "Up", the form shows a where-used analysis.

6.3.5.7 Supply schedule

The Supply schedule form contains a comprehensive view of the future supply and demand – similar to the net requirements but summarized per period and transaction type. As a prerequisite for the use of the supply schedule, set up period templates (*Organization administration> Setup> Calendars> Period templates*) with a period configuration on the tab *Periods*, which determines the columns in the supply schedule.

If you access the supply schedule in the menu item *Master planning> Master planning> Supply schedule*, a filter dialog is shown. In this dialog, enter a filter on the *Plan* (relevant for the display of planned orders), *Period template*, *Item* or *Item allocation key*, and – optionally – inventory dimensions.

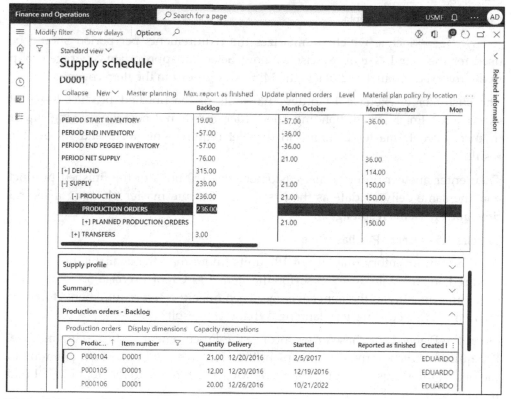

Figure 6-11:   Viewing supply details in the supply schedule

Apart from the menu item, the supply schedule is also available in many other forms. These forms show a respective button in the action pane or the toolbar – for example, the button *Plan/View/Supply schedule* in the released product or the button *Inquiries/Supply schedule* in the net requirements.

In the Supply schedule form, you can view supply and demand details on a tab at the bottom – select a cell in a period column and click the button *Expand/Collapse* in the toolbar for this purpose. With the button *New*, you can manually create planned or actual orders directly in the Supply schedule form. Alternatively, you can start local master planning with the button *Master planning*.

6.3.6   Case Study Exercises

Exercise 6.3 – Min./Max. Principle

A Min./Max. coverage principle should be used for the finished product I-##-F of exercise 5.2. Select an appropriate coverage group in the Released product form, and enter a minimum quantity (500 units) and a maximum quantity (1000 units) in the item coverage of the item.

Then run master planning in the Net requirements form and review the result. In a second step, change the minimum quantity to one unit and execute master planning a second time. Can you explain the new result?

Exercise 6.4 – Period Principle

A coverage principle which summarizes the requirements per period should be used for the item I-##-F of exercise 5.2 now. Select an appropriate coverage group in the released product and delete the Min./Max. record in the item coverage.

The customer of exercise 4.1 orders 100 units of the finished product I-##-F of exercise 5.2. Enter a corresponding sales order, but do not post the packing slip or invoice. Execute master planning in the Net requirements form and review the result.

Then enter another order of that customer with 150 units of the finished product and the same delivery date as the first order. Execute master planning a second time and check the result again.

Exercise 6.5 – Planned Purchase Order

A minimum inventory quantity of 100 units (more than the available quantity) is required in the main warehouse for the item I-##-C1 of exercise 5.1. Enter this minimum quantity in the item coverage. Then open the Net requirements form for the item and execute master planning. What is the result?

Open the Planned purchase order form in the Procurement and sourcing module. If required, switch to the dynamic plan that you have used for master planning in the net requirements. Select the planned order which refers to the item I-##-C1 and transfer it to a purchase order.

7 Inventory and Product Management

The primary responsibility of inventory management is to run the warehouse in terms of quantity and value. In order to meet this task, any update of the inventory quantity has to be registered and posted in a transaction. Most of the transactions are not a result of a business process within inventory, but derive from other areas. For example, posting a product receipt in purchasing generates an inventory transaction for the receipt.

7.1 Principles of Inventory Transactions

Before we start to go into details, the lines below show the principles of transactions in inventory management.

7.1.1 Basic Approach

Inventory management controls the inventory per product (item number). Accordingly, the most important master data in inventory management are the product records of inventoried items. Depending on the dimension groups of the particular product, the quantity and value of the item are controlled at the more detailed level of inventory dimensions. Inventory dimensions include storage dimensions (e.g., warehouse), tracking dimensions (e.g., serial number), and product dimensions (e.g., configuration).

Settings in the storage dimension group and in the warehouse control, if the basic approach for warehouse management or the advanced warehouse management (with license plates/pallets and mobile devices) is used. This chapter explains the basic approach for warehouse management. Details on the advanced warehouse management are given in section 8.1. But except for quarantine management, the features of the basic approach are also available in the advanced warehouse management.

7.1.1.1 Types of Transactions

In order to update the on-hand quantity, you need to post an item transaction. Depending on the direction, the transaction belongs to one of the following types:

> **Item receipt** – Inbound transaction.
> **Item issue** – Outbound transaction.

Item receipts increase the on-hand quantity. They include product receipts in purchasing, customer returns in sales, product receipts in production (reported as finished), positive adjustments in counting, and manual journals in inventory.

© Springer Fachmedien Wiesbaden GmbH, part of Springer Nature 2023
A. Luszczak, *Using Microsoft Dynamics 365 for Finance and Operations*,
https://doi.org/10.1007/978-3-658-40453-6_7

Item issues, which reduce the on-hand quantity, include vendor returns in purchasing, packing slips in sales, picking lists in production, negative adjustments in counting, and manual journals in inventory.

Inventory transfers, which consist of an issue from one dimension value (e.g., warehouse) and a receipt on another (e.g., warehouse), include transfer orders and transfer journals. You use transfer orders to move items from one warehouse to another, particularly if you need a picking list. Unlike transfer orders, transfer journals are not only available for transfers from one warehouse to another, but also for other dimensions (e.g., for changing a serial number in inventory).

7.1.1.2 Transactions from Other Areas

Most of the inventory transactions are not originally entered in inventory but derive from other areas in Dynamics 365. The transaction origin in the other module (e.g., a product receipt in purchasing) has to contain all data which are required to post the inventory transaction (e.g., warehouse, quantity, and cost price). In a posted inventory transaction, you can view the reference to the transaction origin, including the voucher number and date.

7.1.1.3 Inventory Quantity and Value

In order to grant an accurate inventory valuation, Dynamics 365 differentiates the physical transaction (which determines the on-hand quantity) and the financial transaction (which determines the financial value). For illustration purposes, Figure 7-1 shows the physical and the financial part of an inventory transaction related to a purchase order line.

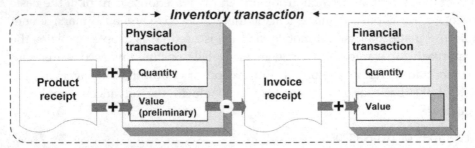

Figure 7-1:   Physical and financial transaction in inventory for a purchase order line

The physical transaction in Dynamics 365 causes a change of the on-hand quantity. An example of a physical transaction is the product receipt in purchasing. In terms of the inventory quantity, the transaction is already completed when you post the product receipt. But inventory valuation only receives a preliminary cost price. For this reason, the value of the product receipt is shown in the field *Physical cost amount* of the inventory transaction details, separate from the field *Cost amount* that contains the financial inventory value.

The second step in processing an inventory transaction is the financial transaction, which determines the cost amount for the invoiced quantity. An example of a financial transaction is the purchase order invoice. Posting the vendor invoice reverses the related posting of the preliminary cost amount of the product receipt (physical amount) and posts the final cost amount of the invoice. The invoice quantity and amount are subsequently included in the financial inventory value.

7.1.1.4 Posting Inventory Transactions

The differentiation between the physical and the financial transaction applies to each inventory transaction, no matter in which module it is generated. But the way of posting a transaction depends on the origin.

For receipt transactions in purchase orders, posting the product receipt generates the physical transaction, and posting the vendor invoice the financial transaction. In production, reporting the manufactured item as finished generates the physical transaction. The financial transaction is posted by ending the production order.

For issue transactions in sales orders, posting the packing slip generates the physical, and posting the invoice the financial transaction (similar to purchasing). In production, posting a picking list generates the physical transaction for BOM lines (materials). The financial transaction for BOM lines is posted in parallel to the financial transaction for the manufactured item when ending the production order.

Unlike the other transactions, journals in inventory management do not generate the physical and the financial transaction in two separate steps, but in parallel.

7.1.1.5 Inventory Closing

For receipt transactions, the financial value is posted finally – apart from later manual adjustments – with the invoice or with production order ending. But for issue transactions, the financial inventory value sometimes is not known – and therefore not final – when posting the invoice. You can, for example, receive the purchase invoice with the final cost price of an item after you have posted a sales invoice with the item. If there is a price on the purchase invoice which is different from the preliminary price in the product receipt, the final costs of the sold item, and therefore the profitability of the sales transaction, are modified. Depending on the date of the purchase invoice receipt, it is even possible that this change is not posted in the same period as the original sales invoice.

Except for items with a standard cost price or a moving average valuation, you need to execute inventory closing to re-evaluate issue transactions. The main purpose of inventory closing, usually a month-end procedure, is to recalculate the financial value of issue transactions based on the final value of receipt transactions.

7.1.1.6 Ledger Integration

Based on the deep integration of finance with the business processes in all areas of Dynamics 365, the inventory journal transactions are posted to ledger accounts in the same way as inventory transactions in other modules (see section 9.4).

7.1.2   At a Glance: Inventory Journal Transactions

Inventory journals are a way to update the on-hand quantity of items manually –
separate from orders in purchasing, sales, or production. The example below
shows a manual item receipt in an inventory adjustment journal. In regular
business, such transactions are an exception, since problems (or missing end-to-
end business processes) in most cases are the reason for receiving an item without
reference to a purchase order, production order, or customer return.

When you open the Inventory adjustment list page (*Inventory management> Journal
entries> Items> Inventory adjustment*), it shows all open adjustment journals which
are not posted yet. If you want to view posted journals, adjust the filter on the
column *Posted* (you can use the filter pane, the grid column filter, or the advanced
filter). A corresponding icon in the column *In use* indicates if somebody is currently
working in a particular journal. If you want to access the details of a journal, click
on the journal ID shown as a link in the grid.

In order to register a new transaction, click the button *New* in the action pane of the
list page. In the *Create inventory journal* dialog which is shown next, select a journal
name in the field *Name* and optionally enter a *Site* and a *Warehouse* (used as default
value for the lines). If you want to support later analysis, enter a short text that
explains the use of the journal in the field *Description*. The journal number in the
field *Journal* derives from the applicable number sequence.

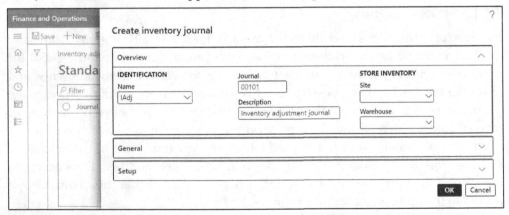

Figure 7-2:   Creating a new journal in the Inventory adjustment journal form

Once you click the button *OK* in the dialog, Dynamics 365 creates the journal
header and switches to the Journal detail form in the Lines view. If you want to
view the complete journal header, switch to the Header view (click the button
Header below the action pane).

In the Lines view, click the button *New* in the toolbar of the tab *Journal lines* to
insert a line. Select the item number in the new line before you enter the site,
warehouse, and other inventory dimensions as specified in the dimension groups
of the item. In order to control the dimension columns that are displayed in the

lines, click the button *Display dimensions* in the toolbar of the journal lines. You can also enter the dimension values on the sub-tab *Inventory dimensions* of the tab *Line details*. On the other sub-tabs, you can enter further details as applicable.

If you enter a positive quantity, the transaction is a receipt. A negative quantity creates an issue. Default values for the warehouse, quantity, and cost price derive from the default order settings of the released product. The default for the quantity is 1.00 if the default order settings do not specify a default inventory quantity.

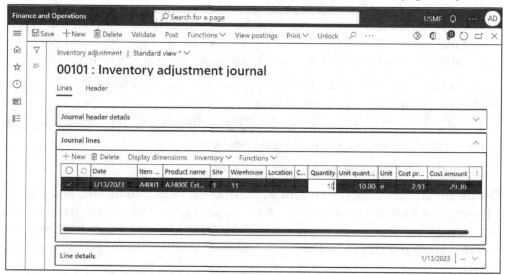

Figure 7-3:   Registering a journal line

Unlike a receipt transaction in purchasing, the inventory journal transaction is not split into a physical transaction (product receipt) and a corresponding financial transaction (invoice). Inventory journals generate the physical and the financial transaction in one step. For this reason, make sure that journal lines with a positive quantity (i.e., item receipts) contain a correct cost price when you post the journal.

Once you have entered the last journal line, post the journal with the button *Post* in the action pane of the Inventory adjustment journal list page or detail form.

Before posting, you can optionally click the button *Validate* to check potential issues.

7.2   Product Information Management

Since business processes, which refer to inventory, require inventoried products, product data represent the core area of master data in supply chain management.

The data structure of products in Dynamics 365 includes two levels – the shared products with basic item data that are common in all companies, and the released products with company-specific item data.

The product table contains all physical items – raw materials, components, semi-finished products, and finished products. But the product table also includes non-inventoried items like service items or phantom items. These items do not exist physically, but you can use them in order management or in bills of materials.

If you need to manage product versioning and engineering changes, you can use engineering change management features.

In various areas of Dynamics 365, for example in the order lines in purchasing and sales, the label "Item" is used for released products.

7.2.1   General Product Data

Details on product data with regard to purchasing, sales, production, and master planning are included in section 3.3, 4.3, 5.2.1 and 6.3.4. The current section does not include the topics which are covered in these sections. Apart from general features in the shared product and in the released product, the focus in this section is on item data in inventory, and on inventory valuation.

7.2.1.1   Structure of Product Data

In Dynamics 365, all products in the companies of a common enterprise are included in the shared product table. In order to be available in a company, the shared product has to be released to the particular company. It is not necessary to release a product to all companies at the same time – you can also release a product to some companies earlier and to other companies later.

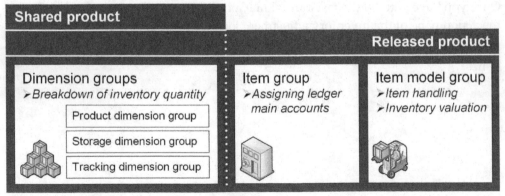

Figure 7-4:   Main control groups of a product

The shared product table contains product data that are common in all companies. These data include the *Product number*, the *Product type* ("Item" or "Service"), the *Product subtype* ("Product" or "Product master"), the *Product name* and *Description*, and the dimension groups. Apart from the *Product dimension group* for product masters, the dimension groups are not mandatory in the shared product – you can leave the dimension groups empty and enter them at the company level in the released products.

Most product details are specified at the company level in the Released product form. Required fields in the released product include the dimension groups (if not specified in the shared product), the item group, the item model group, and the units of measure.

7.2.1.2 Entering Shared Products

Depending on the requirements, there are two ways of creating a new product (compare section 3.3.2):

➢ **Start with the shared product** – Create a shared product and release it.
➢ **Start with the released product** – Create a product in the Released product form (automatically generating a shared product in the background).

In order to view the list of all shared products, open the menu item *Product information management> Products> All products and product masters*. The list pages *Products* (for items without configurations or variants) and *Product masters* (for items with variants) show a filtered view of all shared products.

If you want to create an item in the shared products (*Product information management> Products> All products and product masters*), click the button *New* in the action pane. You can subsequently release the product to one or more companies – click the button *Release products* in the action pane and select applicable companies in the *Release products* wizard for this purpose.

In order to access the released products, open the menu item *Product information management> Products> Released products*. Alternatively, you can access a released product directly from the shared product. For this purpose, click on the link in the field *Item number* on the right of the FactBox *Released to companies* and – in the *Product information* dialog, which is shown next – click on the link in the field *Item number* there.

The workspace *Released product maintenance* is another place, from which you can access the released products. In the center section of this workspace, the list *Recently released* shows the items which have been released in the past days (specify the date range with the button *Configure my workspace*) and the related validation result (missing field values).

There are two ways to create a released product: You can create and release a product in the shared products (*Product information management> Products> All products and product masters*), and you can create the released product with the button *New* directly in the Released product form. The *New released product* dialog, which includes data for the shared and for the corresponding released product (with all mandatory fields of the released product), then creates the shared product and the released product in parallel. If there are templates for released products, the additional field *Apply template*, in which you can select an appropriate template, is shown in the dialog.

You can also apply templates for released products at a later stage – click the button *Product/Maintain/Apply template* in the released product for this purpose. The template then overrides the data in the released product with data from the template. If you want to create a template in the Released product form, click the button *Product/New/Template*.

Note: Creating a product works different if your enterprise uses engineering change management (see section 7.2.5).

7.2.1.3 Product Numbers and Names

The *Product number*, which identifies the shared product, has to be unique across all companies. It is assigned automatically to new products if the number sequence for products numbers (*Product information management> Setup> Product information management parameters*, section *Number sequences*) does not require a manual assignment.

The *Item number*, which identifies the items at the released product level, usually is identical to the shared product number. As a prerequisite, the number sequence for item numbers (*Inventory management> Setup> Inventory and warehouse management parameters*, tab *Number sequences*) in relevant companies must be set to "Manual".

When you create a shared product, the default for the *Search name* derives from the *Product name*, but you can override it. In addition, you can enter a longer product description in the field *Description* on the tab *General* of the (shared) Product detail form. The *Product name* and *Description* are both entered in the system language (default language specified in the System parameters, see section 10.3.4). If there are different product names and descriptions in foreign languages, click the button *Product/Languages/Translations* in the shared product and enter the appropriate text in other languages.

Product name and description are only editable at the shared product level. The *Search name* in the shared product is a default for the released products, which you can override in the Released product form.

7.2.1.4 Product Type and Subtype

The *Product type* controls if a product is an inventoried item. Whereas the product type "Item" characterizes a regular item, the product type "Service" specifies an item without inventory control in any company of the enterprise.

The *Product subtype* controls whether the item has got variants. Whereas the product subtype "Product" applies to a regular standard item, the product subtype "Product master" characterizes a base item for assigned product variants.

For the *Product type* "Service", you can select the *Product service type* "Warranty" for selling extended warranty in the Retail and commerce module (in case the related feature is activated in the feature management).

7.2.1.5 Product Masters

For a product with the product subtype "Product master", the product number alone does not uniquely identify the item in inventory. In transactions with this item, you have to enter the product variant which distinguishes the different versions, styles, sizes, colors, or configurations of the product.

When you create a product master (a product with the product subtype "Product master"), the *Product dimension group* – one of the dimension groups described in section 7.2.2 below – is shown in the *Create product* dialog. The product dimension group of the shared product determines which of the dimensions *Version*, *Style*, *Size*, *Color* and/or *Configuration* are used for the product.

The product dimension *Version* is designated for product versions in engineering change management (see section 7.2.5).

The *Configuration technology*, which is the second mandatory field when creating a product master, determines the way to create product variants.

If you select the configuration technology "Predefined variant", you have to enter the dimension values for the product variants in the Product dimension form. Click the button *Product dimensions* in the action pane of the shared product to access this form, which shows the dimensions of the product (in line with the selected product dimension group) in the left pane.

Once you have entered the applicable product dimension values in the Product dimension form, specify the valid variants (dimension value combinations) in the Product variant form. In order to access this form, click the button *Product variants* in the shared product. The button *Variant suggestions* in the Product variant form facilitates creating new variants. But if, for example, a product is not available in all colors for each size, you might want to create the variants manually. If a product only includes one active product dimension or if all dimension combinations are valid, set the slider *Generate variants automatically* in the (shared) Product detail form to "Yes" before you enter product dimension values – with this setting, you don't have to care about entering the variants (dimension value combinations).

Before you can select a product variant in a transaction, you have to release it to the respective company. Click the button *Release products* in the action pane of the shared product for this purpose and select the variants, which you want to release, in the *Release product* wizard. Apart from releasing product variants in parallel to the product master, you can also release variants separately at a later stage. An alternative way for releasing a variant is to create a released product variant (based on the shared product variant) manually in the Released product variant form. You can access the Released product variant form with the button *Product/Product master/Released product variants* in the released product.

If applicable, you can specify a default variant for order lines and transactions on the tab *Product variants* in the Released product detail form.

If there are common variants for multiple products, you can use variant groups to populate the product dimensions. Create a variant group for sizes (*Product information management> Setup> Dimensions and variant groups> Size groups*), colors, or styles with the related dimension values for this purpose, and select the size group, color group, or style group in the (shared) Product detail form. The dimension values of the variant group are used as the default value in the product dimensions of the shared product.

Default order settings for product masters are available at the level of dimension values and variants in the released product. You can, for example, specify a default warehouse for the size "Large" and a different default warehouse for the color "Red". For an item with the size "Large" and the color "Red", the priority of settings is given by the field *Rank* in the default order settings.

7.2.1.6 Core Settings in Released Products

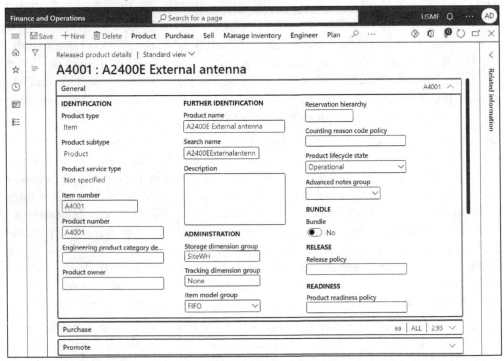

Figure 7-5:   Managing an item in the Released product form

Whereas the shared products (*Product information management> Products> All products and product masters*) only include a limited number of fields, the Released product form contains a wide range of details which characterize the item.

Only a few fields in the released product are mandatory, including the unit of measure, the item group, the item model group (see section 7.2.3), and – either at shared product level or at released product level – the dimension groups (see section 7.2.2). You can click the button *Product/Maintain/Validate* in the released product to check whether a released product contains all mandatory data.

Apart from these mandatory fields, further important data in the released product include the item sales tax groups and the cost price (see section 7.3.3).

7.2.1.7 Units of Measure

When you release a product, Dynamics 365 applies the default unit of measure which is specified in the Inventory parameters (field *Unit* in the section *General*). As long as no transaction with the item has been registered, it is possible to change the inventory unit of a released product.

If an item requires different units of measure in purchasing, sales, and inventory, enter the appropriate units on the tabs *Purchase*, *Sell* and *Manage inventory* of the Released product form (e.g., if you manage inventory in pieces, but purchase pallets). The selected unit in the released product initializes the unit in transactions with the item, for example in a sales order line. In the transaction, you can still override the unit. But a unit conversion between the inventory unit and the other unit needs to be specified.

Units of measure are shared across companies. If you need a new unit of measure, set it up in the menu item *Organization administration> Setup> Units> Units* before you assign it to a released product. The *Unit class* (e.g., "Quantity" or "Mass") categorizes the unit of measure. In one unit per unit class, you can set the slider *System unit* to "Yes", which means that this unit is used for quantity fields without a related unit of measure. The field *Net weight* in the Released product form is an example of such a quantity field. Order lines do not use the system unit, but contain a separate field for the quantity and for the related unit.

The button *Unit conversions* in the Units form provides access to the unit conversions. Conversions on the tab *Standard conversion* are independent of the product (e.g., the conversion between minutes and hours). On the tab *Intra-class conversions*, you can enter conversions per item number within a *Unit class*, and on the tab *Inter-class conversions* you can enter conversions across unit classes (e.g., between the weight and the quantity).

In the (shared) Product form and in the Released product form, you can access the unit conversions for an item with the button *Product/Set up/Unit conversions*.

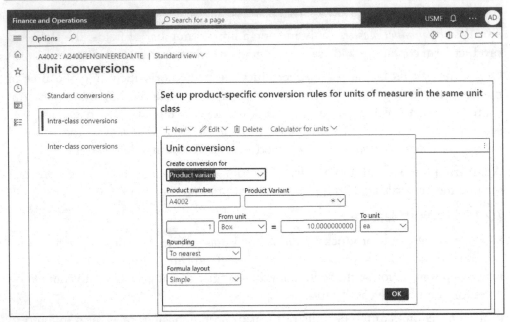

Figure 7-6:   Entering an intra-class conversion at variant level

If you want to specify unit conversions at variant level (e.g., if the number of products in a box is depending on the product dimension "Size"), set the slider *Enable unit of measure conversion* in the shared product to "Yes" (applicable for a product masters). For these products, you can optionally select the option "Product variant" in the lookup *Create conversion for* when setting up an intra-class or an inter-class conversion.

7.2.1.8 Item Groups

The main purpose of item groups (*Inventory management> Setup> Inventory> Item groups*) is to collect products, which post to a common main account in the general ledger. For this reason, you need to set up at least as many item groups as there are different stock and revenue accounts for inventoried items. You can find more details on the posting setup in section 9.4.2.

When releasing a product, you have to keep in mind that you should not change the item group on the tab *Manage costs* of the released product once the first transaction is registered. Dynamics 365 displays a warning on possible issues with inventory reconciliation in finance if you do not carefully check the consequences of changing the group. But you can still change the item group, if necessary.

Item groups are not only used for ledger integration settings in the posting setup, but they also serve as filter and sorting criterion in many reports.

7.2.1.9 Non-Inventoried Items and Services

Apart from regular products, which you want to track in inventory, there are items (e.g., services or office supplies) which are not included in inventory.

In Dynamics 365, there are two separate ways to specify whether inventory control applies to a product:

➢ **Product type** – Option "Item" or "Service".
➢ **Item model group** – Checkbox *Stocked product*.

Depending on the combination of both settings, inventory control works differently (see Table 7-1).

Table 7-1:   Options for the inventory control of products

Product type Item model group	Item	Service
Stocked product	Inventory transactions, inventory quantity	Inventory transactions, no quantity
Non-stocked product	No transactions	No transactions

The product type "Service" is used for products, which do not apply inventory control in any company of the enterprise. But if the released product is assigned to an item model group for stocked products, it still generates inventory transactions. This setting is required for intangible items and services which are part of a BOM.

If you select an item model group, in which the checkbox *Stocked product* is cleared, in a released product, there are no inventory transactions for the item. Since the item model group is assigned to the released product, this setting makes it possible to deactivate inventory control for an item at the company level.

7.2.1.10 Product Lifecycle State

In the field *Product lifecycle state* on the tab *General* in the Released product form, you can select the lifecycle state of the item. At product variant level, you can select the lifecycle state in the Released product variants form.

The setup of the required product lifecycle states (*Product information management> Setup> Product lifecycle state*) includes the slider *Is active for planning*, which you set to "No", if items with the respective state should not be included in master planning (which is the appropriate setting for obsolete items).

If engineering change management (see section 7.2.5) is enabled, the Product lifecycle state form contains the additional tab *Enabled business processes*. On this tab, you can block or enable business processes like sales orders or purchase orders for the respective lifecycle state.

With the periodic activity *Product information management> Periodic tasks> Change lifecycle state for obsolete products*, you can update the lifecycle state – usually to a state "Obsolete" – of items which have not been created recently and which are not used in a recent transaction.

Note: For engineering products (products with an *Engineering product category*), the field *Product lifecycle state* is not editable and you can only change the lifecycle state with the button *Engineer/Engineering change management/Change lifecycle state*.

7.2.1.11 Catch Weight Products

A catch weight product (*CW product*) is an item with weight as the primary unit of measure, and a secondary unit (catch weight unit) for a countable number (e.g., pieces) in parallel. The weight per unit is variable, and as a result, there is no fixed unit conversion between the weight unit and the catch weight unit. In the order lines of purchase orders, sales orders, or batch production orders, only the catch weight quantity (the countable number) is editable. When you register an inventory transaction, both, weight and catch weight quantity, have to be entered in parallel.

The catch weight functionality originates from the process industries. Examples of catch weight products are animals (or parts of animals) in food industry which require to show the counted number and the weight in parallel. Catch weight items usually apply batch numbers or serial numbers.

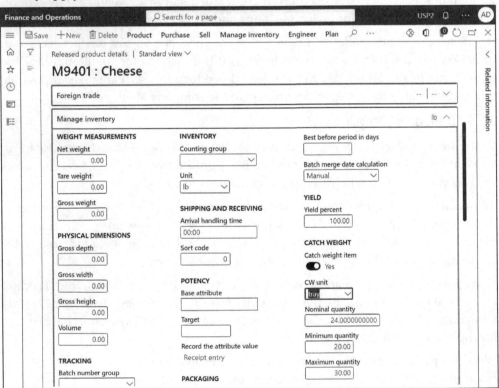

Figure 7-7:   Entering the catch weight settings in the released product

In Dynamics 365, the catch weight functionality is generally available in inventory, in purchasing, and in sales – all applicable forms contain additional fields for the catch weight. The usage in production is limited to batch orders, since only formulas, but not regular bills of materials, may include catch weight items. Because of its complexity, you should only use catch weight if you actually need to track the weight and the catch weight quantity separately.

In order to set up a catch weight item, set the slider *Catch weight* (*CW product*) to "Yes" when creating the shared product. Then click the button *Product/Set up/Unit conversions* in the shared product and enter an *Inter-class conversion* between the inventory unit (weight) and the catch weight unit (pieces). The catch weight unit has to be a unit without decimals (*Decimal precision* = "0" in the unit).

When you release the product, the inventory unit of the item has to be a weight unit (in applicable companies, the default unit in the Inventory parameters usually is a weight unit). On the tab *Manage inventory* in the Released product form, select the catch weight unit in the field *CW unit* and enter the *Minimum quantity* and the *Maximum quantity*, which determine the range of allowed conversion (weight per unit). Then enter further data, including the item model group, item group, and dimension groups, in the same way as in any other product.

If you want to create a catch weight item directly in the released product form, you can also select the slider *Catch weight* in the *New released product* dialog and enter the details in the Released product form as described above.

When you register a purchase order line, enter the catch weight quantity (countable number) in the column *CW quantity*. The column *Quantity*, which is not editable for a catch weight item, shows the quantity according to the regular unit conversion. When you receive the item in the Registration form or in an item arrival journal (see section 3.5.3), you have to enter the CW quantity and the inventory quantity (default from the unit conversion) separately.

CW quantity and the quantity in inventory unit have to be entered separately in all inventory transactions, including sales order picking and inventory journals. Inquiries on the current inventory show both, weight and catch weight quantity.

7.2.2   Inventory Dimension Groups

Inventory dimensions control the breakdown of the inventory quantity within released products. With dimensions, you can split the inventory quantity and the transactions to a more detailed level than the item number.

7.2.2.1   Available Dimensions

The dimension groups of an item determine the inventory dimensions which you have to enter in an inventory transaction. If, for example, the dimension "Batch number" is active in the tracking dimension group of an item, you have to enter a batch number when you post a transaction with this item.

In Dynamics 365, there are the following groups which classify the inventory dimensions:

➤ **Product dimensions** – Version, style, size, color, and configuration subdivide an item based on product characteristics (only available for product masters).
➤ **Storage dimensions** – Site, warehouse, location, inventory status, and license plate represent inventory structures.
➤ **Tracking dimensions** – Batch and serial number control tracking options. The dimension "Owner" refers to vendor consignment (see section 7.4.8).

7.2.2.2 Dimension Groups and Settings

In order to set up a storage dimension group, open the menu item *Product information management> Setup> Dimension and variant groups> Storage dimension groups*. The menu items for product dimension groups and for tracking dimension groups are included in the same menu folder. The different dimension group forms look similar, except for the applicable dimensions which are specific to the particular form.

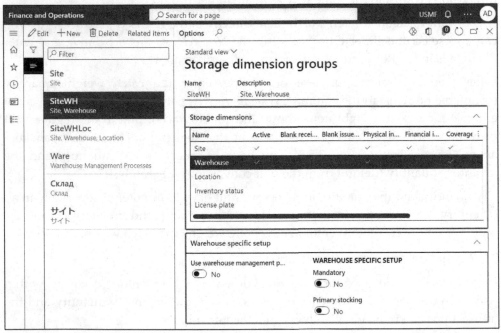

Figure 7-8:   Managing a storage dimension group

The example in Figure 7-8 shows the Storage dimension group form with the list of dimension groups in the left pane. In the right pane, you can edit the inventory dimension settings of the dimension group that is selected in the left pane.

If you need an additional dimension group, create a new record with the required inventory dimension settings (the checkbox settings are explained in Table 7-2 below).

Table 7-2:   Overview of the settings in the dimensions of a dimension group

Parameter	Explanation
Active	Dimension is used in transactions of the item
Active in sales process	Only in tracking dimension groups, for simplified serial number control in sales
Primary stocking	Dimension is mandatory in reservations; displayed as default dimension in the on-hand inquiry
Blank receipt allowed	Dimension is not mandatory receipt transactions
Blank issue allowed	Dimension is not mandatory in issue transactions
Physical inventory	Item availability per dimension value (depending on the item model group, no negative inventory, e.g., per batch number)
Financial inventory	Inventory value per dimension value (necessary for calculating the value and cost price, e.g., per warehouse)
Coverage plan by dimension	Separate item coverage in master planning per dimension value (see section 6.3.4)
For purchase prices	Dimension available for purchase price agreements
For sales prices	Dimension available for sales price agreements (see section 4.3.2)
Transfer	Only in tracking dimension groups, for consignment inventory

In storage dimension groups, the dimension *Site* (see section 10.1.6) is always active, which is why a site has to be entered in every inventory transaction. On the tab *Warehouse specific setup*, the slider *Mandatory* controls whether the warehouse has to be entered already when inserting an order line (or any other transaction) or if the warehouse may remain empty until posting. The slider *Use warehouse management processes*, which activates the inventory dimensions *Inventory status* and *License plate*, controls whether products with this group use the advanced warehouse management.

In product dimension groups, only the columns *Active*, *For purchase prices*, and *For sales prices* are available.

When you create a product, you have to select dimension groups with dimension settings which are in line with your requirements. You can, for example, only view the on-hand quantity per location, if the dimension *Location* is active for the respective item. If you need a particular dimension for some, but not for all transactions of an item, a possible way is to use a dummy dimension value for transactions in which the dimension is not applicable. If locations are only used in some warehouses, accordingly you can use dummy locations as default value in all warehouses without locations.

7.2.2.3 Dimension Groups in the Released Product

In order to assign the applicable inventory dimensions to a released product, click the button *Product/Set up/Dimension groups* in the released product. A dimension group, which is already entered in the shared product, is not editable in related released products.

In order to avoid invalid dimension values in posted transactions, it is not possible to change inventory-related settings in a dimension group once a transaction refers to the dimension group (or to change the dimension group of an item if the quantity is not Zero and there are no open transactions).

If you need to change the dimension settings of an item, post transactions which completely consume the current inventory physically and financially. Before can assign the new group, you still have to execute inventory closing.

7.2.2.4 Number Groups for Tracking Dimensions

In the Released product form, the *Tracking dimension group* controls, if batch numbers or serial numbers are used for the item. For batch number- or serial number-controlled items, you need to record the batch or serial number in all transactions. As a prerequisite to enter a batch or serial number in a transaction, this number has to be included in the batch number table (*Inventory management> Inquiries and reports> Tracking dimensions> Batches*) or the serial number table.

If your company is in charge of assigning the batch or serial numbers to the physical products (e.g., if you produce them) you can set up tracking number groups (*Inventory management> Setup> Dimensions> Tracking number groups*) to generate batch or serial numbers automatically. On the tab *General* in the Tracking number group form, you can specify the structure of the batch/serial numbers and select a *Number sequence code* for the automatic numbers (if you want to use a number sequence, set the slider *Number sequence No.* to "Yes"). If you set the slider *Reference No.* to "Yes", the order number related to a product receipt in inventory will be included in the respective serial or batch number. Settings on the tab *Activation* determine which transactions actually generate numbers. In order to assign a tracking number group for batch or serial numbers to an item, select it in the field *Batch number group* or *Serial number group* on the tab *Manage inventory* in the Released product form.

If you generate batch or serial numbers, make sure to attach a label with the serial/batch number to the physical product in order to be able to physically track the item with the serial/ batch number.

7.2.2.5 Simplified Serial Number Control in Sales Processes

If you need to track serial numbers along the whole supply chain, the tracking dimension *Serial number* has to be active. For items that are linked to a tracking dimension group with this setting, inventory transactions are split by serial number (which causes a high number of transactions). If serial number tracking is only required for warranty purposes in sales, there is no need to split inventory transactions by serial number in purchasing and other areas.

In this case, you can simplify the inventory processes by tracking serial numbers only in sales. With the sales serial number feature, there is only one inventory transaction record for all serial numbers in a transaction. The serial numbers of the transaction are stored in a separate table, which is linked to the inventory transaction. Sales serial numbers are only available for sales orders and return orders, not for other transactions (e.g., transfer orders). Serial number labels are physically attached to the item in inventory, but not tracked within Dynamics 365 until the order is shipped to or returned from the customer.

The sales serial number functionality is controlled by the tracking dimension group. If you want to use sales serial numbers, set up a dimension group in which the checkbox *Active in sales process* is selected for the dimension *Serial number*.

You can register sales serial numbers when you post the picking list registration, the packing slip, the sales invoice, or – in the advanced warehouse management – a sales transaction on the mobile device.

If you want to register serial numbers for items with sales serial number control when posting the packing slip, open the *Packing slip posting* dialog (e.g., with the button *Pick and pack/Generate/Packing slip* in the sales order). On the tab *Lines* of the posting dialog, click the button *Update line/Register serial numbers* to access the Serial numbers form. In the Serial numbers form, which supports the use of scanners, enter or scan the serial numbers one by one. If a serial number label on the physical item is missing or not readable, click the button *Not readable* for the particular item. Once you have registered all serial numbers, close the registration form and post the packing slip.

If you work with two-step picking (see section 4.5.2), you can also use the button *Register serial numbers* on the tab *Lines* in the Picking list registration form.

If you do not post a picking list or packing slip, but ship the item with the sales invoice, open the serial number registration from the *Posting invoice* dialog.

If you want to know which serial numbers have been shipped, open the serial number inquiry in the related journal. In case of a packing slip, click the button *Inquiries/Serial numbers* in the toolbar of the tab *Lines* in the packing slip journal. Tracking of sales serial numbers is also possible in the Item tracing form (*Inventory management> Inquiries and reports> Tracking dimensions> Item tracing*).

7.2.2.6 Dimension Display Settings

The primary setting for the display of dimension columns in the grid of forms is specified on the tab *Inventory dimensions* in the parameters of each relevant module. For example, the default inventory dimensions in the sales order lines are specified in the Accounts receivable parameters (*Accounts receivable> Setup> Accounts receivable parameters*, section *Inventory dimensions*).

In all forms which contain inventory dimension columns, an appropriate button – e.g., the button *Sales order line/Display/Dimensions* in the toolbar of the sales order lines, or the button *Display dimensions* in the toolbar of the inventory journal lines – provides access to a dialog which controls the dimensions that are displayed.

If you display an inventory dimension in an inquiry that shows the inventory quantity or value, take into account that the output is only reliable if the selected dimensions comply with the dimension setup. You should, for example, only report the inventory value and the cost price per warehouse, if the checkbox *Financial inventory* is selected for the dimension *Warehouse* in the applicable storage dimension group. If there is a different setting, the inventory valuation does not offset the item issue transactions with the receipt transactions at the warehouse level, which is why there is no correct cost price at the warehouse level in this case.

7.2.3 Item Model Groups

Item model groups contain settings on the valuation method and on item handling. The number of required item model groups is depending on the requirements for processing items. In a usual Dynamics 365 implementation, there are at least two groups – one for inventoried items and one for service items. In the item model group for service items, the ledger integration should be deactivated.

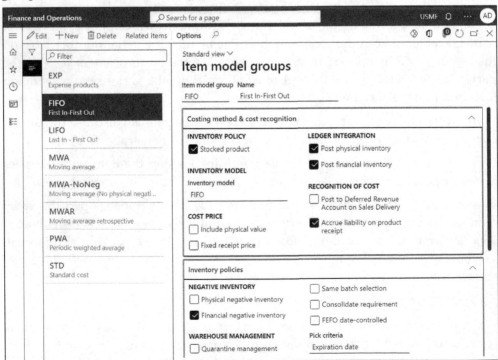

Figure 7-9:   Settings in the item model group

If you change the settings in the *Inventory model* or for the *Ledger integration* of an item model group after posting related item transactions, reconciliation of inventory and finance might become difficult. Before you modify any of these settings, you should carefully consider the consequences.

In the Item model group form (*Inventory management> Setup> Inventory> Item model groups*), the list pane on the left displays the list with the available groups. In the right pane, you can edit the settings of the group that is selected in the left pane.

7.2.3.1 Settings on Item Handling

In item model groups for inventoried items, the checkbox *Stocked product* needs to be selected. Products that are assigned to a group, in which this checkbox is cleared, do not generate inventory transactions. For non-inventoried products like service items (except for subcontracted production services), this is a valid option.

On the tab *Inventory policies*, the checkbox *Quarantine management* controls whether quarantine orders (see section 7.4.6) are created automatically when posting an item receipt.

The checkbox *Registration requirements* on this tab controls, if you have to post an inventory registration (in the Registration form, or the item arrival journal, or a mobile device transaction), before you can post the product receipt in purchasing (see section 3.5.3). The checkbox *Picking requirements* in a similar way controls posting the pick transaction before posting the packing slip in sales.

The checkboxes *Receiving requirements* and *Deduction requirements* control, if you have to post a product receipt in purchasing or a packing slip in sales before posting the invoice.

7.2.3.2 Negative Inventory

In most cases, you do not allow a negative physical inventory for inventoried items, but you do accept a negative financial inventory. A negative financial inventory is a result of posting a sales invoice before posting the purchase invoice.

Settings on negative inventory in the item model group depend on the dimension group settings: Dynamics 365 controls negative physical (or financial) inventory only at the level of the inventory dimensions, for which the checkbox *Physical inventory* (or *Financial inventory*) is selected.

7.2.3.3 Inventory Model

The selected option in the field *Inventory model* (FIFO, LIFO, weighted average, moving average, or standard cost) determines the inventory valuation method. The valuation method is the way in which issue transactions are assigned to receipt transactions in terms of valuation.

You can find more details on inventory valuation methods in section 7.3 of this book, more details on ledger integration in section 9.4.2.

7.2.4   Transactions and Inventory Quantity

Transaction inquiries and inventory quantity inquiries are included in the Released product form. But you can also access both inquiries from the order lines or journal lines in a filtered view on the current record (e.g., with the button *Inventory/ Transactions* or *Inventory/On-hand inventory* in the toolbar of the sales order lines).

The list page *Inventory management> Inquiries and reports> On-hand list* gives an overview of the on-hand quantity for multiple items (selected in a filter dialog).

7.2.4.1   Inventory Transactions Inquiry and Cost Entries

If you want to view the inventory transactions of a released product, click the button *Manage inventory/View/Transactions* in the Released product form. The Inventory transaction inquiry then shows all transactions of the selected item. The columns *Reference* and *Number* display the original voucher.

In order to view the details of a transaction, click the button *Transaction details* in the action pane.

In addition to posted transactions, the Inventory transaction form also shows future transactions which are not posted yet. These transactions include quotation lines and order lines in sales, purchasing, and production, for which no packing slip/product receipt or invoice has been posted. You can recognize such lines by the receipt status "Ordered" or the issue status "On order" ("Reserved physical" in case there is a reservation) and by the empty physical and financial date.

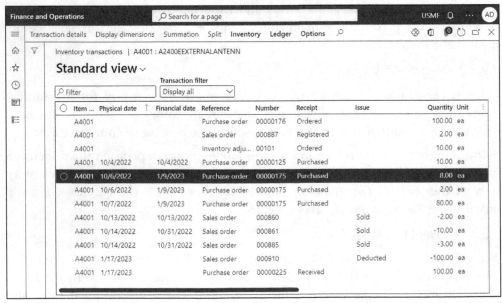

Figure 7-10:   Inventory transaction form with the transactions of an item

The cost entries of an item show a cost-oriented view of inventory transaction data. You can access the cost entries with the button *Manage costs/Cost transactions/Cost entries* in the released product.

7.2.4.2 Physical and Financial Transaction

When you post a product receipt in purchasing, a packing slip in sales, a picking list in production, or a report as finished journal, Dynamics 365 populates the *Physical date* in the inventory transaction with the posting date. In parallel, the status of the transaction changes to "Received" or "Deducted". In the Transaction detail form, the field *Physical cost amount* on the tab *Updates* shows the preliminary inventory value of the transaction.

The *Financial date* in an inventory transaction is updated when you post the related invoice in purchasing or sales, or when you end the production order. The status of the transaction then changes to "Purchased" or "Sold", and the inventory value of the transaction is shown in the column *Cost amount*.

Dynamics 365 does not change the posted financial cost amount anymore. If there is a later adjustment of the inventory value, which is posted with inventory closing or a manual adjustment, the posted difference is shown separately in the field *Adjustment* on the tab *Updates* of the Transaction detail form.

7.2.4.3 Inventory Picking and Registration

Inventory registration in purchasing (see section 3.5.3) and picking in sales (see section 4.5.2) are additional steps when processing an inventory transaction. They update the on-hand quantity of the item and the status of the inventory transaction, but unlike product receipt and packing slip transactions, inventory registration and picking do not generate an unchangeable voucher.

The date of the inventory registration (or picking) is shown in the field *Inventory date* on the tab *General* in the Transaction detail form, and it remains there when posting the packing slip in sales or the product receipt in purchasing. But if you do not proceed the regular way (post a product receipt after registration, or post a packing slip after picking), but cancel the registration, it is not possible to view the original picking or registration transaction in the inventory transactions anymore.

7.2.4.4 Transaction Details and Ledger Integration

Further details on the inventory transaction are shown on the tab *Updates* of the Transaction detail form. The fields on this tab are separated into the field groups *Physical, Ledger, Financial,* and *Settlement*.

The field group *Physical* includes the date, number and preliminary value of the product receipt or packing slip. Invoice data are shown in the field group *Financial*.

If the value of a transaction is modified after posting the invoice (as a result of inventory closing, or with a manual adjustment), the value difference is shown in the field *Adjustment*. The original financial *Cost amount* does not change anymore, all later adjustments are added in the field *Adjustment*.

The field group *Settlement* indicates if an inventory transaction is already settled by inventory closing. If the quantity of a transaction is completely settled with offsetting item issues or receipts, inventory closing populates the field *Financially closed* with the closing date and closes the transaction (the field *Value open* on the tab *General* then shows "No"). Registering a manual adjustment of a closed transaction reopens it again.

The slider *Physically posted* on the tab *Updates* of the transaction details shows if the product receipt or packing slip has been posted to the general ledger. As a prerequisite, ledger integration for physical transactions has to be activated in the item model group of the particular item.

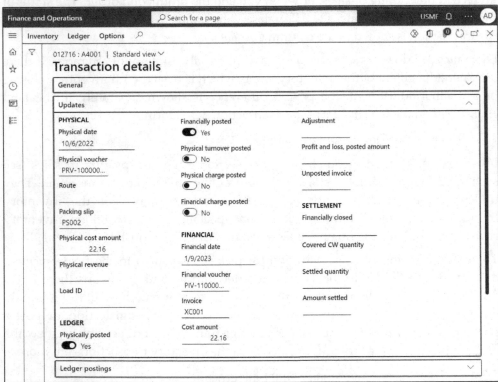

Figure 7-11:   Physical and financial data in the inventory transaction details

If ledger integration is activated for financial transactions, the option "Yes" in the slider *Financially posted* indicates that the invoice related to the inventory transaction has been posted. For purchase invoices, the slider is set to "Yes" after invoice posting even if ledger integration is not active for an item. This has got the reason that a purchase invoice for items always generates a ledger transaction: To a stock account (for the receipt transaction in case ledger integration is active) or to an expense account (for immediate financial consumption otherwise).

7.2.4.5 On-Hand Inventory Inquiry

In order to view the current inventory quantity of an item, click the button *Manage inventory/View/On-hand inventory* in the Released product form.

The related list page shows a list with the inventory quantity of the item on the different sites (or other inventory dimensions which are selected as primary dimensions for the item). For a catch-weight item, you can select the option "Catch weight quantities" instead of "Inventory quantities" in the lookup field above the grid if you want to view the quantity in catch weight units.

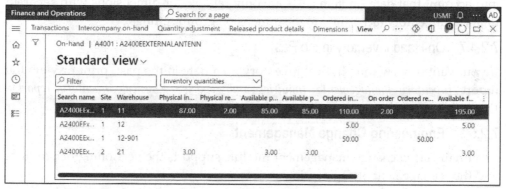

Figure 7-12: On-hand overview with the inventory quantity of an item

If you want to view the quantity at the level of other dimensions, click the button *Dimensions* in the action pane of the on-hand inquiry to open the *Dimension display* dialog, in which you can select dimensions which you want to view as columns in the inquiry. If you select, for example, the batch number in this dialog, the on-hand inquiry lines display the quantity per batch number. If you want to view the grand total quantity of the item, clear all checkboxes in the *Dimensions display* dialog.

7.2.4.6 On-Hand Inventory Details

In order to view the details of a line in the on-hand inquiry, open the On-hand detail form with a click on the link in the column *Search name* of the list page. Apart from the *Physical inventory*, which is the current quantity in inventory, the detail form shows the item availability and the current cost price (average cost price, except for items with a standard cost price or a fixed receipt price).

The physical inventory of an item is the total of the transactions with the following status:

➤ **Posted quantity** – Invoiced quantity (purchase invoices minus sales invoices).
➤ **Received** – Product receipts in purchasing, added to the posted quantity.
➤ **Deducted** – Packing slips in sales, deducted from the posted quantity.
➤ **Registered** – Registration and item arrival, added to the posted quantity.
➤ **Picked** – Picking in sales, deducted from the posted quantity.

Apart from transactions in purchasing and sales, the transactions with the related status in production and all other areas are also included in the calculation.

All data shown in the On-hand detail form refer to the dimensions of the line in the list page from which you open the detail form. In the example of Figure 7-12, the dimensions in the line of the list page are the site "1" and the warehouse "11". In line with this selection, Dynamics 365 will apply a filter on this site and warehouse when you access the related on-hand details to view the detailed quantity and cost amount information. When you review the cost price and the cost amount, take into account that data on item costs are only reliable for dimensions with separate financial inventory (according to the dimension group settings).

7.2.4.7   On Hand Inventory in the Past

If you want to view the physical inventory on a date in the past, print or view the report *Inventory management> Inquiries and reports> Physical inventory reports> Physical inventory by inventory dimension.*

7.2.5   Engineering Change Management

The Engineering change management module supports the versioning of products and the management of engineering changes.

Different from the standard way of creating a product, you start from the released product – and not from the shared product – when creating an engineering product. The shared product is automatically created in parallel (like for a regular released product). If you want to release an engineering product to other companies, you do not start from the shared product, but from the released product in the engineering company (or from an engineering change order).

Product versions of an engineering product are managed with *Engineering versions*. If it is necessary to know the product version in the individual transactions, the engineering product has to be set up as product master with an active product dimension "Version".

7.2.5.1   Required Setup for Engineering Change Management

As a prerequisite for using the engineering change management, it must be enabled in the feature management and in the license configuration. In order to use the product dimension "Version", additionally enable the feature "Product dimension version" in the feature management and in the license configuration.

Engineering companies, in which engineering products are created initially, are set up in the form *Engineering change management> Setup> Engineering organizations.*

If product versions should be tracked in inventory, one or more product dimension groups (see section 7.2.2) with an active dimension "Version" are required. With version number rules (*Engineering change management> Setup> Product version number rule*), you can specify how to generate version numbers. If the option "Auto" is selected in the field *Number rule* of this form, version numbers are automatically created as specified in the field *Format*. If the option "List" is selected, consecutive version numbers have to be specified on the tab *Version* which is shown then.

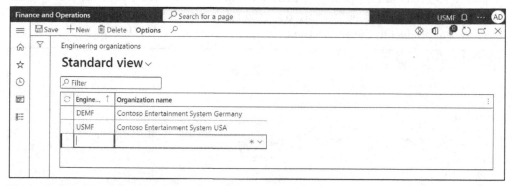

Figure 7-13: Managing the engineering organizations

The product lifecycle state (see section 7.2.1) is used to track the state and to control allowed transactions.

You can set up one or more release policies in the menu item *Engineering change management> Setup> Product release policies*. In the policies, specify for each company to which you release engineering products, if the BOM and the route should be copied (not available, if you select the *Production type* "None" in the release policy), and if/which item should be used as template.

The engineering product categories (*Engineering change management> Setup> Engineering product category details*) are a core setting for engineering change management. When creating an engineering product, the settings in the selected engineering product category determine core item characteristics like the product type, the product subtype, the product dimensions, the version number rule, and the product release policy. If the slider *Track version in transactions* is selected in the category, only *Product dimension groups* with an active dimension "Version" are available. The field *Engineering organization* in the category determines the company, in which you can use the category. If no engineering product category is assigned to a company, it is not possible to create engineering products initially in that company – you can only release engineering products from another (engineering) company to the company.

Engineering change categories (*Engineering change management> Setup> Engineering change management> Engineering change categories*) and engineering change priorities (*Engineering change management> Setup> Engineering change management> Engineering change priorities*) are mandatory in engineering change orders.

In the Engineering change management parameters, the lookup field *Product acceptance* controls whether it is necessary to accept products, BOMs and routes after they have been released from an engineering company. The parameter of the receiving company is relevant in this case.

7.2.5.2 Creating an Engineering Product

It is not possible to create an engineering product starting from a shared product. In order to create an engineering product, open the Released product form in an engineering company (engineering organization) and click the button *Product/New/Engineering product* in the action pane.

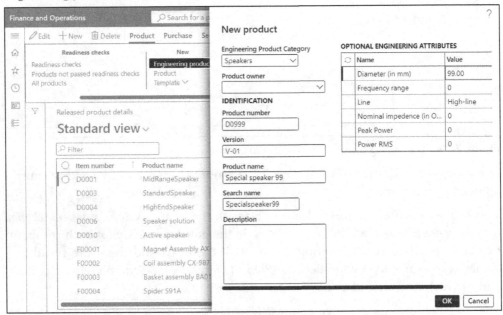

Figure 7-14: Creating an engineering product in the company DEMF

In the *New product* dialog, first select the *Engineering product category* which determines core item characteristics like the product type or the initial version (from the version number rule). Depending on the settings in this category, the product is a product master and the assigned product dimension group applies the product dimension "Version" (for tracking the version in inventory transactions). Apart from the settings which derive from the engineering product category, you can use the other fields and settings in the released product like for any other standard product, including the BOM and the route as applicable.

If you do not want to use the product only in the engineering company, but also in other companies of your enterprise, release the product to the applicable companies. For this purpose, click the button *Product/Maintain/Release product structure* in the Released product form. In the wizard which is shown next, select the applicable product (mark in the column *Select*) and optionally check the details (including BOM and route) with the button *Release details* on the first page. Then select the applicable companies in the next page before you confirm releasing. Depending on the Engineering change management parameter *Product acceptance*, the released product (including BOM and route, depending on the product release policy) is immediately available in the other companies, or only after approval in the form *Engineering change management> Common> Product releases> Open product releases*.

7.2.5.3 Working with an Engineering Product

The product lifecycle state, which you can update with the button *Engineer/ Engineering change management/Change lifecycle state* in the Released product form, controls the allowed transactions for the product (e.g., if sales orders are possible).

If the *Engineering product category* of the item determines that the product is a product master with an active product dimension "Version", the version has to be specified in all transactions and order lines – similar to the other product dimensions (e.g., the size).

7.2.5.4 Version Changes of an Engineering Product

The engineering versions of a product, which you can access with the button *Engineer/Engineering change management/Engineering versions* in the Released product form, can be used for both, for simple products without version control in inventory, and for product masters with an active product dimension "Version". Simple products are easier to work with, but only with the product dimension "Version" you got full control of the version in transactions (e.g., if you want to know which version has been shipped to a customer in case two product versions are available in parallel).

If there are changes on the product design (e.g., if you replace a component in the BOM), create a new product version (engineering version). For this purpose, enter and process an engineering change order. The engineering change request, which you can process as a prior step, is optional.

You can start an engineering change request in several forms, for example in the engineering versions of a released product. In order to create the change request there, click the button *Product/Engineering change request/New engineering change request* in this form In the Change request form, enter a *Title*, a *Priority* and a *Category* (change category, default from the Engineering change management parameters) and make sure that the respective product (including applicable product dimension values) is added on the tab *Products* of the form. If the change request should result in a change order, enter an explanation as a note on the tab *Information* and click the button *Change request/Change status/Approve* before you click the button *Change request/Engineering change order/Copy link and products*. In the following dialog *Add the engineering change request to an engineering change order*, click the button *New* to create a change order.

The change order, which you can also create directly in the form *Engineering change management> Common> Engineering change management> Engineering change orders*, is there to manage the release of new product versions in a structured way. In the engineering change order, you can add and edit the concerned products on the tab *Impacted products*. The column *Impact* in this tab controls if to create a new version or a new product. The new version or new product is shown on the tab *Product details* then. On the sub-tab *Bill of materials* and *Route,* you can manage the BOM and the route for the new version or product.

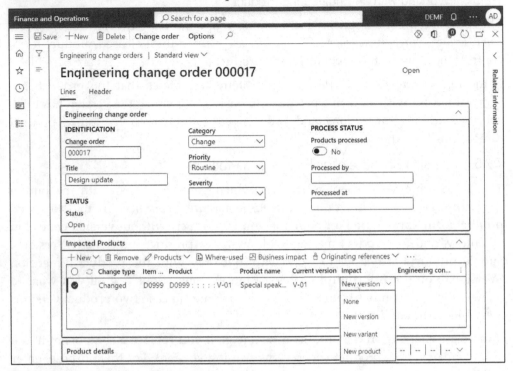

Figure 7-15: Managing an engineering change order

In order to create the new version or product, approve the change order with the button *Change order/Change status/Approve* and *Change order/Change status/Process.* In the next step, the product (including BOM and route, depending on the product release policy) can be released to other companies – like when initially creating an engineering product, but this time with the button *Change order/Product releases/ Release product structure* in the Engineering change order form.

7.2.6 Case Study Exercises

Exercise 7.1 – Dimension Groups

In order to review the functionality of dimension groups, create a new storage dimension group DS-## and a tracking dimension group DT-## (## = your user ID). Set up the dimension groups in a way that the dimensions *Site, Warehouse,* and *Batch number* are required in every transaction. For the warehouse dimension, separate financial inventory valuation should apply.

Exercise 7.2 – Item Model Group

As a preparation for the next exercise, create a new item model group T-## (## = your user ID) with FIFO valuation (inventory model "FIFO"). The ledger integration for physical and financial inventory should be active. The item model group is used for stocked products, and a negative financial inventory is allowed. All other checkboxes remain cleared, approved vendors are not required.

Then set up a second item model group S-## with standard cost valuation, which has got the same settings as the first group, except that the inventory model is "Standard cost" and a negative physical inventory is allowed.

7.3   Inventory Valuation and Cost Management

Based on the deep integration of the entire application, Dynamics 365 provides a very accurate calculation of inventory values. In addition to the valuation methods for moving average and standard costs, there is the option to use an end-to-end FIFO or LIFO valuation.

Relevant modules in this context are the Inventory management module, which contains all data on inventory quantity and value, and the Cost management module with forms and features related to inventory costing and valuation.

7.3.1   Valuation and Cost Flow

Inventory transactions update the physical inventory quantity and the financial inventory value.

In addition to the transaction in the Inventory management module, which contains the complete physical and financial record, the transaction also generates a cost entry, which only contains cost-related data. Cost entries are not generated for inventory transfers with no impact on the inventory value.

7.3.1.1   Basics of Inventory Valuation

The basis for inventory valuation is a simple principle:

➢ **Receipt costs** – The value of receipts is specified in the receipt transaction.
➢ **Issue costs** – The value of issues is calculated according to the valuation model.

The receipt transactions determine the cost price of related consumption (issue transactions). The principle for linking issue and receipt transactions is given by the valuation model (FIFO, LIFO, average cost). It is not possible to enter the cost price or the cost amount in an issue transaction.

The standard cost price, which specifies an inventory value that is irrespective of the actual costs, means an exception to this principle. In Dynamics 365, there are two options for standard cost valuation:

➢ **Standard cost** – Inventory value according to a predefined item cost price.
➢ **Fixed receipt price** – Similar to standard cost, but determining the receipt price.

The option "Fixed receipt price" is available in combination with the valuation methods FIFO, LIFO, and average cost. The fixed receipt price sets the cost price for receipts to a predefined value, which means that the cost price does not change with an actual transaction.

Unlike the fixed receipt price, the inventory model "Standard cost" constitutes a true standard cost valuation. The standard cost price of an item is immediately used in all issue and receipt transactions.

The difference between the methods "Standard cost" and "Fixed receipt price" is obvious when changing the standard cost price of an item. With the standard cost method, an adjustment of the current inventory value is immediately posted. With the fixed receipt price method, there is no adjustment of the current inventory value. The new price is only used for later receipts and the current inventory is issued with the old price until it is completely consumed.

The valuation method for an item is given by the field *Inventory model* in the item model group of the item. In the inventory model, the following options for the valuation method are available:

➢ **FIFO** – First in, first out (the value of the first receipt is consumed first).
➢ **LIFO** – Last in, first out (the value of the last receipt is consumed first).
➢ **LIFO date** – LIFO, consuming only receipts with a posting date before the issue.
➢ **Weighted average** – Average of receipts per period, calculated at the time of inventory closing/recalculation.
➢ **Weighted average date** – Average price per day.
➢ **Standard cost** – Predefined standard cost price.
➢ **Moving average** – Keeps the average cost price.

7.3.1.2 Valuation of Item Receipts

The final value of an item receipt is set by the related financial transaction (invoice). Except for items with standard cost or fixed receipt price valuation, which use a predefined cost price, the cost price in the receipt transactions is calculated as follows:

➢ **Purchase order receipt** – Amount of the invoice line including related item charges. If specified in the costing sheet, indirect costs are added.
➢ **Production receipt** – Cost amount of the production order (total costs of BOM item consumption and resource utilization, including applicable indirect costs).
➢ **Sales return** – Original value of the returned item (if assigned to an original sales order), otherwise the return cost price that is entered in the return order.
➢ **Other receipt** – Cost amount entered in the journal line.

7.3.1.3 Valuation of Item Issues

When you post an item issue (e.g., a sales packing slip), the – preliminary – cost price of the issue is given by the current average cost price (except for items with a standard cost price or a fixed receipt price). Depending on the setting in the checkbox *Include physical value* of the respective item model group, this average cost price is only based on financial transactions (invoices), or includes the preliminary value of item receipts that are not invoiced yet.

The valuation method is used with inventory closing. Based on the assigned receipts, inventory closing calculates the exact cost price of the issue transactions. For this reason, the issue price and amount are not final until you have posted the financial transaction (invoice) of all assigned receipts and inventory closing has been executed. The assignment of issues to receipts is determined by the inventory model (FIFO, LIFO, or average).

In general, the financial date (invoice date) is the basis for the chronological assignment of issue and receipt transactions. The physical date is used for items with the inventory model FIFO or LIFO if the checkbox *Include physical value* in the respective item model group is selected.

In order to determine the correct cost price and inventory value, inventory closing is required for all items – except for items with following valuation methods:

➢ **Standard cost price** – The standard cost price is immediately used in issue and receipt transactions.
➢ **Moving average** – Keeps the cost price of issue transactions (current average cost price at the time of posting) and does not require inventory closing.

These two valuation methods determine the final cost price of consumption already when the consumption is posted.

7.3.1.4 Standard Cost Price

Items with the inventory model "Standard cost" do not require inventory closing because all receipt and issue transactions immediately apply the standard cost price that is specified in the Item price form (see section 7.3.3).

When you activate a new standard cost price, Dynamics 365 immediately posts an adjustment of the current stock value in inventory and in the general ledger. Therefore, the new standard price is immediately used in issues of the current stock.

7.3.1.5 Fixed Receipt Price

The checkbox *Fixed receipt price* in the item model group is only used in combination with the valuation methods FIFO, LIFO, or average cost. With a fixed receipt price, the cost price in the Released product form or in the Item price form specifies the fixed cost price for receipt transactions. The cost price in issue transactions is calculated in line with the valuation method. But as long as you do not change the item cost price, this cost price will match the fixed receipt price of the item.

When you change the item cost price, issue and receipt transactions apply the new cost price immediately. But since there is no revaluation of the current inventory when you change a fixed receipt price, the financial value of the current inventory still complies with the old price. As a result, inventory closing is required for the option "Fixed receipt price" in order to adjust the cost amount of issue transactions to the old price according to the valuation method (until the inventory that has been received with the old price has been consumed completely).

7.3.1.6 Moving Average Price

For items with the inventory model "Moving average", receipt transactions are posted with the cost price of the transaction. When you post a vendor invoice, the financial transaction is depending on whether the quantity that is covered by the invoice is still on hand:

➢ **Complete quantity still on hand** – The total amount of the purchase invoice – including possible differences to the order – is posted as financial cost amount in inventory.
➢ **Part of the quantity already consumed** – For the quantity that is not in stock, the difference between the physical cost amount and the financial cost amount is posted as an adjustment to a price difference account.

When you post an issue transaction (e.g., a sales packing slip), the average cost price at the time of posting is used. This cost price does not change anymore, which is why inventory closing is not required.

7.3.1.7 Inventory Value Calculation

The Table 7-3 below explains the available valuation methods in Dynamics 365.

Table 7-3:   Inventory models with the valuation methods in Dynamics 365

Inventory model	Explanation
FIFO (*First In First Out*)	Item issues are assigned to the oldest item receipt still in stock
LIFO (*Last In First Out*)	Item issues are assigned to the newest item receipt in stock (including all transactions before the date of inventory closing)
LIFO date	Like LIFO, limiting the assignment of issues to receipts before the particular issue
Weighted average	The cost price of item issues in a period is the average cost price of all receipts (including the beginning balance) in this period, calculated when executing inventory closing
Weighted average date	The cost price of item issues is the average cost price, calculated separately for each day
Standard cost	The cost price of item issues and receipts matches the active standard cost price of the item
Moving average	The cost price of item issues is the average cost price of the inventory quantity at the time of posting the issue

In the following example, you can view the cost price calculation for the valuation methods that are based on the actual costs. Standard cost valuation with a pre-defined item price (independent of actual receipts) is not included in the example.

Table 7-4: Posted transactions for the comparison of valuation methods

Date	Transaction	Quantity	Cost amount
July 1	Receipt	10	100
July 2	Receipt	10	200
July 3	Issue	10	(to be calculated)
July 4	Receipt	10	300

The basis of the example are three receipt transactions with different cost prices and an issue transaction in between as shown in Table 7-4. Table 7-5 below shows the cost amount of the issue transaction after inventory closing. This cost amount is depending on the valuation method.

Table 7-5: Valuation of the item issue in Table 7-4

Inventory Model	Amount	Explanation
FIFO	100	From the receipt on July 1
LIFO	300	From the receipt on July 4
LIFO date	200	From the receipt on July 2
Weighted average	200	Average of all receipts
Weighted average date	150	From the receipts on July 1 and July 2
Moving average	150	Current average when posting the issue

7.3.1.8 Financial Inventory Dimensions and Inventory Marking

In addition to the inventory model, the inventory dimension settings have got an impact on the cost amount calculation of item issues. An assignment of an issue to a receipt is not possible across dimensions with a separate financial inventory (according to the dimension group settings).

If a separate financial inventory is, for example, activated for the dimension *Warehouse*, issues of a warehouse "20" are only assigned to receipts in warehouse "20" (including transfers). If a separate financial inventory is not activated for the dimension *Warehouse*, the assignment only complies with the date sequence – irrespective of the warehouse in the transactions.

Marking is another option with an impact on the automatic assignment according to the inventory model. Marking works as a batch for inventory valuation and assigns the cost amount of a particular receipt to a specific issue. You can use it, for example, in vendor returns (see section 3.7.1). If you want to mark a transaction, click the button *Inventory/Marking* in transactions inquiries, order lines, or journal lines.

7.3.1.9   Inventory Value Report and Cost Explorer

The inventory value report is a configurable report with the option to set up multiple report versions. As a prerequisite for this report, you have to set up at least one value report version with the report layout (*Cost management> Inventory accounting policies setup> Inventory value reports*). The settings in the layout determine which inventory value data are shown in the columns and lines of the report version. When you print the inventory value report (*Cost management> Inquiries and reports> Inventory accounting - status reports> Inventory value*), select the report layout in the field *ID* of the print dialog.

The cost explorer is an inquiry that shows the assignment and the adjustments (posted with inventory closing) of issues and receipts. In order to open the cost explorer, click the button *Inventory/Costing/Cost explorer* in an inventory transaction that has been financially posted (invoiced). You can access the inventory transactions in various ways, for example with the button *Manage inventory/View/ Transactions* in the released product.

7.3.2   Inventory Closing and Adjustment

At the time when you post an issue transaction, Dynamics 365 always applies the current average cost price (except for items with a standard cost price or a fixed receipt price). In order to calculate the final cost price and the inventory value according to the valuation method of the item, you have to close inventory. Only items assigned to the inventory model "Standard cost" or "Moving average" are not included in inventory closing.

7.3.2.1   Inventory Closing

You need to close inventory periodically – usually in the course of month end closing in finance – in order to show correct item costs in finance and to close the inventory transactions. After inventory closing, it is not possible to post inventory transactions in the closed period. If you have to post a transaction in a closed period, the only option is to reverse inventory closing.

Inventory closing is executed in the form *Inventory management> Periodic tasks> Closing and adjustment*, which by default shows the active (i.e., posted) closings. In order to close a period, usually the past month, click the button *Close procedure* in this form. The first and second option in the close procedure, the check of open quantities and the check of cost prices, generate reports that help assessing inventory transactions. You can run these reports to take corrective actions (e.g., resolve issues with missing or wrong transactions) before you actually close the period. But it is not required to complete these steps. With the button *Close procedure/Close inventory* in the Closing and adjustment form, closing is finally posted. Depending on the number of transactions, it might be useful to run closing as a batch job in the nighttime.

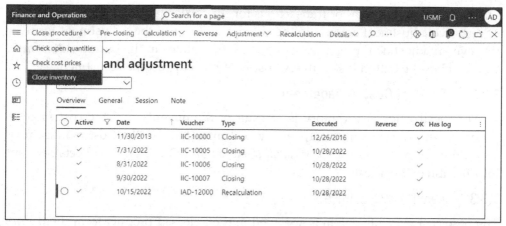

Figure 7-16:   Closing inventory for a past month in the Closing and adjustment form

As a prerequisite for closing a period in inventory, the accounting period in the ledger calendar has to be open. As far as possible, you should post all vendor invoices which refer to item receipts in purchasing, and end all production orders which are reported as finished. The corresponding product receipts in purchasing and in production then already include the financial cost amount (instead of the physical cost amount which is shown before invoicing), which minimizes the number of open transactions.

Once you have finished inventory closing, you can view the posted adjustment transactions with the button *Details/Settlements* in the Closing and adjustment form. If you have to reverse inventory closing, click the button *Reverse* in the Closing and adjustment form.

Sometimes, you want to execute the calculation and posting of inventory closing without actually closing a period – in particular, if you don't want to wait for month end closing to know the final inventory value and cost margins in line with the inventory model of the items. For this purpose, you can click the button *Recalculation* in the Closing and adjustment form.

7.3.2.2   Manual Adjustment of Inventory Value

If you want to adjust the inventory value of an item manually, use the *Adjustment* feature which includes the following options:

➢ **Adjustment/On-hand** – Adjusts the cost price and cost amount of the current financial inventory at the level of inventory dimensions (e.g., for a warehouse).

➢ **Adjustment/Transactions** – Adjusts the cost amount of particular, financially posted, receipt transactions.

➢ **Adjustment/Revaluation for moving average** – Adjusts the cost price and cost amount of the financial inventory for items with a moving average valuation.

In the Adjustment form, which you access with the related buttons in the Closing and adjustment form, click the button *Select* to open the filter dialog in which you select the respective items or transactions for the adjustment. Then enter a positive or negative adjustment amount in the column *Edit now* of the Adjustment form, or retrieve an adjustment proposal with one of the options in the button *Adjustment*. Finally, click the button *Post* in the Adjustment form to post the adjustment.

7.3.3   Product Cost Management

The financial value of inventory is a result of the quantity and the cost price of products. In order to support inventory cost management, the Cost management module with the workspaces *Cost administration* and *Cost analysis* collects relevant information on item costs.

7.3.3.1   Item Base Cost Price

The base cost price of an item is specified in the Released product form (field *Price* on the tab *Manage costs*). This base cost price is used as a default value for the cost price of item receipts in inventory journals and in counting journals (in case there is no site-specific cost price in the Item price form). In order to avoid transactions without (or with a wrong) cost price, make sure that the base cost price is correct.

If the slider *Latest cost price* on the tab *Manage costs* of the released product is set to "Yes", the base cost price in the released product is updated with each financial receipt transaction (e.g., purchase order invoice) of the item. In addition to the cost price in the Released product form, the Item price form (access with the button *Manage costs/Set up/Item price* in the released product) also shows this price update. If you want to track the history of price updates in the Item price form, activate the price history (Inventory parameters, slider *Last price history* in the section *Inventory accounting*).

The base cost price is not used for items with the valuation method "Standard cost". Standard cost price items require an active cost price in the Item price form.

7.3.3.2   Costing Versions and Item Price Form

You can manage the cost price per site (in parallel to the purchase price and the sales price per site) in the Item price form, which you access with the button *Manage costs/Set up/Item price* in the Released product form.

Before you can enter a record in the Item price form, an appropriate costing version (*Cost management> Inventory accounting> Costing versions*) has to be set up. Costing versions contain separate versions of prices and provide the option to set up different calculation principles. Items with standard cost valuation use a costing version with the *Costing type* "Standard cost". The costing type "Planned cost" refers to the other valuation methods. You can set up additional costing versions – for example, if you need to calculate prices in a simulation with other settings. In order to enter a new cost price in the Item price form, switch to the tab *Pending prices* and click the button *New*. In the new cost price, select the *Price type* "Cost" and, in the column *Version*, the applicable costing version. You have to select the

Site if it is not specified in the costing version. Apart from the *Price* itself, the Item price form contains additional details like the *Price quantity* and the *Price charges* (similar to corresponding settings in the Released product form, see section 3.3.3).

For manufactured items with a bill of materials, you can click the button *Calculate item cost* in the Item price form to run a cost calculation. Once you have entered or calculated the pending price, click the button *Activate pending price(s)* to activate it.

Only active prices are used as cost price for inventory valuation. They are shown on the tab *Active prices* in the Item price form.

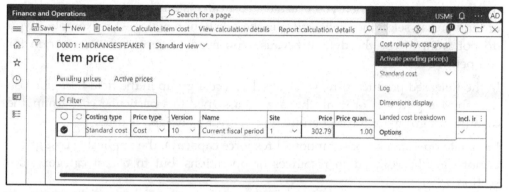

Figure 7-17: Activating a pending price in the Item price form

For product masters, cost prices are available at the product variant level, if the slider *Use cost price by variant* on the tab *Manage costs* in the released product is set to "Yes".

7.3.3.3 Calculation Groups

Calculation groups determine the basis for the calculation of cost prices and sales prices.

You can set up calculation groups in the menu item *Cost management> Predetermined cost policies setup> Calculation groups*. The default calculation group is specified in the Inventory accounting policy parameters (*Cost management> Inventory accounting policies setup> Parameters*, field group *Calculation*). At item level, you can select a *Calculation group* on the tab *Engineer* in the Released product form.

7.3.3.4 Cost Groups

Cost groups classify the different types of costs in the cost calculation on the one hand, and specify different margins for the sales price calculation on the other hand. You can edit the cost groups in the menu item *Cost management> Inventory accounting policies setup> Cost groups*. The field *Cost group type*, which determines the basic costing structure, includes the following options:

➢ **Direct materials** – For material consumption.
➢ **Direct manufacturing** – For route operations (consumption of resource capacity).

> **Direct outsourcing** – For purchased subcontracting services.
> **Indirect** – For overhead margins.
> **Undefined** – For unspecific cost classifications.

For each cost group type, you can specify a default cost group – set the slider *Default* in one cost group per *Cost group type* to "Yes" for this purpose.

Margins for the sales price calculation are specified on the tab *Profit* in the Cost group form – you can enter up to four lines with the *Profit-setting* (in general, "Standard" is selected as default value in the Cost management parameters) and the *Profit percentage*. When you execute a cost calculation or estimate a production order, you can select the *Profit-setting* in the calculation dialog – for example, if you do not want to use the default because you need to apply a lower margin for competitive reasons.

In the Released product form, you can select a cost group in the field *Cost group* on the tab *Manage costs*. For items that are not assigned to a particular cost group, the default cost group for the cost group type "Direct materials" is used.

For route operations (consumption of resource capacity), the applicable cost group is not directly assigned to resources or operations, but to a cost category (see section 5.3.3).

7.3.3.5 Costing Sheet

The costing sheet (*Cost management> Ledger integration policies setup> Costing sheets*) is there to establish a clear structure of item costs. It is used for estimation (cost estimation in production orders) and for costing (when ending production orders and in the general item price calculation), and has got two different purposes:

> **Cost classification** – Classification by cost groups.
> **Overhead costs** – Specification of rules for the calculation of overhead costs (used for both, manufactured and purchased items).

For classification purposes, the costing sheet constitutes a multi-level structure of the different costs. Apart from the cost groups, which are the bottom level in the structure, the costing sheet can contain nodes for totals at multiple levels.

Directly below the node *Root*, you can set up two primary nodes with the *Node type* "Price" – one with the *Type* "Cost of goods manufactured" (for manufactured items) and one with the *Type* "Costs of purchase" (for purchased items).

When you set up the costing sheet, make sure that the cost groups, which are assigned to manufactured items, are below the node with the *Type* "Cost of goods manufactured". The node with the *Type* "Costs of purchase" and the elements below are an optional structure, which you can use to add indirect costs in the costing sheet to the item cost price in purchase orders.

If you want to enter a new node in the costing sheet, select the higher-level node and click the button *New* in the action pane. The lowest level in the costing sheet are the nodes that are assigned to a cost group. When you can create a node for a cost group, select the option "Cost group" in the field *Select node type* of the *Create* dialog. Then select the appropriate *Cost group* on the tab *Edit* in the new node.

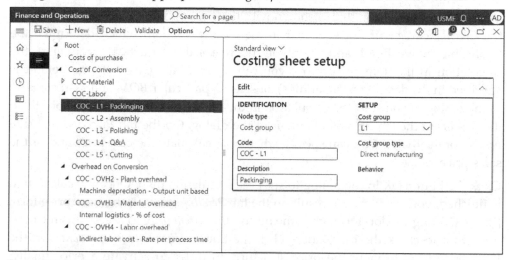

Figure 7-18: Editing the costing sheet

If you want to define overhead costs in the costing sheet, select or create a node with a *Cost group* that refers to the *Cost group type* "Indirect". Sub-nodes of such a node determine the calculation rules for overhead costs. When you create a sub-node for overhead cost calculation, select the applicable *Node type* ("Surcharge", "Rate", "Output unit based", or "Input unit based") in the dialog before you specify the basis for the calculation on the tab *Absorption basis* in the new sub-node. For a node with the type "Surcharge", enter the percentage for indirect costs on the tab *Surcharge*. For the other node types, enter an amount for indirect costs on the tab *Rate*. Then activate the indirect costs with the button *Activate* in the toolbar of this tab. Main accounts for the general ledger transactions for the indirect costs have to be entered on the tab *Ledger postings*.

Before you close the costing sheet, save the changes with the button *Save*.

7.3.3.6 Item Price Calculation

For manufactured items, you can run a price calculation that is based on the bill of materials and the route. There are two different options to execute this calculation:

➢ **Item-specific calculation** – Calculate the price of an item in the Item price form (e.g., when entering a new item).
➢ **Collective calculation** – Calculate the price of multiple items in the Costing version form (e.g., if you want to calculate all item prices once a year).

In order to calculate the price of a particular item, open the Item price form with the button *Manage costs/Set up/Item price* in the released product, switch to the tab *Pending prices* and click the button *Calculate item cost*. For a collective calculation of multiple (or all) items, open the Costing version form (*Cost management> Inventory accounting> Costing versions*), select the appropriate costing version and click the button *Calculation*.

In the calculation dialog that is shown with this button, you can select the *Site* and the *Calculation date* (if not specified in the costing version) which determine the applicable active BOM and route of the released products. If you start the calculation in the Item price form, you can override the *Quantity* (the default is specified in the default order settings), or select a particular *BOM* and *Route number* in the dialog. If you start the calculation in the costing versions, you can specify an item filter on the tab *Records to include* of the dialog. On the tab *Price recordings in version* of the dialog, you can specify whether to calculate the cost price and/or the sales price.

Click the button *OK* in the dialog to start the calculation then. Once the calculation is finished, you can view the result on the tab *Pending prices* in the Item price form (in the Costing version form, click the button *Price/Item price* to access this form). If you want to check the calculation, click the button *View calculation details* in the Item price form to view the price structure. In order to activate a price finally, select the respective pending price in the Item price form and click the button *Activate pending price(s)*.

7.3.4   Case Study Exercises

Exercise 7.3 – Product Records

As a basis for viewing the impact of settings in the dimension groups and in the item model group, create the following items in the Released product form:

➢ Item I-##-S with standard cost valuation (item model group S-## of exercise 7.2).
➢ Item I-##-T with FIFO valuation (item model group T-## of exercise 7.2).

For both items, select the product subtype "Product" and the storage/tracking dimension group which you have set up in exercise 7.1. Enter an item group for merchandise and select an item sales tax group for purchasing and for sales which refers to the standard tax rate. The unit of measurement is "Pieces". The base purchase price and the base cost price is USD 50. The base sales price is USD 100. For purchasing, inventory, and sales, enter the main site and the main warehouse in the *Default order settings*.

For the item I-##-S, you have to enter and to activate a standard cost price. Specify a standard cost price of USD 50 for the main site in the Item price form.

Note: If the number sequence for product numbers is set up for automatic numbering, don't enter a product number.

Exercise 7.4 – Inventory Value of Receipt Transactions

Enter and confirm a purchase order with the vendor of exercise 3.2. This order includes 100 units of the first item and 100 units of the second item of exercise 7.3, both at a purchase price of USD 60.

Check if you can post a product receipt without a batch number. Then open the batch table (use the option *View details* in the batch number column) and create the batch B001 for both items. Insert this batch number in both purchase order lines.

In the next step, post the product receipt and the invoice receipt for the complete quantity. If you look at the item transactions and the on-hand quantity, can you explain the different cost amount and cost price of the two items?

Note: In order to facilitate the tracking of inventory valuation, update the vendor with a sales tax group which does not apply sales tax before you enter the order.

Exercise 7.5 – Valuation after a Second Purchase Order

You want to receive 100 units of the first and of the second item of exercise 7.3 from the vendor of exercise 3.2 again. Create an appropriate purchase order and enter the batch number B001 and a purchase price of USD 80 in both order lines.

Once you have entered the order, confirm it and post the product receipt and the vendor invoice with the entire quantity. In the *Product receipt date* (on the tab *Setup* of the *Posting product receipt* dialog), and in the *Posting date* (in the vendor invoice), enter the day after the posting date of exercise 7.4 (e.g., July 2, if you have posted the transactions in exercise 7.4 with July 1).

Once you have posted the invoice, check the inventory transactions, the inventory quantity, and the inventory value (cost amount) of the two items.

Exercise 7.6 – Valuation of Sales Orders

The customer of exercise 4.1 orders 150 units of the first and 150 units of the second item of exercise 7.3. Enter a corresponding sales order with the batch number B001 in both order lines. Then post the invoice for the entire order. In the *Invoice date* on the tab *Setup* of the posting dialog, enter the day after the posting date of exercise 7.5 (e.g., July 3, if you have posted the transactions in exercise 7.5 with July 2).

Once you have posted the invoice, check the inventory transactions, the inventory quantity, and the inventory value (cost amount) of the two items again.

Exercise 7.7 – Inventory Closing

Run a *Recalculation* in the Closing and adjustment form to calculate the correct inventory value according to the valuation method. In the Recalculate inventory dialog, set the recalculation date to the posting date of exercise 7.6 (e.g., July 3) and enter a filter which restricts the calculation to the two items of this exercise.

For the selected items, check the cost price and the inventory value (cost amount) in the inventory transactions and in the on-hand inventory. Which changes are caused by the recalculation? Can you explain the result?

7.4   Business Processes in Inventory

The only way to change the inventory quantity of an item is to post an inventory transaction. Business processes, which change the inventory quantity and do not originate in inventory management, but in other functional areas like purchasing, sales, or production, generate these transactions automatically in the background.

Business processes in other areas are shown in the corresponding chapter of this book. The lines below cover the business processes within inventory in the basic approach for warehouse management. But except for the quarantine management, the functionality of the basic approach is also available in the advanced warehouse management (see section 8.1). With the advanced warehouse management, inventory transactions are registered on mobile devices in most cases, but you can, if you enter all required inventory dimensions, also post the related transactions with an inventory journal.

7.4.1   Inventory Structures and Parameters

As a prerequisite for inventory transactions, the setup in inventory management and in product management has to be finished.

7.4.1.1 Warehouse Setup

Dynamics 365 includes three storage dimensions which group the inventory according to the physical warehouse structure within the current company – *Site*, *Warehouse*, and *Location*. Depending on the applicable dimension group, you need to record these dimensions in each inventory transaction.

In order to set up a new warehouse, open the menu item *Inventory management> Setup> Inventory breakdown> Warehouses* and click the button *New*. In the new record, enter the warehouse ID, the *Name* and the *Site*. The site (see section 10.1.6) is a mandatory field that groups the warehouses within the company from a geographical and financial point of view.

The lookup field *Type* determines whether the warehouse is a regular warehouse (*Type* "Default"), or a quarantine warehouse, or a transit warehouse. Transit warehouses are used in transfer orders (see section 7.4.4), and quarantine warehouses in quarantine orders (see section 7.4.6).

The slider *Use warehouse management processes* on the tab *Warehouse* of the Warehouse form controls, whether the selected warehouse is subject to the advanced warehouse management. If it is, a further breakdown of the warehouse with the storage dimension *Location* is required (see section 8.1.1).

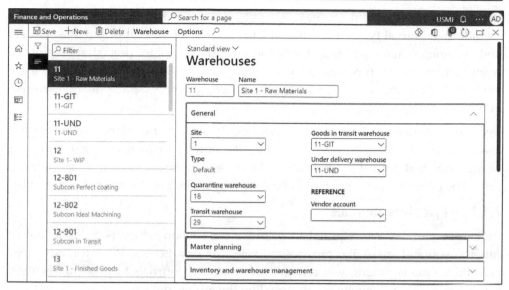

Figure 7-19: Editing a warehouse in the Warehouse form

Note: In addition to the warehouse types which are described above, there are the types "Goods in transit" and "Under delivery" used in the Landed costs module.

7.4.1.2 Storage Dimensions

When you set up warehouse structures, be aware that the storage dimension groups of the released products control the required inventory dimensions in an inventory transaction. If you need locations in a particular warehouse, the storage dimension groups of all involved items have to contain an active dimension *Location*. Since this setting requires locations for all warehouses, you need to set up at least one (dummy) location for each warehouse in this case.

7.4.1.3 Inventory Parameters and Journal Setup

If you want to enter a manual transaction in inventory, you have to use an inventory journal. Apart from sites and warehouses, inventory journal names are another required setup for the use of inventory journals. You can divide the journals in inventory among two groups:

➢ **Inventory journals** – For general transactions.
➢ **Warehouse management journals** – For receipts that are related to orders.

Inventory journals are used to register general transactions – not related to an order – like quantity adjustments, item transfers, or inventory counting. In order to set up the inventory journals, open the menu item *Inventory management> Setup> Journal names> Inventory* and enter at least one journal name for each *Journal type* (see section 7.4.2) which is used in transactions. The number sequence in the lookup field *Voucher series* provides the option to apply a separate number sequence per journal.

Warehouse management journals are used for order-related item receipts and include two journal types: Item arrival journals (for the receipt of purchase orders and customer returns) and production input journals (for the receipt of manufactured items in production). In order to create the warehouse management journals, open the menu item *Inventory management> Setup> Journal names> Warehouse management*.

Inventory parameters (*Inventory management> Setup> Inventory and warehouse management parameters*) contain settings for the number sequences, the default unit of measure, and default journal names. In the section *Inventory dimensions*, you can select the dimensions which should be shown by default in the inventory journals.

7.4.2   Inventory Journals

Inventory journals are required to record a transaction which is independent of other functional areas like purchasing, sales, or production. With the advanced warehouse management, you can still use inventory journals to post transactions, but the transactions usually are recorded on the mobile device.

7.4.2.1   Journal Structure

Since inventory transactions have an impact on finance, the voucher principle applies: First you have to enter a journal completely, before you can post it in a second step.

There are different journals for general inventory transactions, for item arrivals, and for item counting. They have got a common structure, but are divided among the following journal types:

➤ **Inventory adjustment** – Manual updates of the on-hand quantity.
➤ **Movement** – Like inventory adjustment, but with a user-defined offset account.
➤ **Transfer** – Between warehouses or other inventory dimensions.
➤ **Bill of materials** – Consume components and receive the manufactured item.
➤ **Inventory ownership change** – Financial transfer of consignment stock.
➤ **Counting** – Register the actual on-hand quantity and post adjustments.
➤ **Tag counting** – Tags as preparation for counting.
➤ **Item arrival** – Receipt related to a purchase order or sales return order.
➤ **Production input** – Receipt of manufactured items related to a production order.

The journal name setup in the inventory management includes two more journal types, which are used in other modules: The journal type "Project" for item consumption journals in the Project accounting module, and the journal type "Fixed assets" for journals that transfer items from inventory to fixed assets in the Fixed assets module.

When you open an inventory journal, the related list page with the open – not yet posted – journals is shown. If you want to view the posted journals, apply an appropriate filter on the column *Posted* (you can use the filter pane, the grid column filter, or the advanced filter). You can open the Journal detail form, which contains a Header view and a Lines view, with a click on the journal ID shown as a link in the grid.

7.4.2.2 Movement Journals and Inventory Adjustment Journals

If you want to record manual changes of the item quantity in inventory, you can use a journal with the type "Movement" or "Inventory adjustment". The difference between movement journals and inventory adjustment journals is the assignment of the offset account.

Movement journals show the field *Offset account*, in which you select the expense account for the item consumption (or the revenue account for the item receipt). In inventory adjustment journals, the offset account derives from the posting setup and is not shown in the journal lines. You use movement journals, for example, if you want to apply a particular expense account for the item consumption of a department. Since you can enter a default offset account in the journal setup (journal names), you can set up multiple journal names with the related offset account for the different use cases to facilitate the registration.

Section 7.1.2 at the beginning of the current chapter explains how to register and to post a transaction in a journal with the journal type "Inventory adjustment".

The list page *Inventory management> Journal entries> Items> Movement* shows the journals with the journal type "Movement". In order to register a new movement journal, click the button *New* in this page and select a *Name* (journal name) in the *Create* dialog. In the field *Offset account* on the tab *General* of the dialog, optionally enter a default for the offset account in the journal lines before you close the dialog with the button *OK*. In the detail form that is shown in the Lines view next, enter one or more journal lines with the posting date, item number, appropriate inventory dimension values, and quantity (a negative quantity for item issues). In the receipt transactions (with a positive quantity) of items that are not subject to a standard price valuation, the cost price is editable (default value is the base cost price in the released product or the applicable active price in the Item price form). Make sure to select an appropriate main account in the column *Offset account* before you post the movement with the button *Post* in the action pane.

7.4.2.3 Transfer Journals

Unlike movement journals and inventory adjustment journals, which record item issues and receipts, transfer journals are used to register the transfer of inventory from one dimension-combination to another. In most cases, this is the transfer from one warehouse or location to another. But you can also use a transfer journal to change batch numbers, serial numbers, or product dimension values (e.g., the color).

In order to register an item transfer, open the menu item *Inventory management> Journal entries> Items> Transfer* and create a journal with one or more journal lines (similar to an adjustment journal). But in addition to the data entered in inventory adjustment journal lines, you have to enter the applicable inventory dimensions to which the item should be transferred.

The *Quantity* should be entered with a negative sign to issue the item from the "from-dimensions" and to receive it at the "to-dimensions".

Once you have completed the journal lines, post the journal with the button *Post* in the action pane of the Journal list page or detail form.

Although you enter only one line for a transfer in the transfer journal, there are two posted inventory transactions. For example, a transfer between warehouses creates one transaction for the item issue from the shipping warehouse and one transaction for the item receipt at the receiving warehouse.

7.4.2.4 BOM Journals

Bill of materials journals (BOM journals) are used to post the receipt of a manufactured item together with the consumption of the components.

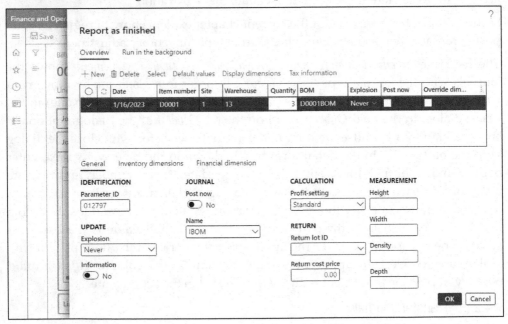

Figure 7-20: *Report as finished* dialog, accessed from the bill of materials journal

It is also possible to use bill of materials journals the other way around – to record the disassembly of a manufactured item together with the receipt of the components. But be aware, that the cost price of the components is not adjusted in this case (which can cause an adjustment of the inventory value).

In order to register a BOM journal, open the menu item *Inventory management> Journal entries> Items> Bills of materials* and create a journal. In a BOM journal, it is not required to enter journal lines manually – you can click the button *Functions/ Report as finished* in action pane of the BOM journal to create the journal lines.

In the *Report as finished* dialog, insert a line with the manufactured item that you want to receive in inventory. If the checkbox in the column *Post now* is selected, the BOM journal is posted immediately after closing the *Report as finished* dialog with the button *OK*. If the checkbox *Post now* is cleared, the manufactured item and its component are transferred to the BOM journal lines, and you can subsequently edit the journal lines before you post the journal with the button *Post*.

7.4.2.5 Item Arrival Journals

Item arrival journals are used to post an initial item receipt related to a purchase order (see section 3.5.3) or a customer return (see section 4.7.1). Production input journals, which work similar to item arrival journals, can be used to post the receipt of manufactured items related to a production order.

In order to register an item arrival journal, open the menu item *Inventory management> Journal entries> Item arrival> Item arrival* and create a journal (similar to an adjustment journal). In order to specify the reference to a purchase order, switch to the tab *Default values* in the *Create* dialog (or in the Header view of the detail form), and select the option "Purchase order" in the lookup field *Reference* before you enter the order number in the field *Number*. For customer returns, select the *Reference* "Sales order" and enter the *RMA number*. If you want to use quarantine management, make sure that the applicable slider in the field group *Mode of handling* is set to "Yes".

Once you have created the journal header, you can optionally click the button *Functions/Create lines* in the action pane of the list page or detail form to retrieve journal lines with default values for the item numbers, the inventory dimensions, and the open quantity from the purchase order lines (or the return order lines).

In order to post the arrival journal finally, click the button *Post* in the action pane of the Journal list page or detail form. Unlike inventory journals, which immediately post the physical and financial transaction, arrival journals require posting the product receipt and the invoice of the corresponding purchase order (or return order) to generate physical and financial transactions.

7.4.3 Inventory Counting

In order to determine the actual quantity in inventory, you have to execute physical inventory counting (stocktaking) in the warehouse. Depending on legal and other requirements, periodical counting is necessary to make sure that the posted quantity in Dynamics 365 is in line with the actual on-hand quantity as physically counted.

In Dynamics 365, you can either use inventory journals with the type "Counting" or – in the advanced warehouse management – mobile device transactions (see section 8.1.4) for item counting.

When you post an item counting journal, the difference between the counted quantity and the quantity in Dynamics 365 is posted as item issue or receipt – similar to the transactions in an inventory adjustment journal. The basic posting setup which determines the stock account and the offset account (expense account for a negative discrepancy or revenue account for a positive discrepancy) is the same as for adjustment journals, but you can override the offset account with a reason code (see below).

Since the counting difference is calculated as of the counting date, you do not need to stop other transactions in inventory while counting. But if required for organizational reasons, you can lock inventory – set the slider *Lock items during count* in the section *General* of the Inventory parameters to "Yes" for this purpose. In this case, a lock is set at the level of warehouse items.

7.4.3.1 Counting Journals

In order to register a counting journal, click the button *New* in the list page *Inventory management> Journal entries> Item counting> Counting*. On the tab *Counting by* in the *Create* dialog, select the inventory dimensions which are the basis for the counting journal. Once you have created the journal header, there are two ways to create the journal lines for inventory counting:

➢ **Manually** – Enter counting journal lines manually.
➢ **Automatically** – Create counting journal lines from a proposal.

You can manually enter the counting journal lines with the counting date (in the column *Date*), item number, site, warehouse, and other inventory dimensions as required. The counted quantity has to be entered in the column *Counted*. The column *On-hand* shows the corresponding inventory quantity in Dynamics 365 as of the counting date. The discrepancy between the counted and the on-hand quantity is shown in the column *Quantity*. This quantity is posted as an adjustment when posting the counting journal – depending on the sign with an issue or with a receipt transaction. In case of a positive adjustment (receipt transaction), you should review the *Cost price* in the line details, which you can update if required (except for items with standard cost valuation).

If you want to create the counting lines automatically, click the button *Create lines/ On-hand* (which creates lines for items and related inventory dimension values that are, or have been, on hand) or the button *Create lines/Items* (which creates lines for all items) in the action pane of the counting journal. In the *Create* dialog, specify a filter on the tab *Records to include* (e.g., for counting a particular warehouse). Other parameters in the dialog provide the option to restrict counting on items or on inventory dimensions (e.g., in combination with a filter on a warehouse) with an inventory transaction after the last inventory counting.

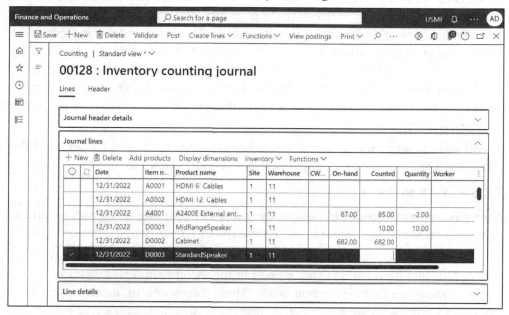

Figure 7-21: Entering the counted quantity in a counting journal line

After creating the counting journal lines manually or automatically, you can optionally print a counting list with the button *Print/Counting list* in the action pane of the counting journal (before and after entering the counted quantity).

Once you have completed the registration and the review of the counting journal, post it with the button *Post* in the action pane of the Journal list page or detail form.

7.4.3.2 Warehouse Items

Warehouse items are the level, at which the counting status is tracked and at which items are blocked while counting (in case locking is activated in the Inventory parameters). If there are multiple warehouses and you want to lock inventory while counting, create a warehouse item per released product and warehouse.

You can access the warehouse items of a released product with the button *Manage inventory/Warehouse/Warehouse items* in the Released product form. A warehouse item at the general level (with empty inventory dimensions) is automatically created when you create a released product. In order to create a warehouse item for an item and a particular warehouse, click the button *New* in the Warehouse item form and select the warehouse on the tab *General*. If you create a counting journal line with this item and warehouse later on, the counting journal is shown on the tab *Counting status* of the warehouse item until the journal is posted. If there is no warehouse item for the respective warehouse, counting is tracked in the warehouse item at the general level (with empty inventory dimensions).

7.4.3.3 Counting Groups

In order to support selecting the items in the dialog for creating counting lines, you can filter on counting groups. Counting groups (*Inventory management> Setup> Inventory> Counting groups*) are not only used for grouping and sorting purposes, but they also contain particular settings for counting. A core setting is the *Counting code*, which controls when to execute counting (periodically, when equal to or below minimum stock, or when there is no stock). You can assign a counting group at the level of the released product (on the tab *Manage inventory*) or in the warehouse item.

If you want to apply the counting code when creating counting lines, set the slider *Activate counting code* in the dialog for creating counting lines to "Yes".

7.4.3.4 Reason Codes for Counting

You can use reason codes to classify the causes of counting discrepancies and to specify particular offset accounts for posting the discrepancy in the general ledger.

If you want to use reason codes, first set up the required reason codes with ID, *Description*, and (optionally) *Offset account* in the menu item *Inventory management> Setup> Inventory> Counting reason codes*. Then create one or more reason code policies (*Inventory management> Setup> Inventory> Counting reason code policies*), in which you select whether a reason code is optional or mandatory, and assign the relevant reason code policy to the warehouses (click the button *Warehouse/Set up/ Counting reason code policy* in the Warehouse form) or the released products (click the button *Product/Set up/Counting reason code policy* in the Released product form).

If counting reason codes are set to be mandatory, you have got to select a reason code in the counting journal lines.

7.4.3.5 Tag Counting

Tag counting (*Inventory management> Journal entries> Item counting> Tag counting*) is an option to pre-register counting lines. The principle of tag counting is to attach numbered tags to the warehouse locations. When you execute counting, write the item number, quantity, and applicable inventory dimensions (e.g., warehouse and serial number) on each tag. Then collect the tags and register them in the tag-counting journal. When you post the tag-counting journal, there is no posting of inventory transactions, but a transfer of the lines to a regular counting journal.

7.4.4 Transfer Orders

Whereas inventory transfer journals move the items immediately and without shipping documents, transfer orders provide the option to manage transport times, to track the quantity which is in transit, and to print shipping documents.

7.4.4.1 Setup for Transfer Orders

As a prerequisite for the use of transfer orders, you have to set up at least one warehouse with the type "Transit" in the Warehouse form. This transit warehouse holds the items for the time of the transport. In addition, you have to assign a transit warehouse to each regular warehouse, from which you issue transfer orders.

If the dimension *Location* is activated in the applicable storage dimension groups, specify a *Default receipt location* and a *Default issue location*, usually a dummy location, in the transit warehouse (on the tab *Inventory and warehouse management* of the Warehouse form).

Delivery date control is an optional feature in transfer orders (similar to the options in sales orders, see section 4.4.3).

7.4.4.2 Processing Transfer Orders

In order to create a transfer order, open the menu item *Inventory management> Inbound orders> Transfer order* (or *Inventory management> Outbound orders> Transfer order*) and click the button *New* in the action pane. The transfer order consists of a header, in which you have to enter the *From warehouse* and the *To warehouse*, and lines, which contain the items that are transferred.

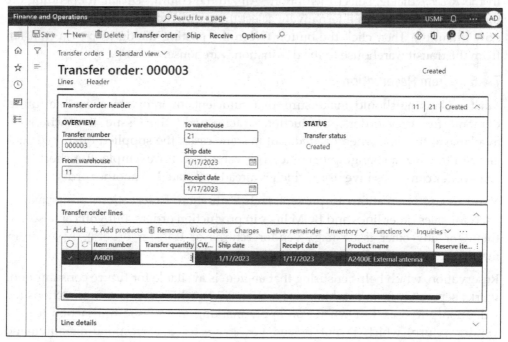

Figure 7-22: Entering a line in a transfer order

When you select the *From warehouse* in the header, the transfer order retrieves the related transit warehouse (shown on the tab *General* in the Header view). In the transfer order lines, enter one or more records with the item number, transfer quantity, and inventory dimensions as applicable.

Similar to sales order processing, you can execute picking with the basic warehouse processes (see section 4.5.2) or the advanced warehouse processes (see section 8.1.3). If picking is not mandatory (depending on the setup), you can immediately post the shipment.

In order to post the shipment (corresponding to a packing slip in sales), click the button *Ship/Operations/Ship transfer order*. In the upper pane of the *Shipment* dialog, select the option "All" in the column *Update* to ship the complete quantity (depending on the prior steps, you can alternatively select the picked quantity or the ship-now quantity). The checkbox *Print transfer shipment* provides the option to print a shipping document. When you click the button *OK* in the dialog, a transfer to the transit warehouse is posted.

When you receive the item at the destination warehouse, post the receipt. You can optionally post an inventory registration or an item arrival – similar to the options in a purchase order (see section 3.5.3) – before posting the receipt.

In order to post the transfer receipt finally (corresponding to a product receipt in purchasing), click the button *Receive/Operations/Receive* in the Transfer order form. In the *Receive* dialog, select the option "All" in the column *Update* (depending on the prior steps, you can alternatively select the registered quantity or the receive-now quantity). Then click the button *OK* in the posting dialog to post a transfer from the transit warehouse to the destination warehouse.

7.4.5   Item Reservation

Master planning should make sure, that sufficient inventory to cover the future demand for sales orders, production orders, and other issue transactions is available at the time when needed. But in some cases, the supplied quantity is not enough to cover a changing demand. This can occur, for example, if a short-term sales order consumes inventory which is already allocated to another order.

You can use reservations to prevent such a situation. Reservations are primarily used for sales order lines and BOM lines in production orders, but you can also use them for any other issue (e.g., vendor returns or transfer orders). Apart from manual reservations, there are automatic reservations.

Reservation, which helps ensuring that an item is available for future consumption, works separately from marking (see section 3.7.1), which connects transactions for valuation purposes. But when you apply marking in an issue transaction (e.g., a vendor return) which is not posted yet, it creates a corresponding automatic reservation.

7.4.5.1 Setup for Reservation

Reservation works at item number and inventory dimension level. Dimensions that are selected as *Primary stocking* in the dimension group (see section 7.2.2) have to be specified when you enter a reservation. A reservation at the lower level of further active inventory dimensions is optional, and you can still change reservations at that level later. If you use the advanced warehouse management, additional settings in reservation hierarchies are required (see section 8.1.1).

In addition to the current on-hand quantity, reservations may refer to future receipts of purchase orders or production orders. As a prerequisite for reserving quantities which are not in stock yet, the reservation of ordered items must be enabled in the Inventory parameters (slider *Reserve ordered items* in the section *General*).

If you enter a sales order line with the setting "Automatic" in the field *Reservation* on the sub-tab *Setup*, there is an automatic reservation. The default for the reservation setting in a sales order line is specified in the item model group (field *Item sales reservation*) of the item. If the selected reservation setting in the item model group is "Default", the reservation setting in the order line receives the default from the corresponding field in the order header, which again receives its default from the Accounts receivable parameters (section *General*, tab *Sales default values*, lookup field *Reservation*).

For the BOM lines in a production order, automatic reservation is controlled by the lookup field *Reservation* on the tab *Setup* in the production order header. The related default value is specified in the Production control parameters (on the tab *General*), but it is possible to override this general default with a default from the item model group (checkbox *Override item production reservation*) of the manufactured item. Unlike sales order lines, production BOM lines are not reserved automatically when creating the order, but when estimating, scheduling, releasing or starting (depending on the reservation option that is selected in the order header).

7.4.5.2 Working with Reservations

If you want to create a manual reservation in a sales order, click the button *Inventory/Reservation* in the toolbar of the sales order lines.

In the Reservation form which is shown next, you can manually enter the reserved quantity in the column *Reservation*. Alternatively, you can create the reservation with the button *Reserve lot* in the action pane of the Reservation form. With the button *Display dimensions* in the toolbar of the tab *On-hand quantities*, you can show applicable inventory dimensions for a more detailed control of the reservation at dimension level. If required, you can change or delete the quantity in the column *Reservation* and enter a quantity in another reservation line. Depending on the related Inventory parameter setting, you can only reserve from the current on-hand inventory or also from open orders.

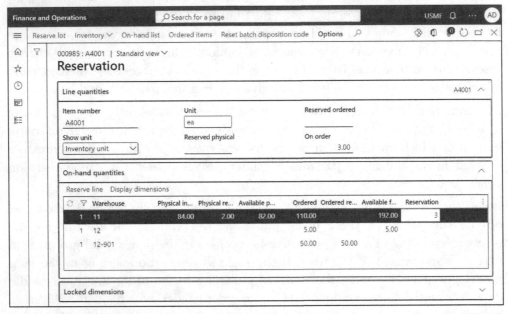

Figure 7-23:   Reserving inventory for a sales order line

Automatic reservations are generated in the background, but you can edit the reservation in the Reservation form in the same way as a manual reservation. If you enter an order line with automatic reservation and the available quantity is not sufficient to cover the automatic reservation, the *Autoreservation* dialog immediately shows the problem.

After reservation, the reserved quantity is shown with the status "Physical reserved" ("Ordered reserved", if a future receipt is reserved) in the inventory transaction and in the on-hand inquiry. The reserved quantity is not available for any other transaction.

7.4.5.3   Removing a Reservation

If the on-hand inquiry is showing a reserved quantity which you need for any other purpose, you can remove the reservation. In the on-hand inquiry (*Inventory management> Inquiries and reports> On-hand inventory*), which you can also access with the button *Overview* in the *On-hand* dialog of transaction lines (e.g., the sales order lines), you can open the inventory transactions with the button *Transactions* in the action pane. Select the respective inventory transaction with the issue status "Reserved physical" and click the button *Inventory/View/Reservation* to access the Reservation form, in which you can update the reservation as required (e.g., set the reserved quantity in the column *Reservation* to zero).

7.4.6 Quarantine and Inventory Blocking

If you want to exclude a particular quantity of an item from the available stock (e.g., because of the test results in quality control), you can alternatively use the following options:

➤ **Inventory blocking** – Temporary blocking (e.g., for the time of quality testing).
➤ **Quarantine management** – Transfer to a quarantine warehouse.

Inventory blocking, which is primarily used with quality inspection, generates a temporary inventory transaction for blocking.

Quarantine management is based on quarantine orders, which post a transfer to a quarantine warehouse. You can create quarantine orders manually whenever necessary, or automatically with each item receipt. When working with quarantine warehouses, keep in mind that only the quarantine order blocks inventory. Just posting an item transfer to a quarantine warehouse does not block inventory.

In the advanced warehouse management, inventory blocking is controlled by the inventory status. Quarantine orders are not available for warehouses with advanced warehouse management.

7.4.6.1 Setup for Quarantine Management

As a prerequisite for the use of quarantine management, set up at least one warehouse with the *Type* "Quarantine" in the Warehouse form. If you want to use automatic quarantine for item receipts, select the applicable *Quarantine warehouse* in each regular warehouse which applies quarantine.

Automatic quarantine applies to released products, which are assigned to an item model group with a checkmark in the checkbox *Quarantine management*.

7.4.6.2 Manual Quarantine

The Quarantine order list page (*Inventory management> Periodic tasks> Quality management> Quarantine orders*) shows the open quarantine orders. If you also want to view ended quarantine, select the checkbox *View ended* at the top of the page.

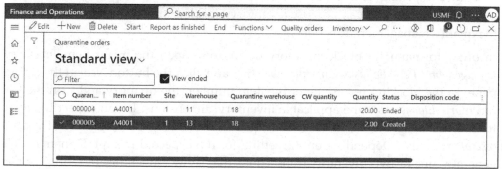

Figure 7-24: Managing quarantine in the Quarantine order form

In order to create a new quarantine order, click the button *New* in the action pane and enter the item number, quantity, site, warehouse, and other inventory dimensions as applicable. On the tab *Quarantine inventory dimensions*, the default for the quarantine warehouse is the quarantine warehouse of the initial warehouse in the quarantine order. The other quarantine inventory dimensions receive the default from the initial dimension values of the quarantine order.

In the next step, click the button *Start* in the Quarantine order form to transfer the quantity to quarantine. Starting quarantine includes transferring the item to the quarantine warehouse, generating inventory transactions for the future transfer back to the initial warehouse and, in order to block other consumption, reserving the item for the transfer back.

If you want to scrap the quarantined quantity partly or completely, click the button *Functions/Scrap* in the Quarantine order form.

In order to end quarantine, with or without prior scrapping of a partial quantity, click the button *End* in the Quarantine order form. Ending quarantine posts the transfer back to the initial warehouse and makes the quantity available again.

If you want to post the completion of inspections as an intermediate step, click the button *Report as finished* in the quarantine order. The item is not available in inventory before ending the quarantine order, which is why reporting a quarantine order as finished usually is only done if the transfer back to the initial warehouse should be posted separately.

7.4.6.3 Automatic Quarantine

When you post an item arrival journal, a production input journal, or a product receipt, Dynamics 365 automatically creates and starts a quarantine order for items that are assigned to an item model group with selected *Quarantine management*. The further processing of quarantine works similar to manual quarantine.

7.4.6.4 Inventory Blocking

Inventory blocking is typically used in combination with quality orders (see section 7.4.7). But you can also use inventory blocking manually, independently of the quality management functionality.

In order to manually block inventory of an item, open the menu item *Inventory management> Periodic tasks> Inventory blocking* and click the button *New* in the action pane. In the blocking record, enter the item number, the quantity and – on the tab *Inventory dimensions* – the applicable inventory dimensions. If you expect the item to become available again (like in a quarantine order), set the slider *Expected receipts* to "Yes". Depending on the setting for the expected receipt, Dynamics 365 generates one or two inventory transactions that show "Inventory blocking" in the column *Reference*. If you want to end inventory blocking, simply delete the line in the Inventory blocking form.

7.4.7 Quality Management

Quality management in Dynamics 365 is integrated into the supply chain and helps managing quality processes and issues. It consists of two components:

➢ **Quality control** – Manage quality orders with quality tests.
➢ **Non-conformance** – Manage quality issues.

Apart from the non-conformance functionality in quality management (*Inventory management> Periodic tasks> Quality management> Non conformances*), you can use the case management (see section 10.5.2), which is a more flexible solution, to manage quality issues. For this reason, the focus in this section is on quality control.

7.4.7.1 Setup for Quality Control

As a prerequisite for the use of the quality control functionality, quality management has to be enabled in the Inventory parameters (slider *Use quality management* in the section *Quality management*). For the tests in quality control, the following additional setup is required:

➢ **Tests** – Measure individual characteristics of the tested quantity.
➢ **Test variables** – Only for tests with results from a list of values.
➢ **Test groups** – Sequence of tests which have to be executed in a quality order.

In order to set up a test, open the menu item *Inventory management> Setup> Quality control> Tests* and insert a line with test ID, *Description*, *Type* ("Fraction" for numbers with decimals, "Integer" for whole numbers, "Option" for distinct values), and *Unit* (for the *Type* "Fraction" or "Integer"). For tests with the *Type* "Option", you have to create a test variable (*Inventory management> Setup> Quality control> Test variables*) with the list of possible results, which you enter in the test variable outcomes (access with the button *Outcomes* in the Test variable form).

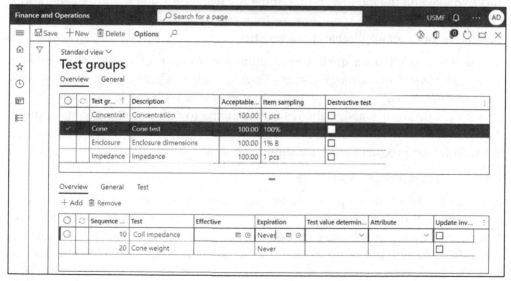

Figure 7-25: Setting up a test group

Once the tests and the applicable test variables are set up, you can create one or more test groups (*Inventory management> Setup> Quality control> Test groups*). For a test group entered in the upper pane of the Test group form, assign the individual tests in the lower pane. When you enter a test with the type "Option" in the lower pane, select the *Test variable* and the *Default outcome* on the tab *Test* in this pane. For the other test types, specify the standard value and the tolerances in the field group *Test measurement values* on this tab. If it is not possible to utilize the tested quantity after the test, select the checkbox *Destructive test* in the upper pane.

If it is required to generate quality orders automatically, set up item sampling and quality associations.

Item sampling (*Inventory management> Setup> Quality control> Item sampling*) determines the test quantity in quality orders that are generated automatically. In the field *Quantity specification*, you can select to test a percentage or a fixed quantity. As long as a quality order is not finished, the test quantity is blocked by inventory blocking (see section 7.4.6). Set the slider *Full blocking* on the tab *Process* of the Item sampling form to "Yes", if it is required to block the complete quantity of a transaction, irrespective of the percentage that is actually tested. Once you have completed the item sampling setup, you can assign item sampling to test groups (in the column *Item sampling* of the Test group form).

Quality associations (*Inventory management> Setup> Quality control> Quality associations*), which are based on items and test groups, control the automatic generation of quality orders. When you set up a quality association, select the *Reference type* (e.g., "Purchase" for purchase receipts, or "Sales" if you want to execute tests before sales shipping), the item selection (with the options "Table"/ "Group"/ "All"), and the *Test group* (on the tab *Specifications*). The fields *Event type* and *Execution* on the tab *Process* determine the trigger for quality order generation. On the tab *Conditions*, you can restrict the quality association to vendors, customers, or other applicable characteristics.

If you want to set up a quality association for a group of items, create quality groups (*Inventory management> Setup> Quality control> Quality groups*) and – with the use of *Item quality groups*, which you can access with the button *Items* in the Quality group form – assign the respective items to one or more quality groups. Alternatively, you can click the button *Manage inventory/Quality/Item quality groups* in the Released product form for assigning an item.

7.4.7.2 Processing Quality Orders

If you want to create a quality order manually, open the menu item *Inventory management> Periodic tasks> Quality management> Quality orders* and click the button *New* in the action pane. In the *Create* dialog, select the *Reference type* ("Inventory" is the default value) and, if applicable, further reference data before you enter the *Item number*, *Test group*, *Quantity*, and the required inventory dimensions. The quality order header is subsequently shown in the upper pane of the detail form, the tests as specified in the test group in the lower pane. The tested quantity is blocked by inventory blocking.

Once you have finished a test, click the button *Results* in the toolbar of the lower pane and enter the *Result quantity* and the related result (*Outcome* for the test type "Option", otherwise the *Result value*) in one or more lines of the Results form. Depending on the results of the particular test and on the *Acceptable quality level*, which is specified on the tab *Test* of the quality order, the column *Test result* on the tab *Overview* in the lower pane of the quality order indicates whether the test is passed or not. Once the last test is finished, click the button *Validate* in the action pane of the quality order. Depending on the results, the column *Status* in the quality order header then shows "Pass" or "Fail". Inventory blocking is removed, and the quantity is available again (in case the test is non-destructive).

If you need to make sure, that the quantity in the quality order is blocked further on in the event of a failed test, set the slider *Quarantine upon validation failure* in the dialog when validating the quality order to "Yes". A related quarantine order, which blocks the quality order quantity, is generated with the validation in this case. As an alternative to the use of quarantine for blocking in case of a failed test, a blocking inventory status (used with advanced warehouse management, see section 8.1.1), which is set automatically for failed quality orders, can be specified on the tab *General* in the Test group form.

If there is an applicable quality association, quality orders are automatically generated when you post the related event (e.g., a product receipt). The *Item sampling* in the quality association determines the quality order quantity. Depending on the setting *Full blocking* in the item sampling, the complete quantity or only the quality order quantity is blocked. Processing a quality order that is generated automatically works similar to a manual quality order.

7.4.8 Consignment Inventory

The consignment inventory feature in purchasing helps to control the inventory of items that are still owned by a vendor, but physically stored in your company.

The following menu items cover the business processes for consignment inventory:

➢ **Consignment replenishment orders** – For the initial product receipt.
➢ **Inventory ownership change** – Journal, in which you post the transfer of the ownership from the vendor to your company (automatically generating a purchase order as a basis for the vendor invoice).

The features, which are currently available, are limited to the core functionality. Consignment inventory is only available for items with the inventory model "Standard cost" or "Moving average" (models without inventory closing). Catch weight is not supported, and restrictions apply to master planning, advanced warehouse management, and reservation (only possible after ownership change).

Consignment inventory in sales, which means that inventory is stored at the customer site but still owned by your company, does not require a special functionality. For sales consignment, you can simply set up a warehouse "Warehouse at customer site" which you replenish with a regular transfer order.

7.4.8.1 Setup for Consignment Inventory

As a prerequisite for vendor consignment inventory, the inventory dimension *Owner* has to be activated in the tracking dimension groups (see section 7.2.2) of the relevant items. In addition, create a record in the menu item *Inventory management> Setup> Dimensions> Inventory owner* for each vendor who supplies consignment inventory (with the vendor number in the column *Vendor account*). A record with an empty vendor account is created automatically for the current company.

In the inventory journals (*Inventory management> Setup> Journal names> Inventory*), at least one journal name with the *Journal type* "Ownership change" is required.

7.4.8.2 Working with Consignment Inventory

A consignment replenishment order (*Procurement and sourcing> Consignment> Consignment replenishment orders*) with the respective vendor, which works similar to a purchase order, is the basis for the physical receipt of consignment inventory. But different from purchase orders, consignment replenishment orders have to be manually entered since it is not possible to generate such an order in master planning. For this reason, assign a coverage group with the coverage code "Manual" (see section 6.3.4) to the items that apply consignment inventory if you do not want master planning to generate regular purchase orders.

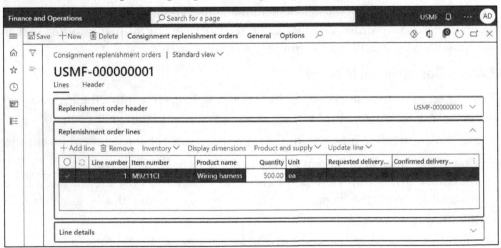

Figure 7-26:   Entering a consignment replenishment order

When you create a consignment replenishment order, enter the order lines with the item number, quantity, site, warehouse, and other inventory dimensions as applicable. At the time you receive the items, you can optionally post the inventory registration in an item arrival journal. Once you post the product receipt with the button *Consignment replenishment order/Generate/Product receipt* in the action pane of the replenishment order, the *Order status* in the Header view shows "Completed".

The product receipt of a consignment replenishment order does not generate ledger transactions. In the on-hand inquiry and in the inventory transactions, consignment inventory is shown as available quantity with the vendor as *Owner* (in the applicable tracking dimension) and no inventory value. In the vendor collaboration portal, the list page *Vendor collaboration> Consignment inventory> On-hand consignment inventory* (in a filtered view also available for applicable vendors) gives an overview of the current consignment inventory.

Before posting the inventory ownership change, the use of consignment quantity is restricted to picking list journals in production orders.

In order to post the inventory ownership change, open the menu item *Inventory management> Journal entries> Items> Inventory ownership change* and create a journal (similar to a transfer journal, see section 7.4.2). When you select the applicable vendor number in the column *From owner* of a journal line, the current company is shown in the column *To owner*. If you have already consumed vendor-owned consignment inventory for production, you can generate the ownership change journal lines based on the picked quantity (click the button *Functions/Create journal lines from production orders* in the action pane of the ownership change journal).

Posting the ownership change journal posts a transfer of the tracking dimension *Owner* to the current company and generates a purchase order with the status "Received", which is the basis for the later vendor invoice. Similar to the situation after posting a regular product receipt in a purchase order, the on-hand inquiry and the inventory transactions show the status "Received" for the related quantity, and ledger transactions for the physical receipt are posted (if ledger integration is activated for product receipts in purchasing).

7.4.9   Case Study Exercises

Exercise 7.8 – Journal Transaction

You find 100 units of the item I-## of exercise 3.5 in the main warehouse. Post an appropriate transaction in an inventory adjustment journal.

Exercise 7.9 – Transfer Journal

The quantity which you have received in exercise 7.8 is transferred to another warehouse. Register and post this transaction in an inventory transfer journal. Then check the transactions and the quantity of the item in the selected warehouse.

Exercise 7.10 – Inventory Counting

You are asked to execute inventory counting for the item I-## of exercise 3.5 in the main warehouse. The counted quantity is 51 units. Create a counting journal with a line, which you either insert manually or generate automatically (with a filter on the item and the main warehouse). Once you have entered the counted quantity, post the journal and check the on-hand quantity.

Exercise 7.11 – Transfer Order

A transfer of 60 units of the item, which you have moved to another warehouse in exercise 7.9, back to the main warehouse is required. This transfer should be processed in a transfer order. Before you create the transfer order, make sure that a transit warehouse is assigned to the warehouse from which the item is shipped. Then enter the transfer order and post the shipment. After the shipment, check the inventory transactions and the inventory quantity of the item in all warehouses. Then receive the item transfer in the main warehouse.

Exercise 7.12 – Manual Quarantine

Because of reported quality issues, you want to block the quantity in the main warehouse which you have transferred in exercise 7.11. Enter a manual quarantine order and select an appropriate quarantine warehouse. Check the on-hand quantity of the item and start the quarantine order.

After some time, you get to know that there is no problem with the item. End the quarantine and check the inventory quantity before and after ending.

Exercise 7.13 – Manual Quality Order

In order to prevent further quality issues, you want to perform quality tests. Create a new test T-## to measure the length of items in centimeters (including decimals). Then create a test group G-## which only includes this test. The standard length is 100 cm with a tolerance of 10 percent above and below.

Enter and process a quality order with this test to examine 10 units of the item I-## of exercise 3.5 in the main warehouse. The length of all tested items is 105 cm.

8 Warehouse and Transportation Management

Depending on the requirements, you want to use mobile devices and to manage detailed transactions in the warehouse. For this purpose, the advanced warehouse management in Dynamics 365 provides the necessary functionality.

Transportation management helps managing carriers and external transports. It is linked to the advanced warehouse management, but can be used independently.

In this chapter, you get to know the core functionality of the advanced warehouse and transportation management. There are additional features for a variety of further processes – e.g., packaging and containerization, shipment consolidation, purchase and sales returns, cross-docking, or quality management integration.

8.1 Advanced Warehouse Management

The advanced warehouse management in Dynamics 365, which allows registering warehouse transactions with pallets or boxes on mobile devices, is an enhancement of the basic warehouse management. Compared to the basic warehouse features, the advanced warehouse management adds the following functionality:

- ➢ **Mobile device support** – *Warehouse Management* app for small-screen devices.
- ➢ **Detailed tracking** – Using inventory transactions within the warehouse.
- ➢ **Flexible setup** – Based on location directives and work templates.
- ➢ **Picking waves** – Combine warehouse work for shipments.
- ➢ **Flexible reservation** – With reservation hierarchies.
- ➢ **Packing** – Special features for item packing.
- ➢ **Inventory status** – Storage dimension for the status of units (e.g., "Damaged").
- ➢ **License plate** – Storage dimension for handling units (e.g., pallets).

The transactions in the advanced warehouse management are regular inventory transactions. Applicable transaction types include the inventory registration (item arrival) in purchasing, picking in sales, and similar transactions in production and transfer orders. In the entire process, these transactions are prior steps to the physical transaction with the product receipt or the packing slip (see section 7.2.4).

If activated in the feature management and in the license configuration, you can use the Material handling equipment interface module to connect an external automated storage system to the advanced warehouse management.

8.1.1 Core Setup for Warehouse Management

Before you can use the advanced warehouse management, you have to complete the related setup (in addition to the setup of the basic inventory management).

© Springer Fachmedien Wiesbaden GmbH, part of Springer Nature 2023
A. Luszczak, *Using Microsoft Dynamics 365 for Finance and Operations*,
https://doi.org/10.1007/978-3-658-40453-6_8

Advanced warehouse management is only used if both conditions are met: The item is assigned to a storage dimension group, in which the advanced warehouse management processes are enabled, and the warehouse is also enabled for advanced warehouse management processes.

8.1.1.1 Parameters and Mobile Device Access

As a preparation for registering warehouse transactions on a mobile device, install the *Warehouse Management* mobile app for Dynamics 365 on your device (available for Android and for Windows). In the app, enter the required settings for the connection to the applicable Dynamics 365 environment.

For testing purposes, you can emulate the mobile app with the address *https://XXX.com/?mi=action:WHSWorkExecute&cmp=YYY* (*XXX.com* = Dynamics 365 URL, *YYY* = Company) in the web client. The web client requires signing in with a Dynamics 365 user before the separate login for a warehouse work user is shown.

The Warehouse management parameters (*Warehouse management> Setup> Warehouse management parameters*) contain basic settings for the Warehouse management module, including the number sequences in warehouse management.

Note: The *Warehouse Management* mobile app for Dynamics 365 replaces the former *Warehousing* app (which has been deprecated in April 2021) without changes to the underlying framework.

8.1.1.2 Inventory Status

The storage dimension "Inventory status" indicates the status or condition of inventory (e.g., "Good", "Damaged", or "Used"). It is only available for items with a storage dimension group, in which the advanced warehouse management processes are enabled. In warehouses with advanced warehouse management processes, the inventory status is the usual means for blocking inventory of items (quarantine management is not available for these warehouses).

As a minimum setup, a status for available inventory has to be created in the Inventory status form (*Warehouse management> Setup> Inventory> Inventory statuses*). This status is required even if there is no need to block inventory with the inventory status. Optionally, set up further status values as required. The checkbox *Inventory blocking* in the Inventory status form controls whether the status blocks inventory (you can still move the blocked quantity within the warehouse).

You can specify a default value for the inventory status of transactions at multiple levels: At the company level (in the Warehouse management parameters, section *General*, tab *Inventory status*), at the site level (in the Site form), at the warehouse level (in the Warehouse form), and in the Default item status form (*Warehouse management> Setup> Inventory> Default item status*).

Blocking via inventory status is making use of the regular blocking feature in inventory (see section 7.4.6). Details on how to change the inventory status for blocking or unblocking an item are provided in section 8.1.4.

8.1.1.3 Warehouse-Related Settings

Before you can create a warehouse that uses the advanced warehouse management processes, the following setup is required:

> ➢ **Location formats** – Specify the structure of location IDs.
> ➢ **Location types** – Indicate the purpose of a location.
> ➢ **Location profiles** – Core setting for locations.
> ➢ **Sites, warehouses, locations** – Show the physical structure of the warehouses.

Figure 8-1:   Setting up a location profile

Location formats (*Warehouse management> Setup> Warehouse> Location formats*) provide a flexible setup for the structure of location IDs. You can, for example, compose the location ID as a combination of the aisle, rack, and position ID. Since it is a required setup, you need to create at least one format with its segments.

Location types (*Warehouse management> Setup> Warehouse> Location types*) are used for filtering and grouping purposes. At least a location type for final shipping locations, which has to be selected in the Warehouse management parameters (section *General*, tab *Location types*, field *Final shipping location type*), is required. If you use staging or packing, additionally set up the related location types and select them in the Warehouse management parameters. Other location types are optional.

Location profiles (*Warehouse management> Setup> Warehouse> Location profiles*) group locations with common characteristics. These characteristics include the location format and settings on license-plate tracking, mixed items, mixed inventory status, and cycle counting.

When you create a location profile, select the applicable *Location format*. In location profiles for regular locations, the slider *Allow cycle counting* should be set to "Yes" to make counting possible. In location profiles for locations on which you want to track the quantity per license plate (required to track, e.g., pallets), the slider *Use license plate tracking* needs to be set to "Yes". For the assigned locations, all receipt and issue transactions have to include the license plate.

The location profile for user locations is selected in the Warehouse management parameters (section *General*, tab *Location profiles*). Location profiles for shipping or for staging locations have to include the *Location type* for shipping or for staging (as selected in the Warehouse management parameters).

Warehouses (*Warehouse management> Setup> Warehouse> Warehouses*) and the settings in the Warehouse form are described in section 7.4.1. In addition to the general settings, the tab *Warehouse* contains the settings for advanced warehouse management. In order to create a warehouse that uses the advanced warehouse management processes, insert a record in the Warehouse form and immediately set the slider *Use warehouse management processes* to "Yes". Then open the related warehouse locations with the button *Warehouse/View/Inventory locations* in the Warehouse form.

In the Location form, you can click the button *Location setup wizard* to create multiple locations in a convenient way. For each location, the selected location profile determines the characteristics of the location (e.g., the format of the location ID, the location type, or settings whether to allow different items in one location).

In a typical warehouse, you can find at least the following types of locations:

➢ **Receiving location** – Intermediate location for purchase receipts.
➢ **Shipping location** – Last location for sales shipping (bay door).
➢ **Buffer locations** – Storage locations for pallets and bulk items (bulk area).
➢ **Floor locations** – Storage locations for single items (picking area).

If there is the need to prepare shipments on separate locations before transferring to the shipping location, set up one or more staging locations with the appropriate location type.

User locations are automatically generated when you create a warehouse user. They are used as intermediate locations for the time between picking from one location and putting to the other location (handling time, e.g., for forklift driving).

Once you have completed the location setup, close the Location form and select a *Default receipt location* for the warehouse on the tab *Inventory and warehouse management* in the Warehouse form.

In the Site form (*Warehouse management> Setup> Warehouse> Sites*), set the slider *Allow users on mobile devices to receive at another warehouse* to "Yes" if it should be possible to receive purchase orders in a warehouse which is different from the warehouse specified in the order line (within the same site).

8.1.1.4 Basic Setup for Warehouse Work

Activities in the warehouse are reflected by "warehouse work" in Dynamics 365. In general, warehouse work consists of a pair of activities – picking from one location and putting to another location. There are two basic types of warehouse work in Dynamics 365:

> **Predefined work** – For predefined activities, like processing a sales shipment, work is generated in advance (based on work templates). Warehouse workers report the actual execution of the planned work later.
> **Unprompted work** – Unprompted work, like a manual quantity adjustment, is created and reported at the time when you execute the activity.

Unprompted work does not require a specific setup. For predefined work, the following setup is necessary:

> **Work classes** – Group and characterize work.
> **Work templates** – Determine what to do (e.g., "Pick" or "Put").
> **Location directives** – Determine where to pick or put (e.g., location "01-001").

Work classes (*Warehouse management> Setup> Work> Work classes*) for predefined work represent the different types of work that are processed on mobile devices. The field *Work order type* groups the work classes by source document type (e.g., "Raw material picking"). The work classes link mobile device menu items with work templates:

> **Mobile device menu items** – In mobile device menu items for work registration, the work class determines which work you can register with the menu item.
> **Work templates** – In the work templates for predefined work, the work class is a mandatory field which links the work template to mobile device menu items.

Work templates (*Warehouse management> Setup> Work> Work templates*) are the basis for automatically generating predefined work. When you open the Work template form, first select a *Work order type* (e.g., "Purchase orders" for item arrival related to purchase orders) in the lookup field at the top of the form. If you want to create a new work template, click the button *New* in the action pane. The upper pane subsequently shows a new record with the next available *Sequence number*. If you need to specify filter criteria, which are used for the selection of a work template when automatically creating predefined warehouse work, click the button *Edit query*. Since the sequence number, which is an editable field, determines the search sequence for the applicable template when creating work, templates with more specific criteria should be first in the sequence.

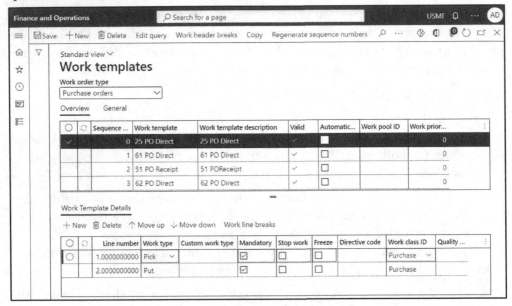

Figure 8-2:   Setting up a work template for purchase put-away

Once you have saved the work template header, switch to the tab *Work template details* and enter a line with the *Work type* "Pick" and a line with the *Work type* "Put". If required, enter additional lines – for example with the *Work type* "Print".

Location directives (*Warehouse management> Setup> Location directives*) determine the location on which the warehouse work has to be executed. Examples are the location directives for the *Work order type* "Purchase orders" and the *Work type* "Put", which determine the location to which to put an item after receiving a purchase order in the warehouse.

In the Location directive form, select the relevant *Work order type* at the top of the list pane on the left first. The related location directives are subsequently shown below. On the tab *Location directives* in the right pane, you can view the *Work type* ("Pick" / "Put") of the location directive that is selected in the list pane on the left. The fields *Site* and *Warehouse* on this tab, and the filter criteria in the dialog that you can access with the button *Edit query* in the action pane, control which location directive is selected automatically for a source document (e.g., a purchase order line with its warehouse and item).

On the tab *Lines*, you can enter an additional filter on quantity and units. The column *Unit* refers to the from/to quantity columns. If you want to set up a directive for a particular unit, select the checkbox *Restrict by unit* and enter the unit in the form, which you access with the button *Restrict by unit* in the toolbar of the tab *Lines*. In this way you can, for example, enter a line which moves full pallets to buffer locations and another line which moves individual units to floor locations.

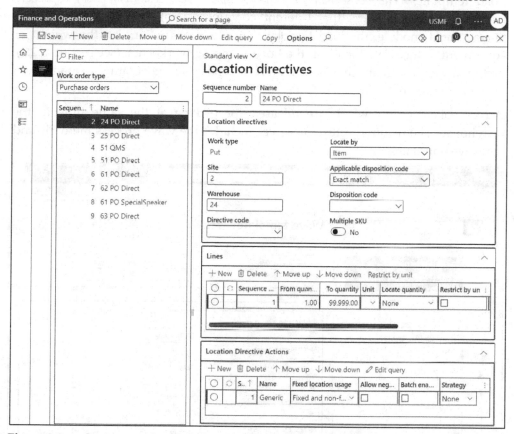

Figure 8-3: Setting up a location directive for purchase put-away

The tab *Location Directive Actions* contains the setting, to which location(s) to put (in directives with the *Work type* "Put") or from which to pick (in directives with the *Work type* "Pick"). The filter criteria, which determine these locations, have to be entered in the filter dialog, which you access with the button *Edit query* in the toolbar of this tab. In the filter dialog, you can also specify sorting criteria on the tab *Sorting* (e.g., referring to the column *Sort code* in the warehouse locations).

If there are products with batch numbers, select the checkbox *Batch enabled* in the location directive action of directives for the work type "Pick" (in an additional line, if you got some items with and other items without batch control).

The *Sequence number* of the location directives (and of the *Lines* within a directive, and of the *Location directive actions* within a line) is an editable field that determines the search sequence for the applicable record when automatically creating work. For this reason, directives, directive lines, and location directive actions with more specific criteria should be first in the sequence.

8.1.1.5 Basic Setup for Shipments

Load templates (*Warehouse management> Setup> Load> Load templates*) represent transportation units (e.g., the different container sizes). In the Transportation management module, the load template initializes restrictions on the weight or equipment of the related loads in the Load planning workbench (see section 8.2.2). In the warehouse management, they are the basis for generating a load in an outbound shipment.

Waves collect orders which are released for picking at the same time in the warehouse. The required setup for waves includes the wave process methods and the wave templates.

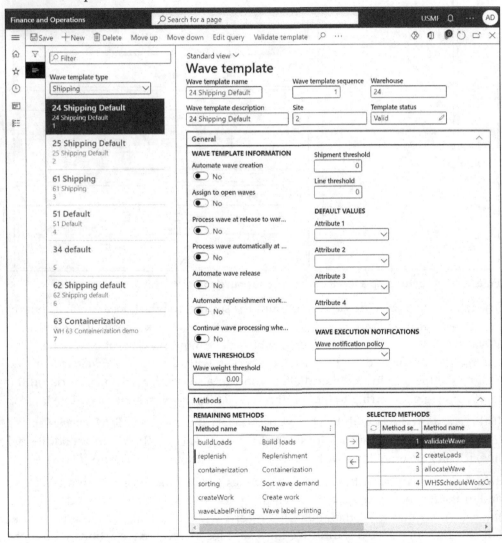

Figure 8-4:   Managing a wave template (updated for manual wave creation)

Wave process methods (*Warehouse management> Setup> Waves> Wave process methods*), which are generated by the application, determine the available steps for wave processing. In a new company or after implementing additional methods, initialize the methods with the button *Regenerate methods* in the Wave process methods form.

Wave templates (*Warehouse management> Setup> Waves> Wave templates*) contain settings for the picking work with reference to the grouping of work, to automated steps, and to applicable methods. In wave templates that specify an automatic wave creation (the slider *Automate wave creation* in the template is set to "Yes"), you can click the button *Edit query* to specify filter criteria that are used for the search of the applicable template when automatically creating a wave. For these templates, the sorting (field *Wave template sequence*) controls the search priority (like in work templates and location directives).

8.1.1.6 Setup for Mobile Devices

Before you can view menus and menu items in the Warehouse Management app on mobile devices, the corresponding setup needs to be completed. You can set up multiple menus and submenus in line with the requirements in the warehouse, and assign each warehouse worker to a respective menu.

The required mobile device setup in Dynamics 365 includes the following items:

➢ **Mobile device menu items** – Determine the available forms on mobile devices.
➢ **Mobile device menus** – Determine the menu structures.

Mobile device menu items (*Warehouse management> Setup> Mobile device> Mobile device menu items*) determine the forms that are available on mobile devices. The primary setting for a menu item is the lookup field *Mode*: The mode "Work" refers to warehouse work (the registration of transactions), the mode "Indirect" includes inquiries and common features (like logging off).

For menu items with the mode "Work", the slider *Use existing work* determines whether the menu item is used to register predefined work (work, which has been created already on the basis of a work template before) or unprompted work.

In a menu item that creates work (unprompted work that is not predefined), set the slider *Use existing work* to "No" and select the applicable work item in the field *Work creation process* on the tab *General* (e.g., "Adjustment in").

In menu items for existing work (required to execute predefined work), set the slider *Use existing work* to "Yes". The lookup field *Directed by* in this case controls whether the system (*Directed by* = "System directed") or the warehouse worker (*Directed by* = "User directed") selects which work to execute. For *User directed* work, the warehouse worker has to enter or scan the work ID of the executed work (which means that he decides on the selection), whereas for *System directed* work the device (mobile device menu item) shows which work to do next. With reference to the option "System directed", you can click the button *System Directed Work Sequence Queries* to enter sorting and filtering criteria for the work.

In case the option "User grouping" or "System grouping" is selected in the field *Directed by*, the worker can register multiple work lines with pick-transactions on the mobile device, then click the button *Done*, and finally register one common or multiple separate put-transactions (controlled by slider *Group put away*).

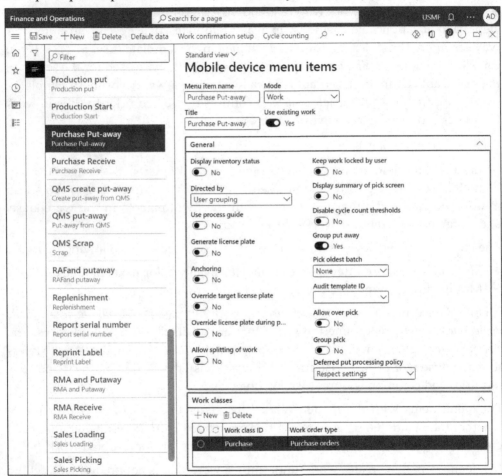

Figure 8-5:   Setting up a mobile device menu item for purchase put-away

The work classes selected on the tab *Work classes* in menu items for existing work determine the work which you can register with the particular menu item. If there is, for example, only one line with a work class "Purchase" on this tab, you can only execute work that is generated from a work template line with the work class "Purchase" (and not a "Sales" work).

Mobile device menus (*Warehouse management> Setup> Mobile device> Mobile device menu*) control the menu structure of the mobile device menu items. You can set up multiple menus and submenus.

8.1.1.7 Warehouse Worker and Work User

It is not required to set up the users of the Warehouse Management app as regular users in Dynamics 365. But you should set up the users of mobile devices in the warehouse as workers in the Human resources module (see section 10.2.2).

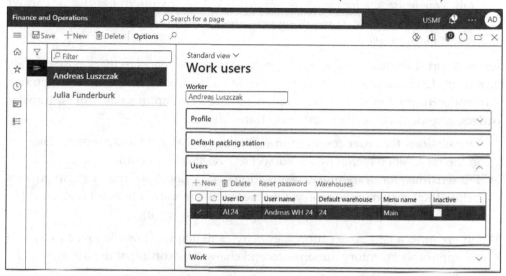

Figure 8-6: Setting up a warehouse worker

Based on the worker record in human resources, you can create the company-specific warehouse workers in the menu item *Warehouse management> Setup> Worker*. For each worker, enter one or more work users on the tab *Users*. The *User ID* and the password of the work user are used for the login on the mobile device. The *Default warehouse* determines the assigned warehouse, and the *Menu name* the available menu and menu items.

If you create multiple users for a worker, you can assign different menus and warehouses to the worker (who has to log in with the respective User ID in this case). For work users who should switch between warehouses, click the button *Warehouses* in the toolbar of the tab *Users* to open the Allowed warehouses form in which you enter the warehouses.

Creating a work user automatically creates a location (used as an intermediate location while executing warehouse work) on the warehouses of the user.

8.1.1.8 Product-Related Settings

In the released product, the following setup is required for the advanced warehouse management:

➢ **Storage dimension group** – Enables advanced warehouse management.
➢ **Reservation hierarchy** – Controls the inventory dimensions for reservation.
➢ **Unit sequence group** – Controls the available units of measurement for warehouse transactions.

The storage dimension group in the released product controls, whether the item is subject to the advanced warehouse management. At least one storage dimension group (*Product information management> Setup> Dimension and variant groups> Storage dimension groups*), in which the slider *Use warehouse management processes* on the tab *Warehouse specific setup* is set to "Yes", is required for the advanced warehouse management. This setting activates the inventory dimensions *Inventory status* and *License plate*.

Reservation hierarchies (*Warehouse management> Setup> Inventory> Reservation hierarchy*) determine for products that use the advanced warehouse management, which inventory dimensions are available for reservation in sales orders, transfer orders, shipments, and other outbound transactions:

➢ **Dimensions for order reservation** – Dimensions above the dimension *Location* in the reservation hierarchy are subject to a reservation in order lines.

➢ **Dimensions for warehouse reservation** – The location and the dimensions below the location in the reservation hierarchy are subject to a reservation in the warehouse (reserving when generating warehouse work).

When creating a new reservation hierarchy, a dialog is shown in which you can select applicable inventory dimensions and change the sorting of the dimensions.

The selected dimensions in the reservation hierarchy of an item have to comply with the active storage and tracking dimensions of the item. For this reason, the setup of the reservation hierarchies depends on the inventory dimensions which are used. The reservation hierarchy is primarily important for items with batch or serial numbers, because it controls whether you reserve the batch or serial numbers already in the order line (in the hierarchy, the batch/serial number is above the location), or later in the warehouse (the batch/serial number is below the location). For batch-controlled items, you can additionally select the checkbox in the column *Allow reservation on demand order* of the reservation hierarchy if you want to enable optionally reserving a batch number in an order line (relevant for hierarchies with the batch number below the location).

Unit sequence groups (*Warehouse management> Setup> Warehouse> Unit sequence groups*) control for the assigned items, which units of measurement you can use for moving and storing the product within the warehouse. The available units in a unit sequence group have to be entered on the tab *Line details* of the Unit sequence group form. The checkboxes *Default unit for purchase and transfer* and *Default unit for production* in the unit sequence group determine the unit that is used as default value when receiving an assigned item. With the default unit, you can, for example, specify to receive a particular item in pallets. The checkbox *License plate grouping* controls whether a separate license plate per unit (e.g., pallet) or one license plate for the whole quantity (in the selected unit) is generated when receiving an item. As a prerequisite for the use of this grouping, the slider *License plate grouping* has to be set to "Yes" in the applicable mobile device menu items.

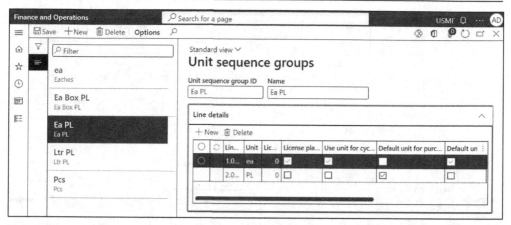

Figure 8-7: Setting up a unit sequence group with the units "ea" and "PL"

When you create a released product (*Product information management> Products> Released products*) that should use the advanced warehouse management, select an appropriate storage dimension group (for advanced warehouse management), a reservation hierarchy (edit with the button *Product/Set up/Reservation hierarchy*), and a unit sequence group (field *Unit sequence group ID* on the tab *Warehouse*). Depending on the units in the selected unit sequence group, related unit conversions are required for the item.

Apart from the weight and the physical dimensions (depth, width, height) on the tab *Manage inventory* in the released product, there is the Physical dimension form (access with the button *Manage inventory/Warehouse/Physical dimensions* in the released product) in which you can enter the physical dimensions of the item in the different units (in particular, the units of the unit sequence group). Weight and physical dimensions can be used to calculate the utilization of location capacity and transportation loads.

Note: If activated in the feature management and in the license configuration, you can use the advanced warehouse management also for catch weight items.

8.1.2 Core Warehouse Processes

Warehouse transactions include inbound processes (e.g., purchase order receipts, transfer order receipts, or product receipts in production) and outbound processes (e.g., sales order shipments, transfer order shipments, or picking in production).

Figure 8-8 below gives an overview of the warehouse layout and the structure of the warehouse work, which is used as a basis for the warehouse transactions.

In the overall process, the mobile device transactions are another way for recording the inventory registration in purchasing (see section 3.5.3), the picking list in sales (see section 4.5.2), and equivalent transactions in production and transfer orders.

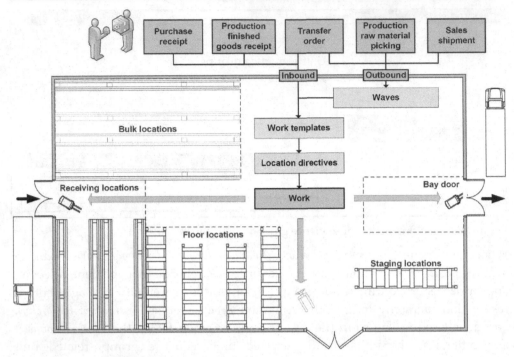

Figure 8-8:   Warehouse layout and the structure of warehouse work

8.1.2.1 Purchase Order Receipt

The starting point for a purchase order receipt in the warehouse is a purchase order line with a product and a warehouse which both are enabled for advanced warehouse management. The receipt process then includes the following steps:

➤ **Initial receipt** – Receive the item in the default receipt location.
➤ **Put away** – Move the item from the receipt location to the final location.
➤ **Product receipt** – Post the product receipt in the Dynamics 365 web client.

In section 8.1.3, you can find a description of further options for purchase receipts on the mobile device.

The initial receipt of a purchased item is not based on work that is created upfront, but generates work when posting the receipt. Applicable mobile device menu items include the following settings: *Mode* = "Work", *Use existing work* = "No", *Work creation process* = "Purchase order line receiving" (enter the order number and line number when receiving) or "Purchase order item receiving" (enter the order number and item number when receiving).

In order to record the initial receipt in the warehouse, open the corresponding menu item <u>on the mobile device</u> and enter or scan the purchase order number and the line number (or the item number). The default for the *Unit* in the receipt is specified in the unit sequence group, but you can select a different unit which is included in the unit sequence group, and you can reduce (split) the quantity.

Depending on settings in the mobile device menu item (slider *Generate license plate*), the license plate that identifies the handling unit (e.g., a pallet, a box, or an individual piece) has to be entered/scanned manually in the field *LP* (from a pre-printed tag), or is generated from a number sequence (which in the end requires to print the tag when receiving). Dynamics 365 then receives the item on the default receipt location of the warehouse.

Posting the initial receipt generates warehouse work for the second step, the put-away work (picking the item from the receipt location and putting it to the final bulk or floor location). The applicable work template and location directive determine the details of this work. The work lines, which are to be registered on a mobile device, are shown in the menu item *Warehouse management> Work> All work*.

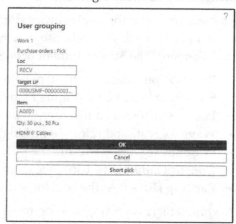

Figure 8-9: Registering the initial receipt and the separate picking for the put-away in the mobile app emulation on the web client

In order to register the put-away work on a mobile device, open an applicable menu item on the device (required settings: *Mode* "Work", *Use existing work* "Yes", *Work class* as specified in the work template that has been automatically selected when generating the work). Depending on the setting in the field *Directed by* of the menu item, the mobile device displays the next work (if "System directed"), or you have to enter/scan the work ID or the license plate (if "User directed") of the put-away work. After you have finished picking on the receipt location, the mobile device shows the put location (based on the location directive). Depending on settings for the work user (slider *Allow put location override* on the tab *Work* in the Work user form), you can override the put location.

Once the registration of the inbound transactions on the mobile device is finished, the product receipt has to be posted in the Dynamics 365 web client (see section 3.5.4). But whereas a purchase order confirmation is not required for the inventory registration, the order has to be confirmed before you can post the product receipt.

When you post the product receipt in the purchase order or in a summary update, select the option "Registered quantity" or "Registered quantity and services" in the lookup field *Quantity* of the posting dialog to make sure that the product receipt refers to the quantity that has been registered on the mobile device. Apart from the options for posting the product receipt in the Procurement module, which require entering a *Product receipt* number in the *Posting product receipt* dialog, there is the menu item *Warehouse management> Periodic tasks> Update product receipts* which you can submit to a batch process. This periodic task does not require entering a product receipt number, but a load ID must be assigned to the order line (if applicable, you can activate the slider *Automatically create at purchase order entry* in the section *Loads* of the Warehouse management parameters to create a load per purchase order automatically).

8.1.2.2 Sales Order Shipment

The starting point for a sales order shipment in the warehouse is a sales order line with a product and a warehouse which both are enabled for advanced warehouse management. The basic shipment process then includes the following steps:

➢ **Reservation** – Reserve the item before shipment.
➢ **Shipment** – Create the shipment and include the item.
➢ **Load** – Create a load for external transportation (before or after the shipment).
➢ **Wave** – Create and release a picking wave with the shipment.
➢ **Warehouse work** – Execute the picking work on the mobile device.
➢ **Confirm shipment** – Close the shipment.
➢ **Packing slip** – Post the packing slip in the Dynamics 365 web client.

A shipment is collecting one or more lines of one or more orders for the same destination address within a load. A load consists of one or more shipments with a common transport (e.g., truck).

Before processing a shipment in the advanced warehouse management, you have to make sure that the item is reserved. The inventory dimensions for the reservation in the sales order are controlled by the reservation hierarchy of the item. You can manually reserve an item in the Reservation form, which you can access with the button *Inventory/Reservation* in the toolbar of the order line. Depending on the settings for reservation, there is an automatic reservation.

Shipments (*Warehouse management> Shipments> All shipments*) represent separate deliveries within a load. If you want to ship a complete sales order, you can create the shipment with the button *Warehouse/Actions/Release to warehouse* in the Sales order form. Alternatively, there is the batch job *Warehouse management> Release to warehouse> Automatic release of sales orders* to create shipments. This batch job applies the setting for the *Sales order fulfillment policy* in the Accounts receivable parameters (section *Warehouse management*) and in the Customer detail form (on the tab *Warehouse*) as minimum criteria for releasing. Creating the shipment sets the *Release status* of the sales order (shown in the corresponding column of the Sales order list page) to "Released".

If there is a load already before you create the shipment (e.g., for transportation planning purposes), open the Load planning workbench (see section 8.2.2) and create the shipment from the load.

A load (*Warehouse management> Loads> All loads*) represents an inbound or outbound transportation unit (e.g., a container or a truck). It consists of one or more shipments. You can also split a single order line into multiple shipments and loads (for example, if the transportation unit is too small to cover the complete order line quantity). For creating a load, there are the following options:

➢ **After creating the shipment** – Create the load in the Shipment form.
➢ **Before creating the shipment** – Create the load in the Load planning workbench.
➢ **Skip creating the load** – Processing the wave in a later step creates the load automatically in this case.

Another option is to create loads automatically at sales order entry (activated in the section *Loads* of the Warehouse management parameters).

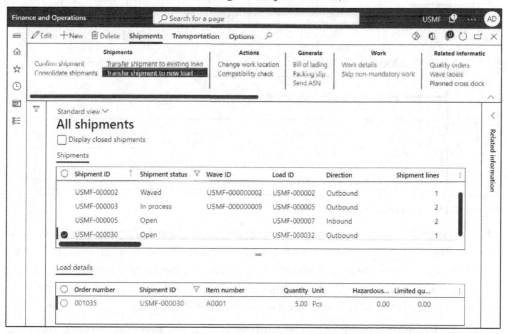

Figure 8-10: Creating a load in the Shipment form

If you want to create a load from a shipment, click the button *Shipments/Shipments/Transfer shipment to new load* in the Shipment form. In the dialog which is shown next, select the load template which characterizes the transportation unit for the load (e.g., the container size) before you click the button *OK*. If you want to ship multiple orders together, add them to a common load (click the button *Shipments/Shipments/Transfer shipment to existing load* in the Shipment form).

A wave (*Warehouse management> Outbound waves> Shipment waves> All waves*) is a group of shipments which are to be processed together in the warehouse. Depending on settings in the applicable *Wave template*, waves are created and processed automatically.

If you need to create the wave manually, click the button *New* in the Wave form and select a wave template in the *Create* dialog. Then click the button *Wave/Wave/Maintain shipments* in the Wave form to open the *Maintain shipments* form. The tab *Shipments not on a wave* in the Maintain shipments form shows all shipments which you can add to the wave. Click the button *Add to wave* in the toolbar of this tab to add a shipment to the wave. Shipments, which are already included in the selected wave, are shown on the tab *Wave lines* in the Maintain shipments form and in the Wave detail form (you might need to refresh the form to display a new shipment).

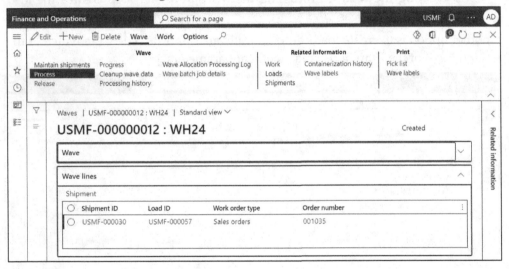

Figure 8-11:   Processing a shipment wave

The workspace *Outbound work planning* is another place for creating a wave. For the *Warehouse* that you select in the upper pane of the workspace, shipments without wave assignment are shown in the list *Shipments needing attention* in the center section. Select one or more shipments and click the button *Add to new wave* in the toolbar of the list to create a wave with these shipments.

In the next step, the wave has to be processed. If wave processing is not executed automatically (specified in the wave template), click the button *Wave/Wave/Process* in the Wave form. Depending on the parameter *Process waves in batch* (Warehouse management parameters, section *General*, tab *Wave processing*), processing is done in a batch job.

Processing a wave generates the warehouse work. You can view this work in the Work form, which you can access in the menu item *Warehouse management> Work> All work* or with the button *Wave/Related information/Work* in the action pane of the

Wave form. But at this stage, the *Wave status* of the wave is "Held", and the work is blocked (shown in the column *Blocked* of the Work list page). Before you can start to execute the actual warehouse work, you have to release the wave with the button *Wave/Wave/Release* in the Wave form.

Depending on the wave template, some or all of the described steps for creating and processing a wave are executed automatically and are not to be done manually for this reason. In case of errors in wave processing (e.g., because of a missing location directive), the list page *Warehouse management> Work> Work exceptions log* will show the relevant messages.

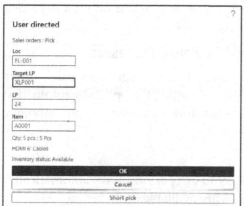 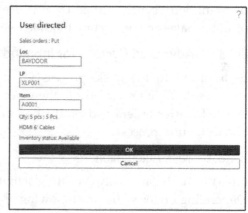

Figure 8-12: Registering the pick transaction and the put transaction in the mobile app emulation on the web client

In order to process the wave in the warehouse, open a menu item for sales order picking on the mobile device (required settings: *Mode* "Work", *Use existing work* "Yes", *Work class* as specified in the work template that is selected automatically when processing the wave). Depending on settings in the work template (field *Directed by*), the next picking work is shown (if "System directed"), or you have to enter or scan (usually scanning from a printed work list) the work ID of the work. After picking the item from the displayed location (specified in the location directive for the work type "Pick"), put the item to the displayed final shipping location or staging location (specified in the location directive for the work type "Put"). Depending on settings specified in the Work user form, you can override the pick location and the put location. Settings in the work template and in the wave template control, whether there are additional steps for staging or for replenishment. Putting an item to the final shipping location as the last step on the mobile device sets the status of the inventory transaction to "Picked".

Once you have finished the warehouse processes on the mobile device, confirm the shipment. Confirming closes the shipment and the load. Apart from automatically confirming (see section 8.1.3), there are the following options for manually confirming a shipment:

➢ **In the Shipment form** – Button *Shipments/Shipments/Confirm shipment* (if the load does not contain multiple shipments).
➢ **In the Load form** – Button *Ship and receive/Confirm/Outbound shipment*.
➢ **In the Load planning workbench** – Button *Ship and receive/Confirm/Outbound shipment* in the toolbar of the tab *Loads*.

Once the shipment is confirmed, post the packing slip with the button *Shipment/ Generate/Packing slip* in the Shipment form (select the checkbox *Display closed shipments* if the shipment is not shown). Alternatively, you can post the packing slip in the Load form (button *Ship and receive/Generate/Packing slip*), or in the Load planning workbench (button *Generate/Packing slip* in the toolbar on the tab *Loads*), or in the Sales and marketing module (see section 4.5.4).

8.1.3   Advanced Options for Inbound and Outbound Processes

In addition to the basic process for purchase order receipts and sales order shipments, there are variants of these processes, including the option to automatize steps. Transfer orders and production orders are further variants of the inbound and outbound processes.

8.1.3.1   Task Automation

Apart from the manually executing activities, you can perform tasks automatically. Depending on the setup, the following options are available:

➢ **Work execution** – Automatically execute warehouse work.
  o **Automatically process** – Select the checkbox *Automatically process* in the work template to execute the work automatically when releasing a wave (e.g., for bulk items not tracked in detail).
  o **Work confirmation setup** – Click the button *Work confirmation setup* in the respective mobile device menu item to open the Work confirmation form, in which you can select the checkbox *Auto confirm* in lines with the *Work type* "Put" (you only register the pick work on the mobile device in this case).
➢ **Picking process** – Automatically create/release shipments/loads/waves.
  o **Release to warehouse** – Automatically create shipments with the batch job *Warehouse management> Release to warehouse> Automatic release of sales orders* (specify the required *Fulfillment policy* on the tab *Warehouse* in the Customer form or, at a general level, in the section *Warehouse management* of the Accounts receivable parameters).
  o **Automatically create waves** – The slider *Automate wave creation* in the wave templates controls automatic wave creation when releasing to warehouse.
  o **Automatically process waves** – Sliders in the wave templates control automatic wave processing when releasing to warehouse or when reaching the threshold in the wave template (online or in a batch job, as specified with the Warehouse management parameter *Process waves in batch*).

- o **Automatically release waves** – The slider *Automate wave release* in the wave templates controls automatic wave releasing.
- o **Automatically create loads** – Slider in the section *Loads* of the Warehouse management parameters; independently of this setting, loads are created automatically when processing a wave for which no load has been created before.
- ➢ **Confirming shipments** – Automatically confirm outbound shipments.
  - o **Work audit template** – Using a work audit template (see below).
  - o **Periodic task** – Execute the task *Warehouse management> Periodic tasks> Process outbound shipments* (enter a filter on the *Load status* = "Loaded").

Reservation is automatically executed when entering a sales order line if the general parameters for reservation are set up accordingly (see section 7.4.5). Apart from the general settings, the tab *Warehouse* in the Warehouse form includes the sliders *Reserve inventory at load posting* (reserving when releasing to warehouse from the Load planning workbench) and *Reserve when orders are released by a batch job* (reserving in parallel to releasing with the periodic task *Warehouse management> Release to warehouse> Automatic release to warehouse*) which provide further options for the automatic reservation in the advanced warehouse management.

With work audit templates (*Warehouse management> Setup> Work> Work audit template lines update*), you can assign additional actions to a mobile device menu item. If you select an audit template that contains a line with the *Function* "Event" and the *Event* "Shipping confirmed" in a mobile device menu item for sales shipments, each shipment for which you execute the warehouse work with this menu item is automatically confirmed. Further features in the audit template lines include the option to display and to print data.

8.1.3.2 Options for Purchase Receipts

In the advanced warehouse management, there are the following options for purchase order receipts:

- ➢ **Two-step order receipt** – Receive with reference to the purchase order number and separately put away in a second step (described in section 8.1.2).
- ➢ **Load item receipt** – Receive with reference to a load (instead of the order).
- ➢ **License plate receipt** – Receive with reference to a license plate (preferably if you import a vendor ASN with e.g., pallet numbers).
- ➢ **One-step receipt** – Receive and put away in one step.

A load item receipt is based on an inbound load, which includes one or more purchase orders. As a prerequisite for load item receipts, set up a mobile device menu item with the *Work creation process* "Load item receiving". If you enter a purchase order and create a load in the Load planning workbench (see section 8.2.2), you can select the *Load ID* (instead of the purchase order number) when registering the receipt with this mobile device menu item. Receiving generates put away work, which has to be executed in the same way as a purchase order receipt.

Apart from the two-step receipt, which requires posting the initial receipt on the default receipt location and the put-away to the final location in two separate menu items on the mobile device, you can execute a one-step receipt to move the item to the final location immediately. As a prerequisite for one-step receipts, create a mobile device menu item with the *Work creation process* "Purchase order item receiving and put away", or "Purchase order line receiving and put away", or "Load item receiving and put away". With these menu items, receiving and putting away is done in one common transaction.

Note: If you want to leave the items on the (default) receipt location and prevent generating and executing work for putting them to a final location (based on work templates and location directives), set up a work policy (*Warehouse management> Setup> Work> Work policies*) with the *Work order type* "Purchase orders", the applicable *Work process* (e.g., "Purchase order item receiving (and put away)"), the *Work creation method* "Never", and, on the tab *Inventory locations*, the (default) initial receipt location(s).

8.1.3.3 Storage Utilization and Limits

When Dynamics 365 searches a location for a put transaction (e.g., for the put away of a purchase receipt), it selects the first location with available storage capacity. The search sequence is specified on the tab *Sorting* in the query that is assigned to the applicable location directive (on the tab *Location Directive Actions*). For the definition of the capacity of a location, there are two different options:

➢ **Location stocking limits** – In the menu item *Warehouse management> Setup> Warehouse> Location stocking limits*, you can enter the maximum quantity of a unit (unit in the unit sequence group) per location. This maximum quantity can be specified at various levels – e.g., for a location profile (this record determines the maximum quantity for all locations with that profile).

➢ **Dimension settings in the location profile** – On the tab *Dimensions* in the location profile, you can specify the capacity of the locations in terms of weight and physical dimensions (depth, width, height).

If the dimension settings in the location profile are used, the available capacity of locations and the required capacity of released products (weight/volume, specified on the tab *Manage inventory* or in the Physical dimension form, see section 8.1.1) are the basis for calculating if there is capacity on a location for storing a product.

Other settings in the location profile (e.g., the slider *Allow mixed items*) control whether it is possible to put an item to a location with current inventory.

If you want to get an overview of the available capacity, run the report *Warehouse management> Inquiries and reports> Warehouse monitoring reports> Warehouse utilization*.

8.1.3.4 Directive Codes

When generating warehouse work, Dynamics 365 searches for the applicable work template and for the location directive separately. With directive codes, you can link a work template to a location directive. This is useful, for example, if some items should be subject to a work template which includes staging as a separate step that has to be done on a special location.

The following setup is required for the use of directive codes:

➢ **Directive code** (*Warehouse management> Setup> Directive codes*) – Create a code.
➢ **Work template** – Select the *Directive code* in applicable work template lines (only in "Put" work template lines of outbound processes).
➢ **Location directive** – Select the *Directive code* in location directives as needed.

When you create work that is based on a work template with an assigned directive code, Dynamics 365 searches the location directive with the same directive code.

8.1.3.5 Staging

Staging, an optional step after picking, enables collecting and preparing shipments on separate locations before transferring them to the final shipping location, on which you execute loading (e.g., truck loading).

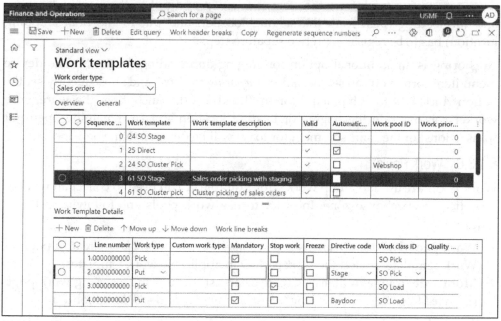

Figure 8-13: Work template for staging

In addition to the basic configuration for sales order shipments, the following setup is required for staging:

➢ **Directive code** – Additional directive code for staging.
➢ **Work template** – Contains work lines for staging and for loading.

➢ **Location directive** – Location directive to put the items to the staging location.

➢ **Mobile device menu items** – Contain the *Work class* of the work template lines.

In order to link the "Put" work template line for staging to the related location directive, enter a directive code in this work template line. In the "Pick" line below this "Put" line, select the checkbox *Stop work* to prevent that picking from the staging location is shown as next activity on the mobile device immediately after putting to the staging location.

In addition, set up a location directive (with the directive code of the "Put" work) for putting to the staging location. If there is no common location directive (without directive code) for putting to the final shipping location, which you can use after staging, create a separate directive code and location directive for this final put work.

In a similar way to the sales order picking process without staging, you can execute the outbound process with staging: Create the shipment, the load, and the wave, and release the wave (applying the work template for staging). The work created from the wave includes four steps in case of staging: Picking from the storage location, putting to the staging location, picking from the staging location, and putting to the final shipping location. On the mobile device, the warehouse work for staging (pick from the storage location and put to the staging location) and for loading (pick from the staging location and put to the final shipping location) has to be registered in two separate steps.

Anchoring is an additional option for staging and loading: In the Mobile device menu item form, you can set the slider *Anchoring* to "Yes" and subsequently set the option *Anchor by* to "Shipment" (or to "Load"). With anchoring, the warehouse worker can override the staging or loading location and all remaining open put transactions for the same shipment (or load) will be directed to the new location.

8.1.3.6 Work Pools

Work pools are used to group work – for example, if you need to collect all work in a particular warehouse zone. In order to use work pools, the following setup is required:

➢ **Work pool** (*Warehouse management> Setup> Work> Work pools*) – Create a pool.

➢ **Work template** – Select the *Work pool ID* in applicable work templates.

➢ **Mobile device menu items** – Create or adjust menu items for using work pools (*Directed by* = "System grouping", *System grouping field* = "WorkPoolId").

In the work records (*Warehouse management> Work> All work*), the work pool is an editable field which is initialized from the work template.

On the mobile device, the work pool (instead of the work ID) is shown when opening a menu item which is configured to use work pools. The work is grouped by work pool in this case.

8.1.3.7   Transfer Orders

Transfer orders (see section 7.4.4) are used to move items from one warehouse to another. While you can process transfer orders from and to a warehouse with or without advanced warehouse management, the way to process the transfer order is different for the different scenarios. Shipping a transfer order from a warehouse with advanced warehouse management works similar to shipping a sales order, and receiving a transfer order on a warehouse with advanced warehouse management works similar to receiving a purchase order.

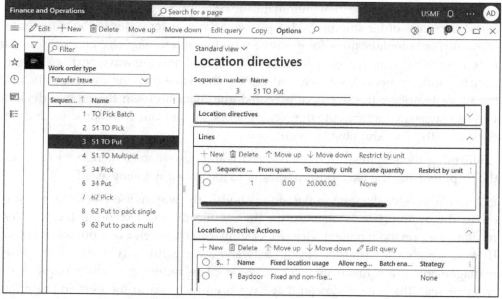

Figure 8-14:   Location directive for transfer issues ("Put" work to the shipping location)

In order to process transfer orders in a shipping or receiving warehouse with advanced warehouse management, the following setup is required (similar to the setup for purchase order receipts and sales order shipments):

> **Item, warehouse(s)** – Enabled for advanced warehouse management (for a transfer between two warehouses with advanced warehouse management, a transit warehouse with advanced warehouse management is required).
> **Work classes, work templates, location directives** – For the work order types "Transfer issue" and "Transfer receipt".
> **Mobile device menu items** – for the work on the mobile device.
>   o **Transfer issue** – *Mode* = "Work", *Use existing work* = "Yes", work class for transfer issue.
>   o **Transfer receipt** – *Mode* = "Work", *Use existing work* = "No", *Work creation process* = "License plate receiving" or "License plate receiving and put away" ("Transfer order line receiving", if the advanced warehouse management is not enabled on the from-warehouse).

o **Transfer receipt put-away** – *Mode* = "Work", *Use existing work* = "Yes", work class for transfer receipt (only required for two-step receipts).
➢ **Wave template** – In case you don't want to use the template for sales shipments.

The transfer order process in the advanced warehouse management starts with creating a transfer order (*Inventory management> Inbound orders> Transfer order*) that ships from or to a warehouse with advanced warehouse management.

If the advanced warehouse management is enabled on the from-warehouse, the first step is to reserve the item (automatically or manually). Then create a shipment (similar to sales order shipments) by releasing the transfer order to the warehouse manually or automatically – for example with the button *Ship/Operations/Release to warehouse* in the Transfer order form. Create the load and the wave next, assign the transfer order, process the wave, and release the wave (depending on settings in the wave template, the steps are executed automatically). On the mobile device, you can subsequently execute the picking work in the from-warehouse (including putting to the final shipping location).

Confirming the shipment in the advanced warehouse management, which closes the shipment and the load, posts a transfer to the transit warehouse.

In order to receive the item in the to-warehouse, the warehouse worker has to log on to the appropriate warehouse on the mobile device. Executing the transfer receipt work on the mobile device works similar to the receipt of a purchase order. If you receive a transfer from a warehouse with advanced warehouse management, use a menu item for "License plate receiving", which requires to enter or scan the license plate(s) that have been assigned to the item in the prior shipping process. If the advanced warehouse management is not enabled on the from-warehouse, use a menu item for "Transfer order line receiving" (or "Transfer order item receiving"), which requires to enter or scan the transfer order number.

If you ship from a warehouse, on which the advanced warehouse management is not enabled, you have to execute the standard transfer order process there (see section 7.4.4). If the advanced warehouse management is not enabled on the to-warehouse, the standard transfer order process has to be executed for receiving.

8.1.3.8 Production Orders

In a production environment, you can use the advanced warehouse management for material picking and for the receipt of manufactured items.

As a prerequisite for processing production orders in the advanced warehouse management, the following setup is required (similar to the setup for purchase order receipts and sales order shipments):

➢ **Items** – Materials and manufactured items enabled for advanced warehouse management.

➢ **Warehouse** – Enabled for advanced warehouse management; one or more warehouse locations in the production area; *Default production finished goods location* in the Warehouse form.

➢ **Production input location** – On the resource, the resource group, or the warehouse (specifies the location from which raw material is consumed, which means that this is the "Put" location for warehouse work).

➢ **Work classes, work templates, location directives** – For the work order types "Raw material picking" and "Finished goods put away".

➢ **Wave template** – Separate from the sales shipment templates (select the option "Production orders" in the left pane of the Wave template form).

➢ **Mobile device menu items** – for the work on the mobile device.
  o **Material consumption** – *Mode* = "Work", *Use existing work* = "Yes", work class for raw material picking.
  o **Finished product receipt** – *Mode* = "Work", *Use existing work* = "No", *Work creation process* = "Report as finished" (or "Report as finished and put away").
  o **Finished product put-away** – *Mode* = "Work", *Use existing work* = "Yes", work class for finished product receipt (only required for two-step receipts).

In order to use the advanced warehouse management in manufacturing, create and process a production order (*Production control> Production Orders> All production orders*) as described in section 5.4.2. Depending on the settings for automatic reservation (field *Reservation* on the tab *Setup* in the Production order detail form), you might need to reserve the raw materials manually after estimation.

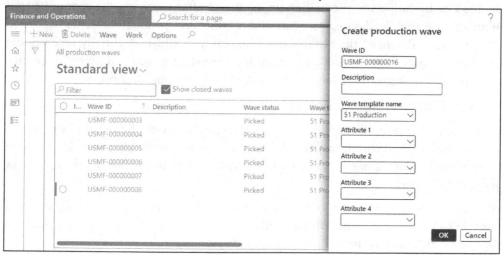

Figure 8-15: Manually creating a production wave

Once the production order is released, create a production wave (*Warehouse management> Outbound waves> Production waves> All waves*), assign the production order (button *Wave/Wave/Maintain productions*), process the wave, and release the wave. Depending on the settings in the applicable production wave template, these steps are executed automatically. Processing the wave creates warehouse work for raw material picking, which you can view with the button *Wave/Related information/Work* in the Wave form.

On the mobile device, you can execute the warehouse work for raw material picking (transfer to production input locations) in the next step. Depending on the setting for the *Issue status after raw material picking* (field on the tab *Inventory and warehouse management* in the Warehouse form), the material is immediately consumed (inventory status "Picked") or only reserved (inventory status "Reserved physical") after putting the item to the production input location. In the Dynamics 365 web client, you can subsequently start the production order and post the picking list that refers to the registered warehouse work.

In order to receive the manufactured item, open the menu item for "Report as finished" or – for one-step receipts – "Report as finished and put away" on the mobile device (which work similar to a purchase order receipt). The mobile device transaction posts a report as finished journal in production, and receives the product on the *Default production finished goods location* of the warehouse (or, in case of a one-step receipt, directly on the final floor or bulk location). In case of a two-step receipt, the initial receipt on the mobile device generates warehouse work for the put-away to the final location, which has to be executed in a separate menu item on the mobile device.

In order to update the production order status to "Reported as finished", click the button *Production order/Process/Report as finished* in the Production order form.

Instead of updating the production order status after receiving the manufactured item on the mobile device, you can also update the production order status to "Reported as finished" first. In this case, reporting as finished initially receives the item and – based on the work template for "Finished goods put away" – creates warehouse work for the put-away to the final bulk or floor location.

8.1.3.9 Canceling Warehouse Work

If the warehouse work is still open, you can cancel it with the button *Work/Work/Cancel work* in the Work form (*Warehouse management> Work> All work*). In case you only want to block a particular work temporarily, click the button *Work/Work/Block work* in this form.

You can also cancel open work on the mobile device. For this purpose, create a mobile device menu item with the with the *Mode* "Indirect" and the *Activity code* "Cancel work" and include it in the mobile device menu.

Once the warehouse work has been executed (*Work status* = "Closed"), it is not possible to cancel it in the Work form or on the mobile device. Administrators can use the menu item *Warehouse management> Periodic tasks> Clean up> Cancel work* to cancel work that is in progress or closed.

After loading a sales order shipment, it is possible to reverse the warehouse work with the button *Loads/Work/Reverse work* in the Load form if the load has not been confirmed yet (*Load status* = "Loaded") – in a subsequent dialog you can select in which location the items are received back. If it has been confirmed, you can reverse the confirmation with the button *Ship and receive/ Reverse/Reverse shipment confirmation* in the Load form. And if the packing slip has been posted already, you can cancel it with the button *Ship and receive/Reverse/ Cancel packing slips* in the Load form (which sets the status back to a confirmed load with *Load status* = "Loaded").

8.1.4 Tasks within the Warehouse

Apart from inbound and outbound transactions, warehouse operations include internal transactions (like counting and movements between locations) and tasks (like inventory blocking).

8.1.4.1 Inventory Blocking

The purpose of inventory blocking is to stop transactions – e.g., prevent shipping a pallet (license plate) with quality issues. In the advanced warehouse management, you can block inventory by changing the dimension value of the storage dimension *Inventory status* for an on-hand quantity. This blocking applies the inventory blocking feature in inventory management (see section 7.4.6).

Changing the inventory status, which blocks or unblocks inventory, generates an inventory transaction, which you can view later on.

After blocking a quantity in inventory, outbound transactions are not possible. If you receive a purchase order line with the status "Blocked", the quantity is blocked after the receipt.

In order to use the inventory status for blocking, the following setup is required:

➢ **Inventory status** – Status value with "Inventory blocking" (see section 8.1.1).
➢ **Disposition codes** – For status changes in parallel to warehouse transactions.
➢ **Mobile device menu items** – For changing the inventory status/disposition code on the mobile device.

If you want to be able to change the inventory status in a separate step on the mobile device, create a mobile device menu item with the setting *Mode* = "Work", *Use existing work* = "No", *Work creation process* = "Inventory status change", and include it in the mobile device menu.

It is not possible to directly update the inventory status in parallel to a warehouse transaction on the mobile device, but you can use the disposition code for this purpose. Each disposition code (*Warehouse management> Setup> Mobile device> Disposition codes*) can be assigned to an inventory status. If you want to be able to update the inventory status (via the disposition code) when registering the initial receipt in an inbound arrival, set the slider *Display disposition code* in the applicable mobile device menu items to "Yes". If the location for the put away of the received items depends on the disposition code, create a particular location directive with the disposition code (e.g., a location directive for the *Work order type* "Purchase orders" and the *Work type* "Put" to store damaged items on separate locations).

Apart from changing the inventory status with the mobile device menu item on the mobile device, you can update the inventory status in the Dynamics 365 web client:

➢ **Inventory status change** *(Warehouse management> Periodic tasks> Inventory status change)* – With flexible filter options.
➢ **Warehouse status change** *(Warehouse management> Periodic tasks> Warehouse status change)* – For blocking/unblocking at warehouse level (select the warehouse and the new status in this form, then click the button *Details* to access the individual items or locations).
➢ **On-hand inquiry** *(Warehouse management> Inquiries and reports> On hand by location)* – Button *Inventory status change* in the toolbar of the tab *On hand* in the on-hand inquiry by location.
➢ **Quality order** – Automatically change the inventory status from a quality order if specified in the test group *(Inventory management> Setup> Quality control> Test groups*, slider *Update inventory status* on the tab *General*).

On a license plate, a mixed inventory status with partly blocked and partly unblocked inventory is not possible. If you want to block a partial quantity of a license plate, move the required quantity to another license plate and block it there. For locations, you can specify in the location profile whether a mixed inventory status is allowed.

8.1.4.2 Movements and Adjustments

Movements and adjustments are manual transactions in inventory. Apart from registering these transactions on a mobile device, you can use regular inventory journals (see section 7.4.2) and enter all required inventory dimensions manually.

Warehouse adjustments are used for manual changes of the item quantity. In that respect, adjustments generate inventory counting journals that post the inventory transaction. The journal name for these journals is specified in the adjustment type *(Warehouse management> Setup> Inventory> Adjustment types)*.

The following setup is required for registering adjustments on the mobile device:

➢ **Adjustment types** – For grouping, specify the inventory journal name.
➢ **Mobile device menu item** – *Mode* = "Work", *Use existing work* = "No", *Work creation process* = "Adjustment in" or "Adjustment out".

In order to record an adjustment on the mobile device, select the menu item for "Adjustment in" or "Adjustment out" and enter the transaction quantity by which you want to change inventory. The quantity is always a positive number, in case of an item issue you have to use a menu item "Adjustment out". The default value for the *Adjustment type* is specified in the mobile device menu item, or in the Warehouse management parameters (section *General*, tab *Adjustments*).

Whereas adjustments change the on-hand quantity, movements are used for manual transfers from one to another location. As a prerequisite for registering movements on the mobile device, a mobile device menu item with the required settings (*Mode* = "Work", *Use existing work* = "No", *Work creation process* = "Movement") has to be set up and included in the mobile device menu.

```
                                                    ?
  Movement

  Movement
  From Information
  Loc
  [ FL-001 ]

  LP
  [ 24 ]

  Item
  [ A0001 ]
  HDMI 6' Cables
  Physical inventory (in Pcs)
  [ 82 ]

  Qty
  [ 3 ]

  Unit
  [ pcs            v ]

  ━━━━━━━━━━ OK ━━━━━━━━━━
  [            Cancel            ]
```

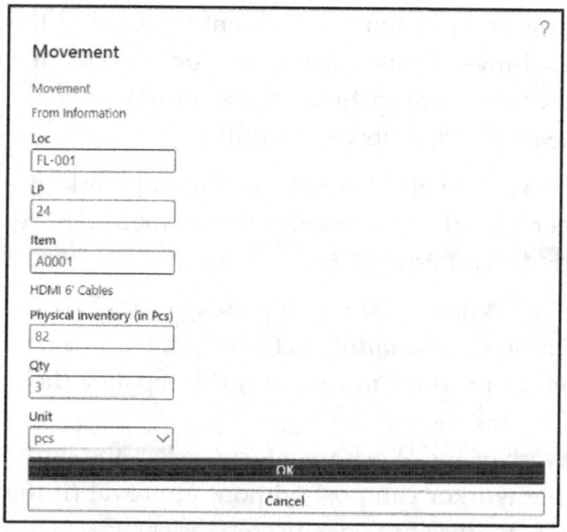

Figure 8-16: Registering a movement in the mobile app emulation on the web client

If required, you can use location directives to suggest the put location in a movement (e.g., for the movement from a quality test location to a storage location). For this purpose, the following setup is required:

➤ **Mobile device menu item for creating work** – *Mode* = "Work", *Use existing work* = "No", *Work creation process* = "Movement by template", *Create movement* = "Yes".

➤ **Work class, work template, location directives** – For the work order type "Inventory movement".

➤ **Mobile device menu item for executing work** – *Mode* = "Work", *Use existing work* = "Yes", work class for inventory movement.

8.1.4.3 Inventory Counting

The purpose of counting is to audit the physical quantity of items, and to adjust the quantity in case of discrepancies. The discrepancies, which are calculated based on the counting transactions on the mobile device, are posted in a regular inventory counting journal. The Warehouse management parameters determine the adjustment type, and with the adjustment type the journal name, for the counting transaction.

In the advanced warehouse management, there are following options for counting:

➢ **Periodic counting** – In a periodic interval (e.g., annual stocktaking).
➢ **Threshold counting** – Counting when inventory reaches the threshold limit.
➢ **Spot counting** – Ad-hoc counting on the mobile device.

The following setup is required for inventory counting on mobile devices:

➢ **Location profile** – In the location profile of all locations that are subject to counting (e.g., not for user locations), set the slider *Allow cycle counting* to "Yes".
➢ **Parameters** – In the section *Cycle counting* of the Warehouse management parameters, enter a default work class and a default adjustment type. Select the checkbox *Remove reservations* in the settings of this adjustment type to avoid that reservations in sales orders (and other issue transactions) block counting.
➢ **Unit sequence group** – Controls the available units for counting.

Periodic counting has got the purpose to create and to execute counting work in a regular interval. In addition to the general setup for counting on the mobile device, the following setup is required for periodic counting:

➢ **Mobile device menu item** – *Mode* = "Work", *Use existing work* = "Yes", work class for cycle counting; with the button *Cycle counting* in the action pane, access additional settings – e.g., how often to re-count in case of a discrepancy (field *Number of attempts*).
➢ **Warehouse worker** – On the tab *Work* in the Work user form, select the limits for counting discrepancies which the worker can post without approval (if the worker is a supervisor, no approval is required to post discrepancies).
➢ **Cycle count plan** (*Warehouse management> Setup> Cycle counting> Cycle count plans*) – Basis for periodic counting, with filter options on items and locations.

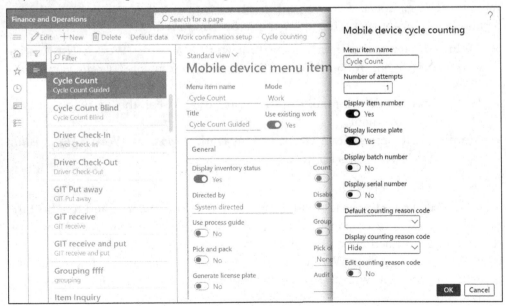

Figure 8-17:   Settings for cycle counting in the mobile device menu item

The first step in the process of periodic counting it to generate the counting work. You can create this work (based on cycle count plans) with the button *Schedule plan* in the menu item *Warehouse management> Cycle counting> Cycle count scheduling* (or with the button *Process cycle counting plan* in the Cycle count plan form). If you want to create counting work independently of cycle count plans, execute the periodic activity *Warehouse management> Cycle counting> Cycle count work by location* or *Warehouse management> Cycle counting> Cycle count work by item*.

Once the counting work is created, you can execute counting on the mobile device with the menu item that is set up for cycle counting. Enter the quantity (including "0") in all counting units per item and location, and confirm the quantity in case of discrepancies (depending on the settings in the menu item). Depending on settings in the work user, discrepancies between the counted quantity and the current quantity in Dynamics 365 are posted immediately in order to adjust the current quantity. Discrepancies, which are not posted immediately, are shown in the menu item *Warehouse management> Work> Warehouse> Cycle count work pending review*. In this form, the button *Work/Work/Cycle counting* provides access to the Cycle counting transactions form in which you can click the button *Accept count* to post the inventory adjustment (if applicable).

Threshold counting is a strategy to execute counting automatically when inventory reaches the threshold limit. As a prerequisite for threshold counting, set up a cycle counting threshold (*Warehouse management> Setup> Cycle counting> Cycle count threshold*). With the buttons *Select items* and *Select locations*, you can specify filter criteria for the threshold. Registering an outbound transaction on the mobile device (e.g., picking) then triggers threshold counting if the quantity on the location reaches the cycle counting threshold. If the slider *Process cycle counting immediately* in the cycle counting threshold is set to "No", Dynamics 365 generates cycle counting work which has to be executed later on the mobile device (similar to periodic counting work). If this slider is set to "Yes", a dialog for counting is immediately shown when registering an outbound transaction.

Spot counting is an ad-hoc counting on the mobile device. As a prerequisite for spot counting, a mobile device menu item (required settings: *Mode* = "Work", *Use existing work* = "No", *Work creation process* = "Spot cycle counting"; access additional counting parameters with the button *Cycle counting*) has to be set up. With this menu item, you can execute spot counting in a similar way to periodic cycle counting (but you can select any location). Posting the counting transactions and resolving discrepancies also works similar to periodic counting.

8.1.4.4 Replenishment

The aim of replenishment within the warehouse is to prepare an efficient picking process by moving the required items from buffer locations to picking locations. In Dynamics 365, there are two basic strategies for replenishing locations:

➢ **Based on minimum/maximum quantities** – Uses minimum and maximum stocking limits at location level.

➢ **Based on demand** – Replenishing required quantity on picking locations, triggered by the picking process for outbound orders.

Minimum/maximum replenishment is used to fill a location to the maximum if the current quantity is below the minimum (e.g., as first work in the morning). For a minimum/maximum replenishment, the following setup is required:

➢ **Replenishment template** (*Warehouse management> Setup> Replenishment> Replenishment templates*) – *Replenishment type* "Minimum or maximum", one or more template details lines with the min/max quantity for the selected items and locations (buttons *Select products* and *Select locations to replenish*).

➢ **Work class, work template, location directives** – For the work order type "Replenishment".

➢ **Fixed locations for items** (*Warehouse management> Setup> Warehouse> Fixed locations*) – Required if you want to refill empty locations.

➢ **Mobile device menu item** – *Mode* = "Work", *Use existing work* = "Yes", work class for replenishment.

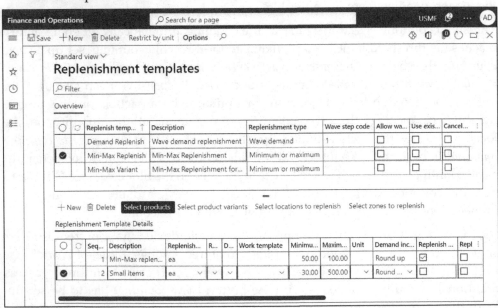

Figure 8-18:   Setting up a min/max demand replenishment template

If you use minimum/maximum replenishment, run the replenishment batch job (*Warehouse management> Replenishment> Replenishments*) to generate replenishment work. In the warehouse, execute the replenishment on the mobile device with the menu item for replenishment.

Wave demand replenishment – unlike minimum/maximum replenishment, which is refilling locations independently of current picking processes – is refilling locations when processing a wave. Wave demand replenishment is only created if there is no available quantity on the location that is selected by the location directive for picking.

If you want to use wave demand replenishment, the following setup is required in addition to the regular setup for sales shipments:

➢ **Replenishment template** – With the *Replenishment type* "Wave demand" and a *Wave step code*.

➢ **Wave template** – With the additional method "replenish" and the wave step code of the replenishment template.

➢ **Work class, work template, location directives** – For the work order type "Replenishment" (match "Put" locations in the replenishment location directive with "Pick" locations in the sales order picking location directive).

➢ **Mobile device menu item** – *Mode* = "Work", *Use existing work* = "Yes", work class for replenishment (you can use the same menu item as for minimum/maximum replenishment).

If the wave template for sales order shipments is set to automatically release waves, set the slider *Automate replenishment work release* in the wave template to "Yes" (replenishment has to be released and executed before sales picking).

In order to execute wave replenishment, create the shipment, the load, and the wave for sales order picking (applying the wave template for replenishment), assign the sales order, process the wave, and release the wave (depending on settings in the wave template, the steps are executed automatically). If no quantity is available on the picking location, a replenishment wave with replenishment work is created when processing the wave for sales order picking. The sales order wave is automatically blocked until the replenishment work is finished. On the mobile device, execute the replenishment work before sales picking and loading.

Load demand replenishment is another type of demand replenishment apart from the wave demand replenishment. The difference between these two replenishment types is, that wave demand is processed automatically (if specified in the wave template) whereas load demand replenishment needs to be calculated with a batch job that can sum the demand for several loads.

Warehouse slotting, which is another option to refill locations in preparation of picking, is a replenishment before releasing orders to the warehouse – in contrast to the wave demand replenishment, which creates the replenishment not before the picking wave is released. For warehouse slotting, a slotting template (*Warehouse management> Setup> Replenishment> Slotting templates*) for each respective warehouse is required. In order to generate the replenishment work for the slotting template, execute the batch job *Warehouse management> Replenishment> Run slotting* or click the corresponding buttons in the Slotting template form (*Generate demand, Locate demand,* and *Run replenishment/Create replenishment work*).

8.1.4.5 Warehouse Inquiries

You can use inquiries on the mobile device to view the current quantity in inventory. In order to set up such a mobile device inquiry (e.g., an inquiry on the on-hand quantity per item), create a mobile device menu item with the *Mode* "Indirect" and the *Activity code* (e.g., "Item inquiry"). On the mobile device, you can access the inquiry in the appropriate menu item and – in the item inquiry – enter or scan the item number to view the quantity on the different locations.

In the Dynamics 365 web client, the inquiry *Warehouse management> Inquiries and reports> On hand by location* is one of the main pages for viewing the current inventory in the advanced warehouse management. In order to show the locations with the item quantities, select a warehouse and refresh the page (or select the checkbox *Refresh across locations*). If you want to change the inventory status of a selected quantity, click the button *Inventory status change* on the tab *On hand*.

8.1.5   Case Study Exercises

Exercise 8.1 – Warehouse Setup

In order to investigate the options for the warehouse setup, create a new location format L-## (## = your user ID) with two segments: A segment with a length of one digit, followed by the separator "-" and a 3-digit segment.

Then set up a location profile F-## for floor locations and a location profile B-## for bulk locations. Both location profiles refer to the new location format L-## and allow cycle counting, but only floor locations use license plate tracking. Accept the default settings in the other fields of the Location profile form.

Once the basic setup is done, create a warehouse WH-## which applies advanced warehouse management processes. This warehouse has got the receiving location "RECV", the shipping location "SHIP", three floor locations ("F-001" to "F-003"), and six bulk locations ("1-001" to "2-003). Floor locations and bulk locations refer to the appropriate location profiles which you have created before. The location "RECV" is the *Default receipt location* in the warehouse.

Exercise 8.2 – Work Template, Location Directive, Wave Template

The purchase put-away work for the warehouse WH-## of exercise 8.1 should be registered in separate menu items on the mobile device. Create a new work class PO-## for this purpose.

Then create a work template for purchase orders with one line for pick work and one line for put work, which only refers to the warehouse WH-## and this new work class. In addition, create a work template for sales orders which is only used in this warehouse and contains one line for pick work and one line for put work (no staging). The work template lines refer to an existing sales order work class.

In order to use the warehouse in purchasing and in sales, related location directives are required. Create a location directive for the warehouse WH-##,

which specifies putting purchase order receipts to bulk locations in case of full pallets and to floor locations otherwise. Then enter a location directive for sales picking which should pick full pallets from bulk locations. Other units should be picked from floor locations first, and in the second line from bulk locations (if all floor locations are empty). The sales order directive should put items to the location "SHIP".

Finally set up a wave template T-##, which does not apply any automatic action, for the warehouse WH-##.

Exercise 8.3 – Mobile Device Menu and Work User

A new mobile device menu is required for the warehouse work in the following exercises. Create the following mobile device menu items for this purpose:

➢ Menu item "##-PO-Receive" for the initial receipt of purchase shipments (with the *Work creation process* "Purchase order line receiving").
➢ Menu item "##-PO-Put" for the transfer from the default receipt location to the final location in purchase receipts (referring to the work class created in exercise 8.2 and *Directed by* = "User directed").
➢ Menu item "##-SO-Direct" for sales order picking (referring to the sales order work class selected in exercise 8.2 and *Directed by* = "User grouping").

Then set up a new mobile device menu "##-Main" with these menu items. In addition, the menu should include a menu item "About" and a menu item for logging off.

In the next step, set up a warehouse worker who is linked to any worker employed in the current company. On the tab *Work users* of the Work user form, enter a user with the user ID X-##, the menu name which you have created in the current exercise, and the warehouse WH-## of exercise 8.1.

Exercise 8.4 – Warehouse Management Settings in the Released Product

In order to apply the advanced warehouse management to a product, you need an appropriate storage dimension group, a reservation hierarchy, and a unit sequence group. In this exercise, you can use an existing storage dimension group. But you want to create a new reservation hierarchy R-##, which does not contain tracking dimensions, and a unit sequence group U-##, which includes pieces and pallets (pallets are the default unit for purchasing).

Then create the item I-##-W with the name "##-AdvWarehouseMgmt" in the Released product form. It is a stocked product without variants or batch numbers, but you want to use the advanced warehouse processes. Select an item group for merchandise and an item model group with FIFO-valuation. The item does not require approved vendors. The base purchase price and the base cost price is USD 50. The base sales price is USD 100. The unit of measurement for the item is "Pieces" in all areas except purchasing. In purchasing, the default unit for the item is pallets (1 pallet = 10 pieces). Make sure to choose the same units of measurement which you have selected in the unit sequence U-##. Assign the new item to the unit sequence group U-## and to the reservation hierarchy R-##.

Note: If the number sequence for product numbers is set up for automatic numbering, don't enter a product number.

Exercise 8.5 – Warehouse Management Processes in Purchasing

Enter a purchase order with 34 units of the item I-##-W of exercise 8.4 and any vendor (e.g., the vendor of exercise 3.2) for a receipt in the warehouse WH-## of exercise 8.1. Confirm the order and check the inventory transaction which refers to the purchase order line.

Log on to the mobile device with the work user X-## of exercise 8.3. Open the menu item for receiving the purchase order and post the receipt for the complete quantity of the purchase order.

Which status do the inventory transactions of the item show afterward? Open the inquiry "On hand by location" in the *Warehouse management* menu, select the warehouse WH-## and take note of the license plate with the posted quantity.

In the next step, open the mobile device menu item for the put-away of the purchase receipt and post the transaction (refer to the license plate shown in the previous inquiry).

If you review the inventory transactions and the inquiry "On hand by location" for the warehouse WH-## again, what is different now? Finally, post the product receipt based on the mobile device transactions of the current exercise.

Note: In order to register transactions on the mobile device, use the *Warehouse Management* app (make sure that the *Connection settings* in the app provide access to the training company), or use the form *WHSWorkExecute* which you can access with the web address *https://XXX.com/?mi=action:WHSWorkExecute&cmp=YYY* (*XXX.com* = URL of the Dynamics application, *YYY* = Training company).

Exercise 8.6 – Warehouse Management Processes in Sales

A customer (e.g., the customer of exercise 4.1) orders 12 units of the item I-##-W, which you have purchased in the previous exercise. Enter an appropriate sales order that is shipped from the warehouse WH-##, reserve the quantity, and create the shipment. What is the status of the inventory transactions now?

Create a load for the shipment. Then enter, process, and release a wave which is based on the wave template T-## of exercise 8.2. Take note of the *Work ID* of the warehouse work that has been generated when processing the wave. Check the inventory transactions of the item again, what is different now? Review the inquiry "On hand by location" for the warehouse WH-## and take note of the license plate shown for the floor location.

In the next step, log on to the mobile device with the work user X-## of exercise 8.3 and open the mobile device menu item for sales order picking. Post the pick transaction that is related to the work ID and – when you pick from the floor location – to the license plate noted before.

Check the inventory transactions and the on-hand quantity in the warehouse WH-## again. What is different now? Finally, post the packing slip for the sales order based on the mobile device transactions of the current exercise.

8.2 Transportation Management

The purpose of the transportation management in Dynamics 365 is to select external freight carriers for inbound and outbound shipments and to manage these inbound and outbound shipments. Transportation management is based on the advanced warehouse management, but it is also possible to use it independently.

Based on the load (e.g., a truckload), the origin address, and the destination address, you can run a calculation of transportation routes and costs, and create a route based on this calculation (or enter it completely manually). Transportation tenders, dock appointments, and the reconciliation of the freight invoice with the route are further options in the transportation management.

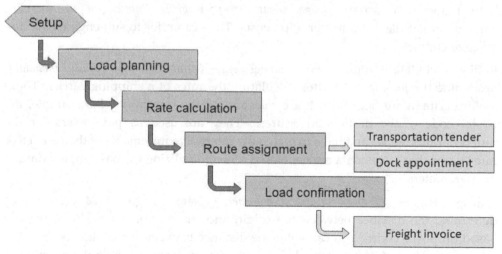

Figure 8-19: Overview of the transportation management functionality in Dynamics 365

Note: For inbound shipments, you can use the Landed cost module instead of the transportation management if you got goods in transit and take the ownership of items before receiving them in the warehouse (often in international trade).

8.2.1 Core Setup for Transportation Management

Before you can perform the processes in the transportation management, you have to complete the required setup.

8.2.1.1 Transportation Engines

Transportation engines, which include rate engines and transit time engines, are calculation routines that compute the price and the time for transportation. Engines include a .NET assembly and work like plug-ins for the individual carrier contracts. While it is easy to integrate additional transportation engines, the standard application includes a few default engines.

The engines are divided into the following types:

➢ **Rate engines** – Calculate the transportation rate.
➢ **Generic engines** – Simple engines that calculate the result (e.g., the distribution of costs for a load) on the basis of call parameters. They are used by other engines.
➢ **Mileage engines** – Calculate the distance between origin and destination.
➢ **Zone engines** – Calculate the zone of the origin and the number of zones between origin and destination.
➢ **Transit time engines** – Calculate the transportation time.
➢ **Freight bill types** – Used for automatic freight bill reconciliation.

Rate engines (*Transportation management> Setup> Engines> Rate engine*) are the core engines for calculating transportation costs. They can refer to sub-engines like the mileage engines.

Rating metadata (*Transportation management> Setup> Rating> Rating metadata*) determine the lookup criteria for calculating the rates of a shipping carrier. These lookup criteria are fields which are relevant for the transport – for example, the postal code of the destination address. They are used as parameters for the different rate engines and have to match the internal requirements of the respective rate engine. Basic metadata are generated when initializing the base engine data in the parameters.

Mileage engines (*Transportation management> Setup> Engines> Mileage engine*) determine the distance between the origin and the destination address, usually based on postal codes. You can enter the distance between the postal codes of the relevant origin and destination addresses on the tab *Details* of the mileage engines. The button *Metadata* provides access to the definition of available and mandatory fields for entering distances. If you add or change a field in the metadata, the related column is subsequently shown in the mileage engine. But be aware that the field selection has to match the requirements of the engine.

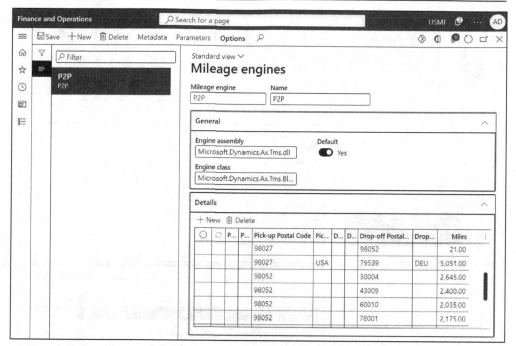

Figure 8-20: Entering distances in the mileage engine

Transit time engines (*Transportation management> Setup> Engines> Transit time engine*) determine the required time for the transport between addresses. The setup is similar to the mileage engine, except that you enter days (instead of miles in the mileage engine) and that the transit time is depending on the carrier service.

8.2.1.2 Transportation Methods and Shipping Carriers

Transportation methods (*Transportation management> Setup> Carriers> Transportation methods*), which include categories like "Air" or "Ground", and transportation modes (*Transportation management> Setup> Carriers> Mode*), which include categories like "Truckload" or "Parcel", differentiate the kinds of transport. They are a basis for the rate calculation definition in the parameters and engines. The transportation method is a required field in the shipping carrier service.

If you want to set up a carrier, open the menu item *Transportation management> Setup> Carriers> Shipping carriers* and insert the carrier. In order to activate the carrier for transportation, set the sliders *Activate shipping carrier* and *Activate carrier rating* to "Yes". The field *Vendor account* assigns the carrier to a vendor for freight invoice matching and posting (see section 8.2.2). On the tab *Services* in the Shipping carrier form, enter one or more transportation services that are provided by the carrier. When you insert a carrier service, a new *Mode of delivery* is created automatically in the line.

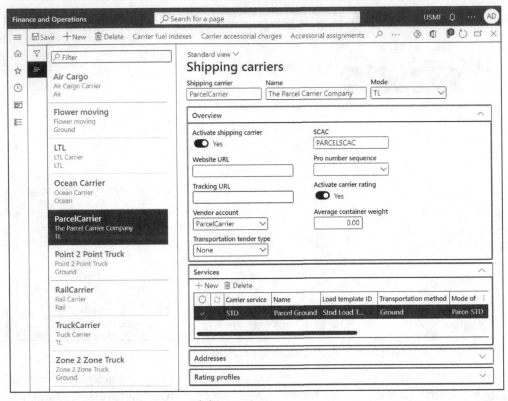

Figure 8-21:   Entering a carrier with his service

8.2.1.3   Break Masters, Rate Masters and Rating Profiles

Break masters, rate masters and rating profiles are the core setup for calculating the carrier rates.

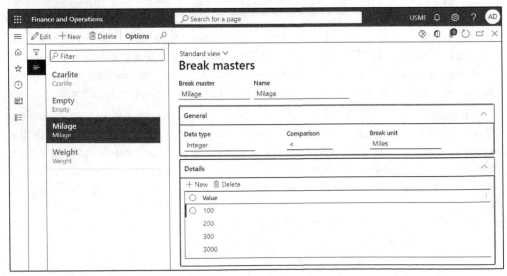

Figure 8-22:   Setting up a break master

Break masters (*Transportation management> Setup> Rating> Break master*) determine the steps (intervals) and the unit (e.g., miles) for the rate. If there is, for example, a different price for transports up to 100 miles and for longer distances, enter a break master with a step "100" and a step "9999" (or another maximum distance).

Rate masters (*Transportation management> Setup> Rating> Rate master*) contain the pricing structure and the prices of the particular carriers. When you create a rate master, select the *Rating metadata ID* (which determines the columns on the tab *Rate base assignments*) on the tab *Overview*. Then click the button *Rate base* and enter the rate bases for the rate master. Rate bases contain the prices of the rate master. They use the steps or intervals of the *Break master* (selected on the tab *General* in the rate base) as columns on the tab *Details*, in which you can enter the respective prices.

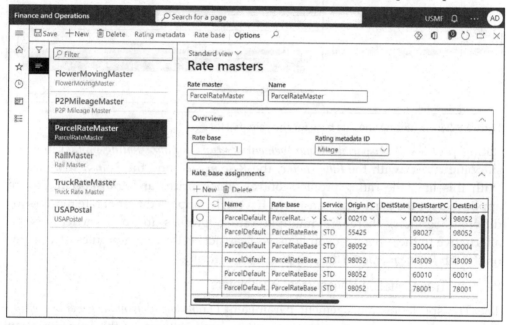

Figure 8-23: Setting up a rate master

Once you have finished the setup of the rate base, return to the Rate master form and, on the tab *Rate base assignment*, enter lines with the rate base (created for the rate master as described above) and the origin/destination address area. The selected *Rating metadata ID* in the rate master controls the columns (e.g., postal codes or zones) for the origin/destination address areas on this tab.

The rate base assignment makes the rate master available for calculating the transportation price from/to the applicable addresses.

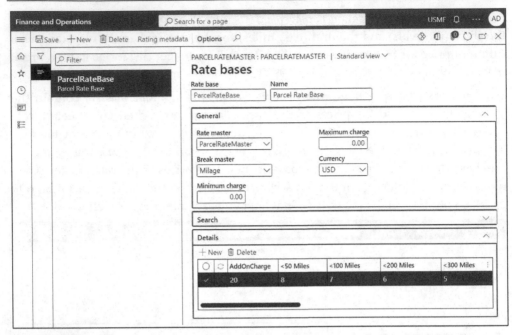

Figure 8-24: Entering the rate base for the rate master

Rating profiles (*Transportation management> Setup> Rating> Rating profile*) link the shipping carrier with the *Rate engine*, the *Rate master*, and the *Transit time engine*. With this link, the rating profiles control which prices and transport times are applicable for the particular transports. If a carrier applies different rate masters for different services, there are multiple rating profiles for one carrier. As an alternative to the separate menu item, you can access the rating profiles of a carrier on the tab *Rating profiles* in the Shipping carrier form.

8.2.1.4   Transportation Management Parameters

The Transportation management parameters (*Transportation management> Setup> Transportation management parameters*) contain basic settings for the Transportation management module, including the number sequences in transportation management. The button *Initialize base engine data* in the toolbar of the tab *General/ Engines* in the parameters provides the option to initialize the engine setup data for the available base engines.

8.2.1.5   Load Templates and Load Posting Methods

Load templates (*Transportation management> Setup> Load building> Load templates*), which are also required for advanced warehouse management (see section 8.1.1), represent the different inbound and outbound transportation units (e.g., regular vs. refrigerated trucks, or different container sizes).

If you want to specify a default load template which is used when creating a load, open the form *Warehouse management> Setup> Load> Item load mapping* and enter the default *Load template ID* for each applicable item group there.

Load posting methods (*Warehouse management> Setup> Load posting methods*) are a prerequisite for generating shipment waves from the load planning workbench. In a new company or after implementing additional methods, initialize the methods with the button *Regenerate methods* in this form.

8.2.1.6   Settings in the Released Products

In the Released product detail form, the slider *Use transportation management processes* on the tab *Transportation* controls whether transportation management is used for the item. This slider is always set to "Yes" if the item is subject to the advanced warehouse management (as specified by the storage dimension group).

For items that use the basic warehouse management, the slider *Use transportation management processes* is set to "No" by default, but you can manually set it to "Yes". In order to use the transportation management when processing a sales order without advanced warehouse management, create and confirm a shipment (without a wave) for a warehouse that is enabled for advanced warehouse management. In the Load planning workbench, execute rating and routing as usual.

8.2.1.7   Check of the Rate Calculation

You can check the rates for transportation, which are calculated with the current transportation setup, in the Rate route workbench (*Transportation management> Planning> Rate route workbench*): Enter a From-address and a To-address on the tab *Criteria* and click the button *Rate shop* in the action pane to view all available transports with the related price on the tab *Route results*. If you deselect the checkbox *Hide Exceptions*, transport options which are not available with the selected settings are also shown. For these transports, you can click the button *View exception details* to view details on the missing setup.

8.2.2   Managing Transportation Processes

Transportation management can be used in inbound and in outbound processes. Apart from sales orders, it covers purchase orders and transfer orders.

8.2.2.1   Core Transportation Process

The starting point for the transportation process is a sales order, a purchase order, or a transfer order with a product that is enabled for transportation management.

The next step is planning the transportation in the Load planning workbench, which you can access in the menu item *Transportation management> Planning> Load planning workbench* or with the button *Warehouse/Loads/Load planning workbench* in the sales order. In the Load planning workbench, select the respective order line(s) on the tab *Sales lines* and add it to a new load (click the button *Supply and demand/Add/To new load* in the action pane) or to an existing load (which you select in the lower pane first). If you add to a new load, a dialog is shown, in which you select an applicable load template. In the lower pane of the dialog, you can edit (reduce) the *Quantity* which is shipped with the load (e.g., if the quantity in the order line is more than the load capacity) and, on the other tabs, view the required and the remaining load capacity in terms of weight and volume. Once you create the load with the button *OK* in the dialog, the new load is shown in the lower pane of the Load planning workbench.

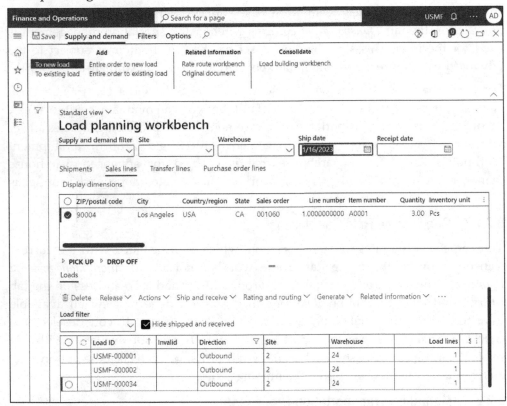

Figure 8-25:   Adding a sales order line to a new load in the Load planning workbench

If the slider *Plan by shipment* in the Transportation management parameters (section *General*, tab *Shipment*) is set to "Yes", the tab *Shipments* is shown in the Load planning workbench. In this case, you can add a sales order line to a load also after it has been released to the warehouse – in other words, add the shipment for a sales order line to a load.

In order to calculate the rate and the time for transportation, select the respective load on the tab *Loads* in the lower pane of the Load planning workbench and click the button *Rating and routing/Rate route workbench* in the toolbar of this tab to open the Rate route workbench.

In the Rate route workbench, click the button *Rate shop* to calculate all available transport options with the particular prices (the button *Rate* only shows the least expensive transport). Once you have decided on the transport, select the respective line on the tab *Route results* and click the button *Assign* in the toolbar of this tab. Assigning creates a route and links this route (which you can also view in the menu item *Transportation Management> Planning> Routes*) to the load.

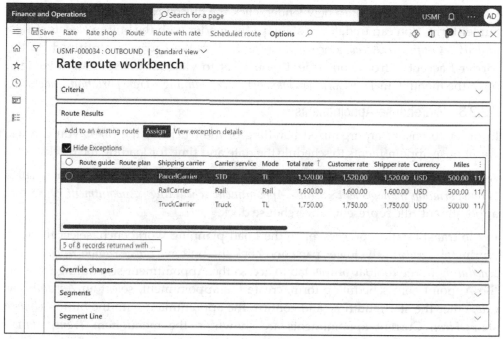

Figure 8-26: Assigning a route in the Rate route workbench

If you want to create a route with a manual price (instead of calculating the price in the Rate route workbench), click the button *Rating and routing/Manual rating* in the toolbar of the lower pane in the Load planning workbench.

In order to initiate warehouse picking next, select the load on the tab *Loads* in the lower pane of the Load planning workbench and create the shipment with the button *Release/Release to warehouse* in the toolbar of this tab. Once all warehouse processes are finished, and the items are received on the final shipping location, you can confirm the shipment and the load (see section 8.1.2). The confirmation tells the carrier that the load has been shipped. The load status changes to "Shipped" and by default, the load is not shown in the Load planning workbench anymore.

8.2.2.2 Transportation Tenders

A transportation tender is an agreement with a carrier on a particular transport. It includes the transportation date and the rate. In the Shipping carrier form (*Transportation management> Setup> Carriers> Shipping carriers*), the field

Transportation tender type on the tab *Overview* controls whether transportation tenders are updated manually or via EDI.

In the transportation process, access the transportation tenders from the respective route in the Route form (*Transportation Management> Planning> Routes*, button *Transportation tenders*), or from the load in the Load form (*Transportation Management> Planning> Loads> All loads*, button *Transportation/Transportation tenders*). In order to create a new tender, click the button *New* in the Transportation tender form. You can update the status of the tender with the button *Update status> Submit / Confirm / Accept* once it is submitted to the carrier / confirmed by the carrier / accepted from your side. If you want to view all transportation tenders, open the menu item *Transportation management> Planning> Transportation tenders*.

8.2.2.3 Warehouse Appointments

In order to ensure an organized handling of the trucks at the dock, you can use warehouse appointments to schedule the date and time for loading the truck.

As a prerequisite for warehouse appointments, set up appointment rules (*Transportation management> Setup> Appointment scheduling> Appointment rules*). An appointment rule represents a warehouse dock.

In the transportation process, open the Load planning workbench, select the load on the tab *Loads* in the lower pane and click the button *Transportation/Appointment scheduling* in the toolbar of this tab to access the Appointment scheduling form. In the Appointment scheduling form, create the appointment, select an *Appointment rule*, enter the start/end time and confirm the appointment with the button *Update status/Firm*. Current appointments are shown in the menu item *Transportation management> Planning> Dock appointment scheduling> Appointment scheduling*.

When the truck arrives, register the driver check-in and check-out in the menu item *Transportation management> Planning> Dock appointment scheduling> Driver check-in and check-out*. Alternatively, you can register the check-in/check-out in the Appointment scheduling form, or on a mobile device in the warehouse (in the applicable mobile device menu items).

8.2.2.4 Transportation Constraints

Transportation constraints restrict the available options for transportation – for example, to prevent that a particular carrier transports a particular item number.

In order to set up transportation constraints, open the menu item *Transportation management> Setup> Routing> Constraints* and enter the disallowed combinations of items, shipments, and carriers. The field *Constraint action* controls whether to create a warning or an error.

When routes are calculated in the Rate route workbench, a constraint (disallowed combination) that is applicable to a particular transport generates an exception. The exceptions are shown in the column *Constraints*.

8.2.2.5 Segmented Transports

Segmented transports apply if you want to change the carrier within a transport. Hub masters represent the hubs where you can switch carrier for this purpose.

As a prerequisite for segmented transports, the following setup is required:

➤ **Hub types** (*Transportation management> Setup> Routing> Hub types*) – Different types of hubs (e.g., harbors or airports).

➤ **Hub masters** (*Transportation management> Setup> Routing> Hub masters*) – Places with an address (e.g., different harbors), on which you can switch carriers.

➤ **Route plans** (*Transportation management> Setup> Routing> Route plans*) – Sequence of transports from the origin to the first hub, from the first hub to the next hub, and between all following hubs. The rate per segment is the result of the regular rate calculation based on the hub addresses, or, if applicable, a spot rate that you enter for the segment (click the button *Spot rates* on the tab *Details*).

➤ **Route guide** (*Transportation management> Setup> Routing> Route guides*) – With criteria for the *Origin* and *Destination*. Enter the route plan on the tab *Result*.

In order to calculate rates with segmented transports, click the button *Route with rate* in the Rate route workbench. If you want to view the transport segments with the rate, select the route on the tab *Route results* and switch to the tab *Segments*.

8.2.2.6 Customer Rate Adjustment

Rate engines calculate the base rate for transportation as described above. If you want to charge a freight rate to a customer, which is different from the base rate calculated by the rate engine, there are the following options:

➤ **Freight discounts** – For the *Discount type* "Customer".

➤ **Override charges** – Customer rate independent of the actual transport.

➤ **Transportation templates** – If selected in the Rate route workbench.

With freight discounts (*Transportation management> Setup> Rating> Discounts*), you can adjust the rates that derive from the base rate. The discounts are available for the rate paid to the carrier (*Discount type* "Shipper") and for the rate charged to the customer (*Discount type* "Customer"). When you set up a freight discount, select the *Discount type* and, on the tab *Dates*, the start/end date. Additional fields in the Discount form enable restrictions which serve as a filter – for example, if a discount should only apply for a particular *Shipper carrier*. In order to enter the discount value, expand the tab *Discount*, select the *Result type* ("Percentage" or "Amount") and enter the rate discount percentage or the rate discount amount. Positive discounts reduce the freight rate, and negative discounts increase the rate. When calculating a rate in the Rate route workbench, the amounts in the columns *Customer rate* and *Shipper rate* deduct the discount from the base rate (*Total rate*).

With override charges (*Transportation management> Setup> Rating> Override charges*), you can enter a fixed price or apply the charges of a fixed carrier irrespectively of the selected route. For a fixed price, set the slider *Manual* on the tab *Charge* of the

Override charges form to "Yes" and enter the price on the tab *Charge manual rates* which is shown then. If you want to apply the charges of a fixed carrier, irrespectively of the actual carrier (e.g., if the customer pays only truck charges), select the *Shipping carrier* on the tab *Charge*. When you calculate the freight rate for the customer in the Rate route workbench, the *Customer rate* shows the rate as specified in the override charges.

Transportation templates (*Transportation management> Setup> Carriers> Transportation templates*) work similar to override charges, but the rate calculation only respects a transportation template if it is selected in the respective field on the tab *Criteria* in the Rate route workbench.

8.2.2.7   Charging Freight to the Customer

If applicable, you can automatically include transportation costs in sales orders. For this purpose, the following setup is required:

➢ **Charges code** (*Accounts receivable> Charges setup> Charges code*) – Set up a charges code with the posting type combination *Customer – Ledger* (for adding the charges to the order total) or *Ledger – Ledger* (for internal posting).

➢ **Charges assignment** (*Transportation management> Setup> Rating> Miscellaneous charges*) – Create a miscellaneous charges assignment with the *Miscellaneous charge type* "None" which links the miscellaneous charges code in accounts receivable with freight charges in transportation management.

➢ **Delivery terms** (*Sales and marketing> Setup> Distribution> Terms of delivery*) – Delivery term(s) with the slider *Add transportation charges to orders* set to "Yes".

In order to generate the charges in a sales order, enter the order, create the load, calculate the rate, and create/assign the route. Then create the shipment ("Release to warehouse") and execute the warehouse processes. When you confirm the shipment, the freight charges are added as miscellaneous charges to the order line.

8.2.2.8   Freight Invoice Matching

When receiving a freight invoice from a carrier, you can enter or import it and match it with the related route. As a prerequisite for freight invoice matching, the following setup is required:

➢ **Bill types** (*Transportation management> Setup> Freight reconciliation> Freight bill type*) – Required to link freight invoice processing to the transportation engine, define the parameters that control the mandatory fields for finding a match.

➢ **Bill type assignments** (*Transportation management> Setup> Freight reconciliation> Freight bill type assignments*) – Assign bill types to carriers and transportation modes.

➢ **Reconciliation reasons** (*Transportation management> Setup> Freight reconciliation> Reconciliation reasons*) – Are used when there is no exact match to a freight bill. For the deviation, they categorize reasons and specify the ledger posting.

> **Audit masters** (*Transportation management> Setup> Freight reconciliation> Audit master*) – For automatic freight reconciliation (optional for manual reconciliation), contain tolerances and reconciliation results.
> **Billing groups** (*Transportation management> Setup> Freight reconciliation> Billing groups*) – Group carrier services for billing purposes. Select the respective *Billing group ID* per service in the Shipping carrier form.
> **Transportation management parameters** – Section *General*, tab *Vendor invoice*.

In the transportation process, freight invoice matching is based on routes which have been completed (the shipment/load is confirmed).

If you want to manually register the freight invoice that you receive from the carrier, open the Load planning workbench, deselect the checkbox *Hide shipped and received* on the tab *Loads* in the lower pane, and select the respective load. Then click the button *Related information/Freight bill details* in the toolbar of this tab to access the Freight bill details form. In this form, select the applicable freight bill in the list pane on the left before you click the button *Generate freight bill invoice* and enter the invoice number in the subsequent dialog.

An alternative way to record a freight bill is to open the Freight invoice details form (*Transportation management> Inquiries and reports> Freight invoice details*) and to enter the invoice with the header and line details manually.

In order to match and to approve the freight invoice subsequently, click the button *Match freight bills and invoices* in the Freight invoice details form. In the form *Freight bill and invoice matching* that is shown next, switch to the tab *Unmatched freight bill details*, select the respective freight bill, and click the button *Match* in the toolbar of this tab. In the Freight invoice details form that is shown after closing the *Freight bill and invoice matching* form, click the button *Submit for approval* in the action pane (if the freight invoice matches the details of the route).

After approval, you can click the button *Vendor invoice journals* in the Freight invoice details form (deselect the checkbox *Hide approved* to view the approved invoice) to access and, if necessary, to post the vendor invoice journal that has been created for the freight invoice.

8.2.3 Case Study Exercises

Exercise 8.7 – Shipping Carrier and Transportation Method

You want to manage the transportation from warehouse WH-## of exercise 8.1 to the customers. As a prerequisite, enter an address for the warehouse.

A new shipping carrier who offers transportation by drones is accepted. Set up a transportation mode M## (## = your user ID) with the name "##-Drone", and a transportation method T## with the name "##-Drone".

Next, create a vendor for the carrier with any name (starting with your user ID), a primary address of your choice, and an appropriate vendor group for domestic vendors. Then create the shipping carrier C## with the transportation mode M##. The carrier name should match the name of the vendor which you have created before. Activate the carrier and the carrier rating, and link the carrier with the corresponding vendor. Finally, enter a service S## with the transportation method M## and the billing group "Freight" for the carrier.

Exercise 8.8 – Shipping Rates and Transit Time

The carrier of exercise 8.7 offers transportation by drone at a price of USD 5 per mile for distances up to 100 miles, and at a price of USD 3 for longer distances.

Create a break master D## (## = your user ID) with the name "##-Drone price steps" for this pricing. Next, set up a rate master DR## with the name "##-Drone pricing" and the rating metadata "Milage" for this offer. In the rate bases for this rate master, insert a rate base DB## with the break master D## and the given prices. Then enter a rate base assignment with this rate base, the service S## of exercise 8.7, the postal code of the warehouse W-## of exercise 8.7 as origin, and the postal code of the customer of exercise 4.1 as destination. Assign the new rate master to the carrier of exercise 8.7.

Exercise 8.9 – Mileage and Transit Time Setup

The distance from warehouse W-## of exercise 8.7 to the customer of exercise 4.1 is 2.300 miles. The transit time for a truck is 5 days, a transport by drone takes 1 day. Enter the required settings for transporting from the postal code of the warehouse to the postal code of the customer in the transportation management setup.

Then check the results for a shipment from the warehouse to the customer in the Rate Route workbench.

Exercise 8.10 – Transportation Process

The customer of exercise 4.1 orders one unit of the item I-##-W of exercise 8.4. The item should be shipped from the warehouse W-## of exercise 8.7. Enter a sales order, check the available quantity in this warehouse, and reserve the item.

Then you want to start transportation planning: Create a load, execute the rate calculation, and create the route. Because of the short transit time, the carrier of exercise 8.7 should do the transport. In the next step, release the load to the warehouse (which creates the shipment). Then enter, process, and release a wave for the shipment as required and execute the warehouse work (like in exercise 8.6). Finally, confirm the shipment and post the packing slip.

Exercise 8.11 – Freight Bill

The carrier of exercise 8.7 transmits the freight invoice "FR001" for the transportation of exercise 8.10. Enter and process the carrier invoice until it is ready for payment.

9 Financial Management

The primary responsibility of finance and accounting is to control and to analyze the transactions that change the financial value in any area of the enterprise. These transactions are generated in business processes all over the organization.

Finance management is the core area of business management solutions. In Dynamics 365, there is a deep integration of finance with all business processes. As a result, accurate financial figures are immediately available all the time.

9.1 Business Processes in Finance

Before we start to go into details, the lines below give an overview of the business processes in finance.

9.1.1 Basic Approach

The core task of finance and accounting is to manage the general ledger with its accounts, which is the basis for the balance sheet and the income statement (profit and loss statement). Apart from the general ledger, there are subledgers – e.g., accounts receivable, accounts payable, fixed assets, projects, and inventory. These subledgers contain detailed data for the related transactions in the general ledger. Inventory management, for example, includes the inventory transactions which reflect the details of changes for the stock accounts in the general ledger.

Whenever you post a subledger transaction that has got a financial impact (e.g., an invoice in sales, or a counting difference in inventory), there is a transaction in the general ledger. If you post a sales order invoice that includes a stocked item, there are transactions in, at least, the following ledgers:

➢ **Inventory** – Financial value (in the transaction and the on-hand quantity).
➢ **Accounts receivable** – Customer debt (customer transaction).
➢ **General ledger** – Stock account, revenue account, COGS account (cost of goods sold), customer summary account.

The ledger integration is one of the core characteristics of Dynamics 365. It provides traceability of all financial vouchers back to the origin in other modules. Depending on the settings for subledger batch transfer in the General ledger parameters, subledger transactions are immediately posted to the general ledger.

For processing transactions in Dynamics 365, the voucher principle applies: In all areas of the application, you have to register a voucher before you can post it. After posting, it is not possible to modify a voucher anymore. If you want to cancel a transaction, you have to post a reversing transaction.

© Springer Fachmedien Wiesbaden GmbH, part of Springer Nature 2023
A. Luszczak, *Using Microsoft Dynamics 365 for Finance and Operations*,
https://doi.org/10.1007/978-3-658-40453-6_9

9.1.2   At a Glance: Ledger Journal Transactions

In order to record a manual ledger transaction in Dynamics 365, you use a journal. The lines below show how to post a single-line transaction in a general journal.

In the General journal list page (*General ledger> Journal entries> General journals*), which shows all open journals that are not posted yet, click the button *New* to create a new journal header. Alternatively, you can open the workspace *General journal processing* and create a journal header with the tile *New journal* there.

In the next step, select a journal name for the new journal in the column *Name* of the Journal list page and optionally enter a text that explains the transaction in the column *Description*. If the transaction is subject to sales tax or VAT, the slider *Amounts include sales tax* on the tab *Setup* of the journal header controls whether the debit (or credit) amount in the journal lines includes tax.

In order to switch to the journal lines, click the button *Lines* in the action pane (or click on the *Journal batch number* shown as a link in the grid of the list page). In a transaction that does not refer to subledgers, leave the default option "Ledger" in the column *Account type* of the journal lines and select the account number with the financial dimensions in the column *Account* (using segmented entry control). If you want to post to a subledger, select the respective *Account type* instead of the type "Ledger" and enter the related account number in the column *Account* – for example, the vendor number in a line with the *Account type* "Vendor".

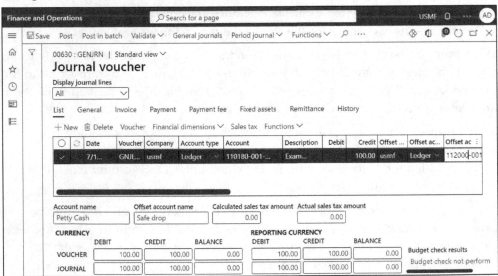

Figure 9-1:   Registering a journal line in a general journal

In a single-line transaction, you can enter the account and the offset account (including applicable financial dimensions) in the one common journal line. Once you have completed the line, post the journal with the button *Post* in the action pane of the journal header or lines.

9.2   Core Setup for Finance

Since settings in finance are a core prerequisite for the whole application, you have to complete the basic financial configuration before you can set up other modules and before you can post a transaction in any part of the application.

The basic configuration in finance includes the following items:

➢ **Fiscal and ledger calendars** – Specify the financial periods.
➢ **Currencies and exchange rates** – Specify the monetary units.
➢ **Charts of accounts** – Specify the ledger accounts.

Charts of accounts, fiscal calendars, currencies, and exchange rates are shared across companies. The Ledger form determines the accounting currency, the chart of accounts, and the calendar that is used in the current company. If you want to manage a separate chart of accounts or calendar per company, set it up and assign it accordingly in the Ledger form of each company.

9.2.1   Fiscal and Ledger Calendars

The primary purpose of fiscal calendars is to determine the fiscal year. Within a fiscal year, the financial periods are specified with the start date and the end date. The ledger calendar, which is based on a fiscal calendar, controls at the company level which financial periods are open for transactions.

9.2.1.1   Fiscal Calendars

Fiscal calendars are shared across the companies within a common Dynamics 365 environment. The field *Fiscal calendar* in the Ledger form (*General ledger> Ledger setup> Ledger*) determines the applicable fiscal calendar for the current company. Selecting the fiscal calendar is part of the initial company setup.

Within the fiscal years of a fiscal calendar, there are the accounting periods with start date and end date. The length of the individual accounting periods depends on the reporting requirements of the company.

In order to edit the fiscal calendars, open the menu item *General ledger> Calendars> Fiscal calendars*. If you want to create a new fiscal calendar, click the button *New calendar* and enter the calendar ID together with the settings for the first fiscal year (start date, end date, name, period length, and unit – be sure to select the unit "Months" in case of monthly periods) in the drop-down menu for the calendar.

If you want to add a fiscal year to an existing fiscal calendar, select the calendar in the lookup field *Calendar* at the top left before you click the button *New year* in the action pane. In the related drop-down menu, select to copy the settings from the last year (set the slider *Copy from last fiscal year* to "Yes"), or – if you select not to copy – manually enter the end date, the period length, and the unit for the new year. Then click the button *Create* in the dialog to create the new year with its accounting periods.

9.2.1.2 Opening Periods and Closing Periods

Apart from regular operating periods (with the *Type* "Operating"), there are two period types which are not available for regular transactions – the types "Closing" and "Opening". If required, you can attach multiple closing periods to each operating period.

Closing periods contain period-end or year-end transactions. You can only register and post these transactions in a closing sheet (*General ledger> Period close> Closing period adjustments*) in the course of period closing.

Opening periods contain the opening transactions for a fiscal year. Once the previous year is closed, you can create the opening transactions in the menu item *General ledger> Period close> Year end close* based on the closing transactions.

9.2.1.3 Ledger Calendars

As a prerequisite for posting a transaction in Dynamics 365, the posting date of the transaction has to be included in a ledger period with the period status "Open". The required period status is controlled at the company level in the ledger calendar, not in the shared fiscal calendar.

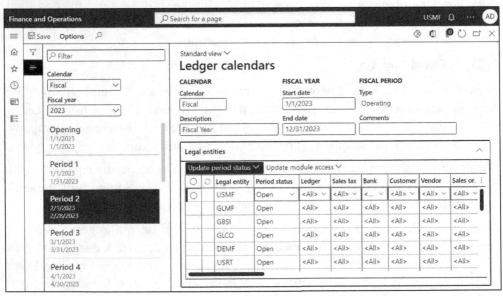

Figure 9-2:   Managing the period status in the ledger calendar

The ledger calendar (*General ledger> Calendars> Ledger calendars*) contains the periods of the fiscal calendar that is assigned to the current company (selected in the Ledger form). For the (fiscal) *Calendar*, the *Fiscal year*, and the period that is selected on the left of the Ledger calendar form, the tab *Legal entities* on the right shows all assigned companies with their period status. You can open or close periods for individual companies (select the respective option in the column *Period status*) or in common (select the applicable companies and click the button *Update period status*).

If the period status is "Open", you can post transactions in that period. The period status "On hold" blocks posting. The status "Permanently closed" also blocks posting, but whereas it is possible to reopen periods that are on hold, this is not possible for permanently closed periods. For this reason, only close a period permanently when it is definitely closed in accounting (after reporting to the authorities).

With the button *Update module access* and the related columns, you can set a module-specific blocking of transactions and exclude user groups from blocking.

In order to support period closing, the workspace *Financial period close* shows a list of tasks. You can set up these tasks in the menu item *General ledger> Period close> Financial period close configuration*.

9.2.2 Currencies and Exchange Rates

The value and the amount in financial transactions – general ledger transactions and subledger transactions (e.g., inventory or customer transactions) – refer to currencies. A transaction is always recorded in the accounting currency of the company, and, if applicable, additionally in a foreign currency. For this reason, the setup of currencies is a prerequisite for posting any transaction in Dynamics 365.

9.2.2.1 Currencies

In order to facilitate the currency management in multi-company organizations, the currency table is shared across all companies within a common Dynamics 365 environment. For the currency that you select in the list pane on the left of the Currency form (*General ledger> Currencies> Currencies*), the tabs on the right show the related settings for this currency. This includes the definition of the rounding precision on the tab *Rounding rules*.

9.2.2.2 Exchange Rates

Exchange rate types (*General ledger> Currencies> Exchange rate types)* enable multiple parallel exchange rates between currencies. You can use two exchange rate types, for example, if you want to apply different exchange rates for budget entries and for current transactions.

In order to access the Currency exchange rates form, click the button *Exchange rates* in the Exchange rate types form, or open the menu item *General ledger> Currencies> Currency exchange rates*. For the *Exchange rate type* selected at the top left in the Currency exchange rate form (see Figure 9-3), the related currency relations are shown in the list pane below. If you need an additional relation (e.g., for a currency which has not been used before), click the button *New* in the action pane and enter the details in the upper area of the right pane. The *Conversion factor* specifies the applicable factor for the exchange rate calculation.

The tab *Add or remove exchange rates* on the right shows the exchange rates for the currency relation that is selected in the list pane on the left. The filter *From date* and *To date* determines the date range for displaying exchange rates. In order to enter an exchange rate for a new date, click the button *Add* in the toolbar of the tab. The column *Exchange value* shows the conversion result. In daily business, enter or import (*General ledger> Currencies> Import currency exchange rates*) new exchange rates regularly to use a correct conversion of foreign currency transactions.

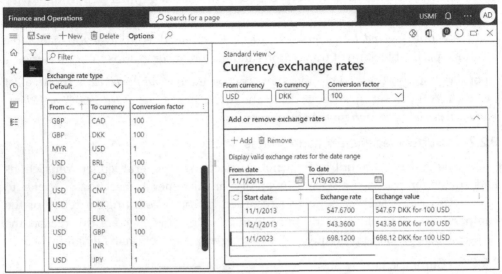

Figure 9-3:   Managing exchange rates in the Currency exchange rate form

Currency exchange rates and exchange rate types are shared across all companies. If you need to keep separate exchange rates per company, select a different exchange rate type for each company in the Ledger form.

9.2.2.3 Currency Settings in the Ledger Form

The *Accounting currency* on the tab *Currency* in the Ledger form (*General ledger> Ledger setup> Ledger*) determines the local currency of the current company. This currency is used in all financial transactions. If required for reporting purposes, you can additionally select a *Reporting currency* in the Ledger form. It is not possible to change the accounting currency or the reporting currency of a company once transactions are registered.

The *Accounting currency exchange rate type* in the Ledger form determines the default exchange rate type for foreign currencies in regular transactions. In addition, there are separate exchange rate types for the reporting currency and for budget transactions.

The main accounts for exchange rate gains and losses in the current company are specified on the tab *Accounts for currency revaluation* in the Ledger form.

9.2.3 Financial Dimensions

In addition to the main accounts that are specified in the chart of accounts, the financial dimensions (like "Cost center" or "Department") are further levels in the structure of financial transactions. The required financial dimensions in a ledger transaction depend on the account structures that are assigned to the current company.

Financial reporting is not only possible at the level of company and main account, but also at the level of financial dimensions. This is, apart from other reporting requirements, also useful with reference to the multisite functionality: If you assign a financial dimension to the inventory dimension "Site" (see section 10.1.6), you can, for example, report the income statement per subsidiary within a legal entity.

9.2.3.1 Setup of Financial Dimensions

In Dynamics 365, financial dimensions and dimension values are shared across the companies within a common Dynamics 365 environment.

Financial dimensions are not limited to standard dimensions like department, cost center, and purpose, but you can easily set up individual financial dimensions. With regard to the ease of use and the probability of wrong entries, you should not set up more dimensions than effectively required.

If you want to set up a new financial dimension, open the menu item *General ledger> Chart of accounts> Dimensions> Financial dimensions* and click the button *New*. Then select the origin of the related financial dimension values in the lookup field *Use values from*:

➢ **<Custom dimension>** – Create a dimension without reference to other tables.
➢ **One of the other options** – Link the dimension to other entities in the application (e.g., customers, item groups, or departments).

If you select, for example, the option "Departments" in the field *Use values from*, the financial dimension is linked to operating units with the type "Department". In this case, each department that is entered in the organization management (*Organization administration> Organizations> Operating units*) is synchronously available as financial dimension value for this dimension.

If you select the option "<Custom dimension>" in the lookup field *Use values from*, you must enter the financial dimension values manually.

Once you have created a new dimension, a system administrator or a user with appropriate privileges has to activate the dimension (click the button *Activate* in the Financial dimension form).

After activation, you can optionally set the slider *Copy values to this dimension ...* to "Yes" if the dimension is linked to an entity like the customer table or the project table. In this case, Dynamics 365 does not only create a dimension value with each new record in the respective main table (e.g., new project), but also assigns the dimension value as default value to the new record (e.g., for projects on the tab *Financial dimensions* in the Projects form). This way you can run financial reporting on, e.g., project numbers without manually creating or assigning a financial dimension value to new projects.

Note: You can only activate financial dimensions when the system is in the maintenance mode.

9.2.3.2 Financial Dimension Values

You can access the dimension values of a financial dimension with the button *Financial dimension values* in the Financial dimension form. For custom dimensions, you have to create the *Dimension values* manually. For other financial dimensions, you can edit the dimension value details, but you cannot create records (since the dimension values derive from a different table).

For the dimension value which you select in the list pane on the left, the related details are shown on the right. The tab *General* on the right contains shared settings that apply to all companies which use the dimension. If you want to block future transactions that refer to the selected dimension value, set the slider *Suspended* to "Yes" or enter applicable dates in the field *Active from* or *Active to*. On the tab *Legal entity overrides*, you can enter further blocking at the company level.

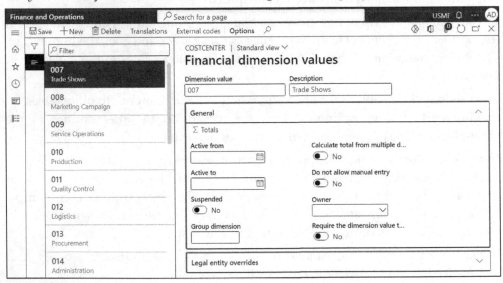

Figure 9-4:   Managing dimension values for a financial dimension

9.2.3.3 Using Financial Dimensions

A financial dimension has to be included in the account structures or the advanced rule structures which are assigned to the current company before you can use it in transactions and inquiries. Settings in the applicable account structure or advanced rule structure also determine, if and which dimension value is optional or required when posting to a particular account.

In master data forms (e.g., in the Customer form or in the Released product form), the tab *Financial dimensions* shows all financial dimensions that are included in the account structures and the advanced rule structures of the current company. A dimension value, which you enter on this tab, is used as default dimension value when registering an order or a journal line.

In the ledger journal lines and in all other forms with a ledger account field, financial dimensions are not shown as separate fields. Using segmented entry control (see section 9.3.1), the financial dimensions are to be entered together with the main account in one – segmented – field.

9.2.3.4   Balancing Financial Dimension and Interunit Accounting

Interunit accounting, an optional feature in Dynamics 365, ensures a balanced balance sheet for a selected financial dimension – the balancing dimension. The following settings are required for the use of interunit accounting:

➢ **Accounts for automatic transactions** – Enter appropriate main accounts for the *Posting type* "Interunit-debit" and "Interunit-credit" in the accounts for automatic transactions (see section 9.2.4).
➢ **Balancing financial dimension** – Selected in the Ledger form.

If a dimension is selected in the field *Balancing financial dimension* in the Ledger form, you have to enter a dimension value for this dimension in each transaction. If the from-value for the balancing dimension in a transaction is different from the to-value, Dynamics 365 posts additional balancing transactions to the main accounts "Interunit-debit" and "Interunit-credit". These balancing transactions are posted together with the ledger transaction from, e.g., one department to another (if departments are the balancing dimension).

9.2.4   Account Structures and Chart of Accounts

Account structures, charts of accounts, and main accounts determine the core structure in finance. They are shared across companies in Dynamics 365. In a company, the chart of accounts that is selected in the Ledger form determines the applicable main accounts. The applicable financial dimensions are controlled by the assigned account structures.

9.2.4.1   Ledger Account and Main Account

The ledger account field in a financial transaction includes the main account and the applicable financial dimensions. The account structure, which is assigned at the level of company and main account, controls the financial dimensions which are included in the ledger account.

9.2.4.2   Charts of Accounts

Depending on the structure of your organization and the number of legal entities, there is one common or multiple independent charts of accounts. The Chart of accounts form (*General ledger> Chart of Accounts> Accounts> Chart of Accounts*) shows all available charts of accounts in the list pane on the left. For the chart of accounts that you select on the left, the main accounts are shown on the right. If you expand the *Related information* pane on the right, the FactBox *Ledgers* will show the ledgers and legal entities which use the selected chart of accounts.

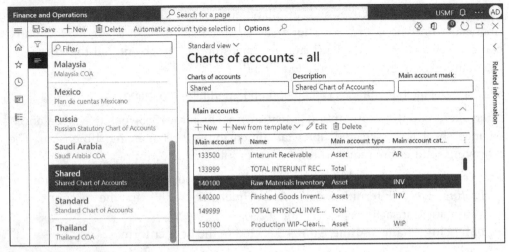

Figure 9-5:   Editing a chart of accounts

If you want to create a completely new chart of accounts, click the button *New* in the action pane. In order to create a main account, click the button *New* or *Edit* in the toolbar of the tab *Main accounts*. In the Main accounts form which is shown then, you can insert or modify the main accounts of the selected chart of accounts.

9.2.4.3 Settings in the Ledger Form

Settings in the Ledger form (*General ledger> Ledger setup> Ledger*) determine the chart of accounts and the account structures which are assigned to the current company. These settings are required before you can register any transaction.

You can use one common chart of accounts in multiple companies – select the same *Chart of accounts* in the respective field of the Ledger form in all applicable companies. Once the first transaction has been posted in a company, it is not possible to change the chart of accounts assignment anymore.

The tab *Account structures* in the Ledger form contains the account structures that are assigned to the current company. In order to add an account structure, click the button *Add* in the toolbar of this tab. Since the account structures determine the available financial dimensions when posting to a ledger main account, each main account which is included in the chart of accounts has to be uniquely assigned to one account structure without overlapping or missing assignments.

If you use interunit accounting, select the balancing financial dimension of the company in the Ledger form. If selected, this dimension has to be included in all account structures of the company.

9.2.4.4 Account Structures

The page *General ledger> Chart of Accounts> Structures> Configure account structures* shows all account structures of the enterprise. If you want to access the details of an account structure, click on the respective field *Name* shown as a link in the grid. Alternatively, open the Account structures detail form from the Ledger form (button *Configure account structures* in the toolbar of the tab *Account structures*).

If you want to create a completely new segment combination that consists of the main account and financial dimensions, click the button *New* in the Account structure list page to create a new account structure. In the drop-down menu that is shown next, the slider *Add main account* usually remains set to "Yes" in order to include the main account as the first segment. You can set this slider to "No" if you want to use a financial dimension, and not the main account, as the first segment – e.g., if your organization has got divisions and you want to apply the division as the first segment in transactions. Once you click the button *Create* in the dialog, the Account structures detail form with the new account structure is shown.

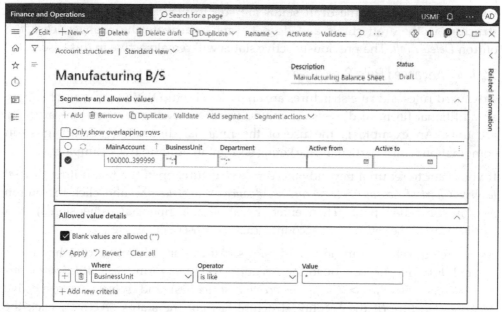

Figure 9-6: Configuring an account structure in the detail form

When you create a new or edit an existing account structure, it has got the status "Draft". In order to add dimensions to the account structure, click the button *Add segment* in the toolbar of the upper pane in the detail form. Then select a segment (financial dimension) in the *Add segment* dialog. Once you close the dialog with the new segment, the related column is shown in the upper pane of the detail form. You can subsequently enter a filter for the segment (an advanced filter in the field itself, or, in an easier way, on the tab *Allowed value details*). If you select the checkbox *Blank values are allowed* for a segment, the dimension is optional, and you are not required to select a dimension value when entering a transaction for a ledger main account which is covered by the account structure.

The example in Figure 9-6 shows an account structure for the main accounts "100000" to "399999", which contains the financial dimensions "BusinessUnit" and "Department" and does not restrict the available dimension values for the dimension "BusinessUnit".

If applicable to the account structure, you can add one or more lines for a segment – including the segment with the main account – with appropriate filters that prevent overlapping definitions. In this way, you can specify multiple allowed dimension value combinations.

Once you have finished the setup of an account structure, click the button *Activate* to put the updated account structure into place. The status is "Active" then. If you want to edit an account structure later, click the button *Edit* in the action pane. The account structure status then switches to "Draft". For the transactions that are posted until the new draft is activated, the settings in the account structure before you have switched to the draft status are still in place. If you edit the account structure in the draft status and do not want to activate the changes, click the button *Delete draft*. The previously active status will remain active in this case.

9.2.4.5 Advanced Rule Structures

Advanced rules and rule structures are an optional setup that you can use to apply an additional financial dimension only to transactions of one or a few particular accounts. An example is the use of the financial dimension "Campaigns" in combination with a particular marketing account in order to track campaigns.

If you want to set up a new advanced rule structure, open the menu item *General ledger> Chart of Accounts> Structures> Advanced rule structures* and click the button *New* in the action pane. Then enter the applicable financial dimension(s) in a similar way to the setup of an account structure (described above).

As a prerequisite for an advanced rule structure, an advanced rule has to be created. For this purpose, open the Account structures form (*General ledger> Chart of Accounts> Structures> Configure account structures*) and select the respective account structure (if the account structure has got the status "Active", click the button *Edit* to switch to the status "Draft") before you click the button *Advanced rules*. In the Advanced rules form, click the button *New* and enter the ID and name for the new advanced rule in the drop-down menu. In order to specify the main accounts which are assigned to the advanced rule, click the button *Add new criteria* on the tab *Advanced rule criteria* of the Advanced rules form.

Then click the button *Add* on the tab *Advanced rule structures* to assign the advanced rule to an advanced rule structure. Activating the account structure, to which the advanced rule is assigned, activates the advanced rule in parallel.

9.2.4.6 Main Accounts

The structure and the format of the main accounts in the chart of accounts only depend on the internal requirements of your company. For reporting purposes (balance sheet, income statement, and other reports in finance), you can set up and use financial reports (*General ledger> Inquiries and reports> Financial reports*) with a structure that is separate from the structure of the chart of accounts.

If you want to edit the main accounts, open the menu item *General ledger> Chart of accounts> Accounts> Main accounts* and click the button *Edit*. Alternatively, you can access the main accounts from the Chart of accounts form (button *Edit* in the toolbar of the tab *Main accounts*).

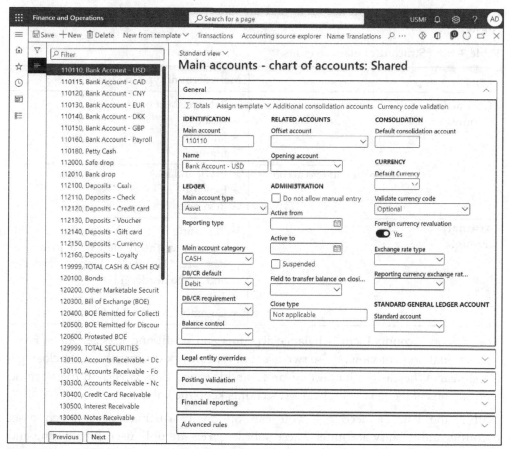

Figure 9-7: Editing a ledger main account

The Main accounts form shows the chart of accounts that is assigned to the current company. The name of this chart of accounts is shown in the header on the right. In case this chart of accounts is assigned to multiple companies, keep in mind that changes on main accounts in this form also affect the other companies.

If you want to create a new account, click the button *New* in the action pane and enter a unique *Main account* number, a *Name*, and a *Main account type*. If you want to enter a translation of the account name, click the button *Name Translations* in the action pane.

In the structure of the main accounts, you have to distinguish between transaction accounts and auxiliary accounts. The core difference between transaction accounts and auxiliary accounts is that you can only use a transaction account in a financial transaction. Auxiliary accounts serve to establish a clear structure of the chart of accounts, but they are not necessarily required.

The *Main account type*, a lookup field in the Main accounts form, divides the accounts into transaction accounts and auxiliary accounts as shown in Table 9-1 below.

Table 9-1:   Structure of main accounts

Type		Main account type in Dynamics 365
Transaction accounts	Balance accounts	➢ Balance sheet ➢ Asset ➢ Liability ➢ Equity
	Profit and loss accounts	➢ Profit and loss ➢ Expense ➢ Revenue
Auxiliary accounts		➢ Reporting (options in the related field *Reporting type* are "Header", "Empty header", and "Page header") ➢ Total ➢ Common (required in China)

Transaction accounts include balance accounts and profit and loss accounts. From a functional point of view, these two account types work differently when closing a fiscal year: Whereas the balance of profit and loss accounts is zero in the opening transactions of the next year, balance accounts keep the balance.

Within the balance accounts, you can optionally distinguish between asset accounts and liability accounts. These subcategories are only used for filtering and sorting purposes. The same way in which you can subcategorize balance accounts, you can split profit and loss accounts into expense accounts and revenue accounts.

In addition to the main account type, the lookup field *Main account category* on the tab *General* of the Main accounts form provides another classification of main accounts. Main account categories (*General ledger> Chart of accounts> Accounts> Main accounts categories*) can be used as a basis for financial reports.

When setting up a ledger main account which receives transactions from other modules (e.g., a summary account for vendor liabilities), select the checkbox *Do not allow manual entry* to block manual transactions on this account.

In further fields on the tab *General* in the Main accounts form, and on the tabs *Posting validation* and *Financial reporting*, you can specify default values and restrictions for transactions. On the tab *Legal entity overrides*, you can block a ledger main account or enter default values for financial dimensions at the company level.

9.2.4.7 Transaction Inquiry and Trial Balance

The inquiry *General ledger> Inquiries and reports> Voucher transactions* shows all posted ledger transactions as selected in the filter dialog. In the Main accounts form, you can click the button *Transactions* in the action pane to view the ledger transactions of the selected account. A button for viewing related ledger transaction is also available in other forms – e.g., in the Trial balance form.

In the Transactions form, the following buttons provide access to further details:

> **Voucher** – Shows the complete voucher (all general ledger transactions that are posted with the selected voucher).
> **Transaction origin** – Shows the related transactions in all modules.
> **Original document** – Provides the option to reprint a document.
> **Audit trail** – Shows the user and the actual time of posting.

If you want to view the balances of the main accounts, open the Trial balance form (*General ledger> Inquiries and reports> Trial balance*) and specify the period that is used for calculating the account balances in the *Parameters* pane at the top of the form. Then click the button *Calculate balances* in this pane to execute the calculation.

9.2.4.8 Accounts for Automatic Transactions

Settings in the *Accounts for automatic transactions* are used for ledger transactions that are posted automatically and for which there is no other setting – e.g., for invoice discounts.

If you want to enter a new account for automatic transactions, open the menu item *General ledger> Posting setup> Accounts for automatic transactions* and insert a record with the posting type and the assigned main account. You can generate a basic set of posting types, for which you enter the default accounts, with the button *Create default types*. Core settings in the accounts for automatic transactions include:

> **Error account** – Used in case of missing account settings.
> **Penny difference in accounting currency** – For small payment differences.
> **Year-end result** – Account for profit/loss when closing the fiscal year.
> **Order invoice rounding** – Sales invoice rounding.
> **Vendor invoice rounding-off** – Purchase invoice rounding.
> **Vendor invoice discount** – Main account for purchase order total discounts.
> **Customer invoice discount** – Main account for sales order total discounts.

If the slider *Interrupt in case or error account* in the General ledger parameters is set to "Yes", Dynamics 365 will display an error message instead of posting to the error account (in case there is a transaction for which no main account is specified in the integration settings).

9.2.4.9 Default Descriptions

Default descriptions (*General ledger> Journal setup> Default descriptions*) determine a default text for transactions which are posted automatically (based on the ledger integration). If you want to enter a new default description, select the transaction type in the field *Description* first. Then enter the *Language* ("user" for a generic description) and the *Text*. The *Text* may include variables – available variables are shown at the bottom of the right pane.

9.2.5 Customers, Vendors, and Bank Accounts

When entering a ledger transaction in a journal line, you can – apart from a ledger account – select a customer, a vendor, a project, a bank account, or a fixed asset in the account field and in the offset account field.

9.2.5.1 Bank Accounts

Before selecting a bank account in a transaction, set it up in the Bank accounts form (*Cash and bank management> Bank accounts> Bank accounts*). In order to create a new bank account, click the button *New* and enter the (internal) bank account ID, the *Routing number* (identifies the bank), the *Bank account number* (as specified by the bank), and the *Name* for the bank account. In the field *Main account*, enter the main account that is assigned to the particular bank account.

The field *Currency* specifies the currency of the bank account. If you want to enable transactions in multiple currencies, set the slider *Allow transactions in additional currencies* to "Yes". The tab *Additional identification* contains the fields for IBAN and SWIFT/BIC.

If your company has got multiple bank accounts at a particular bank, you can create a bank group (*Cash and bank management> Setup> Bank groups*) with general bank data like routing number, address, and contact information. If you select a bank group in the related field on the tab *General* of the Bank accounts form, the bank account is initialized with these data.

9.2.5.2 Vendors

In order to manage vendors in Dynamics 365, open the list page *Accounts payable> Vendors> All vendors* and edit the vendor data as described in section 3.2.1. If you want to view the vendor transactions (invoices and payments), select the vendor and click the button *Vendor/Transactions/Transactions* in the action pane. If the vendor is shared across companies (see section 3.2.1), click the button *Vendor/ Transactions/Global transactions* to view the vendor transactions in all companies.

Apart from the invoice or payment amount in the column *Amount*, the column *Balance* in the Vendor transactions form shows the open, not yet settled amount.

9.2.5.3 Settlement of Vendor Transactions

If you want to apply a posted payment to an invoice, click the button *Invoice/Settle/ Settle transactions* in the Vendor form to access the open vendor transactions. In the *Settle transactions* dialog, select the checkbox *Mark* in the transaction lines which you want to settle. You can settle one or more invoices with one or more payments or credit notes. If there are transactions in foreign currencies, you can specify the settlement date (for calculating exchange rate gain or loss) in the field group *Settlement posting date* at the top of the dialog. The field group *Date used for calculating discounts* determines the date for cash discount calculation. It includes the following options:

> **Transaction date** – Select the transaction line that contains the date for discount calculation and click the button *Mark as primary payment* in the toolbar.
> **Selected date** – Enter the discount calculation date in the date field on the right.

Before you post the settlement with the button *Post* in the dialog, check the balance of the marked transactions on the tab *Totals* at the bottom of the dialog.

If you do not want to post the settlements as a separate step, you can register the settlement already when entering a payment (see section 9.3.3).

In case you have to cancel a posted settlement, open the Closed transactions form with the button *Invoice/Settle/Undo settlement* in the Vendor form. In the Closed transactions form, you can reverse settlements.

9.2.5.4 Customers

You can find details on customer records (*Accounts receivable> Customers> All Customers*) in section 4.2.1 of this book. The way to execute transaction inquiries and to settle transactions (on the action pane tab *COLLECT*) for customers is similar to the procedures in vendor management.

9.2.6 Customer Credit Management

The Credit and collections module includes the credit management for the credit limit of customers and the collections management for payment reminders.

Below you can find a description of the core functionality for credit management. The credit management adds various enhancements to customer credit limits, including the option to flexibly set and manage holds for sales order, or features for credit limit adjustments and shared credit limits.

9.2.6.1 Credit Management Setup

Blocking rules (*Credit management> Setup> Credit management setup> Blocking rules*), which control the credit holds for orders (similar to regular order holds, see section 4.4.3), are a core setting for credit management. The different areas or triggers for blocking are reflected in the sections on the left of the Blocking rules form – e.g., blocking based on overdue invoices or on the total amount of the sales order.

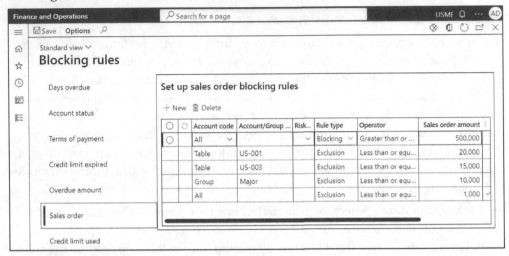

Figure 9-8:   Setting up a blocking rule for high-value sales orders

Apart from blocking rules with the *Rule type* "Blocking", you can enter blocking rules with the *Rule type* "Exclusion" – e.g., to prevent blocking of low-value orders. If you select the checkbox in the column *Release sales order* (only available for the *Rule type* "Exclusion"), applicable sales orders will be released regardless of any other rule that may block the order.

Apart from the blocking rules, which set credit holds as applicable (including a possible hold with the trigger "Credit limit used"), the Credit and collections parameters (*Credit management> Setup> Credit and collections parameters*, section *Credit*, tab *Credit limits*) include an additional setting which can stop transactions when exceeding the credit limit. If the parameter *Check credit limit for sales order* is set to "Yes" and the parameter *Message when exceeding credit limit* is set to "Error", an error message will prevent posting the order confirmation or other documents when exceeding the credit limit. Depending on the parameter *Credit limit type*, this credit limit check only includes unpaid invoices, or also open packing slips, or additionally open orders.

Settings on the tabs *Credit holds* and *Credit management checkpoint* of the Credit and collections parameters control how blocking rules are processed.

A credit management reason (*Credit management> Setup> Credit management setup> Credit management reasons*) with the *Reason type* "Hold", "Release", or "Status" is mandatory when manually setting or releasing a credit hold, and optional when updating the account status.

The account status (*Credit and collections> Setup> Credit management setup> Account statuses*) is an optional setting that characterizes the credit standing of customers and that you can use as trigger in the blocking rules.

If enabled in the Credit and collection parameters (Section *Credit*, tab *Credit holds*, slider *Check customer credit groups credit limit*), you can specify a common (shared) credit limit for customers by the use of customer credit groups (*Credit management> Customers> Customer credit groups*). If a credit limit is also specified on the individual customer, the lower of both will be used for the customer – except if the customer has got unlimited credit limit (applicable result: unlimited credit limit), or if the customer credit limit is zero and the slider *Mandatory credit limit* for the customer is set to "No" (applicable result: credit limit of the group).

In the Customer detail form, settings on the tab *Credit and collections* (see section 4.2.1) include the options *Unlimited credit limit* and *Exclude from credit management*, the *Credit management group*, the *Credit limit*, the *Credit limit expiration date*, and the *Account status*. For the credit limit and other core customer fields, you can enable an approval process (similar to the vendor approval, see section 3.2.1).

9.2.6.2 Working with Credit Holds

When you post a sales document – e.g., a sales order confirmation – and this document is defined as checkpoint in the Credit and collections parameters (*Credit management> Setup> Credit and collections parameters*, section *Credit*, tab *Credit management checkpoint*), a credit hold will be set automatically if a blocking rule with the with the *Rule type* "Blocking" applies.

You can view this hold in the Credit management hold list (*Credit management> Credit management hold list> Open credit holds*), which you can also access with the button *Credit management/Credit management/Credit management hold list* in the Sales order form. In the Credit management hold list, you can check the *Blocking reasons* in the related FactBox (alternatively, click the button *Blocking reasons*).

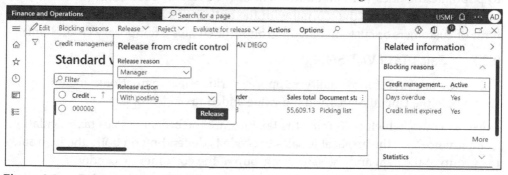

Figure 9-9: Releasing a credit hold

If you want to manually release blocking, click the button *Release* in the Credit management hold list and select a *Release reason* in the related drop-down. If you select the *Release action* "With posting", the posting that has triggered the hold will be executed when releasing the hold. Otherwise, only the hold is released and posting the original document has to be executed separately. As an alternative to manually releasing, you can click the button *Evaluate for release/Process blocking rules* in the Credit management hold list to execute a check whether the original blocking reason is still valid. If the circumstances have changed accordingly (e.g., with a customer payment), the hold will be released automatically (with or without posting, depending on the setting *Automatically release* in the section *Credit* of the Credit and collection parameters).

If you want to manually set a credit hold in a sales order, click the button *Credit management/Credit management/Force credit hold* in the Sales order form and select the hold reason in the following dialog.

9.2.6.3 Adjusting the Credit Limit

You can manually edit the field *Credit limit* in the Customer detail form, which automatically populates the field *Credit limit change date* accordingly.

Unlike the regular credit limit, the temporary credit limits, which you can access with the button *Credit management/Related information/Temporary credit limits* in the Customer form, are not editable. You can only update temporary credit limits with a credit limit adjustment journal.

Credit limit adjustment journals (*Credit management> Credit limit adjustments> Credit limit adjustments*) are used to insert or update the regular credit limit or a temporary credit limit. In a similar way to managing a trade agreement journal (see section 4.3.2), you can create a new journal with the button *New* in this form. Then select the *Credit limit adjustment type* ("Credit limit" or "Temporary credit limit") and click the button *Lines* to access the Journal lines form. In the journal lines, you can manually enter a new credit limit or a temporary credit limit per customer or customer credit group. Alternatively, you can click the button *Generate* to populate the lines with an adjustment of the current credit limit (fixed amount or percentage). Posting the journal with the button *Post* updates the current credit limit of customers or customer credit groups (or creates a temporary credit limit).

9.2.7   Sales Tax / VAT Settings

The sales tax/VAT functionality supports various tax regulations, including the sales tax in the United States and the value added tax in Europe.

Sales tax codes, which determine the tax rate, are the basis for sales tax calculation. In an invoice line, the applicable sales tax code is depending on both, the item sales tax group of the item and the sales tax group of the customer or vendor.

9.2.7.1 Sales Tax Parameters

A primary setting for the tax calculation is whether sales tax is used: If your company is subject to taxation with sales tax (and not with VAT), set the slider *Apply sales tax taxation rules* in the General ledger parameters (*Tax> Setup> Parameters> General ledger parameters*, section *Sales tax*) to "Yes". Further parameters for sales tax include a default *Item sales tax group* or the setting whether cash discounts reduce sales tax.

9.2.7.2 Sales Tax Authorities

In the setup of sales tax calculation, enter the authorities (*Tax> Indirect taxes> Sales tax> Sales tax authorities*) with ID, *Name*, and *Report layout* for tax reporting first.

9.2.7.3 Sales Tax Settlement Periods

Applicable periods for tax reporting (usually monthly periods) are specified in the menu item *Tax> Indirect taxes> Sales tax> Sales tax settlement periods*.

When you create a settlement period definition with ID and description, assign the applicable *Authority* and enter the period length (*Period interval unit* and *Period interval duration*) on the tab *General*. Then switch to the tab *Period intervals* and click the button *Add* in the toolbar to enter the first period manually (e.g., Jan 1 – Jan 31). Create further periods with the button *New period interval* in the toolbar of this tab.

9.2.7.4 Ledger Posting Groups

Sales tax ledger posting groups control the main accounts for sales tax transactions (depending on the sales tax code of the invoice transaction).

In order to create a sales tax ledger posting group, open the menu item *Sales tax> Setup> Sales tax> Ledger posting groups* and click the button *New*. Enter the group ID and description before you select the main account for the *Sales tax payable*, for the *Sales tax receivable*, for the *Use tax expense*, and the *Use tax payable* as applicable. The *Settlement account* specifies the balance account for the payment to the authorities.

Note: Depending on the setting *Apply sales tax taxation rules* in the General ledger parameters, not all fields in the Ledger posting groups form are shown.

9.2.7.5 Sales Tax Codes

Sales tax codes (*Tax> Indirect taxes> Sales tax> Sales tax codes*) control the tax rate and the calculation basis. On the tab *General* in the Sales tax code form, assign the *Settlement period* and the *Ledger posting group*. Detailed calculation parameters are available on the tab *Calculation*. In order to specify the tax rate, click the button *Sales tax code/Sales tax code/Values* in the action pane and enter the applicable rate in the column *Value* of the Sales tax code values form.

Once you have created a sales tax code, assign it to applicable sales tax groups and item sales tax groups. Dynamics 365 determines the sales tax code of an invoice line from the sales tax code, which is included in the settings of both – the item sales tax group of the item, and the sales tax group of the customer or vendor.

In order to apply, for example, a tax code "AV_CAST" to a sales invoice line, the line has to comply with both of the following conditions:

➢ **Item sales tax group** – The item sales tax group of the item contains the sales tax code "AV_CAST".

➢ **Sales tax group** – The sales tax group of the customer contains the sales tax code "AV_CAST".

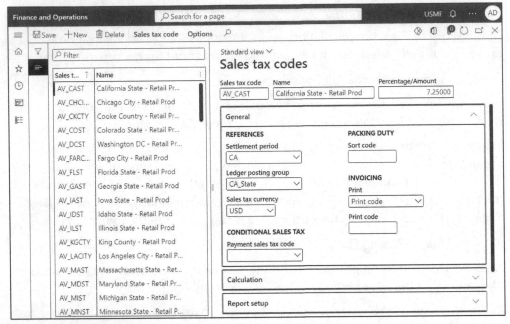

Figure 9-10: Managing the sales tax codes

9.2.7.6 Sales Tax Groups and Item Sales Tax Groups

If you want to set up a new sales tax group, open the menu item *Tax> Indirect taxes> Sales tax> Sales tax groups* and click the button *New*. Enter the ID and the description on the tab *Overview* before you switch to the tab *Setup*. On this tab, insert all applicable sales tax codes for the customers or vendors with this group.

In order to assign the sales tax group to a customer or vendor, open the Customer form (or Vendor form) and select the *Sales tax group* on the tab *Invoice and delivery* in the detail form – usually when creating a customer or vendor. Default values for the sales tax group are specified in the customer group (or vendor group).

The menu item *Tax> Indirect taxes> Sales tax> Item sales tax groups* provides access to the item sales tax groups, which apply to the released products. Setting up an item sales tax groups works similar to setting up a sales tax group.

In order to assign item sales tax groups to an item, open the Released product form and select the *Item sales tax group* for sales (on the tab *Sell*) and for purchasing (on the tab *Purchase*) in the detail form. Default values for the item sales tax groups are specified on the tab *Setup* in the Item group form. If you are using product categories in order lines, assign applicable item sales tax group to the categories in the Procurement category form and in the Sales category form.

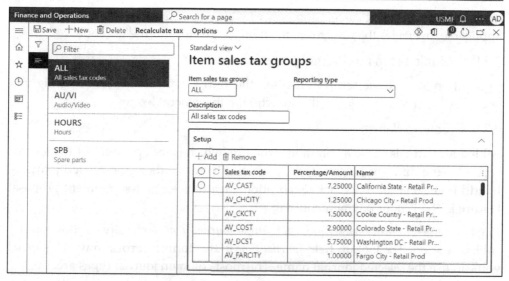

Figure 9-11: Managing the item sales tax groups

9.2.7.7 Sales Tax Transactions

When you enter a transaction in a journal line or in an order line, Dynamics 365 initializes the sales tax code based on the item and the customer/vendor. In order to view the calculated tax before posting, click the button *Sales tax* in the action pane or in the toolbar. This button is available in journal lines, sales and purchase order headers or lines, and posting dialogs (e.g., for the sales invoice).

If necessary, you can change the sales tax groups or the sales tax code in a journal line or order line before posting. When posting an invoice, Dynamics 365 generates a transaction for the sales tax in the general ledger (according to the ledger posting group assigned to the sales tax code) and a sales tax transaction in the tax ledger.

9.2.7.8 Tax Calculation Service

The tax calculation service, which is available for cloud-hosted environments, provides the option to execute the tax calculation as a separate service on Microsoft Azure. It offers a better performance and an improved compliance with ever-changing tax regulations in various countries.

As a prerequisite for using the tax calculation service, activate it in the feature management, install and configure the Tax Calculation add-in in the Lifecycle Services (LCS) and in the Regulatory Configuration Service (RCS). Then enable the service in the parameters (*Tax> Setup> Tax configuration> Tax calculation parameters*).

If the tax calculation service is enabled, transactions like a sales order initially receive the sales tax group, the item sales tax group, and the tax code from within the transactional Dynamics 365 environment. When the tax calculation is triggered, for example with the button *Sell/Tax/Sales tax* in the Sales order form, the required data are sent to the tax calculation service which calculates the tax amount and, if applicable, overrides the tax group, the item tax group, and the tax code.

9.2.8   Basic Setup for Journal Transactions

In addition to the basic setup in finance, the journal names have to be configured before you can register a journal transaction in the general ledger.

9.2.8.9   Journal Names

All ledger journals show a common structure, which is independent of the journal type. But the different journal types enable different fields in the related journals. In addition, some journals include additional features – e.g., the payment proposal feature in the vendor payment journal.

Journal names (*General ledger> Journal setup> Journal names*) classify transactions by subject matters. The lookup field *Journal type* in this form controls, in which journal you can use the selected journal name. The most common journal types are:

> **Daily** – General journal.
> **Periodic** – Periodic journal.
> **Vendor invoice recording** – Invoice journal in accounts payable.
> **Vendor disbursement** – Vendor payment.
> **Customer payment** – Payment of customers.

Depending on the transactions in your company, journal names with further journal types are required – e.g., a journal with the journal type "Post fixed assets" for fixed asset transactions. If you want to use the invoice register and the invoice approval journals in accounts payable, you need a journal name with the journal type "Invoice register" and a journal name with the journal type "Approval".

If you select different number sequences in the field *Voucher series* of journal names, you can distinguish different journals by the voucher number. The default for the offset account in journal lines is specified in the fields *Account type* and *Offset account* of the journal names. Another important setting in the journal names is the slider *Amounts include sales tax*. If this slider is set to "Yes", amounts that you enter in the journal lines include sales tax or input tax (if applicable). Otherwise, the entered line amount is a net amount to which Dynamics 365 adds the sales tax.

9.2.8.10 Journal Approval

There are two options in the journal name setup which enforce an approval of journals before posting:

> **Journal approval system** – Enabled in the field group *Approval*.
> **Approval workflow** – Enabled in the field group *Approval workflow*.

If you want to activate the journal approval system for a journal name, set the slider *Active* in the field group *Approval* to "Yes". Then select the responsible user group for approval in the corresponding lookup field *Approve*.

If you want to apply the other option for approval, the approval workflow, an appropriate general ledger workflow has to be configured in the menu item *General ledger> Journal setup> General ledger workflows*. The workflow type "Ledger daily journal workflow" determines approval workflows for daily journals. You can find more details on workflows in section 10.4 of this book.

9.2.8.11 Posting Layers

When you create a journal name, the default value for the field *Posting layer*, which determines the posting layer of transactions with this journal name, is "Current". If you need to keep particular ledger transaction separate (e.g., to cut off transactions that refer to local tax regulations), you can create journal names with the posting layer "Operations", or "Tax", or one of the custom layers.

You can subsequently select the appropriate posting layer in the closing sheet (when executing the fiscal year closing) or in a journal transaction (indirectly via the journal name) to record transactions, which should not be included in regular reports that are based on the layer "Current". In order to analyze and to report the transactions in the other layers, you can set up additional versions of financial reports which include the transactions in these layers.

9.2.8.12 General Ledger Parameters

The General ledger parameters (*General ledger> Ledger setup> General ledger parameters*) contain further settings for journal transactions. One of these settings is the parameter field *Check for voucher used*, which you should not set to "Accept duplicates" in order to avoid confusion with the voucher number of documents.

9.2.9   Case Study Exercises

Exercise 9.1 – Main Accounts

The following main accounts are required in your company (## = your user ID):

> Main account 111C-##, Name "##-Petty cash", Account type "Balance sheet".
> Main account 111B-##, Name "##-Bank", Account type "Balance sheet".
> Main account 6060-##, Name "##-Consulting", Account type "Expense".
> Main account ZZ##, Name "##-Account structure test", Account type "Balance sheet".

Create these accounts in the chart of accounts of your training company.

Exercise 9.2 – Account Structures

Unlike the other main accounts that you have created in exercise 9.1, the main account ZZ## is not included in an account number range which is covered by any account structure. For this reason, set up a new account structure which only refers to this main account.

Create and activate a new account structure ZS## with two segments – the main accounts and the financial dimension for business units (and in case of interunit accounting, additionally the balancing dimension). The main account ZZ## is the only applicable main account in this account structure. Assign the account structure to your company.

Exercise 9.3 – Bank Accounts

Your company opens a new bank account. Create a bank account B-## with any routing number and bank account number of your choice. Assign the main account 111B-## of exercise 9.1 to this bank account.

Exercise 9.4 – Journal Names

You want to register the transactions of the next exercises in your own journals. For this purpose, create a journal name G-## (## = your user ID) with the type "Daily", a journal name I-## with the type "Vendor invoice recording", and a journal name P-## with the type "Vendor disbursement". Select an existing number sequence in all these journal names.

9.3   Transactions in Finance

Each business process with an impact on financial values generates general ledger transactions. Most of the ledger transactions are not initially created in accounting but derive from transactions in other areas like purchasing, sales, or production. Transactions in these areas generate ledger transactions in the background.

Apart from the derived transactions, some ledger transactions originate from activities in accounting. You can record these ledger transactions in a journal in the General ledger module.

9.3.1   General Journals

If you want to post manual transactions in the general ledger, use a general journal (*General ledger> Journal entries> General journals*).

General journals refer to the journal type "Daily". Apart from the general journals, there are financial journals that are assigned to other journal types – for example, the invoice journals in the Accounts payable module, or the payment journals in the Accounts payable and the Accounts receivable module. If you do not need the advanced functionality of the specific journals (e.g., payment proposals in payment journals), it does not matter whether you register a transaction in the specific journal or in the general journal.

9.3.1.1   Journal Header

Journals are vouchers and therefore consist of a header and at least one line. The header contains common settings and default values for the corresponding lines. In each line, you can subsequently override the default values that derive from the corresponding header field (e.g., the offset account).

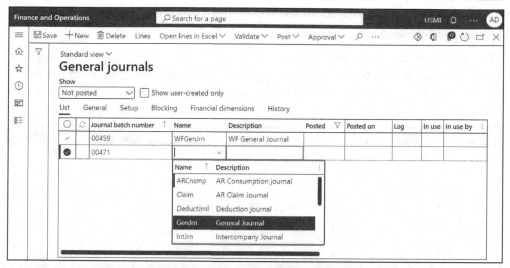

Figure 9-12: Selecting a journal name in a new general journal header

The selected option in the lookup field *Show* at the top of the General journal list page determines whether open or posted journals are shown. In order to register a new journal, click the button *New* and select a journal name.

On the tab *Setup* of the journal header, you can override the default values which derive from the journal name (e.g., the offset account). The columns *In use* and *In use by* in the journal header display if somebody is currently working in the lines of the particular journal.

9.3.1.2 Journal Lines

In order to switch to the journal lines, click the button *Lines* in the action pane or click on the *Journal batch number* shown as a link in the grid of the Journal list page. In a new line, the default for the posting date is the current session date. The voucher number derives from the number sequence of the journal name which you have selected in the header. Depending on the option selected in the column *Account type*, you have to enter a ledger account, a vendor, a customer, a bank account, or a fixed asset in the column *Account*.

If you enter a ledger account in the field *Account*, segmented entry control applies (see below). With segmented entry control, the main account usually has to be entered in the first segment of the ledger account field. If and which financial dimension segments are available and need to be entered is depending on the applicable account structure for the selected main account. The lookup in the account field shows the available values for the segment that is currently selected.

Once you have registered the account, you can enter the amount in the column *Debit* or *Credit*. In a single-line transaction, which applies the same amount (with a different sign) to the debit and the credit account, enter the *Offset account type* and the *Offset account* (including segments for financial dimensions as applicable) in the appropriate columns of the journal line.

The columns *Company* and *Offset company* provide the option to register intercompany transactions. As a prerequisite, intercompany accounting (*General ledger> Posting setup> Intercompany accounting*) has to be configured for the respective companies.

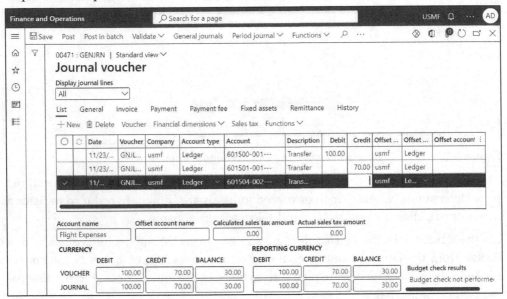

Figure 9-13: Registering the journal lines of a voucher with multiple offset lines

In order to support data entry, a separate pane at the bottom of the lines shows the voucher balance of the selected line and the balance of the complete journal. Before you can post a journal, the balance of the individual vouchers (lines with the same voucher number) and the balance of the complete journal have to be zero.

If you prefer entering data in Excel over the Journal line detail form, you can use the Office integration: Click the button *Open lines in Excel* in the journal header and enter or edit the journal lines in Excel.

In case you need to enter a transaction with more than one offset account, you can record one voucher in multiple lines. In this case, do not enter an offset account in the first line, but in one or more separate journal lines for the offset transactions. As long as the balance of the voucher is not zero, Dynamics 365 retrieves the same voucher number as in the previous line. Once the voucher balance is zero, the next line shows a new voucher number (as a prerequisite, the option "In connection with balance" has to be selected in the field *New voucher* of the journal name).

Note: If the "One voucher" requirement is active (which means that the slider *Allow multiple transactions within one voucher* in the section *Ledger* of the General ledger parameters is set to "No"), it is not possible to post one common voucher for multiple lines with different subledger accounts (e.g., different customers).

9.3.1.3 Segmented Entry Control

When you enter a ledger account in an account field, segmented entry control applies. Since the main account and applicable financial dimensions are merged into a single ledger account field, this field includes the complete posting information as required by the account structure.

The lookup when entering a ledger account refers to the currently active segment of the ledger account field. In order to search a segment value, enter the search content – the first characters of the identification or the name – in the applicable segment of the ledger account field before or after opening the lookup with the lookup button ⊡ or the shortcut *Alt + Down*.

In the example of Figure 9-14, you can view the segment lookup that is shown after entering the characters "sp" in the second segment of the ledger account field. This lookup contains the list of business units that start with the characters "sp" in the ID or the name.

Figure 9-14:   Segmented entry for the main account and applicable financial dimensions

The sequence and the number of segments is depending on the account structure that is assigned to the selected main account (see section 9.2.4). If the account structure allows a blank for a particular segment (or does not include any financial dimension), it is not required to enter a corresponding segment value.

9.3.1.4   Posting Financial Journals

Once you have completed the journal lines, you can post the journal with the button *Post* or *Post/Post* in the action pane of the journal header or lines. If there are issues, an error message is shown and it is not possible to post the transaction.

If you click the button *Post/Post and transfer* (instead of *Post/Post*) in the journal header, only vouchers with correct data are posted. Vouchers in the journal with incorrect data are transferred to a new journal, in which you can enter corrections.

9.3.1.5   Global General Journals

If you want to view the general journals across companies, open the menu item *General ledger> Journal entries> Global general journals*. In the Global general journals list page, the first column shows the company in which the respective general journal has been registered. If you click the button *New journal* in this form, a drop-down is shown in which you select the company and the journal name for the new general journal.

9.3.1.6   Journal Approval System

If a journal approval – either the journal approval system or the approval workflow – is activated for the selected journal name, it is not possible to post the journal before obtaining the required approval.

In case of the journal approval system, you can click the button *Approval/Report as ready* in the journal header to request approval. The responsible person for approval then clicks the button *Approval/Approve* to release the journal for posting.

9.3.1.7   Periodic Journals and Voucher Templates

If you need to register a particular transaction repeatedly, you can use one of the two options for recurring registration:

> **Periodic journals** – If the transaction recurs on a regular basis.
> **Voucher templates** – If you only want to use a copy template.

Periodic journals are used to register transactions which are repeated on a regular basis (e.g., an office rent, or monthly installments). In order to create a periodic journal, open the form *General ledger> Journal entries> Periodic journals* and enter a journal header and journal lines (similar to a general journal). An alternative way for creating a periodic journal is to copy a general journal to a periodic journal (click the button *Period journal/Save journal* in the lines of a general journal). The column *Date* in the lines of a periodic journal determines the start date for the periodic transactions. The frequency of the transaction (e.g., monthly) has to be specified in the columns *Units* and *Number of units* (also shown on the tab *Periodic*).

In order to post the transactions for a periodic journal, you have to create related general journals on a regular basis. In the lines of such a general journal, retrieve the periodic journal with the button *Period journal/Retrieve journal*. Once the periodic journal lines are transferred to the general journal, you can edit and post the lines in the general journal as usual. In the periodic journal, the column *Date* in the lines is – at the time when you retrieve the journal lines – updated with the next posting date. This date is calculated by adding the frequency period to the last posting date that has been retrieved. The column *Last date* in the periodic journal lines indicates when the journal has been retrieved the last time.

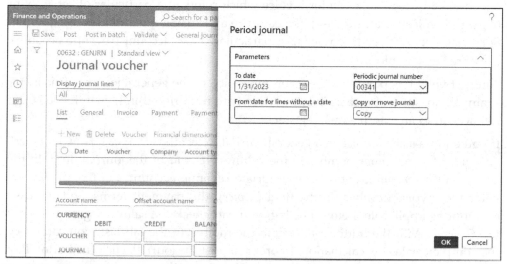

Figure 9-15:   Retrieving a periodic journal into the lines of a general journal

Apart from periodic journals for general journals, you can also use periodic journals as a basis for invoice journals in accounts payable.

Unlike periodic journals, voucher templates are templates for simply copying journals, without a periodic interval. In order to create a voucher template, select a journal line in a general journal (or in an invoice journal) and click the button *Functions/Save voucher template* in the toolbar of the journal lines. The template will include all journal lines with the same voucher number as the selected line. In the dialog that is shown when saving the template, select the *Template type* "Percent" in case you want to apply a proportional distribution of line amounts.

If you select this voucher template in the template dialog that you open with the button *Functions/Select voucher template* in a journal, a second dialog is shown in which you can enter the amount that you want to distribute across the lines according to the proportion in the template.

9.3.2 Invoice Posting

Depending on the particular invoice, there are different ways for registering and posting the document. In Dynamics 365, there are the following options:

➤ **Sales order invoice** – For items shipped to customers (see section 4.6.1).
➤ **Free text invoice** – For sales invoices not related to items (see section 4.6.3).

➢ **(Pending) Vendor invoice** – For items (or procurement categories) received from vendors, with or without reference to a purchase order.

➢ **Vendor invoice journal** – For invoices not related to items or categories.

➢ **General journal** – For manual purchase or sales invoices (not to be printed).

9.3.2.1 Invoices in the General Journal

If you want to register a vendor invoice which refers to a particular offset account (e.g., an invoice for an expense), the easiest way is using a vendor invoice journal. For customer invoices that refer to a particular offset account (revenue account), use a free text invoice.

Alternatively, it is possible to register an invoice in the general journal. This is, for example, an option for sales invoices which are not printed in Dynamics 365 (e.g., invoices from an external cash register).

If you enter a sales invoice in a general journal, select the *Account type* "Customer" and enter the customer number in the column *Account* of the journal lines. In the column *Offset account*, enter an appropriate revenue account. On the tab *Invoice*, enter the invoice number (in the field *Invoice*), the payment terms, and the cash discount as applicable. Before posting, you can check the sales tax groups on the tab *General*. With the button *Sales tax* in the toolbar of the tab *List*, you can check the complete sales tax calculation. In order to post the journal, click the button *Post* or *Post/Post* in the action pane of the journal header or the journal lines.

Registering a vendor invoice in a general journal works similar to the sales invoice – for a vendor invoice, select the *Account type* "Vendor" (instead of "Customer").

9.3.2.2 Options for Vendor Invoice Posting

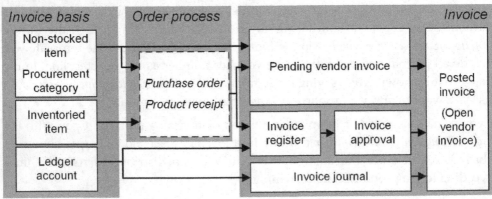

Figure 9-16:   Options for processing vendor invoices

Depending on whether a vendor invoice refers to a purchase order or not, there are the following ways to process the invoice:

➤ **Purchase order invoice** – Purchase orders and purchase order invoices include only lines with products or procurements categories.
➤ **Invoice without order assignment** – Depending on whether you want to select an offset ledger account manually, there are two types:
   ○ **With non-stocked products or procurements categories** – Posting is similar to purchase order invoice posting, but without purchase order assignment.
   ○ **With ledger accounts** – Register and post an invoice journal, usually for particular subjects like office rent or legal services.

You can register a vendor invoice – with or without reference to a purchase order – in the Pending vendor invoice form (*Accounts payable> Invoices> Pending vendor invoices*, see section 3.6.1). The invoice lines in the Pending vendor invoice form contain products and procurement categories. If the invoice which you enter in the Pending vendor invoice form does not refer to a purchase order, you can only select non-inventoried items and procurement categories. But there is no field for manually entering the offset ledger account.

In order to register a vendor invoice that does not refer to an item number or a procurement category, but directly to a ledger account (e.g., for office rent) or to a fixed asset (acquisition), enter a journal transaction. In the Accounts payable module, the following journals are available for recording an invoice:

➤ **Invoice journal** – Main form for vendor invoices in accounts payable.
➤ **Global invoice journal** – Like the invoice journal, but across companies.
➤ **Invoice register** – In conjunction with the *Invoice approval journal*.
➤ **General journal** – As described above.

If you want to apply an approval workflow to invoice journals, set up an appropriate workflow with the workflow type for the respective journal type in the menu item *Accounts payable> Setup> Accounts payable workflows* and assign it to the journal name.

For purchase order invoices, there are two options for recording and processing an invoice that requires approval:

➤ **Approval workflow in the Pending vendor invoice form** – Enter and post the invoice in the Pending vendor invoice form, with activated approval workflow.
➤ **Invoice register journal** – As a prior step to the Pending vendor invoice form, you can first post the invoice to interim accounts in the invoice register journal, followed by recording an invoice approval journal (or an invoice pool) which finally opens the Pending vendor invoice form.

From a financial perspective, the main difference between the vendor invoice approval workflow and the invoice register journal is that the invoice register journal already posts an invoice, which is subject to tax calculation, when starting the approval process.

The Open vendor invoice page (*Accounts payable> Invoices> Open vendor invoices*) shows all invoices that are not yet paid, irrespective of the way of posting the invoice. In the action pane of this form, the options in the button *New* provide an alternative way to access the different vendor invoice journals and the Pending vendor invoice form. Similar options are available in the workspace *Vendor invoice entry* and in the Vendor form (on the action pane tab *INVOICE*).

9.3.2.3 Invoice Journals

The invoice journal (*Accounts payable> Invoices> Invoice journal*), which you can also access from the workspace *Vendor invoice entry*, is the main form in the Accounts payable module for registering invoices which do not refer to a purchase order.

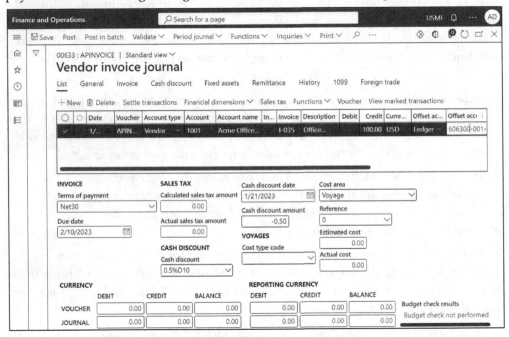

Figure 9-17:   Registering an invoice journal line

In order to register invoices in the invoice journal, create a header record in the list page before you switch to the lines. Enter the invoice lines with the vendor number (in the column *Account*), vendor invoice number (column *Invoice*), transaction text, amount, offset account, terms of payment, approver (*Approved by* on the tab *Invoice*) and other data like sales tax and cash discount as applicable. Then post the invoice with the button *Post* or *Post/Post* in the action pane of the journal header or lines.

9.3.2.4 Invoice Registers

The invoice register (*Accounts payable> Invoices> Invoice register*) provides the option to pre-register vendor invoices. Posting an invoice register includes posting the vendor transaction, the applicable sales tax transactions (depending on Accounts payable parameter settings), and the ledger transactions (to interim accounts).

The structure of the invoice register with journal header and lines is similar to the structure of the general journals, but the account type is restricted to "Vendor". In the journal lines, also enter the responsible employee for approval (*Approved by* in the lower pane of the journal lines), the terms of payment, the cash discount, and sales tax groups as applicable. If the invoice refers to a purchase order, select the purchase order number in the column *Purchase order* of the journal lines to facilitate later approval. In order to post a journal in the invoice register, click the button *Post* or *Post/Post* in the action pane of the journal header or lines.

Posting a journal in the invoice register creates a regular vendor transaction, which you can access with the button *Vendor/Transactions/Transactions* in the Vendor form. The slider *Approved* on the tab *General* of this transaction is set to "No", which is why the invoice is not included in payment proposals.

The ledger transactions of the invoice register are posted to interim accounts. These interim accounts are specified in the vendor posting profile (*Accounts payable> Setup> Vendor posting profiles*, field *Arrival* and *Offset account* on the tab *Setup*).

In the Accounts payable parameters, the lookup field *Time of sales tax posting* (on the tab *Sales tax* in the section *Ledger and sales tax*) determines for invoice register transactions, if sales tax is already posted with the invoice register, or later with the invoice approval.

9.3.2.5 Invoice Approval Journals

Once the invoice is posted in an invoice register, the responsible person for approval can approve it in the invoice approval journal.

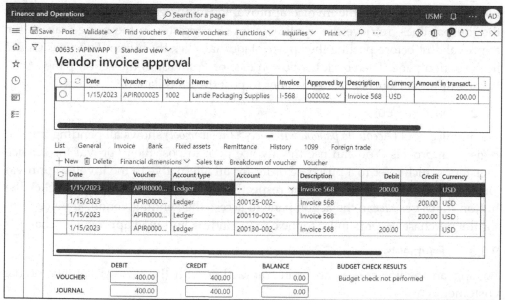

Figure 9-18: The invoice approval journal lines after fetching an invoice register

In order to start processing invoice approval, create a new header in the invoice approval journal (*Accounts payable> Invoices> Invoice approval*). Then switch to the journal lines and click the button *Find vouchers* in the action pane to retrieve a posted invoice register. The *Find vouchers* dialog shows all not yet approved invoice registers in the upper pane. With the button *Select* in this dialog, you can select one or more invoices for approval. Once you close the dialog with the button *OK*, the selected invoice(s) are transferred to the approval journal lines.

If you want to remove a selected invoice from the approval journal lines before posting, click the button *Remove vouchers* in the action pane of the invoice approval.

The following steps are depending on whether the invoice refers to an order:

➢ **Not related to a purchase order** – In this case, select a ledger account (e.g., an expense account) in the lower pane of the invoice approval journal lines (first line in the lower pane of Figure 9-18). The expense amount does not include sales tax. If multiple expense accounts apply, enter multiple lines that share the total amount. In order to post the approval, click the button *Post*.

➢ **Related to a purchase order** – In this case, click the button *Functions/Purchase order* to access the Pending vendor invoice form for the purchase order. In the Pending vendor invoice form, post the invoice as usual (see section 3.6.1).

9.3.2.6   Rejecting Invoice Approval

If you do not want to approve a vendor invoice, which has been posted in the invoice register (e.g., because it does not match the applicable purchase order, or because of other reasons), you have to post a cancellation.

For this purpose, open the invoice approval journal, create a new header, and in the journal lines, retrieve the applicable invoice register in the same way as for approval. But before posting the approval journal, click the button *Functions/Cancel* in the action pane. Then click the button *Post* or *Post/Post* in the action pane of the invoice approval journal header or lines to post the cancellation.

9.3.2.7   Invoice Pool

The invoice pool (*Accounts payable> Invoices> Invoice pool*) shows all pending invoice register approvals. You can use the invoice pool to post the approval for invoice registers, which refer to a purchase order (as an alternative to the invoice approval journal). For this purpose, select the respective line in the invoice pool and click the button *Purchase order* in the action pane to access the Pending vendor invoice form for the purchase order (similar to the corresponding button in approval journals).

9.3.3   Payments

Posting an invoice creates an open transaction with the vendor liability or the customer debt.

9.3.3.1 Open Transactions

In order to view the open transactions, click the button *Collect/Settle/Settle transactions* in the Customer form or the button *Invoice/Settle/Settle transactions* in the Vendor form. The button *Customer/Transactions/Transactions* in the Customer form or *Vendor/Transactions/Transactions* in the Vendor form opens the Transactions form that shows all transactions (you can select the option "Open" in the lookup *Show* above the grid to apply a filter on open transactions).

If you want to print the open transactions, use the report *Accounts receivable> Inquiries and reports> Open transactions report* for customers and the report *Accounts payable> Inquiries and reports> Vendor open transactions report* for vendors.

9.3.3.2 Customer Payments

If you want to register a customer payment which you have received, open the customer payment journal (*Accounts receivable> Payments> Customer payment journal*, or from the workspace *Customer payments*).

In the customer payment journal, create a record in the journal header and switch to the lines. In the lines, enter the payment with the customer number (in the column *Account*), the transaction text (column *Description*), the payment amount (column *Credit*), and the offset account. If the customer has paid to your bank account, select the *Offset account type* "Bank".

If you want to settle the invoice that is paid when entering a payment line, select the invoice number in the column *Invoice* of the journal line – the journal line then receives the payment data (including the amount) from the invoice. Alternatively, you can enter the customer in the column *Account* and click the button *Settle transactions* in the toolbar of the lines to apply one or more invoices to a payment line. In the *Settle transactions* dialog, the checkboxes in the column *Mark* determine the invoices which are paid. Once you have marked all applicable invoices, click the button *OK* in the dialog.

Apart from entering a payment in the journal lines, you can use the button *Enter customer payment* in the journal header to open the Enter customer payment form. In this form, you can select open invoices for the payment and, with the button *Save in journal*, create and settle the payment lines. Another option for creating payment lines, which you can use for direct debiting (withdrawing from the customer bank account), is the customer payment proposal in the payment journal lines (similar to the vendor payment proposal, see below).

Once you have completed the payment lines, post the customer payment journal with the button *Post* or *Post/Post* in the action pane of the journal header or lines

9.3.3.3 Vendor Payments

In a similar way to customer payments, you can record payments to vendors in a payment journal (*Accounts payable> Payments> Vendor payment journal*).

Manually registering a vendor payment works like registering a customer payment (including the settlement option). But in most cases, outgoing payments require additional support and control. In Dynamics 365, the payment proposal and the payment status are available for this purpose. In addition, you can set up the process automation for vendor payments (*Accounts payable> Payment setup> Process automation*) to create payment journals automatically.

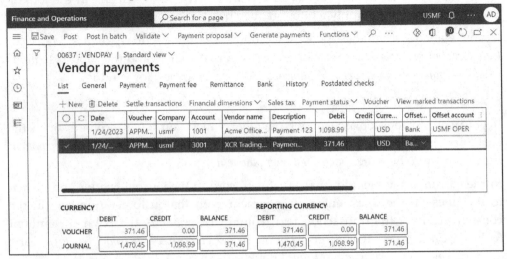

Figure 9-19: Entering a payment line in a vendor payment journal

If you want to prevent paying a particular invoice, open the vendor transaction in Edit mode and switch to the tab *General*. On this tab, you can set the slider *Approved* to "No" or enter an *Invoice payment release date*. The payment proposal does not include the invoice until you set the approval in the transaction to "Yes", or until the release date has passed.

9.3.3.4   Methods of Payment

Methods of payment (*Accounts payable> Payment setup> Methods of payment*) are an important setting for processing vendor payments. Usually, there are at least two methods of payment: One for manual transfers and one for electronic banking.

In payment methods for electronic payment, the option "Approved" or "Sent" should be selected in the field *Payment status* to prevent posting a payment before the payment export file has been generated. More settings for electronic payments (e.g., file formats) are included in the further tabs of the Payment methods form.

The lookup field *Period* in the upper pane of the Payment methods form specifies whether the invoices that are selected in a payment proposal are collected to one payment (e.g., *Period* = "Week" for one payment per week, or *Period* = "Total" for one payment which covers all selected invoices) or if you want to generate a separate payment per invoice (*Period* = "Invoice").

The field group *Posting* on the tab *General* of the Payment methods form controls the bank account or the ledger account from which you pay. This account is the default for the offset account when you select the payment method in a payment journal. If you want to facilitate the bank reconciliation by posting to a bridging account (see below), set the slider *Bridging posting* to "Yes" and enter the bridging account number.

In the Vendor form, you can select the *Method of payment* for the vendor on the tab *Payment*. The payment method of the vendor is the default for purchase orders, vendor transactions, and payment journals.

9.3.3.5 Vendor Payment Proposals

The purpose of payment proposals is to support selecting vendor invoices for payment. In order to run a payment proposal, click the button *Payment proposal/ Create payment proposal* in the action pane of the vendor payment journal.

In the *Vendor payment proposal* dialog, select the applicable option in the field *Select invoices by* (options "Due date", or "Cash discount date", or both) and enter a date range for this date (*From date* and *To date*) to select the invoices which should be paid. If you select the option "Cash discount date" in the parameter *Select invoices by*, invoices without cash discount are not included in the proposal. In the field *Minimum payment date*, you can enter a date (e.g., tomorrow's date if preparing the payment for the next day) to make sure that the payment date in the proposal is on or – for invoices with a later due date or cash discount date – after that date.

On the tab *Records to include* of the dialog, you can filter on vendor and transaction data. The *Summarized payment date* on the tab *Advanced parameters* in the dialog is used if the method of payment refers to the *Period* "Total".

Once you close the dialog with the button *OK*, a second dialog is shown in which you can check and edit the payment proposal. In this dialog, the payment date (from the invoice due date, or the cash discount date, or the *Minimum payment date*) is shown in the column *Date to pay*. You can remove invoices or change the *Date to pay* (you can edit the *Due date* or the *Cash discount date*) as applicable before you click the button *Create payments* to transfer the proposal to the payment journal.

The payment proposal applies a settlement for the selected invoices. Depending on the method of payment in the particular invoices, there is one payment line for multiple invoices or a separate payment line per invoice.

Before posting the vendor payment, you can still edit the proposal – click the button *Payment proposal/Edit invoices for selected payment* for this purpose.

9.3.3.6 Exporting and Posting Payments

In order to check the payment before generating and posting it, you can optionally print the payment journal with the button *Print/Journal* in the header or lines.

If an export file for electronic payment is required, make sure to generate the file before posting the payment. For this purpose, click the button *Generate payments* in the payment journal lines once you have completed the lines. When generating the payment, Dynamics 365 sets the payment status of the journal lines to "Sent". If required, you can also update the payment status in the appropriate column manually (or with the button *Payment status* in the toolbar of the lines).

Finally, click the button *Post* or *Post/Post* in the action pane of the journal header or lines to post the payment from the selected bank or ledger account.

9.3.3.7 Bridging Transactions

Bridging transactions are required if you want to keep the payment on a separate account for the time between posting the payment and recognizing the transaction on the bank account (e.g., useful if you send a check).

In this case, the payment is not directly posted to a bank account when posting the payment journal, but to a bridging account. Settings in the payment method – the slider *Bridging posting* and the *Bridging account* – control whether bridging transactions are generated.

When you recognize the transaction on the bank account (e.g., in the course of reviewing the bank statement), you should post a transfer from the bridging account to the bank account. In order to register this transfer, create a journal in the general journals (*General ledger> Journal entries> General journals*). In the action pane of the general journal lines, click the button *Functions/Select bridged transactions* to access a dialog in which you can select the applicable bridged transactions. For the selected transactions, you can subsequently post the transfer in the general journal.

9.3.3.8 Centralized Payments

Centralized payments are required in a company structure with a head office that processes the payments of an affiliated group. Before you can use centralized payments, you have to set up intercompany accounting (*General ledger> Posting setup> Intercompany accounting*) for the concerned legal entities. In addition, appropriate permission settings in an organization hierarchy with the purpose "Centralized payment" are required.

Payment journal lines and payment proposals show the column *Company* (*Company accounts*). When you post a centralized payment, you can settle invoices in other companies.

9.3.4   Transaction Reversal and Reversing Entries

In Dynamics 365, there are two different types of transaction reversals: Reversals that you enter manually (for corrections) and automatic reversals (for accruals).

9.3.4.1 Transaction Reversal

The transaction reversal, which is available for ledger transactions, vendor transactions, and customer transactions (including free text invoices), is a simple way to correct wrong vouchers in finance.

The transaction reversal is not available for transactions which refer to inventory, purchase orders, or sales orders. In order to reverse these transactions, register an appropriate document in the original module – for example, a return order in the Sales and marketing module.

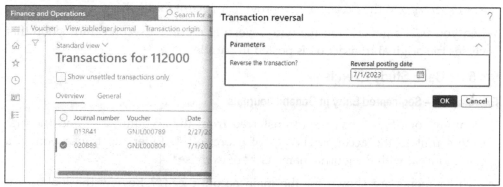

Figure 9-20: Reversing a ledger transaction from the transaction inquiry

You can start the transaction reversal from the transaction inquiry. In order to access the customer transaction inquiry, click the button *Customer/Transactions/ Transactions* in the Customer form. For the vendor transactions, click the button *Vendor/Transactions/Transactions* in the Vendor form. For the ledger transactions, open the form *General ledger> Inquiries and reports> Voucher transactions* or click the button *Transactions* in the action pane of the Main accounts form. In the transaction inquiry, select the original transaction and click the button *Reverse transaction* or *Reverse/Reverse transaction* (for a customer payment, *Reverse/Cancel payment*). In the dialog that is shown next, you can edit the *Reversal posting date*. If you want to reverse a vendor invoice or customer invoice that has been settled already, cancel the settlement (see section 9.2.5) before reversing the invoice.

If you want to reverse a complete journal, you can start from the original journal. For this purpose, open the lines of the posted journal (general journal, invoice journal, payment journal) and click the button *Reverse entire journal* in the action pane.

The transaction reversal posts a new transaction that offsets the original transaction. If required, you can reverse a reversal.

Note: As a prerequisite for reversing entire journals, the feature "Mass reversals for multiple documents" needs to be activated in the feature management.

9.3.4.2   Automatic Reversal with Reversing Entries

Unlike manual transaction reversals, which are used to correct wrong transactions in most cases, reversing entries are transactions that are generated automatically for the reversal of accruals in a later period.

Reversing entries are available in the general journals (*General ledger> Journal entries> General journal*). In order to generate a reversing entry, select the checkbox *Reversing entry* and enter a *Reversing date* in the rightmost columns of the journal lines when entering the original transaction. In the journal header, the checkbox *Reversing entry* and the *Reversing date* provide a default for the lines.

When you post a general journal with reversing entries, a second transaction that reverses the original transaction is posted in parallel.

9.3.5   Case Study Exercises

Exercise 9.5 – Segmented Entry in General Journals

An amount of USD 50 has been transferred from the account ZZ## and the first business unit to the account 111C-## of exercise 9.1. Enter the transaction in a general journal with the journal name G-## of exercise 9.4.

Which segments are shown for the main account ZZ##? Review the lookup for these segments. Then post the journal and check the balance and the transactions of both accounts of the current exercise.

Exercise 9.6 – General Journal Transaction

You withdraw USD 100 from the bank account B-## of exercise 9.3 and put it to the petty cash account 111C-## of exercise 9.1. Register this transaction in a general journal with the journal name G-##.

Before posting, check the balance and the transactions for the bank account and the petty cash account. Then post the journal and check the balances and the transactions again.

Exercise 9.7 – Vendor Invoice

The vendor of exercise 3.2 submits the invoice "VI907" with a total of USD 50. This invoice covers expenses, for which you have created the main account 6060## in exercise 9.1.

Record the invoice in an invoice journal with the journal name I-## of exercise 9.4. The invoice applies the terms of payment and the cash discount of exercise 3.1.

Before posting, check the vendor transactions and the vendor balance and – for the expense account – the ledger transactions and the ledger balance. Then post the invoice and check the balances and the transactions again.

Exercise 9.8 – Vendor Payment

The invoice "VI907", which you have posted in the previous exercise, needs to be paid. Register the payment in a vendor payment journal with the journal name P-## of exercise 9.4. Pay from the bank account B-## of exercise 9.3. The payment amount should be reduced by the applicable cash discount.

Before posting, check the vendor balance and the bank account balance. Then post the payment and check the balances, the voucher transactions, and the transaction origin for the payment.

Exercise 9.9 – Transaction Reversal

Your vendor of exercise 3.2 now submits the invoice "VI909" which is similar to the invoice "VI907" of exercise 9.7, but with a total of USD 30. Register and post this invoice.

After posting, you notice that the posted transaction is incorrect. You want to reverse it for this reason. Before reversing, check the vendor transactions and the vendor balance and – for the expense account – the ledger transactions and the ledger balance. Then reverse the invoice and check the balances and the transactions again.

9.4 Ledger Integration

One of the main advantages of an integrated business solution like Dynamics 365 is, that business transactions registered anywhere in the application are available in all other areas. Posting, for example, a sales order invoice does not only create the required document, but it also generates the following transactions:

> **Inventory transactions** – Affecting the inventory value.
> **General ledger transactions** – Revenue, COGS, stock, and customer accounts.
> **Customer transaction** – Open invoice in accounts receivable.
> **Sales tax transactions** – As applicable.

Depending on the transaction, invoice posting may include additional areas like commission, discount, or cash payment.

9.4.1 Basics of Ledger Integration

Ledger integration – the integration of the general ledger in finance with the other areas of the application – is one of the core characteristics of an integrated business solution (ERP solution). In Dynamics 365, a transaction in any area that is relevant to finance (e.g., sales, purchasing, inventory, or production) posts a transaction to the general ledger automatically.

9.4.1.1 Basic Settings

Several settings control, whether and which main accounts apply to the different transactions in business. For the areas of purchasing, sales, inventory, and production that are covered in this book, the following settings are relevant:

> **Summary accounts for vendor liabilities and customer debts** – In the posting profiles in accounts payable and accounts receivable.
> **Main accounts for inventory transactions** – In the posting setup.
> **Main accounts for resource usage in production** – In resources, cost categories, and production groups.

In addition, there are specific settings for particular transactions like sales tax, cash discount, indirect costs, or miscellaneous charges.

9.4.1.2 Vendors and Customers

Vendor posting profiles control the assignment of summary accounts for vendor transactions. Customer posting profiles for customer transactions work similarly. You can find more details on posting profiles in section 3.2.3.

9.4.1.3 Subledger Accounting

Subledger accounting in Dynamics 365 decouples posting in subledgers (e.g., in accounts payable) from posting to the general ledger. In this context, the subledger journal entry functionality provides the option to execute the transfer to the general ledger either asynchronous or in a batch job, and either detailed or summarized. Subledger accounting does not apply to all subledger transactions, but to some particular document types including:

> **Free text invoices** – See section 4.6.3.
> **Product receipts** – Purchase order receipt, see section 3.5.4.
> **Vendor invoices** – Purchase order invoice, see section 3.6.1.

In the General ledger parameters, settings on the tab *Batch transfer rules* control the subledger transfer per company and document type. The *Transfer mode* specifies, when a subledger transaction is posted to the general ledger:

> **Asynchronous** – Posting as soon as sever capacity is available.
> **Scheduled batch** – In a separate batch job (e.g., in the nighttime), with the option to view subledger transactions before the transfer to the general ledger. With this option, it is possible to summarize accounting entries.

If you set the option *Summarize accounting entries* in a batch transfer rule to "Yes", the ledger transactions of a batch are summarized per account and transaction type which means that you can't inquire the ledger transactions at the level of an individual invoice or product receipt.

Until the transfer to the general ledger (particularly for documents that use the scheduled batch transfer), you can view the posted subledger transactions in the menu item *General ledger> Periodic tasks> Subledger journal entries not yet transferred.* With the button *Transfer now* (for an immediate transfer) or *Transfer in batch* (for a scheduled transfer) in this form, you can immediately post the subledger transactions to the general ledger.

The button *View accounting* in the Subledger journal entries form and in applicable source documents (e.g., free text invoices) provides access to the complete accounting information including all applicable financial segments.

Note: The *Transfer mode* "Synchronous" in the batch transfer rules is not available anymore.

9.4.2 Ledger Integration in Inventory

When you post inventory receipts and issues to the general ledger, there are two different types of transactions in Dynamics 365 (see section 7.1.1):

➢ **Physical transaction** – Posted with the product receipt or packing slip.
➢ **Financial transaction** – Posted with the invoice.

Depending on the structure of the chart of accounts in your company, you can use the same main accounts or different main accounts for the physical and for the financial transaction.

9.4.2.1 Physical Transactions

It is an option, and not compulsory, to post physical transactions (product receipts and packing slips) to the general ledger. The following settings control whether ledger posting is activated for physical transactions:

➢ **Item model group** – Checkbox *Post physical inventory*.
➢ **Accounts payable parameters** – Slider *Post product receipt in ledger* (in the section *General*, tab *Product receipt*).
➢ **Accounts receivable parameters** – Slider *Post packing slip in ledger* (in the section *Updates*, tab *Packing slip*).

For transactions in production control, you can find the relevant settings in the section *General* of the Production control parameters. Physical transactions in production control are picking lists and report as finished transactions.

Irrespective of the parameter settings, physical transactions of items with the inventory model "Standard costs" are always posted to the general ledger.

9.4.2.2 Financial Transactions

For financial transactions, the checkbox *Post financial inventory* in the item model group determines whether inventory transactions are posted to the general ledger.

If this checkbox is cleared in an item model group, ledger integration is not active for the assigned items. For items with this setting, the purchase invoice does not post a ledger transaction to the stock account for inventory, but to the expense account for consumption. Accordingly, the sales invoice does not post a ledger transaction for inventory consumption. This is the appropriate setting for service items.

9.4.2.3 Posting Setup

The posting setup (*Cost management> Ledger integration policies setup> Posting*, or *Inventory management> Setup> Posting> Posting*) determines the main accounts for inventory transactions. It includes the following tabs with account settings:

➢ **Sales order** – Packing slips and invoices in sales.
➢ **Purchase order** – Product receipts and invoices in purchasing.
➢ **Inventory** – Journal transactions in inventory.
➢ **Production** – Picking lists, reporting as finished, and costing in production.
➢ **Standard cost variance** – Standard cost variances in inventory transactions.

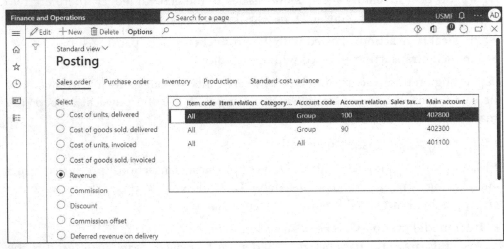

Figure 9-21:   Viewing the posting setup with the account settings for revenue posting

Each of these tabs shows a list of available transaction types in the left pane. In order to view the related main accounts in the right pane, select the respective transaction type in the left pane. The posting setup is primarily depending on the combination of two relations:

➢ **Item relation** – Items or categories.
➢ **Account relation** – Customers or vendors.

In addition, main account settings optionally include the sales tax group and – for standard cost variance transactions – the cost group as applicable dimensions. In the item relation and the account relation (customer on the tab *Sales order*, vendor on the tab *Purchase order*), there are three levels for the assignment of accounts:

➢ **Table** – Particular item, customer, or vendor.
➢ **Group** – Item group, customer group, or vendor group.
➢ **All**– All items, customers, or vendors.

The *Item code* "Category" – an additional option in the item relation for sales and for purchasing – enables settings at the product category level.

When posting a transaction, Dynamics 365 always searches for the most specific setting ("Table") first, then for the group setting, and finally for the general setting ("All"). When you post, for example, a sales invoice, settings for the particular customer and item have the highest priority, followed by group settings. Settings in the Accounts receivable parameters (section *Ledger and sales tax*, tab *General*) control, whether the search should primarily use the item or the customer dimension. For purchasing, similar settings are available in the Accounts payable parameters.

As an alternative to the menu item, you can also access the Posting setup form with the button *Posting* in the Item group form, or with the button *Setup/Item posting* in the Customer group form or the Vendor group form. When you access the posting setup from a group form, it shows the main account settings filtered on the selected group.

9.4.2.4 Transaction Combinations and Ledger Reconciliation

The transaction combinations (*Cost management> Ledger integration policies setup> Transaction combinations*) control the available assignment levels in the posting setup.

Since reports for the reconciliation of the general ledger with inventory – for example, the inventory value report (*Cost management> Inquiries and reports> Inventory accounting - status reports> Inventory value*, see section 7.3.1) – are usually based on item groups, the item group relation is usually activated in the transaction combinations.

9.4.2.5 Example – Transactions Related to Sales Order Processing

The following example for the automatic posting of ledger transactions based on ledger integration settings shows the transactions in sales order processing with activated ledger integration for packing slip and invoice posting (physical and financial transactions).

With the packing slip for the sales order, Dynamics 365 posts a ledger transaction that debits the account *Cost of units, delivered* and credits the account *Cost of goods sold, delivered* as specified in the posting setup. When posting the invoice, the ledger transactions that have been posted with the packing slip are reversed, and a ledger transaction is posted that debits the account *Cost of units, invoiced* and credits the account *Cost of goods sold, invoiced*. In parallel, a ledger transaction that credits the customer summary account (specified in the posting profile) and debits the account *Revenue* and – if applicable – the sales tax account is posted.

If the posting setup includes a setting for the transaction type *Discount*, sales line discounts are posted to this account. Otherwise, the discount is not posted separately but reduces the revenue amount.

9.4.2.6 Standard Cost Price and Moving Average

For items with an inventory model "Standard cost" (see section 7.3.1), essential settings are specified on the tab *Standard cost variance* of the posting setup. On this tab, you can find the main accounts for posting the difference between the actual cost price given by purchase order invoices (or production order costing) and the standard cost price (split by posting type, e.g., *Purchase price variance*).

For items that are assigned to an inventory model with a fixed receipt price, settings for posting a price difference are specified on the tabs *Purchase order* and *Inventory* of the posting setup.

For items with an inventory model "Moving average", settings for posting a price difference (for quantities that are not in stock anymore when posting the purchase invoice) or a revaluation are specified on the tab *Inventory* of the posting setup.

9.4.2.7 Service Items and Non-Stocked Items

Items that are not tracked in inventory (e.g., office supplies or consumables) can be linked to the product type "Service" and a particular item group and item model group for service items. In the item model group, ledger integration for physical and financial transactions should be deselected.

If you post a purchase invoice with such an item, a ledger transaction is posted that credits the expense account for consumption (instead of a stock account).

If you post a sales invoice, there is only a ledger transaction that credits the customer summary account and debits the revenue account (and no ledger transaction to the accounts *Cost of units, invoiced* and *Cost of goods sold, invoiced*).

You can assign non-stocked items to an item model group with a cleared checkbox *Stocked product* (see section 7.2.1). This setting prevents inventory transactions and deactivates the ledger integration for physical and financial transactions. But physical items and service items, which are included in a bill of materials, have to be assigned to an item model group in which the checkbox *Stocked product* is selected.

9.4.2.8 Changes of Settings

In order to avoid issues in the reconciliation of the general ledger with inventory, you should not change ledger integration settings in the item model group, in the parameters, and in the posting setup for items, which are in stock or which have got open inventory transactions. This includes both, changing the setup itself and selecting a new item group in an active item.

9.4.3   Ledger Integration in Production

Unlike ledger transactions that are generated in purchasing, in sales, or in inventory, ledger transactions that are generated in production include the cost of resource operations (primarily from the working time).

9.4.3.1   Production Control Parameters

In line with this constraint, the lookup field *Ledger posting* in the section *General* of the Production control parameters includes the following options:

➢ **Item and resource**
➢ **Item and category**
➢ **Production groups**

The setting in the Production control parameters, which is not available in the Production control parameters by site, is the default for production orders. It is possible to override this default value in the individual production order – for example, if you want to apply specific settings for prototype production.

If the option "Item and resource" is selected in the *Ledger posting* parameter, item transactions apply the main accounts that are specified in the posting setup. For route consumption (resource usage), the main account settings in the resource (*Production control> Setup> Resources> Resources*, tab *Ledger postings*) or – for transactions at the level of a resource group – in the resource group are used.

If the option "Item and category" is selected in the *Ledger posting* parameter, item transactions also apply the main accounts that are specified in the posting setup. But for route consumption, the account settings in the applicable cost category (*Production control> Setup> Routes> Cost categories*, tab *Ledger postings*) are used.

If the option "Production group" is selected in the *Ledger posting* parameter, the account settings in the production group (*Production control> Setup> Production> Production groups*) are used for item transactions and for route consumption. Production orders show the applicable production group on the tab *General* in the detail form (initialized from the tab *Engineer* in the released product).

9.4.3.2   Ledger Transactions in Production

When you process a production order and post a transaction, the following ledger transactions are posted (the main accounts are depending on the selected option in the *Ledger posting* parameter):

➢ **Picking list** – Account *Estimated cost of materials consumed* against *Estimated cost of materials consumed, WIP* (WIP = "work in process").
➢ **Resource usage** – Account *Estimated manufacturing cost absorbed* against *Estimated manufacturing cost consumed, WIP*.

➢ **Report as finished** – Account *Estimated manufactured cost* against *Estimated manufactured cost, WIP*.

➢ **Indirect costs** – Settings in the costing sheet: *Estimated indirect costs absorbed* against *Estimated cost of indirect cost consumed, WIP*.

The ledger transactions are posted when posting a production journal (picking list, route card, job card, report as finished).

Costing the production order reverses all these transactions and posts the final financial receipt of the manufactured item, the consumption of materials and resources, and indirect cost transactions to main accounts that are depending on the selected option in the *Ledger posting* parameter and on the related settings.

10 Core Setup and Essential Features

The organization of an enterprise determines the setup of its business application. For this reason, there needs to be an implementation project which includes the setup of the organization and of other core parameters before starting to work in Dynamics 365.

10.1 Organizational Structures

If you want to set up a new Dynamics 365 environment with its own database, you have got to access the Microsoft Dynamics Lifecycle Services. From the Lifecycle Services, you can deploy a cloud-hosted environment (hosted in Microsoft Azure) or an on-premise environment (hosted in your datacenter).

Within a Dynamics 365 environment, the organization model represents the structure of the enterprise and its business processes. For this reason, it has to be configured according to the operational and statutory structure of the enterprise. You can divide the organizational structures into the following types:

➢ **Statutory organization structures for legal reporting** – Hierarchies which comply with the regulations of public authorities (e.g., for tax purposes).
➢ **Operational organization structures for management reporting** – Hierarchies which comply with the management requirements (e.g., divisional structures).
➢ **Informal structures** – Independent of organizational hierarchies.

In order to comply with the different reporting requirements, large enterprises oftentimes have got multiple organizational structures and hierarchies in parallel. You can, for example, set up a hierarchy that matches the structure and the purpose of legal entities, another hierarchy that represents the divisional structure, and a third hierarchy that complies with regional structures.

For other enterprises, one simple hierarchy may be sufficient for all purposes.

10.1.1 Organization Model Architecture

The organization model in Microsoft Dynamics 365 meets the requirements of the different kinds of organizations. Depending on the requirements, the organization setup includes multiple organization hierarchies in parallel (e.g., for decoupling the operational organization from the statutory organization), or only one simple hierarchy that is used for all purposes.

© Springer Fachmedien Wiesbaden GmbH, part of Springer Nature 2023
A. Luszczak, *Using Microsoft Dynamics 365 for Finance and Operations*,
https://doi.org/10.1007/978-3-658-40453-6_10

10.1.1.1 Organization Types

The organization model includes the following organization types:

> **Legal entities** – Represent the statutory organization.
> **Operating units** – Represent the operational organization.
> **Teams** – Represent informal structures.

Only organization units with the type "Legal entity" and "Operating unit" are available in organization hierarchies. The type "Team" characterizes an informal type of organizations, which is not included in hierarchies.

10.1.1.2 Using the Organization Model within Dynamics 365

Apart from a representation of the company organization, the organization model is used in many areas of the application, including the following purposes:

> **Company structure** – Legal entities are linked to companies in Dynamics 365, which is why you have to set up companies as legal entities.
> **Financial dimensions** – Since legal entities and operating units are available as a basis for financial dimensions, it is possible to use them in financial reporting.
> **Data security** – Based on the organization hierarchy purpose *Security*, you can restrict the user access to organizations separately from the company structure.
> **Business policies** – Business rules for areas like approval processes and centralized payments can apply a structure which is different from the hierarchy of legal entities.

Legal entities and operating units are not only part of the organization hierarchies, but they are also included in the global address book (see section 2.4). For this reason, the addresses and contact details of legal entities and operating units are managed in the global address book.

10.1.2   Organization Units

The organization model includes organization units with the type "Legal entity", "Operating unit" and "Team". Legal entities and operating units are the basic elements in the organizational hierarchies of an enterprise.

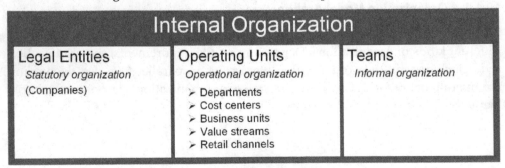

Internal Organization		
Legal Entities	**Operating Units**	**Teams**
Statutory organization	*Operational organization*	*Informal organization*
(Companies)	➢ Departments	
	➢ Cost centers	
	➢ Business units	
	➢ Value streams	
	➢ Retail channels	

Figure 10-1:   Organization units in the organization model

The list page *Organization administration> Organizations> Internal organizations* shows all organization units with their type. Forms that are tailored to the specific requirements of the different organization types are available in the other menu items of the folder *Organization administration> Organizations*.

10.1.2.1 Legal Entities

Legal entities (*Organization administration> Organizations> Legal entities*) are company accounts in Dynamics 365 (see section 10.1.4 below). They are the bottom level for legal reporting. Tax reports and financial statements like balance sheets and income statements are usually based on legal entities.

If multiple legal entities, typically the companies of an affiliated group, work in a common Dynamics 365 environment, you can manage the relations between these legal entities. Depending on the requirements, you use the following features:

➢ **Financial consolidation** – Manage financial consolidation of companies in an affiliated group.

➢ **Intercompany** – Automate business processes between the legal entities of a multi-company organization.

➢ **Organization hierarchies** – Use legal entities in the organization model (e.g., for the setup of data security or approval processes).

10.1.2.2 Operating Units

Operating units (*Organization administration> Organizations> Operating units*) are used for reporting and for the internal control of business processes. The types of operating units that you use (e.g., business units as representation for divisions or regions) are depending on the requirements of the enterprise.

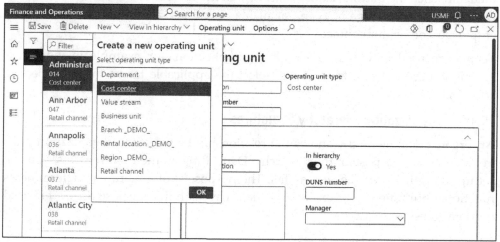

Figure 10-2:   Creating a cost center in the Operating unit form (with Contoso demo data)

In a standard Dynamics 365 environment, there are following operating unit types:

> **Department** – Functional classification (e.g., "Finance"), also used in human resources.
> **Cost center** – For budgeting and expenditure control.
> **Value stream** – For production flows in lean manufacturing.
> **Business unit** – For strategic business objectives (e.g., divisions).
> **Retail channel** – Related to the Retail and commerce module.

When you create a new operating unit in the Operating unit form, select the *Operating unit type* in the drop-down menu first. Then enter additional data like the name, address and contact details in the detail form.

Once an operating unit is assigned to one or more hierarchies, you can click the button *View in hierarchy* to check the allocation within organizational structures.

If you want to report on the financial performance of operating units, link the operating units to financial dimensions (see section 9.2.3).

10.1.2.3 Teams

Teams (*Organization administration> Organizations> Teams*) represent an informal organization of an enterprise. A team simply is a group of people. There is no hierarchical organization structure that links the different teams.

Team types, which you can access with the button *Team types* in the Teams form, restrict the team members to different kinds of people (e.g., system users, employees, or vendor contacts).

When you create a new team, select the team type first. In order to assign people to the team, click the button *Add team members* in the toolbar of the tab *Team members*. Depending on the team type, available members are Dynamics 365 users, employees, or vendor contacts.

Teams are used in various areas of the application, for example in the access permission setup for address books (select the applicable teams in the respective address books).

10.1.3   Organization Hierarchy Structures

An organization hierarchy shows the relationship between the organization units in line with the purpose of the hierarchy. Depending on the requirements, you can set up multiple hierarchies in parallel. The purpose(s) of a hierarchy determine its functional utilization – for example, a hierarchy with the purpose *Security* is used for data access permissions.

10.1.3.1 Organization Hierarchies

The organization hierarchies in your enterprise are shown in the menu item *Organization administration> Organizations> Organization hierarchies*. If you want to create a new hierarchy, click the button *New* and enter the *Name* of the hierarchy.

Then click the button *Assign purpose* on the tab *Purposes* to assign one or more hierarchy purposes to the hierarchy.

In order to view the hierarchy with its elements, click the button *View* in the action pane. In the hierarchy designer that is shown then, you can navigate within the hierarchy and switch the focus with a click on the respective element. You can change the hierarchy in the Edit mode and insert or remove organization units with the respective button in the toolbar. With the buttons *Cut* and *Paste*, you can move a unit and its subunits within the organization hierarchy.

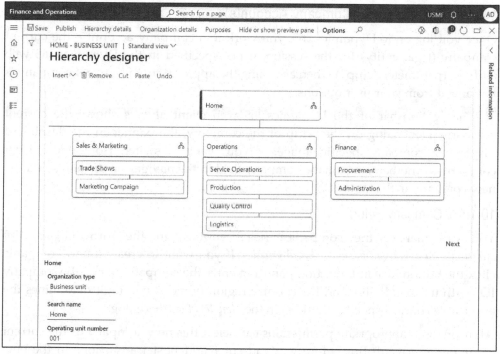

Figure 10-3: Editing an organization hierarchy in the hierarchy designer

Once you have finished editing the organization hierarchy, click the button *Publish* to activate the update. If you want to keep changes in a draft version, do not publish the update but save the changes with the button *Save*.

The organization structure is using validity periods, which is why you enter an effective date when you publish the hierarchy after editing. It is not possible to change the published version anymore – you can only publish another version with a later date. For this reason, you should not publish a hierarchy with a future date as long as it is still possible that there are further changes in the hierarchy.

10.1.3.2 Organization Hierarchy Purposes

In case your enterprise requires different hierarchies for the different purposes, set up multiple organization hierarchies. The organization hierarchy purposes (*Organization administration> Organizations> Organization hierarchy purposes*) refer to functional features in Dynamics 365. For this reason, available purposes (e.g., *Centralized payments* or *Security*) and the allowed organization types per purpose are determined by the application.

In order to assign the applicable organization hierarchy or hierarchies to a purpose, select the respective hierarchy purpose in the left pane of the Organization hierarchy purposes form and click the button *Add* on the tab *Assigned hierarchies* in the right pane. Depending on the requirements, you can assign one or more hierarchies to one purpose, and one hierarchy to one or more purposes.

10.1.4 Legal Entities (Company Accounts)

Once you log on to Dynamics 365, you work in a company account – the current company (legal entity) for the session. If not specified in the Dynamics 365 web address (parameter "cmp") when accessing the application, the current company is initialized from your user options.

The navigation bar of the Dynamics 365 web client always shows the current company. Depending on the setup of the company, the banner in the dashboard displays a company-specific image. If you want to switch from one current company to another, click on the company field in the navigation bar and select the new company in the lookup.

10.1.4.1 Company Setup

You can manage the companies (legal entities) in the form *Organization administration> Organizations> Legal entities*. If you want to create a new company, click the button *New* in the action pane and enter the company name, the company ID (with up to 4 digits), and the country/region (which by default determines the applicable country-specific features) in the *New legal entity* dialog.

All users with appropriate permissions can select this new company as the current company afterward. But before you can enter and post transactions in the new company, the setup of the company in all applicable areas and modules (like general ledger, accounts payable, and accounts receivable) has to be finished. A checklist of basic settings is given in the appendix of this book.

Core data in the Legal entity form include the company name (which is printed on documents and reports) and further settings like the primary company address. In order to enter the primary address or an additional address (e.g., for invoicing or delivery), click the button *Edit* or *Add* on the tab *Addresses*. An example of an additional address is a default delivery address that is different from the primary company address. This delivery address is the default for purchase orders (if no address is specified for the site or warehouse in the order header).

The tab *Contact information* contains the contact data of the company. Since the global address book includes the legal entities, company addresses and contact data are shown in the global address book.

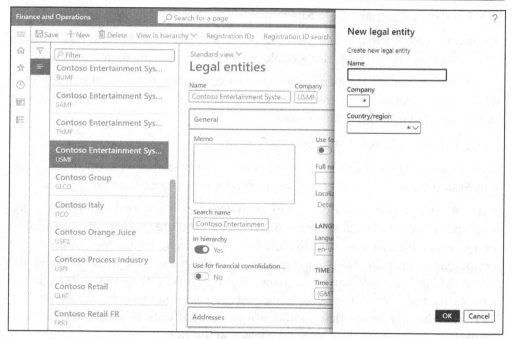

Figure 10-4: Creating a company in the Legal entity form

Further important settings in the Legal entity form include the primary bank account on the tab *Bank account information*. In a company located in the European Union, enter the VAT registration number (VAT exempt number) on the tab *Foreign trade and logistics*.

10.1.4.2 Companies in the Data Structure

You can set up multiple company accounts (legal entities) within a Dynamics 365 environment. Except for shared application data like parties or products, company accounts establish a separate set of data within the database. The company is a key field in all relevant Dynamics 365 tables.

The company "DAT" is a special company. Dynamics 365 automatically generates this company, which holds system data, when creating the environment. You cannot delete it, and you should not use it as a test or operational company in order to clearly distinguish company data from data that are not related to a particular company.

10.1.4.3 Company Banner in the Dashboard

In the Legal entity form, you can select a picture that is shown in the dashboard and another picture that is printed on reports. In order to specify the dashboard image, switch to the tab *Dashboard image* in the Legal entity form, select the option "Banner" or "Logo" in the field *Dashboard company image type* and upload a picture with the button *Change* in the toolbar. The company image on reports is specified on the tab *Report company logo image* of the Legal entity form.

10.1.5 Cross-Company Data Sharing

In Dynamics 365, there are some areas in which data are shared across legal entities – e.g., parties in the global address book, charts of accounts, or shared products.

Sometimes, common data management across companies is required in additional areas – e.g., if you want to ensure uniform payment terms. For this purpose, you can use the cross-company data sharing.

10.1.5.1 Setup of Cross-Company Data Sharing

In order to set up, which tables are shared in which companies, open the menu item *System administration> Setup> Configure cross-company data sharing*.

If you want to create a new collection of shared data, click the button *New* in the action pane and enter a name for the data collection before you save the record. For each shared table that you want to include in the collection, click the button *Add* in the toolbar of the pane *Tables and fields to share*, select the *Table name* and click the button *Add table* in the drop-down menu. If you expand a node with a table in the pane *Tables and fields to share*, you can adjust the selection of fields that are shared. Then add the companies that should use the shared data collection in the pane *Companies which share the records in these tables* on the right.

In order to activate data sharing for a table collection, click the button *Enable* in the action pane of the Configure cross-company data sharing form.

10.1.5.2 Working with Cross-Company Data Sharing

If you insert, update or delete records in a table and in a company, which is included in a shared table collection, the update of table data immediately applies to all companies in the table collection.

10.1.6 Sites

Unlike company accounts, which represent legal entities, sites are a representation of subsidiaries within a company. Since sites are an inventory dimension (storage dimension), they are available in all areas of the supply chain management within Dynamics 365.

In order to calculate financial results at the site level, you can link the inventory dimension "Site" to a financial dimension. With a filter on the financial dimension, you can, for example, generate an income statement per subsidiary then.

10.1.6.1 Multisite Functionality

The multisite functionality in Dynamics 365 includes the following options:

➢ **Master planning** – Per site or per company.
➢ **Bills of materials** – Per site or per company.
➢ **Production control parameters** – Per site or per company.
➢ **Item data (Released products)** – Default order settings per site or per company.

> **Transactions** – Sites in all inventory transactions, sales orders, purchase orders and production orders.
> **Financial reporting** – Optionally for sites (if linked to a financial dimension).

10.1.6.2 Setup of Sites

In order to create a site in the current company, access the menu item *Inventory management> Setup> Inventory breakdown> Sites* and click the button *New* before you enter the ID, the name, and optionally the address. On the tab *Financial dimensions*, which is shown in case the inventory dimension "Site" is linked to a financial dimension, you can enter a dimension value for this dimension. This is mandatory if the dimension link is activated.

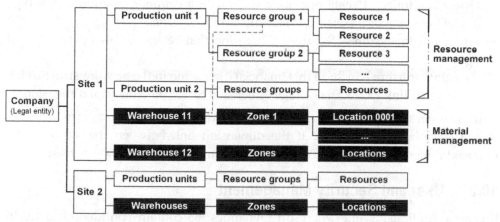

Figure 10-5: Organization structure in resource management and material management

The link between the inventory dimension "Site" and a financial dimension is specified in the menu item *Cost management> Ledger integration policies setup> Dimension link*. In Edit mode, you can select a financial dimension that you want to use for sites. In order to use the dimension value that is entered in the Site form as a default in the financial transactions with the particular site, activate the link with the button *Activate link* in the action pane of the Dimension link form. With the button *Lock link*, you can prevent overriding the dimension value in a transaction.

Sites are a mandatory storage dimension that is automatically activated in all storage dimension groups. For this reason, every inventory transaction includes a dimension value for the site. In addition, each warehouse has to be linked to a site.

If sites are not required in the organization of your enterprise, set up a single site which is the default in all transactions. You can enter this site as default in applicable settings – for example, in the *Default order settings* of released products. More details on inventory dimensions are given in section 7.2.2 of this book.

10.1.6.3 Production Units

In the organization structure for material management, the storage dimension *Site*, which groups the warehouses, is the level below the legal entity (company). In resource management, the *Production unit* is an additional level in the structure of resources and resource groups. Each production unit is linked to a site and represents a plant in master planning.

10.1.6.4 Linking Sites to the Organization Model

It is not possible to include sites directly in the organization model (see section 10.1.3). But you can link sites to a financial dimension, and financial dimensions to organization units, which in the end shows sites in the organization model.

In order to use sites in finance and in the organization model, complete the following implementation steps:

> **Operating units** – Create operating units with a common operating unit type (e.g., *Department* or *Business unit*) for the individual sites.
> **Financial dimension** – Set up a dimension that refers to this operating unit type.
> **Account structure** – Include this financial dimension in the account structure(s).
> **Dimension link** – Link the storage dimension *Site* to this financial dimension.

You can enter the name of the organization unit in the related site to visualize sites in the organization hierarchy. If the dimension link between the site and the financial dimension is activated, you can perform financial reporting per site.

10.2   User and Security Management

Business applications like Microsoft Dynamics 365 contain confidential data. In order to protect sensitive information, access to the application has to be limited in compliance with the requirements of the particular enterprise.

10.2.1   Access Control

Access control in Dynamics 365 is based on two elements:

> **Authentication** – Identification of users.
> **Authorization** – User permissions.

As a prerequisite for authenticating a user in Dynamics 365, a system administrator has to create and to enable a Dynamics 365 user who is linked to the Microsoft Azure Active Directory account of the user. User authentication is not only required for permission control. It is also the basis for logging user transactions and data updates. Further settings with reference to the Dynamics 365 user include the favorites, the user options, and the usage data, which enable a personalized workspace in Dynamics 365.

Dynamics 365 is using a role-based security model for authorization, which means that security roles control the access to application elements (e.g., menu items). A user in Dynamics 365 can have one or more roles, and these roles determine his permissions.

Permissions for application elements are not directly assigned to a role, but to duties and privileges. Duties and, below duties, privileges establish a grouping level for permissions in the structure of the security model.

The extensible data security framework additionally provides the option to restrict access based on effective dates or application data (e.g., based on sales territories).

10.2.2 Users and Employees

Each person who accesses Dynamics 365 has to be set up as a Dynamics 365 user.

10.2.2.1 Entering User Accounts

In order to create a Dynamics 365 user, open the list page *System administration> Users> Users* and click the button *New*. In the new record, enter the *User ID* within Dynamics 365, the *User name*, the *Provider* (tenant of your organization in the Azure Active Directory) and the *Email* (Azure Active Directory user ID) and make sure that the slider *Enabled* is set to "Yes" (enabling the user to log on to Dynamics 365).

Apart from creating users manually, you can use the import wizard (click the button *Import users* in the action pane) to import Dynamics 365 users from the Azure Active Directory.

10.2.2.2 Security Roles and Permission Assignment

In order to specify the permissions of the particular user, switch to the tab *User's roles* in the User detail form and assign the applicable security roles. Alternatively, you can use form *System administration> Security> Assign users to roles* to associate users with roles. In this form, you can also set up rules which assign new users automatically to security roles.

In the User detail form and in the list page, the security roles of the selected user are shown in the FactBox *Roles for the selected user* on the right. If a user is assigned to multiple roles, the permissions of all selected roles apply to the user. In case of overlapping permission settings for an object, the higher access level applies.

You can restrict the security roles of a user at the organization level. For this purpose, select the user in the User detail form first. Then select the role that you want to restrict on the tab *User's roles*, and click the button *Assign organizations* in the toolbar of this tab. In the *Assign organizations* form, you can enable global access with the selected role, or restrict the role access to particular organizations. For permissions at the level of organizations, select legal entities (or elements of an organization hierarchy with the purpose *Security*) in the upper pane of the *Assign organizations* form and click the button *Grant* in the toolbar of the lower pane.

10.2.2.3 User Options

The button *User options* in the User form provides access to the user options of the selected user. Apart from the access from the user management, users with appropriate permissions can access their personal user options with the button

Settings ⚙ */User options* in the navigation bar. Accessing the user options from the user management is a way to predefine settings like the language or the default for the current company.

10.2.2.4 Assigning Employees to Users

Apart from being a user, people who access Dynamics 365 are an employee, a contractor, or a contact person at an external party (e.g., customer). The global address book contains both, workers (employees and contractors) and external contact persons.

In order to assign a Dynamics 365 user to a person in the global address book (worker or external contact), open the User detail form and, in the field *Person*, select the person that you want to assign to the user. The button *Maintain versions* provides the option to enter an effective date and an expiration date.

The worker assignment is used throughout the whole application. Examples are purchase requisitions, project accounting, human resources, case management, and sales order management. Once a user is assigned to a worker who is employed in the current company, the worker ID is used in all areas. It is, for example, the default for the field *Sales taker* in the order header when creating a sales order.

10.2.2.5 Employee Management

The User form contains the user settings for the access to Dynamics 365. Separately from the user setup, the Worker form is there to manage the enterprise staff.

Workers include employees and contractors, no matter whether they are Dynamics 365 users or not. Worker records are shared across companies, and the contact details are included in the global address book. The employment of a worker determines his assignment to one or more companies.

The Worker list page (*Human resources> Workers> Workers*) shows all employees and contractors who are currently employed in any company of the enterprise. In order to view only current employees (workers with the type "Employee") in the current company, open the Employee list page (*Human resources> Workers> Employees*). If you want to view the workers who have been employed in the past, or workers with an employment in the future, click the button *As of date* in the Worker form or the Employee form and select the respective date.

General worker data are shared across companies, but some data – including the employment – are company-specific. In the FactBox *Employment history* on the right, and in the Employment form which you open with the button *Worker/ Versions/Employment history*, you can view the current and past employments of the selected worker. The tab *Employment* in the Worker detail form, which is only displayed if the worker has got an employment in the current company, shows the company-specific employment data in the current company.

In order to create a new worker, click the button *New* and, in the *Hire new worker* dialog, enter the *First name*, the *Last name*, the company (*Legal entity*) employing the worker, the *Personnel number* (if not deriving from a number sequence), the *Worker type* (employee or contractor), and the *Employment start date*.

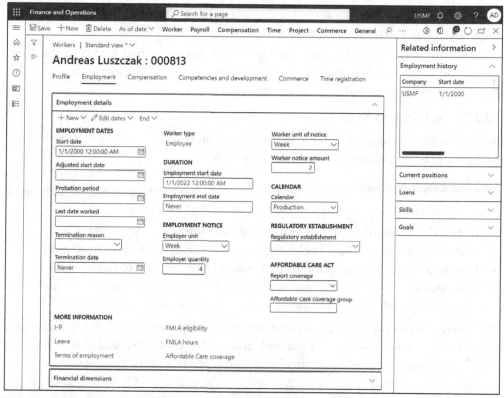

Figure 10-6: Managing employment data in the Worker detail form

The default for the employing company is the current company. On the tab *Employment* in the Worker detail form, you can edit the employment in the current company or add an employment if the worker changes from this company to another company of the enterprise (or if he has got a parallel employment in another company of the enterprise).

The required detail data for a worker primarily depend on the Dynamics 365 modules that are used in your organization. These details include data for project accounting, human resources, and expense management.

10.2.2.6 Online Users

If you want to know the users who are currently logged on to Dynamics 365, open the menu item *System administration> Users> Online users*. This inquiry shows all client sessions that are connected to the application. If you have got appropriate permissions, you can click the button *End sessions* in the toolbar of the tab *Client sessions* to log off a user.

10.2.2.7 User Groups

User groups (*System administration> Users> User groups*) are not used in the role-based security setup, but for some particular settings. You can, for example, open ledger periods, which are on hold, for a specific user group. In workflows or financial journals, you can optionally apply user groups for the workflow task assignment, for approval, and for posting restrictions.

In order to assign users to a user group, select the respective group in the User group form and switch to the tab *Users*. On this tab, assign the applicable users by moving them from the left pane to the right pane.

10.2.3   Role-Based Security

In line with the security model in Dynamics 365, permissions are not directly assigned to individual users, but to security roles.

10.2.3.1 Security Model

The role-based security model includes the following elements:

➢ **Role** – Group of duties required for a job function (e.g., "Accountant").
➢ **Duty** – Group of privileges necessary for a task (e.g., "Maintain fixed assets").
➢ **Privilege** – Permissions at the level of objects (e.g., "Post fixed assets journal").
➢ **Permission** – Low-level access restriction to securable objects (user interface elements, reports, tables and fields, service operations).

The assignment of a user to one or more roles (depending on his job functions) determines his permissions. In general, roles refer to duties, and duties refer to privileges. But if required, you can also assign a privilege directly to a role.

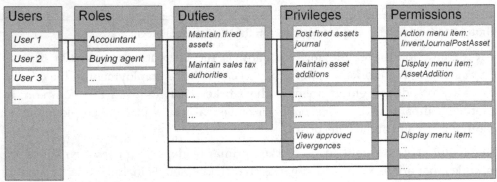

Figure 10-7:   Components of the security model

A role is a set of access permissions that are required to perform a job function. Apart from functional roles, which refer to the functional tasks, there are additional role types. In general, we can divide the roles into following types:

➢ **Functional roles** – For example, "Buying agent".
➢ **Organizational roles** – For example, "Employee".
➢ **Application roles** – For example, "System user".

The role "System administrator" has got access to all areas of the application. The access settings for this role are not editable.

10.2.3.2 Managing the Security Configuration

You can manage the security roles, duties, and privileges in the form *System administration> Security> Security configuration*. This form contains the tabs *Roles, Duties* and *Privileges* with the related security elements.

On the tab *Roles*, the left pane shows the available roles in your environment. For the selected role in the left pane, you can view the duties and directly assigned privileges with a click on the respective element in the pane *References* in the middle of the form. If you want to add a duty or privilege to the selected role, select the respective node (e.g., "Duties") in the pane *References* and click the button *Add references* in the toolbar of the tab. If you want to create a completely new role, click the button *Create new* (or the button *Copy* that is shown after a click on a role).

A duty is a group of privileges that are required for a particular task – e.g., for maintaining fixed assets. If you want to view or edit the duties, switch to the tab *Duties* of the Security configuration form. Select a duty and click on the respective element in the pane *References* in the middle of the form to view the related privileges (and roles). If you want to add a privilege to the selected duty, select the respective node *Privileges* in the pane *References* and click the button *Add references* in the toolbar of the tab.

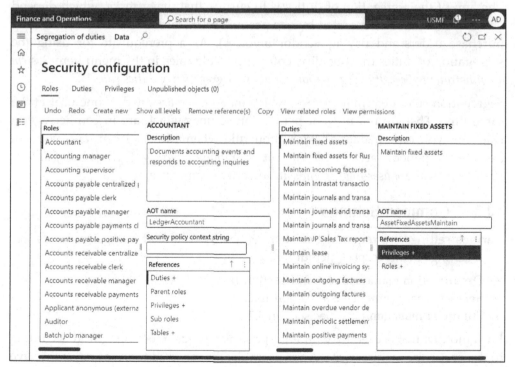

Figure 10-8:   Viewing the duties of the security role "Accountant"

A privilege contains all permissions that are required for a particular application object. You can view and edit the security privileges on the tab *Privileges* of the Security configuration form. Select a privilege and click on the respective element in the pane *References* to view the related application objects (e.g., *Action menu items*). If you want to add a permission to the selected privilege, select the node in the pane *References* and click the button *Add references* in the toolbar of the tab.

Permissions specify the access restrictions at the lowest level, based on application objects. The permissions, which you can select in the security privileges, are determined by application development.

While editing the security configuration, updated elements are shown on the tab *Unpublished objects*. In order to activate the changes, click the button *Publish all* (or *Publish selection*) in the toolbar of this tab.

10.2.3.3 Security Diagnostics

In all Dynamics 365 forms, the button *Options/Page options/Security diagnostics* displays a dialog that shows which roles, duties, and privileges grant access to the respective form. The button *Add roles to user* in the dialog provide access to the form *Assign users to roles* (if a role is selected in the dialog). If you select a duty, you can assign a role, and for a privilege, you can assign a duty.

10.2.3.4 Segregation of Duties

The aim of the segregation of duties is to ensure, that major tasks, which depend on each other, are not executed by one person but by different users (e.g., creating purchase orders and paying vendor invoices). As a prerequisite for using the segregation of duties functionality, enter applicable rules in the menu item *System administration> Security> Segregation of duties> Segregation of duties rules*.

Segregation rules determine duties, which may not be assigned to one user at the same time. They do not prevent permission settings which are in conflict with a rule. But you can validate a segregation rule when you set it up, and you can execute the periodic activity *System administration> Security> Segregation of duties> Verify compliance of user-role assignments* to verify compliance.

10.3   Common Settings

Various settings are required before an enterprise can start using Dynamics 365. Core settings in this respect include:

➢ **Organization management** – See section 10.1.
➢ **Security management** – See section 10.2.
➢ **Financial management** – See section 9.2.

Each module that is used by your enterprise also needs to be configured according to the particular requirements. As an example, the required terms of payment have to be set up in purchasing and in sales. In addition, there are some basic settings that are used in all areas of the application. You can find a short description of these settings below.

10.3.1 Number Sequences

Number sequences control the allocation of numbers throughout the whole application. In particular, number sequences are used in the following data areas:

> **Master data** – For example, vendor numbers.
> **Journals and orders** – For example, purchase order numbers.
> **Posted transactions** – For example, invoice numbers.

Dynamics 365 includes company-specific number sequences and number sequences on the enterprise level. The scope parameters of a number sequence control, whether it is shared or specific to a company.

10.3.1.1 Number Sequence Setup

In order to manage the number sequences, open the menu item *Organization administration> Number sequences> Number sequences*. The FactBox *Number sequence segments* on the right of this page shows the company and other segments of the selected number sequence as applicable. If you want to create a new number sequence, click the button *Number sequence/New/Number sequence* in the action pane. Then enter a unique *Number sequence code* and a *Name*, and switch to the tab *Scope parameters* of the detail form. On this tab, you can specify whether the number sequence is shared, or restricted to a company or organization unit.

On the tab *Segments* of the detail form, specify the number format for the number sequence. Segments of a number include the following types:

> **Alphanumeric** – Number which increases every time the number sequence is used, replacing the number signs (#) in the format with the next number. The length of the alphanumeric segment must cover the largest number (specified on the tab *General*).
> **Constant** – Segments for prefixes (e.g., for a format "INV#####" or "12#####") and for suffixes (e.g., for a format "#####-INV"). In general, prefixes are preferable since they are easier to use (e.g., for filtering).
> **Other types** – Segments with the type *Company, Legal entity, Operating unit* or *Fiscal calendar period* are only available if they are included in the *Scope* of the number sequence.

When you set up number sequences for document and transaction numbers, it is a good idea to avoid overlapping number sequences for the different documents in order to facilitate the tracking of transactions.

10.3.1.2 Number Sequence References

The number sequence references determine for a number sequence, to which master data or transactions it is assigned. In order to edit the number sequence references, switch to the tab *References* in the Number sequence detail form, or access the section *Number sequences* in the Parameters form of each module.

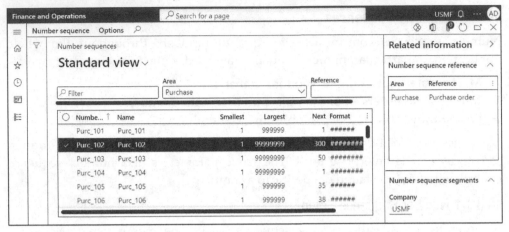

Figure 10-9:   Viewing the FactBox *Number sequence reference* in the Number sequence form

A single number sequence can be assigned to multiple number sequence references at the same time. You can, for example, assign one common number sequence to invoices and credit notes. This setting does not generate duplicate numbers, but assigns numbers to invoices and credit notes in line with the chronological order of the transactions.

10.3.1.3 General Settings in Number Sequences

The numeric first (*Smallest*) and last (*Largest*) number of a number sequence are specified on the tab *General* of the Number sequence detail form. The field *Next* shows the next number that will be provided by the number sequence. You can change the next number, but make sure to avoid duplicate keys and gaps in continuous numbers.

The slider *Manual* controls whether numbers are entered manually. If the slider *To a lower number* or *To a higher number* is set to "Yes", you can change the numbers that are assigned from the number sequence. Gaps in a number sequence are prevented with the slider *Continuous*. Set this slider only in number sequences to "Yes", which actually require continuous numbers. Voucher numbers often require continuous numbering, since it is a statutory requirement in many countries.

10.3.1.4 Preallocation of Numbers

On the tab *Performance* in the Number sequence detail form, you can set the slider *Preallocation* to "Yes" to enable preloading numbers from the database to the computer memory. This should not be selected for continuous numbers, but for other number sequences it will improve the system performance. With the button *Number sequence/Administration/Status list*, you can check the preallocated numbers. In order to remove (free) the preallocated numbers, select the applicable option in the button *Number sequence/Administration/Manual cleanup*.

10.3.2 Calendars

As a prerequisite for posting any transaction in Dynamics 365, an open ledger period that covers the respective posting date is required.

10.3.2.1 Ledger Calendars

Ledger calendars (*General ledger> Calendars> Ledger calendars*), which refer to the fiscal calendar that is linked to the current company, determine the open periods in which you can post transactions (see section 9.2.1).

10.3.2.2 Other Calendars

Apart from the calendars in finance, other areas within Dynamics 365 apply additional period and calendar definitions.

The form *Organization administration> Setup> Calendars> Working time templates* (or *Production control> Setup> Calendars> Working time templates*) contains default settings for the weekly working times. Working time templates are a basis for the calendars in the menu item *Organization administration> Setup> Calendars> Calendars* (see section 5.3.1). These calendars are used in all areas of the supply chain management – including master planning, production, purchasing, sales, and inventory management.

The Project accounting module uses separate calendars, which you can access in the menu item *Organization administration> Setup> Calendars> Period types*. These calendars are a basis for project invoicing and required for estimates, invoice subscriptions, and the project-related employee setup.

10.3.3 Address Setup

The address setup is a prerequisite for entering and printing addresses correctly. In order to access the address setup, which is shared across companies, open the form *Organization administration> Global address book> Addresses> Address setup*.

On the tab *Country/region* of the Address setup form, you can view the available countries. Microsoft Dynamics 365 already includes a standard list of countries, but you can enter additional countries with the button *New* in the toolbar of this tab.

On the tab *Parameters*, sliders specify whether *ZIP/postal code*, *District* or *City* are validated when entering an address. If set to "Yes", you cannot enter an address with, for example, a new ZIP code before the new ZIP code is entered on the tab *ZIP/postal codes* in the address setup.

The address format on the tab *Address format* determines the way in which street, ZIP/postal code, city, and country are shown in the address field of addresses. In order to comply with the regulations in different countries, an individual format per country is possible. The field *Address format* in the country setup (on the tab *Country/region* in the address setup) controls the address format per country.

If you want to set up a new format, click the button *New* in the toolbar of the tab *Address format*. In the pane *Configure address component* on the right, enter the way in which the address segments (including *Street* and *City*) should be shown on printed documents. The segment selection is also used when you enter an address – only fields, which are included in the address format of the particular country, are shown.

When you set up address formats, take into account that not only the individual fields of the address are stored, but also the formatted address. If you change the address format and there are already addresses with the old format, you can update the existing addresses with the button *Update addresses* in the toolbar of the tab *Address format* in the Address setup form.

10.3.4   Parameters

Parameters are basic settings which select the way, which fits best to your organization, from the supported business process options in Dynamics 365.

The definition of correct parameter settings is a core task when implementing Dynamics 365. Depending on the respective parameter, it is not easily possible to change a parameter setting at a later stage. Before you change any basic setting in an operational environment, make sure that you are aware of the consequences. Depending on the circumstances, read the online help or ask an expert to avoid data inconsistency or other issues.

The System parameters (*System administration> Setup> System parameters*) contain global parameters like the system language (default language for language texts in shared data, like product descriptions), or the default basic currency.

In addition, a parameter form that controls the company-specific settings is included in each module of the application. In order to access the parameters of a module, open the respective menu item in the folder *Setup* of the module – for example, the Accounts payable parameters in the menu item *Accounts payable> Setup> Accounts payable parameters*.

10.4   Alerts and Workflow Management

A workflow, which is a sequence of operations in a routine business process, contains the necessary activities for processing a document. Typical examples of workflows are approval processes – e.g., for purchase requisitions.

Microsoft Dynamics 365 provides the required functionality for configuring and processing workflows, including automated workflow processes. You can, for example, configure workflows in a way that low-value purchases are approved automatically while high-value purchases require manual approval.

Alerts within Dynamics 365 are automatic notifications that are based on alert rules and triggered by selected events (e.g., inserting a record). Compared to workflows, which support a sequence of activities including automatic actions, alerts are simple notifications without further options.

10.4.1 Alert Rules and Notifications

If you want to notify a user of an event that occurs within Dynamics 365, create an alert rule in the respective form. You can, for example, set up a rule to notify the responsible person when an agreed delivery date has passed, or when a new vendor is created.

10.4.1.1 Alert Rules

In order to create an alert rule, click the button *Options/Share/Create a custom alert* in the action pane of detail forms and list pages. A dialog is shown next, in which you can enter the details of the alert rule.

In the field *Event* of the dialog, select the trigger for the alert – for example, creating or deleting a record, or modifying the content of a particular field. In alert rules that refer to a field, select the respective field in the lookup *Field* of the dialog. If the basis of an alert rule is a date field, the field *Event* provides the option to generate alerts when the date is due.

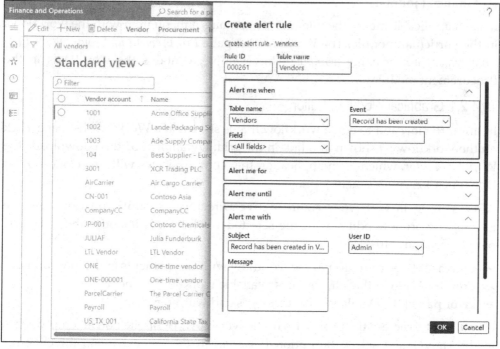

Figure 10-10: Entering details in the dialog for a new alert rule

If you want to edit existing alert rules, click the button *Options/Share/Manage my alerts rule* in the action pane. Administrators can use the menu item *System administration> Setup> Alert rules*.

10.4.1.2 Alert Processing and Notifications

Alert notifications are only shown after executing the periodic activity *System administration> Periodic tasks> Alerts> Change based alerts* or, for alert rules that refer to a due date for a date field, *System administration> Periodic tasks> Alerts> Due date alerts*. These activities are usually periodic batch jobs.

Once an event triggers an alert, a notification is sent to the action center (message center). Click the button ▣ (*Show messages*) in the navigation bar, which indicates the number of unread notifications, to view the notification. In the notification, a link to the alert origin provides access to the record that has triggered the alert.

10.4.2   Configuring Workflows

Workflows are available in many areas of Microsoft Dynamics 365, including but not limited to:

> **Purchase requisitions**
> **Purchase orders**
> **Vendor invoices**
> **Free text invoices**
> **Financial journals**

In each applicable menu, the folder *Setup* contains a menu item with the workflows in the particular module. The Workflow list page *Procurement and sourcing> Setup> Procurement and sourcing workflows*, for example, contains the workflows in the Procurement module.

10.4.2.1 Graphical Workflow Editor

In order to view and to edit a workflow that is shown in a Workflow list page, click on the workflow *ID* shown as a link in the grid. Dynamics 365 then downloads the *Workflow Editor*, which is an application that communicates with the cloud-hosted Dynamics 365 environment.

After signing in with your Azure Active Directory account, you can view the graphical workflow editor with the selected workflow. It includes the following panes (see Figure 10-11):

> **Canvas** [1] – Area to design the workflow with the elements and connections.
> **Toolbox** [2] – On the left, contains available workflow elements.
> **Error pane** [3] – Displays error messages and warnings.

If you want to access the properties of the workflow, right-click on an empty space in the canvas and select the option *Properties* in the context menu (or click the button *Properties* after selecting an empty space in the canvas). Basic workflow settings include the *Owner* of the selected workflow.

In the toolbox on the left of the workflow editor, the workflow elements are grouped by type (e.g., *Approvals* and *Tasks*). Depending on the selected workflow, the toolbox contains different elements. You can hide or to show the toolbox with the button *Toolbox* in the action pane.

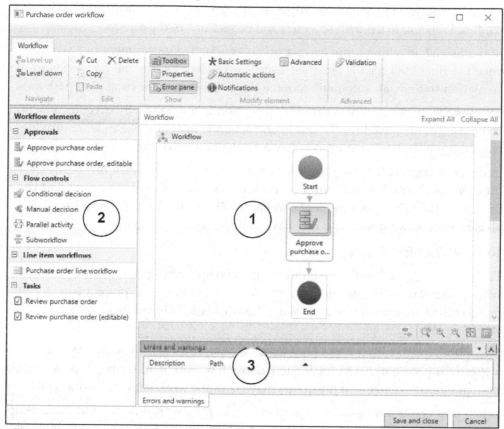

Figure 10-11: Editing the purchase order workflow in the Workflow editor

If you want to add a workflow element to the workflow, click the respective element in the toolbox and drag it to the canvas. In order to edit the properties of the element, select the option *Properties* in the context menu (right-click the element to open the context menu for the respective element) or click the appropriate button in the button group *Modify element* of the action pane. The available options for the element are depending on the element type.

For elements that require a manual activity (e.g., *Tasks* or *Manual decision*), the properties include a tab or button *Assignment* for assigning responsible persons. The *Assignment type* defines the search path for the responsible person. Applicable assignment types are "Participant" (related to user roles and user groups), "Hierarchy" (related to the position hierarchy in human resources), "Workflow user" (related to the user who starts or owns the workflow), "User" (direct assignment of respective usernames), or "Queue" (work item queues, see below).

Workflow elements with the type "Approval" contain a lower workflow level with the approval steps. The responsible persons for approval are assigned at the level of approval steps. In order to access the approval steps, double-click the particular approval element or click the button *Level down* in the action pane of the workflow editor. If you want to access the upper level again, click the button *Level up* or click the link *Workflow* in the path shown in the header line of the canvas.

In the *Escalation* settings, you can set up an automatic reassignment of a work item once the time limit for the assigned user is exceeded. On the tab *End action* in the escalation settings, an automatic action is specified in case the escalation path fails.

Settings for *Automatic actions* provide the option to automatically execute an action if the condition entered for the automatic action is met – for example, approving a requisition if the total amount is below a predefined maximum.

In order to connect the workflow elements in the canvas, create a line between the different elements. For this purpose, click on the border of one element and drag the line to the subsequent element (similar to Microsoft Visio). In a valid workflow, all elements between *Start* and *End* have to be linked.

10.4.2.2 Work Item Queues

The option "Queue" in the assignment of the responsible person is only available with particular workflow element types (e.g., *Tasks*). As a prerequisite for the queue-based assignment, set up work item queues (*Organization administration> Workflow> Work item queues*).

Work item queues are used to pool workflow activities and to assign an activity to a group of people instead of a single person. If a work item is assigned to a work item queue, all members of the queue may claim the work item and work on it.

When you create a new work item queue, select the workflow type in the lookup field *Document* to specify the workflows in which the work item queue is available. Once the status of the work item queue is set to "Active", you can use it in the applicable workflows.

Apart from manually adding users to a work item queue (on the tab *Users* of the work item queue), you can apply an automatic assignment that is based on filter criteria. In order to access the setup for automatic assignment, click the button *Work item queue assignment rule* in the Work item queue form, or open the menu item *Organization administration> Workflow> Work item queue assignment rules*.

10.4.2.3 Workflow Versions

When you save a workflow with the button *Save and close* in the workflow editor, Dynamics 365 creates a new version. For this reason, a dialog is shown in which you select whether to activate the new version or to keep the previous version activated.

If you want to access the versions of a workflow, click the button *Workflow/ Manage/Versions* in the Workflow list page. In the *Workflow versions* dialog, you can activate a new version or an old version as applicable.

The active version is used in new workflows, which are submitted after activation. Work items of workflows in progress have to be finished with the original version.

10.4.2.4 Entering Workflows

In order to create a new workflow in a Workflow list page, click the button *New* in the action pane. A dialog is shown next, in which you have to select the applicable *Workflow type* (e.g., "Purchase requisition review") before you access the graphical workflow editor that is described above.

If there are two workflows of the same type in the Workflow list page, you can click the button *Workflow/Manage/Set as default* to specify a default.

10.4.2.5 Basic Setup for Workflows

Workflow processing is an asynchronous batch job, which is why the next activity in a workflow is not available immediately, but only after the respective workflow element has been processed. Depending on the batch configuration, this may take some time.

In order to set up the workflow infrastructure initially, an administrator can use the menu item *System administration> Workflow> Workflow infrastructure configuration*. This wizard generates batch jobs which are shown in the menu item *System administration> Inquiries> Batch jobs*. As a prerequisite for the use of workflows, these batch jobs have to be processed repeatedly.

10.4.3 Working with Workflows

If there is an active workflow related to a Dynamics 365 form, the button *Workflow* is shown in the action pane of this form. This button indicates that workflow processing is necessary and provides the option to start workflow processing.

When working with workflows, you should keep in mind that the workflow system processes workflow tasks in a batch process. For this reason, work items are not available before the batch process has processed the submitted workflow.

10.4.3.1 Start of Workflow Processing

Once you have entered a record in a form that is assigned to a workflow, you can start workflow processing with the button *Workflow/Submit* in the action pane (e.g., in the purchase requisitions shown in Figure 10-12). In the following dialog, you can optionally enter a comment before you click the button *Submit* at the bottom. Submitting starts workflow processing, which generates work items that are based on the workflow elements of the workflow (specified in the workflow editor).

After starting the workflow, the button *Workflow* does not show the option *Submit* anymore, but other options which are depending on workflow settings and on the current status of the workflow.

If you want to check the current status of workflow processing, click the button *Workflow/Workflow history* in the action pane. In the Workflow history form, you might want to refresh the screen with the shortcut *Shift+F5* or with the button 🔄 (*Refresh*) in the action pane from time to time – in particular, if the workflow batch job has not processed the workflow yet.

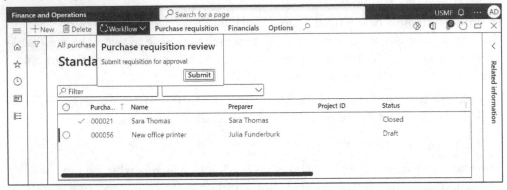

Figure 10-12: Submitting a purchase requisition for approval (starting a workflow)

10.4.3.2 Work Items in Approval Workflows

Depending on the settings of the related workflow element, work items are either assigned to a work item queue or to individual users.

If necessary, you can change the assigned approver (appropriate permissions required). For this purpose, open the Workflow history form and click the button *Reassign* on the tab *Work items*.

The work items that are assigned to a user are shown in the left pane of the dashboard and in his work item list (*Common> Work items> Work items assigned to me*). Available options in the button *Workflow* of the Work item page are depending on the workflow element properties of the selected work item (as specified in the workflow editor on the tab *Advanced settings/Allowed actions* in the *Properties* of the respective workflow element). Possible options include:

➢ **Approve** – Approve the request.
➢ **Reject** – Reject the approval finally (which does not prevent re-submitting).
➢ **Request change** – Reject, but promise approval if the request is changed.
➢ **Delegate** – Transfer the decision to another user.

The additional option "Recall" is not available to the approver, but to the person who has submitted the request. Recalling is an option to stop workflow processing before approval (e.g., if you want to modify the request).

If you are approver and need to know more details before deciding on approval, you can access the original request straight from the Work item form – click the button *Open* in the action pane or click on the request ID shown as a link in the column *ID*. In the original request (e.g., the purchase requisition), you have got the same approval options as in the Work item list page.

Depending on the settings in the particular workflow (specified in the workflow editor), there are additional workflow activities or multiple approvers.

10.4.3.3 Working with Work Item Queues

If a work item is assigned to a work item queue, it is shown in the list page *Common> Work items> Work items assigned to my queues*. As a prerequisite, you have to be a member of the work item queue to which the work item is assigned.

In the work item queue, you can click the button *Workflow/Accept* in the action pane to claim a work item on which you want to work. Accepting a work item moves the item to your work item list (among the other work items that are directly assigned to you) and prevents other queue members to work on the same item.

In the work item list (*Common> Work items> Work items assigned to me*), you can execute applicable workflow actions like in any other directly assigned work item. In addition, the workflow button contains the options *Reassign* (for reassigning the work item to other persons) and *Release* (for releasing it back to the queue).

10.5   Other Features

Advanced features, which are available across the whole application, include the document management, the case management, and the task guides.

The license configuration and the feature management determine the features that are available in Dynamics 365.

10.5.1   Document Management

In daily business, you are working with structured data represented by data records in the business application (e.g., customers records). In parallel, there are data with reference to these records which are only available in an unstructured format (e.g., files or emails). These unstructured data oftentimes are hard to find.

With the document management in Microsoft Dynamics 365, you can solve this issue by appending files to data records. Attached files are directly accessible from within Dynamics 365. If you use the document management to attach, for example, all related notes and files to the respective customer in the Customer form, Dynamics 365 provides access to all relevant data on the customer – business data within Dynamics 365 as well as related files – directly from the Customer form.

10.5.1.1 Document Types and Document Management Setup

As a prerequisite for accessing the document management in the Attachment form, the slider *Enable document handling* in the user options (on the tab *Miscellaneous* in the section *Preferences*) has to be set to "Yes" for the users who work with the document management. In addition, the required document types have to be configured in the menu item *Organization administration> Document management> Document types*.

The document types are divided into the following classes:

➤ **Simple note** – For plain text, which you enter directly in the Attachment form.
➤ **Attach file** – For attaching a file.
➤ **Attach URL** – For a web link, entered in the field *Description* of the document.

You can create multiple document types per class. The field *Class* in the document type determines whether assigned documents are notes, attachments, or URLs. For the class "Attach file", the selected option in the field *Location* determines whether attached files are stored inside the Dynamics 365 SQL database, or in the Azure Blob storage, or in SharePoint.

Core parameters for document management (*Organization administration> Document management> Document management parameters*) include the number sequence for documents in the section *Number sequences* of the Document parameter form, and, in the section *File types*, the file types which are available in document management (providing the option to exclude possibly malicious file types like EXE-files). If the slider *Use active document tables* in the section *General* of the parameters is set to "Yes", document management is only available for the tables that are included in the active document tables (*Organization administration> Document management> Active document tables*).

10.5.1.2 Attachment Form for Document Handling

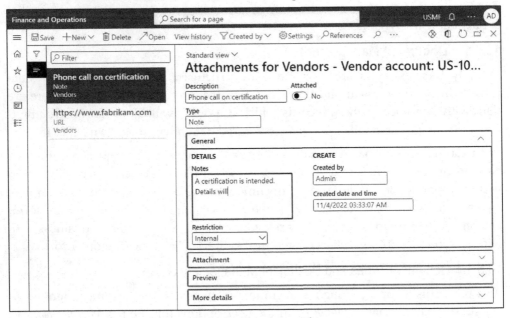

Figure 10-13: Entering a simple note in the Attachment form

In every list page or detail form, you can access the Attachment form for document handling with the button 🗨 in the action pane (the icon shows the number of attached documents) or with the shortcut *Ctrl+Shift+A*. In the Attachment form, you can edit notes and append documents as applicable. The documents are attached to the record that has been selected in the original form when opening the Attachment form.

If you want to create a new document in the Attachment form, insert a new record with the button *New* in the action pane. The *Type* that you select for the new record in the drop-down menu determines if the document is a note, a file attachment, or a URL. If the type is a file attachment, you can upload the document in a dialog that is shown next. If the type is a note, you can enter a multiline text in the field *Notes* on the tab *General*. In the field *Restriction* on tab *General*, select the option "External" if the document should be visible for external parties and printed on external documents (e.g., sales invoices).

In case the document is an attachment, you can view the attached document with the button *Open* (which downloads the attachment) or directly on the tab *Preview* in the Attachment form.

10.5.1.3 Document History and Recycle Bin

In the Document management parameters, the slider *Enable document history* in the section *General* activates tracking of document handling activities. If enabled, you can view the past activities with the button *View history* in the Attachment form.

The slider *Deferred deletion enabled* in the Document management parameters activates a recycle bin for document handling. If enabled, you can view the recycle bin with the button *Deleted attachments* in the Attachment form.

10.5.2 Case Management

The purpose of case management in Dynamics 365 is to manage any kind of question or issue centrally. You can use it in many areas – for example, in customer service, collections, purchase management, and product management.

10.5.2.1 Setup for Case Management

Apart from the number sequence for cases, there is the following setup for the case management:

> **Case categories** – Classify cases by functional area.
> **Case processes** – Specify the activities for processing a case (optional).

Case categories (*Organization management> Setup> Cases> Case categories*) group cases in a hierarchical structure. In order to set up a new case category, click the button *New* in the action pane and select the *Category type*. If you do not select the top-level node in the left pane, but an existing category group, the new category is a subcategory with the category type of that group. On the tab *General* of the category, you can enter default values for the owner and for the *Case process*. These defaults are used when creating a case with the respective category.

Case processes (*Organization management> Setup> Cases> Case processes*), which are an optional setup, determine the necessary steps for processing a case. When you set up a new case process, enter the *Name*, the *Description*, and make sure that the *Type* is "Case process" (if you don't create a case process for another type) before you save the record. The slider *Active* should be set to "Yes" to activate the case process. In order to define the steps (stages) for case processing, click the button *Process/View/Details*. In the process details, you can create a process stage with the button *New/Create level* (enter the name of the stage in the field *Purpose* then). If required, you can create a multi-level hierarchy of stages.

For a simple case process, it may be sufficient to set up stages. But if required, you can create activities (e.g., *Appointments*) for the stages in the process details. Click the button *New/Create appointment* (or one of the other options in the *New* button) for this purpose and – in case you want to make sure, that a particular activity is executed when working on a case – set the slider *Required* in the activity to "Yes". In case of required activities, additionally set the slider *Check for required activities* on the tab *Exit criteria* of the related stage to "Yes".

10.5.2.2 Processing Cases

You can create a new case with the appropriate button in the action pane of any list page or detail form that refers to case management – for example, in the Sales order form (click the button *General/Customer/Cases/Create case*), the Customer form, the Vendor form, or the Released product form.

Cases which you create in a sales order are assigned to the respective customer and to the order. In the *New case* dialog, select the *Case category* (only categories with the category type "General" or "Sales" are available) and enter a *Description*. On the tab *Other* of the dialog, you can override the default values for the *Employee responsible* (owner), the *Service level agreement* and the *Case process* that are retrieved from the selected *Case category*.

If you want to follow up on a case, open the list page *Common> Cases> All cases* and click on the respective case ID (shown as a link in the column *Case ID*) to switch to the detail form. Assignments of the case (e.g., to a sales order) are shown on the tab *Associations*. If there are later additional associations, you can add them on this tab in the Case form – for example, if you want to assign a return order case also to the original sales order. The FactBox *Process tree* displays the process steps as specified in the applicable case process. The current status of the stages is shown in the Case process form, which you can access with the button *Case/Process/Case process* in the action pane of the Case form.

When you start working on a case, click the button *Case/Maintain/Change status/In process* in the Case form (if this status has not been selected when creating the case).

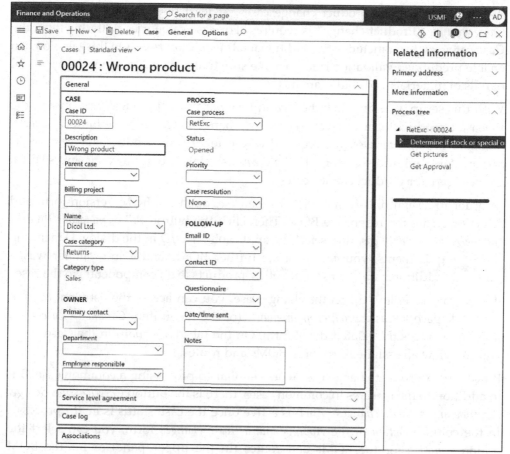

Figure 10-14: Editing the details in a case associated with a sales order

If the case is attached to a *Case process* and you proceed with the case, click the button *Case/Process/Case/Change stage* and select the applicable stage, to which you want to move. If the case process includes activities (e.g., *Appointments*), click the button *General/Activities/Activities/View activities* in the Case form (or open the menu item *Common> Activities> All activities*) to access the related activities. Required activities of a case have to be completed by the responsible person.

On the tab *Case log*, you can view all interactions (e.g., a product receipt) that refer to the case. The case log facilitates getting an overview of the status of a case.

In order to close a case, click the button *Case/Maintain/Change status/Closed* in the Case form.

10.5.2.3 Product Change Cases

If you don't want to use the comprehensive Engineering change management module (see section 7.2.5), you can alternatively use the product change cases to manage a common approval of multiple bills of materials and routes.

As a prerequisite for product change cases, at least one case category with the *Category type* "Product change" is required. For case categories with this type, the Case category form includes the additional tab *Validation rules*. On this tab, you can enable predefined validation rules to make sure that all conditions for the approval of bills of materials and routes are met.

With this setup, you can click the button *Engineer/Product change/Create case* in the Released product form to create a product change case – <u>not</u> the button *General/ Maintain cases/Create case* (the required case category for product change cases is not available with this button). In the *New case* dialog, enter a *Name* and select a *Case category* for product change cases.

In order to assign bills of materials to the case, open the BOM version form and select or create the respective BOM. Then click the button *Bill of materials/Product change/Associate with case* and select the applicable *Case ID* in the dialog. Depending on the requirements, you can associate further BOMs and – in a similar way – routes. In addition, you can associate other products (e.g., components) to the case.

If you want to follow up on the change case, you can access the list *Open cases* in the workspace *Released product maintenance* (or the menu item *Common> Cases> All cases*) and access the related detail form. On the tab *Associations* in the Case form, you can view all assigned products, BOMs and routes.

Processing a product change case works similar to processing a common case. But in addition to the features in common cases, there is the button *Case/Product change/ Approve and activate changes* which is active once the case status is in "In process". In the column *Action* of the *Approve and activate changes* form, you can select the option *Approve* for the BOMs and routes (in the upper pane) or for the BOM versions and route versions (in the lower pane, with the additional options *Activate* and *Expire*). With the button *Set action* in the toolbar of the upper or lower pane, you can initialize the column *Action* in multiple lines. In order to execute the action that is selected in the lines, click the button *Apply actions* in the action pane.

10.5.3   Task Recorder and Task Guide

Task guides are step-by-step instructions that explain how to perform a business process in Dynamics 365. In order to create a task guide, use the task recorder.

You can open the task recorder with the button ⚙ */Task recorder* in the navigation bar. In the *Task recorder* dialog, click the button *Create recording* to create a recording. Then enter a *Recording name* in the next dialog and click the button *Start*. Once the recording is started, execute the steps which you want to record in the Dynamics 365 web client. You can edit the instructions with the button ✎ next to each step in the task recorder pane.

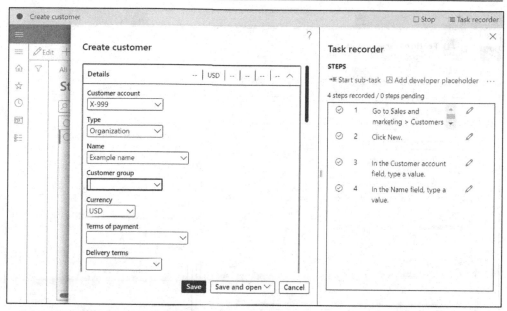

Figure 10-15: Recording a guide in the task recorder

Once you have finished the recording, click the button *Stop* in the task recorder banner at the top. The task recorder subsequently shows a dialog with the option to save the recording to your PC, to the Lifecycle Services, or to export it as a Word document. When you are finished, click the button *Return to main menu* at the bottom of the dialog to return to the task recorder pane.

If you want to play a recording as a task guide, click the button *Play recording as guide* in the task recorder pane and open the recording that has been saved to your PC or to the Lifecycle Services. If you have saved the recording to a Business Process Library in the Lifecycle Services that is selected on the tab *Help* in the System parameters, you can view the recording on the tab *Task Guides* in the help pane of the pages that are covered by the recording.

10.5.4 Feature Management and License Configuration

When a new feature has become available with a Microsoft service update, it is shown in the Feature management workspace. In this workspace, which you can access with the corresponding tile in the dashboard, the drop-down below the workspace name provides the option to enable new features automatically. Usually, it is set in a way that new features are only available after they have been manually enabled with the respective button in the workspace.

The feature management is intended to delay the availability of new features temporarily – for example, if you don't want to use the Planning Optimization until you are ready to use it.

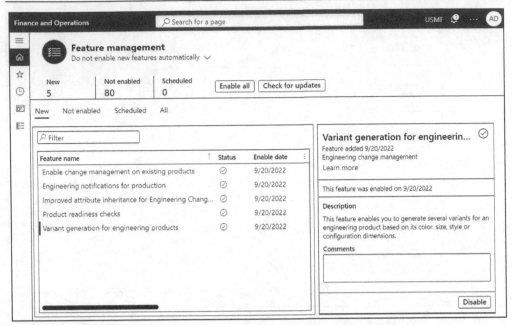

Figure 10-16: Managing new features in the Feature management workspace

Unlike the feature management, the license configuration is designed to control the available functional components on a long-term basis. If, for example, your enterprise doesn't need the catch weight functionality and wants to get rid of the related fields and functions, deselect the corresponding configuration key. Changing the license configuration is only possible in the maintenance mode.

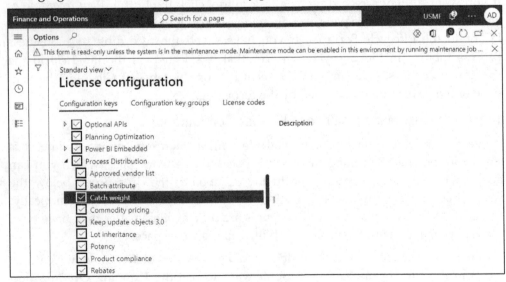

Figure 10-17: Viewing the active license configuration

Appendix

Setup Checklist

The checklists below show the essential setup of Dynamics 365 for Finance and Operations. The tables on the basic setup include the necessary configuration steps for the functional areas that are covered by the book. They have to be finished before you can start to work in any module. Master data and other essential settings of the individual modules are included in the subsequent tables. Depending on the requirements, additional setup is necessary in most cases.

Table A-1:   Basic system setup

No.	Name	Menu Item	Section
1.1	Configuration	*System administration> Setup> License configuration*	10.5.4
1.2	Parameters	*System administration> Setup> System parameters*	10.3.4
1.3	Legal entities	*Organization administration> Organizations> Legal entities*	10.1.4
1.4	Users	*System administration> Users> Users*	10.2.2
1.5	Features	Workspace *Feature management*	10.5.4

Table A-2:   Basic setup of a legal entity

No.	Name	Menu Item	Section
2.1	Operating units	*Organization administration> Organizations> Operating units*	10.1.2
2.2	Dimensions	*General ledger> Chart of accounts> Dimensions> Financial dimensions*	9.2.3
2.3	Fiscal calendars	*General ledger> Calendars> Fiscal Calendars*	9.2.1
2.4	Currencies	*General ledger> Currencies> Currencies*	9.2.2
2.5	Rate types	*General ledger> Currencies> Exchange rate types*	9.2.2
2.6	Exchange rates	*General ledger> Currencies> Currency exchange rates*	9.2.2
2.7	Chart of Accounts	*General ledger> Chart of accounts> Accounts> Chart of accounts*	9.2.4
2.8	Account structure	*General ledger> Chart of accounts> Structures> Configure account structures*	9.2.4
2.9	Ledger	*General ledger> Ledger setup> Ledger*	9.2
2.10	Sites	*Inventory management> Setup> Inventory breakdown> Sites*	10.1.6
2.11	Warehouses	*Inventory management> Setup> Inventory breakdown> Warehouses*	7.4.1
2.12	Dimension link	*Cost management> Ledger integration policies setup> Dimension link*	10.1.6

© Springer Fachmedien Wiesbaden GmbH, part of Springer Nature 2023
A. Luszczak, *Using Microsoft Dynamics 365 for Finance and Operations*,
https://doi.org/10.1007/978-3-658-40453-6

No.	Name	Menu Item	Section
2.13	Bank accounts	*Cash and bank management> Bank accounts> Bank accounts*	9.2.5
2.14	Address setup	*Organization administration> Global address book> Addresses> Address setup*	10.3.3
2.15	Address book parameters	*Organization administration> Global address book> Global address book parameters*	2.4.2
2.16	Number sequences	*Organization administration> Number sequences> Number sequences*	10.3.1
2.17	Units	*Organization administration> Setup> Units> Units*	7.2.1
2.18	Unit conversion	*Organization administration> Setup> Units> Unit conversions*	7.2.1

Table A-3:   Basic setup for general ledger and sales tax

No.	Name	Menu Item	Section
3.1	Default descriptions	*General ledger> Journal setup> Default descriptions*	9.2.4
3.2	Accounts for aut. transactions	*General ledger> Posting setup> Accounts for automatic transactions*	9.2.4
3.3	Tax posting group	*Tax> Setup> Sales tax> Ledger posting groups*	9.2.7
3.4	Tax authorities	*Tax> Indirect taxes> Sales tax> Sales tax authorities*	9.2.7
3.5	Sales tax settlement periods	*Tax> Indirect taxes> Sales tax> Sales tax settlement periods*	9.2.7
3.6	Sales tax codes	*Tax> Indirect taxes> Sales tax> Sales tax codes*	9.2.7
3.7	Sales tax groups	*Tax> Indirect taxes> Sales tax> Sales tax groups*	9.2.7
3.8	Item sales tax groups	*Tax> Indirect taxes> Sales tax> Item sales tax groups*	9.2.7
3.9	Journal names	*General ledger> Journal setup> Journal names*	9.2.8
3.10	Parameters	*General ledger> Ledger setup> General ledger parameters*	9.2.8

Table A-4:   Basic setup for procurement and accounts payable

No.	Name	Menu Item	Section
4.1	Terms of payment	*Accounts payable> Payment setup> Terms of payment*	3.2.2
4.2	Vendor groups	*Accounts payable> Vendors> Vendor groups*	3.2.3
4.3	Posting profiles	*Accounts payable> Setup> Vendor posting profiles*	3.2.3
4.4	Accounts payable parameters	*Accounts payable> Setup> Accounts payable parameters*	
4.5	Procurement parameters	*Procurement and sourcing> Setup> Procurement and sourcing parameters*	

Table A-5:   Basic setup for sales and accounts receivable

No.	Name	Menu Item	Section
5.1	Terms of payment	*Accounts receivable> Payment setup>Terms of payment*	3.2.2
5.2	Customer groups	*Accounts receivable> Setup> Customer groups*	4.2.1

No.	Name	Menu Item	Section
5.3	Posting profiles	*Accounts receivable> Setup> Customer posting profiles*	4.2.1
5.4	Form setup	*Accounts receivable> Setup> Forms> Form setup*	4.2.1
5.5	Accounts receiv. parameters	*Accounts receivable> Setup> Accounts receivable parameters*	
5.6	Sales and markt. parameters	*Sales and marketing> Setup> Sales and marketing parameters*	

Table A-6: Basic setup for product and inventory management

No.	Name	Menu Item	Section
6.1	Storage dimension groups	*Product information management> Setup> Dimension and variant groups> Storage dimension groups*	7.2.2
6.2	Tracking dimension groups	*Product information management> Setup> Dimension and variant groups> Tracking dimension groups*	7.2.2
6.3	Item groups	*Inventory management> Setup> Inventory> Item groups*	7.2.1
6.4	Transaction combinations	*Cost management> Ledger integration policies setup> Transaction combinations*	9.4.2
6.5	Posting setup	*Cost management> Ledger integration policies setup> Posting*	9.4.2
6.6	Item model groups	*Inventory management> Setup> Inventory> Item model groups*	7.2.3
6.7	Costing versions	*Cost management> Inventory accounting> Costing versions*	7.3.3
6.8	Inventory journal names	*Inventory management> Setup> Journal names> Inventory*	7.4.1
6.9	Warehouse journal names	*Inventory management> Setup> Journal names> Warehouse management*	7.4.1
6.10	Parameters	*Inventory management> Setup> Inventory and warehouse management parameters*	

Table A-7: Basic setup for production control

No.	Name	Menu Item	Section
7.1	Production units	*Production control> Setup> Production> Production units*	5.3.2
7.2	Cost groups	*Cost management> Inventory accounting policies setup> Cost groups*	7.3.3
7.3	Working time templates	*Production control> Setup> Calendars> Working time templates*	5.3.1
7.4	Calendars	*Production control> Setup> Calendars> Calendars*	5.3.1
7.5	Route groups	*Production control> Setup> Routes> Route groups*	5.3.3
7.6	Shared categories	*Production control> Setup> Routes> Shared categories*	5.3.3
7.7	Cost categories	*Production control> Setup> Routes> Cost categories*	5.3.3
7.8	Resource capabilities	*Production control> Setup> Resources> Resource capabilities*	5.3.2
7.9	Resource groups	*Production control> Setup> Resources> Resource groups*	5.3.2

No.	Name	Menu Item	Section
7.10	Resources	*Production control> Setup> Resources> Resources*	5.3.2
7.11	Journal names	*Production control> Setup> Production journal names*	5.5.1
7.12	Calculation groups	*Cost management> Predetermined cost policies setup> Calculation groups*	7.3.3
7.13	Costing sheet	*Cost management> Ledger integration policies setup> Costing sheets*	7.3.3
7.14	Parameters	*Production control> Setup> Production control parameters*	
7.15	Parameters by site	*Production control> Setup> Production control parameters by site*	

Table A-8:   Basic setup for master planning

No.	Name	Menu Item	Section
8.1	Coverage groups	*Master planning> Setup> Coverage> Coverage groups*	6.3.4
8.2.	Forecast models	*Master planning> Setup> Demand forecasting> Forecast models*	6.2.2
8.3	Master plans	*Master planning> Setup> Plans> Master plans*	6.3.3
8.4	Forecast plans	*Master planning> Setup> Plans> Forecast plans*	6.2.2
8.5	Parameters	*Master planning> Setup> Master planning parameters*	6.3.3

Table A-9:   Other key settings

No.	Name	Menu Item	Section
9.1	Employees	*Human resources> Workers> Workers*	10.2.2
9.2	Terms of delivery	*Procurement and sourcing> Setup> Distribution> Terms of delivery*	3.2.1
9.3	Modes of delivery	*Procurement and sourcing> Setup> Distribution> Modes of delivery*	3.2.1
9.4	Cash discounts	*Accounts payable> Payment setup> Cash discounts*	3.2.2
9.5	Payment methods (Purchasing)	*Accounts payable> Payment setup> Methods of payment*	9.3.3
9.6	Activate trade agreements (Purchasing)	*Procurement and sourcing> Setup> Prices and discounts> Activate price/discount*	4.3.2
9.7	Vendor price/ discount groups	*Procurement and sourcing> Prices and discounts> Price/discount groups> Vendor price/discount groups*	4.3.2
9.8	Trade agreement journal names	*Procurement and sourcing> Setup> Prices and discounts> Trade agreement journal names*	4.3.2
9.9	Item discount groups	*Procurement and sourcing> Prices and discounts> Price/discount groups> Item discount groups*	4.3.2
9.10	Price tolerance setup	*Accounts payable> Invoice matching setup> Price tolerances*	3.6.1
9.11	Activate trade agrmt. (Sales)	*Sales and marketing> Setup> Prices and discounts> Activate price/discount*	4.3.2

No.	Name	Menu Item	Section
9.12	Customer price/ discount groups	*Sales and marketing> Prices and discounts> Customer price/discount groups*	4.3.2
9.13	Charges codes (Purchasing)	*Accounts payable> Charges setup> Charges code*	4.4.5
9.14	Charges codes (Sales)	*Accounts receivable> Charges setup> Charges code*	4.4.5
9.15	Return action (Purchasing)	*Procurement and sourcing> Setup> Purchase orders> Return action*	3.7.1
9.16	Disposition codes (Sales returns)	*Sales and marketing> Setup> Returns> Disposition codes*	4.7.1
9.17	Category hierarchies	*Product information management> Setup> Categories and attributes> Category hierarchies*	3.3.1
9.18	Procurement categories	*Procurement and sourcing> Procurement categories*	3.3.1
9.19	Sales categories	*Sales and marketing> Setup> Categories> Sales categories*	4.3.1
9.20	Document management parameters	*Organization administration> Document management> Document management parameters*	10.5.1
9.21	Document types	*Organization administration> Document management> Document types*	10.5.1
9.22	Workflow configuration	*System administration> Workflow> Workflow infrastructure configuration*	10.4.2

Table A-10: Master data

No.	Name	Menu Item	Section
10.1	Vendors	*Accounts payable> Vendors> All vendors*	3.2.1
10.2	Customers	*Accounts receivable> Customers> All customers*	4.2.1
10.3	Products	*Product information management> Products> All products and product masters*	7.2.1
10.4	Released products	*Product information management> Products> Released products*	7.2.1
10.5	Bills of materials	*Product information management> Bills of materials and formulas> Bills of materials*	5.2.2
10.6	Operations	*Production control> Setup> Routes> Operations*	5.3.3
10.7	Routes	*Production control> All routes*	5.3.3

Commands and Keyboard Shortcuts

Table A-11: Basic commands and keyboard shortcuts

Shortcut	Button in the action pane	Description
Alt+N	*New*	Create a record
Alt+Del (*Alt+F9*)	*Delete*	Delete a record
Alt+S (*Ctrl+S*)	*Save*	Save record (in Edit mode)
F2	*Edit* (or *Options/Edit/Read mode*)	Switch between Read mode and Edit mode
Esc		Close form (optionally without saving)
Shift+Esc		Close form and save record
Ctrl+Shift+F5	*Options/Edit/Revert*	Restore record (Undo pending changes)
Shift+F5	⟳ (*Refresh*)	Refresh (Save and synchronize record)
Ctrl+F2	(Click on the *Related information* pane on the right of the form)	Show the FactBoxes
Ctrl+Shift+H	*Header* (in the title line)	Switch to the Header view (in transaction forms)
Ctrl+Shift+L	*Lines* (in the title line)	Switch to the Lines view (in transaction forms)
Ctrl+F10	(Right-click)	Open the Dynamics 365 context menu
Ctrl+G	(Click the column header)	Open the grid column filter for the current column
Ctrl+F3	▽ (in the sidebar on the left)	Open the filter pane
Ctrl+Shift+F3	*Options/Page options/ Advanced filter or sort*	Open the advanced filter
Ctrl+Shift+A	📎 (*Attach*)	Document management
Alt+F1	≡ (in the sidebar on the left)	Show the navigation pane
Alt+G	🔍 (in the navigation bar)	Open the navigation search
Ctrl+?	❓/*Help* (in the navigation bar)	Help on forms

The option *View shortcuts* (in the context menu of controls like a field name or a button in a form) and the Dynamics 365 help explain all available keyboard shortcuts.

Bibliography

Literature

Murray Fife: Configuring Supply Chain Management within Dynamics 365: Dynamics 365 Bare Bones Configuration Guide (Independently published, 2022)

Ludwig Reinhard: Special Finance Applications in Microsoft Dynamics 365 for Finance and Operations (Independently published, 2019)

Scott Hamilton: Master Planning in Manufacturing using Microsoft Dynamics 365 for Operations (Scott Hamilton, 2017)

Simon Buxton: Extending Microsoft Dynamics 365 Finance and Supply Chain Management Cookbook (Packt Publishing, 2020)

Other Sources

Microsoft documentation (https://learn.microsoft.com/dynamics365/finance/ and https://learn.microsoft.com/dynamics365/supply-chain/)

© Springer Fachmedien Wiesbaden GmbH, part of Springer Nature 2023
A. Luszczak, *Using Microsoft Dynamics 365 for Finance and Operations*,
https://doi.org/10.1007/978-3-658-40453-6

Index

A

Account (General ledger) 401, 405
Account for aut. transactions 142, 401, 407
Account structure 400, 403
Accounting currency 398
Action center 22, 464
Action message 269, 272
Action pane 13, 14, 15
Address 37, 56, 130
   Delivery address 80, 130, 148
   Invoice address 129, 149
Address book 45, 47
Address format 48, 461
Address setup 48, 461
Adjustment (Cost price) 313
Adjustment type 370, 372
Advanced notes 88, 132
Advanced rule structure 404
Alert rule 463
Approval
   Bill of materials 201, 204
   Customer 129, 411
   Invoice register 427
   Journal transaction 416, 422
   Payment 106, 430
   Purchase order 84, 274
   Purchase requisition 119
   Vendor 58
Approval workflow 108, 417, 425
Approved vendor 71
Arrival overview 95
Attachment 131, 470
Audit trail 407
Authentication 5, 452
Authorization 452
Azure 5, 31, 259

B

Balance sheet 393
Balancing dimension 401, 402
Bank account 408

Banner 10, 449
Batch number 292, 294, 347
Batch processing 34, 89, 467
Bill back agreement 185, 186
Bill of materials (BOM) 200
   Activation 204
   Approval 201, 204
   Version 200
Blanket order 116, 143
Block
   Inventory blocking 334, 336, 342, 369
   Item (Product) 71
   Payment 427, 430
   Period 396
   Product 134
   Vendor 55
BOM designer 206
BOM level 201, 274
BOM line 203, 246
Bridging posting 432
Broker contract 188
Business Intelligence 3
Business unit 446

C

Calculated delay 266, 270, 272
Calendar 208, 461
Cancel
   Inventory registration 95
   Order 85, 147
   Packing slip 167
   Picking List 163
   Product receipt 97
   Rebate 187
   Warehouse work 368
Capability (Resource) 214, 222, 226
Capacity 212
   Available capacity 230
   Finite capacity 214, 231
Capacity unit 213, 221
Case management 471
Cash discount 62, 409

© Springer Fachmedien Wiesbaden GmbH, part of Springer Nature 2023
A. Luszczak, *Using Microsoft Dynamics 365 for Finance and Operations*,
https://doi.org/10.1007/978-3-658-40453-6

Cash on delivery 61
Catch weight 68, 250, 290, 301, 353
Category 65, 69, 134, 439
Centralized payment 432
Change management 75, 84, 274
Charge (Surcharge) 81, 115, 155, 189, 390
    Charges code 155
    Price charge 73
Chart of accounts 401
Client performance options 11, 13, 35
Collective invoice 107, 170
Color (Product) 292
Company account 9, 37, 445, 448
Configuration (Product) 292
Confirmation request 87
Connected windows 17
Consignment 293, 337
Consumption (Production) 234, 236, 242
Contact information 46, 58
Co-product 250, 252
Copy
    Bill of materials 204
    Purchase order 82
Cost category 214, 220, 441
Cost center 399
Cost entry 299, 307
Cost explorer 312
Cost group 221, 246, 315
Cost price 71, 199, 314
Costing 243
Costing sheet 229, 244, 308, 316
Costing version 221, 314
Counting (Inventory) 325, 371
Coverage code 267
Coverage group 268
Create dialog 18, 67, 128
Credit hold 409
Credit limit 131, 409
Credit management 409
Credit note
    Purchasing 112
    Sales 174
Cross-company data sharing 59, 128, 450
Currency 397
Custom field 40
Customer 128, 409
Customer classification 163

Customer portal 5

D
Dashboard 6, 10, 449, 468
DAT company 449
Database log 43
Decoupling point 262, 269
Default order settings 71, 134, 199, 286
Default order type 71, 199
Delete 20
    Order 86, 147
Deliver remainder 85, 98
Delivery alternative 153
Delivery date 149, 329
Delivery note 165
Delivery schedule 82, 147
Delivery term 56
Demand forecast 255, 258
Department 399
Detail form 14, 18
Dimension (Financial) 173, 399
Dimension display 295, 301
Dimension group 68, 292, 321, 352
Direct delivery 179
Discount 136, 154
    Freight 389
    Line discount 139
    Multiline discount 141
Discount group 135
Document handling 14, 131, 470
Document routing agent 31
Document template 36
Drop-down menu 21, 27
Due date 61
Duplicate address 47, 48, 55, 128
Duty 456, 457

E
Edit mode 12, 18, 19, 37
Employee 351, 454
Engineering change management 302
Engineering change order 305
Error account 407
Error message 22
Estimation (Production order) 229
Excel 32, 34, 38
Exchange rate 137, 397
Explosion (BOM) 152, 203, 274

F

FactBox 13, 15
Favorites 8
Feature management 3, 475
Field group 21
FIFO 308
Filter 13, 23
    Advanced 25
    Save 26
Filter pane 24
Finalize order 84
Financial dimension 173, 399, 421, 444
Financial transaction 278, 299, 437
Firming time fence 269
Fiscal calendar 395, 461
Fiscal year 395
Fixed receipt price 307, 309, 440
Flushing principle 200, 203, 235, 242
Forecast 255
    Forecast model 255, 256
    Forecast plan 257
Form (Detail form) 14, 18
Form setup 88, 131
Formula 250
Free text invoice 172, 433, 436
Freight discount 389

G

Gantt Chart 233
General journal 418
General ledger 393
Global address book 45, 55, 80, 128, 444
Global general journal 422
Grid column filter 22, 25
Grid footer 38
Gross requirement 259

H

Header view 17, 82
Help 28
    Customize 29
Hierarchy designer 446

I

Income statement 393
Indirect costs 244, 308, 317, 442
Input tax 56, 63, 81, 412
Intangible item 65, 68, 80
Intercompany 420, 432, 445

Interunit accounting 401, 402
Inventory closing 300, 312
Inventory dimension 291, 342, 352, 451
    Coverage 270
    Financial inventory 311
    Pricing 137, 293
Inventory forecast 259
Inventory model 297, 308, 312, 440
Inventory picking 160, 299
Inventory registration 75, 92, 176, 299
Inventory status 342, 369
Inventory transaction 80, 94, 100, 298
Inventory unit 70, 352
Inventory valuation 114, 178, 307
Inventory value report 312
Invoice 423
    Free text invoice 172, 433, 436
    General journal 424
    Purchase invoice 103, 409, 424, 436
    Sales invoice 168, 424
Invoice account 129, 149
Invoice approval 427
Invoice discount 136, 141, 142
Invoice inquiry 110, 169
Invoice journal 424, 426
Invoice matching 108
Invoice pool 425, 428
Invoice register 425, 426
Item (Product) 67, 69, 134, 198, 282
Item allocation key 257
Item arrival journal 94, 96, 176, 325
Item coverage 71, 199, 270
Item group 288, 438
Item model group 198, 289, 296
    Inventory model 297, 308, 312, 440
    Ledger integration 437
    Picking requirement 160
Item price form 72, 314
Item receipt 277, 308
Item return 97, 112, 175

J

Job (Route) 231
Job card 239
Job scheduling 231
Journal
    Bill of materials 324
    General ledger 416, 418

Inventory 321, 323
Invoice 424
Payment 429
Production 236, 241
Journal type 416

K
Keyboard shortcut 17, 482
Keyword search 147

L
Landed cost 379
Language 37
Lean manufacturing 193, 211
Ledger account 22, 401, 421
Ledger calendar 313, 396, 461
Ledger form 395, 398, 402
Ledger integration 63, 142, 155, 237, 435
Legal entity 9, 445, 448
License configuration 476
Lifecycle services 3, 29, 443
LIFO 308
Line number 80
Line type (BOM) 203
Link (shared) 9
List page 12, 18
List pane 15
Load 356, 361, 385
Load template 348, 384
Location 292, 320, 344
Location directive 346, 359, 363, 369
Location profile 344, 370, 372
Login 5
Lookup 21, 25, 27
Lookup field 21
Lump sum agreement 185

M
Main account 22, 401, 405, 421
Main account category 406
Make-to-stock 262
Manufacturing execution 234, 236
Margin alert 153
Marking 114, 178, 226, 311, 330
Master data 4, 49, 123, 193, 277
Master plan 264
Master planning 253, 260, 271
    Dynamic plan 262
    Static plan 261, 266

Material handling interface 341
Material requirements 50, 194
Material where-used 207
Message bar 22
Minimum quantity 268, 271
Mobile app 5
Mobile device (Warehouse) 342, 349, 354
Mobile device menu item 345, 349, 360
Mode of delivery 56, 157, 381
Module 7
Moving average 310, 440
Multisite functionality 450

N
Navigation bar 10
Navigation pane 6
Negative inventory 297
Net requirement 152, 272, 274
Network printer 31
Notification 464
Number sequence 459
Numeric field 21

O
Office integration 34
One-plan strategy 262, 266
One-time vendor 58
Open transaction 61, 114, 409, 429
Operating unit 445
Operation 204, 216
Operation relation 216, 219, 223
Operations planning 253
Operations scheduling 210, 230
Order confirmation 60, 87, 157
Order hold 148, 409
Order type 77, 83, 146
Organization hierarchy 446
Origin (Transaction) 102, 110, 169, 407
Overdelivery 99
Overhead margin 317
Owner 338

P
Packing slip 165
Packing slip inquiry 167
Pallet 341
Parameters
    General 462
    Production 226, 441

Partial delivery 97
Party 45, 55, 128, 444
Party type 45, 47, 55
Payment 428
    Approval 106, 430
Payment method 430
Payment proposal 431
Payment term 61
Period 395, 461
Periodic journal 422
Permission 452, 456, 458
Personalization 11, 38
Phantom item 199, 203, 230
Physical transaction 278, 299, 437
Picking 159, 160, 299, 349, 359
Picking list
    Production 235, 237, 366
    Sales 161
Picking workbench 163
Planned order 50, 273
Planning method 263, 271
Planning Optimization 253, 261, 263
Post and print 34, 87
Postal address 46, 56, 80, 130
Postal code 57
Posting dialog 87
    Direct delivery 180
    Invoice 168
    Order confirmation 157
    Packing slip 166
    Product receipt 95
    Vendor invoice 104
Posting layer 417
Posting profile 63, 128, 436
Posting setup 63, 436, 438
Price calculation 229, 243
    Calculation group 315
Price group 153
Price quantity 138
Price variance 107
Pricing 72, 153
Print 31
    Print archive 33
    Print preview 33
Print management 88, 90, 157
Print Management 131
Privilege 456, 458

Pro forma document 88
Process manufacturing 193, 250
Procurement category 65, 67, 80, 424
Product
    Change case 198, 473
    Information dialog 22, 283
    Inventory 282, 351
    Product master 67, 285, 315
    Production 198
    Purchasing 67
    Sales 134
Product category 66, 69, 134, 439
Product dimension 69, 270, 285, 293, 302
Product lifecycle state 289, 303
Product receipt 91, 95, 278, 436
Product receipt inquiry 101
Product type 284, 440
Product version 302
Production group 441
Production journal 236
Production order 225, 252, 366
    End 243
    Release 234
    Start 234
    Status 225
Production papers 234
Production type 198, 250
Production unit 210, 451
Prospect 144
Purchase agreement 116
Purchase inquiry 60, 87
Purchase order 74, 76
Purchase order status 100, 109
Purchase requisition 50, 118
Purchase type 77, 83, 113
Purchasing policy 118, 119

Q
Quality management 335
Quality order 336, 370
Quantity on hand 301
Quarantine 297, 333, 342
Queue (Work item) 466, 469
Quick filter 23
Quotation 144

R
Rate engine (Transportation) 380

Rating metadata 380, 383
Rebate 182
Rebate management 190
Receipt
　Invoice 103
　Product 91
Receipts list 75, 92
Receive now 96, 98
Recent 8
Record template 43, 284
Reduction key 269
Reduction principle 256, 266, 269
Refund 114, 178
Registration (Inventory) 75, 92, 176, 299
Release order 117
Release picking 161, 162
Released product 69, 270, 283, 351, 385
Rename 43
Replacement (Credit note) 112, 176
Replenishment (Location) 373
Report as finished 240, 241, 366
Report dialog 32
Reporting 3
Reprint 90
Request for quotation 50, 120, 274
Requirements (Material) 50, 194, 274
Requisition purpose 118, 265
Reservation
　Capacity 230
　Item 114, 152, 163, 230, 330, 352, 361
Resource 212, 441
Resource consumption 203, 210
Resource group 210, 212
Returned order 113, 175
Reversal (Transaction) 433
RFQ (Request for quotation) 120
Role (Party role) 48
Role (Security) 453, 456
Route 215
　Complex sequence 218
　Simple sequence 217
Route card 239
Route group 220, 231, 235, 239
Route network 217, 219
Royalty agreement 189
Run time (Route) 221

S
Sales agreement 143
Sales category 65, 134
Sales forecast 255
Sales order 143
Sales price 135
Sales quotation 144
Sales tax 412, 416
Save record 19
Saved views 41
Scenario 256, 261
Scheduling parameter 215, 226
Scrap 178, 203, 219, 240, 242
Scrollbar 13
Search (Action) 14
Search (Navigation) 8
Secondary operation 212, 218
Security role 453, 456
Segmented entry control 22, 401, 421
Segregation of duties 458
Serial number 292, 294
　Active in sales 294
Service item 198, 246, 285, 289, 440
Session date 10, 21
Settlement
　Customer transaction 409, 429
　Inventory transaction 300
　Vendor transaction 61, 114, 409
Setup time 221
Shipment 356, 359, 360, 387
Shipping carrier 381
Simulation 262
Site 71, 292, 320, 399, 450
Size (Product) 292
Sort records 27
Staging 344, 363
　Anchoring 364
Standard cost price 307, 309, 440
Status
　Approval 75, 84, 100
　Order 100, 109, 166, 225
Stocktaking 325, 371
Storage dimension 451
Subcontracting 245
Subledger accounting 102, 110, 436
Sub-production 203, 230
Subsidiary 450

Summary account 63, 436
Summary update
  Invoice 170
  Printing 88
  Product receipt 96
  Purchase order 89
Supplier 54
Supply forecast 259
Supply schedule 275
System language 462

T
Tab 15
Table reference 22
Tag counting 328
Task guide 29, 474
Task recorder 474
Team 446
Template 43, 284, 423
Term of payment 61
Tile 12
Toolbar 16
Total amount 107
Total discount 136, 141, 142
Trade agreement 72, 136
Trade allowance 182
Transaction
  Inventory transaction 100, 298
  Ledger transaction 407, 418
Transaction combination 438
Transaction data 4
Transaction origin 102, 110, 169, 407
Transaction settlement 61, 409, 429
Transfer journal 323
Transfer order 328, 365
Transportation 379
Transportation constraint 388
Transportation template 390
Transportation tender 387
Trial balance 407
Two-plan strategy 262, 266

U
Underdelivery 99
Undo (Reverse) 20
Unit conversion 287
Unit of measure 70, 287, 352
Unit of time 213

Unit sequence group 352, 354, 372
URL parameters 5
Usage data 26, 37, 44
User 453
User (Warehouse) 342, 351, 355, 372
User group 456
User options 5, 18, 21, 36, 453
User template 44

V
Valuation method 308, 312
VAT (Value added tax) 56, 412
VAT Reg No 56, 449
Vendor 54, 408
Vendor collaboration 60, 87, 339
Vendor group 63
Vendor invoice 103, 409, 424, 436
Vendor rebate 72, 189
View details 22
Voucher principle 4, 51, 195
Voucher template 423

W
Warehouse 292, 320, 344
Warehouse item 327
Warehouse slotting 375
Wave 349, 358, 367, 374
Wave template 349, 360, 367, 375
Weighted average 308
WIP (Work in progress) 195, 237, 243
Work (Warehouse) 345, 349, 355, 358
Work audit template 361
Work item 467
Work item queue 466, 469
Work policy (warehouse) 362
Work template 345, 360, 363, 375
Work user 342, 351, 355, 372
Worker 351, 454
Workflow 464
Workflow editor 464
Workflow history 467
Working time registration 239
Working time template 209
Workspace 11, 18, 40

Z
ZIP code 57

Printed in the United States
by Baker & Taylor Publisher Services